A Comprehensive Christian Appraisal

MODERN PSYCHOTHERAPIES

SECOND EDITION

Stanton L. Jones
& Richard E. Butman

WITH CONTRIBUTIONS BY Sally Schwer Canning, Kelly Flanagan, Tracey Lee, Michael W. Mangis, Mark R. McMinn, Laura Miguélez, David Van Dyke, Michael J. Vogel, Robert Watson and Terri Watson

IVP Academic
An imprint of InterVarsity Press
Downers Grove, Illinois

InterVarsity Press
P.O. Box 1400, Downers Grove, IL 60515-1426
World Wide Web: www.ivpress.com
E-mail: email@ivpress.com

InterVarsity Press® is the book-publishing division of InterVarsity Christian Fellowship/USA®, a movement of
students and faculty active on campus at hundreds of universities, colleges and schools of nursing in the United States
of America, and a member movement of the International Fellowship of Evangelical Students. For information
about local and regional activities, write Public Relations Dept., InterVarsity Christian Fellowship/USA, 6400
Schroeder Rd., P.O. Box 7895, Madison, WI 53707-7895, or visit the IVCF website at <www.intervarsity.org>.

All Scripture quotations, unless otherwise indicated, are taken from the Holy Bible, New International Version®.
NIV®. Copyright ©1973, 1978, 1984 by International Bible Society. Used by permission of Zondervan Publishing
House. All rights reserved.

While all stories in this book are true, some names and identifying information in this book have been changed to
protect the privacy of the individuals involved.

Design: Cindy Kiple
Images: Cargo/Getty Images

ISBN 978-0-8308-2852-4

Printed in the United States of America ∞

Library of Congress Cataloging-in-Publication Data

Jones, Stanton L.
  Modern psychotherapies: a comprehensive Christian approach /
Stanton L. Jones & Richard E. Butman; with contributions by Sally S.
Canning . . . [et al.].
    p. cm.
  Includes bibliographical references and index.
  ISBN 978-0-8308-2852-4 (casebound: alk. paper)
  1. Psychotherapy—Religious aspects—Christianity. 2.
Christianity—Psychology. 3. Pastoral psychology. I. Butman, Richard
E., 1951- II. Title.
  BV4012.J65 2011
  261.5'15—dc23

                                                              2011023124

P	20	19	18	17	16	15	14	13	12	11	10	9	8	7	6	5	4	3	2	1
Y	28	27	26	25	24	23	22	21	20	19	18	17	16	15	14	13	12	11

Our little systems have their day;
They have their day and cease to be:
They are but broken lights of Thee,
And Thou, O Lord, art more than they.

Alfred Tennyson,
"In Memoriam"

*Twenty years ago, we dedicated the original version of this text
to our children. We retain that dedication, noting that God has
allowed each to grow into adulthood and has answered our prayers
for their lives beyond what we could have ever dreamed.*

*To
Jenny, the gentle spirit;
Brandon, full of sensitive brightness;
and Lindsay, an effervescent sprite—
in hopes that you will each grow up to know
the fullness of God's love.*

*And to
Ashley Elizabeth, aglow with wonder—
in hopes that you will continue to manifest God's grace
in the lives of those you touch.*

CONTENTS

The Systemic Psychologies

ACKNOWLEDGMENTS

❖

*R*eformed Christian thinkers often assert that in pursuing truth, we attempt to "think God's thoughts after him." We cannot be so confident to claim that we are presenting "God's thoughts" in this book, but it has been exciting to pursue that goal in this project. As we wrote, we were acutely aware of those who have been friends, conversation partners and mentors to us in some form or another along the paths of our development. In some sense, much of what might be good in all that follows is due to their influence—we have been thinking "their thoughts" as well as God's thoughts. What is inadequate in what follows is due to our own weaknesses.

Our acknowledgments in the original version of this book need to be retained, because the basic contours of our thinking as influenced by our friends and collaborators endures in this new, revised edition. Twenty years ago we thanked, and continue to thank, the following individuals: scholars C. Stephen Evans and Alan Tjeltveit, who read the first draft of the first manuscript in its entirety; colleague Michael Mangis, who did the initial draft of the "Contemporary Psychodynamic Psychotherapies" chapter for us; colleagues Dennis Okholm, Frances J. White, Siang Yang Tan, Robert Roberts, H. Newton Malony, Kirk Farnsworth, Don Bosch, Drew Loizeaux, Brian Van Dragt and Jon Peterson, who offered critiques of individual chapters at various stages of development; our first editors at InterVarsity Press, Michael Maudlin and Rodney Clapp; our secretaries at Wheaton College, Carol Blauwkamp and Geraldine Carlson; and several generations of research assistants including Joel Arp, Karen Crow Blankenship, Rose Buier,

David Dodd, Michael Gillis, Kathy Hobson, Todd Keylock, Kathleen Lattea, Stephen Moroney, Grace Ann Robertson, Lauren Strickler, Trudy Walk, Elizabeth Watson, David Wilcox, Don Workman and Chris Zang. Our thanks go out yet again for the gracious hosting twenty years ago of our respective first sabbaticals: for Stan, to the recently deceased Don Browning and the faculty of the University of Chicago Divinity School, and for Rich to H. Newton Malony and the faculty, students and staff of the Graduate School of Psychology at Fuller Theological Seminary.

The passing of twenty years and the completion of a new revision of this volume offers a whole new array of persons and things for which to give thanks. At the broadest level, this book bears the imprint of the marvelous institution at which we work. As we write, the journal *First Things,* a forum for discussion of the impact of religion in the public sphere, in its November 2010 issue has just declared that "Wheaton College in Illinois is the single best place to go to college in America" (p. 3). While there is certainly room to challenge their methodology, their rankings of the various colleges in America are based on the confluence of three major variables: academic seriousness, social healthiness, and spiritual and theological integrity and thoughtfulness. Their ideal college would be a place where students are mentored by quality faculty at the forefront of their disciplines, where the campus atmosphere encourages growth into responsibility and maturity rather than degeneration into debauchery, and where resources are offered to facilitate growth in Christlikeness. Such a college environment that is healthy for students is equally healthy for the professionals blessed to serve there. Such is Wheaton College.

Since the first version of this book was completed in 1990, dramatic changes have occurred in the study of psychology at Wheaton College. The department has doubled in size, moving from a department of six undergraduate faculty and three graduate faculty serving undergraduate majors and students pursuing a master's degree in clinical psychology to a department of seventeen individuals serving undergraduate and master's students but also a cadre of students pursuing a doctorate in clinical psychology. The addition of so many capable faculty colleagues has multiplied the riches for conversation and reflection on what it means to be a Christian psychologist.

There have also been personal changes for the two of us. Rich moved long ago from the undergraduate faculty to the graduate faculty, focusing increasingly on the teaching of psychopathology and psychological assessment. Stan, after a too brief, one-year stint as the Rech Chair of Psychology and Christian Faith, moved in 1996 to his current role as provost of Wheaton College. While these transitions have continued to foster our reflections on matters of the relationship of psychology and Christian faith, neither one of our positions have allowed us to continue to teach the survey courses in Christian approaches to psychotherapy that formed the basis of our first version of this book.

Thus, this new revision has become a community project. As we began to consider revision of this book, it became abundantly clear that we needed to reach out for help to the extraordinary community of scholars around us who are teaching these different psychotherapy approaches to tap their rich integrated understandings of the various approaches. As is noted in the list of authorship on the table of contents, each colleague took one of our original chapters and revised and updated it. This eventually led to a substantial reorganization of the material of the book. We also added a new chapter on community psychology to broaden our understandings beyond the typical dyadic counselor-client relationship to see broader possibilities for constructive change using the tools of psychology. Our heartfelt thanks go out to our coauthors for their friendship, their expertise and their patience during the long revision process.

Portions of chapter one in the current volume are based on S. L. Jones (2010), "An Integration View," in E. Johnson (Ed.), *Psychology and Christianity: Five views* (2nd ed., pp. 101-128), Downers Grove, IL: InterVarsity Press; used by permission. Portions of chapters five and six were originally based on S. Jones (1988), "A Religious Critique of Behavior Therapy," in W. Miller and J. Martin (Eds.), *Behavior therapy and religion* (pp. 139-170), Newbury Park, CA: Sage; used by permission.

Handling the issue of gender in writing is an ever-troublesome matter. We have chosen to use inclusive terms wherever it did not torture the language to do so. In places where it was not stylistically pleasing to use neutered terms, we have attempted to alternate references to females and males. We were not compulsive in the process, so some unintentional inequities may remain, but we hope not.

Stan will be eternally grateful to Brenna, with profound gratitude for her support, love, patience and encouragement; without her this revised book would never have been completed. Thank you for being excellent in all that you do.

Rich would like to express his deep gratitude to both his immediate and extended families that have stood with him in the good times—and in the difficult and challenging times. Recently, this has included his graduate teaching assistants, Tamara Koch and Stalin George, and his clinical colleagues, Tim Brown, Alex Tsang, Sandy Johnston Kruse, Victor Argo, Terri Watson, William Struthers, Gary Burge, Don Kerns and Rob Ribbe. Finally, he wants to acknowledge the support of his mountaineering friends, who have faced together seemingly innumerable changes, losses and transitions over a span of nearly four decades.

COLLABORATORS

Sally Schwer Canning is associate professor of psychology at Wheaton College and a clinical psychologist at Lawndale Christian Health Center.

Kelly S. Flanagan is a child clinical psychologist, and assistant professor of psychology and Psy.D. program director at Wheaton College.

Tracy Lee is a clinical psychologist working in private practice in Columbus, Ohio, specializing in the area of psychological assessment.

Michael W. Mangis is a clinical psychologist and professor of psychology at Wheaton College.

Mark R. McMinn is a clinical psychologist and professor of psychology at George Fox University.

Laura C. Miguélez is an ordained deacon and works as an adjunct assistant professor of theology at Wheaton College.

David J. Van Dyke is a marriage and family therapist and an associate professor at Illinois School of Professional Psychology.

Michael J. Vogel is pursuing a doctoral degree in clinical psychology from George Fox University.

Robert A. Watson is a clinical psychologist who maintains a clinical and consulting practice in the Chicago area.

Terri S. Watson is a board certified clinical psychologist and an associate professor of psychology at Wheaton College.

INTRODUCTION

❖

*T*his book attempts to appraise each of the current major psychotherapy approaches or theories in the mental health field from the perspective of evangelical Christianity. It is a dialogue between the supposedly nonreligious therapeutic psychologies and the Christian religious and theological tradition. But it is a dialogue where one side of the conversation, that of the Christian faith, is presumed to have the ultimate standing as truth. Nevertheless, we presume that the various psychologies have much to teach us and may in fact lead us to see certain truths of the Christian tradition in a different light.

In 1977, I (Stan) was in the first year of graduate school and while struggling with issues of faith in the context of a highly secular program came across a book written in the 1950s relating Christian faith to the field of psychology. It was authored by one who was at that time one of the most eminent scholars in the field of clinical psychology, someone whose enduring legacy continues to this day. I wrote an enthusiastic letter to this scholar, asking if he had written more in this area. He graciously replied, saying that he was no longer a Christian; he was not sure where he stood religiously, but it was probably closest to Zen Buddhism. But he also added that while he no longer had a personal commitment to the presuppositions from which he wrote in the 1950s, he nevertheless felt that the earlier book was logically sound; that is, the form and content of his analysis stood even though he no longer believed the foundations for what he wrote at that time. Unlike this scholar, we remain passionately committed to the truth of the Christian faith, but consistent with his answer, we seek to provide here a thoughtful analysis of the psychotherapy enterprise that will assist fellow believers in approaching psychotherapy from a distinctively Christian perspective, and which may also yield helpful reflections for nonbelievers on the philosophical and assumptive foundations of their approaches to helping persons change.

Because of our presumption of the truth of the orthodox Christian tradition, this book may be perceived as parochial by some, as it represents only one religious tradition. Our intended audience is students, pastors, mental health professionals, and interested and informed laypersons in the evangelical Christian tradition. But in line with the story of the previously mentioned scholar, we would argue that the form of our analysis stands even if one is not an evangelical Christian. Christians of other stripes, and perhaps even those of non-Christian faith traditions, will, we hope, find this book helpful in outlining the religious implications of the various psychotherapy traditions and in suggesting how religious faith might interact with and revise the way we think about personality and psychotherapy.

When we were writing the first edition of this book in the late 1980s, the "integration of psychology and Christianity" movement was just gaining momentum. In the decade of the 1980s, very few Christian institutions of higher learning had graduate programs in applied psychology, and only two had doctoral programs in clinical psychology (Fuller Theological Seminary and Rosemead School of Psychology at Biola University). At the same time, signs of openness were only beginning in the field of psychology to consideration of religious and spiritual factors affecting the field, and indications of continuing hostility toward religious faith among many in the mental health fields were remarkable.

How things have changed! The integration movement has continued to grow in its volume, complexity and breadth (this is more thoroughly developed in chap. 1). Notably, movements critical of the idea of integration such as the biblical counseling movement have continued to hold sway in certain parts of the conservative Christian church. At the same time, a vibrant movement to endorse a distinct "Christian psychology" approach is prospering, and the integration movement continues as well (all discussed ably in Johnson, 2010). Helpful anthologies tracing the development of these conversations have been published (Stevenson, Eck & Hill,

2007). Training programs in the mental health field have proliferated amazingly; by the mid-1990s, our own Wheaton College had initiated our doctoral program in clinical psychology, and now quite a number of Christian institutions of higher learning are host to doctoral training programs that embody Christian distinctiveness in various ways.

In the meantime, the conversation has changed in the mainstream, secular discipline. We are pleased to have played some role in this process. In 1994, Stan published a key article (Jones, 1994) in what is regarded as the "flagship journal of the American Psychological Association (APA)" (Stevenson et al., 2007, pp. 94-95) arguing for a major shift in professional attitudes toward religion, specifically for a move to consider religion as a partner in constructive dialogue in both the scientific and professional practice dimensions of the discipline of psychology. Whether this article was crucial in what followed or not, its publication marked an opening for a different kind of engagement by the APA with spirituality and religion, namely, that "Prior to this article, the topic of religion (including integration) had been virtually ignored in APA publication materials. Since its publication, the APA has published a number of books and articles (in APA's own journals) stressing the centrality and predictive importance of religious faith in psychological functioning" (Stevenson et al., 2007, p. 95; see for example Shafranske, 1996, and Miller & Delaney, 2005). In short, a good bit of the hostility and resistance to the role of religion and spirituality in life has been ameliorated, replaced by an unprecedented dialogue about the role of such factors in human well-being.

Even so, the degree and nature of this openness should not be overestimated or misunderstood. Our summary judgment is that there is much more openness to generic, humanistically grounded spirituality than there is to substantive religious faith, especially as that religious faith is grounded in formal creeds and ecclesiastical institutions. There is a growing trend in the field to view religious faith and spirituality as a natural human capacity that exists and persists because it serves basic human needs despite its ultimately illusory nature. A recent journalistic account (Azar, 2010) captures this well in its subtitle: "Religion may fill the human need for finding meaning, sparing us from existential angst while also supporting social organization, researchers say." The traditional Christian has every reason to believe that true religion does indeed serve basic human needs, and we would argue that it does so because it is ultimately grounded in a true account of reality; the secular psychology accounts, however, serve to subtly erode such understandings.

This resistance to more formalized versions of religious faith, at times seeming especially directed toward orthodox Christianity, is often subtle, but not always. At this writing, two different court cases, winding their way through the appeals courts, have resulted from graduate students who are traditionalist Christians with conservative moral views of sexuality (particularly homosexual conduct) being ejected from graduate training programs in counseling (i.e., counseling per se as defined by the American Counseling Association, and as differentiated from counseling psychology) for holding views deemed incompatible with and not acceptable in the counseling profession. Even though there is a good case to be made that scientific findings have done little to invalidate the moral concerns of traditional Christians (Jones & Yarhouse, 2000; Jones & Kwee, 2005), and despite the ostensible moral neutrality of the APA and the various other mental health professional organizations, there are signs of movement toward similar reactions against Christian moral stances (also shared by traditionalist Jews, Muslims and Buddhists) in the discipline of psychology (APA, 2009); these moves have been contested (Jones, Rosik, Williams & Byrd, 2010). These are just some of the signs of tension in the relationship between religion and psychology broadly construed. The seeming openness of the field to spirituality should not be engaged naively.

In each of the chapters, we cite recent literature that examines the particular issues and psychotherapies we are addressing. Often this literature will be from the growing and increasingly sophisticated integration literature; at other times it may reflect literature that is a part of the more generic spirituality dialogue of the broader field. In composing this book we and our coauthors have been able to build on the work of many able scholars, to whom we are each heavily indebted.

Before embarking on our study, we will briefly examine the nature of psychotherapy and counseling, since it is vital to have a general picture of the nature of what we are appraising before we focus on the details.

WHAT IS PSYCHOTHERAPY AND COUNSELING?

The topics we will examine in this book are germane to the concerns not just of professional psychologists, but to all mental health workers, pastoral counselors and pastors, and indeed to the concerns of informed laypeople who desire to be effective in their interpersonal ministries. But despite the number of people involved in this endeavor, defining psychotherapy and counseling is quite complicated.

The Problem of Diversity

Psychotherapy is a generic term that covers a wide variety of theories and techniques, all of which have articulate spokespersons and supporters and make claims of success. The varied theories and techniques are derived, for the most part, from clinical experience and reflection rather than deductively from scientific axioms or from systematic empirical research. This helps to explain the proliferation of therapy approaches. They emerge from each theorist's unique experiences of the type of people he or she has seen for counseling, the types of problems they manifest, the cultural context of the therapist, his or her assumptions about how people change, and the core beliefs that shape the therapist's life philosophy. This understandably leaves wide room for diverse approaches to people-helping.

There are an incredible array of approaches. Not only are there numerous major theories, but each seems to have a number of variations as well. Even twenty-five years ago, leading experts had identified 260 distinct schools of psychotherapy (Strupp & Binder, 1984); since then, many of these have drifted into obscurity only to be replaced by other unique approaches. Certainly, many of these approaches are kissing cousins rather than truly unique approaches.

Since many approaches to psychotherapy claim impressive results, it is difficult to evaluate critically the ultimate worth of a particular theory or technique. One must get the broad perspective when assessing the value of a specific system: Who is working with whom, under what conditions and assumptions, and on what particular problems and concerns? There is an ever-present danger of the overenthusiastic extrapolation of a theory or technique to client populations or problems for which it was never intended, or for which there is little or no reason to suggest its effectiveness. For example, the unquestionable effectiveness of behavior modification with many autistic children (Lovaas, 1987) has little bearing on its use with adults struggling with the meaning of life. Likewise, counselors should be appropriately humble in their pronouncements about their theories and techniques, though we don't know of a single counseling approach that hasn't in some form claimed to be the true and best way.

Defining Psychotherapy and Counseling

In light of all this diversity, it is not surprising that academicians, clinicians and researchers have found it difficult to agree on a specific definition of counseling and psychotherapy. As London (1964) noted, many find it easier to practice the art and science of people-helping than to describe it.

Still, across theories and techniques there appear to be some common features. In fact, many theoreticians and researchers today argue that these common factors influence, or even determine, the likelihood of a successful therapeutic outcome. Some approaches to understanding these common factors focus on the common techniques that all psychotherapists seem to use (though with differing frequencies). A classic work from thirty years ago (Garfield, 1980) concluded that most psychotherapy comprises varying mixtures of four basic interventions offered by the therapist or counselor: (1) offering reassurance and support, (2) desensitizing the client to distress, (3) encouraging adaptive functioning, and (4) offering understanding and insight. While clearly there are some intervention strategies that don't fit in any of these categories, this analysis still has some validity. Understanding these common features can be helpful as one tries to define counseling.

Another recent approach to the investigation of common-factors focuses is not on technique but on variables that seem to determine or shape the outcome of any counseling approach. As we will explore more in chapter eleven, McMinn and Campbell (2007) interpret the best meta-analytic empirical research on psychotherapy to indicate that the key variables that influence positive outcome include specific psychotherapeutic techniques, but more importantly expectancy effects (the degree of hopefulness and optimism versus pessimism of the client), the quality of the relationship between the counselor and client, and the degree of contextual or situational support (or lack thereof, or even stressfulness and aversiveness) in the person's immediate environment.

We would describe individual counseling or psychotherapy as a dyadic (two-way) interaction between a client who is distressed, and perhaps confused and frightened, and a professional helper whose helping skills are recognized and accepted by the client. The two engage in an ongoing, private, collaborative encounter that is structured as to time, place and overall purpose in a way that informal friendships are not. The relationship is likely to rely heavily on verbal communication of the client's thoughts, feelings, attitudes and behaviors. The client comes to believe in and develop hope from what happens in therapy, in part because the therapist appears to have a theory for understanding and explaining the client's distress as well as having intervention techniques for reducing it. In a supportive atmosphere with an empathetic and caring therapist, the client begins to disclose and reevaluate feelings and behavior patterns, to understand and accept previously rejected aspects of herself, to take risks, to become more open and honest about herself, to learn new methods of living with self and others, and to gain new satisfactions from life. With the client having less need for the psychotherapy, the process is usually terminated by mutual consent with the therapist (adapted from Frank, 1961; Garfield, 1980; and particularly Goldenberg, 1983, pp. 172ff.). While this definition assumes that the client is an individual, increasingly practitioners of psychotherapy are open to the client being a couple, a family, a group or a larger system.

Given that counseling and psychotherapy is so intensely personal and yet is regarded as a professional rather than personal relationship, how is psychotherapy and counseling different from friendship? As is commonly observed, a lot of good counseling goes on over cups of coffee, in the barber shop or over a backyard fence; perhaps a lot more than goes on during any given day in the offices of psychotherapists (Matarazzo & Wiens, 1972). There are some important differences, though. Ideally, the therapist is able to avoid undue emotional involvement with the client so as to be more objective, allowing the client to more freely communicate his thoughts and feelings (Copans & Singer, 1978). The therapist's personal qualities and the environment she creates encourage risk taking and facilitate the acquisition of skills and sensitivities that will foster the development of health and wholeness. Perhaps the most important distinction between psychotherapy and friendship is that the former is by definition a one-way relationship emotionally and psychologically, and it is the client who is supposed to derive good from the interchange. The growth and healing of the therapist is not the purpose of this limited and purposeful relationship (Korchin, 1976). Friendships, on the other hand, are ideally mutually beneficial emotionally and psychologically, and are not structured intentionally for the benefit of only one of the parties involved. It is obvious, though, that we cannot say that psychotherapists derive no benefit from the therapeutic relationship, as financial, professional and social benefits certainly can and do accrue to the psychotherapist who is effective.

Are Psychotherapy and Counseling Different?

An important and often hotly debated question that is no more settled today than it was thirty years ago is how psychotherapy and counseling are to be differentiated (McLemore, 1974). The traditional distinction promulgated by doctoral-level practitioners has been that counseling is done by less comprehensively and intensively trained professionals (e.g., pastors, school guidance counselors) and by paraprofessionals (lay counselors or mental health volunteers). It is done with less seriously disturbed groups of persons, such as those struggling with decisions of what career to pursue, whether or not to get married and so forth. Counseling has often been regarded as relying heavily on the giving of wise advice as a major mode of intervention.

Historically, psychotherapy was thought to be more appropriate for "deeper" problems and was most often done by more highly trained or certified therapists. The focus was on significant personality change rather than adjustment to situational and life problems. It is sometimes said that psychotherapy attempts significantly to change the personality of clients, often paying less attention to specific current life problems, while counseling works within existing personality structures to help people adjust to the current demands on them.

Although some authors still prefer to make a distinction between counseling and psychotherapy, we have chosen to use the terms interchangeably in this text for two main reasons. The first is that clinical and counseling psychology, which were once substantially different disciplines and arose out of different historical roots, have grown closer together over the last several decades. The distinctions between the two subdisciplines were hard to make out twenty-five years ago (see Altmaier, 1985) and are even harder today. Notably, among the doctoral-level faculty in our own clinical psychology faculty at Wheaton College are a number of respected colleagues whose doctorates are in counseling psychology.

Perhaps more importantly, we will not make the distinctions here because the very same theories are utilized as guides for the change process by psychotherapists and counselors. Survey textbooks for counseling theories and methods, and for psychotherapy theories and methods, contain almost identical content. While there can be different emphases in books to the two professional populations, the basic theories are not different.

STRUCTURE OF THE BOOK

Our perspective in this book is decidedly psychological and spiritual. In taking this perspective we do not wish to minimize the clear importance of the biological/physical perspective on mental health, nor of the sociological/sociocultural perspective (Yarhouse, Butman & McRay, 2005). But our focus will be on the current interactional psychotherapies. We believe that a careful critique of these approaches is important for the Christian world today.

We also believe that psychologists do not have the final word in understanding humanness, suffering and growth. If anything, psychologists have been saying too much and the populace has been listening too much. It is no wonder that many today describe psychologists as the "secular priests" of our age. We believe that the centrality of religious reflection must be reasserted, as well as the value of philosophical, artistic, literary and other facets of our human ways of knowing.

Psychotherapy has assumed a position of high visibility and importance in many sectors of our American society. Our goal is to come to a new understanding of this field in order that we might more effectively participate in the work that God is doing in and through his church. The needs of contemporary society are creating new and potentially challenging roles for Christians who desire to minister in the name of Christ to a hurting world. We believe strongly that a greater awareness and knowledge of both the assets and liabilities of the major psychotherapy approaches can contribute in a significant way to the larger mission and work of the church.

As we mention in our acknowledgments, the most significant change in this book, as we move from the first edition to the second, is our indebtedness to numerous coauthors who have worked to create new versions of each chapter in this book. We believe the diverse perspectives that these coauthors bring added new richness and vitality to our work.

This book is structured in three parts. In the two introductory chapters we have outlined a summary of our view of what it means to relate or integrate the Christian faith with a field like psychology or psychotherapy theory.

Chapter one discusses this process in general terms and deals with some important and frequently expressed objections (at least in conservative circles) to such an approach. Since an examination of psychotherapy from a Christian perspective must proceed from a foundational Christian understanding of persons, chapter two focuses specifically on the broad strokes of our Christian view of persons. Having clarified our method and the Christian view of persons, we then proceed into the heart of our appraisal.

Chapters three through ten cover a variety of approaches to psychotherapy. The four major paradigms in the field today are the psychodynamic, the cognitive-behavioral, the humanistic, and the family approaches; in a real sense, we devote two chapters to each of these four major paradigms. The most important representatives of each of these traditions are examined from our Christian perspective. Each chapter will begin with a summary presentation of each model; the interested reader can get a more exhaustive presentation of these approaches by consulting the volumes suggested for further reading at the end of this introduction and at the end of each chapter.

The book will conclude with an examination of how one can profitably draw from more than one approach in elaborating one's approach to counseling (chap. 11) and a discussion of what it means to be a Christian counselor (chap. 12). Our main premise in these concluding chapters is that there are many ways to counsel Christianly. But it is not and cannot be the case that "anything goes." We hope that our suggestions in these concluding chapters will help the process of putting it all together for the reader.

This volume is offered in fervent hope that it will instigate and support the rigorous development of thoroughly Christian mental health professionals who will manifest and embody biblical truth as they serve those in need of quality mental health services.

FOR FURTHER READING

Browning, D. S., & Cooper, T. D. (2004). *Religious thought and the modern psychologies* (2nd ed.). Minneapolis, MN: Fortress.

Corey, G. (2009). *Theory and practice of counseling and psychotherapy* (8th ed.). Belmont, CA: Thomson/Brooks Cole.

Corey, M. S., & Corey, G. (2011). *Becoming a helper* (6th ed.). Belmont, CA: Brooks/Cole.

Corsini, R. (2008). *Current psychotherapies* (8th ed.). Belmont, CA: Brooks/Cole.
   Some of the many accessible textbooks providing broad overviews of the current theories and practices in psychotherapy and counseling.

Johnson, E. F. (Ed.). (2010). *Psychology and Christianity: Five views* (2nd ed.).
   Downers Grove, IL: InterVarsity Press.
   The best "one-stop shop" to read about the dialogue over how Christian faith
   and psychology can relate.

McMinn, M., & Campbell, C. (2007). *Integrative psychotherapy: Toward a comprehensive Christian approach.* Downers Grove, IL: IVP Academic.

Tan, S. Y. (2011). *Counseling and psychotherapy: A Christian perspective.* Grand
   Rapids, MI: Baker Academic.
   Representative samples of the kinds of rigorous Christian engagement avail-
   able in reflecting on psychotherapy.

REFERENCES

Altmaier, K. (1985). Counseling psychology. In D. Benner (Ed.), *Baker encyclopedia of psychology* (pp. 252-254). Grand Rapids, MI: Baker.

APA Task Force on Appropriate Therapeutic Responses to Sexual Orientation.
   (2009). Report of the Task Force on Appropriate Therapeutic Responses to
   Sexual Orientation. Retrieved from www.apa.org/pi/lgbt/resources/therapeutic
   -response.pdf.

Azar, B. (2010, December). A reason to believe. *APA Monitor on Psychology*,
   41(11), 52-55.

Copans, S., & Singer, T. (1978). *Who's the patient here?* New York, NY: Oxford
   University Press.

Corey, G. (2009). *Theory and practice of counseling and psychotherapy* (8th ed.). Belmont, CA: Thomson/Brooks Cole.

Corey, M. S., & Corey, G. (2011). *Becoming a helper.* (6th ed.). Belmont, CA:
   Brooks/Cole.

Corsini, R. (2008). *Current psychotherapies* (8th ed.). Belmont, CA: Brooks/Cole.

Frank, J. (1961). *Persuasion and healing.* Baltimore, MD: Johns Hopkins University Press.

Frank, J. (1973). *Persuasion and healing.* (Rev. ed.). Baltimore, MD: Johns Hopkins University Press.

Garfield, S. (1980). *Psychotherapy: An eclectic approach.* New York, NY: Wiley-
   Interscience.

Goldenberg, D. (1983). *Contemporary clinical psychology* (2nd ed.). Monterey, CA:
   Brooks/Cole.

Johnson, E. F. (Ed.). (2010). *Psychology and Christianity: Five views* (2nd ed.). Downers Grove, IL: InterVarsity Press.

Jones, S. L. (1994). A constructive relationship for religion with the science and profession of psychology: Perhaps the boldest model yet. *American Psychologist, 49*(3), 184-199.

Jones, S., & Kwee, A. W. (2005). Scientific research, homosexuality, and the church's moral debate: An update. *Journal of Psychology and Christianity, 24*(4), 304-316.

Jones, S., Rosik, C. H., Williams, R. N., & Byrd, A. D. (2010). A scientific, conceptual, and ethical critique of the Report of the APA Task Force on Sexual Orientation. *The General Psychologist, 45*(2), 7-18.

Jones, S., & Yarhouse, M. (2000). Homosexuality: The use of scientific research in the church's moral debate. Downers Grove, IL: InterVarsity Press.

Korchin, S. (1976). *Modern clinical psychology.* New York, NY: Basic Books.

London, P. (1964). *The modes and morals of psychotherapy.* Washington, DC: Hemisphere.

London, P. (1986). *The modes and morals of psychotherapy* (2nd ed.). Washington, DC: Hemisphere.

Lovaas, O. (1987). Behavioral treatment and normal educational and intellectual functioning in young autistic children. *Journal of Consulting and Clinical Psychology, 55*(1), 3-9.

McLemore, C. W. (1974). *Clergyman's psychological handbook.* Grand Rapids, MI: Eerdmans.

Matarazzo, J., & Wiens, A. (1972). *The interview: Research on its anatomy and structure.* Chicago, IL: Aldine.

McMinn, M., & Campbell, C. (2007). *Integrative psychotherapy: Toward a comprehensive Christian approach.* Downers Grove, IL: IVP Academic.

Miller, W. R., & Delaney, H. D. (Eds.). (2005). *Human nature, motivation, and change: Judeo-Christian perspectives on psychology.* Washington, DC: American Psychological Association.

Shafranske, E. (Ed.). (1996). *Religion and the clinical practice of psychology.* Washington, DC: American Psychological Association.

Stevenson, D. H., Eck, B. E., & Hill, P. C. (Eds.). (2007). *Psychology and Christianity integration: Seminal works that shaped the movement.* Batavia, IL: Christian Association for Psychological Studies.

Strupp, H., & Binder, D. (1984). *Psychotherapy in a new key.* New York, NY: Basic Books.

Yarhouse, M., Butman, R., & McRay (2005). *Modern psychopathologies: A comprehensive Christian appraisal.* Downers Grove, IL: InterVarsity Press.

THE INTEGRATION OF PSYCHOLOGY AND CHRISTIANITY

Stanton L. Jones and Richard E. Butman

Christian counselors and psychotherapists are vitally concerned with understanding the human condition, fostering human flourishing and alleviating human suffering. Our field has arisen in a time when it is painfully obvious that improving our standard of living and our physical health does not guarantee anyone a sense of personal well-being. Far too many people are in emotional, mental or spiritual pain.

Out of a desire to improve the human condition and alleviate suffering, many Christians today are interested in the mental health fields. There is a strong desire to enrich Christian ministry by drawing upon the resources of the evolving field of psychology and its related disciplines. What thoughtful pastor or counselor would not want to use all available knowledge and techniques to make his or her people-helping as effective as possible?

But there is also considerable ambivalence about and outright opposition to drawing upon the strengths of psychology among some conservative Christians. Some describe the field of psychotherapy as "satanic" or "completely secularized" and "unredeemable." While in graduate school, one of us (Stan) spoke to Jay Adams, the founding father of "Biblical Counseling." I asked if he had any words of guidance for Christians studying psychology, to which Adams responded, in essence, "Drop out of graduate school. If you want to serve God as a counselor, you can only do so by going to seminary, studying the Word of God rather than the words of men, and becoming a pastor."

Neither one of us took Dr. Adams's advice. We have, however, tried to maintain our foundational commitments to Jesus Christ in our work as psychologists. This book is the fruit of the working out of that goal. It covers a significant aspect of what we believe it means to be a Christian psychologist, mental health professional, counselor or psychotherapist.

This book is about thinking Christianly about contemporary approaches to psychotherapy and counseling. We strongly believe that it is not enough simply to pray for clients, or to refrain from discouraging their spiritual sensitivities, or to have high ethical standards while the Christian psychotherapist otherwise uses the methods and practices of theories and methods derived from secular sources. Every theory or method of people-helping carries with it a system of beliefs, a way of seeing or understanding people: who they are, why they experience what they do, how they can change and what they should be aiming for in life. As Browning and Cooper (2004) put it, psychological science (and particularly the applied psychologies) "cannot avoid a metaphysical and ethical horizon" (p. xiv). These theoretical suppositions may or may not conflict with direct assertions of the Christian faith or with more indirect implications of the faith. *It is because we feel that these theories of psychotherapy have often been either summarily dismissed or uncritically embraced by Christians that we have attempted to provide a balanced appraisal of these views from a Christian perspective.*

In this first chapter we want to set our foundations by grappling with the core of how a religious faith should interact with the seemingly "secular" and "scientific" field of psychotherapy. Since this task is often called "the integration of psychology and Christianity" or of "psychology and theology," the core of this chapter is a discussion of what *integration* means. We approach this in two stages, discussing first the general stance of the Christian toward "secular knowledge," then moving to the more specific issue of our stance toward "psychological knowledge and science." We will then briefly discuss criticisms from various directions of the integration movement and conclude with a discussion of the specific integration methodology we will use to appraise or critique the various approaches to psychotherapy.

HOW DOES CHRISTIANITY RELATE TO "SECULAR KNOWLEDGE"?

Being a Christian is easy when faith is contained in a "spiritual" corner of one's life. But the living God has a mind of his own. Not being content with such limits, he often breaks out into the rest of our lives and lays claim to territory we had not yet thought about deeding over to him.

Often he first lays claim to our moral lives, with the result that we discover that being a Christian entails confronting and struggling with our selfishness, jealousy, anger, pettiness or rebelliousness. This often has implications for our vocational lives, such as when we must curtail unethical practices or when we must reassess the values that have energized us for years.

But God can lay claim to our thought lives as well. Do we need to think differently about politics, science, art, philosophy and indeed all areas of life as a result of our faith? Indeed we do. The claims of the gospel are all-inclusive, spanning every dimension of our private and public lives, because Christ has been declared the Lord of all (Col 1:15-20).

What does it mean for sincere Christians to relate their religious beliefs and faith to an area not overtly or obviously religious or theological? There is a distinctive Christian position on the nature of God and of salvation, but is there a correct Christian position on literary criticism, on thermodynamics, on the nature of human memory, on the fundamental motivations of human personality or on the nature of depression? Answering this general question on the relation of faith and scholarship or science has absorbed the energies of many Christian thinkers over the centuries.

This is not a new question. Thanks to the work of faithful believers over at least three millennia, we have abundant examples to follow in answering this question, examples that are too little known among Christian students today. Let's begin with the Old Testament's description of the "wise man" or "sage."

Derek Tidball (1986) points out that in ancient Jewish society, before the coming of Christ, there were three types of "pastors": priests, prophets and wise men. "The objective of the wise men was to provide down-to-earth counsel about the ordinary affairs of life" (Tidball, 1986, p. 43); thus, it seems to us that there are many parallels between the wise man role in ancient Jewish life and the role mental health professionals serve in contemporary American life. Tidball suggests that the wise men did not often provide their counsel according to explicit divine revelation; they were grappling with practical matters which simply were not a preoccupation of God's revelatory energies. In other words, they dealt with matters for which no simple recourse to "the Bible says X" was possible. "Their approach was to consider, with steady logic, the truth which was hidden within human nature and creation in order to discover the regularities which could form the basis of their lives and counsel" (Tidball, 1986, p. 43). The provision of such wisdom is a prime duty of the Christian psychotherapist, for whom it is vital to remember, as did these wise men, that true wisdom begins with "the fear of the LORD" (Prov 1:7).

Tidball seems to suggest that there are two primary elements of the wise man's or sage's methodology: grounding their approach in God's word in the Scriptures, and then searching in human experience with "steady logic" for enduring truth. In a recent volume Coe and Hall (2010a, b) also urged that Christian psychology be founded on following the model of the sage, and, like Tidball, seem to suggest the same two methodological elements. On this basis Coe and Hall argue that "the Old Testament sage's psychology is not an act of integration; rather, it is one single, though complex, act of doing a science or psychology" (2010b, p. 155). Unfortunately, Coe and Hall are simply wrong that the work of the sage is not an act of integration in nature, and their specific citation of Proverbs 24 as a prototype of the work of the sage is helpful in establishing why.

Coe and Hall seem bothered that the integrationist turns to and engages secular sources of wisdom to expand our knowledge, striving to make sense of such secular knowledge within our deeper Christian intellectual commitments. But it turns out that this is *exactly* what the Old Testament sage or wise man did. In addition to being grounded in God's Word and using steady logic about what we observe of human nature, the very Old Testament sages that wrote Proverbs and Ecclesiastes did what we are here calling integration.

The author of Ecclesiastes, thought by many scholars to be King Solomon, calls himself "Qoheleth," which can be translated teacher, preacher or sage.[1] And in explaining his own methodology, he writes "He pondered and searched out and set in order many proverbs. The Teacher [i.e., Qo-

---

[1]Treier (forthcoming) argues compellingly that the best translation of Qoheleth is Sage.

heleth] searched to find just the right words, and what he wrote was upright and true" (Eccles 12:9-10). Just how far-reaching was that search for proverbs by Qoheleth? Quite extensive, it turns out. Proverbs 24, as well as Proverbs 31 and other passages in these two wisdom books, are heavily influenced by pagan wisdom literature. As I argued elsewhere (Jones, 2011), it turns out that the sages who wrote the Old Testament wisdom literature were well grounded in the Hebrew Scriptures and skilled in steady logic, but also facile in the pagan, secular literature of the day. The sages who composed Proverbs were discerning editors and compilers, integrationists who appropriated good ideas from secular literature, adapted them and built on them.

Recognition that Proverbs 24 is just such a passage is so widespread that it has made its way into the notations of prominent evangelical study Bibles. The *English Standard Version Study Bible* notes that Proverbs 22:17–24:22 or "The Thirty Sayings of 'The Wise'" reflects "an awareness of the Egyptian wisdom text, *The Instruction of Amenemope*, dated to about 1250 B.C. Clearly [the sage/author] did not slavishly copy *Amenemope*, but there are many affinities in content" (p. 1173; see also the *New International Version Archeological Study Bible*). Far from slavishly copying, theologian Daniel Treier argues that the sage/author always adapted what he drew from secular literature to godly purposes: "the most important features for interpreting particular proverbs [drawn from pagan sources] concern their recontextualization within or relation to the fear of YHWH, Israel's God" (forthcoming, p. 113 in ms.; see also Waltke, 2004, 2005). So we have evidence already in the Old Testament of the value of appropriating secular wisdom to God's purposes, if that work is done with due diligence to remain faithful to God's revealed Word.

Let us now move into the New Testament era, the era of the church. Among conservative Christians today, many assume that a "Bible only" stance of antagonism toward "secular knowledge" is what has marked "real Christians" for two millennia. Often unwittingly, they adopt a posture mimicking one of the most prolific early church fathers, Tertullian (c. A.D. 160-220), who wrote (taking "Athens" as a metaphor for secular Greek philosophical wisdom and "Jerusalem" for the wisdom of the Bible as directly inspired by God):

What indeed does Athens have to do with Jerusalem? What concord is there between the [philosophical] Academy and the Church? What between heretics and Christians? . . . Away with all attempts to produce a mottled Christianity of Stoic, Platonic, and dialectic composition! We want no curious disputation after possessing Christ Jesus, no inquisition after enjoying the Gospel! With our faith, we desire no other belief. For this is our palmary faith, that there is nothing which we ought to believe besides. (in Geehan, 1971, p. vi)

Sadly, Christians who adopt such a stance are unaware that Tertullian was himself a brilliant product of a broad, humanistic education in the very Academy he mocks in this quote, and that he drew capably and well on that broad background in service of the gospel as he wrote apologetics and theological works. In this quote he was engaging in a bit of preacherly hyperbole to make a particular point; the quote in isolation considerably exaggerates his true position on the value of secular knowledge.

It is more important to note that the early church never systematically embraced any such repudiation of secular knowledge. Indeed, engagement with secular knowledge has always been important to the church. Philosopher Arthur Holmes's *Building the Christian Academy* (2001) gives an exceptionally readable introduction to this fascinating history. Holmes discusses how the earliest Christian liberal arts academy was established in Alexandria, Egypt, in the third century. The term *liberal arts* in the ancient world had nothing to do with today's political liberalism. It was an ancient Greek term by which they distinguished the type of technical education suitable for slaves, whose job was to do specific tasks, from the education suitable for *liberated* peoples—the free citizens of the state, whose role was to guide the civic order by their wisdom and breadth of learning. As opposed to technical education, the liberal arts centered on the *trivium* (the three arts of language—grammar, logic and rhetoric or persuasion) and the *quadrivium* (the four mathematical arts—arithmetic, geometry, astronomy and music). A liberal arts education was presumed applicable to everything; it ideally equipped the student to reflect deeply and critically on the current state of affairs, preparing the citizen to lead.

According to Holmes (2001), the first Christian liberal arts academy was established almost eighteen centuries ago for four reasons, reasons as relevant today as then: (1) to interact with the best thinking of unbelievers for the sake of evangelism and apologetics to reach nonbelievers with the gospel, (2) to learn from non-Christian thought, since clearly nonbelievers can think rigorously and well, and it would be arrogant of Christians to think that they have nothing to learn from non-Christian thought, (3) to worship and honor God, who is truth in himself and the source and the author of everything, by thinking broadly and well, and (4) to provide a holistic education of both mind and character, fostering growth both in intellect and in personal maturation, out of recognition that we are unitary beings whose minds are interconnected with our hearts and souls.

Holmes (2001) summarizes some of the high points of the Christian academy over the ensuing centuries. He mentions the great monasteries of the medieval period, where monks that loved God and loved knowledge preserved learning through the Dark Ages. There were direct connections between such monasteries and the establishment of the first great universities at Bologna, Paris, Oxford and Cambridge, universities that began as training schools for clergy, yet were comprehensive in their curricula; the founders of these institutions originally saw learning as an outgrowth of sincere Christian faith and a liberal arts education as necessarily done in the context of Christian reflection on the subject matter.

Theologian Don Browning (2010) recently sketched one particularly pivotal moment in the church's engagement with secular knowledge. For centuries the great thinkers of the church had focused on the writings of Plato for their dialogue with secular thought, but one millennium ago in Spain and Sicily, the medieval intellectual world was shaken and revitalized by the rediscovery of the texts of Aristotle. These texts had been lost in the Christian world but preserved in the Islamic world, and as these two worlds collided in Spain and Sicily, the texts of Aristotle became the focus of an intellectual dialogue among Islamic, Jewish and Christian scholars. This rich dialogue spurred forward the explosive progress of science and the humanities in the following centuries. The work of Thomas Aquinas, whom many consider the greatest mind ever to work in the Christian tradition, is clearly indebted to the fruits of this religious dialogue.

Returning to Holmes (2001), his next focus for discussion of the Christian academy is on the heroes of the Protestant Reformation, whose indebtedness to their engagement with secular learning is remarkable. John Calvin, for example, is often described today as a theologian, but in truth he was educated in the humanities (liberal arts) and specifically in the field of law. So also Jonathan Edwards, whom many regard as the most capable scholar America has ever produced, was deeply shaped by his liberal arts education.

In the following two centuries Christianity in general and Protestantism in particular fostered the development of modern science by (1) providing a theological foundation for an embrace of physical reality as good and worthy of study, (2) emboldening the search for universal laws by construing the physical world as the engineering of a universal law-giver who had left imprinted on the world the traces of his rational mind, (3) inspiring empirical research by emphasizing God's free will in creating, such that the structure of the world could not be deduced by the armchair philosopher but had to be discovered by the empirical researcher, and (4) providing personal motives for scientists such as improving the world to bring glory to God or helping to provide rational evidence for God's existence (Brooke, 1991). In this early period of what is often called modernism, faith was not seen as antagonistic to science, rationality or knowledge at all, and so it was common for great figures in science such as Francis Bacon, Nicholas Copernicus, Galileo Galelei, Blaise Paschal, Isaac Newton and many others to be devout Christians of various sorts while standing as dominant figures in their scientific fields.

But it is in the 1800s and 1900s that we begin to see why it makes sense to talk about "integration," because during this period faith and learning became disintegrated and fragmented from each other. In the late modern period the intellectual movement called the Enlightenment drove a deep wedge between faith and reason. For very complicated reasons, religion, tradition and authority came to be seen as the enemy of knowledge (Toulmin, 1990). What emerged over time was a view that "facts" were produced by logic or by empirical science, whereas religion was ultimately about values, ethics or about some other undeniable, ethereal aspect of human experience that had nothing to do with the world of facts (Johnson, 2010b; Jones, 2010). Increasingly, faith was seen as the enemy of knowledge, ushering in our situation today where so many of the "new atheists," such as Richard Dawkins, trumpet science as the antithesis of religious faith. And these developments have had a profound impact on educational institutions as well; whereas the original mentality in the great universities of the world was that theology was the "queen of the sciences," today, religion has been driven from, or to the periphery at, most of the universities, and these schools are often experienced by Christians as communities of great hostility toward orthodox faith (e.g., Marsden, 1994).

HOW DOES CHRISTIANITY RELATE TO SECULAR PSYCHOLOGY? THE INTEGRATION VIEW

It is in this intellectual context that contemporary psychology has come to maturity (or what passes for maturity). As Jones (1994), Johnson (2010b) and many others have discussed, almost every movement in psychology has had a facet of antagonism toward, dismissal of or the impulse to explain away religious faith in general and often Christianity in particular. The psychologies of Sigmund Freud, B. F. Skinner, Carl Rogers and others are often explicit (and contemptuous) in their dismissal of Christianity, and thus appropriation of what is of value from these approaches takes great care and discernment.

Even though Christians ought to approach the topic of psychology believing in and celebrating the unity of all knowledge in Christ, the practical reality we encounter is a field of knowledge that has become disintegrated and fragmented. Vast swaths of the discipline of psychology contain implicit or explicit commitments antagonistic to Christian faith, as the chapters that follow in this book will illustrate. The task of the integrationist in this present circumstance is to bring back together that which God intended as a seamless whole but which in present reality lies fragmented.

We use this term *integration* even though we regard it as problematic. The word implies that things that don't naturally mix must willfully be brought into connection, to be integrated. This is surely not the vision of faith and scholarship that we are advocating, as we believe that faith and scholarship naturally and inevitably interrelate.

We will not often refer to the integration of psychology and *theology* (i.e., the academic discipline), because this implies that the goal is the fusing together of what are and should properly be two distinct conceptual disciplines. Surely integration is misguided if it is directed at creating a new academic discipline, such as "psychotheology" or "theopsychology."

There are a number of different approaches to understanding the integration of Christian faith with the discipline of psychology.[2] Indeed, a plethora of articles and books have been dedicated to sorting and resorting these approaches. Years ago Jones (1986) characterized the main three approaches to integration as (1) *ethical integration*, the focus on the application of faith-based moral principles to the *practice* of science (including, in this case, the professions of psychotherapy); (2) *perspectival integration*, the view that scientific and religious views of any aspect of reality are independent, with the result that scientific/psychological views and religious understandings complement but don't really affect each other (e.g., Jeeves, 1976; this view has come to be called the levels-of-explanation view); and (3) *humanizer or Christianizer of science integration*, an approach that involves the explicit incorporation of religiously based beliefs as the control beliefs that shape the perceptions of acts, theories and methods in social science (e.g., Evans, 1977, 1989; or Van Leeuwen, 1985). Let us use this same grid to understand the basic layout of the discussion of the relationship of psychology and Christianity today, but broaden the final category of humanizer or Christianizer approaches into two groups as follows.

- *Ethical integration*. Practitioners of variations of the ethical approach have found particular expression recently among Anabaptist Christians. For instance, out of their basic theological commitments, Jacobsen and Jacobsen (2004) suggest that the primary goal of the Christian scholar should be to "strike up the friendships [with secular scholars] that might lead to mutual respect and cooperation" (p. 24). Relationships become the primary ethical imperative for the Christian scholar. Any approach to scholarship that is not first premised on an imperative of cooperation, in this view, is suspect. These authors emphasize the contours of friendship over truth claims of Christian faith, arguing that "Christian

---

[2]Much of the discussion of these issues of integration has been influenced by recent developments in the philosophy of science. We wish to acknowledge immediately that the field of psychotherapy does not conform in all ways to the common meaning of the term *science*. In other words, we are not treating the terms *science, psychology* and *psychotherapy* as equivalent. But we would argue, on the other hand, that the most central issues in relating religious faith to a putatively nonreligious area of scholarship have been illuminated by discussions of the hardest case, that of science, since science is supposedly the human activity with the least to do with other ways of human knowing. What we are after in this section are the lessons that have been learned about the general character of integration from the dialogue about relating faith to science generally and the scientific discipline of psychology in particular. These lessons will form the context for our specific discussion of psychotherapy.

scholars will probably need to develop a range of new, less grandiose ways of relating faith and learning that are more attuned to contemporary scholarly practices" (p. 28). They seem to prioritize cooperation and acceptance, and to be averse to conflict with the secular academy.

Another Anabaptist ethical work is the proposal of Dueck and Reimer (2009) for a "peaceable psychology." While much more open than the Jacobsens to conflict with the secular academy (indeed, they are adamant in their criticisms of the field of psychology), Dueck and Reimer are not at all prone to propose that we seek out approaches to Christian scholarship that conform to secular standards. Indeed, they call Christians to construct a distinctive psychology, both theoretical and therapeutic, that is driven by its allegiance to Christ in its being marked by ethical commitments to peacemaking and reconciliation. Their approach clearly is driven by its ethical dimension.

The levels-of-explanation and Christianizer approaches are well on display in Johnson (2010a), who in *Psychology and Christianity: Five Views* portrays the levels-of-explanation view and two variants of the humanizer or Christianizer of science approach, namely (1) integration, and (2) Christian psychology (in three variations).

- *Levels-of-explanation.* Myers (2010) defends the levels-of-explanation view, arguing that scientific and religious views of any aspect of reality are to some degree independent. Myers is particularly motivated to defend the integrity of science as a unique and successful method to develop knowledge. Myers argues first that much of religious discourse—the teachings of Scripture and of theology—is less about empirical reality (the particular domain of science) and more about the values, purposes, morality, meanings and significance of our experiences. Where the teachings of Scripture and of theology touch on the world of facts, those teachings are simply too vague, imprecise or inconsistent to substantively guide science. The result is that scientific/psychological views and religious understandings complement but don't really affect each other. We will jump over the integration view, returning to it later.

- *Christian psychology.* Three examples of Christian psychology approaches are presented: Roberts and Watson (2010) present what they

term the Christian psychology view, Coe and Hall (2010a) the transformational psychology view, and Powlison (2010) the biblical counseling view. What marks these views in common is their claim that the
unique resources of the Christian tradition, including the Scriptures
themselves and the great theological resources of the church, including
the pastoral and psychological works of many of the great thinkers of
the church, can provide some definitive starting points for shaping and
determining our fundamental starting points in constructing an approach to psychology such that we can develop a (emphasis on the singular) distinctive Christian approach to psychology. The biblical counseling approach (Powlison, 2010) is marked by yet further independence
from secular psychology in comparison to the other Christian psychology views, such that while academic psychology might be of some intellectual value, in the applied world of counseling for hurting persons
resources from the psychological disciplines are deemed as having almost no value whatsoever in favor of the sufficient resources that can be
gleaned from the Bible itself.

- *Integration approach.* So how is the integration view different? What
  defines it? Jones (2010) argues that what is right about the levels-of-
  explanation view is its high valuing of science properly conducted and
  the knowledge that we obtain from it. What is right about the Christian psychology and biblical counseling approaches is their high valuing
  of the truth we obtain about the human condition from the Scriptures
  and the Christian tradition, and also their insistence that these truths
  from Christian sources should shape the contours of our understandings of persons and thus influence how we do psychological science and
  how we practice the mental health professions.

Further details about concerns an integrationist has with the other
views can be found in the specific responses Jones wrote to each in the
Johnson (2010a) volume. But at the broadest level the integration view
contrasts with the levels-of-explanation view in arguing that even how we
conduct and interpret science will be shaped by our Christian convictions.
Christians must ask then whether they can absorb unfiltered the products
of secular scientific inquiry, and further ask if Christian understandings of
the person might lead us to ask different questions, develop different hy-

potheses, utilize different methods of inquiry and start from different fundamental convictions than unbelieving scientists.

More subtle to grasp are the differences between the integration view and the Christian psychology approaches. These other views argue for a specific approach that emerges as "the" Christian approach to understanding persons, "the" Christian approach to psychology, whereas the integration view posits that the result of our Christian engagement will be a family of views that share a sibling resemblance to each other based in their common commitments to biblically grounded truths. We are tempted to argue that the very structure of the Five Views book (Johnson, 2010a) proves our point, in that the three Christian psychology approaches each claim to be "the" Christian approach, and yet each of the three disagree in fundamental ways with each other! What better proof could we produce than while Christian truth can and should guide us, and will be determinative of many aspects of our thought, that nevertheless our best hope should be for a family of views, all shaped by their grounding in Christian truth? The integrationist would argue that rather than *the* view, our aspiration should be to have a civil and progressive conversation with each other, our fellow Christians, about how to progressively sharpen our understanding of persons, a conversation that includes not just theological elements but the fruits of solid scientific study as well!

The heart of the integration approach is a commitment to thinking biblically about our subject matter. Greidanus (1982) argues rightly that the task of the Christian scholar is "to study reality in the light of biblical revelation" (p. 147). Because the claims of the gospel are all-inclusive, and the gospel should penetrate to the core of all who claim the name Christian, the task of integration is that of being distinctively Christian in an appropriate and responsible fashion in one's scholarly pursuits. Specifically, Jones (2010) offers the following definition of the task of integration:

> Integration of Christianity and psychology (or any area of "secular thought") is our living out—in this particular area—of the Lordship of Christ over all of existence by our giving his special revelation—God's true Word—its appropriate place of authority in determining our fundamental beliefs about and practices toward all of reality and toward our academic subject matter in particular. (p. 102)

So how do we approach this task?

Destructive and Constructive Modes of Integration

The work of integration is open-ended and dialogical. The work begins with a determined but humble embrace of Christian perspectives on our subject matter, in this case of human personality and character. Grounded in Christian truth, we nevertheless recognize that even our understandings of biblical truth are subject to our finiteness and sinfulness as human beings, and thus are potentially correctable by knowledge from any source, including the findings of science. Just as we know that Jesus' pronouncement that "You are the salt of the earth" (Mt 5:13) does not mean that we are literally made of salt because our rational capacities grounded in our experiences of reality recognize this exclamation as a metaphor rather than a scientific pronouncement, so also, for instance, the expanding findings of science challenge us to sort through what is metaphorical and theological as opposed to scientific in the first chapter of Genesis. So also the scientific fruits of studying psychology may help us to discern better what Scripture is teaching about humanity.

But the reverse is also true. Our commitments to biblical truth demand that we sort bad science, or anti-Christian philosophy masquerading as science, from good science. When classic Freudian psychology posits that humans are fundamentally irrational and driven by libidinal and death-seeking motivations, or radical behaviorism claims humans are nothing but material creatures shaped by learned associations, it is our commitment to Christian truths that will lead us to challenge such pronouncements.

Integration can be performed with either an essentially destructive or constructive stance toward relating the Christian faith to the life of the mind, with very different results. Many of the classic opponents of integration (such as Adams, 1979; Bobgan & Bobgan, 1979, 1987; Kilpatrick, 1985) assume a destructive stance toward non-Christian thought in psychology, feeling this is the only viable option. They approach the study of psychotherapy theories with the assumption that each therapy model is a vision of human nature that is in direct competition with the Christian faith. Thus the approach must be deconstructed, disproved by finding critical flaws in it so that it can be rejected. This certainly appeared to be the main method of Adams (1970) in *Competent to Counsel*, where he dismissed the theories of Freud and Rogers after showing that the assumptions on which they are built were in places incompatible with Christian faith.

This destructive mode of functioning is vital, in many ways, for Christians today. There are times when the best response of the Christian is to "demolish arguments and every pretension that sets itself up against the knowledge of God" (2 Cor 10:5). But we contend that the appropriate time for such apologetic efforts is when the views actually are raised up against God. In other words, when the views of humanist Carl Rogers, for instance, are presented as ultimately satisfying answers to the major questions of life, the right Christian response is to point out critical flaws in the approach and to reject his views. This is what we appreciate about the critics of psychotherapy—they take matters of faith so seriously that they are zealous to protect it from distortion or perversion. Surely it is right and good to have such a concern.

But there is a constructive side of relating Christian faith to human scholarship that is unrecognized by the critics of psychotherapy (from Stoker, 1971). A believer who strives to stand upon a distinctive commitment to the truths of the living Christian faith and build an understanding of persons that is true, broad and more complete can validly engage in a constructive dialogue with the psychotherapy theories. The Bible, although containing God-inspired revelation that is infallible and authoritative, is nevertheless of limited scope (i.e., Scripture doesn't cover everything). Thus it is not unfaithful to search out how to reasonably expand our understanding beyond what God chose to reveal in the Bible.

In discussing the value of secular learning to the Christian thinker earlier, we were already laying a foundation for this approach. Christian intellectuals have long sought to build beyond the basic structure of the fundamental truths of Scripture to answer questions only tangentially addressed in the Bible. Christian theologians engage in this sort of constructive interaction when they gain enlightenment from secular philosophers for resolving nagging theological problems (e.g., Allen, 1985). In fact, Christian theologians sometimes even derive benefit from the study of other religions! The late Anglican bishop and theologian Stephen Neill (1984) summarized a respect-worthy position on this matter: "The Christian faith may learn much from other faiths; but it is universal in its claims; in the end Christ must be acknowledged as Lord of all" (p. 284). We can profitably learn from other thought systems that are not explicitly Christian if we retain the distinctiveness of our faith commitments to Christ in the process.

Yet, even this constructive approach should embody some elements of the more critical spirit of the destructive approach. While appropriating what is good in a particular theory, we must also discern the erroneous baggage it carries. Christians who get naively excited about some superficial compatibilities of a psychotherapy theory with the faith and turn off their critical faculties can be led astray. Christians examining the psychotherapy theories with a constructive motive (as we will try to do) should retain an attitude of careful, constructive criticism, and should note problems encountered in order not to fall prey to error. But neither should they summarily dismiss an entire system because of the problems encountered.

In summary, if our goal is, for instance, to show how Skinnerian behaviorism is an inadequate life philosophy, then our stance must be destructive, showing how the Skinnerian metaphysical system is an impoverished and unsatisfying materialistic deception. But if our task is a constructive one of building the truest distinctively Christian view of psychotherapy possible, or even the more modest but positive applied goal of developing the most effective method to alter the self-destructive behavior of a severely autistic child, we would look at and learn from Skinnerian behaviorism after taking a firm stand on the foundation of the orthodox Christian faith and tradition. This would be especially the case if God had given us a burden for a population where behavioral methods have been shown to be effective.

The Two Stages of Constructive Integration

There are two stages in constructively integrating Christian scholarship with secular thought. The first is critical evaluation, where we engage in a dialogue with secular thought to find what may be of value in models that are not easily and obviously compatible with a Christian stance. This phase is essentially one of sorting through the approaches of others to retain the good and discharge the bad. We must recognize, however, that the end product of this phase alone will be a rather disjointed conglomeration of useful insights and helpful tidbits that hardly form a powerful and cohesive system of thought.

Critical evaluation needs to be followed up with the second stage, theory building. After Christian scholars have discerned the advantages of secular models with which they have interacted in the critical evaluation phase, they need to develop new and different theories to incorporate these insights. They need to propose new hypotheses and theories for scholarly examination, ones that bear the imprint of the Christian presuppositions. We would contend that good integrators must not only review research but do research as well. This implies active involvement in the process of doing science, informed by enlightened notions of philosophy of science (Evans, 1989; Jones, 1994, 1996). Good integrators must be committed to evaluation and assessment of their endeavors. Currently, the community of Christian psychologists demonstrates only modest strength in this area, though there are some promising signs of growth (Jones, 2010).

Our hope is that readers of this volume will contribute to the theory-building enterprise from a Christian presuppositional base. This is critical because, as we will argue in chapter twelve, the work of the mental health field significantly overlaps with the healing and reconciling work of the church. It is vital that Christian scholars develop thoroughly Christian approaches to counseling. The work of the church has suffered from those who promote either hastily baptized versions of secular models or superficial renderings of "biblical" models.

While developing a tested family of Christian psychotherapy approaches is our dream, we know that this book represents only the first stage, the critical evaluation phase, of constructive scholarship. We do not offer a powerful new theory but hope to encourage the development of thoroughly Christian thinking by offering a critique of existing secular theories. In other words, we believe the place to start is to appraise the thinking of the secular theorists who have gone before us. We believe that carefully listening to them from the perspective of the Christian tradition is an essential first step.

We anticipate that a thoughtful reader will find this book inadequate, in that we will end with finding none of the approaches adequate for understanding human nature, while pointing out many benefits of most of the approaches. We challenge such a thoughtful reader to join in the dialogue of developing the comprehensive Christian approach that we all so need!

The Dangers of Integration

The process of integration is complicated in part because in many areas, and especially in psychology, adequate scholarship requires interacting with scientific theories and clinical models that are questionable from a

Christian standpoint. We believe that the field of psychology in general and psychotherapy in particular can be a slippery path for Christians to walk. Why do we regard the study and practice of psychotherapy as a different and riskier endeavor compared to other areas such as forestry, dentistry or physics?

First, many of the major proponents of secular approaches to psychotherapy were (or are) non-Christian thinkers, with many having large axes to grind against religion generally and Christianity in particular. In this field of study, one inevitably encounters direct and indirect jabs against the Christian faith. Some of the major psychotherapy systems have been set up as competing life views that are religious in scope and content. Research has shown that psychologists as a group tend to be socially and politically more liberal and less traditionally religious than the general population (Lovinger, 1984, chap. 1). Thus it is not uncommon to have the type of encounter one of us had when he began his graduate studies: In the opening moments of the first class, the professor gave a five-minute diatribe against Christianity! And as Jones (1994) argued, psychology has often been overtly imperialistic toward religious faith, stretching to claim that it has explained and hence explained away religious experience. We concur with Dueck and Reimer (2010) when, with reference to secular psychology, they argue that "Secularity and Christianity are not only two traditions, they are *competing* social projects with different cultural aims and practices" (p. 84).

More often the antagonism against Christianity is subtle, demonstrated more in the silence about religion in psychology texts, papers and classes than in open antagonism. Kirkpatrick and Spilka (1989), for instance, have documented the almost total neglect of religion as a meaningful human phenomenon in major psychology texts. We are convinced that this conspiracy of silence about things spiritual can be more deadly than open antagonism. Christians are seduced into lowering their guard and being lulled into a secular mindset where faith is neither good nor bad, true nor false, but simply irrelevant. (This has not always been the case. In the first half century of American psychology—1880-1930—religion was a major area of investigation for the field [Spilka, Hood & Gorsuch, 1985].)

Second, we believe that psychology in general and psychotherapy in particular are especially prone to subtle errors or departures from truth.

As theologian Emil Brunner (1946) suggested, sin biases and distorts not only our moral behavior but also our thoughts (this is called the noetic effect of sin by theologians). Brunner went on to argue that sin would have a more subtle and profoundly disturbing effect on belief the closer one gets to the "center of existence," where one is struggling with the core truths of human life. Proportionally, the further one is away from this core, the less the influence sin has on thought. Thus when one is studying the nocturnal migration behavior of the notch-winged red-bellied thrush (if there is such a species), one is not grappling with quite the same core issues that one encounters in grappling with the central motivations and needs of human life.

The closer one gets to this core of existence, the further one gets from the facts or data of experience and the more one depends on speculation. Data can be seen as a restraint on speculation (being held accountable to clear and irrefutable facts); in the absence of such close restraint, when the scholar is attempting to propose a grand theory of personality and therapy, one may be freer to drift from the facts into pure speculation and hence error. We are not, however, arguing that science can only function with pure facts or that Christians should only deal with pure facts; actually, contemporary philosophers of science have shown that there really is no such thing as a pure fact. All facts rest in a web of interpretation of some kind; it is simply the case that some human assertions are more interpretation than others (see Wolterstorff, 1984).

Third, as we will develop more fully in our last two chapters, we believe that there are some very seductive elements of the profession of psychotherapy that can ensnare the immature or unwise Christian. Psychotherapists take great pride in being in a "people-helping" profession and, in most circles, are accorded respect for their skills and professional activities. One can subtly begin to believe that helping people on an interpersonal dimension is all there is to caring for others. It is all too easy to become enamored of the powerful position one occupies in relation to one's clients and to the financial rewards possible in the field (though these have been greatly exaggerated), which can open the door to great error.

We have offered these points as what we feel are realistic warnings about some dangers of the task of integration. Critics of integration go beyond these warnings to voice concerns they claim render the entire task of integration illegitimate. We will summarize their core concerns, show-ing that every concern has a kernel of truth but has been exaggerated be-yond reasonable and biblical bounds.

CRITICISMS OF THE WORK OF INTEGRATION

Criticism of the integration approach is abundant, and we should always listen to our critics with care. We will summarize and respond briefly to three major sets of criticism: that integration is unscientific, unbiblical and hyper-rationalistic.

Integration Is Unscientific

The late Harvard scientist and intellectual Stephen Jay Gould (1999) of-fered a provocative and terse argument for why science and religious belief should never interact with each other. His argument is embedded entirely within his opening definitions: "Science tries to document the factual character of the natural world, and to develop theories that coordinate and explain these facts. Religion, on the other hand, operates in the equally important, but utterly different, realm of human purposes, meanings, and values" (p. 4). If these definitions are true, then indeed science and reli-gious belief should never interact.

But if these definitions are flawed, as indeed they are, then the argu-ment falls apart. Science, it turns out, is not best understood as comprising exclusively facts woven into theories. Rather, it is now broadly acknowl-edged that even the most basic empirical observations do not occur in a contextless void. Humans make even the most basic observations from the context of preunderstandings of reality that influence what we see. For this reason it is now commonly said that all facts are "theory laden" or, as we argued earlier, that facts always reside in a web of belief. And scientific judgments about theories are never a mechanical, syllogistic process but rather are human judgments that are indeed rational, but inclusive of aes-thetic and value-laden aspects of judgment.

On the other hand, Christianity (we will leave others to deal with ge-neric religion) is not merely about "purposes, meanings, and values." Christianity is in part about purposes, meanings and values, but these are in turn based on the claim that God has revealed himself in history and acted in history in ways that are every bit as factual as anything else humans can claim as facts. If God really said that murder is immoral, then the declaration "murder is immoral" is as fundamental a fact of the universe as $E = MC^2$. And claims that Christ turned water to wine and rose from the grave after dying are claims about the real state of affairs of the universe, about facts, not merely about values.

Putting these together, if science is much more complicated than Gould's (1999) simplistic description, and if Christianity is about real events and universal truths about reality, then there is room—indeed an obligation—to examine how science and Christian faith interact. For more on these complicated issues, see Jones (1994, 2010) and Wolterstorff (1984).

Briefly, we must examine an additional concern about integration and science, expressed this time by conservative Christians rather than secular scientists. This is the claim that while Christians indeed should pay attention to good science, to facts, that this does not justify engagement with bad science. Psychology, they argue, and particularly psychotherapy, is bad science. Surely the vain speculations and philosophies of mere humans (2 Cor 10:5) do not merit a place in our beliefs alongside God's Word (Bobgan and Bobgan, 1987, pp. 29-30).

In response, let us first address an implicit claim in the argument. We deny the fundamental premise that Christians can only derive knowledge from two sources of facts, authoritative revelation or science. Revelation merits the most fundamental place among human ways of knowing, and science also merits a place as well. Properly understood, all human routes to knowledge deserve an appropriate place in the cognitive life of the believer. Authority (including revelation), experience, intuition and reason—the four commonly described ways of knowing—all have legitimate roles to play (Foster & Ledbetter, 1987). On the basis of the foregoing, then, we reject the simplistic assertion that Christians need heed only authoritative revelation and science. If only life were that simple!

Is psychology "bad science"? This argument is usually pressed quoting historian and philosopher of psychology Sigmund Koch saying that "psychology cannot be a coherent science" (Koch, 1981, p. 262). This statement is taken to mean that psychological research is incoherent. What Koch was actually arguing, however, is that psychology covers too broad a span of reality (from the neurons of insects to the psychology of human communities) to ever have one model of scientific methodology govern all areas of study. Thus if the requirement for coherence as a science is a uniform methodology, then psychology will never be a coherent science. We must use different methods to study neurons and multiple personalities.

Koch further argues that some scientists would have a rigid, restricted list of methods for what counts as science, but that psychology can never be captive to such a list. Koch argued that investigators in some areas of study should properly distance themselves from the rigidly empirical methods traditionally associated with hard science, such as physics and chemistry, if these investigators are to do justice to their areas of study. In these areas, psychologists may properly use methods traditionally associated with history, anthropology or even literary scholarship in their pursuit of truth. In other words, being "nonscientific" in some areas of psychology is a virtue to Koch. Psychology is an amazingly broad discipline that cannot be easily defined by one model of science and suffers from confusion and lack of clarity regarding standards for properly scientific methodology (see Koch & Leary, 1985).

Psychology is not necessarily bad science. Christians should carefully look at any way of knowing that helps us better understand the human condition, even if that way of knowing does not conform to some narrow definition of "good science." On the other hand, we must acknowledge that some areas of psychotherapy (and some of what passes for theology) are neither good science nor good reasoning, good intuition nor anything else; they are rather examples of slipshod argumentation and speculation.

Integration Is Unbiblical

There are two core variations of the "integration is unbiblical" argument that traditionally have been advanced. They are:

1. The assertion that the Bible declares itself (in passages such as 2 Tim 3:16-17; 2 Pet 1:4; 3:14-18) to be sufficient to meet all human needs. Thus, to argue that one should study anything other than the Bible (such as psychology) in order to better meet human needs is tantamount to declaring the holy Scriptures to be inadequate to equip the servant of God and also to rejecting God's own claims for his revelation (Bobgan & Bobgan, 1987, p. 11; Adams, 1979, p. 46).

2. The belief that "the Bible's position is that all counsel that is not revelational (biblical), or based upon God's revelation, is Satanic" (Adams, 1979, p. 4; see also Bobgan & Bobgan, 1987, p. 32). Thus to decide to

listen to and learn from a non-Christian in an area where God has revealed his will (i.e., in psychology) is to "walk in the counsel of the wicked" (Ps 1:1).

In response, first, we affirm the sufficiency of the Bible. At the same time, we must remember that it is God, not the Bible itself, who is declared to be all-sufficient, to provide all that pertains unto life (2 Pet 1:4; 3:14-18). Christians should courageously claim and proclaim whatever authority and power that the Scriptures declare for themselves—no less and no more.

Second Timothy 3:16-17 teaches that Scripture is inspired (God-breathed), but is not declared to be the only and all-sufficient source for every bit of knowledge that will ever be needed by anyone for any purpose related to human need. Rather, it is called "useful." We do not look to Scripture for guidance for theoretical physics or surgery; nor should we for distinguishing schizophrenia from autism.

Paul teaches that Scripture is essential to the forming of our character, which, if shaped and molded by God's living Word, can prepare us for beginning any good work, though the accomplishment of that good work may also depend on the mastery of other key skills. Thus, though the Bible is an essential foundation for a Christian approach to psychotherapy, it is not an all-sufficient guide for the discipline of counseling. The Bible is inspired and precious, but it is a revelation of limited scope, the main concern of which is its presentation of God's redemptive plan for his people and of the great doctrines of the faith. The Bible doesn't claim to reveal everything that human beings might want to know.

Second, all truth is from above (Jas 1:17). Correspondingly, Satan is the father of lies, ranging from out-and-out fabrications to lies that are subtle twists and perversions of the truth. In addition, humanity is fallible, fallen and finite. Thus our theologies, our confessional heritages, our Bible teachings (not the Bible itself) and our prayers are filled with subtle and sometimes blatant falsehoods and imperfections. We are not right in all that we believe, though by God's grace through the Holy Spirit and the influence of the body of Christ, we are guided into sufficient truth to be able to actually relate to God and understand something of his nature, and to even be able to proclaim our faith as the truth.

The flip side is that Christians are not the sole possessors of truth. Just as the rain falls on the just and the unjust, so too does truth, by the process that theologians call God's common grace. Romans 1 speaks of God even revealing central truths about his nature to unbelievers (Rom 1:19). John Calvin, that great figure in the Protestant Reformation, stated it well when he said, "The human mind, however much fallen and perverted from its original integrity, is still adorned and invested with admirable gifts from its Creator. . . . We will be careful . . . not to reject or condemn truth wherever it appears" (*Institutes of the Christian Religion*, 2.2.15).

Thus, God's counsel is not always synonymous with the counsel of a Christian, and Satan's counsel is not synonymous with the counsel of a non-Christian. Rather, we should identify God's counsel with the truth, and Satan's counsel with falsehood. Sometimes a so-called secular approach to understanding a given topic may be nearer the truth than the distorted understanding of a particular Christian person. If we understand God's counsel to be truth, we will be committed to pursuing truth wherever we find it. And we may sometimes find it in the careful and insightful writings of unbelievers. (For more on responding to this general criticism, see Jones, 2001.)

Integration Is Hyper-Rationalistic

In a postmodern context, some scholars emphasize the personal. Jacobsen and Jacobsen (2004) criticize the integration approach as overly rationalistic, attributing this to a bias toward Reformed (Calvinistic) theology. They question whether "faith supplies the believer with a full-blown Christian worldview" and then ask a series of rhetorical questions:

> Is Christian revelation personal or propositional? Does revelation supply us with a complete vision of the world, or is revelation more piecemeal, offering important clues about the origins, meaning, and purpose of the universe but never spelling things out in fine detail? Do Christians possess extrafactual knowledge about the world, or is the addition of Christian revelation primarily a matter of values and attitude? (p. 28)

Their rhetorical questions risk serving as a pretext for the dismissal of a controlling function of special revelation over the cognitive life of the Christian scholar. Take two key assertions they seem to make—that to focus on the rational is a Reformed theological bias, and that one must decide between knowledge as personal or propositional. We can challenge both questions at the same time by turning to the non-Reformed theologian Pope John Paul II, who said, in *Fides et Ratio*, "What is distinctive in the biblical text is the conviction that there is a profound and indissoluble unity between the knowledge of reason and the knowledge of faith" (II.16.4). Further, "Belief is often humanly richer than mere evidence, because it involves an interpersonal relationship and brings into play not only a person's capacity to know but also the deeper capacity to entrust oneself to others, to enter into a relationship with them which is intimate and enduring" (III.32.1). John Paul II sees the interpersonal *enriching* the knowing process and not counterposed against it; he sees the human capacity to know cognitively as complementary to the capacity to know interpersonally. It is not "personal or propositional," rather, it is personal *and* propositional.

The Jacobsens have created a straw man. A worldview may not be a "complete vision of the world" and yet still be worthwhile, just as a map can be an imperfect and incomplete representation of reality yet still be good enough to guide us. Knowledge from the Bible that is partial can nevertheless be knowledge secure enough to serve to organize our thoughts. The issue is whether we have a word from God that has relevance for our work as scholars. Integrationists agree that revelation does not constitute our disciplines; Scripture does not exhaust what humans know or can know. But if God has spoken and acted, and if his spoken or enacted Word has relevance for our area of academic study, what could possibly be our rationale for ignoring that Word?

METHODOLOGY FOR CHRISTIAN APPRAISAL

To evaluate models of counseling and psychotherapy, we must think clearly about our theological commitments, our views of humanity and our moral standards. While we must be careful about being overly dogmatic and rigid, good evaluation is brutally honest about the realities of the human condition in all their tragic complexities.

The following are the major guidelines we intend to pursue in critiquing the theories in this book.[3]

---

[3]Our colleague Robert C. Roberts at Wheaton has derived independently criteria for the evaluation of therapy systems that are similar to our own. Roberts (1985, 1987) has argued for what he calls the "virtues approach to integration." He starts the examination of an approach to

Philosophical Assumptions

We begin each chapter looking carefully at the philosophical assumptions or presuppositions that ground each approach to counseling. Ideas about human character and personality do not arise in a vacuum. As Browning and Cooper (2004) say, "the modern psychologies function within larger contexts of meaning about the way the world is" (p. 87). The approaches vary widely in terms of how explicitly they articulate their philosophical assumptions. Behaviorism has been an easy target for Christian critique over the years because Skinner was so transparent about his assumptions (see chap. 5). The originators of some other approaches have not been so explicit, resulting in the need for careful work in unearthing their presuppositions.

No common philosophy unifies the many diverse and varied approaches. Each has a different view of reality, truth, purpose, personhood and the like. These assumptions and presuppositions are of crucial importance for the Christian academician, clinician or researcher, as these convictions directly or indirectly affect every phase of science and of the people-helping process. Theory significantly affects practice, whether or not this relationship is acknowledged.

A distinctively Christian approach to counseling and psychotherapy will have theological and philosophical underpinnings compatible with Christian faith. It will look at the task of the psychotherapist from both eternal and temporal perspectives and will fully acknowledge the reality of the supernatural. Sin and the consequences of the Fall will be taken seriously, as well as the reality of supernatural evil.

Model of Personality

We must also examine the personality theory or model of humanity on which an approach is built. Every theory must build on an understanding of what defines human character and action. These approaches vary widely

---

psychotherapy by looking at the virtues that the approach strives to cultivate. This is similar to our criterion of a model's vision of ideal humanness or wholeness. Roberts argues in turn that each virtue is embedded in a network of assumptions that he calls the "grammar" of the virtue (alluding to the way that verbal ideas are nested in linguistic grammar systems). Minimally, this grammar system includes a concept of human nature (similar to our criterion of the view of personality), an explanation for the failure to achieve virtue (a theory of abnormality), and some ideas for how change toward the development of the virtues of the system can be facilitated (prescriptions for change).

in terms of their understandings of human motivations, personality structure and core characteristics. As Tjeltveit (1989) says, "Models of human beings—explicit or implicit, complex or simple, internally consistent or inconsistent, . . . open to change or static—shape society, the actions of every human being, and every individual's worldview. . . . [They are] part of every psychotherapy session" (p. 1).

Our understandings of persons and personhood must be grounded in the words of Scripture, but also in Christian experience in the context of our confessional communities and the historic teachings of the church. The purpose of Scripture is to present a record of God's redemptive dealings with persons throughout history, to present a plan of salvation and discipleship, and to provide us with the knowledge necessary to guide us into productive life. The Scriptures were never intended to be a textbook of all psychological conditions and disorders, although they should anchor and condition our metaphysical and ontological assertions about persons and provide a practical foundation for moral guidance.

We begin by asking if each theory of personality is compatible with Christian truth. Is it clear yet comprehensive? Does it do justice to what is known about human behavior and experience, and does it reflect diverse gender, socioeconomic and sociocultural contexts? Is the personality theory concerned with all dimensions of human behavior and experience—cognitive, affective, interpersonal, spiritual, physical and behavioral? Is the theory elegant and parsimonious, given the complexity of the subject? Does it generate serious research and study? Does it directly inform clinical practice and theory? In short, is the theory valuable at multiple levels of inquiry (i.e., theory, research and practice)?

Model of Abnormality

We will look with care at each theory's understanding of human abnormality. To discuss a theory of personality is usually to presume that one also understands deviations from normal personality development. To suggest how one can change human action is to presume that one has some understanding as to the processes that explain how it came to need changing in the first place.

How compatible is the view of abnormality with the Christian faith? Are the core concepts like human accountability, responsibility and sinfulness compatible with the model? Is faith itself classified as pathological?

Are the Christian virtues viewed as abnormal? Is there a balance between personal causation of distress ("because of my sins") and systemic causation of distress ("because I live in a fallen world")?

Model of Health

Every theory has an explicit or implicit vision of human wholeness which complements its view of abnormality. To discuss the change one intends to engender in the client's life is to presume a direction that one is going to move in, a goal one is moving toward. Even theoreticians who are aiming to be value neutral by saying that they are just trying to decrease pain are working from an implicit hypothesis that minimizing pain is part of human wholeness.

The goals and views of normalcy within a particular psychotherapy tradition should be closely examined. What does the theory propose the truly healthy individual will be like? What are the explicit and implicit notions of maturity, wellness, wholeness or health being advocated? Methods of therapy are often intimately intertwined with the theory of normalcy of the approach. For instance, a therapist may use emotional catharsis ("discharge") techniques because the therapist's view of normalcy includes emotional expressiveness as one of the criteria for health. Further, unless theorists or therapists are clear about where they are headed, therapy tends to become directionless and unfocused. Goals for change should be explicit and communicated to clients at the beginning of therapy.

Model of Psychotherapy

We need to look at the prescribed methods of change to gauge their essential credibility. Some proposed change methods are quite similar to intuitive or lay understandings of the process of growth, while others can be so radically different as to require substantial support merely to make them look credible. Do the counseling processes and techniques provide real resources for healing? Are the techniques proposed ethical and moral?

As Tan (1987) has observed, a distinctively Christian approach to people-helping will emphasize the primacy of warm, empathic and genuine relationships, stressing the relevance of *agape* love. Such compassion should extend to the clinician's personal and professional relationships with others. A distinctively Christian approach will take the role of the Holy Spirit seriously, as well as the many spiritual resources available to the Christian counselor (see chapters eleven and twelve). Large contextual factors like familial, societal, religious and cultural influences will not be minimized, and appropriate community and church resources will be mobilized when necessary. We have to be more than pragmatists (using whatever works), being sure to employ techniques that are consistent with biblical truth and with the wisdom and discernment of the confessional community.

Demonstrated Effectiveness

Finally, as a matter of Christian stewardship, it behooves us to look not merely at the five more conceptual criteria already listed, but also at what the scientific research says about the effectiveness of a particular approach. There has been a huge movement within clinical psychology over the last two decades toward what are widely called "empirically validated treatments." The research literature on psychotherapy and counseling is vast and yet deserves the serious consideration of the Christian would-be people-helper. A full-fledged literature review of effectiveness studies for every approach is beyond the scope of the present volume, but we will try at least to provide the reader with a summary of the state of the empirical literature for each major approach today.

CONCLUSION

The business of evaluating psychotherapy theories is complex, and healthy (but not paranoiac) caution is in order. What at first may seem like clear compatibilities between faith and a particular theory can hide radical incompatibilities. On the other hand, superficial incompatibilities can distract the Christian professional from perceiving deep and striking areas of compatibility between the faith and the theory. Only sustained, lucid analysis in the context of a thoughtful community of faith can save us from errors on either side. It is our prayer that this volume, which emerges from the discussions and interactions of our particular Christian intellectual community, will advance that cause.

FOR FURTHER READING

Browning, D. S., & Cooper, T. D. (2004). *Religious thought and the modern psychologies* (2nd ed.). Minneapolis, MN: Fortress.

Browning, D. S. (2010). *Reviving Christian humanism: A new conversation on spirituality, theology and psychology.* Minneapolis, MN: Fortress.

Though written from a self-described liberal Christian perspective and requiring much theological sophistication to fully digest, the first of these valuable works explores the religious implications of many of the major therapy systems we will examine in this book, and the second the broad contours of Christian engagement with the world of ideas.

Johnson, E. F. (Ed.). (2010a). *Psychology and Christianity: Five views* (2nd ed.). Downers Grove, IL: InterVarsity Press.

The best "one-stop shop" to read about the debate over how Christian faith and psychology can relate.

Koch, S., & Leary, D. (Eds.). (1985). *A century of psychology as science.* New York, NY: McGraw-Hill.

A massive and challenging overview of the status of psychology as a discipline. Probably not readable by the nonpsychologist, it has inadequate coverage of applied psychology, especially the area of psychotherapy.

Miller, W. R., & Delaney, H. D. (Eds.). (2005). *Judeo-Christian perspectives on psychology: Human nature, motivation, and change.* Washington, DC: American Psychological Association.

This and Shafranske are two of the more fascinating compilations of articles discussing religion and psychology published by the American Psychological Association, indicating burgeoning interest in this topic.

Shafranske, E. (Ed.). (1996). *Religion and the clinical practice of psychology.* Washington, DC: American Psychological Association.

Stevenson, D. H., Eck, B. E., & Hill, P. C. (Eds.). (2007). *Psychology and Christianity integration: Seminal works that shaped the movement.* Batavia, IL: Christian Association for Psychological Studies, Inc.

This volume honoring the fiftieth anniversary of the Christian Association for Psychological Studies contains, as the title indicates, a plethora of key historic articles in the movement of integration.

Wolterstorff, N. (1984). *Reason within the bounds of religion* (2nd ed.). Grand Rapids, MI: Eerdmans.

A classic, readable and intriguing discussion of contemporary philosophy of science from a Christian perspective.

REFERENCES

Adams, J. (1970). *Competent to counsel.* Grand Rapids, MI: Baker.

Adams, J. (1979). *More than redemption: A theology of Christian counseling.* Phillipsburg, NJ: Presbyterian & Reformed.

Allen, D. (1985). *Philosophy for understanding theology*. Atlanta, GA: John Knox Press.

Bobgan, M., & Bobgan, D. (1979). *The psychological way/The spiritual way*. Minneapolis, MN: Bethany Fellowship.

Bobgan, M., & Bobgan, D. (1987). *Psychoheresy: The psychological seduction of Christianity*. Santa Barbara, CA: Eastgate.

Brooke, J. H. (1991). *Science and religion: Some historical perspectives*. Cambridge: Cambridge University Press.

Browning, D. S. (2010). *Reviving Christian humanism: A new conversation on spirituality, theology and psychology*. Minneapolis, MN: Fortress.

Browning, D. S., & Cooper, T. D. (2004). *Religious thought and the modern psychologies* (2nd ed.). Minneapolis, MN: Fortress.

Brunner, E. (1946). *Revelation and reason* (O. Wyon, Trans.). Philadelphia, PA: Westminster Press. (Original work published 1938).

Coe, J. H., & Hall, T. W. (2010a). A transformational psychology view. In E. Johnson (Ed.), *Psychology and Christianity: Five views* (2nd ed., pp. 199-226). Downers Grove, IL: InterVarsity Press.

Coe, J. H., & Hall, T. W. (2010b). *Psychology in the Spirit: Contours of a transformational psychology*. Downers Grove, IL: InterVarsity Press.

Dueck, A., & Reimer, K. (2009). *A peaceable psychology: Christian therapy in a world of many cultures*. Grand Rapids, MI: Brazos.

Evans, C. S. (1977). *Preserving the person*. Grand Rapids, MI: Baker.

Evans, C. S. (1989). *Wisdom and humanness in psychology*. Grand Rapids, MI: Baker.

Foster, J., & Ledbetter, M. (1987). Christian anti-psychology and the scientific method. *Journal of Psychology and Theology, 15*, 10-18.

Geehan, E. (Ed.). (1971). *Jerusalem and Athens*. Phillipsburg, NJ: Presbyterian & Reformed.

Gould, S. J. (1999). *Rocks of ages: Science and religion in the fullness of life*. New York, NY: Ballantine.

Greidanus, S. (1982). The use of the Bible in Christian scholarship. *Christian Scholar's Review, 11*, 138-147.

Holmes, A. F. (2001). *Building the Christian academy*. Grand Rapids, MI: Eerdmans.

Jacobsen, D., & Jacobsen, R. (2004). *Scholarship and Christian faith: Enlarging the conversation*. New York, NY: Oxford University Press.

Jeeves, M. (1976). *Psychology and Christianity: The view both ways*. Downers Grove, IL: InterVarsity Press.

John Paul II. (1998). *Fides et ratio: On the relationship between faith and reason*. Retrieved from www.catholic-pages.com/documents/fides_et_ratio.pdf.

Johnson, E. F. (Ed.). (2010a). *Psychology and Christianity: Five views* (2nd ed.). Downers Grove, IL: InterVarsity Press.

Johnson, E. F. (2010b). A brief history of Christians in psychology. In E. Johnson (Ed.), *Psychology and Christianity: Five views* (2nd ed., pp. 9-47). Downers Grove, IL: InterVarsity Press.

Jones, S. (1986). Relating the Christian faith to psychology. In S. Jones (Ed.), *Psychology and the Christian faith* (pp. 15-34). Grand Rapids, MI: Baker.

Jones, S. L. (1994). A constructive relationship for religion with the science and profession of psychology: Perhaps the boldest model yet. *American Psychologist, 49*(3), 184-199.

Jones, S. L. (1996). Reflections on the nature and future of the Christian psychologies. *Journal of Psychology and Christianity, 15*(2), 133-142.

Jones, S. (2001). An apologetic apologia for the integration of psychology and theology. In T. R. Phillips & M. R. McMinn (Eds.), *The care of the soul: Exploring the intersection of psychology and theology* (pp. 62-77). Downers Grove, IL: InterVarsity Press.

Jones, S. L. (2010). An integration view. In E. Johnson (Ed.), *Psychology and Christianity: Five views* (2nd ed., pp. 101-128). Downers Grove, IL: InterVarsity Press.

Jones, S. L. (2011). Psychology and Christianity in 3-D. *Christian Scholar's Review, 40*(3), 267-81.

Kilpatrick, W. (1985). *The emperor's new clothes: The naked truth about the new psychology.* Westchester, IL: Crossway.

Kirkpatrick, L., & Spilka, B. (1989, August). *Treatment of religion in psychology texts.* Paper presented at the annual Convention of the American Psychological Association, New Orleans, LA.

Koch, S. (1981). The nature and limits of psychological knowledge. *American Psychologist, 36*, 257-269.

Koch, S., & Leary, D. (Eds.). (1985). *A century of psychology as science.* New York, NY: McGraw-Hill.

Lovinger, R. (1984). *Working with religious issues in therapy.* New York, NY: Jason Aronson.

Marsden, G. M. (1994). *The soul of the American university: From Protestant establishment to established nonbelief.* New York, NY: Oxford University Press.

Myers, D. G. (2010). A levels-of-explanation view. In E. Johnson (Ed.), *Psychology and Christianity: Five views* (2nd ed., pp. 49-78). Downers Grove, IL: InterVarsity Press.

Neill, S. (1984). *Christian faith and other faiths.* Downers Grove, IL: InterVarsity Press.

Powlison, D. (2010). A biblical counseling view. In E. Johnson (Ed.), *Psychology and Christianity: Five views* (2nd ed., pp. 245-273). Downers Grove, IL: Inter-Varsity Press.

Roberts, R. C. (1985). Carl Rogers and Christian virtues. *Journal of Psychology and Theology, 13*(4), 263-273.

Roberts, R. C. (1987). Psychotherapeutic virtues and the grammar of faith. *Journal of Psychology and Theology, 15*(3), 191-204.

Roberts, R. C., & Watson, P. J. (2010). A Christian psychology view. In E. Johnson (Ed.), *Psychology and Christianity: Five views* (2nd ed., pp. 149-178). Downers Grove, IL: InterVarsity Press.

Spilka, B., Hood, R., & Gorsuch, R. (1985). *The psychology of religion: An empirical approach*. Englewood Cliffs, NJ: Prentice-Hall.

Stoker, H. (1971). Reconnoitering the theory of knowledge of Professor Dr. Cornelius Van Til. In E. Geehan (Ed.), *Jerusalem and Athens* (pp. 25-70). Phillipsburg, NJ: Presbyterian & Reformed.

Tan, S. Y. (1987). Intrapersonal integration: The servant's spirituality. *Journal of Psychology and Christianity, 6*, 34-39.

Tidball, D. (1986). *Skillful shepherds: An introduction to pastoral theology*. Grand Rapids, MI: Zondervan.

Tjeltveit, A. (1989). The ubiquity of models of human beings in psychotherapy: The need for rigorous reflection. *Psychotherapy, 26*, 1-10.

Toulmin, S. (1990). *Cosmopolis: The hidden agenda of modernity*. Chicago, IL: University of Chicago Press.

Treier, D. J. (forthcoming). *Brazos theological commentary on the Bible: Proverbs and Ecclesiastes*. Grand Rapids, MI: Baker/Brazos.

Van Leeuwen, M. (1985). *The person in psychology*. Grand Rapids, MI: Eerdmans.

Waltke, B. K. (2004). *The book of Proverbs chapters 1–15*. Grand Rapids, MI: Eerdmans.

Waltke, B. K. (2005). *The book of Proverbs chapters 15–31*. Grand Rapids, MI: Eerdmans.

Wolterstorff, N. (1984). *Reason within the bounds of religion* (2nd ed.). Grand Rapids, MI: Eerdmans.

2

A CHRISTIAN VIEW of PERSONS

Stanton L. Jones, Laura Miguélez and Richard E. Butman

O̲ur task is to critically evaluate the major secular psychotherapy theories in light of Christian revelation and faith. But what is "the" Christian view, particularly of human beings, by which we are going to grade the secular psychotherapy approaches? Is there a Christian personality theory hidden in the pages of the Bible?

The purpose of this chapter is to highlight what we believe the Christian Scriptures assert about human beings, as these beliefs will be the backdrop or plumb line against which all else will be evaluated. It is our contention that the Scriptures and Christian theology do not teach a theory of personality as understood by contemporary psychology. We are grounding our position in the Reformed understanding of the perspicuity (clarity) of Scripture, namely, that the Bible is clear in its central message of salvation and holiness and capable of being understood by any literate person. Scripture teaches us the way to eternal fellowship with the Creator-Father-God, and everything we need to know about ourselves and our predicament to obtain salvation and to grow as persons. It records God's redemptive dealings with his people throughout the ages. But it teaches us less than we need to know (or less than it would be edifying to know) to understand why individual persons have the characteristics they do (for instance, why a particular person struggles with obsessive tendencies or another is blessed with incredible strength of character). Scripture also teaches us less than we need to know to help many individuals move beyond the pain and confusion they feel.

What the Scripture does teach about persons lacks the specificity and precision necessary for qualifying either as a formal scientific theory of personality or as a clinically useful heuristic model for understanding personality functioning. ("The general judgment of theologians has been that the Bible gives us no scientific teaching on man, no anthropology, which should or could concur with scientific anthropological research on man" [Berkouwer, 1962, p. 194]). Even in ancient times, pastoral theologians found it necessary to develop models for understanding personality that were built on but went beyond scriptural revelation in order to develop guidelines for pastoral care. In doing this, Christian pastoral thinkers have frequently turned to contemporary nonreligious scholarship about dimensions of personhood to construct more complete models of ministry (Clebsch & Jaekle, 1975; Oden, 1984). While some seem to regard this as heresy (e.g., Adams, 1979), as discussed in the previous chapter, we regard this as a strength as long as the distinctives of the Christian faith are preserved and given preeminence.

But if we are not searching for a personality theory, what in the Scriptures can we reasonably expect to find? In brief, we believe that our foray into theological and biblical anthropology will give us the essential foundation for a more true and more complete understanding of persons by giving us "control beliefs" (Wolterstorff, 1984) or presuppositions. These control beliefs are the "givens," the foundational assumptions that control or shape all other thought. We can then use these control beliefs to build a theory of personality with greater Christian distinctiveness.

Before embarking on this task, we would endorse a number of basic hermeneutical principles (from Greidanus, 1982) that undergird orthodox biblical interpretation.

First, since God is the Creator, there can be no ultimate conflict between knowledge from special revelation (God's specific self-disclosure, especially in Christ and Scripture by means of the Holy Spirit) and general revelation (God's self-disclosure in creation or nature). There can be and often has been, however, conflict between interpretations of special revelation and interpretations about the facts of the created order. In such cases of conflict, our interpretation of either special or general revelation, or possibly both, can be wrong.

Second, "the Bible is the Word of God addressed to the heart of man" (Greidanus, 1982, p. 140). Hence a sincere submission to the Lord who speaks through the Scriptures and is revealed in them by his Holy Spirit enables us to see reality, however imperfectly, from God's perspective, the only proper perspective. Special revelation is specific, and that is why Calvin suggested that the Scriptures can function as spectacles that correct our vision of God's creation when sin has distorted our understanding.

Third, the Bible is a historical book recording God's interactions first of all with a particular people in their culture at a certain time and for particular occasions and purposes. Thus the biblical message to us today cannot be understood properly without understanding its historical and cultural context. With a proper appreciation of these factors, we can confidently expect that we will hear God's voice speak to us through his words to ancient peoples.

Fourth, the Bible was written using phenomenological language, including commonly accepted concepts of the day. In other words, historical and scientific matters were addressed in terms of how they appeared to the authors. Care must be taken not to apply twenty-first-century standards of exactness and science to these ancient texts. For example, when Scripture speaks of the sun standing still (Josh 10:13), this is not a scientific statement but a descriptive one in much the same way as people today speak of the sun "rising."

Similarly, many of the verses often cited as teaching formal psychological concepts cannot responsibly be interpreted scientifically because they were meant as descriptions. The folk psychology in the verses is merely a vehicle by which to teach the main point of the verse. For instance, Paul's use of "spirit, soul and body" (1 Thess 5:23) connotes the whole person, every aspect of the believer, and does not necessarily mean that Paul was authoritatively teaching a tripartite (three-part) view of personhood (see further discussion of this matter later in this chapter). The danger here is expecting from Scripture something God did not intend to provide.

Fifth, biblical passages must be understood in light of the author's intention or meaning, and in the light of the totality of the biblical revelation. It is especially important to remember the Reformers' judgment that Scripture is to interpret Scripture. Since God is the source of all of Scripture, obscure or unclear biblical passages should be interpreted in light of clearer, more unequivocal passages, and deference must be given to the cumulative weight of many passages over one seemingly clear text if there is apparent conflict.

Our overview of humanity derives from Augustine's classic understanding, articulated in his *Enchiridion* (CXVIII; 1961), of humanity's four stages of the Christian life: (1) Prefallen humanity was created *posse non peccare* (able not to sin). (2) Fallen humanity became *non posse non peccare* (not able not to sin) and thus were slaves to sin. (3) Redeemed humanity, by the Holy Spirit's regeneration and the work of God's grace in Christ, are once again *posse non peccare*. (4) Glorified humanity will one day be *non posse peccare* (not able to sin).

HUMANITY IN ITS CREATED STATE: *POSSE NON PECCARE*

Intelligibility, Meaning and Value

"In the beginning God created the heavens and the earth" (Gen 1:1). Historically, the Christian doctrine of creation *ex nihilo* (creation from or out of nothing) is derived from the first chapter of the Bible. Though some scholars today view these opening verses as referring to God's organizing the created order rather than his creating ex nihilo, most evangelical scholars continue to accept this doctrine based on statements elsewhere in Scripture (Ps 33:6; Heb 11:3). Consequently, God's creating *ex nihilo* has assumed a place of priority in all the historic creeds (e.g., the Apostles' Creed: "I believe in God, the Father Almighty, Maker of heaven and earth") and doctrine.

The first biblical information we have about humanity occurs later in the creation story, where we find, "Then God said, 'Let us make man in our image, in our likeness'" (Gen 1:26). Humanity and the entire created order were made by the purposeful actions of the sovereign God of the universe. Far from being the chance products of blind causal forces with lives that are thereby unintelligible and meaningless, we were created intentionally. Our understanding of ourselves begins here. Our basic identity will remain confused until we see ourselves as part of God's creation.

In his book *Maker of Heaven and Earth*, theologian Langdon Gilkey (1985) examines the myriad implications of this central Christian doctrine. Prominent among these implications is the notion that being created, rather than having simply come to exist by naturalistic processes operating without purpose or meaning, is the foundation of intelligibility and meaning for our lives. Our lives are intelligible precisely because we can have faith that our existence is the result of the actions of an all-knowing, intelligent God. Our lives have meaning because God meant or intended for us to be. His plan or purpose remains sovereign throughout history.

In addition to having meaning, we accrue value in at least three ways. First, being the creation of the all-perfect Lord imputes value to us in the same way that all creation has value; we are the work of the Lord, and all of God's works have value. It would be contempt toward God to suggest that any of his creations are without value (as is said in our vernacular, "God doesn't make junk"). Second, we have special value in that we are the only aspect of creation specifically said to be created in God's image. Finally, and getting a bit ahead of ourselves, we have value because God chose to send his Son in complete human form, a high priest who is able to sympathize with our weaknesses, and who in every respect has been tempted as we are, yet without sin (Heb 4:15), to live, suffer, die and rise again for us and our salvation. Surely, God would not waste the life of his dear Son on beings that are without value. We gained value through the acts of the incarnation, the life, suffering, death and resurrection of Jesus Christ. Thus God's mighty works both give us value and reveal that we had and have value. These realities form the basis for our psychological perception of value.

As one final implication of being created, we should note that if we were made by God out of nothing, then we are different from and separate from God, though we are continually dependent on him as the ultimate ground of our very being. As Gilkey (1985, pp. 58ff.) has noted, it is an undeniable implication of Eastern monism (the doctrine that the universe is of one indivisible essence; everything is God) and pantheism (God is everything) that humans are part of God and thus finiteness (being less than God) and individuality (being a creature separate from others, including God) are illusory and evil.

For Christians, separateness from God and others is real and good. We belong in relationship to God and others, but this relatedness is not meant to consume and destroy our separateness. Union with God is a theme of

Scripture, but nowhere are we taught that we cease being ourselves in the process of this union. As in marriage, two persons become one without the loss of their personal identities; so it is with our union with God. An image of heaven as a time when we will merge and become one with the Godhead, losing our individuality in the process, is a perversion of the Christian view of heaven; this distortion stems from the influence of non-Christian Eastern religions pervasive in Western understandings of spirituality today.

The Image of God

The scriptural teaching that human beings are made in the image of God (the *imago Dei*) is utterly foundational to a Christian understanding of persons, but there is ambiguity about what this doctrine means. A number of authors (e.g., Beck & Demarest, 2005) have classified views of the *imago Dei* in three basic categories: substantive, functional and relational.

The substantive understandings of the *imago Dei* focus on what we *are*. Since only humans are noted in Genesis as made in the *imago Dei* (Gen 1:26; cf. 1:20), this view proposes that what makes humans distinctive is what we are made of or possess, whether that is a substance (such as spirit) or a capacity (such as reason, understood to be a function of the spirit), distinct from the rest of the created order. According to classic Reformed teaching, humans image God in their capacity for *rationality* and *morality:* the possession of a spirit or soul is how people image God in their very being.

The functional understandings of the *imago Dei* focus on what we *do*. Humans are understood to be made in God's image because we relate to the rest of the created order in a way that represents or reflects God. One common example is the argument that in obedience to God's command to humanity to exercise "dominion" over creation as God's stewards and representatives (Gen 1:28), we mirror God's dominion over the entire cosmos.

Drawing from the statement in Genesis that God made humans male and female (Gen 1:27), the relational understanding of the *imago Dei* focuses on our *unique relationship to God:* "to be in the image of God is to be related to God in the way that other creatures are not, and so related to the other creatures differently from the way in which they are related to one another" (Gunton, 2002, p. 42). This relational understanding is also extended to include our ability to relate to others, whether in marriage (Barth understood the image as being most exemplified in our male and femaleness) or relationships within society (Brunner's position).

Our point here is that even for this most central of doctrines about what it means to be a human being, ambiguity remains about the exact meaning of this key concept. A spiritual component or dimension is what, ultimately, distinguishes the uniqueness of human creation. Unlike plants and animals, which are created "according to their kinds" (Gen 1:12, 25), God's image is imprinted on human beings. We are not created after our own kind, but are made in God's kind! And the reader can probably see that all three views—the substantive, functional and relational—interact. Just picking out one strand of each view, one could argue that we are rational because we are God's children, that God made us rational so we could exercise dominion and be in relationship with him, and that we are fully rational only when we are in relationship with him and doing the dominion work he set for us to do. Dominion and relating are part of the total picture, but the reason humans are able to exercise dominion and have relationships with God and one another is precisely because they are made in God's image.

Reducing the *imago Dei* to either being rational or exercising dominion or relating limits the image only to those who are healthy and able to exercise it and excludes certain people. For example, an infant is made in God's image though she has limited rational powers and is unable to exercise dominion; an autistic child is made in God's image even though he may be unable to relate fully to those in his environment.

Thus, to be made in the image of God is to bear his imprint on our very spirit, or soul. A scriptural understanding of human flourishing indicates that we fulfill our human created purpose best when we love and serve the Lord God with all our heart, soul, mind and strength (Deut 6:5; Mt 22:37), love others (Lev 19:18; Mt 22:39)—as per the relational view—*and* care for the created order in which God has placed us—as per the functional view.

Compound Beings

Scripture presents us with some challenges in understanding the basic constituent elements of human nature, the substance(s) of which we are made. The basic options boil down to three: monism, dichotism and trichotism (see Beck & Demarest, 2005, pp. 119-141). Monists believe that humans are made of one substance, with some believing we are exclusively physical beings and others some form of spirit. Dichotomists believe we are composed of two substances—our physical bodies and some type of nonphysical soul/spirit. Trichotomists believe that soul and spirit are different substances, distinct from the physical and from each other, so that we are rightly understood to be composed of three substances.

There are good arguments, grounded in Scripture and in human rationality, for each of the positions, with the dichotomist position being the most widely held in church history. When we add in other passages that speak of four elements (heart, soul, mind, strength [Mk 12:30]), or note the flexibility with which Scripture often speaks about psychological phenomena (invoking psychological functions of the heart, bowels, kidneys and so forth), we are driven to be cautious in advancing dogmatic, scientifically precise formulations of biblical teachings about our constituent elements.

Historically, the trichotomist position has based its understanding on Scriptures such as 1 Thessalonians 5:23 and Hebrews 4:12, which speak of our "spirit, soul and body." Irenaeus (as well as the Scofield Bible notes) reflects this trichotomist view. The dichotomist position draws its support from passages such as Matthew 10:28 and James 2:26, which speak of the possible separation of soul (or spirit) from body. Another key body of texts that undergird this position point to an intermediate state, a state of provisional happiness (or judgment) until Christ returns. Jesus' statement to the thief on the cross in Luke 23:43 ("today you will be with me in paradise") seems to indicate an immediacy to the thief's presence with Christ. So too Paul's statements in Philippians 1:22-23 ("I desire to depart and be with Christ") and 2 Corinthians 5:6 ("as we are at home in the body we are away from the Lord"—and vice versa) suggest that though at the time of death we die physically, we nonetheless live spiritually to God in Christ who is the Giver of eternal life to those who believe in him (Jn 11:26).

More recently, at least three developments have caused some evangelicals to adopt a monistic view of the human person. First, science has confirmed an intense and close interconnection between physical and psychological aspects of humanness, supporting the idea that people are truly purely material beings. For example, the findings that electrical stimulation to certain parts of the brain may elicit emotional reactions, memories or movements suggest profound physicality of our most "purely" cognitive experiences. Dichotomists such as Cooper (2000) and others counter by noting that by God's design our bodies and souls/spirits are so intertwined that both are naturally affected when one is strongly affected. Neural stimulation may elicit reactions, but so also subjects instructed to think about certain things are noted to create patterns of brain activity that represent clear changes from their preintervention state. The fact that the two aspects of our humanity—the physical/brain and the mental/psychological—are highly correlated does not mean the mental collapses into the physical.

A second argument in favor of monism criticizes the idea of the immortality of the soul as nothing but an adoption of the Greek view rather than a scriptural understanding of resurrection. These monists note, with some merit, that the traditional Christian view does not attribute to the human soul the attribute of immortality on its own strength or by its very nature. That is, while Plato may have believed that souls are simply things that have and will exist eternally, Christians have believed instead that souls come to exist in the womb, live out their course of life on this earth and then have everlasting life either as beings resurrected for heavenly communion with God or hellish judgment. Dualists like Cooper respond that this is exactly the traditional view of immortality: the soul's immortality has traditionally been understood as ongoing existence beyond physical life based on our coming resurrection, our physical rising from death at Christ's return or parousia.

Third, Green (1998) and other monists reinterpret Paul's statements about "being absent from the body is to be present with the Lord" in an eschatological sense, as if these statements refer only to the end of the ages. This position requires a rereading of Scripture that many regard as too imaginative; for instance, requiring Christ's assurance to the thief that he would be with him that day in paradise as presupposing a "soul sleep" between the moment of death and the thief's eventual resurrection.

Three important facets of this matter deserve special emphasis. First, though our position is that the biblical data best support a bipartite view, the biblical emphasis is always on the unity of the person. As McDonald (1982) says, persons are "constituted of a unity of these two entities" (p. 78), and hence it is not true that one aspect (the soul-spirit or the body) is the real person and the other part an add-on. We are embodied soul-beings.

This is why we prefer the term *bipartite* rather than *dichotomous* for this view, since the latter term might imply that the two elements are fundamentally opposed and irreducibly separate and noninteracting (Hoekema [1986] uses "psychosomatic unity" and Cooper [2000] "holistic dualism" to make the same point). The former term, however, implies that while the two elements are distinguishable in the human person, full human identity is vested in the union of the two aspects. We can never say, "That was my body that did that, not my spirit," or vice versa.

Often, biblical words for the various aspects of our being are used to refer to the whole person from a certain perspective. Nevertheless, there is a center to our persons, and the biblical term *heart* (Mt 15:18; Lk 16:15; Acts 14:17; 2 Cor 5: 12) is most consistently used to describe this core of what psychologists and philosophers often call our self. The scriptural emphasis on "heart" teaches us the importance of understanding ourselves as a unity.

Second, this recognition of two distinct essences cannot be used to make a hard differentiation in value between the two essences (as when many Christians are exposed to teachings emphasizing soul over body). In spite of passages suggesting that our temporal existence is of lesser importance (e.g., Mt 10:28; 2 Cor 12:3), ultimately people are their bodies and soul-spirits in unity. The value of bodily existence is unquestionably assumed in the creation (God made us bodily beings), the incarnation (God became a bodily being), and in Christ's and our own bodily resurrection (through which we will remain bodily beings, albeit perfected bodies, for eternity). As McDonald (1982) said, "Thus does the biblical view of man represent him as consisting of two principles, the cosmic and the holy, which unite the individual into a free and personal oneness of being" (p. 78).

Finally, one tendency that can be quickly noted among secular (and Christian) thinkers is that of exaggerating one end or the other of our compound natures (Evans, 1990). Some so emphasize or exaggerate the immaterial side of our being as to deify humanity and deny that we are inevitably conditioned by our physical existence. We will see this tendency among the humanistic psychologists (chaps. 7, 8). The other extreme is to emphasize or exaggerate our temporal existence so as to make us mere physical machines that are just another biological phenomenon caught up in the grand mechanistic universe. Behavioral and classical psychoanalytic thought make this mistake (chaps. 3, 5).

A Christian view of the person balances these diverse aspects of personhood, emphasizing our unity and respecting that we are at the same time embodied spirits and enspirited bodies, embodied souls and ensouled bodies. Over the last few decades something like this unified vision has been embraced in the secular discipline in the form of what has been called the biopsychosocial model (Engel, 1977). This model argues that psychological health outcomes (see Straub, 2006) are influenced by what are understood as the three primary dimensions of human existence: the biological (most often understood as the physiological dimension of the body studied by biologists), the psychological (understood as the psychological experiences such as consciousness, cognition and affect studied by psychologists) and the sociological (the relationships between humans and their interaction with culture studied by sociologists). The causal influence is presumed to go both upward and downward. Within psychology the biopsychosocial model seeks to avoid narrow understandings of human beings by requiring that they nearly always be understood as biological and psychological beings existing within nested social networks. This model might appear to be common sense to most because of its intuitive acknowledgment that people exist across these multiple dimensions, but there often is a bottom-up flavor to it. There are numerous examples of research into psychopathology using brain imaging studies or genetics findings that, despite reference to a biopsychosocial model, manifest a reductionistic approach to psychopathology. Such studies unilaterally explore the impact of biology on the "higher" psychological and social factors, but ignore the fact that this model also allows for a "downward" flow of causal influence as well. Research has shown clearly, for instance, that sociological stressors can exert negative influence on psychological states (such as depression) and also affect negatively immune functioning.

The development of the biopsychosocial model opens room for conversation about Christian understandings of the unity of persons, but there are limitations to the approach as well. Within the context of this model, religion is often treated as a social factor and spirituality is understood as a psychological process. Christian scholars must be cautious about the reductionism inherent in such a conceptualization: personal faith is more than mere psychology (it involves a living relationship with Christ), and our corporate Christian faith is more than mere sociology (it involves participation in the living body of Christ). Even so, the biopsychosocial understanding, complemented by fully developed Christian understandings of religious faith, give us a fuller understanding of what it means to be a unified human being. All of these dimensions of our personhood are crucial, and all have a causal influence on our lived experience. The influence can be "upward": brain damage or immunological issues may very well influence a person's ability to be empathetic or to feel close to God. The influence may be "downward": as the spiritual life of an individual grows and deepens, it can impact his or her social relationships, mental health, immunological status and even modify synapses in the brain. A fully developed biopsychosocial-spiritual model of persons would direct the Christian psychotherapist to assess the interrelationships of the multiple dimensions and systems that contribute to our personhood, ranging from the genetic to the spiritual. By understanding the reciprocal relationships between the various levels and how they constantly affect (or fail to affect) psychological problems, a more realistic and holistic view of pathology and recovery can be developed.

Human Agency

As we put together the diverse elements that we have uncovered so far concerning our essential natures, we begin to see an emerging pattern of humans as persons with capacities and qualities unique among the created order. One of the premier capacities of personhood merits special attention, that of responsibility, limited freedom or agency.

Evans (1977) put it well in saying that "human beings are first and foremost agents. Their lives do not merely consist of a string of happenings or events, but constitute a series of choices and decisions about what they will do" (p. 144). C. S. Lewis (1963), in discussing this matter, said, "Yet, for us rational creatures, to be created also means 'to be made agents.' We have nothing that we have not received; but part of what we have received is the power of being something more than receptacles" (p. 50).

One way Reformed doctrine views human agency is by understanding humans as "created persons" (Hoekema, 1986, p. 5). We are "created" and therefore completely dependent on God for our being; but we are also "persons" with a sense of responsibility to God. To be a human being is to reflect God in our capacity to act responsibly, and to act responsibly may require some freedom but not perfect freedom.

It is not necessary to a Christian view of freedom to argue that a person always and in every instance reacts with complete and unbounded freedom. Some events in our lives may be so powerful as to cause us to react involuntarily, which may occur, for example, when a young woman sexually abused since childhood reacts with fear and revulsion when approached by an aggressive young man interested in a date. In such instances, she may have practically no freedom to respond as she might rationally choose. At other times, we may be characterized as having limited freedom, as when the abused woman has struggled with and reflected on her experience and can make some choices of thought and action as an adult that will at least partially reshape her responses to men. Finally, there may be some instances wherein people act with almost total freedom, when they have few powerful forces impinging on their choices and they freely choose their actions. A pastor whose marriage is relatively stable but who chooses to have an affair to experience the excitement of rebellion against "rules and regulations" might be such an example.

The Christian view of persons requires that people have some responsibility in life, not that we always act without influence or constraint. Precisely how this influence interacts with human responsibility and agency is a profound mystery. The fact that we are so profoundly influenced by God's providence, by our biological inheritance, our families, our communities, our cultures and by the idiosyncratic events that happen in the course of life only adds to the mystery.

Personhood

Our understanding of humanness is also affected by the continually changing attitudes toward sexuality, gender and race.

Sexuality. The Christian Scriptures present a positive and cohesive portrait of our sexuality (Jones & Hostler, 2005), teaching that:

1. Our physical bodies are good. God made us physical beings; we do not just *have* bodies, we *are* bodies though we are more than just bodies.

2. God made us sexual beings, male and female, and our sexuality is good.

3. We are made for relationship; in Genesis 2:15-24 we learn that even the perfect man—in the perfect environment and in perfect relationship with

God—is insufficient by himself. God declares that it is not good that the man be alone; human beings are made for relationship with a complementary version of human being, a man for a woman and a woman for a man.

4. Humans are created capable of "becoming one flesh" through the joining of their bodies, and the resulting capacity for reproduction in marriage is blessed by God and a blessing from God.

5. Humanity rebelled against God and in the process broke God's beautiful gift of sexuality, along with all of his other gifts to us. As a result, we are rebellious, broken, twisted.

6. God is at work redeeming our sexuality in two crucial ways: God has revealed his standards or rules for how we are to conduct our sexual lives (and his laws are for our own good [Deut 10:12-13]), and then he offers us a living relationship with him through the death and resurrection of his Son, Jesus Christ, so that we are actually capable of living our lives in a way that gives him pleasure and moves us toward the holiness he intended for us.

7. The Scriptures reveal to us that sexual intercourse has a meaning fixed and determined by God: it creates a one-flesh union between a man and a woman, a union that is to knit them together in a way that's supposed to remain permanent through life (and thus this teaching is the foundation for Jesus' condemnation of divorce in Matthew 19 and Paul's condemnation of sexual immorality in 1 Corinthians 6).

Gender. Storkey (2007) has noted the plethora of work done by evangelicals in the past quarter century investigating how gender engages with the breadth of Christian doctrine (Trinity, Christology, soteriology, personhood, eschatology, Godhead language). Out of this discussion (or at times, acrimonious debate) have emerged two primary schools, with many gradations in between: the complementarian view and the egalitarian view. The key divide is over ordination to official offices of the church and the issue of headship and authority in marriage. The debate is grounded in a strong commitment to scriptural authority on both sides. But fueling the debate is the complexity and at times mysteriousness of the scriptural witness on these matters. For example, the apostle Paul on the one hand commends Junia (a feminine proper name in Greek) as one of the apostles (Rom 16:7) and yet grounds his prohibition on women teaching in seemingly absolute terms in the creation account (1 Tim 2:12-14). Thus, the scriptural position is far from clear, despite strong statements from both schools.

Part of the importance of this discussion is that historically some Christians have grounded arguments against women's ordination or for male headship in assertions about women being the "weaker" or lesser sex, only to see these views subsequently used to mistreat women or deprive them of basic human rights and dignity. Fortunately, today the primary exponents of both the complementarian and egalitarian positions together affirm women as made fully in God's image, as equally given the dominion mandate to carry out alongside men, as redeemed equally by Christ Jesus, and as indwelt fully by the Holy Spirit, the giver of all gifts. They are also united in recognizing increasingly that both the Old and New Testaments present views of women that were uniquely empowering, affirming and respectful in the context of their contemporary cultural contexts. Despite those who insist that Scripture is univocal on this issue, to avoid further division in the church over this matter the wisest course may be to hold one's position with humility given the lack of biblical consensus.

Race. The realities of globalization provide tremendous opportunities for realizing the promise made to Abraham that all nations would be blessed through him (Gen 12:3). The "Christian family" today is profoundly multiracial and multiethnic. For too long in the Western world, theology was viewed as being properly understood only through Western eyes, yet there is an increasing awareness today of careful and Christ-honoring theological work being done not only in North America and Britain/Europe, but also in Africa, Asia and Latin America. Though agreeing on the foundations of theological belief—the triune God, the authority of Scripture, the fallenness of humanity, salvation being provided through Jesus Christ—this intercultural conversation is helping Christians everywhere appreciate better what aspects of their "Christian" views derive from Scripture and which derive from culture. There is an increasing recognition that because all humans are made in the image of God and will one day, together, come and worship the Lord (Rev 15:4), we have much to learn from one another during the early earthly part of our sojourn as well.

Human Motivations in Creation

The Bible gives no direct message about the nature of human motivation, but that does not mean that we are left drifting on this important point. We find it highly instructive to study carefully the first two chapters of the

Bible to see the tasks that the first persons were assigned in the beginning. If we believe that God created our first parents as a perfect match for the role they were intended to fill in the Garden, then perhaps part of the matching would be that we are motivated at a fundamental level to live out the tasks assigned to us.

As noted earlier, part of human flourishing calls us to image God in our roles of dominion and relating to God and others. In Genesis 1:26 we read that we were made to rule over all of creation. We were also made male and female, and in being blessed by God we were instructed to be "fruitful and increase in number" (Gen 1:28). God then repeated the instruction that we are to rule over all living things, plant and animal. In Genesis 2 the charge to rule reoccurs in the instruction to cultivate and keep the Garden of Eden (Gen 2:15). Further, Old Testament scholars point out the additional significance of Adam naming the animals, since naming was a function of authority in ancient times, signifying one who owns or controls. In the creation of Eve we learn that God himself uttered the words that "it is not good for the man to be alone" (Gen 2:18). We learn that it was God's creational intent to provide a partner for the man, one for whom he was to separate from his family, to whom he was to cleave and with whom he was to become one flesh (Gen 2:24).

Two themes emerge. The first is the theme of *responsible dominion*. Humans were meant to rule on God's behalf, in dependence on him. Our vocations, our callings, are a primary vehicle through which we rule. Even seemingly mundane work such as gardening is a manifestation of our capacity for exercising dominion. We are God's stewards in this world, and all persons are meant to live out their Godlikeness in exercising responsible dominion over their part of the created order. Our contention is that this command entails a human need for *purposeful activity in life, a need for meaningful work and the realization of purpose outside of ourselves.*

The second theme is that of *loving relatedness.* Though there are scholars who view the use of the plural pronoun in Genesis 1:26 (God said, "Let us make man in our image, in our likeness") as primarily reflecting the language of royal theology common to the ancient Near Eastern world, and thus as being a reference to those in God's court (such as angels), we stand with many others who view these plural statements as reflecting God's triune nature. God has always related to himself. This is what divine perfection means. He did not need to create us, for he already had triune fellowship, but he chose to create. And it is clear that we were created for fellowship with God. Like our Creator, human beings are intrinsically relational and social beings. God's greatest gift to us at the beginning was not the order of creation or the beauty of the Garden, but the fellowship of his own person and the capability to enter into that fellowship. The Scriptures talk about our relationship with him in terms of a covenant or marriage contract. As Paul so eloquently notes, "Christ loved the church and gave himself up for her, that he might sanctify her, having cleansed her by the washing of water with the word, so that he might present the church to himself in splendor, without spot or wrinkle or any such thing, that she might be holy and without blemish" (Eph 5:25-27 ESV). This is the Christian's individual and corporate destiny. Yet the web of relatedness intended by God reaches up not only to the sovereign Lord, but also out to our fellow believers in marriage by our capacity to become one with another who is separate and different from us. In this union we image God in having the capacity for procreation, a reflection of God's much more profound capacity for creativity and generativity. Having children anchors us in cross-generational relationships of loving acceptance and discipline. But we also image God more broadly by our relational capacity reflected in the rich possibilities of celibate friendship through which the individual, whether single or married, can live a life of love and sharing in the community of the people of God. Such relatedness with our Christian brothers and sisters is vital for all of the heavenly Father's children. Obviously, generating biological children is not the only means of our reproducing ourselves. Adoption and cross-generational ministry are among the many profound ways of passing on one's riches to the next generation.

It bears special emphasis in these times that a Christian view of persons will emphasize family as fundamental to what it means to be human, not the least of which includes our local communities of worship, our true family created by our brother Christ who has provided a means for us of becoming children of our heavenly Father by his indwelling Holy Spirit. Families are webs of relationships in which we are imbedded throughout life, for better or for worse, in much the same way that God who created us remains in relationship with us, his fallen and wayward people. And family is a profound metaphor for our interrelating in Christ. This creation mandate of relatedness suggests that a fundamental human motive will be the establishment and maintenance *of meaningful relationships characterized by intimacy and unity even while we celebrate our uniqueness.*

HUMANITY IN ITS FALLEN STATE: *NON POSSE NON PECCARE*

Though we were created for dominion and relatedness, we managed to corrupt both capacities in the Fall. We were given the task of accountable dominion over the earth and were given the freedom and the abilities to discharge those responsibilities, but there were limits to the dominion marked by God, and we violated those guidelines in prideful disobedience. Though created to be in loving relationship with the Father, we betrayed his faithfulness and love toward us with our rebellion and deceitfulness. We betrayed the loving Father who had only our good at heart. Created to be open and responsive to God, we became willful, accountable rebels against God, and as Hubbard (1979) said, "at that moment God's scepter of glory became his gavel of justice" (p. 78).

This is seen as unpopular and harsh language in certain evangelical circles, but biblical realism takes sin seriously, and we must do the same. Fallen and under divine wrath, we became alienated from God. As a further result, we became disoriented within ourselves; in theological terminology, this is known as the noetic effect of sin, that sin affects even the way we think. We all have a rather predictable tendency to deceive ourselves and others, and we often attempt to deceive our Creator. Perhaps the most powerful literary rendering of this capacity and tendency for self-deceit is C. S. Lewis's (1956) brilliant novel *Till We Have Faces,* in which the main character, who had spent her whole life justifying her actions, realizes her unreadiness to confront her Judge and asks rhetorically, "How can they meet us face to face till we have faces?" (p. 294). In other words, how can we meet God face to face when we spend so much of our lives deceiving ourselves about who and what we really are and hiding our true faces from ourselves and God? Our alienation from God and disorientation within ourselves are regarded as the twin facets of the Fall.

The divine wrath that we are under is not only an expression of God's justice and dignity; it is an expression of his love. Where such vast capacity for fellowship exists, the capacity for hurt is enormous, not unlike that of a broken marital covenant. "What we were made to do and what we were best at doing are now our sharpest and clearest failures" (Hubbard, 1979, p. 79).

The Nature of Sin

Sin as state and act. Sin is dealt with in very complex ways in the Scriptures, and getting a clear handle on this slippery concept is difficult. Christians often think of sin as isolated acts that violate moral standards. We think this or that act was a sin. Yet in Scripture sin refers not just to acts but to a state of being. Individual sins testify that we have a "sin nature," which predisposes us to those individual acts of violation against God's law. (Mark 7:20-23 states that individual acts proceed out of a heart of corruption.) As Bloesch (1984) states, "Sin is not just a conscious transgression of the law but a debilitating ongoing state of enmity with God" (p. 1012).

Yet sin is even more than a disposition in our natures; it is something palpable beyond ourselves; it is "a power that holds us in bondage" (Morris, 1986, p. 57). Among the New Testament writers, Paul especially seems at times to reify sin as a transpersonal "force" acting against God and his purposes (Rom 6–7). Because we are now fallen, we are only able to choose according to our fallen natures—our choices consistently align us against God. As a result of the Fall we have lost our human freedom, the freedom to do God's will. We have lots of choices, but in our own strength they all drive via different roads away from God. So sin is at once acts of transgression, a nature or disposition, and a force in opposition to God.

Rebellion or anxiety? What is the nature of our sinfulness? Why do we commit sins and have a sinful nature? The classic orthodox answer to this question has been to highlight our human rebelliousness against God. Bloesch (1984) states that

> in Reformed theology, the core of sin is unbelief. . . . Hardness of heart, which is closely related to unbelief, . . . means refusing to repent and believe the promises of God (Psalm 95:8; Hebrews 3:8, 15; 4:7). It connotes . . . stubborn unwillingness to open ourselves to the love of God (2 Chronicles 36:13; Ephesians 4:18). (p. 1012)

In this formulation sin is a culpable rejection by humans of their rightful submission to God's sovereignty. It is a willful abuse of the freedom God imparted to us.

Another major current understanding of the nature of sin might be characterized as "neo-orthodox." Originating with Niebuhr and Tillich, this view suggests that sin originates in the "union between man's dependence as a creature and his free spiritual life" (Gilkey, 1985, p. 231). Confronted with the awesome responsibility of managing the tension between our human finiteness and contingency (dependence on God for our very existence), on the one hand, and our capacity for freedom and transcendence, on the other, we experience anxiety of an existential nature. We don't want to be dominated by our temporal existence, but neither do we want the responsibility of choice. The righteous response to this dilemma is to balance the tension and choose to live in humble submission to the Creator as a dependent being with responsible choice. But the sinful response is to evade the human responsibility of managing this tension by either denying our freedom and living life dominated by the cares of this world (plunging oneself into sensuality with the cry "I can't help myself," for example), or denying our dependence on God and trying to become gods unto ourselves (thus rebelling against God's laws and saying, "No one is going to legislate my life for me!"). Both of these imbalanced responses are regarded as sin, as both shrink from responsibly living out life in the way God created it to be.

There are actually many other understandings of sin (see Bloesch, 1984). Liberation theology, for example, rightly recognizing that sin can and often does become institutionalized, emphasizes the exploitative, oppressive, greedy nature of corporate sin. And many of these views are not mutually exclusive; it is not hard, for instance, to see the Reformed and neo-orthodox views as complementary truths, and orthodox Christians can sadly concur that sin is often institutionalized, while also insisting that there is an inescapable individual aspect of sin.

A Christian understanding of sin that is truly biblical must maintain a balance between seeing sin as a violation of law and as a violation of relationship, of sin as individual and sin as corporate, of sin as driven by rebellion and sin as driven by anxiety, of sin as something we are in bondage to and are yet responsible for.

Moral evil, natural evil, finitude and the satanic. Ethicists commonly make the distinction between moral and natural evil. Moral evil is the result of moral choice—such as intentional theft, for instance. Some things, though, are bad but are not the result of a culpable choice. The accidental injury of a young child who falls down a set of stairs is such a natural evil, as are most instances of disease, decay and death. They may be no one's fault, but they are bad nevertheless, a part of life's reality in a fallen world.

Theologically, the origin of both moral and natural evil is humanity's fall from grace. In Adam and Eve's original choice to turn from God's command and partake of the forbidden fruit (Gen 3:6) lies the beginning of human moral evil. As our first parents chose, now so we choose. Natural evil's origin may be seen in God's judgment on Adam and Eve. They who were given responsibility to care for the garden have the judgment on them extended to the garden that now will produce thorns and thistles (Gen 3:18). Natural evil, therefore, is now understood as nature, the created order, working against human flourishing. Important to note in this discussion is that the temptation to both Adam and Eve, who were created good, arose not from their own natures but from the serpent, or Satan, who was already in the garden. (Genesis 3:1, Revelation 12:9 and Revelation 20:2 identify Satan with the "ancient serpent" of Genesis.)

We can also distinguish moral and natural evil from our finitude, our limitedness as human beings. Our human limitations exist because we are not gods, and thus finitude existed in creation prior to either moral or natural evil. There is much that is beyond our possible reach physically, mentally, emotionally and spiritually. Adam could not run a two-minute mile, will immediate emotional changes, know the future or in any way exceed the capacities God had given him. Humans must confront their finitude and achieve some reconciliation with their limitations. Limitations are not necessarily flaws or sins; they are simply the limits of the raw material from which we are to forge who we are and who we are to become. Thus finitude is part of our God-ordained creatureliness that we might learn to depend and rely on the One in whose image we have been made.

These distinctions become important when sorting out our understanding of human problems. Some human difficulties are due exclusively to human moral evil—sometimes our own, sometimes that of others, but most often both. If we deceive ourselves and engage in immoral behavior, we will bear the consequences.

But many human problems are essentially natural evils rather than moral evils. Chemical brain imbalances appear to be predisposing factors in such disorders as schizophrenia, and are probable factors in other serious disorders. Alternatively, we may experience problems because of our finitude without that problem being a sin. The college student struggling with the difficulty of making decisions about careers is confronting the reality of her finitude—no one knows the answers to all the questions one could ask about careers and the future, and it is not sin not to know these answers and to struggle with the decision.

We must also mention another significant instance of moral evil, that of the active opposition against God's purposes and goodness by the "forces of wickedness" and darkness (Eph 6:12 NASB). Satanic and demonic evil are real. The personal evil of the supernatural forces in rebellion against God must be taken seriously by all Christian mental health workers. Shuster (1987) has argued that there is a demonic element to all evil, and that Scripture suggests that these personal forces of evil have infiltrated all aspects of human life. This further complicates our understanding of moral evil, natural evil and finitude when we grapple with how forces of darkness corrupt our experience and contribute to the evil we are exposed to and commit. Usually, all these elements—the moral evil of ourselves and those about us and of the demonic world, natural evil and human finitude—are involved in the problems of the person who comes for psychotherapy.

We can see the complexity of the human condition as we recognize how all of these aspects of our human experience come together for all of us. A child faces life in the context of human finiteness with a limited capacity to deal with trauma. Perhaps that child is exposed to such unfortunate events (natural evil) as the loss of a mother to cancer. The child's surviving parent, out of his own weakness and fallenness, sinks into alcoholism and begins physically abusing his son in frustration and grief. The demonic forces seek to use these events to pull this child away from any openness to a loving Father God. As that child grows into a young man, he may continue to experience natural evil (a girlfriend killed in a car accident) and moral evil perpetrated against him (the father's abuse turns into chronic emotional abusiveness). In his finiteness he has only so much capacity to strive to overcome all he has experienced but now begins to contribute his own moral evil as he abuses substances to cope and responds abusively to women. And again, supernatural forces for evil seek to use all of this to turn this young man from seeking healing from God.

Johnson (1987) suggested the designation of "moral fault" to describe instances where both moral evil and "weakness" (his term for what we are calling finitude) are involved. We prefer a three-component designation as developed earlier, but his concept of moral fault is a good one, which suggests that often, perhaps almost always, problems involve all these components of moral evil, natural evil, finitude and the satanic.

Sin and Human Freedom

The state of human freedom after the Fall is a topic of mind-boggling complexity. Humanity is now burdened with an impaired capacity for freedom to please and follow God, in that sin now infuses our very being and clouds our every choice. The desperate cries of Paul in Romans 7 are repeated by all Christians who find their desire to follow God in righteousness frustrated by a continual bondage of the will to sin. We can all testify to our impotence to obey God perfectly and to follow him wholeheartedly. And yet God holds us responsible for our disobedience. In short, we have the dual experience of choice *and* bondage, culpability *and* an incapacity to do otherwise. This experience matches the scriptural puzzle of our seeming inability not to sin coupled with our undeniable culpability for sinning.

We can offer no easy resolutions to this matter (see McDonald, 1982, pp. 57-67, 92-100). According to Scripture, God's general revelation in nature (Rom 1:20) and the human conscience (Rom 2:15) hold us accountable to God. Yet though this revelation in the created world is indeed part of God's self-disclosure to humanity, it is clear that only by means of God's special revelation, his specific disclosure in Jesus Christ, are humans able to submit to God by his Word, grace and Holy Spirit.

Historically, theological discussion of the matter of free will has usually centered on a specific, crucial choice: the person's choice to become a Christian. Both Calvinists and Arminians hold to a view of theological compatibilism—that God's exhaustive foreknowledge is compatible somehow with humans' exercising responsibility before God. Even so, Calvinists tend to stress the "God" side of the equation, asserting that the act of coming to Christ is wholly the work of God through his grace. They further assert that to believe that any element of being born again is attributable to the person's choice diminishes God's sovereignty, making faith a "work" and thus Christianity a religion of works rather than grace. Arminians, on the other hand, tend to stress the "human responsibility" side, asserting that there is an element of choice or human freedom in becoming a believer. They argue that to assert otherwise is to make humans into moral robots, God into the grand puppet master, and Christianity a deterministic religion. They do not, however, deny our bondage to sin or the central importance of God's work in freeing us from that bondage.

For our purposes here we are not so concerned with the decision of becoming a Christian as we are with the capacity for human freedom in the give-and-take of everyday life. Suffice it to say that in everyday life humans, on a moment-to-moment basis, may not be free to choose the perfect good. Most often this appears beyond our grasp. But the inaccessibility of that choice does not render nonexistent other choices that we can make. For example, we may not be able to choose to be perfectly honest, but we have real choices day by day of particular instances where we can veer either in the direction of being honest or deceitful.

God in his sovereignty may shape human choices to ensure the triumph of his grace and of his redemptive plan for humanity, but human choice is nonetheless real. For example, one of our children may be destined by God to some work of critical importance to God's purposes on earth, and as such God may be guiding our actions toward them, drawing that child toward him, either through our good example and discipline as parents or through the poverty and pathos of our hypocrisy. In either case, we parents still make choices of how to deal with them and are accountable to God for those actions. There are, from eternity's perspective, no small decisions and no unimportant persons.

Human Motivations After the Fall

Earlier we addressed human motivations implied in the creation narrative. There are also implications for our understanding of human motivation to be drawn from the saga of humanity's Fall, both in terms of new motivations we experience and in the distortions of our most basic creation-grounded motivations.

In terms of new motivations, rebellion against God, the desire to be gods ourselves, now becomes an operative motive in all that we do. Whether we admit it or not, we are all rebels. In addition, to the extent that sin is rooted in the ontological anxiety of grappling with our freedom in light of our limitations, the desire to run away from this burdensome responsibility now operates as an ever-present motivation as well. The story of the Fall makes it clear that Adam and Eve tried to cover up their sin by first avoiding God and then attempting to shift blame and abrogate personal responsibility. This awareness of divine judgment and the desire to avoid that righteous judgment now color all that we do. We are motivated to escape culpability for who we are and what we do.

The Fall also contaminates our most basic good motivations. The good motive for meaningful work and to serve good purposes can become twisted into a drive to dominate others, to be number one, to control or even to rebel against the notion that we have purpose in life and to choose to drift meaninglessly. The good motive of relatedness can be twisted into sensualism and an idolatry of sexuality, into pathetic dependence on another, into a loss of identity in the other, or in a retreat from engagement from others. We no longer experience the pristine original motivations of Adam and Eve before the Fall. Scripture's account of humanity's Fall may additionally offer some insight into spiritual warfare: whenever we find ourselves questioning or disbelieving God's Word ("Did God really say?" [Gen 3:1]) or God's goodness ("God knows that when you eat of it, your eyes will be opened, and you will be like God, knowing good and evil" [Gen 3:5]), we need to be wary of these age-old temptations.

All of this immeasurably complicates our understanding of human motivation. Humans experience compound and conflicting motivations as part of their essential unredeemed natures (and even once redeemed as well). For example, as we approach dating and marriage, we may desire another with the good motive of seeking intimacy and the bad motive of desiring someone to exercise power over. In summary, the constellation of our motivations is vastly complicated by our rebellion against God. Our motivations are seldom pure and never simple.

HUMANITY IN ITS REDEEMED STATE: *POSSE NON PECCARE*

Using covenant terminology (after Anderson, 1987), we might say that in the midst of the devastation of the Fall, the marriage between humanity and God had been shattered, but from one side only. Grace for reconciliation is needed. God has offered restoration in the life, death and resurrection of Jesus Christ, the pivotal events in all of history and the only source for our hope and salvation. Receiving this grace may lead to significant transformations in the lives of ordinary people through believing and acting on the truths of the faith.

Life Between the Beginning and the End

It is commonly noted that the experience of the Hebrews in being redeemed from Egypt by the Lord (Exodus through Deuteronomy) is a powerful model of our own redemption process. While the Israelites were oppressed, God raised up for them a savior, Moses (a type of Christ). God through Moses freed them from their bondage and servitude to an alien master, and initially they exuberantly celebrated their freedom. But release from captivity was not immediately followed by entering the Promised Land. Rather, the Israelites had to wander in the wilderness for many years before being ushered into the "land of milk and honey." Christians similarly live between the day of emancipation and the day of final deliverance. A battle has been won but the war is not over. Brunner (1939, p. 114 and throughout) calls this "life in contradiction"—life suspended between our fallen and redeemed natures.

With the coming of Jesus the King, the kingdom of God has been inaugurated. Thus, we now live between the "already" of the kingdom of God that is present and the "not yet" of the kingdom of God that is to come. We must navigate the struggles and tensions of this "in-between" life by depending on God and others who share this journey. We do this by becoming part of a covenant people, by becoming deeply involved with a local body of believers. Only in the context of a healing community can we learn to cultivate and express the fruits of the Spirit, which along with a deep concern and compassion for others should epitomize mature, committed Christians.

The Goal of the Redeemed Life

Paul's central prayer for the Philippians expresses well the central goal of life in Jesus Christ:

> I consider everything a loss compared to the surpassing greatness of knowing Christ Jesus my Lord, for whose sake I have lost all things. I consider them rubbish, that I may gain Christ and be found in him, not having a righteousness of my own that comes from the law, but that which is through

faith in Christ—the righteousness that comes from God and is by faith. I want to know Christ and the power of his resurrection and the fellowship of sharing in his sufferings, becoming like him in his death, and so, somehow, to attain to the resurrection from the dead. (Phil 3:8-11)

According to the apostle Paul, the goal of the Christian life is to know Christ, which entails having a righteousness based on faith, being conformed to (or in some way identifying with) Christ's sufferings and death, and finally attaining eternal fellowship with Christ through the resurrection of the dead.

On our contemporary scene, much has been written about emotional wholeness and Christian holiness. Some authors seem to regard the two as essentially identical. Surely growth in Christ means to become more like Jesus, and the more we are like him, the more holy and whole we must be.

Yet wholeness and holiness are actually very different. We live in a fallen world. It is easy for our conceptions of wholeness to become contaminated with sub-Christian notions of well-being, especially those that emphasize easy accommodation with the world. All too often in psychology the goals for clients are to become well adjusted and do one's best at a purely human level, rather than radical realignment of one's life to the claims of Christ.

Curiously, one recent secular acknowledgment of this tension was contained in a prominent report from the American Psychological Association (2009). That report acknowledged that conflict and tension may exist between psychological and religious perspectives on personhood, stating that "Some religions give priority to *telic congruence* . . . [while in contrast, certain models of] psychology give priority to *organismic congruence*" (p. 18). The term *telic congruence* means that some religions (they clearly had Christianity in mind) formulate the purpose of life to include, against many of our instincts, seeking to reject how we find ourselves to be and striving to become (to develop congruence) with some other goal (Greek *telos*) such as seeking to become like Christ. They contrast this with *organismic congruence,* a psychological valuing of embracing (congruence) what we are already (what is organismic). The APA could not be more on target that this is a fundamental tension—are we okay just as we are, or do we need to be saved from what we are and conformed to something transcendent?

In contrast to such idealized goals as minimizing conflict, total emotional awareness and expression, maximizing life satisfaction and pleasure, and living up to our innate potential, note that Paul prescribes the goals of becoming conformed to Christ's suffering, death and resurrection. Such a calling certainly includes a number of personal experiences that are far from secular psychology's ideals for well-adjusted human living. In short, we are called to a way of life that is often at odds with the ways of the world, a way of life where suffering and pain are an inevitable part of our lot in life, where being holy, which literally means being set apart to God's purposes and manifesting his righteous character, can be difficult and even despised by the world. The Christian life is a way of life in which, as Paul stated, believers know both how to be abased and how to abound, having learned in all circumstances the secret of facing plenty and hunger, abundance and want: "I can do all things through Christ who strengthens me" (Phil 4:12-13 NKJV).

McLemore (1982) cautions that it is quite possible for an individual to be a paragon of mental health, as it is traditionally defined in psychology, yet be living without faith in God through Christ. The peaceful practitioner of Zen Buddhism, unruffled by life's demands as he retreats into an inner world, might be supremely healthy by the definition of some. On the other hand, a "saint" in the local church may be living a life of emotional pain and interpersonal estrangement as she faithfully follows God's calling, thus living a life of holiness that is far from the current psychological understanding of wholeness.

Thus, while there may be much that overlaps between *wholeness* and *holiness* (especially as both are embodied in the concept of Christlikeness), and the two concepts may not be contradictory in any fundamental way, we must be exceedingly careful when we discuss the two terms. The chief danger is that the pursuit of wholeness is so easily and widely approved of in the Western world that it would be easy for Christians to pursue "growth" as defined by some therapy approach while deluding themselves into thinking that they are thus pursuing holiness as well.

Christian clinicians need to think carefully, critically and courageously about the goals that they are advocating in the context of counseling and psychotherapy, to think in the light of what it means for a believer to be "salt and light" in the world and to be "bearing the marks of Christ." It is imperative that these goals include considerations of Christian faith and experience.

Another unfortunate contemporary development is that of substituting the language of the soul with that of the self. The loss of belief in Scripture as God's Word and concern over Platonic construals of the soul has resulted in a shift within much of the psychological literature of referring to one's "self" rather than one's "soul." Yet these words are far from being synonyms. As Boyd (2001, p. 114) notes, to speak of a self is to limit one's perspective to the earthly; to speak of the soul is to acknowledge that there is a life beyond this one and One to whom we must one day give an account.

HUMANITY IN ITS GLORIFIED STATE: *NON POSSE PECCARE*

Perhaps it is appropriate to end this overview where Augustine did, looking to humanity in its glorified state, no longer able to sin but demonstrating complete freedom to please God in all things. As the Westminster Shorter Catechism notes, one day we will achieve our chief end of fully and without sinful impediment glorifying God and enjoying him forever.

As we struggle with various trials, temptations and earthly suffering, we need to remember that the effects of the Fall are temporary; that one day Christ will wipe away every tear from our eyes (Rev 7:17); that the earthly part of our sojourn is the *short* part of our journey; that one day we will cease to walk by faith and will know our Maker fully by sight, no longer seeing in a mirror dimly, but face to face; no longer knowing in part, but knowing fully even as we have been fully known (1 Cor 13:12); that our earthly labor is not in vain but, in Christ, is full of meaning (1 Cor 15:58). Thus we receive John's encouragement: "Dear friends, now we are children of God, and what we will be has not yet been made known. But we know that when he appears, we shall be like him, for we shall see him as he is" (1 Jn 3:2).

This sure hope is what allows us to persevere in the face of our own suffering and that of others.

CONCLUSION

It is essential for Christian pastors, academicians, clinicians and researchers to take Christian worldviews and control beliefs seriously. As McDonald (1986, p. 138) has noted, there is no purely psychological theory of personality that can give an effective account of all the ethical and religious concerns of the human individual. What we have covered here does not constitute a personality theory, but it does form a vision of personhood that should undergird a personality theory acceptable to Christians.

No such theory exists today. Christian psychologists must therefore tentatively work within incomplete personality systems while striving for development of a full-bodied Christian view. As Brunner (1939, p. 62) has argued, there can be no Christian psychology if by that we mean a theory of elemental sensory processes or memory. But when we move to the level of a comprehensive understanding of the *person*, then there will be a distinctively Christian approach to psychology.

Does the faith have implications for how we intervene with persons? Does it specify modes of counseling with troubled people? From surveying the writings of Christian counselors, one sometimes gets the idea that God specifies one and only one way of dealing with all problems and difficulties. As we already argued in chapter one, the problem is that each of the Christian counselors specifies a different set of techniques, claiming that his or her system is the one endorsed by Scripture. One emphasizes exhortation to behavior change, another a change to biblical thinking, another healing prayer, another supernatural intervention and yet another the casting out of demons.

Our position on this matter is that we have much to learn from various forms of pastoral intervention recommended and utilized in the Scriptures. In 1 Thessalonians 5:14, the apostle Paul says, "And we urge you, brothers, warn those who are idle, encourage the timid, help the weak, be patient with everyone." Paul's admonition shows that different types of human problems call for different types of responses from counselors. Many other types of interpersonal helping responses are specified in the Bible, including loving, forgiving, providing material charity, teaching, comforting, grieving with, rebuking, excommunicating and so forth. Clearly what is needed is a flexible repertoire of approaches, grounded in coherent theory and deeply respectful of the complexity and profundity of human struggles.

Almost any form of counseling interaction in the Bible can find its counterpart in the practice of secular psychotherapy. It is interesting, though, that each major school of psychotherapy tends to build its identity around a rather limited number of styles of therapist-client interactions so that cognitive therapists are teachers, person-centered therapists are accepting, psychoanalytic therapists are distant and interpretive, and so forth. No counseling model we know of embodies the diversity of interaction styles that seem to be recommended in Scripture. So, as the Christian therapist moves beyond a secular theory, one needed area of growth is an expanded vision of technique that incorporates the eclecticism found in Scripture.

FOR FURTHER READING

Berkouwer, G. (1962). *Man: The image of God* (D. Jellema, Trans.). Grand Rapids, MI: Eerdmans. (Originally published n.d.).

An excellent Reformed study of theological anthropology, emphasizing the image of God.

Blocher, H. (1997). *Original sin: Illuminating the riddle*. Grand Rapids, MI: Eerdmans.

A penetrating and remarkably interdisciplinary reflection on the nature of sin.

Clebsch, W., & Jaekle, C. (1975). *Pastoral care in historical perspective*. New York, NY: Jason Aronson.

One of the best studies of the history of the pastoral care tradition, including "exhibits" of original writings in pastoral care from throughout history.

Cooper, J. W. (2000). *Body, soul, and life everlasting: Biblical anthropology and the monism–dualism debate*. Grand Rapids, MI: Eerdmans.

An insightful critique of monism from an evangelical perspective.

Hoekema, A. A. (1986). *Created in God's image*. Grand Rapids, MI: Eerdmans.

A solid overview of all facets of theological anthropology from a Reformed perspective.

Lewis, C. S. (1946). *The great divorce*. New York, NY: Macmillan.

A moving and thought-provoking depiction of physical existence after the resurrection.

McDonald, H. (1982). *The Christian view of man*. Westchester, IL: Crossway.

An excellent overview of Christian anthropology.

McMinn, M. R., & Phillips, T. R. (Eds.). (2001). *Care for the soul*. Downers Grove, IL: InterVarsity Press.

A collection of essays from the 2001 Theology Conference at Wheaton College, this compilation offers thoughtful insights about the integration of theology and psychology from a number of perspectives.

REFERENCES

Adams, J. (1979). *More than redemption: A theology of Christian counseling*. Phillipsburg, NJ: Presbyterian & Reformed.

APA Task Force on Appropriate Therapeutic Responses to Sexual Orientation. (2009). Report of the Task Force on Appropriate Therapeutic Responses to Sexual Orientation. Washington, DC: American Psychological Association. Retrieved from www.apa.org/pi/lgbt/resources/therapeutic-response.pdf.

Anderson, R. (1987). *For those who counsel*. Unpublished manuscript, Fuller Theological Seminary, Pasadena, CA.

Augustine (Intro. by Thomas Hibbs). (1961). *Enchiridion on faith, hope, and love*. Washington, DC: Regnery Publishing.

Beck, J. R., & Demarest, B. (2005). *The human person in theology and psychology: A biblical anthropology for the twenty-first century*. Grand Rapids, MI: Kregel.

Berkouwer, G. (1962). *Man: The image of God* (D. Jellema, Trans.). Grand Rapids, MI: Eerdmans. (Originally published n.d.).

Bloesch, D. (1984). Sin. In W. Elwell (Ed.), *Evangelical dictionary of theology* (pp. 1012-1016). Grand Rapids, MI: Baker.

Boyd, J. H. (2001). In defense of the word *soul*. In M. R. McMinn & T. R. Phillips (Eds.), *Care for the soul* (pp. 102-117). Downers Grove, IL: InterVarsity Press.

Brunner, E. (1939). *Man in revolt* (O. Wyon, Trans.). Philadelphia, PA: Westminster Press. (Originally published 1937).

Clebsch, W., & Jaekle, C. (1975). *Pastoral care in historical perspective*. New York, NY: Jason Aronson.

Cooper, J. W. (2000). *Body, soul, and life everlasting: Biblical anthropology and the monism–dualism debate*. Grand Rapids, MI: Eerdmans.

Engel, G. L. (1977). The need for a new medical model: A challenge for biomedicine. *Science, 196*(4286), 129-136.

Evans, C. (1977). *Preserving the person: A look at the human sciences*. Grand Rapids, MI: Baker.

Evans, C. (1990). *Søren Kierkegaard's Christian psychology*. Grand Rapids, MI: Zondervan.

Foster, R. (1985). *Money, sex, and power: The challenge of the disciplined life*. San Francisco: Harper & Row.

Gilkey, L. (1985). *Maker of heaven and earth*. Lanham, MD: University Press of America. (Originally published 1959).

Green, J. (1998). Bodies—that is, human lives: A re-examination of human nature in the Bible. In W. S. Brown, N. Murphy & H. N. Malony (Eds.), *Whatever happened to the soul? Scientific and theological portraits of human nature* (pp. 149–174). Minneapolis, MN: Fortress.

Greidanus, S. (1982). The use of the Bible in Christian scholarship. *Christian Scholar's Review, 11*, 138-147.

Gunton, C. E. (2002). *The Christian faith: An introduction to Christian doctrine*. Malden, MA: Blackwell.

Hoekema, A. A. (1986). *Created in God's image*. Grand Rapids, MI: Eerdmans.

Hubbard, D. (1979). *What we evangelicals believe*. Pasadena, CA: Fuller Theological Seminary.

Jewett, P. (1975). *Man as man and female*. Grand Rapids, MI: Eerdmans.

Johnson, E. (1987). Sin, weakness, and psychopathology. *Journal of Psychology and Theology, 15*, 218-226.

Jones, S., & Hostler, H. (2005). The role of sexuality in personhood: An integrative exploration. In W. R. Miller & H. D. Delaney (Eds.), *Human nature, motivation, and change: Judeo-Christian perspectives on psychology* (pp. 115-132). Washington, DC: American Psychological Association.

Lewis, C. S. (1956). *Till we have faces*. New York, NY: Harcourt Brace Jovanovich.

Lewis, C. S. (1963). *Letters to Malcolm: Chiefly on prayer*. New York, NY: Harcourt Brace Jovanovich.

McDonald, H. D. (1982). *The Christian view of man*. Westchester, IL: Crossway.

McDonald, H. D. (1986). Biblical teaching on personality. In S. Jones (Ed.), *Psychology and the Christian faith: An introductory reader* (pp. 118-140). Grand Rapids, MI: Baker.

McLemore, C. (1982). *The scandal of psychotherapy*. Wheaton, IL: Tyndale.

Morris, L. (1986). *New Testament theology*. Grand Rapids, MI: Zondervan.

Oden, T. (1984). *Care of souls in the classic tradition*. Philadelphia, PA: Fortress.

Plantinga, C. (1988). Images of God. In M. Noll & D. Wells (Eds.), *Christian faith and practice in the modern world* (pp. 51-67). Grand Rapids, MI: Eerdmans.

Shuster, M. (1987). *Power, pathology, and paradox: The dynamics of good and evil*. Grand Rapids, MI: Zondervan.

Storkey, E. (2007). Evangelical theology and gender. In T. R. Larson & D. J. Treier (Eds.), *The Cambridge companion to evangelical theology* (pp. 161-176). Cambridge: Cambridge University Press.

Straub, R. O. (2006). *Health psychology: A biopsychosocial approach* (2nd ed.). New York, NY: Worth.

Webber, R. (1986). *The church in the world*. Grand Rapids, MI: Zondervan.

Wolterstorff, N. (1984). *Reason within the bounds of religion* (2nd ed.). Grand Rapids, MI: Eerdmans.

Wolterstorff, N. (1987). *Lament for a son*. Grand Rapids, MI: Eerdmans.

3

CLASSICAL PSYCHOANALYSIS

Stanton L. Jones, Robert Watson and Richard E. Butman

Although psychoanalysis is the grandparent of all psychotherapeutic methods, it tends to be unpopular in many conservative Christian circles. The specific concerns focus around three troubling themes in classical Freudian psychoanalysis: (1) the emphasis on sexual and aggressive drives as the motivational bases for behavior, (2) the deterministic and naturalistic assumptions of the model, and (3) the direct attacks on religion Freud made in his later writings.

Despite these reservations, many Christian mental health professionals have a profound respect for this tradition (see, for example, Sorenson, 2004; Crabb, 1988; McLemore, 1984; Narramore, 1984; Peck, 1983). Certainly the reservations are legitimate, but to dismiss psychoanalysis as irrelevant to the real problems of life is to fail to see its potential significance for the church and the society (Browning & Cooper, 2004).

Classical psychoanalysis has reemerged in contemporary conversations between neuroscience and psychoanalysts. While there is no clear consensus, a number of key neuroscientists suggest that the basic contours of Freud's view of the mind may serve as a theoretical framework or template that can organize the empirical findings (Kandel et al., 2005). In fact, recent Nobel laureate in physiology and medicine Eric R. Kandel (1999) said that in light of the findings of contemporary cognitive neuroscience, psychoanalysis is "still the most coherent and intellectually satisfying view of the mind" (p. 505). The direct impact of psychoanalysis as a system of thought can be seen in nearly all academic disciplines, including history, literature and philosophy. The more indirect influence on the larger public consciousness can hardly be overestimated (Jones & Wilson, 1987). Thus, Freudian thought continues to be relevant at a cultural level, and its broad impact profound (and despite the legitimate Christian objections we will raise here, we seriously doubt that all the influence has been negative).

Given the brevity of our treatment, we cannot trace the development of psychoanalytic thought over time. Freud's thinking evolved over his productive years; the most striking example of this is his gradual move away from a harshly biological approach to his subject matter, and his widening of his understanding of motivation to include not just the sexual drive but the aggressive/death drive as well (Mitchell & Black, 1995). For the sake of economy, we will present Freud's system as if it were a static whole, though we recognize that this fails to capture the evolution of classical psychoanalytic ideas. We will appraise contemporary derivatives of the classical Freudian analytic tradition (called psychodynamic theories) in chapter four.

DESCRIPTIVE SURVEY

Classic psychoanalysis assumes that all human behavior is determined by the impact of early childhood experiences on the management of psychic energy. In order to make sense of a person's current behavioral patterns, it is necessary to understand the behavior's roots in largely unconscious conflicts and motives. The forces that "move" us are irrational and strong, and are related to aggressive or sexual drives that arise from biological instincts. Consequently, the goal of psychoanalysis is to make the unconscious conscious: to bring into conscious awareness disavowed desires, feelings, fantasies, fears, memories and wishes whose expression has been thwarted. Often, this involves exploration of memories of critical life events in the formative childhood years thought to be related to the psychopathological symptoms and problems in living that emerge throughout the remainder of the lifespan. Only through greater self-knowledge and self-regulation can mature adults increase their capacity to love and work effectively.

This theory is best understood when we grasp the historical-cultural milieu or context of psychoanalysis. We will highlight three aspects of

Freud's historical-cultural context: (1) the Enlightenment worldview of the late nineteenth century, (2) the Darwinian assumptions underlying Freud's anthropology, and (3) his Victorian-era Austrian cultural milieu.

The early modern era, beginning in the early 1600s, brought to an end the medieval era in Europe. For our purposes, this transition marked dramatic shifts in cultural (including theological) views of personhood. Cushman (1995) observed,

> What was once a spiritual being who contained a soul and was embedded within a community that was in turn held in the hand of God, had become an early modern individual who contained a mind which was dependent upon the domination of reason and will over the wild emotions of the body. (p. 93)

The modern, Enlightenment view of persons construed the individual's mind as ruled by reason, but construed the emotions (and the body) as wild and primitive; it also entailed a dramatic shift toward an individualistic view of the self. Order, domination and control emerged as key values in the post-medieval European world that supported its burgeoning market economies, republics and politics. The individual mind and its capacity to bring order, rationality and control over itself (including the body and its passions) preoccupied much intellectual discourse. The use of science and technology to bring a rational sense of order and control over the natural world, human institutions and people groups also became hallmarks of the modern era. Freud was not just an uncomplicated Enlightenment figure, however; the Romantic movement that competed with rationalistic Enlightenment thinking is also reflected in and took inspiration from Freud, who never saw rationality alone as the route to understanding or achieving human wholeness. The emotional realities of the human psyche were irrefutable and inevitable contributors, even determinants, of human experience. Freud never manifested the bland optimism that reason was the answer to all problems, which characterized other Enlightenment figures. Further, with his relentless search *behind* our current conscious experience for hidden explanations in our unconscious, Freud helped set the stage for the development of postmodernism, particularly in terms of the way in which his "hermeneutic of suspicion" (i.e., an instinct that the surface explanation for human experience is rarely the fundamental one) became one of the pillars of postmodern epistemology (Westphal, 1998). Thus, it is probably less accurate to call Freud an Enlightenment thinker, and better to identify him as an exemplar of modernity.

Freud formed his psychoanalytic theory and treatment approach against this historical-cultural backdrop, informed by his work as a research neurologist and clinical psychiatrist. At the center of his theory building, Freud viewed mind as a kind of internal, psychological battleground for the three *modern* forces of the human condition: instincts, rationality and culture (Cushman, 1995). The connection between Freud's model of mind and his context seem clear on this point: his awareness, particularly as an Austrian Jew, of the long history of war, bloodshed, repression and strife in Europe influenced his view of the interior struggles of the individual. For Freud, as a quintessential modern man, "Life is a constant contest, a struggle to determine which aspect of the mind would dominate and which suffer from the consequences of submission" (Cushman, 1995, p. 115). This was, of course, represented theoretically in his structural theory of mind as a battleground between three intrapsychic "agencies" (more on this later).

It is also against this historical-cultural background that Freud's focus on sexuality as central to personality, development and psychopathology developed. The Enlightenment (and Romantic) view of persons suggested that beneath rational civilization and individual mind lays the primitive, pleasure-oriented bestial aspects. Consistent with the cultural perspective of his day, Freud linked pleasure-seeking, primitive instincts and a Romantic view of animals with human sexuality. "Thus, Freud established sexuality as a realm of unfettered pleasure, free from the tyranny of the object and social necessities, a 'nature preserve,' like a zoo in the middle of an urban setting" (Mitchell, 1988, p. 121). For Freud the inevitable conflict in the mind between agencies of rationality, culture and instinct best explains human behavior, development, psychopathology and personality.

The second of the cultural-historical factors influencing the classical psychoanalysts were the Darwinian assumptions underlying Freud's anthropology. Darwin's evolutionary perspective exerted profound influence over the thinking of Freud's late-nineteenth-century European scientific milieu. Consistent with Darwin's emphasis on evolutionary development from primitive (or lower) to advanced (or higher) organisms, Freud considered mental development to follow a similar trajectory. We develop as our "bestial," primitive core is brought under control by our rationality and cultural constraints. Freud made use of the Darwinian shift from the Platonic-Judeo-Christian portrayal of humankind as fallen from harmony with and designed by a divine Creator to humankind evolving from below. "Man was not a fallen angel, a chip off the divine block gone astray, but a more or less refined beast. This reversal provided a fresh and exciting perspective on human nature and experience, and Freud was very much a beneficiary" (Mitchell, 1988, p. 73). This perspective, of course, put classical psychoanalysis on a direct collision course with theistic worldviews of his day (and ours).

The third contextual aspect influencing classical psychoanalysis is the highly repressive and obsessively proper Victorian-era Austrian cultural milieu in which Freud worked and lived. Being an astute clinician and an ethnic outsider, he saw through the superficial propriety and popular piety of the day. His patients' stories reflected darker aspects of everyday human experience: lust, envy, possessiveness, ambivalence, hatred and self-deception—things no one addressed directly in proper conversation. In fact, his clinical work eventually brought him to a conceptual (and personal) crisis: his patients' stories of childhood sexuality, including abuse and seduction, led him to suspect that children from good Viennese families had actually been seduced sexually by parents and parent figures. Ultimately, Freud resolved this crisis in his thinking and practice (in part) by assuming that these stories were, by and large, fantasies generated by his patients when they were *children*. He thus construed these fantasies as not only fearful, nightmarish sexually traumatic fantasies, but also as wish-fulfilling, pleasure-seeking fantasies—that is, as what they as children wanted to experience with their parent(s) emotionally and sexually. What was, of course, lost in this theoretical resolution of the problem was the distinct likelihood that Freud was actually hearing about *real* traumatic memories of sexual abuse—a prospect the magnitude of which he may have been unable to face.

As a result Freud brought into the open what polite Victorian society tried to avoid. And he argued that this very avoidance of what is most primitive, instinctual and uncivilized about us is at the core of psychological problems and symptoms. Cushman (1995) writes,

> [Freud] thought the unthinkable, and uttered the unspeakable; no one was
> safe from his gaze, not mothers, not children. Paul Ricoeur has called psy-

choanalysis a "hermeneutics of suspicion," and for good reason. Freud saw psychopathology as a product of urges, conflicts, and self-deceptions common to all persons, regardless of social class, race, religion, or gender. According to Freud's theory, if peoples' inherent physiological drives are not repressed by the "internalized" norms of society, acts of violence or sexual perversity would destroy society. But repression, in turn, causes its own problems, which are manifested through various psychological symptoms: what is repressed "returns" in creative but ultimately self-destructive or dangerous behavior. (pp. 110-111)

Ironically, while Freud clearly valued the role that culture played in civilizing our base, animal instincts, he also pioneered a worldview and method that helped to bring to an end the Victorian view of persons as rational, pious and civilized at the core.

Philosophical Assumptions and Model of Personality

Philosophically speaking, psychoanalysis reflects the influence of classical empiricism as well as the Enlightenment tradition (cf. Rychlak, 1973). Freud adopted a materialistic or naturalistic worldview as the backdrop for his model. Ultimately, Freud believed that his psychology would be understood in terms of brain physiology. For example, Freud (1914) once opined, "We must recollect that all of our provisional ideas in psychology will presumably one day be based on an organic substructure" (p. 78). Classical psychoanalysis makes at least five core assumptions about persons (Brenner, 1973; Arlow, 1984): (1) topographical, (2) genetic, (3) dynamic, (4) structural and (5) economic.

The *topographical assumption* asserts that there are three levels of consciousness: (1) the conscious experiences we are aware of (e.g., thoughts you have as you read this page), (2) the preconscious experiences that we can voluntarily recall but are not currently cognizant of (e.g., the memory of your best experience in the fifth grade), and (3) the unconscious experiences that are the primary determinant of psychic life but are not directly accessible to conscious examination (e.g., unresolved conflicts from your childhood). All behavior is assumed to have largely unconscious determinants. Although we may be aware of our conscious motives for writing this book (e.g., contributing to the work of the church), at a somewhat deeper and perhaps more powerful level, we may be unconsciously looking for approval from parents or significant others.

The *genetic assumption* essentially asserts that current behavior and experience, but most notably troubling repetitive behavior, is overdetermined by past events. All the influences that we believe to be shaping us in the present (e.g., conflict with a supervisor at work or love for our spouse) have their real power through the unresolved issues of our past (e.g., conflict with a parental figure that was strictly authoritarian or overly permissive). In other words, the experiences that trouble us largely derive their meaning from activating unresolved difficulties from the formative years of childhood. Consequently, psychoanalysis has a strong historical as well as deterministic bias (cf. Ford & Urban, 1963).

The *dynamic assumption* contends that all behavior is ultimately dependent on the interaction of two fundamental human drives. The *libidinal drive* is largely erotic or sexual in nature. Broadly defined, the libido focuses on far more than genital sexual release and pleasure—it includes the desire or urge to create, to develop or maintain intimacy, to love self or others, to form ideals and values, and more (Munroe, 1955). The other major drive is primarily oriented around the twin themes of aggression and death. Both drives have creative or destructive potential (Prochaska, 1979). Libido and the death instinct also are the impetus for attachment and separation behavior. Both drives can be understood as deterministic at the intrapsychic, interpersonal or societal levels. These "life instincts" and "death instincts" are at the core of the Freudian view of human nature and of what drives human behavior.

The *structural assumption* asserts that the psychic apparatus can best be understood in terms of three separate but interdependent psychological entities known as the *id, ego* and *superego*. The id is the repository for our most primitive sexual and aggressive drives and urges. Id processes are assumed to be present at birth and to be largely unconscious, illogical, demanding and relentlessly driving toward personal gratification (this is called the pleasure principle). The ego is reality based and develops as an individual interacts with the external world. The ego is largely conscious and serves a vital role in mediating the primitive urges of the id with the constraints or opportunities of reality. Finally, the superego places restrictive demands on both the id and the ego. It is generally understood as a split-off from the ego and as the repository of the moralistic standards one has absorbed from significant others, most often parents and society.

Often seen as a primitive kind of conscience, the superego is assumed to be only partially conscious.

Finally, the *economic assumption* asserts that human personality can best be understood as a closed or quasi-hydraulic system. In other words, a certain amount of energy is introduced into the psychic system in the form of the basic drives. Exactly how instinctual energy (bodily, primitive instincts) became psychic energy (i.e., that powers the structures of the personality) was never explained by Freud. He, like all thinkers of his time, was limited by the mind-body dualism introduced by Descartes. Since this energy must be released, ways must be found to disperse it in a direct or transformed manner. This is *economic* in the sense that energy is neither gained nor lost; the bank account always balances. The goal of psychoanalytic treatment is to develop the capacity for the release of id energy in socially acceptable and appropriate ways. In contrast, psychopathology is understood as the consequence of a compromise negotiated by the ego between the demands of the superego to comply with the internalized rules of others and of the id to allow for partial gratification of unacceptable wishes (e.g., a psychosomatic symptom that elicits attention and also expresses aggression). At more severe levels, psychopathology may also be understood as gratifying release of id energy with little regard to the constraints of reality or external social norms (e.g., psychotic regression).

For Freud consciousness was only a small part of the total psyche. Although it cannot be studied directly, Freudians believe the existence of the unconscious can be inferred from direct observation of behavior or through conscious experiences such as dreams, slips of the tongue or material derived from free association. Freud hypothesized that all the stored experiences, memories and repressed material of a lifetime can be found in the unconscious. Since unconscious material influences all behavior, the deeper contents of the mind must be explored at some level to achieve any significant measure of health and wholeness. Awareness and insight of this material alone isn't curative—it must be worked through, ideally in the context of a psychotherapeutic relationship.

In the absence of such working through, however, means must be found to deal with the anxiety that develops out of the conflict between the id, ego and superego over the control of the available psychic energy. Ideally, the ego can control the anxiety through direct and rational means, but more often than not the largely unconscious and often primitive ego defense mechanisms must be utilized. These defense mechanisms transform the threatening anxiety into some alternate form the person can deal with and thus help one cope with threatening unconscious conflicts. The more primitive defense mechanisms often result in marginal coping. Most abnormal psychology, personality or psychotherapy textbooks contain summaries of the most important defense mechanisms. The main lesson to be learned about defense mechanisms is that overt behavior rarely means what it seems to, because in transforming the anxiety caused by unconscious conflicts, the true reasons for our behavior become largely inaccessible.

The classic Freudian understanding of the development of personality asserts the existence of a series of psychosexual stages. According to this perspective, the personal and social development that occurs in these critical stages of infancy, childhood and adolescence lays the foundation on which further maturation can be built. Both healthy and unhealthy personality development reflect the manner in which the relevant tasks were accomplished. Each stage is distinguished by the focal area of the body where the gratification of libidinal impulses is concentrated.

The *oral stage* (first year of life) is foundational to later personality development. The caregiver's focus is on feeding and nurturing the infant, and gratification for the baby centers on the mouth; sucking and chewing are primary. Failure to get one's needs met potentially leads to greediness or an unhealthy preoccupation with possessions in later life.

The *anal stage* (ages one to three) centers around the child's experience of parental demands, discipline and expectations, especially as they relate to toilet training. Psychic gratification centers on retention and expulsion of feces and urine. Unresolved issues at this stage potentially lead to unhealthy attitudes about the body or bodily functions. Extremes of orderliness or messiness are also assumed to be related to unresolved issues in this period.

In the *phallic stage* (ages three to six) the focus for gratification moves away from the mouth and anus to the genitals. It is during this stage that the child learns much about sex-role identity and develops an interest in sexual matters. Parental attitudes in particular are communicated verbally or nonverbally, and negative experiences can affect feelings about sexuality throughout the remainder of the life span.

The phallic stage is assumed to be the period in which Oedipal (for boys) or Electra (for girls) conflicts emerge, in which the child develops threatening, erotically charged feelings for the parent of the opposite sex. Freud developed his notions of what happens at this stage for boys to a much greater extent than for girls, so we will focus on those. (The Oedipal crisis was named after the famous Oedipus myth of Greek mythology, in which Oedipus was destined to murder his father and marry his mother.)

The boy, Freud proposed, comes to experience vague libidinal longings for union with his mother. These are rarely experienced consciously. These feelings are often exhibited by intense attachments to mother, jealousy for her attention and so forth. Realizing that the father is a competitor for the love of the mother, the boy first experiences an angry competitiveness with the father, followed by a fearful realization that he cannot, as a child, hope to compete for the attention of the mother (assuming the basic health of the parental relationship). The healthiest resolution to this terrible dilemma is for the boy to identify with the father and actually absorb parts of the father's personality, so that at least the boy can have some sense of special attachment to the mother on a vicarious level by being like the father. Part of what is absorbed becomes the foundation for the superego.

In the *latency stage* (ages six to twelve), increased socialization with other children typically replaces the inwardness of the phallic period. Coupled with new interests in others, the child develops academic, athletic, interpersonal or recreational competencies. These social themes are predominant throughout the prepubescence period.

In adolescence the child moves into the *genital stage* (ages twelve to eighteen) where again sexual impulses become predominant. Interest in the opposite sex develops, often with some sexual experimentation. Ideally, libidinal energies are redirected in socially appropriate activities (e.g., dating friendships). The genital stage is assumed to continue throughout the remainder of life as one searches for a healthy balance between love, work and play.[1]

Even the most ardent critic of psychoanalysis would agree that the approach is comprehensive and that its model of personality has heuristic value (Ryckman, 1985). Unfortunately, the theory all too often lacks pre-

---

[1]Somewhat parallel but complementary understandings of these stages can be found in the work of Erikson (1982) or other major developmental theorists (cf. Berger, 1988).

cision and testability, and runs the risk of leading to "nothing-but," or reductionistic interpretations of behavior (e.g., everything becomes the result of aggressive or sexual drives). Still, as Silverman (1976) has observed, aspects of psychosexual theory can be clinically demonstrated. For example, persons with primitive defenses against aggressive and sexual impulses do seem to exhibit greater rates of neurotic psychopathology, an observation consistent with Freudian theory.

Model of Health

In the psychoanalytic tradition, healthy individuals have enough conscious awareness of their wish-fulfilling aims to have self-control and self-awareness (as Freud [1933] said, "Where id was, there shall ego be. It is a work of culture—not unlike the draining of the Zuider Zee" [p. 80]). Both wish fulfilling and painful and traumatic memories have largely been worked through and are no longer denied or distorted. To a meaningful and significant degree, aspects of the unconscious have been made conscious. Important dimensions of the personality structure have been reconstructed as neurotic processes have been undone, thereby facilitating greater movement toward maturity.

The healthy person has good ego strength. Destructive impulses exert less pressure on the individual so that he or she is increasingly able to make responsible decisions about how to deal with the tasks of everyday living. The clash between the biological urges and the demands of social reality is still there, but effective compromises, choices and commitments have been made. Self-knowledge about these and other tensions are of supreme importance in this tradition, so much so that it is often viewed as a necessary, if not sufficient, condition for growth toward an autonomous and productive life (Korchin, 1976, pp. 326-332).

Maturation, then, is seen as a lifelong process of increasing the capacity to understand and regulate one's self. Obviously, this will require a high level of self-awareness and intelligence, a fair degree of willingness for painfully honest self-assessment, and a strong motivation for change and growth in one's life. Perfection is impossible to reach.

Model of Abnormality

According to this tradition, everyone is pathological, to a greater or lesser degree, due to the inevitable conflicts and fixations that develop in our formative years. The specific symptoms that develop reflect both the psychosexual stage in which the conflicts and fixations first developed and the particular manner in which immature or primitive ego defense mechanisms are utilized to deal with the resulting anxiety. In other words, psychoanalysis assumes that problems in living are universal, since nobody proceeds through the developmental stages without difficulty. At the intrapsychic level, all symptoms "work," in that they help us cope with the demands of everyday living, even though the symptoms may be self-defeating and perhaps even self-destructive.

The model is thoroughly intrapsychic in its assessment of the etiology and maintenance of emotional difficulties. The more intense the conflicts and fixations are, the more severe the psychopathology. Given sufficient environmental or internal stress, the defenses can be overwhelmed and symptoms emerge. These internal threats are typically avoided rather than dealt with directly, and the person is highly motivated to keep unacceptable impulses or childish, primitive anxieties out of direct consciousness at whatever cost. When the avoidance strategy is coupled with often well-meaning attention from family and friends that help continue the unhealthy way of dealing with the conflict, the cycle of avoidance can become a deeply ingrained pattern (what has come to be designated "the neurotic nucleus").

In short, stress stirs up unacceptable wishes and makes the person anxious (i.e., creates internal conflict); the anxiety is avoided at all costs (which can be highly reinforcing); and a vicious cycle becomes established. A more direct strategy of resolving the core conflict itself is not adopted because the deeper unconscious "primary process" is nonlogical (irrational) and atemporal (makes no differentiation with respect to time) (cf. Prochaska, 1979, pp. 34-35).

According to the model, conflict is not incidental to being human. Rather, conflict is intrinsic to human nature and forms the core of our being. At the minimum the positing of two distinct fundamental drives creates the potential for confusion and tension in human motivation. Freud thus differed from later humanistic theorists who consistently see motivational confusion and tension as the result of external interference with the uncomplicated motivations of persons; for Freud, confusion and tension was often intrinsic. But more consistently, the instincts of the id conflict with the repressive dictates of the superego, such that the two seem to do battle, like two powerful horses, with the ego astride them both, trying to get them to cooperate. Consequently, conflict is as much a part of normalcy as it is of pathology.

Anxiety is at the core of all psychopathology, operating largely at the unconscious level. Generally speaking, the person has no awareness of the deeper significance of immediate precipitating events and how they affect the underlying impulses or unresolved conflicts and fixations. As the largely unconscious anxiety intrudes on consciousness, the person tends to experience feelings ranging from a mild sense of dread to feelings of panic. Anxiety at any level serves a signal function: it signifies (painfully) the presence of a threat—from the inside or the outside. Depending on where these conflicts and fixations first developed psychosexually, and the specific ego defense mechanisms utilized to bind the anxiety, the full spectrum of psychopathology takes shape. Obviously, certain responses to immediate precipitating events are healthier than others. But at some level all symptoms are gratifying, even to highly functioning individuals. This inevitable tendency to deny and distort reality is apparently generic to the human condition (cf. Munroe, 1955, for an especially insightful treatment of these themes).

Model of Psychotherapy

For Freud the ultimate goal of psychoanalysis is the complete analysis of all aspects of personality and the resolution of virtually all intrapsychic conflicts (which is the highest and most difficult goal of any system of psychotherapy). In order to accomplish this goal psychoanalysts argue that it is necessary to relive memories of certain painful childhood experiences and work them through. This process is called abreaction or catharsis, but a patient, careful therapeutic focus on the patient's avoidance of these memories via defense mechanisms, precedes it. In making the unconscious conscious, the ego is strengthened, thereby facilitating a greater capacity for managing the demands of the instinctual urges within the constraints of reality. The resulting self-awareness and insight is more than merely intellectual—it is deeply felt and experienced after an agonizingly difficult and often painful process of change, and thoroughly integrated by the patient.

Classical psychoanalysis usually involves multiple appointments every week for at least two or three years, and often more. Obviously, this can be an expensive and demanding commitment. In actual practice, analysts work in diverse and varied ways, depending on their personal styles and the needs of their clients. Despite these differences, concerned analysts early recognized the need to reduce the length of the standard treatment, without sacrificing the technique's unique properties (Korchin, 1976, p. 325).

But it is precisely because of the typical length, expense and intensity of the treatment that psychoanalysis is so widely disparaged in both lay and professional circles. Specifically, it is asserted that psychoanalysis is an elitist therapy, geared toward the rich and self-indulgent who find that talking about themselves to a highly trained analyst a great deal promotes their own sense of well-being. In their defense, classical Freudian psychoanalysts assert that promoting lasting and significant change is of necessity a difficult and time-consuming process. Not only do clients need to unlearn self-defeating coping strategies, but they must also develop new and more effective ones. Further, change is resisted because these same patterns have historically worked for the client, in that they bind anxiety, provide some degree of instinctual gratification, and often lead to attention from others. As Korchin (1976) has summarized it, "the process of character reorganization . . . is about on par with learning a new language to replace one's mother tongue, particularly if the student is ambivalent in his motivation, fighting the new experience while seeking it" (p. 325).

Classical Freudian psychoanalysts usually agree that they should remain *relatively* neutral and personally anonymous to their clients. This way of relating to patients is thought to help by bringing out into the open and into the therapeutic relationship the very psychological conflicts that are related to their psychopathological symptoms. So, for example, if their symptoms are about feeling anxious at work in relation to a critical supervisor, the neutral stance of the analyst may evoke similar feelings of anxiety toward another authority figure (i.e., the analyst) that can be worked through in the therapeutic relationship. They assert that more directive and supportive approaches have lesser value for many patients, in that they tend to promote dependency rather than autonomy. Further, psychoanalysts assert that these therapies run the risk of becoming anti-developmental, in that they tend to lessen the necessity of the "legitimate suffering" that will occur when the client works at self-exploration. Only deep self-awareness and understanding can lead to the kind of insight needed to promote lasting change (see Meissner, 1985). On the other hand, contemporary Freudian psychoanalysts (e.g., Gabbard, 1994) also understand that some patients—typically with more severe psychopathology—cannot tolerate nondirective, highly emotionally stimulating interventions typical of the classical approach. For these patients, directive and supportive interventions are targeted at supporting and scaffolding healthier defenses, coping strategies and overall ego functioning (Gabbard, 1994).

The most basic method of psychoanalysis is free association. Clients are asked to minimize conscious control and tell everything that comes to their minds, with the expectation that more and more significant material bearing allusions to unconscious conflicts will emerge. This basic rule of psychoanalysis is exceedingly difficult to follow even with the best of intentions. Most of us are loathe to speak directly and truthfully, even in the best of situations. This is especially pronounced in the context of a clinical relationship, where difficult and often painful material must be explored and worked through. Resistance to free association often builds in direct proportion to the psychic significance of the unconscious material emerging. Indeed, classical psychoanalysis asserts that the forces that are striving toward recovery are usually met with equally strong opposing ones. And it is the analysis of these blocks or disruptions in free association (i.e., resistances to the process of analysis owing to defense mechanisms) that often give the analyst clues as to the nature of psychic conflicts and fixations. If they can be brought to awareness and effectively dealt with, increased insight can result.

Another major theme in this tradition is the analysis of the transference relationship that occurs between the therapist and the client. Strong, personal feelings of both a positive and a negative nature usually develop between client and therapist that go beyond the actual or real clinical relationship. Specifically, both client and therapist bring to the current relationship issues that are brought forward (transferred) from earlier relationships with significant others. Assuming that the analyst has dealt with his or her own countertransference issues (basic conflicts that might be transformed into feelings, expectations and attitudes toward the client), the focus can be on bringing the client's hidden and repressed conflicts or feelings from the past, which are transferred into feelings about the therapist, into the present where they can be examined, understood and resolved. The neutrality of the therapist encourages the development of transference, as the more unknown the therapist, the easier it is for the client to project his or her internal material on that therapist. Thus client reactions toward the therapist are vitally important. Indeed, they can develop to the point where a transference neurosis will emerge, which then becomes the major focus of therapy. A potential transition between illness and health also becomes possible if the deeper meaning of the neurotic origins of the expressed feelings can be explored and worked through in the context of the client's current difficulties and needs.

Interpreting the client's resistances and defensive maneuvers is another fundamental strategy utilized in psychoanalysis. Good interpretations are appropriate in timing, tact and sensitivity. Specifically, they must be given at the level at which the client can hear, understand, appreciate and incorporate them. They not only make sense intellectually, they *feel* true at a deep emotional level. If the interpretations are premature or inappropriate, they only lead to greater resistance. If they are well-suited, they can contribute to greater understanding and perhaps relief. Ideally, good interpretations help the client to make sense of current thoughts, feelings and behavior in light of his or her past.

Psychoanalysts assert that dream analysis is especially helpful in uncovering important unconscious material. During dreams, normal conscious controls are relaxed, perhaps even more deeply than they are in free association. Through inquiry, inference and eventually interpretation, the meanings of both current and longstanding conflicts or difficulties can be explored and worked through. Although Freud once described dreams as "the royal road to the unconscious," they are "hardly a freeway with unlimited visibility, nor do hidden meanings roll forth with simple clarity" (Korchin, 1976, p. 328). As with free association, resistance and transference, working through the material is hard work that takes time and an extremely high degree of commitment on the part of the psychoanalyst and patient.

In summary, psychoanalysis consists of a variety of methods to make unconscious conflicts conscious so that they can be worked through in the context of the psychotherapeutic relationship. In particular, the "then and there" conflicts and fixations of the formative years of childhood and early adolescence are explored as they relate to "here and now" concerns. These must be "reconstructed, discussed, interpreted, and analyzed" (Corey, 1986, p. 38) with a view toward the strengthening of the reality-oriented ego—one's best hope of lasting change. Since the therapeutic goals are so high and difficult to obtain, and the self-defeating patterns so deeply established with the client, it is inevitable that most treatment be intensive and long-term.

Few clinicians alive today can deny that they have felt the impact of Freudian theory and technique. Hardly any well-developed approach to people-helping lacks a conception of an unconscious, an appreciation of the role of early childhood development, or an understanding of the relevance of such clinical concepts as transference and countertransference, resistance or the ego defense mechanisms. The model stresses biological and instinctual factors to the neglect of other psychosocial, interpersonal or sociocultural factors, but it does speak broadly and deeply to certain dimensions of the human experience. On the other hand, as Alston (1967) has noted (p. 516), psychoanalytic concepts need to be more explicitly stated and anchored in objective criteria if they are going to be the basis for further interdisciplinary dialogue. The works of Hackett (1986), Oakland (1977) and Walters (1973) are good initial examples of such interdisciplinary work.

Contemporary psychotherapists are indebted to the legacy of classical psychoanalysis. While many aspects of Freud's theory—most especially his drive theory—appear to have limited value, many other pieces of classical psychoanalytic theory and technique have held up well over the course of time. Empirical research and vast clinical experience would seem to support ongoing interest in and utility of six clinical concepts grounded in psychoanalysis, namely, the dynamic unconscious, psychological ambivalence, defense mechanisms and resistance, the compulsion to repeat, the centrality of the therapeutic relationship and mourning of illusion.

Dynamic unconscious. That a significant portion of our consciousness is beneath our own awareness is unquestionable from the standpoint of classical psychoanalysis and of contemporary cognitive neuroscience. The remaining questions about the unconscious mental processes revolve around questions of what the content is. For example, neuroscientists working at the interface of psychoanalysis and cognitive neuroscience suggest that Freud's dichotomy of unconscious instinctual life into sexuality and aggression is not comprehensive enough. At present, at least four basic instinctual "circuits" seem to underpin our instincts (Solms, 2004). They are a "pleasure" system (which motivates us toward the pursuit of pleasure), the "anger-rage" system (which is related to aggression associated with fight or flight when threatened), the "fear-anxiety" system (which helps alarm us into action in the face of potential threat), and the "panic" system (which is related to instincts associated with social bonding and attachment). That these systems operate much of the time out of our awareness is fairly obvious—particularly in terms of their motivational aims. Knowing that most of human consciousness is not directly accessible is useful to any clinician. Having a basic map of the terrain of the unconscious is particularly helpful when attempting to understand human behavior.

Ambivalence. Classical psychoanalysis provided us with a basic framework for understanding and working clinically with a fundamental reality of human beings; namely, that we live between what we *wish* for and what we *fear* will happen if we get what we wish for. Freud and the classical psychoanalysts recognized that wishes and fears are linked: you cannot have one without the other surfacing nearby. If a patient feels anxiety about an upcoming family event—a reunion, perhaps—the therapist can safely assume that there are corresponding wishes that are tethered to the fears. For example, the individual anxiously anticipating the event may wish (perhaps unconsciously) that this time she might feel welcomed and secure in her mother's presence. On the other hand, getting what we wish for often triggers unexpected fear or anxiety. For example, the pleasure of a wished-for promotion at work is often followed by feelings of dread regarding whether she can now perform up to a new set of standards and expectations.

Defense mechanisms and resistance. Another enduring contribution from classical psychoanalysis involves methods of psychological self-protection and self-preservation. When examined outside of a relational context (e.g., the psychotherapy relationship), these methods are called defense mechanisms. When explored within a relational context, these are called types of resistance. Defense mechanisms have been cataloged and stratified over many years. Many contemporary approaches cluster individual defense mechanisms from most primitive and least adaptive to most mature and most sophisticated psychologically (see the *Adaptive Functioning Scale* of the American Psychiatric Association, 2000).

Repetition compulsion. One of Freud's most poignant and useful clinical observations is summed up in the following from his 1914/1963 article: "the patient remembers nothing of what is forgotten or repressed, but that he expresses it in action. He reproduces it not in his memory but in his behavior; he repeats it, without of course knowing that he is repeating it" (p. 160). Freud goes on to provide, as an example, the story of the patient who does not remember being defiant and critical of his parents' authority in his childhood, but behaves precisely in that way toward the therapist. This very human propensity to express in action that which is too painful to remember is an essential clinical phenomenon for psychotherapists of all theoretical orientations to understand. It is this dynamic that drives transference phenomena.

Patients that have histories of psychological trauma—particularly *chronic* trauma over many years—are most vulnerable to the compulsion to repeat. In this attempt at self-protection (to not remember) coupled with a wish to "revisit the scene of the crime" to try to have a different outcome in the present, many people unconsciously orchestrate present-day scenarios to reenact their painful historical experiences. This can take the form of trying to please authority figures in the present that are withholding approval, choosing a romantic partner or mate who behaves like an abusive or neglectful figure from childhood, or (unconsciously) choosing a vocation that holds out the promise that the practitioner can finally help people in the present in ways that they could not help their own families in the remote past—a common motivation for people who become psychotherapists!

Centrality of the therapeutic relationship. Classical psychoanalysis was the first psychotherapeutic system to insist that what happens within the therapeutic relationship figures centrally in the outcome of the treatment. The assumption is that patients deliver into the relationship with the therapist the very patterns of thinking, feeling and behaving that caused them to seek treatment. And this aspect of the repetition compulsion (and of the patient's resistance to becoming aware of what is being repeated) is highly significant grist for the mill of what happens in psychotherapy sessions and what ultimately leads to making progress and experiencing healing.

In recent years empirical support for the link between the quality of the therapeutic relationship and the outcome of treatment has been mounting. In fact, the psychotherapy outcome research literature suggests that 30 percent of the variance in courses of psychotherapy with positive results is accounted for by the quality of the therapeutic relationship and other factors common to all therapies. This percentage of the variance is second only to the 40 percent of the variance attributed to "patient qualities and extratherapeutic change" (Lambert & Barley, 2001). While contemporary psychotherapy outcome research does not prescribe a classical psychoanalytic model for the therapeutic relationship, it certainly argues for the potency of the relationship between therapist and patient. And the psychoanalytic tradition clearly is the most thoughtful and comprehensive in its reflection on making use of the therapeutic relationship on behalf of the patient's healing.

The perceived effectiveness of Freud's psychoanalysis was enhanced by the clinical insightfulness he demonstrated in his writings, but according to Storr (1989, pp. 100ff.), while Freud mentioned 133 cases in his writings, he only provided extensive reports on six cases. Of these six, he only saw two for over six months, and only one for a full course of psychoanalysis. This last, full case, the famous "Wolf Man," was "not quite the advertisement for psychoanalysis which Freud might have hoped for" (pp. 106-107). Apparently while Freud reported his analysis to be a complete success, a follow-up study suggested that the Wolf Man's analysis with Freud was only somewhat helpful, allowing him to live a life of moderate maladjustment. Thus, while Freud encouraged a helpful understanding of the therapeutic relationship as central, it is by no means clear that his own clinical work demonstrated a high success rate.

Mourning of illusion. Perhaps Freud's most useful and enduring contribution to contemporary psychotherapists was his elucidation of the relationship between the process of mourning of illusion and growth. In fact, it can be argued that mourning and growth are two sides of the same coin (Shabad, 2001). Freud's clinical work with depressed patients helped him to recognize that the failure to disengage the wishes and desires bound up in one's relationship with, for example, a lost parent sets the stage for a kind of thwarted mourning. In normal mourning the wishes and desires—the emotional attachment to the lost parent—are transferred from the actual person to the memories of that person. In pathological mourning the grieving person is vulnerable to clinical depression if she *psychologically* keeps the lost parent alive in her mind in order to meet psychological needs that she believes she cannot meet apart from the lost parent, like feeling confident or loved. Using a psychological sleight of hand, human beings who cannot let go of the other keep the other alive by identifying with them—in essence, allowing their own self to be *eclipsed* by an internalized version of the other. This attempt to hold onto the relationship leads to one of the characteristic symptoms of thwarted mourning—the self-loathing and anger-turned-inward that many depressed people manifest (Freud, 1915/1957). Listening clinically to this type of self-loathing pretty quickly leads to the conclusion that the very things the depressed person is angry about themselves are actually attributes of the lost other. So, for example, the son who cannot come to terms with the death of his mother finds himself berating himself for being mean-spirited and critical of others' mistakes—a quality clearly more related to his mother's personality and behavior than to his own.

So what does this have to do with mourning of illusion *and* growth? Freud recognized that to grow—to become less conflicted, more integrated, more free to choose—requires that we negotiate well the "necessary losses" (Viorst, 1986) that life presents. And the process of negotiation involves willingness on our part to face reality courageously, to endure the necessary dis-illusionment, and to re-member aspects of our hopes and dreams that have been thwarted by the reality of the loss. This last aspect, re-membering or re-collecting, is the least intuitive piece of the mourning process (Shabad, 2001). It involves intentionally thinking about (and feeling about) how we would have wanted/hoped life to have been if the inevitable loss had not occurred. So, for example, it is essential to the healing of the broken heart of the young woman who prematurely loses her father to cancer that she think about how she would have wanted her graduations, wedding and birth of children in the future to have been with her father present—all the while knowing that he will not be a part of those events. This is a type of re-membering—of joining back to her own heart and soul those pieces that have been torn apart by the loss of her father. It is a costly thing for the mourner, for she comes face to face with the very thoughts that evoke the deepest feelings of grief.

For a person with a Christian worldview it is not difficult to sense something paschal about this psychological formulation: it alludes to the deepest pattern and rhythm of reality—that *death precedes new life*. In this case, facing "death" in the form of what was and will be lost in terms of hopes and dreams is a necessary step toward discovering new life. And this type of psychospiritual pilgrimage takes both faith and hope. This integrative theme will be developed further in the next section.

CHRISTIAN CRITIQUE

As might be evident from the previous section, Freudian thought has come under fire from many sectors. As Hurding (1985) notes, Freud receives criticism "from the academic psychologists for being unscientific, from humanistic and theistic psychologists for being too reductionistic, and from the behaviourists for not being reductionistic enough" (p. 70). Still, a balanced and fair assessment would recognize that we owe much to Freud in assisting us in our efforts to make sense of the often bewildering complexity of our psychospiritual natures.

Philosophical Assumptions

Freud is perhaps best known in religious circles for his attacks on religion. Classical psychoanalysis is essentially an agnostic or atheistic system, since Freud treated religion as a wish-fulfilling illusion. Genuine religious motivation and the spiritual life are ignored or treated negatively in psychoanalysis (Vitz, 1987, p. 66). Exemplified in works like *The Future of an Illusion, Civilization and Its Discontents*, and *Moses and Monotheism*, the essence of Freud's argument is that the religious believer in adolescence or adulthood comes face to face with a cold, ambiguous and threatening universe in which annihilation, isolation or meaninglessness are seen as likely options, and death is the inevitable outcome. This creates overwhelming anxiety. In a primitive, self-protecting gesture, we create a comforting illusion with which to shield ourselves. The illusion we embrace stems from real or distorted memories of our childhood years, when as weak and vulnerable persons we felt nurtured and protected by what we perceived to be omnipotent, omniscient and loving parents, and, specifically, an idealized father.

In a desperate attempt to maintain that sense of security and well-being, and to meet our adult needs and wants, we embrace some form of religion, creating an imaginary deity, a divine father figure. Freud specifically argued that religion fulfilled three needs: "[The gods people believe in] must exorcise the terrors of nature, they must reconcile men to the cruelty of Fate, and . . . they must compensate them for the sufferings which a civilized life in common has imposed upon them" (quoted in Storr, 1989, p. 89). Indeed, the illusions we create for ourselves can also serve as a symbolic means to meet unfulfilled childhood longings as well. From the psychoanalytic perspective religion is seen as a kind of universal neurosis that civilization substitutes for a more authentic personal reality based on scientific (objective) knowledge.

In light of Vitz's (1988) treatment of the deeper motives for Freud's rejection of religion, it seems reasonable to assert that important events in his own life contributed to his antipathy toward matters of faith. In fact, Freud's profound ambivalence about Christianity in particular appears to be as much a function of projection of his own conflicted wishes and fears about God and religion as it is the logical outcome of his theorizing. Vitz suggests, for instance, that the traumatic early loss of a nanny who may have been a devout Catholic believer could have complicated Freud's feeling about religion. Vitz also documents Freud's possible dabbling in matters of the occult. There is apparently more to Freud's contention that religion lacked integrity than his "adulation of the scientific method of the day" (Hurding, 1985, p. 73). His attitudes about Christianity reflected his complex hostility and attraction to a faith that meant something to him at a deeply personal level, at the level of Freud's unconscious.

The analysis by Vitz and Gartner (1984a, 1984b) of Freud's understanding of religion also reveals some interesting weaknesses in the theory. They argue that if one presumes God is an illusion, then the "projection of a father figure" understanding of religion makes sense. But if one starts with a presupposition that God exists, psychoanalysis does equally well in explaining atheism!

How would the denial of a real God happen psychologically if classical psychoanalysis is true? If God is a heavenly "father," then disbelief in God must clearly be attributable to the Oedipal period of development. During this period the child feels infantile rage at the same-sex parent who competes with the child for the love of the opposite-sex parent. If the child does not adequately resolve that unconscious rage at the parent during the genital stage, the unconscious rage might be played out as atheism in adulthood; after all, what better way to get back at (or murder) a father figure than to simply not believe in him! Since one can only go so far in rejecting the earthly parent, a deeper rage, an even more primitive aggressive impulse, can be vented on God by denying his very existence.

This theme was developed in Ernest Becker's (1973) classic text *The Denial of Death*. Becker suggested that, from the point of view of the Christian philosopher Søren Kierkegaard, the real problem identified in Freud's Oedipal formulation was that the child wishes to be the father of himself—to be *causa sui*, self-caused. This hostile denial of fatherhood and contingency, Becker argues, is at the center of Oedipal rage:

> In Kierkegaard's understanding of man, the *causa-sui* project is the Oedipus complex, and in order to be a man one has to abandon it completely. From this point of view Freud still had not analyzed away his Oedipus complex, no matter how much he and the early psychoanalysts prided themselves that they had. He could not yield emotionally to superordinate power or conceptually to the transcendental dimension. (p. 257)

For Becker (1973), it is pride that holds back the Oedipal child and the atheist alike from yielding intellectually or relationally to contingency (the father, the concrete embodiment that I did not create myself) and to the transcendent (the Father).

While interesting in itself, we can also see in this brief sketch that one frequently noted problem of the theory of psychoanalysis is its very adaptability. Psychoanalysis can literally explain anything, as in this case it both explains religion and atheism! This is quite a conundrum, in that a true and comprehensive theory would have to explain all facets of human experience, but a theory that is so flexible that it is impossible to come up with any human facts that refute the theory ceases to be a theory and achieves the status of a worldview or dogma.

This case study of Freud's view of religion also highlights the epistemological problems latent in the theory. Because the theory is deemed to explain everything, and because all human experiencing (including rational reflection on truth) is viewed as shaped and determined by irrational, unconscious forces, it follows that we are ultimately locked in a closed system where everything that humans think or believe can be rendered as a function of early childhood factors. If atheism can be explained in as facile and convincing a fashion as religion, then there is no ultimate hope of ever knowing anything truly. We can all point at each other and say, "Well you believe 'X' because of your unresolved issues with your mother and father." Such an all-encompassing psychologizing of our capacity to know is repugnant to Christians, who believe that we are capable of knowing truly, at least at some level. Positively, it is an asset of psychoanalysis that it deeply understands our profound capacities for self-deception (which we will develop later).

Further, psychoanalysis tends to be thoroughly mechanistic and naturalistic in terms of its core hypotheses, in that it assumes that all mental events are ultimately biological and instinctual in origin. This inevitably leads to reductionistic explanations about religious matters and indeed about all that we regard as distinctively human. Freud is consistent in asserting that biological and physical laws determine every important aspect of human existence. And naturalism was not just a working hypothesis for him: "Freud was dogmatic about it" (Browning & Cooper, 2004, p. 37).

Such a philosophical and scientific commitment allows no room for anything supernatural, for the kind of general or special revelation so central to the Christian faith, nor for a more constructive perspective about our spiritual urgings for deeper meaning and significance in life. Freud's system is a closed system of cause and effect with no room for a transcendent reality. It is at this point that there is no possible reconciliation with the fundamental assertions of the Christian tradition and the dictates of Freudian psychoanalysis. We concur with Hurding (1985), who states:

> The Christian believes in a creator God who brought all that exists into being and who sustains the universe by his power and love; he also declares a redeemer God who has intervened in history in countless ways but supremely in the incarnation, life, death and resurrection of His Son, and in the sending of the Holy Spirit. This is a God who calls man, both individually and corporately, to choose good rather than evil, life rather than death, the Lord's way rather than the Enemy's. This blend of divine determinism . . . and man's freedom to choose . . . is at the heart of biblical revelation and is a far cry from Freud's naturalistic world view. (pp. 74-75)[2]

---

[2]Other helpful treatments from a variety of perspectives on the philosophical tensions between psychoanalysis and Christian theology can be found in Browning and Cooper

Model of Personality

Narramore (1985) argues that the personality concepts in psychoanalysis should stand or fall on whether or not they enable us to make sense of the complexity of human nature in light of biblical revelation and human experience. As with nearly every major theory we will discuss in this book, we contend that it would be a mistake to reject hypothetical constructs because their exact equivalent cannot be found directly in the Scriptures.

Our perspectives on some of the Freudian notions of psychosexual development have changed since our initial exposure to these concepts as undergraduates. Initially, we were quite skeptical, but our experiences since with our own children and clients have taught us that, broadly understood, these developmental themes have some contemporary relevance. As we listen to the struggles of our clients and students, certain themes often emerge, including powerful "feelings towards parents of the opposite sex, . . . guilt over sexual feelings and actions, fears related to sexual intimacy and loving, fears of abandonment, struggles in the area of defining one's own sexual identity, anger and rage in not getting what one wanted as a child, and love/hate conflicts" (Corey, 1986, p. 39). Psychoanalysis speaks directly and deeply to the roots of these concerns. One does not need to accept all the tenets of orthodox psychoanalysis to appreciate the potential contribution of these emphases for our awareness and understanding of our client's difficulties. In fact, most contemporary psychoanalytic perspectives reject the notion of hard-and-fast stages of development in favor of viewing the developmental issues identified in the stage theories from a life-cycle perspective. In other words, the anal wish to be neat, orderly and tidy is understood less as a developmental outcome related to mastery of bodily functions and more as an aspect of the lifelong developmental task of self-regulation and control that spans all phases of one's life.

Psychoanalytic thought is certainly a unifying perspective that stresses the developmental, historical and unconscious dimensions of the human experience. Although we find the approach to be overly deterministic, we share Korchin's (1976, p. 332) assessment that many of the central tenets of Freud's intrapsychic theory are perhaps less biological and universal

---

(2004), Burnham (1985), Irwin (1975), Kristol (1970), Robinson (1985), Wallace (1983) and Wood (1980).

than originally posited, and more overtly interpersonal or sociocultural. This is certainly the direction that psychoanalytic "revisionists" (who added onto Freud's ideas) and "heretics" (who rejected the core of Freud's ideas in favor of their own) took psychoanalysis after Freud's death.

Browning and Cooper (2004) summarize several scholars who suggest that Freud himself was actually quite torn on this point, writing sometimes in a mechanistic, deterministic, individualistic vein, but at other times in an "intersubjective or . . . dialogical one" (p. 39). Several psychoanalytic writers have pointed out that part of the reason why classical psychoanalysis seems so conflicted about this is because the first psychoanalyst never underwent psychoanalysis with another person. Freud was his *own* analyst, and thus didn't experience firsthand the intersubjective, dialogical nature of the therapeutic relationship. It is largely from an emphasis on the nonmechanistic aspects of Freud that the broad popularity of the contemporary psychodynamic theories has grown. There is certainly more possibility for Christian appreciation of psychoanalytic thought when theorists move away from the mechanistic, reductionistic aspects of psychoanalysis; we shall find this to be precisely the case in chapter four.

Freud made his understanding of personality the backdrop for understanding all of existence. By doing so, he presented Christians with an unsatisfactory scheme for understanding the foundations for life. As Browning and Cooper (2004) say, "By taking the position that the psychobiological realm is the only relevant context for human action he has indeed elevated eros [libido drive] and death [aggression drive] to metaphors of ultimacy, that is, to metaphors which represent the only effective and relevant ultimate context of experience" (pp. 43-44).

Are eros/libido and death/aggression the ultimate motivational contexts for life? These id-drives could be described as aberrant and distorted reflections of the relational and dominion motivations we gleaned from Genesis 1-2 (see chap. 2). Biblically, we are seen to be positively motivated to procreate, to create and to love, and certainly the biblical attention paid to the distorted and evil sexual motivations we experience also suggests some centrality to sexual motivation in life. Further, the Scriptures assert very clearly that sinful humanity is bent on death and self-destruction. Aggression is sometimes understood as an aspect of control, making it possible that Freud's "darker drive" is a depraved version of our dominion drive.

We also note (with Van Leeuwen, 1985, 1990) that Freud's description of humans as having two intrinsically opposed core motivations places conflict as central and endemic to being human. Unlike the humanistic theories which say that humans are basically good but "messed up" by external influences, psychoanalysis says that to be human is to be torn by conflict. This darker reading of the human plight is much closer to biblical reality than Romantic humanism. Christianity does not paint the conflict in the same way, but suggests that our conflict is most fundamentally between longing for God and being in rebellion against him. A Christian point of view is not completely incompatible, however, with the psychoanalytic view of motivation.

We appreciate Freud's stress on the reality of dynamic unconscious mental processes. Certainly there is a reality beyond, or perhaps, beneath that which we are immediately aware, perhaps most directly evident in the content of our dreams. In the clinical context both free association and other psychoanalytic techniques strongly suggest that there is a level of thinking, perceiving and feeling beyond direct consciousness. These assertions are not inconsistent with the scriptural understanding of persons.

We share the widespread appreciation for the psychoanalytic understanding of the defense mechanisms, especially as they are developed in clinical treatments (e.g., Meissner, 1985). The Scriptures speak directly to our tendencies to be deceitful to self and others and to avoid facing painful realities (cf. Jer 17:9). As Narramore (1985) says, psychoanalysis's "understanding of the role of the defense mechanisms . . . goes beyond scriptural descriptions of how we avoid facing painful reality but is consistent with that scripturally described process" (p. 900).

Psychoanalysis can contribute much to our awareness of both the unhealthy and healthy ways that conflict and sin can be dealt with in the context of our religious communities. Indeed, the language of the ego defense mechanisms has so widely and thoroughly permeated contemporary Western culture that it is difficult to imagine how we could discuss our avoidant tendencies without such terminology. Psychoanalysis asserts that we can learn more adaptive and goal-oriented means of managing anxiety. The limitation, however, of the psychoanalytic approach is that there are serious constraints on that potential due to our sinful nature (i.e., we are in need of divine intervention; we can't heal ourselves).

Psychoanalysis essentially contends that all behavior is purposeful and motivated. This assertion is not inconsistent with scriptural teachings about the nature of human beings. Nor is the assumption about the crucial importance of early childhood experience. Indeed, the Scriptures assert that the parenting relationship, like the marital relationship, ought to reflect the divine-human encounter (cf. Narramore, 1979; Prov 22:6), with all the inherent risks and responsibilities. The psychoanalytic assertion of the importance of familial, early life experiences alone does not, however, constitute a substantial contact point with Christianity, as any reasonable understanding of human life would emphasize these primary relationships as formative.

Model of Health

It should be evident from the earlier section on Freudian notions of health that the model stresses individualism over and against interdependence. We find this to be a matter of deep concern, since our understanding of the Christian tradition emphasizes a deep awareness of our utter dependence on God and the absolute necessity of developing meaningful and significant relationships with others, both within the body of Christ and in the broader community and society we live in. Our concern is that the insight and self-awareness so deeply valued in the psychoanalytic tradition won't necessarily translate into appropriate other-directed behaviors. Rather, it will remain largely self-directed or self-serving.

Psychoanalysis is actually so oriented to understanding the person as a self-contained psychological system that even for the healthy person, "relationships with other human beings are of value only in so far as they facilitate instinctual gratification" (Storr, 1989, p. 91). Browning and Cooper (2004) noted that a literal interpretation of the Freudian paradigm would inevitably make us skeptical about whether there is such a thing as authentic and legitimate altruistic service toward others that is free of self-serving gain. How could Freudian thought, for example, account for the sacrificial service of Mother Teresa in the slums of Calcutta?

A clearly articulated, stable ethical system is lacking in psychoanalysis (Browning & Cooper, 2004, pp. 48ff.), though like all systems, it actually contains an implicit system in its view of health. The best description of its implicit ethic might be that of a "cautious but fair reciprocity" (p. 49). It is a reciprocity system because Freud recognized that if each person ultimately cares only about his or her own gratification, then we must each trade gratifications to keep everyone satisfied. It is cautious because Freud believed that libidinal energies are ultimately for our own satisfaction. We cautiously give to others so we can get what we want.

But the stance of "cautious reciprocity" stands in stark contrast to the kind of costly discipleship and risk-taking inherent in Christian morality and in a Christian conscience. Authentic love for the other (*agape*) is not based on reciprocity but on our common family membership, on Christ's example and on the Spirit's enablement. Granted, many of our efforts to be loving or distinctively and decidedly Christian in our compassion are less than noble or pure. But the assumption in psychoanalysis is that there is no normative basis for responsible ethical decision-making and action. In particular, psychoanalysis is profoundly skeptical about whether there can be any *genuine* commitment to an absolute like the love of God or the love of one's neighbor that is not ultimately a derivative of the sexual instinct. Its commitments to a Darwinian worldview lead it to view love in survival-of-the-fittest evolutionary terms. Psychoanalysis is brutally honest about our propensity toward extrinsic motivation, but asserts that intrinsic motivation, especially in a religious context, is largely a wish-fulfilling illusion.

Another concern about the Freudian notion of wellness is its extreme emphasis on subjectivity. Self-awareness tends to become a major goal of the maturation process. Our fear is whether a preoccupation with the "inner reality" of one's psychic life will replace any appropriate concern about the "outer reality" of God or the relational obligations to the local church and community. Our worst fear is that the view of persons that classical psychoanalysis prescribes may breed an unhealthy narcissism and self-absorption that removes one from engaging with the world of everyday living. But in practical application this seems an exaggerated concern: Classical psychoanalysis's vision of adult maturity—the capacity to love and work meaningfully and purposefully—seems to be appropriately other-directed and pro-social. Ultimately, though, human beings are motivated at the deepest levels to maximize pleasure and to minimize pain. As such, even the most altruistic behaviors are understood to be self-serving in that they bring pleasure or the avoidance of pain to the individual.

No doubt there is a need for greater self-awareness and understanding in our Christian communities, but this should not develop into an escape from active involvement in the local church or with the lives of suffering persons. Obviously, a healthy balance between escape and engagement is essential. The need to "know thyself" must not replace the command to "love God and others."

What is desperately needed in our Christian communities today are persons who can balance a desire and willingness to know self with an equally strong passion to know God. This accords marvelously with John Calvin's discussion in the first chapter of his *Institutes of the Christian Religion* (1559/1981):

> Our wisdom, in so far as it ought to be deemed true and solid wisdom, consists almost entirely of two parts: the knowledge of God and of ourselves. But as these are connected together by many ties, it is not easy to determine which of the two precedes, and gives birth to the other. For, in the first place, no man can survey himself without forthwith turning his thoughts toward God in whom he lives and moves.... On the other hand, it is evident that man never attains to a true self-knowledge until he has previously contemplated the face of God, and come down after such contemplation to look into himself. (1.1.1-2)

A final fear relates to our concern about the ultimate direction of the maturation process in psychoanalysis. As Christians we must continually remind ourselves that our ultimate salvation comes from without, not from within. There is the distinct danger in psychoanalysis of a kind of gnosticism where self-knowledge is seen as a means to self-salvation (Vitz, 1987, p. 73). From the standpoint of the Christian contemplative tradition, self-knowledge produces humility, not salvation. Specifically, the cultivation and expression of the Christian virtues (Roberts, 1982, 1984) should be seen as the apex of sanctification for the committed believer, not self-awareness and insight. The search for psychological wholeness ought not replace our desire to know God or pursue authentic holiness, but be seen as *one* means of pursuing God and holiness.

A wonderfully helpful example of how concerned and committed Christian theoreticians can correct some of these inadequacies can be found in two articles by Vitz and Gartner (1984a, 1984b). At the core of the Freudian critique of Christianity is the assertion that unresolved Oedipal issues are foundational in the formation of one's superego (e.g., the son tries to take over the role of the father). In contrast, a more theologically informed understanding of the sacrificial love of the Son for the Father and how the obedient death of the Son brings ultimate redemption can illustrate how the life of Jesus becomes a needed corrective for the unresolved issues of the "unredeemed self" caught in unresolved Oedipal tensions. In short, Jesus serves as a kind of anti-Oedipus who finds life by obediently doing his Father's will rather than trying to destroy the Father. Part of the good news of the gospel, then, is the potential power that comes when the perpetual fear and hatred of the Father due to the Oedipal crisis can be replaced by a thorough transformation of the mind through conversion and Christian commitment. The "unredeemed self" studied by Freud can be changed into a "redeemed self" in Christ through the mystery of belief in the incarnation, crucifixion and resurrection of Jesus.

Model of Abnormality

The psychoanalytic approach speaks deeply and meaningfully to the origins and functions of symptoms. It seems foolish to disregard the impact of critical life events in the formative years or to neglect the role of the ego defense mechanisms in the etiology and maintenance of problems in living. On the other hand, it does not necessarily follow that one must dwell exclusively on these matters in order to help clients make sense of the roots of their difficulties.

Psychoanalysis contends that the root of much of our psychopathology can be found in aberrant psychosexual development. In particular, aggressive or sexual impulses are major determinants of our neurotic tendencies. This is not consistent with the thrust of Scripture, where our own drive to be autonomous and godlike (i.e., pride) is seen as a more basic source of maladjustment and sin (Narramore, 1985, p. 900). Sexual or aggressive impulses are sometimes troublesome but have become so because of our rebellion against God.

The Freudian tradition is prone to reductionistic interpretations of the etiology and maintenance of symptoms. This is inconsistent with the thrust of contemporary thought in the human sciences, where etiology is more accurately seen as a function of multiple factors for almost all disorders. Despite its strong emphasis on the biological and instinctual bases for behaviors, Freudian thought has very little to say about more recent advances in biological psychiatry and medicine (e.g., neurotransmitters, chemical imbalances, genetic predispositions and so on). In its defense, psychoanalysis was originally focused on the concerns of reasonably high-functioning neurotics in a particular cultural and historical context. Even so, the theory that emerged from that work has been asserted to have near universal applicability, and the scope of psychoanalytic practice has been considerably broadened since its inception, and thus fundamental revision to incorporate a broader range of concepts is indicated.

Traditional psychoanalysis needs a much broader base of social motivations and dynamics to be closer to a more biblical understanding of persons. The more one views psychoanalysis as not just a tool in the therapist's armamentarium but as a worldview as well, the more difficult it seems to reconcile psychoanalysis and legitimate religious concerns (Wallace, 1983). Indeed, the developments in psychoanalytic thinking and practice of the past sixty years have begun to bridge somewhat the gap between the limited viewpoint of the classical perspective and biblical understandings of persons.

Model of Psychotherapy

Responsible eclectic therapists find psychodynamic concepts like resistance, transference and countertransference, repetition compulsion, mourning of illusion, and the ego defense mechanisms to be extremely useful in exploring current difficulties in a client's life. Further, awareness of the psychoanalytic distinctives probably helps these same clinicians to have a greater depth of awareness and understanding in their efforts to assist their clients. Broadly understood, Freudian thought can be a powerful model for understanding behavior.

Psychoanalysis, when practiced in its strict classical form, is widely perceived as impractical for the majority of mental health settings in this country or abroad. The great time commitment and expense that is involved and the limited availability of highly trained psychoanalysts make this an inefficient approach. Few potential clients have the necessary financial and personal resources (e.g., introspective and verbal skills) and fewer still are willing to make the kind of commitment of those resources that would be necessary for a successful analysis. The lofty goal of personality reconstruction is probably inappropriate and unrealistic for the vast majority of suffering persons.

But there might be ways to transcend certain of these limitations. Klein

(1970), for example, suggests that society should underwrite part of the cost of psychoanalysis for truly needy clients as well as a limited number of future psychotherapists. He suggests that this would contribute much to the continued development of the mental health movement and to the direct well-being of the persons involved. The Institute for Psychoanalysis in Chicago (Desruisseaux, 1983) has been exemplary in offering low-cost psychoanalytic training and treatment to human-service providers (e.g., teachers, child care workers, etc.). By investing in the lives of those persons in the trenches, they are making a long-term contribution to the mental and emotional well-being of the lives their clients will touch. Gabbard (1994) also argues for a place for classical psychoanalytic practice within the current health care system. He advocates for shorter-term treatment, more circumscribed goals for treatment, and interventions along a spectrum from emotionally stimulating (e.g., interpretation) to supportive (e.g., prescriptive strategies like giving therapeutic homework).

We respect the emphasis of this tradition on the training and supervision of future therapists. No major system of psychotherapy takes the personal development of the clinician more seriously than does psychoanalysis. Only after years of personal therapy, specialized coursework and careful supervision of select cases can the psychoanalyst become certified. With the incredible proliferation of people-helpers in our society, the careful and meticulous preparation of the psychoanalyst is certainly to be commended.

Such training, however, is not without its risks. Psychoanalysis is often accused of being an arrogant, exclusive professional guild. But even within that establishment many articulate and vocal critics can be found (e.g., Robert Coles, a committed Christian psychiatrist and Harvard professor). But all too often the professional isolation remains, creating for all practical purposes rather exclusive clubs of the fully initiated "true believers." This has done little to create goodwill with other traditions within the mental health field. The proliferation of managed care in North America over the past twenty years or so served as a bit of an antidote to the arrogance and haughtiness of some of the psychoanalytic community.

We also have a concern that classic psychoanalytic treatment is not necessarily a good model for either clinical or personal relationships. Certainly there is a need for clinicians to listen attentively and respectfully to the stories of their clients. But the risk is that the often cold, distant, anonymous style of the classical Freudian analyst can replace a more balanced and genuinely warm style that we more often associate with authentic Christian love and concern. The anonymous relationship that may be necessary for the formation of a transference neurosis can covertly or even overtly communicate deeper values about relationships in general. As Miller and Jackson (1985) have noted, notions of ideal clinical or personal relationships should be deeply informed by both societal standards and religious belief systems. Psychoanalytic therapy raises tough questions about what it means to care for others and be fully present to them. Specifically, it asserts that there is an essential place for the quiet receptivity of the psychoanalyst (Kovel, 1976). But whether it should be the primary relational modality of the psychoanalyst is a matter of intense debate both within and without psychoanalytic circles. Indeed, the question of the moral dimensions of psychotherapy is a key point of discussion in the psychoanalytic literature and at conferences.

Finally, we sense a certain fatalism and pessimism in intensive and long-term psychoanalytic treatment. Obviously, a tremendous commitment of time, energy and expense is needed to bring about increased self-control and self-regulation through greater insight and self-awareness. Although we agree with Wheelis (1978) that change is all too often painfully slow and agonizingly difficult, the Christian faith commitment raises the possibility of quick, dramatic change in an individual's life (cf. McLemore, 1982). Granted, persons bring their "raw material" into their Christian conversion, but the possibilities for change are certainly greater than classical psychoanalysis would have us believe, although perhaps less dramatic and sudden than many Christians would like to believe. In fact, Freud himself believed that "the end result of analysis was the replacement of neurotic misery by everyday unhappiness" (Breuer & Freud, 1895/1957, p. 305).

It is at this point that the classical psychoanalytic perspective alludes to but does not quite provide a more hopeful vision for human suffering. As mentioned earlier, Freud's brilliant work on the relationship between mourning of illusion and growth offers the Christian mental health professional a framework to understand at least one dimension of the most profound theological mystery—that death precedes new life. While most authentic, devout Christians express earnest belief in this most central piece of our doctrine and history, many fail to recognize the reality of this paschal pattern in their own lives. In fact, one could argue that many theologically orthodox churches in North America have swallowed whole the cultural mandate to avoid loss, pain or legitimate suffering whenever possible. This perspective is promoted because, in subtle and not so subtle ways, we are encouraged to believe that we are entitled not to suffer, that we should be able, somehow, to transcend the pain associated with loss, death, grief and mourning. And so, in many churches, we celebrate Easter morning with joy—having thought (or, more importantly, felt) very little about Good Friday.

The necessity of mourning of illusion calls us back to this basic paschal process, because it insists that in order to grow—psychologically or spiritually—we must be open to the process of mourning. This makes sense when we consider that all change—even the most positive change—necessarily entails loss. These losses may be of relationship, of status, of role, of a stage or era of life. They may even involve the way that we understand God—our own personal working theology. At such times Christians need ways to face their loss courageously, directly, and to feel their grief acutely. And this process happens best in relationship—in community with others. We need, like Mary Magdalene outside the empty tomb of Christ (Jn 20:11-17), to be willing to not cling to what or whom we have loved (i.e., Jesus before ascending to the Father) in order to be given something much better (i.e., the Holy Spirit) (Rolheiser, 2001). We can imagine how wrenching and painful and confusing it must have been for her to let go of her own hopes, dreams, desires and wishes embodied in the man who stood before her on the same morning that she discovered his body was missing and two days after she had watched him murdered by the authorities. Her hope that what he told her was the best thing for both of them, and her faith to see beyond her own grief and disillusionment, together are a powerful example for us to follow. To become people capable of mourning opens us to becoming people available to the Holy Spirit, whose aim is to re-form, form, and transform us.

CONCLUSION

Psychoanalysis deserves to be more than a whipping boy for conservative Christians. It is a comprehensive and exhaustive system of personality, psychopathology and psychotherapy that should be carefully considered by committed and thoughtful persons of faith. Our primary concerns have to do with some of the metapsychological assumptions of the Freudian worldview.

In our judgment psychoanalysis as a therapy is probably inappropriate and impractical for all but a very few carefully selected individuals. The model certainly needs to be more clearly articulated so that the central tenets are amenable to more rigorous clinical and empirical investigation. But we still assert that it is highly advisable to think, on occasion, in psychoanalytic terms so as to give greater structure and direction to our efforts to be effective change agents. On the other hand, the committed Christian needs to offer clearly articulated correctives to some of the deficiencies that can be found in this tradition, especially with reference to the overly deterministic and naturalistic assumptions. We fully suspect that classic psychoanalysis will serve as a springboard for discussion, debate and dialogue for decades to come in Christian counseling circles. Perhaps its most enduring legacy will be that it gave birth to the approaches discussed in chapter four.

FOR FURTHER READING

Becker, E. (1973). *The denial of death.* New York, NY: Free Press.
   Becker critiques classical Freudian psychoanalysis from the perspective of Christian philosopher Søren Kierkegaard.
Gay, P. (1989). *The Freud reader.* New York, NY: W. W. Norton.
   The best of the many edited readers available in print today. Gay is a highly respected Freud scholar.
Mitchell, S. A., & Black, M. J. (1995). *Freud and beyond: A history of modern psychoanalytic thought.* New York, NY: Basic Books.
   An excellent overview of the psychoanalytic tradition that puts Freud's ideas in the context of contemporary psychoanalytic thought.
Storr, A. (1989). *Freud.* New York, NY: Oxford.
   A readable brief introduction to Freudian thought.
Wallace, E. (1983). Reflections on the relationship between psychoanalysis and Christianity. *Pastoral Psychology, 31,* 215-243.
   One of the best of the many introductory articles available that speaks directly to integrative issues.
Westphal, M. (1998). *Suspicion and faith: The religious uses of modern atheism.* New

York, NY: Fordham University Press.

A Christian philosopher helps us to see our own spiritual growth potential by taking the insights of Freud, Marx and Nietzsche seriously.

REFERENCES

Alston, W. (1967). Psychoanalytic theories, logical status of. In P. Edwards (Ed.), *The encyclopedia of philosophy* (Vols. 5-6, pp. 512-516). New York, NY: Macmillan.

American Psychiatric Association. (2000) *Diagnostic and statistical manual* (4th ed.). Washington, DC: American Psychiatric Association.

Arlow, J. (1984). Psychoanalysis. In R. Corsini (Ed.), *Current psychotherapies* (3rd ed., pp. 14-55). Itasca, IL: F. E. Peacock.

Becker, E. (1973). *The denial of death.* New York, NY: Free Press.

Berger, K. (1988). *The developing person through the life span* (2nd ed.). New York, NY: Worth.

Brenner, C. (1973). *An elementary textbook of psychoanalysis.* Garden City, NY: Anchor/Doubleday.

Breuer, J., & Freud, S. (1895/1957). *Studies on hysteria. Complete psychological works, Standard edition, Vol. 2.* London: Hogarth Press.

Browning, D. S., & Cooper, T. D. (2004). *Religious thought and the modern psychologies* (2nd ed.). Minneapolis, MN: Fortress.

Burnham, J. (1985). The encounter of Christian theology with deterministic psychology and psychoanalysis. *Bulletin of the Menninger Clinic, 49,* 321-352.

Calvin, J. (1981). *Institutes of the Christian religion* (H. Beveridge, Trans.). Grand Rapids, MI: Eerdmans. (Original work published 1559).

Corey, G. (1986). *Theory and practice of counseling and psychotherapy* (3rd ed.). Monterey, CA: Brooks/Cole.

Crabb, L. (1988). *Inside out.* Colorado Springs, CO: NavPress.

Cushman, P. (1995). *Constructing the self, constructing America: A cultural history of psychotherapy.* New York, NY: Perseus.

Desruisseaux, P. (1983, January 12). Psychoanalysis: Off the couch and into the streets of Chicago, IL. *The Chronicle of Higher Education.*

Erikson, E. (1982). *The life cycle completed: A review.* New York, NY: Norton.

Ford, D., & Urban, H. (1963). *Systems of psychotherapy: A comparative study.* New York: Wiley.

Freud, S. (1933). *New introductory lectures on psychoanalysis* (W. J. H. Sprott, Trans.). New York, NY: Wiley.

Freud, S. (1957). *Mourning and melancholia. Complete Psychological Works, Standard edition, Vol. 14.* London: Hogarth Press. (Original work published 1915).

Freud, S. (1957). *On narcissism: an introduction. Complete Psychological Works, Standard edition, Vol. 14.* London: Hogarth Press. (Original work published 1914).

Freud, S. (1963). Further recommendations in the technique of psychoanalysis: Recollection, repetition, and working through. In *Therapy and technique.* New York, NY: Macmillan. (Original work published 1914).

Gabbard, G. O. (1994). *Psychodynamic psychiatry in clinical practice: The DSM-IV edition.* Washington, DC: American Psychiatric Press.

Hackett, C. (1986). Psychoanalysis and theology: Two dialectics. *Journal of Religion and Health, 25,* 29-45.

Hurding, R. (1985). *Roots and shoots.* London: Hodder & Stoughton.

Irwin, J. (1975). Reinhold Niebuhr critique of Freudian psychoanalysis. *Journal of Religion and Health, 14,* 242-254.

Jones, J., & Wilson, W. (1987). *An incomplete education.* New York, NY: Ballantine.

Kandel, E. R. (1999). Biology and the future of psychoanalysis: A new intellectual framework for psychiatry revisited. *American Journal of Psychiatry, 156,* 505-524.

Kandel, E. R. (2005). *Psychiatry, psychoanalysis, and the new biology of mind.* Washington, D.C.: American Psychiatric Association.

Klein, G. (1970, August). *Is psychoanalysis relevant?* Paper presented at the annual convention of the American Psychological Association, Miami, FL.

Korchin, S. (1976). *Modern clinical psychology.* New York, NY: Basic Books.

Kovel, J. (1976). *A complete guide to therapy.* New York, NY: Pantheon.

Kristol, I. (1970). God and the psychoanalysts. In A. H. Cohen (Ed.), *Arguments and doctrines.* New York, NY: Harper & Row.

Lambert, M. J., & Barley, D. E. (2001). Research summary on the therapeutic relationship and psychotherapy outcome. *Psychotherapy: Theory/research/practice/training, 38,* 357-361.

McLemore, C. (1982). *The scandal of psychotherapy.* Wheaton, IL: Tyndale House.

McLemore, C. (1984). *Honest Christianity.* Philadelphia, PA: Westminster Press.

Meissner, W. (1985). Theories of personality and psychopathology: Classical psychoanalysis. In H. I. Kaplan & B. J. Sadock (Eds.), *Comprehensive textbook of psychiatry* (Vol. 4, pp. 337-418). Baltimore, MD: Williams & Wilkins.

Miller, W., & Jackson, K. (1985). *Practical psychology for pastors.* Englewood Cliffs, NJ: Prentice-Hall.

Mitchell, S. A. (1988). *Relational concepts in psychoanalysis: An integration.* Cambridge, MA: Harvard University Press.

Mitchell, S. A., & Black, M. J. (1995). *Freud and beyond: A history of modern psychoanalytic thought.* New York, NY: Basic Books.

Munroe, R. (1955). *Schools of psychoanalytic thought.* New York, NY: Holt, Rinehart & Winston.

Narramore, S. (1979). *Parenting with love and limits.* Grand Rapids, MI: Zondervan.

Narramore, S. (1984). *No condemnation.* Grand Rapids, MI: Zondervan.

Narramore, S. (1985). Psychoanalytic psychotherapy. In D. G. Benner (Ed.), *Baker encyclopedia of psychology* (pp. 896-900). Grand Rapids, MI: Baker.

Oakland, J. (1977). The introjected and the intrinsic in psychology and Christianity. *Journal of Psychology and Theology, 5,* 91-94.

Peck, S. (1983). *People of the lie.* New York, NY: Simon & Schuster.

Prochaska, J. (1979). *Systems of psychotherapy: A transtheoretical analysis.* Homewood, IL: Dorsey Press.

Roberts, R. (1982). *Spirituality and human emotion.* Grand Rapids, MI: Eerdmans.

Roberts, R. (1984). *The strengths of a Christian.* Philadelphia, PA: Westminster Press.

Robinson, L. (1985). The illusion of no future: Psychoanalysis and religion. *Journal of the American Academy of Psychoanalysis, 13,* 211-228.

Rolheiser, R. (2001). *The holy longing: The search for a Christian spirituality.* New York, NY: Doubleday.

Rychlak, J. (1973). *Introduction to personality and psychotherapy.* Boston, MA: Houghton Mifflin.

Ryckman, R. (1985). *Theories of personality* (3rd ed.). Monterey, CA: Brooks/ Cole.

Shabad, P. (2001). *Despair and the return of hope.* Northvale, NJ: Jason Aronson.

Silverman, L. (1976). Psychoanalytic theory: The reports of my death are greatly exaggerated. *American Psychologist, 31,* 621-637.

Storr, A. (1989). *Freud.* New York, NY: Oxford.

Solms, M. (2004). Freud returns. *Scientific American Magazine, 290*(5), 82-89.

Sorenson, R. L. (2004). *Minding spirituality.* New York, NY: Routledge.

Van Leeuwen, M. (1985). *The person in psychology: A contemporary Christian appraisal.* Grand Rapids, MI: Eerdmans.

Van Leeuwen, M. (1990). *Gender and grace: Love, work and parenting in a changing world.* Downers Grove, IL: InterVarsity Press.

Viorst, J. (1986). *Necessary losses.* New York, NY: Fawcett Gold Medal.

Vitz, P. (1987). Secular personality theories: A critical analysis. In T. J. Burke

(Ed.), *Man and mind: A Christian theory of personality* (pp. 65-94). Hillsdale, MI: Hillsdale College Press.

Vitz, P. (1988). *Sigmund Freud's Christian unconscious.* New York, NY: Guilford.

Vitz, P., & Gartner, J. (1984a). Christianity and psychoanalysis, Part I: Jesus as the anti-Oedipus. *Journal of Psychology and Theology, 12,* 4-14.

Vitz, P., & Gartner, J. (1984b). Christianity and psychoanalysis, Part II: Jesus as the transformer of the superego. *Journal of Psychology and Theology, 12,* 82-90.

Wallace, E. (1983). Reflections on the relationship between psychoanalysis and Christianity. *Pastoral Psychology, 31,* 215-243.

Walters, O. (1973). Psychodynamics in Tillich's theology. *Journal of Religion and Health, 12,* 342-353.

Westphal, M. (1998). *Suspicion and faith: The religious uses of modern atheism.* New York, NY: Fordham University Press.

Wheelis, A. (1978). *How people change.* New York, NY: Harper & Row.

Wood, B. (1980). The religion of psychoanalysis. *The American Journal of Psychoanalysis, 40,* 13-26.

4

CONTEMPORARY
PSYCHODYNAMIC PSYCHOTHERAPIES

Michael W. Mangis, Stanton L. Jones and Richard E. Butman

*T*he contemporary psychodynamic psychotherapies are those schools of thought influenced by Freud and classic psychoanalysis that have evolved substantially beyond orthodox analytic thought. Christians have not been alone in being dissatisfied with the deterministic and mechanistic assumptions of the Freudian system, which paint a picture of humans as isolated beings irrationally driven by biological, primitive drives welling up within them, their personalities molded by discrete psychic structures interacting mechanically and unconsciously to achieve compromises leading to drive gratification. Christians have also not been alone in seeing the rich possibilities of a system that seeks to understand the profound impact of early relationships on our character, the mysterious way in which we are shaped by unconscious processes, and the pervasive presence of psychological conflict in our lives.

In fact, many argue that Freud himself led the way in attempting to resolve some of the mechanistic and deterministic problems in his own model. The focus of much of Freud's later work was on the ego as presented in *The Ego and the Id* (1923/1961). In his earliest theorizing, when he was working from his seduction theory, Freud emphasized interpersonal environment as the cause of pathology. He quickly moved away from that position to a more "scientific" view where psychological development was seen as an almost entirely internal and self-contained process. The person was seen as controlled by biological instincts and drives, and by the actions and fantasies associated with those drives. The ego had little true efficacy. But in *The Ego and the Id*, Freud began to acknowledge again the role of the environment, of relationships, in the development of the internal workings of the mind.

Some theorists have suggested that Freud intended *The Ego and the Id* to be a major paradigm shift, a new direction in his thinking, but others vehemently disagree. The classical psychoanalytic school (see chap. 3) believes Freud was not overhauling his thought but fine-tuning it. They have remained true to the bulk of Freud's work and see psychological development as being entirely controlled by biological drives; the psychic structures of id, ego and superego; and the effects of psychosexual development. For the traditional psychoanalyst the instinctual drive model was and continues to be the only viable focal point for understanding human nature.

DESCRIPTIVE SURVEY

Whether it was his intent or not, Freud's new thinking about the ego did create a dramatic shift in some psychoanalytic circles, resulting in several new models and paradigms. These neo-Freudian, or post-Freudian, theorists share an appreciation for the way traditional psychoanalysis illuminates the complexity of our conflicting motivations and the influence of unconscious processes. Their key differences with classic psychoanalysis have to do with the ways in which these intricate processes are explained. Generally speaking, their formulations are less biological and mechanistic, and more respectful of cognitive and interpersonal processes, precisely because they have shifted from Freud's emphasis on id and drive to an emphasis on ego, self and relationships. As Guntrip (1969) noted,

> Emphasis has moved away from "instinct entities" and their control, on to the vital problem of how we begin to grow an ego, the core of a personal self, in infancy; and how this growth in personal reality is rooted in the baby's environment of personal relations, first with the mother, then the father, family, neighbours, school, and the ever-widening world around. (p. 326)

Post-Freudian psychodynamic thinking has usually been divided into three camps (Pine, 1988): ego psychology, object-relations theories and self psychology.

Ego psychology, usually dubbed the "American school," stresses the development of personality across the life span. It does not deny that certain conflicts reflect id impulses striving for immediate gratification, but it does assert that the ego strivings for adaptability, competency and mastery are at least as important. The model is mostly an adaptation of Freud's original thought with a heightened emphasis on ego and relationships. Beyond the tensions surrounding sex and aggression, issues of identity, intimacy and integrity become especially striking and salient in this tradition. Erik Erikson, Anna Freud, Heinz Hartmann, Rudolf Lowenstein and David Rapaport are among the major theoreticians in this tradition (cf. Korchin, 1976; Prochaska, 1984).

Object-relations theorists similarly emphasize the outward focus of the ego, reject Freud's narrow range of hypothesized instincts and deemphasize or ignore his main psychic structures. Collectively called the "British school," these theorists concentrate on those first few years of life, where they believe the foundation of the personality is laid. Experiences and relationships in these early years, they assert, leave impressions on the personality that profoundly affect the individual throughout the life span. The main determinant of personality is presumed to be the internalized images that we each carry within us of the primary relational figures in our past ("objects" such as mother and father). Personality is then understood primarily in terms of the relationships among and characteristics of these internalized "objects." These internal images or objects then are the primary psychic structures, replacing id, ego and superego. The interrelations of the objects create our psychological drives, rather than them welling up from the id (Edkins, 1985). The drives themselves are deemed relational rather than crudely sexual and aggressive. Well-known theorists in this tradition include W. R. D. Fairbairn and Otto Kernberg.

Self psychology, established by Heinz Kohut and his followers, also emphasizes the experiences of the early years in the development of a sense of identity after a process of differentiation and integration (to be explained shortly). If early relationships are healthy and nurturing, a stable or "true" self will develop that is capable of mature relationships. If the early environment is characterized by deprivation, however, the resulting "false" self remains limited in its relationship capacity (i.e., the individual cannot value both autonomy and community). A more mature identity is one that is open to input from others without a competing fear of being overwhelmed. Whereas the object-relations school focuses on psychological relations between internalized objects, self psychology goes the further step of positing a strong entity of self that is not a separate psychic structure but rather "might be said [to be] the sum of all these [intrapsychic] entities plus an unnamed integrating function" (Johnson, 1985, p. 1052). Such a cohesive and higher-order entity is quite a departure from Freud's original thought.

Greenberg and Mitchell (1983) point out that the three traditions share a common view of the primacy of cognitive and interpersonal processes as the building blocks of personality. The ego psychologists accommodate classic psychoanalysis by building on it. They modify the classical id-drive model by emphasizing early, formative relationships. A more radical alternative strategy, adopted by the object-relations theorists, requires complete replacement of the drive concept with a strong interpersonal model. Greenberg and Mitchell suggest that a third category, one of model mixing, describes the self psychology of Heinz Kohut and his followers; they have adopted drive-model concepts and mixed them with the relational model.

Our focus in this chapter will be on the commonalities of the psychodynamic models. Because each of the three models, and indeed different theorists within the three traditions, can be radically different from one another, we will stay at a general level in our presentation. Because of the popularity of object-relations theory, we will discuss it more than the other models. In recent years the contemporary psychodynamic models have coalesced somewhat into an eclectic whole. Authors cite theorists from any of the traditions, and practitioners seldom cite one theorist as their primary anchor.

As should be evident from chapter three, many of the fundamental tenets of classic psychoanalysis are simply irreconcilable with an orthodox Christian worldview. It is our judgment, however, that these contemporary variations on Freudian thought deserve a closer inspection because of their rich integrative potential. These contemporary psychodynamic movements have generally inherited the distrust of organized religion because of their roots in traditional psychoanalysis. But there seems to be considerably less overt hostility toward religion in general in the writings of these contemporary theorists than was true of Freud himself.

Hoffman has noted that British object-relations theory, in fact, is particularly grounded in biblical perspectives of the nature of the person. She notes that Fairbairn and Winnicott were especially influenced by their religious upbringing and affiliation. Fairbairn's immersion in the Calvinism of the Scottish Presbyterian Church and Winnicott's involvement in the Wesleyan church greatly influenced their views of the nature of a self and the inherent draw of humans toward relationship, particularly with God. Hoffman (2004) notes that "the study of 'persons in relationship' that emerged not only in object relations, but in the greater British academic culture, was undoubtedly influenced by the prevailing Judeo-Christian narrative, a narrative that made it particularly probable that the personal would make its entry into psychoanalysis by way of that culture" (p. 801).

Psychodynamic psychotherapy has become enormously influential in recent decades. In the judgment of many academicians and clinicians, these approaches have been fertile ground for broad-ranging discussions about personality, psychopathology and psychotherapy. It is not surprising, then, that growing numbers of Christian mental health professionals have found these ever-evolving formulations to be useful in relating their Christian faith and practice with their professional lives. We suspect that the majority of Christian psychologists today would describe themselves as psychodynamic or at least "psychodynamically informed."

Philosophical Assumptions

Few if any of the psychodynamic theorists have made the kinds of broad dogmatic assertions that Freud did, and this makes it difficult to explicate any fundamental philosophical presuppositions in these models. Since all are revisions of Freudian thought, all are likely to share the naturalistic or materialistic assumptions of psychoanalysis. Yet all of the models have rejected the mechanistic metapsychology of Freud and have thus opened up the possibility for a more satisfactory resolution of the determinism/causality issue than was possible with Freud. Nevertheless, none of the models, to our knowledge, have explicitly embraced a limited human freedom stance compatible with Christian belief. We will develop in the later critique how this might, in fact, be attainable.

Workman (1988) convincingly argues that these models share what might be called a "subjective epistemology" that is congruent with contemporary thinking in philosophical epistemology. The core of this view is that knowable reality is a "function of the inner world of experience as perceived" by the person (p. 3). External reality is ultimately unknowable except through the intermediary of psychological experience.

In fact, several approaches to Christian counseling have their roots in this tradition, though this is sometimes not acknowledged. The work of Lake (1966, 1986), called "clinical theology," is fundamentally a derivative from contemporary psychodynamic thought, specifically of the object-relations variety. The "healing of memories" phenomenon (e.g., Linn & Linn, 1978; Seamands, 1985) is best understood as a lay derivative of a psychodynamic understanding of persons, though it proposes a directly supernatural methodology for healing. Hurding (1985) has developed a thoughtful critique of the clinical theology and healing-of-memories approaches. Larry Crabb's widely read book *Inside Out* takes a psychodynamically influenced perspective on the individual's relationship with God (Crabb, 1998).

Model of Personality

Object representations, or introjects, are intrapsychic structures that are significantly affected by interpersonal relations. More specifically, introjects are the mental representations of the self and others (the objects). As mentioned previously, the central tenet of psychoanalysis and of psychodynamic theories in general is that each individual has an internal world that is affected by the past and which, in turn, affects one's functioning in the present, external world. According to object-relations theories the past affects us through internalized memories and images of events and relationships. We are usually not conscious of these imprints, but they influence our daily lives in profound and significant ways.

When we interact with a person we are relating not just to the real person that stands before us but to an internal representation or idea that we have of who that person is. It is seldom possible for that internalized representation of the person to be wholly based on the raw reality of who the person before us is. Rather, our perception is colored by past images of events and people. In a sense, we relate to real people through our internal representations of past relations. For example, a person may look like someone we once knew, or someone may be in a position of authority and therefore stir up memories of our parents; a person's mannerisms or tone of voice may set off other cues, and so forth. In short, we transfer parts of past images of people onto others. If these past images are strong enough, and if our ability to sort out the distortions from the reality is weak enough, we may act and feel in quite unrealistic ways toward this person. We may feel resentful toward others when they have done nothing to anger us. We may feel dependent on them for no apparent reason. Our feelings may vary dramatically toward them in any given encounter or across time.

In addition to these internal representations of others, we have internal representations of ourselves. In our earliest interactions with the important people in our environment we form ideas of who we are. A common example is the "gleam in the mother's eye." When an infant gazes up into his mother's eyes, her expression provides the child with a mirror image of himself. These mirror images form the earliest perceptions of self. If we are treated with adequate nurturing and protection, we will develop a whole and integrated sense of self. This representation will include a realistic awareness of both good and bad qualities coexisting. In an environment where the needs are not adequately met, however, this integrated sense of self cannot develop. Instead, an incomplete or inaccurate sense of who we are is formed.

The development of the mature or integrated self is thought to take place in several stages through the first few years of life. To adequately complete a stage, parents need to meet the needs of the child in a loving and consistent fashion. In their study of young children, Mahler (1968) and her associates (Mahler, Pine & Bergman, 1975) utilized object-relations theory to provide a model of the psychological birth of the child, which is considered to take place over the two years following the biological birth. They suggest that the self develops in three primary stages. From physical birth (or perhaps even within the womb) until approximately two months, the normal infant exists in the autism stage, characterized by what is called "absolute primary narcissism." During this phase infants are aware only of physical sensations they experience as globally pleasant or unpleasant. Children are not able to distinguish between self and external world; they have no sense of identity whatsoever.

In the symbiotic stage, from about two to six months, the infant experiences a sense of oneness or symbiosis with the primary caregiver. The child is presumed to be only aware of the functions that the parent serves in meeting the needs of the infant. Thus, the infant views the parent as something of an "object." The parent's task in this stage is to be readily available and attentive to the needs of the infant. If the parent is "good enough" at meeting these needs, to use Winnicott's well-known phrase, the infant develops the capacity to trust the world and also to look within for some capacity for comfort and meeting of needs.

From six months to two years the child is engaged in the process of separation and individuation, which has several stages. The child first begins to focus externally, rather than on her own bodily sensations. As she begins to move about and explore her world, and is able to affect her world (by grabbing things, etc.), her sense of separateness or differentness from the external world is heightened. This usually results in ambivalence as the child is conflicted between feelings of independence and wonder, on the one hand, and fear, on the other, which results from the loss of the ever-present sense of the parent's reassuring presence. These feelings feed the infant's sense of the parent as good and loving but also bad and frustrating.

Similarly, the child begins in this stage to realize that she, herself, can also be good and bad. For normal development to occur, the parent must walk the fine line of both encouraging independence while continuing to serve as a source of protection and nurturance. Overemphasis on either extreme can result in personality disturbances. If this phase is successfully navigated, the child achieves the optimal resolution of being able to internalize mental representations of parent and self that are stable, realistic (recognizing good and bad in self and parent) and comforting (because the parent's love and protection are with the child even when separated from the parent). The child feels loved and lovable, and has a sense of her capacity for independence and interdependence.

Since we carry around internal images of ourselves and others, relationships are necessarily complicated. Not only are two real people interacting, but one's internal image of oneself is relating to the internal image of the other person, and the same is happening in the other person as well. In a reasonably mature individual, the internal objects, or representations of self and others, have been allowed to develop adequately and come close to external reality. In a person who has been subjected to inadequate or nonexistent parenting there is little ability to discriminate between the reality and the distorted internal objects; this person seems to be responding to an "inner agenda" rather than true interpersonal reality. This function of discriminating between the internal images and the external reality belongs to the ego, and this emphasis on the relation between the internal images and the external reality is the primary difference between contemporary psychoanalysis and its classical ancestry. (This interest in relationships is also what led to the establishment of an object-relations school of family therapy, as discussed in chapter 9.)

Model of Health

As just described, the infant begins the process of maturation essentially unaware of the existence of others. As the child develops, a process of learning to separate and individuate from others takes place. The child learns to differentiate self from other, and can carry on a healthy, interdependent relationship with another person. Such a relationship is characterized by a valuing of other persons for more than their usefulness in meeting needs and desires. Maturity is, then, "the realization of our full potentialities as persons in personal relationships" (Guntrip, 1969, p. 324).

One of the most refreshing aspects of contemporary psychodynamic psychology is its definition of health. This is somewhat ironic since it, like its psychoanalytic counterpart, is essentially a psychology of sickness. This focus on the abnormal is obvious in light of the way the previous discussion of personality theory turned quickly to a discussion of disruptions of development. Psychodynamic theory has been constructed through the clinical experiences of the theorists who practice therapy. Such a system is necessarily skewed toward finding pathology. Nevertheless, by extrapolating from the theories of pathology and by observing the health that is there, as well as the health that develops, a model of maturity can be developed.

The mature adult, according to the relational model, sees self and others in a constant way that deviates only minimally from reality. The adult is, as a result, capable of enjoyable and interdependent relationships. Such individuals have learned to value others for qualities beyond their usefulness (unlike the narcissistic person). They can also view self and others as having an integration of both good and bad qualities without having to either reject or idealize others on the basis of passing moods or pressing needs (unlike the person with a borderline personality disorder).

Since the mature individual perceives the world and other people accurately, there is no need for exaggerated psychological defenses. Defenses are built initially against the real hazards of the world—pain inflicted, accidentally or intentionally, by people or events of our childhood. Later, however, we continue to project the threats of pain onto the world or people in the world when, in reality, those threats do not exist. The mature individual trusts others but remains aware that at times of potential pain the self may need to be defended.

The mature individual is able to build new, creative relationships with other healthy individuals. Immaturity is marked by seeking out unhealthy individuals with whom to engage in pathological relational patterns that repeat old, unresolved interactions. Like its classical counterpart, contemporary psychoanalysis sees the mature individual as freed from the prison of unconsciously and unnecessarily reliving the past.

Model of Abnormality

Given an adequate environment where the parent nurtures the child and meets his needs, the process of maturation is thought to unfold naturally. But for many the necessary nurture is not provided and the resulting immature personality, deprived of such a relationship, remains stuck in the early phase of viewing others for their usefulness in meeting internal needs. The object-relations literature primarily focuses on categorizing and treating the disorders of the personality that can result when the needs of the developing self are not adequately met.

A fragmented internal sense of self most frequently occurs when the primary parent is not healthy enough to provide adequately for the psychological needs of the child. Such a parent never had those needs adequately met for him- or herself. The parent will provide either little or no love, inappropriately intimate attention, love in an unpredictable way or love only when the child acts as the parent wants him or her to act. In such an environment the child's internal sense of self can become distorted in many ways. One common example is an inability to "own" or experience as part of us those aspects that our parents found unacceptable, as when a parent rejects a child when she is needy. This may result in a fragmented psychology wherein the "bad" parts are split off from the acceptable parts, and the person's sense of a coherent identity is damaged.

Freud essentially divided psychopathology into two categories, neurosis and psychosis. Psychosis, the inability of the ego to interact with the reality of the external world, was seen as largely untreatable through traditional psychoanalysis. Neurosis, however, reflected unresolved conflicts from the Oedipal period of development. The individual generally remained cognizant of reality and had established the capacity to develop a transference relationship that was seen as essential for a successful course of psychoanalysis.

Other analysts, working with populations more diverse than those visiting Freud in Victorian Vienna, found that many nonpsychotic patients were untreatable using the techniques of classic psychoanalysis. These patients were not capable of sustaining a consistent sense of self or of others and were, therefore, unable to invest in the necessarily intense analytic relationship. The consistent variable in the personality of such patients was the focus on pre-Oedipal disturbances in their relationships, disturbances rooted in problems before the age of four. The existence of such patients suggested a realm of abnormality between neurosis and psychosis.

Initially, these patients were seen as walking a fine line between neurosis and psychosis, what some called a "borderline" state. In time, psychodynamically oriented clinicians began to view this state as an entirely separate cluster of syndromes, the "personality disorders," with features unlike either the neurotic or psychotic constellation of symptoms.

Disruptions in the early development of object relations are usually considered to lead to the formation of either narcissistic or borderline disorders. What any two theorists mean by either of these terms, however, can vary widely. Stone (1986), for example, identified six different uses for the term *borderline* in describing personality dysfunction. While theorists may disagree as to the number, differentiation and organization of personality disorders, they consistently assert that disruptions in early relationships leave the personality in an immature or incomplete state, largely incapable of forming healthy and mature adult relationships. By definition, an individual with a personality disorder has remained stuck in pre-Oedipal development and is thus always looking for ways to satisfy unmet needs. A neurotic individual, by comparison, has a reasonably well-developed personality but is still unable to effectively manage anxiety in his or her life.

There is disagreement as to whether the infant is born with a complete and unblemished ego or a fragmented ego in need of further development. Relational model theorists agree, however, that the adequate development of the personality depends on the care and nurture provided by the primary parental figure(s). The parent who adequately meets the child's needs, or to use Winnicott's (1965) term, the "good enough parent," provides the child with the necessary raw materials for the development of a consistent and healthy sense of self and the world. As mentioned earlier, the parent whose needs were not adequately met in her or his own childhood probably cannot adequately meet those needs for the child. Instead the child will be provided with conditional love and an inconsistent or negative sense of worth.

The relational model's emphasis on the effects of the behavior and motivations of the parent on the personality of the child has been criticized by feminists and others as "mother-bashing," particularly since the mother is typically the primary caregiver (cf. Van Leeuwen, 1990, pp. 125-143). Indeed, the responsibility for the adequacy of the child's personality is placed disproportionately on the shoulders of the parents. The child is not able to have much volitional control over the development or reparation of his or her personality until late adolescence at the earliest. This certainly places an awesome responsibility on the primary caregiver(s).

Model of Psychotherapy

One of the strengths of the psychodynamic model is the direct link between theory and therapy. The theory is derived from the clinical work of the theorists with their clients. Because we are fundamentally relational beings, healing can only come through relationships. The core assumption is that healthy relationships have therapeutic potential.

In the classical approach to psychoanalysis the patient-analyst relationship is defined by transference and its interpretation. The analyst is an anonymous and blank canvas on which the patient recreates the vicissitudes of his or her past. Any feelings or personal involvement on the part of the analyst are seen as countertransference, the therapist's own unresolved neurotic conflicts. Thus, it is fair to say that the classic analytic relationship is not a real relationship at all.

Greenberg and Mitchell (1983) argue that the relational psychodynamic models see therapy quite differently from the classical model. Therapy is a relationship. The analyst and the patient participate in a dynamic interaction. Transference is an important part, but the therapist cannot be a blank canvas. Who she is as a person will necessarily influence the transference. Countertransference (the reaction of the therapist to the client) also plays an important part. Rather than being seen as the immaturity or "unfinished business" of the therapist, it is understood to be an essential tool and empathetic guide to the patient's inner experience of the world. In a sense the transference and countertransference interact as in a dance, a mutual event. In all likelihood therapy may be the first authentic or consistent intimacy that many patients have encountered. The impersonal and artificial methods of classical analysis had to be discarded because in this model the only hope for real change for the client is through a real relationship, and not through technique:

> The task of the analyst is not to remain outside of a process which is unfolding from within the mind of the patient, because this is theoretically impossible in the terms of the model's basic premises, but to engage the patient, to intervene, to participate in, and to transform pathogenic patterns of relationship. (Greenberg & Mitchell, 1983, p. 390)

Object-relations theories do not prescribe techniques or exercises for therapy. On the contrary, the spontaneity and mutual exploration of the relationship constitute the healing process. The therapist does not keep the theory always in mind. It becomes second nature, "the invisible backdrop, the unseen framework, within which the analyst hears the patient's story" (Greenberg & Mitchell, 1983, p. 15).

Contemporary writers on the psychotherapy process have come to refer to four different modes or channels of listening to the therapeutic relationship. Some have labeled these modes the one-person, one-and-a-half-person, two-person and three-person approaches. The first, or one-person model, describes the classical Freudian approach. The goal of the therapist's personal analysis was complete objectivity. The analyst was believed to be free of countertransference that would distort his or her capacity for providing accurate interpretations of the patient's unconscious defenses. The only person in the room, so to speak, is the one person of the patient. The analyst is more of a reflective object with personal perspectives removed.

Such a confidence in objectivity as Freud's could only have thrived in the modernist ethos of his time. Ricoeur (1970) noted that Freud's very method of observing the depth of the human capacity for self-deception helped demolish all confidence in the capacity of the analyst, or anyone else, for true objectivity. While the contemporary psychodynamic therapist might glean insights from Freud's classical theory, few will hold out any confidence for the analyst's capacities of neutrality, abstinence and anonymity that Freud believed in. Further, since the advent of object-relations theory, few would suggest that such detachment is even desirable.

The one-and-a-half-person mode has been the dominant mode of thinking about therapy for several decades. In this perspective the therapist is half of a person in the equation. Therapeutic relational boundaries and the rules of the therapeutic frame keep the therapist from being fully present. This model proposes the therapist as an empathic tool. By providing empathy, insight and corrective emotional experiences, the therapist brings about change in the patient. But the therapist in never fully present, because the therapeutic relationship is always about the needs of the client.

The two-person mode involves both the therapist and the patient fully in the relationship. But perhaps the circle of those present must be expanded further. Altman (1995) and others have pointed out that psychoanalysis has largely been developed and practiced in a very homogeneous world of privileged Europeans and Americans. Such homogeneity makes it possible to ignore the presence of a "third" person, the intersubjective experience uniquely created by the two people in the room. The idea of this third presence is a strong theme in contemporary relational theorists. The bringing together of two people and their intersubjective worlds is thought to create something entirely unique while also vaguely familiar to both of them. This three-person model of thinking about development and therapy (generally, now referred to as relational psychoanalytic psychotherapy) has become, if not a theory of its own, at least a strong and growingly cohesive tradition. For an excellent overview of theorists and seminal ideas of this tradition, see Mitchell (1999).

For both the two- and three-person models, therapy is thought to provide a context where the vital internal representations of primary figures, which form the core of personality, will begin to emerge. Therapy will focus on past and present experiences to encourage this uncovering. What makes therapy different from other relationships (where internalized representations are just as operative) is that the trained therapist can recognize distortions based on maladaptive inner images and can maintain the relationship in such a way as to allow the client to begin to change these images and come to have a more accurate understanding of self and the interpersonal environment.

The countertransference, or responsive and reactive state of the therapist, is her or his primary tool. Therapy hinges on it (Racker, 1957; Winnicott, 1956). The subtle confrontations or interpretations of the patient's experience of the world are chosen and worded through the matrix of the therapist's experience of the world. In the one-and-one-half-person model, the therapist seeks to limit the distortion of her own perspective by relying on empathic listening and by making the patient's transference the focus of discussion. In the three-person model the therapist actually selectively discloses her experience of the relationship with the patient, even acknowledging mistakes and countertransference reactions to the patient.

A healthy therapist will judge the maturity of the patient's behavior with reasonable effectiveness and accuracy. She can momentarily step outside herself to monitor the countertransference and separate much of what is her internal interpretation of reality from that of the patient. An immature therapist, however, can model a distorted sense of maturity and influence the client to develop according to the therapist's faulty perspective. Little possibility exists, in this theoretical framework, for the therapist leading the patient to a greater level of maturity than the therapist has personally attained.

Unlike the classical model of psychoanalysis that required longer-term therapy with multiple sessions per week, contemporary dynamic therapists are likely to work within more realistic constraints. The Vanderbilt Psychotherapy Study of Strupp and his colleagues, in fact, has demonstrated that the helpful effects of psychodynamic therapy can be experienced in a time-limited context of twenty-six sessions (Strupp & Binder, 1985). Using Strupp's time-limited method the therapist anticipates that each patient suffers from a cyclical maladaptive pattern that interferes with all of his significant relationships. The therapist monitors her relationship with the patient, watching for the emergence of this pattern.

Unlike the classical model that demanded the therapist's objectivity, the emerging relational model assumes that the therapist will, at times, lose all objectivity and become lost in the patient's cyclical relational pattern, enacting past relational failures. This comfort with intersubjectivity is built on the object-relations theorists' trust in the relational process over the therapist's ability to provide constructive interpretation of the patient's unconscious conflicts. The therapist is trusted to help the patient see the cycle they have both fallen into and to disclose her feelings about that experience. This type of immediacy is quite unlike the classical Freudian model of abstinence and anonymity. By breaking free from the morass of the cyclical maladaptive pattern, the patient is thought to receive both a new experience and a new insight that will help him to bring change into other relationships in his life. While capacity for insight is important, some patients are thought to benefit from the experience of healthy immediacy without simultaneous insight into the source of their problems.

CHRISTIAN CRITIQUE

Philosophical Assumptions

In reacting against the scientism and mechanism of classical drive theory, contemporary psychodynamic psychology has adopted a theoretical understanding of human nature based primarily on the analysis of human relationships. Object-relations theorists look first and foremost at the primary attachments made between children and the caregivers in the early developmental years. Other biological, psychosocial and sociocultural variables are deemed as less formative on later personality development and functioning. These influences are not seen as irrelevant, only less uniquely and fundamentally "human." Who we are and who we tend to become, they argue, can best be understood in the interpersonal context.

In basing the foundation of its psychology on the relational rather than biological components of personality, psychodynamic theory has essentially taken a step back into the phenomenological and philosophical realms in which psychology as a discipline began. In embracing such an emphasis and in moving away from a mechanistic model, psychodynamic theorists have removed many major obstacles for Christians who appreciate their model. In particular, as Hoffman (2004) has noted, Fairbairn and

Winnicott—two of the primary theorists to form the contemporary psychodynamic movement—were thoroughly immersed in Protestant worldviews and developed theories consistent with those roots. Because of that influence, object-relations theories lend themselves to questions of human nature, values and subjective experience. Not surprisingly, contemporary psychodynamic theories have become a realm for creative discussion among theologians and Christian mental health professionals.

Object-relations theorists claim that humans have an inherent capacity and need for relationships. Guntrip (1969), for example, suggested "the universe has begotten us with an absolute need to be able to relate in fully personal terms to an environment that we feel relates beneficently to us" (p. 328). Such a statement is reminiscent of the discussion in chapter two about the relational nature of humankind and how some say this is the central feature of what it means to be created in the image of God. Vanderploeg (1981a, 1981b), White (1984), Greenlee (1986) and others have noted how this common ground—an emphasis on the centrality of relationships—provides a foundation for the integration of the relational model and Christian thought. Hoffman (2011), in fact, notably demonstrates the long-unrecognized influence of the "Christian narrative on the theories, clinical practices and history of psychoanalysis" (p. 2).

Further, the notion that we internalize our relationships, that they become part of us, corresponds with Christian belief in marital union (Eph 5), family relatedness in the body of Christ (1 Cor 12) and even the notion of God residing in our very being when we become his child. Surely theirs is a purely psychological understanding of relatedness, but it is at least a step in the right direction.

Since the relational model addresses itself to that which is fundamental to human nature, the place of sin and particularly of original sin plays a prominent role in a Christian critique of its theories. Henderson (1975, 1977) points to a parallel between the object-relations view of the infant's earliest stage of primary narcissism, or egocentrism, with the Judeo-Christian view of original sin as selfishness, a sense of omnipotence or of viewing self as the center of the universe. He suggests, however, "the approach of dynamic psychology, in contrast to that of theology, is to assist the individual ego to search for, discover and know its inherent quantum of badness in the view that a badness which is well-known and familiar is thereby rendered impotent" (1975, p. 114). Christianity, however, goes further by offering forgiveness for and victory over sin, rather than merely rendering it psychologically impotent. Again, though, this is a step in the right direction, and there are almost certainly helpful aspects of this psychodynamic understanding of how we come to overcome our own "badness."

One result of the classic psychoanalytic approach has been a gradual erosion of a concept of sin. What theology had ascribed to sin, Freud ascribed to symptoms of illness, especially to psychological defenses. A person is not "bad" but "ill." Henderson (1977) resists this tendency with the accurate rationale that such a view tends to steer us away from "individual human accountability for the human situation" (p. 427). He suggested "psychotherapists should bring a concept of sin back into their work and emphasize personal moral culpability and accountability as vital to mental health" (p. 432). This is consistent with the view of psychodynamically oriented clinicians such as Peck (1983) and Menninger (1973), and is a move all Christians can applaud.

The importance of individual moral culpability notwithstanding, a psychodynamic perspective may have something to teach us about sin. To search for a psychological factor in some forms of sin does not require a corresponding diminution of personal accountability. Since early deprivation can leave the personality in an immature and vulnerable state, it seems feasible that some means of protecting the self could reflect our sinfulness (cf. Mangis, 2008). This would not equate sin with defense, but some sins could serve a defensive function. Sexual sins, for example, might, in some cases, be motivated by early unmet needs for intimacy. A propensity toward gossip might be motivated by an inner need to feel superior to others. This controversial area of human accountability may provide fertile ground for dialogue between theologians and psychodynamically oriented clinicians. Specifically, greater awareness and understanding of the nature of sinful behavior may aid in more effective (albeit limited) interventions that address it. Obviously, human beings in and of themselves are powerless to ameliorate either the ultimate causes or effects of sin. But they can serve an important and vital role as being agents of reconciliation and renewal in human relationships.

Discussions concerning moral accountability inevitably raise philosophical questions as to the existence of free will. On first glance, contemporary psychodynamic thought, in abandoning or altering the emphasis on biological instincts and drives, appears to have rejected the accompanying assumptions of determinism. In an apparent rejection of determinism, Guntrip (1969) states that

> we have non-dynamic behaviour theories describing human beings as just repertoires of behaviour patterns to be treated by techniques of reconditioning. . . . Over and against this is the dynamic psychology of the psychoanalytic and psychotherapeutic schools, standing for man's basic freedom and right not to be manipulated, but to be supported till he can find his own proper mature selfhood. (pp. 330-331)

While proponents of the relational model may seem to have wholly accepted the concept of free will, it is more likely that most have, in Evans's (1984, 1989) terms, rejected a "hard" determinism, which acknowledges the incompatibility of psychological causation and human freedom, for a "soft" determinism, which simply redefines freedom to make it seemingly compatible with psychological determinism. In both cases, internal forces exert powerful influences on our thoughts, feelings and behaviors.

But the relational models are much more amenable to a "libertarian" perspective on personal responsibility than is classic analysis. Evans (1984) has, in fact, argued forcefully that contemporary psychodynamic theory really has no need to retain the deterministic assumption of psychoanalysis. Eliminating that assumption would eradicate a stumbling block for Christian utilization of this approach. He argues that these approaches are quite compatible with a type of "limited freedom." We exist in the context of our personal histories. We are certainly influenced in powerful and significant ways by past relationships. We do not have to assume, however, that this history forces us to behave in a predetermined way, but rather provides probabilities of how we will act. Within certain boundaries, we have freedom and are, therefore, still accountable for our actions.

Models of Personality and Abnormality

While the emphasis of object-relations theorists is on the parents' impact on the child's personality, they do stress that no parent can be perfect, only "good enough." Kohut even emphasizes the importance of occasional failures by the parents so as to aid the internalization of the child's sense of responsibility for the maintenance of her or his own self-image.

It is difficult to criticize the relational model for its emphasis on the importance of the relationship between parent and child for personality development. If the *imago Dei* (the image of God) is at some level a need for relatedness, it follows that our healthy development would depend largely on adequately meeting that need, and that our earliest and most profound relationships would leave powerful impressions on us. Greenlee (1986) has pointed out that the dynamic of persons deprived of adequate caring in childhood in turn depriving their own children might be seen as a way in which the sins of the fathers are passed on to the succeeding generations (Ex 34:7). Certainly the notion of intergenerational sin and psychopathology deserves more serious attention in our religious circles in light of the alarmingly high rates of childhood trauma (e.g., physical and sexual abuse).

The view of *imago Dei* as "need for relatedness" certainly is not restricted to relations with other humans such as parents. According to a Christian creational perspective, the need itself arises from the fact that humankind was created for relationship with God and others. It is not surprising, then, that being created for a relationship with God and being born into a world where we find only broken and fallible images of God, we should have difficulty finding adequate resources for the building of a mature self capable of healthy relationships. It is also not surprising that we should have just as much difficulty developing a healthy relationship with God as with other human beings. Though created for this relationship, we are nevertheless on this earth separated from God, and thus there will always be a hunger for a greater sense of connectedness with him.

This latter difficulty of relating to God has been a prominent area of discourse between object-relations theorists and Christian theologians. The center of this discussion has been how individuals image or conceptualize God. This area of research developed out of the common and puzzling observation that people have radically different core views of God even within the same religious groups (e.g., God as Daddy, Judge, Distant Originating Cause, Buddy, Cosmic Vending Machine, etc.). Ana-Maria Rizzuto (1974, 1979, 1996) is probably best known for her work in this area. She draws on the object-relations concept of internal representations, developed in early childhood, which later influence our interactions with other people and our world. She suggests that in infancy the child, dependent on the parents for the provision of even the most elemental needs, creates an idealized representation of the parent (primarily mother) as God. While later development will lead to separate representations for the parents, this original God-image remains.

This concept is not new to psychodynamic thought. As discussed in chapter three, Freud saw the child's view of the parents as the origin of belief in God. He employed play on words of the Genesis account of God making humankind in his own image and suggested that, instead, humankind makes God in its own image. Freud saw God as an individual and corporate myth arising out of early relations with our own human fathers. The healthy adult must, therefore, abandon the infantile belief in a supreme being and resign her- or himself to the relative and impersonal nature of the universe.

The object-relations perspective of our image of God is decidedly more tolerant than that of Freud. Rizzuto sees one's image of God as a dynamic and creative part of the self that can grow and change, particularly as our perceptions of our parents, the original models for the God image, grow and change. Guntrip (1969) argued that "'religious experience' is the same kind of 'stuff' as human 'personal relations experience'" (p. 328), and that a relationship with God is the "personal heart of reality" (p. 331). Such a relationship, he suggests, can contribute to the maturation and integration of the developing personality. Rizzuto (1974) did not take her interpretation this far but did suggest that

> such a systematic grasp of the sources and the adaptive or maladaptive potential of internalized God-images within the larger theory of object relations would be, I submit, a useful tool, not just in the hand of the clinician, but also in the hands of the minister, rabbi and priest in their pastoral work as well as in the religious education of children. (p. 98)

But there is still potential here for views that are destructive of true faith as conceived in orthodox Christianity. Guntrip (1969), for example, regards God as an "indefinable term" (p. 331). Similarly, religion as a relationship with God is

> an overall way of experiencing life, of experiencing ourselves and our relationships together; an experience of growing personal integration or self-realization through communion with all that is around us, and finally our

way of relating to the universe, the total reality which has, after all, evolved us with the intelligence and motivation to explore this problem: all that is meant by "experience of God." (p. 326)

An internal relationship with a healthier image of God or the universe will remain, however, a unidirectional relationship. It is relating to an image (even illusion) within. When we form an internal image or representation of our parent, on the other hand, it originates out of an attempt to relate to the real person of the parent. No matter how distorted that internal image of the parent is, the potential always exists for further interactions with the parent and further maturing of the self to lead to a more accurate and reality-based internal image. Such a relationship is bidirectional. We can test aspects of our internal image against the real person, and the real person can take action to attempt to alter our internal image of her or him.

A secular object-relations theory cannot conceive of an internal relationship with an internal image of God as bidirectional. In fact, any belief in a real supernatural world in which the real God exists would be interpreted as "out-of-date dogmas or inadequate symbolisms of worship" (Guntrip, 1969, p. 329), a projection of our own subjective beliefs onto an impersonal external world. If this view were true, then Christianity would subsist purely of personal or collective autobiography, representations and images of God as recorded by our ancestors, together with our individual inner images of God formed in the context of relationships with significant others. Obviously this runs the risk of developing into a theology of personal subjective experience only.

Such a perspective by a secular object-relations theorist could allow for our image of God and our religion to be healthy, important, even artistic and poetic, but could not see it as a real relationship with a real person. The temptation, of course, is to believe that the discovery of the source and the distortion of our image of God is the end, to conclude that "we have discovered God and he is us." It is tempting to see an "almost" relationship with our internal image of God as the same thing as a relationship with God, to confuse sentimentality about vague religious impulses with a true relationship. It seems plausible, after all, that our images of God could be distorted by our experiences with fallen people, especially parents, in a fallen world. The slope can be quite slippery from that point, however.

Having "psychologized" our experience of God, it may then seem logical to conclude that what Christians often interpret as their experience of God is actually the work of the unconscious, and so, perhaps, we should worship the "God image" in all of us. To counter this, more accurate and "objective" concepts of the Creator God must be shaped in the context of Christian worship, education, fellowship and service. We need the input of these external sources for corrective feedback against our subjective and projective tendencies.

The seductiveness of these arguments does not invalidate the possible helpfulness of the object-relations theories. Knowledge of early development may truly inform us about distortions in our images of God; this knowledge could serve to lead us to a truer and more intimate relationship with God and others, just as understanding how our spouse is in reality quite different from our internalized image of "Mommy" or "Daddy" can aid the maturation of our marriages. It can take on an important role in therapy, especially when we know that in Christ we have a current, two-way relationship with a living, objective God both through the Word in us and the written Word, "living and active, sharper than any double-edged sword" (Heb 4:12 ESV).

The relational model of contemporary psychodynamic psychology may also provide helpful insights into how our image of God can grow and become healthier as our capacity for relationships goes through its necessary healing and maturing process (cf. Hoffman, 2011).

We would note in closing that this notion of the God image being profoundly shaped by parental images has been subjected to careful empirical assessment. Spilka, Hood and Gorsuch (1985, p. 81) summarize the results of this research by stating that the complexity and the subtlety of the hypothesis, and the difficult and challenging measurement issues involved, make this a very complicated question indeed. The existing data provide some modest support for the projective hypothesis, suggesting mild similarity in concepts of God and concepts of the same-sex or most-liked parent.

Theory of Health

According to psychodynamic theory, the mature individual values relationships and can maintain a commitment to them, even when the other person is not present. Such maturity requires a valuing of self since our perceptions of others are highly dependent on our internal representation of self. This notion is certainly in accord with the commandment to "love your neighbor as yourself" (Mt 22:39). It is significant, in light of the object-relations view of God, that this is the second greatest commandment. Jesus said that it was like the greatest commandment to "love the Lord your God with all your heart and with all your soul and with all your mind" (Mt 22:37). Our greatest commandment, to love God, places love of self and other second, an impossibility if self and other are real while God is only an internal representation. Perhaps the primary point should be, though, that love is central to what God wants in us when we are fully human, and it is to their credit that these models put the kind of interpersonal bonding that might be called love at the very center of their model of normalcy.

The psychodynamic system, like all psychotherapy systems, contains an implicit ethical system embedded in its understanding of normalcy. Altruism and mutual dependence are valued within the contexts of close (especially family) relationships, but self-sacrifice, giving to the point of allowing pain to be inflicted on the self, would not be highly valued. The hidden ethical vision of this tradition "is that one has a moral obligation to do that which deep down one wants to do. Or to say it differently, it is morally justifiable to do what one is inclined to do because what one is inclined to do is also moral" (Browning & Cooper, 2004, p. 225).

Because of our relational natures we are inclined to care for those close to us because they care for us and nurture us. This view directly parallels that of classic psychoanalysis. Thus a self-sacrificial act would generally be thought of as a self-induced punishment for irrational guilt or the result of an inaccurate view that others are more worthy of love than oneself. While this is probably often true (e.g., the self-styled Christian "doormat"), this model has little place for the reality of Christ's unilateral sacrifice and our commandment to model ourselves after his example (cf. Smedes, 1988). Since contemporary psychodynamic psychology is agnostic regarding the existence of reality or truth outside of this temporal world, it cannot allow for choices or values that call for the sacrifice of the needs of the self. It cannot envision a relationship with a real God that could empower one to make a truly self-sacrificial act.

In calling for the importance of equal and trusting relationships, and in highly prizing interrelatedness, however, it fares decidedly better than some theoretical systems which seem to actively embrace narcissism alone (Browning & Cooper, 2004, chap. 8). Its ethic is still partial and incomplete, but it is an important improvement.

Model of Psychotherapy

Benner (1983), Workman (1988) and others have suggested provocative parallels between the process of psychodynamic psychotherapy and God's work of salvation and sanctification. Salvation and sanctification, it is argued, might be loosely understood as the process by which in intimate relationship with God we grow by the process of God himself, through Christ, taking upon himself our "badness." Through Christ's death, "he is open to receive all our sin, able to contain anything we can project onto him. In this relationship, we are offered the opportunity to become whole persons" (Workman, 1988, p. 21). These authors suggest this is an analog to the psychotherapy relationship wherein the therapist acts as a human mediator who accepts, on behalf of God, the "bad introjects," the "psychic split-offs," that the client must be rid of to become whole.

This conception does parallel our call to be "Christ's ambassadors" (2 Cor 5:20-21), reconciling sinners with God. These authors do not wish to stretch these analogies too far, and we would agree with this caution. The analogies are fascinating, but the dangers of rendering God's work into a purely psychological framework and of elevating the redemptive work of the therapist to a grandiose level are great. The analogies may be helpful, but surely Christ's work is of an entirely different order than anything we can accomplish at a human level.

The psychodynamic methods of therapy may also be criticized for their seeming lack of appreciation for methods for change other than having a curative relationship. The pastoral instruction of the New Testament gives a great deal of attention to removing the characterological barriers to good relationships. We are to lay aside jealousy, envy, malice and so forth. But there is also ample biblical attention paid to other functions such as correcting our thinking, disciplined prayer and seeking restoration of shattered relationships. In the psychodynamic camp such interventions are often regarded as trivial or necessarily ineffectual. Further, these models are subtly humanistic in assuming that all will be well if the client has one really good relationship. The person will, as it were, be able to function autonomously through the direction of the ego once the bad internalized objects are straightened out. What is missing is an understanding of health that includes a long-term relationship with a living God and an appreciation for anchoring self in commitments to the church and God's revelation of himself in the Bible.

From a Christian perspective the faith of the therapist is important, though not the only factor, in determining effectiveness in psychotherapy. The worldview of a Christian is, presumably, substantially different from that of a non-Christian therapist. A non-Christian therapist with a healthy capacity for relationships may do far more good toward the healing of the personality than an immature Christian therapist, and a mature Christian therapist could possibly lead a patient away from true Christlikeness. On the whole, however, the greatest capacity for healing must certainly come from a Christian therapist directed by the Holy Spirit. As people, and in a profound and sobering way as therapists, we are imagers of God. The more that the therapist can be an accurate imager of God and therefore direct the individual to a greater capacity for relationship with God, the more healing will take place. A Christian object-relations therapist would, therefore, realize and help to facilitate the importance of a relationship between the patient and God in which God actively participates.

While the intimate connection between theory and therapy may be considered the strength of contemporary psychodynamic models, those who aspire to a more objective science of psychology will view it as a fatal weakness. Because all knowledge of internal dynamics comes from the therapy process in which the therapist is intimately involved, all conclusions are subject to the interpretations and distortions of the therapist. This might help explain the substantial disagreements between psychodynamic theorists from different schools and different eras. It is impossible to separate the conclusions of the theorist from his or her own individual dynamics.

To the question, Have the premises of contemporary psychoanalytic psychotherapy been adequately researched? the answer has, until recent years, depended on one's theoretical orientation. In a meta-analysis of psychodynamic psychotherapy outcome research, Shedler (2010) notes considerable empirical evidence for the efficacy of psychodynamic psychotherapy. Psychodynamic therapy was found to be as effective as other therapeutic modalities. And he noted that the effectiveness of other therapies is likely rooted, at least in part, in their similarities to the foundational principles of psychodynamic psychotherapy. Further, Shedler found that the effects of psychodynamic therapy were longer lasting than with other approaches, with patients continuing to find improvement after therapy had ended.

The fact that psychoanalytic theory grows out of the personal interactions of theorists with their patients provides an urgent call for Christian psychodynamically oriented therapists. One of the strongest voices in this area was Randall Lehman Sorenson. The thoughtful integration of contemporary psychoanalytic theory with Christian faith was dealt a terrible blow by his untimely death. Respected within both the secular and the Christian psychoanalytic communities, he mentored many practitioners and researchers in the relational psychodynamic tradition. We rely now on his writings and on the wisdom gained from those who were mentored by him (c.f. Sorenson, 1994a, 1994b, 1997, 2004).

CONCLUSION

The psychodynamic psychotherapies are among the broadest, most comprehensive systems in use today. In moving beyond Freud's narrow commitment to a biologically rooted, "scientific" theory, contemporary psychodynamic theorists have developed a system that does not present many of the problems to the committed Christian psychotherapist that classical analysis does.

These models are relational in nature, balance a cautious optimism with a deep appreciation of our capacity for self-deception and have a substantial (though secondary in emphasis) understanding of our rational capacities as humans. The values imbedded in the model are broadly compatible with Christian values, though of course there is not a perfect match.

The observant reader will note that our criticisms of this model were not devastating. Rather, they took the form of cautions. We think it fitting that this is one of the models that many Christian therapists are embracing; it holds much promise as a possible foundation for future elaboration of a thoroughly Christian understanding of human personality.

FOR FURTHER READING

Altman, N. (1995). *The analyst in the inner city.* Hillsdale, NJ: Analytic Press.
Altman challenges the Eurocentric and socioeconomic assumptions of psychodynamic therapies.

Berzoff, J., Flanagan, L. M., & Hertz, P. (1996). *Inside out and outside in: Psychodynamic clinical theory and practice in contemporary multicultural contexts.* Northvale, NJ: Jason Aronson.
This introductory textbook covers the major psychodynamic theories and therapies and examines them from a multicultural perspective.

Browning, D. S., & Cooper, T. D. (2004). *Religious thought and the modern psychologies* (2nd ed.). Minneapolis, MN: Fortress.
Browning's sympathetic analysis of the potential contributions of Kohut and Erikson to a Christian understanding of persons in his chapter eight is a model of scholarly thoroughness, though in the mainline denominational rather than evangelical tradition.

Hoffman, M. (2004). From enemy combatant to strange bedfellow: The role of religious narratives in the work of W. R. D. Fairbairn and D. W. Winnicott. *Psychoanalytic Dialogues, 14*(6), 769-804.
This article explores the faith-based roots of two of the most significant object-relations theorists.

Lake, F. (1986). *Clinical theology.* (Edited and abridged by M. Yeomans). New York, NY: Crossroad.
A readable abridged introduction to the fascinating thought of a dedicated Christian expounding a thoroughly psychodynamic view of the counseling process.

Levenson, H. (1995). *Time-limited dynamic psychotherapy: A guide to clinical practice.* New York, NY: Basic Books.
This application of Strupp's research on time-limited psychotherapy is extremely practical and readable.

Mitchell, S. A. (Ed.). (1999). *Relational psychoanalysis: The emergence of a tradition* (Vol. 14). Hillsdale, NJ: Analytic Press.
Until his untimely death Mitchell was the foremost relational theorist in the contemporary psychodynamic scene. In this volume he gathered some of the seminal works of relational psychoanalysis.

Stark, M. (1999). *Modes of therapeutic action: Enhancement of knowledge, provision of experience, and engagement in relationship.* Northvale, NJ: Jason Aronson.
This readable and practical book utilizes the three modes of listening discussed in this chapter and translates them into very practical advice for psychotherapists.

REFERENCES

Altman, N. (1995). *The analyst in the inner city.* Hillsdale, NJ: Analytic Press.

Benner, D. (1983). The incarnation as a metaphor for psychotherapy. *Journal of Psychology and Theology, 11,* 287-294.

Browning, D. S., & Cooper, T. D. (2004). *Religious thought and the modern psychologies* (2nd ed.). Minneapolis, MN: Fortress.

Crabb, L. J. (1998). *Inside out.* Colorado Springs, CO: NavPress.

Edkins, W. (1985). Object relations theory. In D. Benner (Ed.), *Baker encyclopedia of psychology* (pp. 769-771). Grand Rapids, MI: Baker.

Evans, C. S. (1984). Must psychoanalysis embrace determinism? Or can a psychologist be a libertarian? *Psychoanalysis and Contemporary Thought, 7,* 339-365.

Evans, C. (1989). *Wisdom and humanness in psychology.* Grand Rapids, MI: Baker.

Freud, S. (1961). The ego and the id. In J. Strachey (Ed. and Trans.), *The standard edition of the complete psychological works of Sigmund Freud* (Vol. 19, pp. 3-66). London: Hogarth Press. (Original work published 1923).

Greenberg, J., & Mitchell, S. (1983). *Object-relations in psychoanalytic theory.* Cambridge, MA: Harvard University Press.

Greenlee, L., Jr. (1986). Kohut's self psychology and theory of narcissism: Some implications regarding the fall and restoration of humanity. *Journal of Psychology and Theology, 14,* 110-116.

Guntrip, H. (1969). Religion in relation to personal integration. *British Journal of Medical Psychology, 42,* 323-333.

Henderson, J. (1975). Object relations and the doctrine of original sin. *International Review of Psychoanalysis, 2,* 107-120.

Henderson, J. (1977). Object relations and the psychotherapy of sin. *Canadian Psychiatric Association Journal, 22,* 427-433.

Henry, W. P., Strupp, H. H., Schacht, T. E., & Gaston, L. (1994). Psychodynamic approaches. In A. E. Bergin & S. L. Garfield (Eds.), *Handbook of psychotherapy and behavior change* (4th ed., pp. 467-508). New York, NY: John Wiley.

Hoffman, M. (2004). From enemy combatant to strange bedfellow: The role of religious narratives in the work of W. R. D. Fairbairn and D. W. Winnicott. *Psychoanalytic Dialogues, 14*(6), 769-804.

Hoffman, M. (2011). *Toward mutual recognition: Relational psychoanalysis and the Christian narrative.* New York, NY: Routledge.

Hurding, R. (1985). *Roots and shoots.* London: Hodder & Stoughton.

Johnson, R. (1985). Self psychology. In D. Benner (Ed.), *Baker encyclopedia of psychology* (pp. 1051-1053). Grand Rapids, MI: Baker.

Korchin, S. (1976). *Modern clinical psychology*. New York, NY: Basic Books.

Lake, F. (1966). *Clinical theology*. London: Darton, Longman & Todd.

Lake, F. (1986). *Clinical theology*. (Edited and abridged by M. Yeomans). New York, NY: Crossroad.

Linn, M., & Linn, D. (1978). *Healing life's hurts: Healing memories through five stages of forgiveness*. New York, NY: Paulist Press.

Luborsky, L., Barber, J., & Crits-Christoph, P. (1992). Testing psychoanalytic propositions about personality change in psychotherapy. In J. W. Barron, M. N. Eagle & D. L. Wolitzky (Eds.), *Interface of psychoanalysis and psychology* (pp. 572-585). Washington, DC: American Psychological Association.

Mahler, M. (1968). *On human symbiosis and the vicissitudes of individuation*. New York, NY: International Universities Press.

Mahler, M., Pine, F., & Bergman, A. (1975). *The psychological birth of the human infant*. New York, NY: Basic.

Mangis, M. (2008). *Signature sins: Taming our wayward hearts*. Downers Grove, IL: InterVarsity Press.

Menninger, K. (1973). *Whatever became of sin?* New York, NY: Hawthorne Books.

Mitchell, S. A. (Ed.). (1999). *Relational psychoanalysis: The emergence of a tradition* (Vol. 14). Hillsdale, NJ: Analytic Press.

Peck, S. (1983). *People of the lie*. New York, NY: Simon & Schuster.

Pine, F. (1988). The four psychologies of psychoanalysis and their place in clinical work. *Journal of the American Psychoanalytic Association, 36*, 571-596.

Prochaska, J. (1984). *Systems of psychotherapy* (2nd ed.). Chicago, IL: Dorsey.

Racker, H. (1957). The meanings and uses of countertransference. *Psychoanalytic Quarterly, 26*, 303-357.

Ricoeur, P. (1970). *Freud and philosophy: An essay on interpretation* (D. Savage, Trans.). New Haven, CT: Yale University Press.

Rizzuto, A.-M. (1974). Object relations and the formulation of the image of God. *British Journal of Medical Psychology, 47*, 83-99.

Rizzuto, A.-M. (1979). *The birth of the living God: A psychoanalytic study*. Chicago, IL: University of Chicago Press.

Rizzuto, A.-M. (1996). Psychoanalytic treatment and the religious person. In E. P. Shafranske (Ed.), *Religion and the clinical practice of psychology* (pp. 409-431). Washington, DC: American Psychological Association.

Seamands, D. A. (1985). *Healing of memories*. Wheaton, IL: Victor Books.

Shedler, J. (2010). The efficacy of psychodynamic psychotherapy. *American Psychologist, 65*(2), 98-109.

Smedes, L. (1988). *Caring and commitment*. San Francisco: Harper & Row.

Sorenson, R. L. (1994a). Ongoing change in psychoanalytic theory: Implications for analysis of religious experience. *Psychoanalytic Dialogues, 4*(4), 631-660.

Sorenson, R. L. (1994b). Therapists' (and their therapists') God representations in clinical practice. *Journal of Psychology and Theology, 22*(4), 325-344.

Sorenson, R. L. (1997). Transcendence and intersubjectivity: The patient's experience of the analyst's spirituality. In C. Spezzano & G. J. Gargiulo (Eds.), *Soul on the couch: Spirituality, religion, and morality in contemporary psychoanalysis* (Vol. 7, pp. 163-199). Hillsdale, NJ: Analytic Press.

Sorenson, R. L. (2004). *Minding spirituality*. Hillsdale, NJ: Analytic Press.

Spilka, B., Hood, R., & Gorsuch, R. (1985). *The psychology of religion: An empirical approach*. Englewood Cliffs, NJ: Prentice-Hall.

Stone, M. (1986). Borderline personality disorder. In A. Cooper, A. Frances & M. Sacks (Eds.), *Psychiatry: Vol. 1. The personality disorders and neuroses* (pp. 203-217). New York, NY: Basic Books.

Strupp, H. H. (1993). The Vanderbilt psychotherapy studies: Synopsis. *Journal of consulting and clinical psychology, 61*, 431-433.

Strupp, H. H., & Binder, J. L. (1985). *Psychotherapy in a new key: A guide to time-limited dynamic psychotherapy*. New York, NY: Basic.

Vanderploeg, R. (1981a). Imago dei, creation as election: Foundations for psychotherapy. *Journal of Psychology and Theology, 9*, 209-215.

Vanderploeg, R. (1981b). Imago dei as foundational to psychotherapy: Integration versus segregation. *Journal of Psychology and Theology, 9*, 299-304.

Van Leeuwen, M. (1990). *Gender and grace*. Downers Grove, IL: InterVarsity Press.

White, S. (1984). Imago dei and object relations theory: Implications for a model of human development. *Journal of Psychology and Theology, 12*, 286-293.

Winnicott, D. (1965). *The maturational process and the facilitating environment*. New York, NY: International Universities Press.

Winnicott, D. W. (1956). On transference. *International Journal of Psycho-Analysis*, 386-388.

Workman, D. (1988, April). *An analysis of object-relations theory*. Paper presented at the Christian Association for Psychological Studies convention, Denver, CO.

5

BEHAVIOR THERAPY

Stanton L. Jones, Kelly Flanagan and Richard E. Butman

*T*raditional behavior therapy (BT) is perhaps the most straightforward and direct of all approaches to human change. It has attempted to define a set of problem behaviors (including thoughts and emotions), determine the conditions that cause the problem behaviors to occur, and then intervene to eliminate or decrease the occurrence of those problem behaviors in the most efficient and effective way possible, all using the tools of "scientific psychology" or the "laws of learning."

The history of BT includes several phases. The first phase in the 1950s and 1960s was purely behavioral in focus. BT gained rapid popularity, undoubtedly due to its ability to demonstrate clear empirical success in accomplishing change with certain tightly defined problems. With the recognition that behavioral principles did not deal adequately with the role of thoughts and feelings in patients' mental health problems or with more complex problems, the second phase, beginning in the 1970s, involved the broadening of its models and techniques to incorporate the growing emphasis on cognitive models.

The third phase is an even more dramatic departure from the early foundations of BT. It is now difficult to define BT apart from its cognitive counterpart, as indicated by the (controversial) change in name of the flagship organization from the Association of the Advancement of Behavior Therapy to the Association of Behavior and Cognitive Therapies. Further, to improve the effectiveness of BT, current approaches often consider the role of factors and the use of methods once considered "soft and unscientific" by the movement's founders, factors such as therapeutic relationships, mindfulness, acceptance, personal values and emotional deepening (Hayes, Follette & Linehan, 2004; Tsai et al., 2009). These "third-wave behavior therapies" differ in focus and technology from traditional behavioral approaches that focused solely on basic behavior or learning principles by incorporating consideration of context and combining BT techniques with utilization of a broadened scope of experiential and indirect change strategies (Hayes, 2004; Kohlenberg & Tsai, 1994).

Two examples of mainstream BT today show how dramatically the field has incorporated nonbehavioral elements in therapy. Parent-child interaction therapy (PCIT; Eyberg, 1988) is a parent-training intervention for disruptive behavior problems in young children. The first stage of PCIT is humanistic in approach, seeking to establish warm, loving relationships between parents and children. Only then is more traditional BT offered in the form of instruction in effective behavior management based on behavioral learning principles. Sheila Eyberg, the developer of PCIT, recognized the importance of developing warm and safe therapeutic and parent-child relationships, and thus the intervention is conducted within play interactions between parent and child (Hembree-Kigin & McNeil, 1995).

Similarly, behavioral marital therapy focused on direct behavior change in couple interactions (e.g., replacing fighting with more effective problem-solving behavior) was recognized as having limited effectiveness. Despite immediate reductions in distress, many couples relapse two to four years later (Baucom, Shoham, Meuser, Daiuto & Stickle, 1998). Thus, a new approach was developed. In integrative behavioral couple therapy (IBCT; Jacobson & Christensen, 1996; Jacobson, Christensen, Prince, Cordova & Eldridge, 2000), traditional behavioral marital treatment techniques (e.g., effective communication training, problem-solving, behavioral exchange strategies) are combined with a focus on "acceptance." Specifically, couples are encouraged throughout the therapy to compromise, accept aspects of their spouse that are unlikely to change, and actively collaborate.

The evolution of BT over the past fifty years highlights not only the shortcoming of traditional BT but also the resiliency of this therapeutic model with its ideological focus on learning principles and its strong support within psychology. In this chapter, BT in its older, purer and more stringently behavioristic form will be the focus, with particular attention paid to its foundational principles and to those contemporary practices still defined by their utilization of more classic behavioral techniques. The more cognitive approaches of cognitive-behavior therapy and third-wave therapies focused on mindfulness and acceptance will be discussed in the next chapter.

DESCRIPTIVE SURVEY

Philosophical Assumptions

Behavior therapy is an outgrowth of *behaviorism*, which in turn is a product of two factors: a view of metaphysics, specifically that of naturalism; and a view of science, first that of inductive empiricism and later that of logical positivism (see Van Leeuwen, 1979, for an expanded discussion). Naturalism assumes that the universe is composed exclusively of matter and energy, and hence there are no such things as supernatural entities such as gods or spirits. The human qualities that distinguish us from the rest of the universe (especially "mind"), and which are commonly assumed to transcend nature, are in this view presumed either not to exist or to be understandable by the same physical laws that explain the rest of existence. Human beings are not viewed as special in the sense of transcending these laws of the universe.

Behaviorism took shape under the influence of a particular view of science, that of logical positivism and its predecessor, inductive empiricism. According to logical positivism, all meaningful assertions must be either analytic (statements that are true by definition, such as 2 + 2 = 4) or be *empirically verifiable* or *falsifiable*. Statements such as "God exists" are, in this view, not merely false but rather are meaningless because they are neither analytic nor verifiable by empirical means. In this view, empirical data become the highest court of meaning and hence determine truth. Contemporary philosophers of science have convincingly documented the problems with this view of science and proposed outlines for a better understanding of the process of human knowing (see Evans, 1989; Jones,

1994; and Van Leeuwen, 1982, for Christian analyses: Brown, 1977; and Kuhn, 1996, for a more standard treatment of this issue from the perspective of the philosophy of science; and Berry, 2001, for an intriguing complementary perspective). Further, in postmodern analysis, the validity of truth claims made through empirical study has been called into question, with stark consequences for psychological science (Dueck & Parsons, 2004; Gergen, 2001; Gorsuch, 2002).

If the material universe, understandable only as matter and energy operating according to universal laws, is all that is, then human beings are material beings only and hence explainable by natural laws. Because psychological events were not accessible to empirical study, classic behaviorism eschewed all "mentalism." Philosophical behaviorism was first given clear articulation by John B. Watson. In the 1920s he directly challenged the notion that mind or consciousness ("psyche") was the proper subject matter of psychology because it could not be empirically examined. For Watson the road to progress in psychology was to follow after the natural sciences in dealing only with empirically verifiable constructs (i.e., behavior); thus behavior was understood through its material and causal relationships to other behaviors and environmental events. The specific formulas for understanding behavior were supplied later by the learning theories of Pavlov, Thorndike, Skinner and others.

Behavior therapy has been described, in addition to being an outgrowth of empirical psychology, as also a reaction against "the bizarre, symbolic interpretations of behaviors" offered by psychoanalysis; BT was construed in contrast as a "direct, humble, rational, and empirical" therapeutic approach (Hayes, 2004, p. 2). In general, the leaders in the development of BT were critical of what they viewed as unfounded, vague and poorly researched theories and treatments of mental disorders (Wolpe & Rachman, 1960).

Behaviorism's embrace of naturalism gave rise to what has been called reductionism, the principle of breaking down more complex phenomena into simpler, more elemental ones. Thus, human language became understood as "verbal behavior," operating by the same principles as all overt behavior and reflexes. Thought in turn became "subvocal verbal behavior." These complex phenomena were in turn believed to be understandable in terms of the most elemental processes of learning. In this view, what we call "mental events" (such as thoughts and beliefs) and affect (feelings and emotions) may be part of human functioning, but are important only in their direct ties to overt behavior (e.g., dispositions to engage in behavior, initial cues to ensuing behavior). Everything, it was believed, can be reduced to elemental processes, and human behavior can be understood by breaking it down into parts. Without identification and analysis of these elements, complex human behavior cannot be studied, comprehended or effectively altered.

At the most basic level, then, an additional assumption of behaviorism can be termed *environmentalism*, not in the ecological sense but in the sense that behaviors are caused by factors outside of or external to themselves. All human and animal behavior is viewed as caused by environmental events. Thus, the reading of this chapter by graduate students is seen by the strict behaviorist as having been compelled by reinforcement contingencies exerted on them by the environment (i.e., demanding professors who dole out passing grades only in response to completion of educational tasks) and generated by the stimuli of the book lying on their desk.

The word *compel* signals that we must deal with the concept of determinism as well. Generally speaking, behaviorists accept the notion that all behaviors are the inevitable results of the causally relevant conditions that preceded them (*metaphysical determinism*) (Erwin, 1978). Skinner (1976) stated, "A person is not an originating agent; he is a locus, a point at which many genetic and environmental conditions come together in a joint effect" (p. 185). If the behaviors of human beings are merely part of the stream of natural material events occurring in a mechanistic cosmos, then it can logically follow that all our actions, including even what we call our decisions and choices, are caused in such a way that, as Wolpe (1978) put it, "We always do what we must do" (p. 444).

Although some modern behaviorists view behavior as a result of a system comprising random events (termed *metaphysical probabilism* or *probabilistic determinism*), human choice cannot be an originating source of that variability (Galuska, 2003). In fact, the concept of free will has been labeled "an illusion based on ignorance of the factors determining behavior" (Baum, 1994, p. 15). Thus, in this view human free will is ultimately illusory; our actions are the inevitable results of the causal forces impinging on us.

Model of Personality

Behaviorism is unique in that statements about a view of persons are typically only indirectly made by writers in this tradition. The real focus of the model is on the principles of behavior that apply to all organisms, both animal and human. From the basic philosophical assumptions of behaviorism, to understand persons you only need to understand the laws of learning. Behavioral understandings of the person are generally that the person is a bundle of behavior patterns, reflexes, perceptions and impressions. The self is nothing more, in this view, than the aggregation or composite of the person's empirical characteristics.

In contemporary texts on behavioral assessment (e.g., Bellack & Hersen, 1998; Kazdin, 2001), persons or their personalities are not assessed but rather behaviors and their controlling variables. For example, a primary characteristic of behavioral assessment is that it provides "a hypothesized model of the client" (Haynes, 1998, p. 11). This position can be taken to its logical conclusion that "personality is not a real thing" (Bellack & Hersen, 1977, p. 12) Behavioral views of the person can rightly be described as atomistic; persons are best understood by looking at the "atoms" of their behavior patterns and how these atoms are arranged and related. These atoms are not seen as being held together by or emanating from any comprehensive core of the person that we might call a self. Rather, at the foundation of personhood, the behaviorist considers classical and operant learning processes as the explanation for all behavior, with a core emphasis on environmental influences on behavior. Early researchers focused on delineating theories of learning and the different mechanisms and principles that could explain learning (Krasner, 1990). So it is to these processes we now briefly turn. (These topics are immensely complex and have generated an enormous literature; thus any brief summary is bound to be misleading due to oversimplification and selective attention.)

Classical conditioning. Classical conditioning is the process by which an involuntary response becomes reflexively associated with new eliciting stimuli. All human beings exhibit reflexive, unlearned (or unconditioned) responses to stimuli that elicit these responses from us, as when the smell of food elicits salivation, a puff of air elicits eye blinking, a burn elicits pain, a noxious odor elicits nausea and so forth. These reactions do not demonstrate learning. Instead, we exhibit these responses without prior training. Pavlov showed that these reactions could be associated with new stimuli that themselves had previously not elicited these responses, which is learning at its most basic.

The classic example of this process is Pavlov's dogs, who learned to salivate at the sound of a bell because of the repeated association of the bell with the presentation of food. In this case the food was the *unconditioned stimulus* that elicited an unconditioned response of salivation. After conditioning trials the previously irrelevant bell became a *conditioned stimulus* (i.e., it became a relevant stimulus only through conditioning trials) that could elicit a conditioned response of salivation even when no food was presented.

The procedures of Wolpe's behavior therapy are based on these principles. Wolpe considered anxiety a central feature of most adult psychopathology. Anxiety can easily be conceptualized in terms of classical conditioning. For example, an intense emotional reaction (such as fear) to a "legitimate" or understandable stimulus (e.g., being bitten by a dog) can become associated through the process of classical conditioning with previously emotionally neutral stimuli (e.g., going out of one's house). In an extreme case a person unfortunate enough to make the associations between being bitten and leaving his house might become agoraphobic, profoundly fearful of being away from home and in situations where escape would be difficult. If, in trying to leave the house and overcome the anxiety, he gave into the fear and did not leave, the agoraphobic response would be further reinforced by the powerful relief from the anxiety gained through avoiding what he feared.

This analysis of the dynamics of the establishment of debilitating fears also leads to some fruitful hypotheses about fear reduction. Pavlov demonstrated that most conditioned responses could be changed or "wiped out" through two means: (1) a new response that was incompatible to the previous conditioned response could be conditioned to the conditioned stimulus, or (2) the conditioned response could be extinguished by presenting the conditioned stimulus repeatedly without pairing it with the unconditioned stimulus.

Wolpe pioneered the technique called *systematic desensitization* based on the former process of pairing a new response with the old stimulus. Wolpe understood the phenomenon of anxiety largely in terms of its physical, observable manifestations and thus reasoned that the response most anti-thetical to anxiety was muscular relaxation. Desensitization was developed to provide a way for relaxation to become associated with what had previously been an anxiety-evoking stimulus. A therapist would first teach an anxious client physical relaxation and then have the client slowly and gradually imagine closer and closer approaches to the anxiety-provoking stimulus while the client maintains a relaxed state. After the client is able to maintain physical relaxation while imagining a full approach to the previously feared stimulus, the therapist would then guide the client closer to real-life approaches to the feared stimulus.

Behavior therapists may also utilize Pavlov's latter notion of extinguishing the unwanted response. Extinction for the dogs occurred simply by presenting the bell, which had previously been associated with food, over and over again without any presentation of the food. In this way the salivation response to the bell eventually died out. Similarly, some argue that many forms of anxiety are best extinguished by exposing the client to the feared stimulus or stimuli without the feared outcome occurring. Exposure to a feared stimulus can be gradual or all at once. For example, Marks (1981) reported the case of a woman with a longstanding obsessive-compulsive disorder who had previously not responded to either drugs or several forms of psychotherapy, including psychoanalysis. He worked with the formulation that the fears of germs, sickness, death and so forth were generating avoidance behaviors such as compulsive cleaning rituals and avoidance of social contacts. These avoidance behaviors in turn reduced the anxiety, which reinforced the avoidance. Therapy then consisted of exposing the patient to the feared stimuli, which Marks did in an intensive inpatient treatment program. Marks had the woman touch "contaminated" objects (e.g., dirt, shoes, toilet seats, floors and used eating utensils) all while refraining from cleansing herself; she even was asked to put her soiled fingers in her mouth, to rub her clothes before putting them on and to rub her own eating utensils before using them. Within days, since there was no trauma to keep the conditioned fear alive (since the feared disease and death did not occur), the obsessive-compulsive neurosis and the anxiety causing it slowly diminished (extinguished). At follow-up, she maintained her therapeutic gains.

Operant learning. Operant learning, also called instrumental learning, refers to the modification of spontaneously emitted behavior (in contrast to the elicited behaviors we have just been discussing such as salivation or fear). These emitted behaviors are presumed to exist for the purpose of operating on the environment, hence the term *operant behavior*. Operant learning is the process by which this emitted behavior is modified over time by the *consequences* that follow contingently upon the response behavior and by the stimuli that form the context under which the behavior occurs.

The classic example is, of course, the rat in the Skinner box. Lever pressing or other forms of emitted rat behavior are modified by the consequences arranged to follow the behavior. Responses followed by such events as presentation of food or drink, or by the removal of unpleasant noise or shock, are likely to increase in frequency (*reinforcement*). Responses followed by aversive consequences such as a spray of ice water or shock, or by the removal of food or drink, are likely to decrease in frequency (*punishment*). Rats can attend to and learn to respond to stimuli, such as lights, which signal that reinforcement is available (e.g., lever pressing leads to food when only the green light is on) or unavailable (e.g., lever pressing is ineffective when the red light is on). We are more likely to smile at a passing stranger on the sidewalk if we have received smiles in return from the previous people we have passed.

Whereas classical conditioning does not create new behavior, operant conditioning can lead to new and complex behavior. First, new behaviors never before emitted by the organism can be taught through the process of *shaping*. Shaping involves reinforcing closer and closer approximations to a goal response. For example, a chicken can be taught to peck a piano key by first reinforcing the behavior of being nearer and nearer the piano, then the behavior of touching the piano closer and closer to the keyboard, until a peck on the keys can be reinforced. New complex patterns of behavior can be created by chaining, wherein more and more links between specific behaviors are required to occur together for reinforcement to be delivered, until an entire chain of behavior occurs before the final reinforcement (e.g., the chicken now raises a curtain, moves a stool, and then plays a piano).

Those who practice behavior modification posit that human behavior is largely the result of these operant processes. Human problems occur when (1) people learn maladaptive or inappropriate responses, (2) people fail to learn effective or appropriate responses due to their previous learning environments, or (3) the wrong environmental contingencies are provided in response to maladaptive behaviors. Often the cause is described as the combination of all three factors. The disruptive behavior of the aggressive child in the home and classroom may be the result of previous learning of inappropriate responses of hitting, yelling and tantrums in response to conflict. The child may also have failed to learn appropriate anger management skills and appropriate ways of expressing emotion and interacting with others. Finally, the aggressive behavior may be reinforced by peers, parents and teachers who, perhaps unwittingly, pay attention to the child when misbehavior occurs, allow the child to "get her way," and fail to reinforce appropriate behavior and interactions with peers.

Social learning theory. Learning theory approaches were forced to incorporate much more complex phenomena by the recognition that humans, and even relatively simple animals, learn not just by direct but also by observed or vicarious experience. This was behaviorism's first (and forced) engagement with cognitive phenomena, and a key step toward more clinically relevant strategies to complex human difficulties.

Social learning theory as developed by Bandura (1986) highlights the social context and relationships in which these learning processes take place and the social influences on the development of behavior. Further, social learning theory emphasizes the crucial role of cognition in selectively attending to and encoding information in one's environment, the impact of values and expectations on motivation to engage in various behaviors, and, more broadly, the interaction of cognition and the environment to construct behavior. The influence of this theory is reflected in the assessment, conceptualization of behavior and learning processes, and the clinical approaches (e.g., modeling, skill training) of contemporary BT.

Social learning theory provides a perspective on human learning not addressed by classical and operant learning theories. In particular, the concept of *observational learning* helped describe how we are affected by social influences. We learn not just by direct experience but by observing others; such observations impart information and elicit emotional reactions that influence our beliefs, expectations and self-perceptions. The impact of observational learning was described in Bandura's classic experiments on aggression in children, showing that children exposed to aggressive models behaved more aggressively, while children who viewed prosocial behavior performed by others displayed reductions in aggressive behavior.

Other important concepts embedded in social learning theory include self-efficacy and reciprocal determinism. Self-efficacy refers to how a person's beliefs or perceptions regarding his or her own capabilities to act effectively (or not) influence how he or she later behaves. Reciprocal determinism asserts that we are both the product and the creators of our environments; this in contrast to classic determinism, which emphasizes how an environment causes behavior alone. In reciprocal determinism, behavior is explained through the dynamic and reciprocal interaction of the environment with our personal factors (e.g., sex, ethnicity, temperament, beliefs, self-perceptions) and our behavior.

Notably, social learning theory provides for greater human agency than classical and operant learning processes (Bandura, 2001). Though in this view the individual is not free from the effects of the environment, there is some recognition that the individual has the ability to influence one's own behavior and impact his or her environment. According to social learning theory, humans are shaped by their environment, but are also able to be self-reflective and to engage in forethought and self-regulation of behavior. Thus, cognitive processes are given a greater role in determining behavior than in the foundational learning theories of behaviorism.

Model of Psychotherapy

Believing that behavior is caused by its environment, behavior therapy begins with a careful assessment of the factors that seem to exert influence on the problematic behavior. Modern behavior analysis is typically less mechanistic and uses a form of analysis termed *functional behavior analysis* that assesses behavior in light of its interaction with historical, motivational and situational antecedents and its expected consequences (Haynes & O'Brien, 2000). Note that persons are not assessed but behaviors and the functional relationships and contextual variables that affect behavior.

Two contemporary behavior therapy approaches, functional analytic psychotherapy (FAP) and acceptance and commitment therapy (ACT), take it a step further and assess not only the role of contextual variables but also less easily observed subjective cognitive and affective factors (Callaghan, Gregg, Marx, Kohlenberg & Gifford, 2004) in recognition of the role of intrapersonal and interpersonal experiences in the development and maintenance of clients' problems. Yet the premise of this assessment approach continues to be that a "system's" (i.e., not a person's) behavior and psychological events cannot be understood unless objectively evaluated through systematic investigation (Skinner, 1953). In BT, ongoing assessment should include multimethod, multi-informant and multimodal measurements that are aimed at decreasing bias and are interpreted with the understanding that human behavior will change depending on context, time and contingencies for the behavior. Even in FAP, which utilizes the therapeutic relationship to reinforce more adaptive, effective interpersonal behaviors through differentially responding to the client's in-session behaviors, the therapist continually assesses whether his or her contingent responses result in changes in the client's targeted problematic behaviors and distress (Kohlenberg & Tsai, 1994).

As a general example the temper tantrums of a five-year-old may be seen by the parent as caused by disrespect for authority, low self-esteem or a problem of the sinful heart (as some Christian families have described the problem). The behavior therapist, however, would collect data on the events and situational factors (antecedents) that predict the behavior and the events that reinforce it (consequences). By performing a comprehensive behavioral assessment the therapist discovers that the behavior only occurs when one parent is present and not in the presence of the other (more consistent disciplinarian) parent, that the worst misbehavior occurs when the parent uses abrupt and harsh directives (such as yelling for the child to stop what he is doing), and that the parent responds to misbehavior by yelling without any real punishment. Such cycles often escalate over time as the parent worries about "setting off" another tantrum and becomes unsure of his or her parenting. The analysis may also show that the problem behavior occurs when the parents are engaged in a heated argument and that the child's misbehavior causes the parents to cease their argument, thus allowing the child to have some control over the environment. A BT intervention in such a case occurs at the point at which action will be effective (Skinner, 1976), and might include preparing the child for difficult transitions, providing consistent negative consequences for tantrum behavior and positive consequences for cooperative behavior, and altering the family dynamics when in conflict. Intervention does not occur until a clear conceptualization of the behavior is obtained through thorough analysis.

Due to the commitment to the scientific method, behavior therapists emphasize continuing assessment both throughout and after the intervention period to verify that change is occurring and is maintained as expected. Thus, a strength of BT is the evaluation of treatment effectiveness and the subsequent modification of therapy itself. In general, the therapeutic techniques that emerge out of this model are powerful methods for teaching new behaviors and for arranging environments to make desired behavior more likely and to reduce or completely extinguish undesired behavior. Several examples will illustrate these principles and how they have been effectively used.

One of the dramatic successes of BT has been in the treatment of children with pervasive developmental disorders (PDDs), autism in particular. While the causes of these disorders are still uncertain, BT interventions are the most effective treatments for generating social behavior, everyday adaptive skills and independent functioning (Lovaas & Smith, 2003; Schreibman, Koegel, Charlop & Egel, 1990). BT for children with autism involves intensive training provided consistently for many hours per week. The goal is to modify these children's behavior by altering their environment (and thus the antecedents and consequences) and to encourage the acquisition of new skills. Children are first rewarded with tangible rewards for appropriate behavior at their current level of functioning. New, adaptive behaviors and social skills are slowly developed through shaping and chaining. Extremely dangerous behavior such as self-injurious head-banging may have to be directly punished (e.g., with time-out procedures, verbal reprimands or loss of a privilege), but as much negative behavior as possible is simply ignored with the goal of displacing negative behavior with positive response to more appropriate behavior as the child's functioning improves. Progressing from fundamental behaviors, such as language sounds and attending to others, programs reinforce increasingly more complex and socially skilled behaviors. Early, intensive interventions utilizing these strategies of BT have produced astonishing outcomes for many children with PDDs, who after treatment may display behavior and social functioning similar to children without PDDs (Newsom & Hovanitz, 2006).

Parent training and classroom behavior management programs also reflect contemporary BT practice. Skinner and others argued that the best way to manage behavior is to use positive reinforcement, but this is difficult to implement, particularly in the classroom, because misbehavior so often obtains inordinate amounts of attention from the teacher and other students. Many behavioral programs have been developed that involve direct reinforcement of positive behavior through contingency management systems, such as a reward system in the classroom or home in which children can earn tokens which count as points toward obtaining some desired reward (e.g., school supplies, a special role in the classroom, parties, sleepovers, special privileges, etc.). Because each reward is earned through points in this token economy system, teachers and parents can specify desired behavior and reinforce the child frequently. Adults are also trained to provide differential attention to appropriate behavior and to ignore disruptive and inappropriate behavior. Other students can be trained to model appropriate behavior. Such programs are effective in increasing positive social behavior, compliance and academic performance, and have been used to teach children greater self-control (DuPaul & Eckert, 1997; McMahon, Wells & Kotler, 2006).

A final example of BT is social skills training. Many individuals who report interpersonal difficulties lack critical social skills, and BT teaches clients the social skills necessary to interface more effectively with their social world. Clients are provided with instruction and modeling of specific abilities, as well as support and reinforcement for skill acquisition and practice (i.e., role plays, homework, in vivo practice). The focus is on increasing competence with discrete skills in specific social situations (e.g., enhanced listening, or assertiveness in a job). In general, social skills training with adults and children, in outpatient and inpatient settings, has been found to produce clinically significant effects on outcomes such as social performance, self-esteem and decreased anxiety (Morrison, 1990).

CHRISTIAN CRITIQUE

Philosophical Assumptions

The first philosophical presupposition we mentioned in regard to behavior therapy was naturalism. Obviously, naturalism is at odds with the Christian faith: God exists and is above nature since he is the maker of nature, and therefore dogmatic naturalism is false. There are such supernatural entities as God, angels, the devil and demons. However, this quick dismissal of doctrinaire naturalism is not an endorsement of the opposite belief—that human beings are purely supernatural beings.

Authors such as Boivin (1985) have argued that while Christians must reject a behavioristic worldview that denies the reality of the supernatural, it may be biblical to assert that while there are supernatural entities that interact with the created order, the created order itself (including humanity) is purely naturalistic. Compare the words of Watson (1930), "Man is an animal different from other animals only in the types of behavior he displays" (p. v) with the words of Boivin (1985), "Only our relationship and responsibility to God makes us qualitatively different from animals" (p. 83). Boivin asserts that a Christian understanding of the person does not need to posit more than a natural existence for humanity. He supports this view by pointing to the Hebraic notion of the unity of human existence, to the doctrines of embodied life and to the confusion of traditional Christian anthropology about soul and spirit. He suggests, in short, that naturalism is true with reference to human beings.

We agree that there has been at times a misplaced emphasis on doctrines of disembodied souls in the Christian tradition. Nonetheless, the Christian faith seems to require viewing persons as partially immaterial beings. The naturalism of behaviorism does, however, remind us that humans have pridefully underestimated the extent to which our embodied existence conditions, shapes and even determines some aspects of our experience. As suggested by Browning and Cooper (2004), as long as we are careful not to completely swallow the most dogmatic of philosophical assumptions underlying BT, that of pure naturalism with no acknowledgment of a spiritual nature, self-transcendence and freedom, we can and should take seriously how external reinforcement contingencies do influence our behaviors and personhood. The success of BT in clear cases of conditioned anxiety (phobias) belies our creature nature and the forces of learning on us. But in emphasizing only bodily existence, the behaviorist misses a key aspect of human nature—the interplay of body and soul-spirit and the distinctively transcendent aspects of our natures.

The behavioristic rejection of "mentalism" and its view of the mind are also problematic. If thought is merely a behavioral disposition or a byproduct of physical brain events, then humans cannot transcend the physical order of things. This provides a conceptual grounding for the doctrine of determinism. As we shall see in the paragraphs to come, such determinism is not acceptable. Christian belief does not lead to an easy resolution to the brain-mind issue, though it does set up certain parameters within which to choose proper resolutions to the matter (Jones, 1985). One of these parameters, though, must be some notion that thought is more than just an epiphenomenon, as strict behaviorism presupposes. Christians cannot accept a notion that belief and thought are not effectual causes of behavior.

We have already delineated how behaviorists accept determinism and thus reject the concept of freedom and consciousness. Even so, it is common to read of "freely emitted behavior" and even "freedom" in behavioral writings. Zuriff (1985) is helpful here in noting that the language of freedom or action is used in BT to designate behaviors that are not reflexively elicited or coerced. In this view, a certain action (for example, raising a hand) is free if the behavior coincides with one's desires (as when waving bye-bye to a child) but is not free when it is against one's desires (as when one raises both hands during a robbery or in response to stimulation of the motor cortex of the brain during neurosurgery). Note though that all of the actions in these examples would be regarded by the behaviorist as causally determined; the first two by the "laws of learning" and the last one by neurological stimulation.

What makes the first instance of waving "free" for the behaviorist is not that one could have acted otherwise under the same circumstances; in the behavioral analysis one could not have done so given one's learning history and the current context (e.g., interaction with a child). It was "free," in the view of Skinner and others, because the enacting of that behavior was not unpleasant for the actor and it was in accord with the person's causally predetermined desires at the moment. In other words, the actor had the subjective experience of choice, but the choice and the desires that motivated it were really predetermined by learning history. To the behaviorist all behavior is regarded as inevitable; we can never do other than what we do.

In critiquing this view we must first note that not all psychologists engaged in modern forms of BT use mechanistic forms of analysis that are characteristic of this strict behaviorist assumption. In addition, clients who make an active choice to engage in BT and alter a problematic behavior (rather than those "in charge" of behavior modification plans) are in effect acting on their environment, which in turn will act on their behaviors. Indeed, as mentioned in the introduction of this chapter, modern forms of BT utilize "mindfulness" and "acceptance," indicating that the mental and motivational aspects of our personhood cannot be denied in treatment.

The coupling of environmental influences and freedom can be seen within Christianity as well; we are called to make the active choice of putting ourselves in an environment and in conditions (e.g., community, workplace, social and leisure activities) that encourage "a new way" to promote behavior change and spiritual growth (Browning & Cooper, 2004; Lasure & Mikulas, 1996). Some have argued that the commonalities between behaviorism and Christianity should be given more attention, including the emphasis within behaviorism on improving quality of life and Christian strivings of being free from or avoiding sin (e.g., Rom 7:7-25) (Galuska, 2003). It is further argued that BT could offer resolution to these strivings through behavioral techniques (e.g., self-control, reinforcement) (Galuska, 2003). Though we do not deny the utility of behavioral interventions, as Zuriff (1985) stated, at the core behavioristic psychology "is not . . . compatible with the notion of a free-willed self-initiating agent" (p. 199).

We argued in chapter two that Christian belief requires a rejection of determinism—the view that every human event is the inevitable outcome of preceding events—and requires belief in limited freedom. Though some Christian psychologists (e.g., Bufford, 1981) and some Christian groups embrace such a strong view of God's sovereignty that they could be labeled theological determinists, such a position has not been typical of historic, orthodox Christianity. John Calvin is commonly believed to have denied the freedom of persons, but along with Muller and Vande Kemp (1985), we would argue that his belief in God's sovereignty, divine election, predestination and the depravity of the human will cannot be equated with the philosophical determinism accepted by most behaviorists. Human freedom is even defended in the Calvinistic tradition, as stated in the Westminster Confession of Faith (Leith, 1973): "God hath endued the will of man with that natural liberty, that [it] is neither forced nor by any absolute necessity of nature determined to good or evil."

In most segments of the Christian tradition, human beings are regarded as responsible, as morally culpable. Responsibility for our actions seems to require the capacity to have acted other than we did in a given situation. Thus, from a Christian perspective total determinism is unacceptable and limited freedom is an essential belief (Evans, 1977). The Christian must believe that a person's choices are sometimes the ultimate and deciding factor in the occurrence of an action in order to believe that we are truly responsible beings who can be held accountable for our actions before God.

Yet note that causes do not have to be exclusive. To argue that in a particular instance the person was an ultimate cause does not rule out that other causes also affected the behavioral outcome. Even though we make real choices, we do so as persons with experiences and constraints that exert an effect. Accepting the notion of agent causation does not mean denying the assertion that some or even much of our behavior is determined, or that the true choices of a free agent are shaped, by constitutional or environmental factors.

The Christian concept of limited freedom is not the same as freedom from regularity, freedom from influences on behavior or freedom from finitude. It simply means that the final choices that create behavior were not merely the result of impersonal forces, and the person choosing was not merely a "locus" of influences coming together. Rather, the person decided among real options, influenced by his or her history and constitution. This position has been excellently delineated by Browning and Cooper (2004, p. 102):

> The doctrine of the freedom, transcendence and responsibility of humans does not mean that we are totally free and completely unconditioned by either internal impulse or external reinforcements. In fact, it means just the opposite. It means that in spite of our massive conditionedness by these forces, there is still a sufficient modicum of transcendence over them to make it possible for us to alter, to some meaningful degree, the course of our lives.

It would seem that we are stuck with incompatible perspectives on this topic; determinism and limited freedom do not in fact appear to be reconcilable.

Positively, we can learn from behavior modification that our behavior is influenced and shaped by many factors that we are often unaware of. In

denying determinism Christians are often in danger of embracing a prideful claim that their choices and actions are totally free and unconditioned
by their material existence. We are dangerously close to a self-deifying
view that denies our finitude and dependency. It also seems true that
human beings are a composite of lower and higher capacities, and that we
erroneously want to deny the real role conditioning influences play in our
basic psychological makeup.

Model of Personality

We introduced earlier the atomistic view of the person embedded in behaviorist psychology. In this view there are no necessary interrelationships
between discrete components of the person's behavior. If interrelationships
exist between clusters of behaviors, as when a person tends to lie and to
steal, they are thereby the accident of conditioned association or some such
process. There is no necessary grounding of any particular behavior or
behavior pattern in a self.

A concept of general human responsibility is thus impossible, since each
behavioral pattern has its own specific controlling conditions that bear no
necessary relationship to the person as a whole. There is no "person" to
hold responsible for the behavior exhibited, which is why Skinner (1971)
could call for the abolition of our criminal jurisprudence system; there
really are no persons to be punished but only response patterns to be modified, and thus behavior modification should replace judicial punishment.
Further, one negative behavior pattern (e.g., repeated lying) does not make
the person a bad person; rather, the lying is a behavior pattern that needs
to be modified. There is, in fact, no "good" or "bad" within our characters,
merely behavior patterns that are unrelated to the "person," as the person
does not exist.

There is a certain clinical wisdom and utility to such an approach, in
that the spurious overidentification by a client with a particular negative
aspect of her or his behavior is genuinely problematic. We have known
sincere Christians who ignore many positive areas of discipline and maturity in their lives to focus on one negative pattern ("I've not been able to
kick this bad habit; I am an evil, unlovable person!"). Thus, religious
thinkers can come away from BT with crucial insight: not every behavior
pattern is a true index of the state of the self. One person's rudeness in a
situation may be an accurate index of their arrogance, pride and self-

deification. The exact same act by another person may be an anomaly related to being inattentive to social cues at that moment. Perhaps even behavior patterns that are good indices of the condition of the heart will have to be changed deliberately after the heart changes. Old, sinful habit patterns do not automatically change when the heart changes.

Even so, Christian thought requires the identification of specific behaviors in some significant manner with the unified person, because a person who commits specific behavioral acts that are sins must be capable of validly being labeled a sinner. In a powerful way, a person's behavioral acts often are diagnostic of the inner condition of the "heart," or unified core of the person. As Christ said, "By their fruit you will recognize them" (Mt 7:16). Behaviors are not atoms unconnected with the heart; they are often (but not always) evidence of what lies in the heart. If we deny that persons are unified beings, then there is no one to hold responsible for sin, no unified person to be redeemed and sanctified or punished, and sins are just behaviors which occur in a person's body or in his or her actions, but are unconnected with the person per se. Atomism is thus unacceptable, though instructive, to the Christian.

Every theory of personality has a view of human motivation, though we have dealt only implicitly with it in BT thus far. The behavioral view is both simple and complex. First, BT is simple in proposing that human survival is the driving, evolutionarily based motivation behind our behavior. As Browning and Cooper (2004) and others have pointed out, there are remarkable parallels between Skinner's environmental reinforcement and Darwin's concept of natural selection. For the Darwinian evolutionist nature "selects" species that successfully adapt to their environmental niche. For the behaviorist the environment "selects" behaviors by reinforcing those responses that aid survival and adaptation to the organism's niche in life.

Looking only at rat behavior in Skinner boxes, we often mistakenly imagine reinforcement to be something that others (behavioral engineers or parents) intentionally do because they deliberately want to change the behavior of the subject (rat or child). Yet in the "real world," reinforcement and punishment occur naturally depending on how good of a match the organism's behavior is to the demands of the environment. For example, a particular type of hunting behavior by a predator may be reinforced by a successful kill because the hunting behavior meshed well with nature. To Skinner, individual adaptation to the environment, and hence greater chance of survival, is the motivation for human behavior. One of the distinctives of behaviorism is that it proposes a small list of inherent motivations or instincts that are themselves critical to survival, including such drives as for food, drink and sex (Herrnstein, 1977).

However, the behavioral view of motivation becomes exquisitely complex when we realize that almost anything can become a reinforcer that motivates performance through its association with more primary or basic reinforcers. Things like money or verbal praise become reinforcement through constant association with primary reinforcers such as food, warmth and sexual outlet. In this way we can be led to value (and hence be motivated by) a diversity of stimuli, including financial reward, the praise of our parents and peers, or interpersonal recognition. Further, response patterns like academic excellence, artistic creativity, physical brutality and psychopathic manipulation can become vehicles for obtaining primary reinforcers and hence the response patterns can come to have a positive value in their own right. So in the behaviorist analysis there is no one core human motivation that is easily appealed to in order to understand human behavior. Rather, human motivation is idiosyncratically organized; each person's motivations may be different from those of others.

Christians may applaud the motivational diversity of behavior therapy, but be rightly troubled by its assumption that all effective motivations ultimately depend on basal drives shared with animals. Additionally, moral concepts of altruism and unconditional love of other become mere behavioral reactions to reinforcement. Christians must claim that human beings are capable of acting out of higher motives, such as the desire to serve God, and that these higher motives cannot always be reduced to the drive for tangible reinforcement.

A Christian judgment that human motivations ought to be more noble and higher may be valid; at the same time, appeals to "higher motives" may be ineffective incentives to change a person's behavior. For instance, Christians often object to token economies for their problem children on the grounds that the children ought to obey their parents and do their chores because "it is the right thing to do," not to earn points to purchase video games. But when a disruptive child is motivated only by the avoidance of punishment and rewards, those appetites may be the best avenue for modification of the child's behavior. Such an initial change may establish the very possibility of the child being motivated by other things, such as a respectful and loving relationship with a parent. Having children obey their parents, improve their school performance and attend church to earn tokens to buy toys may be the best way to expose them to activities which they ought to value more, and thus increase the likelihood that they will come to prefer them. Just because Christianity teaches that people ought to value more than material things does not mean they do, and there is no psychotherapy system more humble and realistic about the depth to which human motivation can sink than BT.

The approach also suggests a technology for the alteration of human values and motives through the acquisition of skills and association of events. As Clouse (1985) put it, "God created us as beings who respond to reinforcers and punishers in our environment" (p. 94). Perhaps it is the original sin of human pride and self-reliance more than anything that makes us prone to believe that we supersede all environmental influence. The deliberate structuring of our environments to build up righteous behavior seems a helpful lesson to learn from behavior modification. The New Testament epistles often give instructions not for individual effort and growth, but to the creation of powerful fellowship contexts, which can be effective mechanisms for the modification of individual behavior. Sometimes the best path to personal change is the immersion of the individual into the community, with the person thus being subject to the contingencies of the personal consequences of that community. The behavioral analysis of this influence is, on an ultimate level, unsatisfactory, but it points us to an aspect of personal reality to which we might not otherwise attend.

We can also mention in passing the behavioral view of good and evil (see Browning & Cooper, 2004). For the behaviorist, good and evil as such do not exist, because there are no values that exist outside of human conditioning patterns. Moral codes, to Skinner, are believed to embody codified instructions about how to obtain reinforcement (this is the "good") and avoid punishment (the things that are "bad"). A moral absolute such as "Thou shalt not steal" is behaviorally understood as expressing the normative pattern in a particular culture that persons can generally expect rewards for honesty and diligence, and punishment for theft and cheating. Browning and Cooper (2004) convincingly argue that a close examination of Skinner's work, especially of his famous utopian novel about a behavioristic community, *Walden Two*, shows that beneath Skinner's purportedly purely evolutionary ethic lies a commitment to a radical egalitarian justice ethic that places special emphasis on the "primary goods of liberty and opportunity" (p. 99). Because this detailed examination of Skinnerian ethics is more relevant to Skinner's utopian aspirations rather than to behavior modification as a therapy system, we refer the reader to Browning and Cooper for further information.

One of the most frequent criticisms of BT is that its views of the person are simplistic. However, it is not the case that behaviorists think human behavior is simple. They acknowledge that we are capable of exquisitely complex behavior and that we are affected by complex environments. Complex behavior is attributed to the human capacity for enacting complex chains of behavior, for making fine discriminations between stimuli so that our complex behavior is well tailored to our exact circumstances, and for being guided by symbolic rules. These rules are regarded as mere compound stimuli that shape our behavior. Thus, though the basic processes governing behavior are simple, just as simple brushstrokes of color may grow into paintings of the most exquisite sorts, so simple learning processes can yield behavioral patterns of true complexity.

The core of our complaint then must not be that BT sees human behavior simplistically but rather that by reducing human processes to instances of basic learning concepts, it does irrevocable harm to our view of persons. This is reductionism. The danger is that at some point in reductionistic arguments, what is essential for maintaining a holistic view of what it means to be human will be lost. At the point where the human as a self, as a person, disappears and is replaced by conditioned response patterns, reductionism has gone too far. On the other hand, we must remember that to intervene, or to have science at all, some level of reductionism is necessary. At some point we must determine that our assessment is as complete as necessary or possible, and that we are unable to gain a truly full understanding of the complex and unique person whom we are treating. We must choose an intervention that will most likely focus on only a particular component of our conceptualization. If counselors had to understand clients in all their unique and incredible complexity before intervening, no counseling would ever get done.

The issue is whether in the process of simplification too much gets lost. We would argue that this is indeed the case in behaviorism. Even though basic learning processes can yield startling complexity, it still demeans humanity to regard all behavior as resulting from basic learning processes. (It is not demeaning, however, to suggest that some or even much of our behavior may be shaped by such processes.) The fundamental and irrevocable weakness of behavior modification is that in the process of reducing complexity to fundamental processes, all that is recognizably and distinctly human disappears.

We now turn to a further examination of the concepts of consequence and habit. Remember from chapter two that a Christian view of persons asserts that we were created to exercise purposeful dominion over the earth. We might conclude from this that we are intrinsically goal-oriented beings whose actions are meant to produce tangible outcomes in our world. Hence, it is not nonsense from a Christian point of view to expect human beings to be influenced by the consequences of their actions. Scripture is full, if you will, of direct appeals to act in our own welfare, as C. S. Lewis (1980) pointed out so well in his sermon "The Weight of Glory." God through his revealed Word promises us unimaginable and eternal rewards both now and in the hereafter if we will but become his followers, and unimaginable punishment if we do not (see Piper, 1977). As Bufford (1981) effectively argues, one of the primary ways God deals with humanity is through consequences for our actions, and it would be foolish to deny that human behavior is profoundly shaped by the contingencies we perceive and interact with. Thus, behaviorism has something to remind us of.

However, we cannot simply state that behaviorism is true because rewards are discussed in the Bible. First, in BT, reinforcement (not rewards) is used in a technical sense that entails implications about human behavior and nature that Christians cannot accept. The concept of reward, in the Christian view, often implies moral worthiness to receive the reward, not just manipulation by consequences. Second, any psychological theory can make sense of human beings responding to material incentives; so BT is merely unique in the emphasis on this dynamic rather than being the only theory that recognizes it. Nevertheless, it seems true that by emphasizing this human tendency to respond to incentives, unique and effective means of intervening can be developed, especially with specific populations, such as with children and individuals with profound developmental disabilities, for whom verbal methods are less likely to effect change.

Christian thought is also hospitable to the notion of habit. In fact, the biblical counseling method of Jay Adams is actually built in part around the notion that both sinful and righteous behaviors can and do become habits. Adams (1979, chap. 14) argues that the core of a Christian counseling approach is contained in Ephesians 4:22-24, where we are instructed to lay aside the old self and put on the new self. Adams argues that these terms of self refer essentially to habit patterns formed out of the choices one has accommodated oneself to. Thus, for Adams, laying aside the old self is "dehabituation" and putting on the new self is "rehabituation" (p. 237). Habit is said to be "a great blessing of God that has been misused by sinners" (p. 161). The capacity to respond automatically is misused through its adaptation to perform sinful acts out of habit, as when we train our hearts in greed (2 Pet 2:14; see also Jer 13:23). Adams argues that the believer can also develop godly habits with the help of the Holy Spirit (Heb 5:14), and that these habits can be undermined by, for example, "bad company" (1 Cor 15:33). A Christian view of persons recognizes the place of habit in human life, which behavior modification certainly does. However, Adams would distinguish his approach from behavior modification especially in his assertion that real change only happens with the indwelling of the Holy Spirit, and not through human effort alone.

Model of Psychotherapy

Applied behaviorism has often been criticized with reference to how it might be applied in a utopian attempt to shape humanity. For instance, many regard C. S. Lewis's famous science fiction novel *That Hideous Strength* to have been an early antibehavioristic tract (and a thought-provoking one it is!). More directly, Van Leeuwen (1979b, 1979c) and Browning and Cooper (2004) critique and draw implications from *Walden Two*, Skinner's behavioristic utopian novel. It is a recurrent theme among critics of Skinner that in spite of his deterministic assumptions, he often makes pronouncements that demonstrate his implicit ethical commitment of how we should or must implement behavioral control technology on a society-wide basis if we are to see "what man can make from man" (Skinner, 1971, p. 206).

His critics point out the contradiction of saying on the one hand that "all behavior is determined, everything happens as it must," while at the same time saying, "we must seize the opportunity now to reform and re-shape humanity to save our race and better our plight." Browning and Cooper (2004) are correct in judging Skinner to be endorsing something like societal husbandry to cultivate the types of behavior patterns among the populace that the elite behavior-control experts would judge as being for the common good of our species. Such a system would of necessity become elitist and totalitarian. On the basis of these tendencies many dismiss behavior modification. We will not interact further with how behaviorism might be implemented as social policy and grapple instead with how it is used clinically.

Let us first address what are for many the most troublesome cases in which the recipients of therapy are not able or willing to agree to the change process. What of behavior modification with the developmentally disabled or as applied on inpatient psychiatric wards where patients may be detained against their will? There are some legitimate similarities between behavior modification applied in these situations and the more speculative accounts of how they might be applied in a totalitarian system. First, we must acknowledge that the interventions in these situations are generally applied with the consent of the parent, legal guardian or custodian of the persons in the interest of their best welfare. Second, this particular dilemma is one faced by all coercive applications of therapy methods.

Further, those engaged in BT typically view what they are doing as building necessary behavior changes to equip clients to acquire greater freedom and choice in life. Rebellious adolescents, it could be argued, are actually experiencing diminished freedom because their behaviors are largely being shaped by deviant social cues and reinforcement, and they are missing out on other age-appropriate opportunities. Thus, coercive intervention may be necessary to alter established behavior patterns, as when adolescents engaged in risky or self-injurious behavior must conform to a behavior management system on an inpatient unit or in the home. Hopefully, the new, healthy behavior acquires greater value and the deviant behavior fades. Even highly aversive treatment, such as punishment by shock or physical restraint, may be necessary to disrupt highly destructive behavior such as self-abuse.

Another example of a coercive treatment that demonstrates the effectiveness of BT as well as the values that are implicitly held by this treatment modality is behavioral treatment of children with developmental delays. As described earlier, BT for children with autism and related disorders involves an intensive protocol. As part of the treatment, several coercive techniques might be used to decrease aggressive and self-stimulatory behaviors, including time-out, the shaping of alternative, more socially acceptable behavior, and the provision of a loud "no" or slap on the thigh or hand (Lovaas, 1987). The outcome of these interventions is typically quite good, with the eventual decrease or complete extinction of these unwanted behaviors. BT in this case is used to achieve the goal of creating and enhancing the child's eventual freedom from aggressive and self-stimulatory behaviors, much like the Christian idea of dying to sin in order to experience freedom from sin. To many the outcome of this coercive treatment is desirable and beneficial; however, some argue that this treatment approach is unethical or, at the extreme, that treatment of autism spectrum disorders as a whole are invalid as these individuals (and their behaviors) are inappropriately deemed disordered. Interestingly, the controversy indicates that our view of psychopathology and treatment is ultimately grounded in varying particular beliefs of what good human functioning should resemble.

We can see some legitimacy to the behaviorist's argument that coercive treatment is valid when the suffering person is failing to act in self-enhancing fashions. What compassionate person will accept the strident demands of a twelve-year-old that only her peer group should tell her how to behave? Who will withhold shock punishment from a mentally challenged individual who has a ten-year history of horrible head banging, when this treatment promises to eliminate that behavior in two days?

However, what legitimately frightens skeptical nonbehaviorists is the lack of any sharp and clear delineation in the theory of how practitioners distinguish between incompetent and competent persons, and between adaptive and maladaptive behavior patterns, especially since in the behavioristic view, everyone's actions are determined anyway. Behavior modification is trumpeted as a tool that can be applied to change any behavior. What then will stop abuses such as the application of "behavioral principles" in prisoner-of-war camps where human beings were deprived of sufficient food to make them more responsive to food as a reinforcer for compliance and hard work? The potential for such abuses is frightening.

In the outpatient situation, however, BT is less controversial and has even been referred to as "amoral" (Woolfolk & Richardson, 1984). That is, although behavior modification has values built into its system, as a therapy model it has a much less well-developed notion of human health or perfection than the classic psychoanalytic or humanistic models. Its supporters argue that a less defined ideal allows for greater flexibility of direction and less intrusive influence of the therapy's embedded values. Its application, in other words, is usually put more at the disposal of the client based on the client's values. This argument may be somewhat true, but our concern is that such amorality would simply relocate the influence from a relatively public therapeutic model to a more elusive and idiosyncratic locus (i.e., the personal opinions and values of the therapist). Hence, its techniques can be pointed in many directions, as its abuses show. Without a built-in explicit model of healthy humanness, behavior modification becomes almost a collection of techniques in search of an application, as Tan (1987) has noted.

The fact that behavior modification has developed a diversity of techniques is both a strength and a weakness. On the surface, students of BT often feel they are studying a loosely woven collage of intervention strategies. None of the other therapies rival BT in the degree to which treatment for different persons can be truly individualized because of the many techniques found in the model, and this is a strength. Further, its supporters argue that BT is not a set of techniques but a framework for analysis and modification, based on a purposefully clear and simple approach to theory-development of human behavior (i.e., systematic and ongoing evaluation of behavior and controlling factors). And yet the most frequent complaint against BT is its superficiality, and the appearance of superficiality is certainly strengthened by the chaotic breadth of technologies available. This apparent superficiality may reflect the more profound lack of a central organizing understanding of personhood at the center of the model.

Another reason that BT is judged superficial is that its view of persons is ahistorical; the important determinants of human action (and hence of personality) are almost exclusively in the present. While behavioral therapists use concepts such as learning history, their emphasis is on the current determinants of behavior. The origins of the self-defeating habit pattern are of little intrinsic interest to the therapist; the factors that cue the behavior and currently reinforce it are preeminent.

The issue here is the cause of distress, and the behavior therapists do have a point worth considering, that of how an event from the past can have any causal impact on us now. They argue that past events must be made current in some form to affect us in the present. So if a person is troubled by memories of a traumatic event from the past, the determinants of their current memories must be examined rather than the event in the past. Some Christians might view this present focus as a strength, in that it facilitates accountability and action for growth. Others would view it negatively in that it trivializes a person's sense of history and hence sense of self.

Of all the therapy models the person of the therapist is least important in BT (Tan, 1987). Behavior therapists have been forced by empirical research to admit that the quality of the therapist-client relationship is a powerful determinant of therapeutic outcome, and modern forms of BT reflect their acknowledgment and use of the therapeutic relationship to foster change. BT has evolved with use of the relationship as an important medium through which reinforcement and modeling occur and a source of motivation for the client (Kohlenberg, Hayes & Tsai, 1993). However, this finding has been brought into the model after the fact, and to many behavior therapists, the efficacy of therapy lies in the techniques applied to client problems rather than the relationship being an influential or curative variable in and of itself.

BT corresponds well to the Christian concept of stewardship. Stewardship would dictate that Christian counselors be committed to documenting the effectiveness of their efforts. It is easy for counselors to get a warm feeling that they are helping people, but if hard research would show that the people who talk to those counselors were, three years after the end of therapy, no better off than before entering therapy, then all the warm feelings in the world would not justify the time and expense invested in the counseling.

Behavior therapists are typically more committed than many other practitioners to outcome evaluation, which is actually one of the defining principles that shapes the field. They seek hard documentation for the outcomes they strive for. There exists a large body of evidence from clinical research studies and meta-analyses of the efficacy of BT and cognitive-behavioral therapy for specific psychological problems. On the other hand, there also exist meta-analyses that compare various forms of psychotherapy that have not proven the greater efficacy of BT with general populations or for specific disorders (e.g., Dunn & Schwebel, 1995; Parloff, London & Wolfe, 1986; Smith, Glass & Miller, 1980). BT may be particularly useful for specific populations. For instance, behavior modification has emerged as the most efficacious treatment for children and adolescents (Casey & Berman, 1985; Weisz, Weiss, Alicke & Klotz, 1987; Weiss & Weisz, 1995). Overall, the emphasis on outcome evaluation of psychotherapy in this model should be commended. If counseling were not a profession established on the presumption of effectiveness, this might not matter. But it is built on that presumption, and efforts should be directed at establishing such accountability.

CONCLUSION

The fundamental vision of humanity embedded in the behaviorist tradition is one of humans as temporal beings only, motivated by survival and successful adaption to a challenging environment. Our capacities for learning, which so often serve us well, can go awry with the result that we learn conditioned responses and operant behaviors that interfere with our capacity to deal adaptively with the challenges life throws our way. Despite being determined by our learning histories, human beings can change through their efforts and their interactions with those around them. Through the creative application of techniques based on research in the basic psychology of learning, human problems can be ameliorated.

From a Christian perspective the behaviorist claims of materialism and determinism are easily rejected. Yet the model serves to remind us of our createdness and temporality. While we are transcendent beings, we are not only transcendent. In our temporality and creature nature, the reality of habit, the power of consequences and our environments, and the very "conditionedness" of our existence must be more thoroughly understood and accepted by Christian counselors. Although persons may not be understood as only loose collections of action patterns and potentials, we are beings whose behavior has different degrees of relatedness to the conditions of our hearts. Behavior modification provides effective procedures for dealing with many problems and populations. Nevertheless, though BT may give us a useful account of our creatureliness, it falls far short in appreciating our higher human capacities.

FOR FURTHER READING

Bufford, R. (1981). *The human reflex: Behavioral psychology in biblical perspective.* San Francisco, CA: Harper & Row.

A sympathetic apology for behaviorism by a "Christian behaviorist."

Lattal, K. A., & Chase, P. N. (Eds.). (2003). *Behavior theory and philosophy.* New York, NY: Kluwer.

A recent in-depth exploration of the philosophical roots of behaviorism.

O'Donohue, W. T., Henderson, D. A., Hayes, S. C., Fisher, J. E., & Hayes, L. (2001). *A history of the behavioral therapies: Founders' personal histories.* Reno, NV: Context Press.

An insider's look at the history of behavior therapy as related by the founders.

Woolfolk, R., and Richardson, F. (1984). Behavior therapy and the ideology of modernity. *American Psychologist, 39*(7), 777-786.

A penetrating analysis of how behavior therapy reflects aspects of our Western cultural milieu.

REFERENCES

Adams, J. (1979). *More than redemption: A theology of Christian counseling.* Phillipsburg, NJ: Presbyterian & Reformed.

Bandura, A. (1986). *Social foundations of thought and action.* Englewood Cliffs, NJ: Prentice-Hall.

Bandura, A. (2001). Social cognitive theory: An agentic perspective. *Annual review of psychology,* Vol. 52 (pp. 1-26). Palo Alto, CA: Annual Reviews.

Baucom, D. H., Shoham, V., Meuser, K. T., Daiuto, A. D., & Stickle, T. R. (1998). Empirically supported couple and family interventions for marital distress and adult mental health problems. *Journal of Consulting and Clinical Psychology, 66,* 53-88

Baum, W. M. (1994). *Understanding behaviorism: Science, behavior, and culture.* New York, NY: HarperCollins.

Bellack, A. S., & Hersen, M. (1977). *Behavior modification: An introductory textbook.* New York, NY: Oxford University Press.

Bellack, A. S., & Hersen, M. (Eds.). (1998). *Behavioral assessment: A practical handbook* (4th ed.). Needham Heights, MA: Allyn & Bacon.

Berry, W. (2001). *Life is a miracle: An essay against modern superstition.* New York, NY: Basic Books.

Boivin, M. (1985). Behavioral psychology: What does it have to offer the Christian church? *Journal of the American Scientific Affiliation, 37,* 79-85.

Brown, H. (1977). *Perception, theory and commitment: The new philosophy of science.* Chicago, IL: University of Chicago Press.

Browning, D. S., & Cooper, T. D. (2004). *Religious thought and the modern psychologies* (2nd ed.). Minneapolis, MN: Fortress Press.

Bufford, R. (1981). *The human reflex: Behavioral psychology in biblical perspective.* San Francisco, CA: Harper & Row.

Callaghan, G. M., Gregg, J. A., Marx, B. P., Kohlenberg, B. S., & Gifford, E. (2004). FACT: The utility of an integration of functional analytic psychotherapy and acceptance and commitment therapy to alleviate human suffering. *Psychotherapy: Theory, Research, Practice, and Training, 41,* 195-207.

Casey, R. J., & Berman, J. S. (1985). The outcome of psychotherapy with children. *Psychological Bulletin, 98,* 388-400.

Clouse, B. (1985). Moral reasoning and Christian faith. *Journal of Psychology and Theology, 13,* 190-198.

Dueck, A., & Parsons, T. D. (2004). Integration discourse: Modern and postmodern. *Journal of Psychology and Theology, 32,* 232-247.

Dunn, R. L., & Schwebel, A. I. (1995). Meta-analytic review of marital therapy outcome research. *Journal of Family Psychology, 9,* 58-68.

DuPaul, G. J., & Eckert, T. L. (1997). The effects of school-based intervention for attention deficit hyperactivity disorder: A meta-analysis. *School Psychology Digest, 26,* 5-27.

Erwin, E. (1978). *Behavior therapy: Scientific, philosophical and moral foundations.* New York, NY: Cambridge University Press.

Evans, C. (1989). *Wisdom and humanness in psychology.* Grand Rapids, MI: Baker.

Evans, C. S. (1977). *Preserving the person: A look at the human sciences.* Grand Rapids, MI: Baker Books.

Eyberg, S. M. (1988). Parent-child interaction therapy: Integration of traditional and behavioral concerns. *Child and Family Behavior Therapy, 10,* 33-46.

Galuska, C. M. (2003). Advancing behaviorism in a Judeo-Christian culture. In K. A. Lattal & P. N. Chase (Eds.), *Behavior theory and philosophy* (pp. 259-274). New York, NY: Kluwer.

Gergen, K. J. (2001). Psychological science in a postmodern context. *American Psychologist, 56,* 803-813.

Gorsuch, R. L. (2002). The pyramids of sciences and of humanities: Implications for the search for religious "truth." *American Behavioral Scientist, 45,* 1822-1838.

Hayes, S. C. (2004). Acceptance and commitment therapy and the new behavior therapies. In S. C. Hayes, V. M. Follette & M. Linehan (Eds.), *Mindfulness and acceptance: Expanding the cognitive-behavioral tradition* (pp. 1-29). New York, NY: Guilford Press.

Hayes, S. C., Follette, V. M., & Linehan, M. (Eds.). (2004). *Mindfulness and acceptance: Expanding the cognitive-behavioral tradition.* New York, NY: Guilford Press.

Hayes, S. C., Strosahl, K. D., & Wilson, K. G. (1999). *Acceptance and commitment therapy: An experiential approach to behavior change.* New York, NY: Guilford Press.

Haynes, S. N. (1998). The changing nature of behavioral assessment. In A. S. Bellack & M. Hersen (Eds.), *Behavioral assessment: A practical handbook* (4th ed.). Needham Heights, MA: Allyn & Bacon.

Haynes, S. N., & O'Brien, W. H. (2000). *Principles and practice of behavioral assessment.* New York, NY: Kluwer/Plenum.

Hembree-Kigin, T. L., & McNeil, C. B. (1995). *Parent-child interaction therapy.* New York, NY: Plenum Press.

Herrnstein, R. (1977). The evolution of behaviorism. *American Psychologist, 32,* 593-603.

Jacobson, N. S., & Christensen, A. (1996). *Integrative couple therapy: Promoting acceptance and change.* New York, NY: Guilford Press.

Jacobson, N. S., Christensen, A., Prince, S. E., Cordova, J., & Eldridge, K. (2000). Integrative behavioral couple therapy: An acceptance-based, promising new treatment for couple discord. *Journal of Consulting and Clinical Psychology, 68,* 351-355.

Jones, S. (1985). Mind-brain relationship. In D. Benner (Ed.), *Baker encyclopedia of psychology* (pp. 712-715). Grand Rapids, MI: Baker.

Jones, S. L. (1994). A constructive relationship for religion with the science and profession of psychology: Perhaps the boldest model yet. *American Psychologist, 49*(3), 184-199.

Kazdin, A. E. (2001). *Behavior modification: In applied settings* (6th ed.). Belmont, CA: Wadsworth.

Kohlenberg, R. J., Hayes, S. C., & Tsai, M. (1993). Radical behavioral psychotherapy: Two contemporary examples. *Clinical Psychology Review, 13,* 579-592.

Kohlenberg, R. J., & Tsai, M. (1994). Functional analytic psychotherapy: A radical behavioral approach to treatment and integration. *Journal of Psychotherapy Integration, 4,* 175-201.

Krasner, L. (1990). History of behavior modification. In A. S. Bellack, M. Hersen & A. E. Kazdin (Eds.), *International handbook of behavior modification and therapy* (pp. 3-26). New York, NY: Plenum Press.

Kuhn, T. S. (1996). *The structure of scientific revolutions* (3rd ed.). Chicago, IL: University of Chicago Press. (Original work published 1962).

Lasure, L. C., & Mikulas, W. L. (1996). Biblical behavior modification. *Behavior Research and Therapy, 34,* 563-566.

Leith, J. (1973). *Creeds of the churches: A reader in Christian doctrine, from the Bible to the present.* Atlanta, GA: John Knox Press.

Lewis, C. S. (1980). *The weight of glory and other addresses.* New York, NY: Macmillan. (Ed. by W. Hopper; originally published 1949).

Lovaas, O. I. (1987). Behavioral treatment and normal educational and intellectual functioning in young autistic children. *Journal of Consulting and Clinical Psychology, 55,* 3-9.

Lovaas, O. I., & Smith, T. (2003). Early and intensive behavioral intervention in autism. In A. E. Kazdin & J. R. Weisz (Eds.), *Evidence-based psychotherapies for children and adolescents* (pp. 325-340). New York, NY: Guilford Press.

Marks, I. (1981). *Cure and care of neuroses.* New York, NY: Wiley.

McMahon, R. J., Wells, K. C., & Kotler, J. S. (2006). Conduct problems. In E. J. Mash & R. A. Barkley (Eds.), *Treatment of childhood disorders* (3rd ed, pp. 137-268). New York, NY: Guilford Press.

Morrison, R. L. (1990). Interpersonal dysfunction. In A. S. Bellack, M. Hersen & A. E. Kazdin (Eds.), *International handbook of behavior modification and therapy* (pp. 503-522). New York, NY: Plenum Press.

Muller, R., & Vande Kemp, H. (1985). On psychologists' uses of Calvinism. *American Psychologist, 40,* 466-468.

Newsom, C., & Hovanitz, C. A. (2006). Autistic spectrum disorders. In E. J. Mash & R. A. Barkley (Eds.), *Treatment of childhood disorders* (3rd ed., pp. 455-511). New York, NY: Guilford Press.

Parloff, M., London, P., & Wolfe, B. (1986). Individual psychotherapy and behavior change. *Annual Review of Psychology, 37,* 321-349.

Piper, J. (1977, March). How I became a Christian hedonist. *His, 1,* 4-5.

Schreibman, L., Koegel, R. L., Charlop, M. H., & Egel, A. L. (1990). Infantile autism. In A. S. Bellack, M. Hersen & A. E. Kazdin (Eds.), *International handbook of behavior modification and therapy* (2nd ed., pp. 763-789). New York, NY: Plenum Press.

Skinner, B. F. (1953). *Science and behavior.* New York, NY: Free Press.

Skinner, B. F. (1971). *Beyond freedom and dignity.* New York, NY: Bantam.

Skinner, B. F. (1976). *About behaviorism.* New York, NY: Vintage Press.

Smith, M., Glass, G., & Miller, T. (1980). *The benefits of psychotherapy.* Baltimore, MD: Johns Hopkins University Press.

Tan, S. Y. (1987). Cognitive-behavioral therapy: A biblical approach and critique. *Journal of Psychology and Theology, 15,* 103-112.

Tsai, M., et al. (2009). *A guide to functional analytic psychotherapy: Awareness, courage, love, and behaviorism.* New York, NY: Springer.

Van Leeuwen, M. (1979a). The behavioristic bandwagon and the body of Christ (Part 1): What is behaviorism? *Journal of the American Scientific Affiliation, 31,* 3-8.

Van Leeuwen, M. (1979b). The behavioristic bandwagon and the body of Christ (Part 2): What is behaviorism? *Journal of the American Scientific Affiliation, 31,* 88-91.

Van Leeuwen, M. (1979c). The behavioristic bandwagon and the body of Christ (Part 3): What is behaviorism? *Journal of the American Scientific Affiliation, 31,* 129-138.

Van Leeuwen, M. (1982). *The sorcerer's apprentice: A Christian looks at the changing face of psychology.* Downers Grove, IL: InterVarsity Press.

Watson, J. (1930). *Behaviorism* (3rd ed.). Chicago, IL: University of Chicago Press.

Weiss, B., & Weisz, J. R. (1995). Relative effectiveness of behavioral versus non-behavioral child psychotherapy. *Journal of Consulting and Clinical Psychology, 63,* 317-320.

Weisz, J. R., Weiss, B., Alicke, M. D., & Klotz, M. L. (1987). Effectiveness of psychotherapy with children and adolescents: A meta-analysis for clinicians. *Journal of Consulting and Clinical Psychology, 55,* 542-549.

Wolpe, J. (1978). Cognition and causation in human behavior. *American Psychologist, 33,* 437-446.

Wolpe, J., & Rachman, S. (1960). Psychoanalytic "evidence": A critique based on Freud's case of little Hans. *Journal of Nervous and Mental Disease, 131,* 135-148.

Woolfolk, R., & Richardson, F. (1984). Behavior therapy and the ideology of modernity. *American Psychologist, 39,* 777-786.

Zuriff, G. (1985). *Behaviorism: A conceptual reconstruction.* New York, NY: Columbia University Press.

6

COGNITIVE THERAPY

Mark R. McMinn, Stanton L. Jones, Michael J. Vogel
and Richard E. Butman

*I*f choosing an approach to psychotherapy were based simply on popularity in the scientific literature, then cognitive therapy would be the clear choice. Robins, Gosling and Craik (1999) evaluated scientific trends for four major schools—psychoanalysis, behavioral psychology, cognitive psychology and neuroscience—and concluded that psychoanalysis was virtually absent from psychological science over the previous several decades, behaviorism had waned dramatically from its heyday in the 1950s and 1960s, and neuroscience has shown only a slight increase in the scientific psychology literature.[1] But cognitive psychology showed a striking and consistent increase over the last fifty years of the twentieth century, and was clearly "the most prominent school" (p. 117). The ascendance of cognitive therapy in scientific psychology corresponds with a growing number of Christian adaptations (Backus, 1985; Backus & Chapian, 2000; Cloud & Townsend, 1995; Crabb, 1975, 1977; Johnson & Ridley, 1992; McMinn, 1991; McMinn & Campbell, 2007; Propst, 1988; Schmidt, 1983; Thurman, 2003). But popularity does not ensure orthodoxy, so the astute

---

[1]The popularity of the neuroscience school may have changed since Robins et al. reported their findings in 1999. We suspect neuroscience will be an area of rapid growth in the future. Also, though psychodynamic therapies have been underrepresented in the scientific literature, it is important to note that scientific evidence supports the usefulness of psychodynamic interventions (see Shedler, 2010).

Christian has good reason to question some assumptions of contemporary cognitive therapies.

DESCRIPTIVE SURVEY

Describing cognitive therapy is challenging because history has rendered it a moving target, with its emphasis changing from one decade to the next. When the first edition of *Modern Psychotherapies* was published in 1991, the predominant paradigm was shifting from what Hayes (2004a) describes as the first wave to a second wave in behavioral and cognitive therapies. That is, traditional behavioral therapies were giving way to a form of cognitive therapy that emphasized identifying and changing disturbing thoughts. Because another chapter in this volume is devoted to behavioral therapies, we do not attempt to describe the first wave here. The therapies in this chapter differ from the behaviorist approaches considered in chapter five in that cognitive therapists believe some human behavior is caused by internal or mental events. For the true behaviorist all the ultimate causes of behavior are external to the person; internal events are real but ineffectual epiphenomena, mere temporary conduits for environmental forces. In cognitive therapy internal events are seen as powerful in their own right, and not ultimately reducible to environmental events. In sum, thought is judged to be real and important.

The second wave of cognitive therapy focuses on understanding and changing these internal events. Much of what is still offered in contemporary psychotherapy is second-wave cognitive therapy. Second-wave cognitive therapy involves intervening by helping clients evaluate and change their thoughts, beliefs and assumptions. For example, two skiers of equal experience stand at the top of a difficult slope. One is exuberant about the trip down the mountain; the other is terrified. A cognitive therapist assumes the difference is related to appraisal. One skier is thinking, *This will be great fun*, and the other is thinking about life insurance benefits. One perceives pleasure, the other risk. Cognitive therapy helps people gain perspective and control over negative thought patterns so they can also have greater flexibility with their feelings and behaviors. Prototypes of second-wave cognitive therapy can be seen in the work of Albert Ellis (1962, 1978), Aaron Beck (e.g., Beck, 1976, 1993; Beck, Rush, Shaw & Emery, 1979) and Donald Meichenbaum (1977, 1985). Ellis's model is known as rational emotive behavior therapy (REBT), Beck's as cognitive therapy, and Meichenbaum's as cognitive-behavioral therapy. Collectively, we will call these approaches "cognitive therapy."[2]

Within the past two decades a third wave of therapies has emerged. This movement, though in its infancy, is rather broad and tends to draw from many sources of influence, including contextualism, postmodernism and spirituality (see Hayes, 2004b, for a review). It builds on the foundations of traditional behavior and cognitive therapies (the first and second waves, respectively) while incorporating aspects such as mindfulness and acceptance (Hayes, 2004a). This third wave can be grouped into at least three distinct approaches: acceptance and commitment therapy (ACT; Hayes, 2005; Hayes & Strosahl, 2004; Hayes, Strosahl & Wilson, 1999); mindfulness-based cognitive therapy (MBCT; Segal, Williams, Teasdale, 2002; Williams, Teasdale, Segal & Kabat-Zinn, 2007); and dialectical behavior therapy (DBT; Linehan, 1989, 1993a, b).

Second-wave approaches focus on changing internal mental events—appraisals, meanings, solutions and otherwise—in order to gain greater control over unwanted emotions and behaviors. The third-wave theorists, on the other hand, tend to deemphasize the traditional, mainstream aspects of cognitive focus and instead underscore the significance of attentional and metacognitive processes. They are less concerned with the accuracy of perception and prefer to accentuate contextual and functional aspects of thoughts and behaviors. In other words, they are more interested in the interactional processes—the how—than in content of thoughts or behavior—the what (see Dobson, 2010). The anxious skier atop a steep hill might learn to dispute automatic thoughts in a second-wave therapy. Instead of thinking, *I'm going to die*, the skier might learn to say, *I've skied tough slopes before, and I have never died yet; this will be fun!* In a third-wave intervention the therapist might help the client accept and understand the context of anxious thoughts rather than fighting them. So the skier at the top of the slope may reflect on how these anxious thoughts seem to come whenever something unpredictable lies ahead,

---

[2]In the first edition of *Modern Psychotherapies,* Jones and Butman referred to these as cognitive-behavioral therapy. The change in nomenclature reflects the movement of the cognitive therapies toward incorporating constructivist and interpersonal approaches to therapies (see McMinn & Campbell, 2007; Ryle, 1990; Safran & Segal, 1990; Safran, 1998; Segal, Williams & Teasdale, 2002).

then to accept the anxiety as part of living in an uncertain world, while still choosing to ski down the hill.

As evidenced by the relatively rapid shift from first- to second- to third-wave therapies, the cognitive therapies do not have a unifying personality theory that provides stability and theoretical coherence.

> Despite the increasing popularity of cognitively oriented theorizing in psychotherapy, there is no single, uniform, cognitive theory of personality development, psychopathology, and change, only a host of differing cognitive concepts, many of which appear to be independent and lacking in cohesion. (Safran & Segal, 1990, p. 44)

Cognitive therapy's lack of personality theory is both troublesome and helpful for the Christian clinician. It is troublesome because assessment and interventions can sometimes seem haphazard and lack a coherent rationale. It also makes it difficult to critique cognitive therapy because assumptions made by one therapist may or may not be held by other cognitive therapists. However, there is also some benefit in cognitive therapy not having a systematic personality theory because it leaves a void that can be filled in with a Christian view of persons. McMinn and Campbell (2007) have recently attempted such a venture, using a Christian view of persons as the foundation for an integrative psychotherapy that relies heavily on contemporary cognitive therapy treatment strategies.

One thing that characterizes academic clinical psychology today is the relative neglect of grand personality theories in favor of what might be called "microtheories" of specific phenomena. Researchers today tend to be eclectic about the grand theories they draw inspiration from, being strongly wedded to none of them. Their goal is to develop well-articulated smaller-scale theories about specific phenomena (such as altruism, panic, depression or social skills), not about persons as whole beings. The hope is thus to make these theories more accurate than the grand theories by making the universe of phenomena they attempt to explain smaller. For example, cognitive therapy began as an attempt to understand and treat depression, and then broadened to an approach for dealing with all affective disorders, bringing under its umbrella anxiety as well. It is a theory about pathological emotions and a proposal for effective change methods for altering maladaptive emotional reactions. It is important to note, however, that even microtheories must make general assumptions about human beings that exhibit the phenomenon of study, and thus these approaches are necessarily embedded in grand theories of human personality, though they are often less explicit about those assumptions. This complicates the evaluation of their approaches.

To understand the multifaceted origins of the cognitive therapies, we need to consider the confluence of four factors. The first is the social cognitive approach to human personality of Bandura (1986) and Mischel (1973), which evolved out of traditional behaviorism—what Hayes (2004a) considers the first wave leading to today's cognitive therapy. Whereas behaviorism emphasizes a deterministic relationship between environmental contingencies and human behavior, the social cognitive approaches introduced the possibility of reciprocal determinism (Bandura, 1978). That is, not only does the environment influence the person, but the person also influences the environment. Unlike radical behaviorists, who reduce the person to a set of behaviors, social cognitive theorists acknowledge both behavior and internal factors as important in human personality. Thus the environment, behavior and internal factors are in constant interplay. This "softening" of radical behaviorism created a climate in the scientific psychological community for a cognitive psychology that focused on internal events and mental representations of reality, though a close alignment between social cognitive theory and the clinical practice of cognitive therapy has not materialized. Perhaps this is because most of the major social cognitive theorists are not clinicians, which has prevented a clear and cogent connection between social cognitive theory and clinical application, or perhaps it is due to the growing influence of interpersonal theories on the practice of cognitive therapy.

Cognitive science is a second factor to consider in evaluating the theoretical roots of the cognitive therapies. Cognitive scientists study mental processes such as perception, memory, recall and reasoning. Prevailing paradigms in cognitive science have often paralleled technological advances, so it is not surprising that today's cognitive science is strongly influenced by computer technology and information processing models of understanding human cognition. In an information processing system, certain information is put into the system through the sensory systems (e.g., vision, hearing), then the information is organized, stored and later retrieved. At some point the information emerges out of the system and is expressed through verbal or nonverbal behavior. Information processing theory poses many problems as a philosophical foundation for cognitive therapy (McMinn & Campbell, 2007; Safran & Segal, 1990).

A third factor is what might be considered clinical pragmatism. Both Ellis and Beck were trained in psychoanalytic therapy. They became frustrated with an approach they perceived to be slow and ineffective, and so developed alternative approaches based on their observations of the change process in psychotherapy. In other words, they developed an approach to therapy that removed symptoms quickly, but without doing much theoretical or philosophical work first. Unlike many other psychotherapies, which are built atop a theoretical foundation, Beck's and Ellis's cognitive therapies began with a set of practice behaviors that helped people change. At best, they developed the theory simultaneous to the practice. At worst, the theory was filled in later, after the practice techniques were established. But again, the possibility of filling in a theoretical foundation after practice techniques are established also creates the possibility that a Christian foundation can be established while retaining some of cognitive therapy's effective change strategies.

Fourth, the cognitive therapies have been influenced by constructivist forces in psychology (Mahoney, 1993, 2003; Safran & Segal, 1990; Safran, 1998). Once cognitive therapists wrestled the domain of thoughts away from the behaviorists, so that internal events were deemed important in their own right, it was only a matter of time before psychologists realized that these thoughts are socially constructed—influenced in profound ways by gender, ethnicity, culture and interpersonal relationships. As a result, some of the recent approaches to cognitive therapy reflect a growing distance from behavior therapies and rapprochement with object relations and interpersonal approaches to psychotherapy. As third-wave cognitive therapies have gained momentum, this contextual influence has become more explicitly spiritual, especially related to Buddhist ideas (e.g., Hayes, 2002; Linehan, 1993a). Mindfulness, radical acceptance of one's emotions and openness to suffering are common elements of third-wave cognitive therapies. Hathaway and Tan (2009) note that "these strategies can be found in many cultural contexts, but are highly developed in Eastern spiritual traditions, such as Buddhist Vipassana meditation" (p. 160). Whereas the second-wave therapies were developed apart from religious considerations and then religious adaptations emerged (most often Christian), many of the third-wave therapies have been developed by individuals with training in both psychology and Eastern spirituality.

Philosophical Assumptions

Each of the influencing factors just described comes with philosophical assumptions, though the first two and the third and fourth are similar enough that they can be considered together. The first two overlap substantially with assumptions of behaviorism and the third and fourth with assumptions of relativism.

Social cognitive approaches, cognitive science and assumptions of behaviorism. Social cognitive and cognitive science views share some of the assumptions of behaviorism. This seems reasonable when considering that social cognitive perspectives emerged out of behaviorism, and both cognitive science and behaviorism share a materialistic scientific worldview.

Overlapping assumptions include materialism and atomism, both of which deserve critical evaluation from a Christian worldview. Materialism denies the existence of the spiritual realm and posits that matter is all that matters. Though materialism contributes to spiritual obliviousness, it also serves to remind us of the physicalness and finitude of our existence and the way this conditions all aspects of our being. Historically, Christians have sometimes erred by ignoring the material, veering toward a gnostic understanding of the world, and so it behooves us to consider the inescapably material nature or dimension of existence. Atomism suggests that each person is a loose collection of behavioral and cognitive habits and predispositions. While this undermines notions of personal responsibility (since the person behind the behavior is not necessarily viewed as a moral agent), atomism helps us not to overidentify with our actions.

Some other assumptions of behaviorism can be seen in cognitive therapy, but in muted tones. These include reductionism, determinism and antimentalism. Reductionism is present in cognitive therapy, though the steps of reducing a phenomenon do not seem to go so far in the direction of basic processes as with behavior modification. Instead of reducing all events to operant learning, human phenomena are understood in terms of expectancies, thoughts, assumptions and so forth. Still, this is not a holistic view of persons.

Determinism is modified substantially in cognitive therapy. Remember that the classic behaviorist believes that events outside the person, operating through the laws of learning, totally determine all behavior. We cannot do other than what we do. Bandura (1978) has taken this issue on indepth with his views of reciprocal determinism, and other cognitive theorists and therapists have typically endorsed his formulation of this matter enthusiastically. (Bandura's softer form of determinism is discussed in more detail later in this chapter.)

The antimentalism of behavior modification is altered in an interesting way in cognitive therapy. The view that thoughts are noncausal epiphenomena gives way to the notion of thought patterns being powerful determinants of behavior. At the same time, thoughts are typically regarded as being the result of naturalistic processes. Since these thought patterns are not presumed to operate by the rules of operant and classical learning, cognitive therapists can remain materialists who do not believe in mentalism (in the sense of believing in an immaterial mind or soul), but at the same time can believe that human thought is a complex and causally efficacious phenomenon that is not a simple result of reinforcement. For the behavior modifier, the thought *I should study for my calculus exam tonight* is presumed to be a mere byproduct of the external reinforcement contingencies that produce studying behavior (such as reminders by a professor, the past history of grades and praise, and so on). In cognitive therapy such a thought is seen as an important contributor to studying behavior occurring; it is a causal force in its own right. That is why cognitive therapists are often called "mentalists" by behavior modifiers; this is perhaps the highest insult the behavior modifier can inflict.

Following recent developments in cognitive science and neurobiology, some cognitive theories now borrow from the assumptions of evolutionary theory. This position often overlaps substantially with the above mentioned assumptions, but it seems to have a decidedly more developed, prescribed metaphysical framework. Insofar as evolutionary theory posits a view of the universe in totality, proponents tend to endorse an extreme form of materialism. In doing so they generally assume a monistic, reductionist position wherein the physical universe is all that exists. Anthropological claims from evolutionary theory often follow that the individual is merely a combination of physical elements that comprise the brain, body and emotion, all governed by various physical mechanisms promoting self-preservation and fitness. Human activity is generally considered within a context predicated on biological causation, and therefore adherents to evolutionary theory tend to assume a form of antimentalism and determinism. For Christians the assumptions of evolutionary theory generally, and as they relate to cognitive therapies specifically, deserve careful scrutiny. While some have argued that theistic evolution is amenable to a biblical worldview (e.g., Collins, 2006), others in the Christian community seem to have responded to all evolutionary theory with wholesale rejection, if not contempt. It is daunting for thoughtful Christians to take this on as an integration task, where both science and Scripture are affirmed and valued. Yet this is the task we are called to, which suggests that one needs to understand the scientific foundations of materialistic perspectives while still recognizing that a Christian worldview both affirms the material world and demands a spiritual dimension that cannot be fully explained by materiality.

Clinical pragmatism, constructivism, and assumptions of relativism. The third and fourth influencing factors described earlier—clinical pragmatism and constructivism—also come with philosophical assumptions, one of which McMinn and Campbell (2007) call functional relativism. In most forms of cognitive therapy, the veracity of a client's thoughts are evaluated based on slippery relativistic criteria that are selected because they bring about enhanced mood and functioning. The major tasks of second-wave cognitive therapies are helping the client identify, evaluate and alter irrational thoughts, but who determines what is rational or irrational?

There appears to be three ways to answer this question, each associated with one of the pioneers of cognitive therapy and all heavily steeped in relativism. First, some clinicians define rationality themselves and then pronounce their values to clients. This produces a form of relativism that is highly vulnerable to error because it emerges out of one person's worldview and remains unaccountable to larger systems of determining truth from untruth. Albert Ellis (1962, 2000) used this approach when crafting various lists of irrational beliefs.

A second approach is what Aaron Beck calls collaborative empiricism. Beck often has his clients conduct "experiments" in which they collect data to determine the validity of their thoughts. But in looking closely at these experiments one realizes they are far from objective, and are mostly based on what makes the client feel better; a thought that adds to depression or anxiety is deemed irrational, whereas a thought that leads to greater peace of mind is deemed rational.

A third approach is found in social constructivist views of rationality. Though Donald Meichenbaum's early writings were steeped in behavioral language, he soon moved to an information processing perspective and then to constructive narrative perspective where "humans actively construct their personal realities and create their own representational realities of the world" (Meichenbaum, 1993, p. 203). The job of the therapist, then, is to help the client construct a story that brings a certain degree of peace and hope. This is not necessarily as individualistic and haphazard as it may seem at first glance. Most social constructivists embed an understanding of truth in cultural and community values, thereby broadening the base of accountability beyond the personal values of the client and therapist. The constructivism of second-wave cognitive therapy naturally leads to the contextual, acceptance-based approaches found in third-wave cognitive therapies. From a Christian perspective, social construction is not fully adequate as a basis for truth because it overlooks the possibility of a transcendent God defining and revealing truth.

Model of Personality

Ideally, psychotherapies are connected to personality theories that are, in turn, embedded in well-reasoned metaphysics and supported by scientific findings. Conversely, the most useful personality theories are connected with effective models of psychotherapy. Unfortunately, the connection between personality theory and cognitive therapy is disappointing in both directions.

Here we can make a distinction between bottom-up approaches and top-down approaches. Bottom-up approaches are developed by psychologists with strong philosophical or research interests and then clinical applications are worked out later. Top-down approaches come from clinicians with strong applied interests; the theoretical underpinnings are developed to support new methods of intervention. There is a traditional bottom-up theory by Walter Mischel (1973) that warrants consideration, but it has not reached very far up. In other words, it has not influenced the actual practice of cognitive therapy very much. Similarly, the third-wave work of Steven Hayes (e.g., Hayes et al., 1999) has progressed from a bottom-up approach, though its influence is only budding, and it also has not yet made a grand impact on cognitive therapy. Many of the remaining models of cognitive therapy, both second and third wave, have been developed with a top-down approach, but the theories have not reached very far down. That is, many of the theoretical models developed to describe the work of cognitive therapists are relatively shallow and unsophisticated with regard to metaphysics and connections with psychological science. Nonetheless, they hold core assumptions on which a model of personality could essentially be based. Here we briefly outline the development of these approaches, beginning with their origins and concluding with their contributions to personality theory.

Mischel. Walter Mischel (1973) has suggested that rather than understanding personality from the perspective of universal dispositions or traits, people are better suited to "idiographic analysis" where each person is analyzed individually without reducing individual differences to measurements of universal traits (such as the big five traits of McRae & Costa, 2003). Each person's personality is unique and must be understood as such.

Mischel organizes his idiographic approach to understanding persons around five person variables. These are not traits or psychological structures (such as the id, ego, superego of psychoanalysis), but are categories of processes that can develop differently in different persons. Though Mischel is associated with the social cognitive approach, his person variables also show clear connections with an information processing approach.

The first variable is *cognitive encoding strategies.* All persons sort the raw data of their sensations of the world in different ways. Our encoding strategies transform a perception of a mouth movement of another into either a warm, accepting smile or a judgmental grimace of condescension, for example. Some Christians might look at others in the church and categorize a small group as "real believers" and all others as "hypocrites," while another person may sort persons according to maturity judged by how gracious and loving they seem to be. Persons with sophisticated, broad, adaptable ways of sorting or encoding their experiences will be more adjusted and adaptable than persons with simplistic, rigid and narrow encoding strategies.

Second, Mischel describes *cognitive and behavioral construction compe-*

tencies. In response to the raw data we take in through our senses and our encoded perceptions, we must figure out our world by constructing a cognitive model of it and then go on to construct actions for responding to it. Once we have given a label to experience, we put bits of experience together in a way that seems to make sense. These models may vary from highly accurate and productive (such as the insightful understanding of the politically astute employee in an organization) to highly inaccurate and destructive (such as the paranoid delusions of the psychotic). On the basis of that model and utilizing the skills available, the person then acts. People differ widely in the actions they are capable of exhibiting. For example, married persons differ widely in their capacity to be emotionally sensitive and responsive to their spouses. We all differ in terms of the ways we make sense of our world and the capacities we possess for acting in response to it.

Third, Mischel postulates *subjective stimulus values.* Another dimension on which persons differ is what they value and hence what motivates them. According to Mischel, people build up from the few basic motivations that Skinner allowed (need for food, warmth, water, pleasure, etc.) to almost an infinite array of valued stimuli, which then become incentives for behavior or a focus for motivation. People can then differ immensely on what are motivations for them because of their very different learning histories.

Fourth is *operant and classical conditioning.* Though he has moved beyond traditional behaviorism, Mischel believes that basic learning processes are still influential in human behavior. He does not understand these in the mechanistic manner of a Skinnerian, but believes them to be operative at a cognitive level. For instance, operant learning (changes in behavior based on reinforcement patterns) is understood not as the mechanistic conditioning of operant behavior but as the influencing of choice behavior by the alteration of expectations of reward.

Fifth, Mischel describes *self-regulatory systems and plans.* One of the major contributions of Bandura (1978) and Kanfer (1979) in moving beyond traditional behavioral conceptions of persons was the proposal that persons typically internalize control of their behavior as they develop. Skinner may believe that our environment controls all, but these theorists argued that through memory, expectancy and language we take our environment inside us, and thus the thoughts we engage in become as powerful determinants of our actions as the external environment. While the exam-preparation behavior of a student may be partially due to external contingencies, such as social praise from dorm associates, availability of other activities and so forth, the student can also create alternative forces that influence behavior through, for example, self-statements such as *I must study now or I will flunk out of school,* or *Imagine how my boyfriend will be impressed when I get an A in this course!* The image of the boyfriend conjured up at will can be as powerful a determinant of behavior as the real person. People then differ in their capabilities to regulate their own behavior. People differ according to what behavior they pay attention to in themselves, how they judge that behavior (e.g., stringent versus generous standards of judgment) and how effectively they give overt consequences (*No video games for me tonight; I didn't do my housework!*) or covert consequences (self-statements such as *I did a great job!* or *I'm a hopeless case!*) to themselves.

Mischel's understanding of personality has not resulted in a formal therapy approach per se, but his model provides a framework for understanding the connections between social cognitive approaches, information processing theory and potential therapeutic interventions. His work on self-regulatory systems and plans is related to Bandura's work on self-efficacy. This is the concept that it is not just past consequences of an action that determine its occurrence (as Skinner might argue) or even the expectation of a future consequence (a cognitive event which Skinner would deny the importance of), but it is also our evaluation of our own competency or effectiveness in behaving that determines action. For example, a Skinnerian would say a shy person's reluctance to interact with others is a function of having not been rewarded for such activities in the past and of receiving ongoing rewards for shy behavior. As treatment, the Skinnerian would implement a learning strategy that would positively reinforce outgoing behavior. To this Bandura would add that the shy person must not only expect reinforcement for outgoing behavior, but must also manifest a sense of personal efficacy for those types of behaviors, a sense on confidence about interacting effectively with others.

Ellis. Rational emotive behavior therapy does not have a comprehensive theory of personality per se, but focuses more on a view of emotional disturbance and health. The core assertion of REBT is that a person's *thoughts* are central to understanding that person. Ellis formulated this relationship in an A-B-C format. People often come for therapy because *consequent emotions* (C) are disturbing them (e.g., feeling depressed). It is common for people to attribute their emotional or behavioral consequence to activating events (A), as if there were some necessary and invariant causal relationship between A and C (e.g., "My car is wrecked and I am broke, so I'm depressed"). According to Ellis, people are not really disturbed by events themselves, but by the *beliefs* (B) they hold about those events. So in order for a car accident to result in depression, Ellis postulated that an intervening belief must be brought into play. For example, "It is terrible and awful that I have no money to repair my car." In therapy, Ellis taught clients to *dispute* (D) these irrational thoughts in order to achieve a more hopeful cognitive *effect* (E).

The A-B-Cs of REBT are the core of its approach to personality. As mentioned earlier, a full-fledged theory of personality usually attempts to predict and explain behavior in all or most areas of life. Ellis's A-B-C theory could be pressed to do so, but this would most likely result in weak, ambiguous explanations or predictions such as "my thinking and beliefs led me to act this way." Such loose explanations are largely useless in the scientific study of personality, and so REBT has spawned no serious scientific hypotheses or research regarding the broader aspects of human personality. But for clinical purposes, where the focus is less on predicting or explaining behavior generally and more on the focal explanation and modification of distress, the simplicity of REBT is regarded by its proponents as a virtue, in that simplicity increases the utility of the theory.

The simplicity of REBT has benefited those committed to developing Christian versions (Hauck, 1972; Johnson, 1993a; Johnson & Ridley, 1992). Though Ellis himself was a rather staunch atheist and hedonist (Ellis, 1980), the theoretical shallowness of his approach means that REBT interventions need not be rooted in the worldview assumptions of its founder. One can use Christian principles instead of hedonistic principles to discern what is rational—something Ellis (2000) eventually acknowledged. One religious adaptation of REBT was even coauthored by Ellis himself (Nielsen, Johnson & Ellis, 2001).

Meichenbaum. Meichenbaum's early work (1977), which goes back as far as his doctoral dissertation, was to develop a method for understanding the impact of cognitions on behavior and emotion, and a method for changing the nature of that impact. He proposed a three-stage process for effective change. First, a person must become aware of thoughts relevant to the problem being experienced. Next, therapist and client must determine alternative thoughts (self-statements) that can believably replace thoughts that are causing the person trouble. Finally, the person must implement thought changes and begin to enjoy the benefits of non-destructive cognition.

For example, some of Meichenbaum's work has been with impulsive, hyperactive children. In this population it is assumed that the problems are due in part to a failure to establish the cognitive skills that normal children have to manage their own behavior. Thus impulsive children might be taught initially to define their task and continually remind themselves what to do ("I'm in class and my job here is listening to the teacher"), to use thoughts to cope with distractions or less than optimal performance ("Oops. My mind wandered! Back on track; just pick up where you left off") and to use positive thoughts to reward good performance and perhaps negative thoughts to punish unwanted performance ("Great! I'm doing better. I paid attention for ten minutes in a row!"). Meichenbaum's methods have been applied to such populations as children, schizophrenics, adults with anxiety disorders or chronic pain, and those with explosive tempers (see Meichenbaum, 1985).

Later, Meichenbaum (1993) described three metaphors for his work, progressing from his early career to present. Interestingly, his three metaphors correspond closely with the three waves of cognitive therapy described by Hayes (2004a). The first, just described, represents Meichenbaum's earliest work when cognitive-behavioral therapy was based on the behavioral paradigm of conditioning. Next, Meichenbaum moved toward an information processing paradigm. Here the client is not merely learning new thought processes to modify behavior, but is seen as an active agent in interpreting and reinterpreting life events. From an information processing perspective, people are constantly engaging in transactions with the environment—perceiving, interpreting, remembering, recalling, attributing and so on. Often these transactions involve cognitive errors that cause a person to misperceive a situation. So a depressed person may perceive a minor illness as an awful catastrophe, where someone not prone to depression simply sees it as an unfortunate event. In the third and longest stage of Meichenbaum's career, he has turned toward constructive narrative to understand the change process. This is rooted more in existentialism and hermeneutics than in behaviorism. Each person is living out a story, and the way the story is interpreted and told has powerful effects on how it is lived. The therapist becomes a conarrator, helping clients retell their story in ways that bring hope and meaning to life. These changes in Meichenbaum's perspectives reflect general trends in cognitive therapy—moving away from its behavioral roots toward more existential and interpersonal models of personality.

Beck. Whereas Meichenbaum has moved from a behavioral perspective to information processing and then constructivist narrative, Aaron Beck's model has always been based on an information processing perspective. Over time, Beck's model has become increasingly sophisticated, both as a result of his own work and because of others who have suggested additions and modifications to his theory. Beck has applied his ideas to many different clinical problems, including depression (Beck et al., 1979), anxiety disorders (Beck, Emery & Greenberg, 1985), substance abuse (Beck, Wright, Newman & Liese, 1993), bipolar disorder (Newman, Leahy, Beck, Reilly-Harrington & Gyulai, 2002), personality disorders (Beck, Freeman & Davis, 2003), and marital problems (Beck, 1988). Beck has been a productive clinician and researcher. His work differs from REBT in more fully utilizing cognitive and behavioral methods, in being less doctrinaire in what he regards as rational and irrational (using instead the labels "adaptive" and "maladaptive" beliefs) and most importantly in encouraging a therapeutic style less combative and rigid than Ellis's in favor of a gentler, though direct, Socratic questioning style known as *guided discovery.*

Beck proposes that pathological levels of depression and anxiety are the result of dysfunctional automatic thoughts. It is commonly noted that depressed and anxious people report thoughts that are clearly inaccurate. A depressed man says, "Everything I've ever done has been a failure"; yet friends who know him well reveal that he has done and still is doing many things satisfactorily. An anxious woman says, "There is no way I can handle that situation; it will destroy me"; yet family members disclose that she has in fact handled situations like what she is afraid of in the past, and that what she fears cannot destroy her. Other approaches to counseling view these thoughts as symptomatic of other problems (low self-esteem, projection of unacceptable impulses) and thus see no benefit in directly changing the thoughts. In Beck's model the distorted thinking is not the symptom of the problem, it is the cause of the problem. In a direct fashion, most clearly reflective of the Socratic philosophical tradition, Beck uses persistent but gentle logic and persuasion to alter the person's thinking, and he uses collaborative empiricism—involving the client in collecting evidence to support or undermine beliefs ("Please gather all your employee reviews for the last five years; if you really are a complete failure, there shouldn't be a single positive statement on them").

Beck's model has been criticized for being superficial and overly intellectual, and indeed it is often presented this way by instructors in introductory counseling classes and by clinicians with minimal training in cognitive therapy. In actuality, Beck's model has developed far beyond the superficiality he is accused of. One of the most helpful developments in recent years has been the introduction of *schemas* to the cognitive therapy model (Needleman, 1999; Young, Weinberger & Beck, 2001; Young, Klosko & Weishaar, 2003). A schema is a structure that contains a representation of reality that functions beneath conscious awareness. Whereas dysfunctional automatic thoughts are responses to particular situations, schemas contain more general rules and assumptions about the world. A socially anxious person may have a dysfunctional thought such as, *I am going to turn red and get all flustered when I give my class presentation, and I may even faint and make a fool of myself.* This automatic thought is situation specific, quite accessible to consciousness and easily changed by looking at the evidence (e.g., *I have never fainted before, and it's not terrible to blush when presenting, so I guess it will be okay*). But beneath these automatic thoughts are intermediate beliefs that are more general, less conscious and not so easily changed (e.g., *I must always impress people with my poise and preparation*). Intermediate beliefs are shaped by the deepest and most general beliefs of all, often referred to as core beliefs. Core beliefs are typically unconscious and emerge out of a person's developmental past (e.g., *I am only loved if I perform well*). These various beliefs and related cognitive processes are all part of a person's cognitive schema.

Schemas can be activated and deactivated, depending on life circumstances. A student with a fear of class presentations may function well on a day-to-day basis, but as the date of the presentation comes closer, the fear and apprehension begins to grow as the schema is activated more and more. Schemas can be deactivated in one of two ways: either the circumstances change (e.g., the professor cancels the presentation) or the person learns to exercise conscious control to deactivate the schemas. This, of course, is the point of therapy—to help people gain the necessary self-awareness and skills to deactivate their troublesome schemas.

Cognitive schemas do not function alone. They are also connected with motivational, affective, behavioral and physiological schemas. As the date of the presentation approaches, the anxious student will be more motivated to prepare (motivation), and may spend many hours researching the topic in the library (behavior). A sense of fear also grows (affect) and causes the person to tremble and feel nauseated (physiology). All these can be altered by changing the associated cognitions. Beck (1996) understands cognitive, affective, physiological, motivational and behavioral schemas to exist in packages he calls *modes*. So a person will behave quite differently from one situation to another (note the similarity with Mischel's model here), depending on what modes are functioning. Walking in the wilderness and seeing a poisonous snake is likely to trigger one mode. Sitting next to a close companion at a beautiful symphony is likely to trigger another.

Some of those who criticize Beck for not considering emotions and developmental issues have not kept up with his theoretical developments. Schema theory helps account for the influences of early childhood, and Beck's notion of modes helps explain the connection between emotions and cognitions.

Still, there are inadequacies with Beck's model (McMinn & Campbell, 2007). Any thorough personality theory should account for motivation, and Beck's system does not do this satisfactorily. Though he suggests that motivational schemas exist within modes, he does not explain how motivation affects one's progress through life. Beck's model may help us understand why a person who encounters a deadly snake is motivated to run away, but it does not explain why one loves nature and goes hiking in the first place. It accounts for why a student wants to avoid class presentations, but not for why one attends college, seeks new knowledge, pursues intimate relationships and finds a career (unless these are motivated by dysfunctional beliefs).

Hayes. Steven Hayes (e.g., Hayes, 2004a, 2005; Hayes et al., 1999) developed acceptance and commitment therapy (ACT), a bottom-up approach grounded in functional contextual philosophy (see Hayes, 1993), to explain human suffering and direct the processes of change. Unlike his predecessors in the first and second waves, Hayes deemphasizes some of the mechanistic and formal assumptions dominant in behaviorist and information processing approaches (Hayes 2004a, b; Hayes et al., 1999). In doing so, he dismisses the mechanist's notion of the world as preorganized into an objective and predictable reality; his approach to therapy is no longer about understanding the true elements, relations and forces at work in the lives of clients—the cogs in a machine. Instead, Hayes focuses his attention on the functions of actions (whether behavioral, cognitive, emotional or other), looking to provide a pragmatic, holistic account of events in order to guide the process of therapy—the contexts in which the machine operates. His functional emphasis also departs from the formal considerations at the heart of information processing approaches, so therapy shifts from changing the kind of action to altering its role in a client's context. For instance, modifying an irrational thought is not the clinical focus in ACT, but rather the aim of therapy is to understand and then alter the contexts in a client's life, both internal and external, that permit the thought to function negatively. Thus, by mindfully observing the irrational thought, a shift of internal contexts, its problematic functions loosen and it then becomes acceptable.

Context is king from the perspective of ACT. An initial goal of this approach is therefore to understand the contextual factors that have led an individual to experience suffering, especially those embedded in language and learning (Hayes et al., 1999). Hayes (e.g., 2004a, b) suggests that when these processes go awry they foster psychological inflexibility, the result of which is indiscriminant aversion, cognitive fusion and experiential avoidance. A subsequent goal of ACT is to diffuse the influence of these responses through various metacognitive and attentional strategies (e.g., mindfulness), all of which are in the service of acceptance. When, for example, a client admits to thinking, *I am worthless*, the ACT practitioner might have the client dispassionately repeat aloud the metacognitive observation, "I am having the thought that I am worthless," until it loses its negative effects. Again, the goal is not to replace the cogs and, for instance, substitute worthy for worthless, but instead it is to shift the contexts, this time internal, where the thought *I am worthless* operates in order to undermine its influence. As an eventual goal in ACT, clients are encouraged to construct their values and desired life consequences to function as a dependable guide for future activities (Hayes, 2004a, b; Hayes et al., 1999). In other words, ACT helps clients build a personalized set of guiding beliefs, important to their true sense of self, from which goals can be specified and responsible actions carried out—the commitment aspect. This rightfully may serve to raise the brow of any believer concerned about relativism.

As a theory of personality, ACT is limited. Hayes bases his approach on the *assumption of destructive normality* and tends to suggest that the ordinary state of human psychological processes is dysfunctional. In particular, ACT proposes that human beings are inborn with unique mechanisms for language and learning that form the bases of evaluative knowledge. While originally intended for flourishing, these mechanisms have become corrupted and been misused over time such that the natural state of humankind is now one of fear, self-criticism and deception. In other words, ACT assumes that within language and learning processes lie the origins of pain and despair. The ubiquity of human suffering is not too unlike the Christian doctrine of original sin, and Hayes is quick to draw similarities between his approach and the Bible (e.g., Hayes et al., 1999), even as he also draws comparisons between ACT and Buddhism (Hayes, 2002).

At a grander level ACT assumes that human beings have developed into linguistic, meaning-making (although he calls it "sense-making") organisms through the process of evolution. And although Hayes begins to consider the interactions between biological predispositions, sociocultural influences, environmental pressures and sources of individual motivation, this is the closest that ACT comes to a comprehensive theory of personality. Needless to say, ACT is not based on a comprehensive personality theory. However, its lack of specificity in the area of personality theory may actually appeal to the Christian community, who are now free to establish a more sophisticated, theologically informed view of humankind.

Segal and colleagues. Struck by the need to reduce relapse after cognitive therapy for depression, Zindel Segal, Mark Williams and John Teasdale (2002) set out to provide a modified form of cognitive therapy known as mindfulness-based cognitive therapy (MBCT)—a top-down endeavor. Their quest initially led them to the work of Beck and his colleagues (e.g., Beck, 1976; Kovacs & Beck, 1978), which suggested that individuals acquired persistent attitudes and assumptions following an episode of depression, making them vulnerable to relapse (Segal et al., 2002). However, this rather linear conceptualization, with persistent negative and self-critical thinking patterns giving way to depressed moods, did not seem to adequately explain recurrence for Segal, Williams and Teasdale. They then began to reconsider how activating depressive symptoms (i.e., mood, body, thought) might elicit learned responses and cause relapse (Segal et al., 2002; Williams et al., 2007). A new understanding of the vulnerabilities to depressive relapse began to emerge out of their work, indicating that previous episodes had imprinted particular modes of thought, mood and bodily sensation that were capable of reactivation when only a single element was triggered. (Notice the similarities between this and Beck's notion of modes.)

For example, as an individual with a history of depression feels some sad or unpleasant moods, experiences that were part of previous depressive episodes, associated bodily sensations and thoughts might also become reactivated. Segal and colleagues maintain that once these symptoms re-emerge, the individual will likely begin to ruminate on the negative aspects of self and situation (*What is wrong with me? I have nothing to be upset about, so why am I feeling this way?*). By appraising unwanted emotional and bodily experiences as problematic and in need of immediate resolution or avoidance, the ruminative mind then redirects mental attention from the external world toward the internal problem in a critical, judgmental manner (*I need to stop feeling this way. I must be really messed up inside.*). Segal et al. (2002) suggest this ruminative state of mind might act as a catalyst for relapse. In sum, they drew from Beck's cognitive theory of depression (e.g., Beck et al., 1979) to develop an anatomy of depressive relapse, and then began to explore possible treatment strategies to prevent or disrupt the cycles of rumination and experiential avoidance.

Segal and colleagues enlisted the help of Jon Kabat-Zinn, whose early work in mindfulness-based stress reduction (e.g., 1990) seemed to offer a promising solution for depressive relapse. With the subsequent integration of cognitive therapy and mindfulness, MBCT began to incorporate features of Western and Eastern thought into its core assumptions, especially those related to personality (Segal et al., 2002; Williams et al., 2007). From this perspective the individual evolved into a bipartite mind comprising two broad modes for experiential processing: the doing mode and being mode (see Crane, 2009, for a review). The doing mode, which includes the ruminative mind, emerged as the goal-oriented, problem-solving dimension, narrowly directing attention away from momentary sensations to thoughts about past and future experiences. The advantage of this mode is its analytical prowess within the external world, enabling individuals to detect discrepancies between actuality and desire in order to maximize gains and minimize losses (Segal et al., 2002; Williams et al., 2007). In contrast, the being mode is a psychological mechanism that developed to process momentary sensations rather than to strive toward achievement; it is metacognitive, intentional, experiential and nonjudgmental. Its major advantage is in being able to provide perceptual feedback from events in the immediate sphere of awareness through an attitudinal tone characterized by acceptance, compassion and curiosity.

Distilled from this microtheory is a vague set of materialistic assumptions, not least of which is that humans have emerged through the process of evolution. As mentioned, psychological mechanisms, particularly the doing and being modes, developed and were retained for the advantages they afforded throughout the course of evolutionary history. The bipartite mind exists now because it once promoted fitness and self-preservation, motivations assumed to underlie the whole of human activities. MBCT also assumes that sociocultural influences are at least partially responsible for the prevalent overreliance on the doing mode in Westernized communities. As a theory of personality, MBCT is limited in focus and lends very little to any comprehensive model. As with other theories, Christians are encouraged to view this as an opportunity to thoughtfully plunder the riches in MBCT and incorporate them into a biblical worldview.

Linehan. Marsha Linehan (e.g., 1987, 1989, 1993a, b) originally developed dialectic behavior therapy (DBT) to more effectively treat individuals with chronic suicidality, particularly women with borderline personality disorder (BPD) (Dimeff & Linehan, 2001). Over the next two decades, however, DBT was adapted to serve the needs of various other populations and treatment settings, though it managed to remain the choice treatment for individuals with BPD (see Lieb, Zanarini, Schmahl, Linehan & Bohus, 2004; and Robins & Chapman, 2004, for a review). The clinical versatility of this approach is almost certainly linked to its conceptual sophistication and integrated foundations, which have drawn influence from several diverse approaches to therapy, behavioral science, mindfulness and dialectical philosophy (Dimeff & Linehan, 2001; Koerner & Dimeff, 2007). We focus here, however, on the origins of DBT and its top-down assumptions about personality.

Clinical observations, it would seem, led Linehan to the initial conclusion that BPD was at its core a pervasive disorder of the emotional regulation system (Koerner & Dimeff, 2007; Linehan, 1993a). As such, she saw the problematic behaviors indicative of BPD (e.g., suicidality, dissociation) as failed attempts to self-regulate and tolerate distress. Situating her approach to case conceptualization in biosocial theory, Linehan then suggested that these behaviors had developed from and were maintained by biological and environmental factors; problems arose from an interaction between inborn vulnerabilities and pervasively invalidating environments (Dimeff & Linehan, 2001; Koerner & Dimeff, 2007; Linehan, 1993a, b). Among other things, these experiences inhibited individuals with BPD from effectively managing their cognitive and emotional responses, rendering them easily overwhelmed and incapable of effective self-validation (Robins, Schmidt & Linehan, 2004). In approaching these needs with the traditional cognitive therapies, however, Linehan quickly noticed a therapeutic dilemma: individuals with BPD became suddenly flooded with cognitive and emotional arousal when change was emphasized (as in traditional cognitive therapies), but when change was deemphasized, and suffering in the present situation was accepted, they felt invalidated, enraged and hopeless (Robins et al., 2004). In other words, treatment with an exclusive focus on change was too much, and treatment with an exclusive focus on acceptance was too little.

Dialectic behavior therapy emerged out of this context, firmly rooted in a dialectical philosophy that provided Linehan with both a method of persuasion and a set of worldview assumptions with which to tackle the challenges inherent in the treatment of BPD (Koerner & Dimeff, 2007; Robins et al., 2004). While a comprehensive discussion is beyond the scope of this chapter, the essential idea of dialectics is that each proposition or thesis also contains a contradictory proposition or antithesis. From a dialectical perspective, progress occurs not as a single proposition triumphs over another, but rather it comes from the resolution of opposites—thesis and antithesis blend together to form a synthesis. Linehan (e.g., 1989, 1993a, b) allowed this philosophy to guide her approach in DBT, believing that with enough perspective and the right skills, individuals with BPD might learn to grow—self-regulate, tolerate distress and otherwise—as they begin to synthesize their dialectically opposed experiences, particularly of acceptance and change. The practice of mindfulness seemed to offer just such a synthesis, teaching individuals with BPD the skills to simultaneously observe and engage their experiences—to accept and to change them (Robins et al., 2004). Through a series of training modules DBT incorporates these skills with traditional cognitive and behavioral strategies for emotional regulation, distress tolerance and interpersonal effectiveness.

In terms of personality, DBT offers very little to any normative conceptualization of development; it is a microtheory about disorder. BPD follows a diathesis-stress model, where biological predispositions interact with toxic life circumstances and lead to pathology. At a metaphysical level the emphasis on biology and genetics offers some theoretical rationale for the material dimensions of personality development from the perspective of DBT. However, what relationship, if any, the immaterial dimensions have with the material processes is rather unclear in this approach. It would seem that the incorporation of dialectical philosophy into DBT all but demands the existence of immaterial in direct opposition to the material. The resolution or synthesis of the tension between dualism and monism (as exemplified in the mind-brain dilemma) is of particular interest, though none is offered in DBT. This is curious because Linehan herself studied both contemplative Christianity and Zen Buddhism, both of which demand exploration of the immaterial in relation to the material world. In sum, this approach has strong metaphysical implications for a theory of personality development, but more needs to be done before DBT can offer a complete or satisfying picture of personality.

Models of Health and Abnormality

Because cognitive therapy lacks a comprehensive personality theory that accounts for human motivation, it also tends to be sketchy about defining normalcy and abnormality. Nonetheless, three assumptions about health and abnormality warrant attention—two from traditional approaches and one from the third wave. First, cognitive therapy assumes normalcy is defined by society and by a person's own assessment of his or her level of distress and functioning. Thus cognitive therapy is characterized by what Woolfolk and Richardson (1984) call "amorality," a tendency to go along with the individual's definitions of normalcy and abnormality. If a client comes into a clinic complaining that a pattern is a problem, then for that person it is a problem. This usually meshes well with common sense; no one is going to disagree that agoraphobia or suicidal depression is abnormal. But it leaves open to the individual decision of the therapist and client the normalcy or abnormality of various adjustment problems.

A perhaps extreme example is Lazarus's (1980) work with a woman who reported having married her husband only for the financial rewards he gave her. She had had numerous sexual affairs. She came to therapy because of a developing aversion to sexual relations with her husband. Lazarus's response was not to confront the obvious narcissism of the client or to urge her to work on the marriage. Rather he deemed her aversion to sex in a loveless and pragmatic marriage a worthwhile target for therapy and taught her cognitive techniques to allow her to "turn herself off emotionally" so that she could continue to tolerate sex with her husband while continuing to enjoy her adulterous affairs. While this is an extreme example, it points to the risks of an obscure definition of normalcy.

Second, cognitive therapy assumes that normalcy is achieved by thinking more rationally than the thinking that occurs in an abnormal state. This also fits well with common sense. No one would question that a highly functioning person free from psychological distress is thinking more clearly than a person in the throes of a psychotic episode or profound depression. But what seems obvious when considering this extreme example becomes more troubling when considering the underlying assumption that daily health is achieved through proper thinking and compromised through sloppy thinking. McMinn and Campbell (2007) demonstrate various reasons why this assumption needs to be questioned. We will return to their analysis later in this chapter.

These seem directly tied in with a final assumption, this time offered by third-wave theorists, which suggests cognitive processes, and not merely their contents, can sometimes lead to abnormality. In other words, from this metacognitive, thinking-about-thinking perspective, it is not so much that the substance of thoughts is problematic, but rather it is the activity of thought itself that is disruptive. Health comes by dislodging oneself from socioculturally and individually held truths, rules and requirements, thereby becoming free to step back, take stock and choose a direction that best suits a person. It is also about finding balance between rationality and other forms of experiencing the world. However, a danger of this assumption is that the accountability embedded in communities and shared truth claims is discredited, leaving individuals with the task of constructing relativistic forms of functional truth and reality.

Model of Psychotherapy

In the 1960s, 1970s and early 1980s, cognitive therapy in clinical practice tended to be characterized by short-term interventions targeted at specifically defined problems. Problems were attacked as directly as possible, in a manner some belittled as mere "symptom reduction." The A-B-Cs of Ellis, Beck's early model of change and Meichenbaum's link to behaviorism all lent themselves to rapid, symptom-focused methods of change. Then in the late 1980s and early 1990s more intensive cognitive therapy interventions began emerging. Ellis's model waned in deference to Beck and Meichenbaum—perhaps due to its superficiality or maybe to Ellis's abrasive interpersonal style. (Meichenbaum once quipped that Ellis could only get away with his style because he practices in New York City.) Meanwhile, Beck's model deepened theoretically with the development of schema theory (Young, 1990), which allowed therapists to use cognitive therapy with disorders other than depression and anxiety. Cognitive therapy was extended to more intractable problems such as substance abuse (Beck et al., 1993) and personality disorders (Beck, Freeman & Associates, 1990; Linehan, 1993a; Young, 1990). At the same time, Meichenbaum (1993) and others (Mahoney, 1993) became increasingly intrigued with constructivist, narrative models, which often required lengthier, more in-depth treatment, typically calling the client back to childhood events in order to make sense of present circumstances.

Progress toward interpersonal and contextual considerations in cognitive therapy suffered a setback in the late 1990s when the Society of Clinical Psychology, which is Division 12 of the American Psychological Association (APA), launched an ambitious and controversial project of identifying empirically supported treatment procedures (Chambless & Hollon, 1998). In order to be included on the Division 12 list, a therapy needed at least two double-blind studies demonstrating its effectiveness, and the therapy needed to be manualized to assure that it be delivered in similar ways by various research centers. The longer-term cognitive therapies were dealt a damaging blow as a result, both because they were too new to have a strong research base and because they did not lend themselves to manualization. Vigorous debate followed (e.g., Garfield, 1996; Havik & VandenBos, 1996; Messer, 2004; Silverman, 1996; Wampold & Bhati, 2004), eventually resulting in a more open understanding of evidence-based practice than what initially guided the Division 12 task force (e.g., Norcross, Hogan & Koocher, 2008).

The third-wave therapies have created a useful bridge between the research support garnered for cognitive therapy in early days and the emphasis on contextual factors that began with the constructivist cognitive therapy movement. A number of the third-wave therapies have been evaluated empirically, and though most do not meet the Division 12 criteria exactly (Öst, 2008), they show a reasonable level of efficacy.

McMinn and Campbell (2007) distinguish between symptom-focused, schema-focused and relationship-focused therapy. Symptom-focused therapies rely heavily on therapeutic techniques and are best suited for treating uncomplicated anxiety disorders. Current treatments for anxiety disorders almost always involve a combination of behavioral and cognitive interventions, with a heavy emphasis on the behavioral. Treating panic disorder, for example, involves both exposure to early symptoms of the panic cycle and cognitive restructuring (Craske & Barlow, 2001). Similarly, treating obsessive-compulsive disorder involves cognitive restructuring plus exposing the client to fearful, obsessive thoughts without allowing the corresponding behavioral rituals (Foa & Franklin, 2001). Many symptom-focused interventions are completed within ten to fifteen sessions.

Some other disorders—most notably clinical depression—have a high relapse rate with traditional symptom-focused interventions, and so cognitive therapists are turning to longer-term schema-focused interventions (Young et al., 2001). The first part of these interventions is almost identical to some aspects of symptom-focused interventions as the therapist helps the client evaluate and restructure dysfunctional automatic thoughts. Treatments for depression may also involve behavioral techniques, such as increasing the number of pleasant events in a person's daily routine or learning assertive skills, but there is relatively greater emphasis on cognitive methods than behavioral methods (Young et al., 2001). Unlike symptom-focused treatment, schema-focused treatment does not end once the symptoms are treated. Rather, the therapist and client explore the deeper cognitive structures and the developmental issues that may have given rise to maladaptive schemas. Schema-focused interventions typically require twenty to forty sessions.

Relationship-focused interventions go beyond traditional cognitive therapy, moving in the direction of interpersonal and object-relations therapy and away from the behavioral tradition from which cognitive therapy emerged. The emphasis shifts to the therapeutic relationship more than the specific therapeutic methods the therapist uses.

CHRISTIAN CRITIQUE

The earliest forms of cognitive therapy were closely related to behaviorism, so many of the points made in chapter five also relate to cognitive therapy. But the lack of a comprehensive personality theory has resulted in a drift away from behaviorism to other theoretical perspectives making today's cognitive therapy a loose connection of ideas from behaviorism, contemporary psychodynamic theory, humanism, existentialism, social constructivism and generic forms of spirituality. This makes the task of a Christian critique rather daunting, but it also demonstrates a theoretical flexibility that makes cognitive therapy adaptable to a Christian worldview.

Philosophical Assumptions

As stated in chapter five, the behavioristic presuppositions of materialism, naturalism, atomism, reductionism and scientism are unacceptable for Christians because they exclude God and supernatural activity, and they strip humanity of its God-given rationality and dignity. Let us then turn to the matter of determinism.

As Christians we must believe in limited freedom, as developed in chapter two. And we must reject the kind of materialistic determinism espoused by Skinner. But is reciprocal determinism, as developed by Bandura, adequate as an understanding of limited freedom?

Bandura (1989) says explicitly that "freedom . . . is defined positively in terms of the exercise of self-influence. . . . Self-generated influences operate deterministically on behavior the same way as external sources of influence do. . . . The self is thus partly fashioned through the continued exercise of self-influence" (p. 1182). Note several things about this statement. First, Bandura defines freedom positively rather than negatively, presumably meaning that freedom does not mean the absence of causes. Second, it is clear that Bandura conceives of the working of the self in a mechanical way, suggesting that it develops by universal laws of behavior and is activated by external influences that impinge on the person. For Bandura, human beings are free in the sense that their behavior has an effect on their environment and hence on the changing of their own behavior (which he calls the development of the self). Further, these self-systems are not mere way stations for environmental influence but contribute something to behavior beyond the influence of environment.

Bandura's view can best be understood in terms of the distinction between hard and soft determinism (as discussed in chap. 5; Evans, 1989). Both forms of determinism share the belief that behavior is determined and thus could not have occurred otherwise. Where the two views differ is that the hard determinist (e.g., Skinner) explicitly acknowledges that his view is incompatible with freedom while the soft determinist redefines freedom in such a way as to make it compatible with determinism, thus creating the illusion of freedom. Bandura engaged in just such a redefining move in the previous reference by defining freedom not as the capacity to have acted other than the causal forces dictated but as the exercise of self-influence, even when the exercise of self-influence is itself causally determined to occur! In other words, we have freedom whenever the self exercises its influence, even though the self-system operates by determined rules and thus could not have behaved otherwise. Bandura is clearly a soft determinist.

In Bandura's view we are not free in the sense of having any choices over which we exercise ultimate control as responsible agents. Bandura (1978) himself stated that there is no "psychic agent that controls behavior" (p. 348). For example, according to Bandura honesty may be described as an ability to resist external temptations to steal or lie, but that personality disposition is itself caused by something other than the decision of the person. At a descriptive level Bandura would agree that the person has the perception of making decisions to be honest. But ultimately the development of the characteristic of honesty is caused by factors over which the person has no control. The person learned to define honest and dishonest behavior, to value honesty and to regulate his or her own behavior to be able to resist external temptation by the standard laws of learning. Moral choice becomes just another behavior that is acquired the way all behaviors are acquired. This is why Wren (1982) described the social-learning understanding of persons as "paramechanical." The person never escapes the closed circle of determined acts.

In none of the behavioristic conceptions of the person do we have true limited freedom. All of these models are thus dangerous in that they propose a view of human persons in which we are mechanisms of some sort or another, beings which always do what they must do. This is as true for Bandura's conception of the person as for Skinner's. In the latter, we are noncognitive machines; in the former, we are thinking machines. Such views demean our true nature and undermine our sense (which reflects reality) of our responsibility for our actions.

As cognitive therapy has moved away from its moorings in behavioral theory, it has also moved away from Skinner's hard determinism and even Bandura's soft determinism. Beck's notion of a conscious control system suggests a degree of limited freedom, though Beck himself seems less interested in articulating philosophical presuppositions than making sense of what he observes as a clinician. It is possible that Beck sees the conscious control system as a metaphor for soft determinism, but he gives no reason to suspect this. Ellis and Meichenbaum also seem to assume human freedom—Ellis identifying more with a humanistic understanding of autonomous freedom and Meichenbaum with a postmodern constructivism understanding where one's perceptions influence reality just as surely as reality shapes one's perceptions. All cognitive therapists—perhaps especially those involved in third-wave approaches—emphasize metacognition, which is the ability to think about one's thinking. The very idea of metacognition assumes some degree of human freedom.

Of course, moving away from deterministic views brings other challenges. Ellis's model carries many of the same risks as the humanistic therapies (see chap. 7) where individual freedom and personal happiness are elevated to such a priority that they leave no room for the universal realities assumed in Christianity. For example, the doctrine of sin is central to Christian orthodoxy. To some extent, sin is inescapable and therefore determinative. In Romans 7:14-25, the apostle Paul describes his battle with sin—how he desires freedom in Christ but fights against his sin nature despite his noble wishes.

> So I find this law at work: When I want to do good, evil is right there with me. For in my inner being I delight in God's law; but I see another law at work in the members of my body, waging war against the law of my mind and making me a prisoner of the law of sin at work within my members. (Rom 7:21-23)

This passage implies a degree of determinism, just as the following passage in Romans 8 implies a degree of freedom to choose right over wrong through the transforming power of Christ. Early in his career Ellis (1960) singled out the notion of sin to be the cause of virtually all psychopathology, calling people to rise above these guilt-inducing religious ideas in order to experience true freedom and happiness. He later argued that many religious doctrines, with their confining views of human freedom, are contrary to mental health (Ellis, 1971). Though Ellis (2000) eventually reversed his earlier views of religion, this seemed more a concession to ideological trends in psychology and scientific data that demonstrated his earlier views to be wrong than any real philosophical change in REBT.

Other cognitive therapists have tried to look beyond behavioral assumptions to find explanations for dysfunctional automatic thoughts. This trend has pushed cognitive therapy closer to contemporary psychodynamic thought (Jones & Pulos, 1993; Ryle, 1990; Safran, 1998). A person may be troubled by the thought, *My boyfriend seems distant, and that is terrible.* A relationally oriented cognitive therapist will want to help this person reevaluate how terrible a distant boyfriend really is (i.e., dispute the automatic thought) while also looking deeper to see where the automatic thought originates. Perhaps this person has an intermediate belief: *I must always have a boyfriend to be a complete person.* But where does this intermediate belief come from? Perhaps it springs forth from a core belief, *I am defective and unlovable,* which emerged from childhood years with an enraged alcoholic mother and a passive, distant father. Notice how looking to childhood helps explain the origin of automatic thoughts while also introducing the same deterministic assumptions found in psychodynamic theories. Childhood experiences are determining psychological functioning later in life. Just as linking cognitive therapy with behavioral theory yields a deterministic view of persons, so also does linking cognitive therapy with psychodynamic theory.

On first look the third-wave therapies seem to resist the deterministic impulses found in other forms of cognitive therapy. The emphases on constructing one's own path in life and on mindfulness, for example, seem to suggest a good deal of individual freedom in choosing how one appraises and accepts a situation. Still, the underlying assumptions of evolutionary psychology rest on the deterministic notion that survival dictates human behavior and experience.

Nonetheless, of all the various psychotherapies perhaps the cognitive therapy view, faulty as it is, comes closest to a Christian view of freedom. Most cognitive therapists avoid the radical suggestion of autonomous freedom embraced by the humanistic psychologies, and they stop short of the suffocating determinism of classical psychoanalysis and behavior modification. It fails because only a theistic view of persons which asserts that we are created for moral accountability has an adequate grounding for a full conception of limited freedom.

Cognitive therapists are distinctive among the psychotherapy approaches for being open with clients about the change process and trying to enlist the client as a collaborator, a concept that carries with it a high view of the client's powers of choice and freedom. Compared to psychoanalysis, person-centered therapy and family-systems approaches, which seem to have a low view of the person's capacity for meaningful change apart from expert intervention, cognitive therapy has a high view of the person's capacity for change through self-control and related processes.

Although Beck appears to have no Christian intent, there are similarities between his notion of conscious control and the writings of the apostle Paul, who instructs his readers to transform their identities by the renewing of their minds (Rom 12:1-2) and to form a new identity in Christ (Rom 6:1-14; see also Roberts, 2001). Both Beck and the apostle Paul assume humans can develop self-awareness and the ability to change their views of self in relation to the world. Some Christian psychologists have taken these similarities too far, implying an intrinsic consistency between cognitive therapy and Christianity. But the similarity is limited to how the change process is perceived; their fundamental goals are still different. The goal of cognitive therapy is to help people feel and function better on their own terms and by their own definitions, whereas the apostle Paul's goal was to help people form an identity in Christ regardless of the immediate psychological consequences, and to make progress toward growth in holiness and manifesting Christlikeness as defined by God.

As noted previously, Hayes's assumption of destructive normality bears some resemblance to the Christian notion of original sin. Both have a certain deterministic quality that is viewed alongside the hope of human agency. We are mired in something destructive, but we are also able to gain freedom. How we gain freedom over destructive normality is the place where Christian orthodoxy and ACT part ways, with ACT being informed more by Buddhist spirituality than Christian thought.

Let us now move from the assumption of determinism to the cognitive therapy view of mind. There is no one cognitive therapy view of mind, but the general approach to the mind-brain problem is consistent with that of cognitive science and behaviorism in embracing an implicitly materialistic theory, viewing thought as a naturalistic process rooted in our neurology. But there are options in thinking about the mind-brain distinction that take the physical bases of thought seriously but do not leave us trapped in a deterministic framework. In particular, we can look at the emergentist view of Nobel Prize winner Roger Sperry.

Sperry's (1980) view of mind-brain interaction, in much too brief summary, is that human thought is founded on but transcends in limited ways physical determination. He suggests that human thought, characterized by limited freedom, emerges from the complex neurological building blocks of brain processes, which are fundamentally dependent on their physical substrates yet capable of transcending that physical programming. One of the analogies he uses is that of a rubber tire. By being formed into a tire shape, the rubber molecules behave in ways not predictable from knowledge of just their physical properties. Rolling freely is a property of wheels, not of rubber. Similarly, Sperry argues that thought emerges from—and has properties based on but not completely predictable from—the physical functioning of the brain. This view is intriguing, in that it proposes real freedom (a transcendent property), but not a freedom that ignores or is independent from the physical realities of our created natures.

Problems can occur at different levels of functioning. One person may have an existential crisis (a problem at the highest level of transcendence), which is manifested as anxiety, while another can have a biologically mediated anxiety problem (perhaps as a bad reaction to a prescription medication, a "purely" chemical problem). But most human concerns are multiple-level problems. An example would be a person with a phobia who is biologically predisposed to emotional overreactivity and who is unfortunately exposed to some powerful classical-conditioning experiences with phobic objects and develops distorted thinking patterns and expectancies based on past experience and finally responds to these proclivities in an existentially inauthentic manner (Evans, 1986). This view suggests that we can validly learn from the behavioral approaches in spite of their reductionism, as they give some perspicacious understandings of more primitive aspects of human psychological functioning.

Cognitive therapy does not fully embrace an emergentist view of mind, but it moves in that direction in suggesting that the rules governing the behavior of cognition are not the same rules of learning that govern lower-order animal behavior. And the movement of cognitive therapy toward constructivism (Mahoney, 2003) and mindfulness (Segal et al., 2002) seems to be moving it closer to emergentism. Segal et al. (2002) describe mindfulness training as an important part of cognitive therapy, likening changing one's frame of mind to changing gears on a car:

> We can think of the task of mindfulness training as teaching individuals ways to become more aware of their mode of mind ("mental gear") at any moment, and the skills to disengage, if they choose, from unhelpful modes of mind and to engage more helpful modes. We can describe this process as learning how to shift mental gears. (p. 70)

Clearly implied in this description is a sense of transcendence over material processes. Mindfulness and constructivism hold other problems, such as relativism, but they also bring an autonomous view of the mind that makes cognitive therapy more acceptable to Christians as an integrating view of persons.

Sperry's view suggests that distinctly human characteristics are built on but not wholly reducible to the more basic processes we share with animals. A complicated human phenomenon such as religious conversion can involve basic processes, such as operant and classical conditioning; middle-level phenomena, such as expectancies, encoding strategies and stimulus values; and highest-level processes, such as human responsibility and existential authenticity. Today's cognitive therapy spans much of the gap between operant learning at one extreme and existential choice at the other, reflecting the gamut of processes that are at play in human experience, from the naturalistic to the transcendent.

Finally, the assumptions of relativism found in each of the major models of cognitive therapy warrant consideration. A Christian view differs from the modern psychotherapies in that Christianity asserts that truth is established and revealed by God. Thus, the task of a Christian is to learn the truth and live accordingly; one makes meaning of life because God first ordained that life is meaningful and good. Furthermore, God reveals particular ways of living that maximize life's meaning and goodness. Christians are called to discern God's will and live accordingly—not because God is a cosmic sadist who wants people to plod through lives of joyless obedience, but because God desires people to experience an abundant life now and through all eternity, and knows how this is best accomplished.

In contrast, virtually all cognitive therapies assume that truth and meaning are not revealed by God but are human constructions. One of the most dangerous examples of this can be found in early forms of REBT when Ellis apparently perceived himself capable of determining what thoughts were rational and irrational. For example, Ellis (1962) considered it irrational to become upset over other people's problems. One wonders what he might say of the apostle Paul's instruction to "weep with those who weep" (Rom 12:15 ESV). Even more, one wonders how and why he determined sympathy to be irrational. When truth is defined by a particular clinician, it is vulnerable to the whims of personal circumstances and contemporary trends. Early in Ellis's career he deemed virtually all dogmatic religious thought to be irrational (Ellis, 1971).

Beck's approach may be slightly more responsible in that he collaborates with clients to set up "experiments" which help determine the veracity of a thought. In this way he is grounding rationality in at least two people's ideas (client and therapist), but it often seems that the goal of helping the client feel better becomes the standard of distinguishing rational and irrational thoughts. This may lead to symptom relief, and relieving suffering is a good and high calling, but a Christian worldview does not allow the luxury of defining rationality or truth on the basis of personal comfort.

The most responsible form of relativism is to ground reason in larger communities and cultures. Rather than one person or one therapeutic dyad determining rationality, the values of a larger group are used to define truth. It might be a contemporary community, such as an extended family or an ethnic group, or a historical community, such as a religious tradition. Today's psychology, with its emphasis on multicultural awareness, often draws on this socially constructed view of rationality. Both Meichenbaum's constructivist approach and contemporary third-wave approaches to cognitive therapy emphasize contextual factors more than previous forms of cognitive therapy. At best, this interest in social constructivism and cognitive therapy fits with a collectivist understanding of truth. At worst, in the hands of less responsible clinicians, it can devolve into an individualistic relativism where each person "writes" his or her own story with little regard for the large social values surrounding the person.

Though Christians ultimately reject relativism, it is important to look for a degree of wisdom in social constructivism that values culture and context. For example, not many decades ago it was considered morally unacceptable for Christians in the United States to attend movies, have a glass of wine with dinner or use playing cards. Most Christians now recognize that these were not biblical truths but socially constructed phenomena peculiar to a particular time and culture. More significantly, in centuries past Christians have used the Scripture to justify atrocities such as slavery and oppressive versions of patriarchies, apparently thinking they were following God's truth, without recognizing how they were constructing views of truth according to social and economic values. Some recognition of social construction as a descriptive truth about the impact of our culture on our beliefs is important for thoughtful Christians, but constructivism should not substitute for believing in absolute truth. However imperfect our ability to perceive God's truth may be, Christianity is built on the assumption that reality is bigger and more than social construction.

Believing that God ordained absolute truth still does not guarantee that each individual Christian can interpret that truth correctly. In our fallen state each of us is blinder than we know (Moroney, 2000), and we need the help of a historical and contemporary community to correctly discern truth. A thoughtful Christian worldview calls us to dig deeply and find value in contemporary cultures and historical perspectives, and to do so not because truth is socially constructed but because social communities help us better understand aspects of God's revealed truth that might otherwise slip past our attention.

Models of Personality, Health and Abnormality

Because of the propensity of practitioners in this school of psychology to focus on microtheories of the specific pathologies, there is little we can comment on from a Christian perspective regarding the discipline's overall approach to defining personality, health and abnormality. There are no grand postulates about ultimate human ideals or about motivations among the prominent cognitive therapies.

However, McMinn and Campbell (2007) have recently proposed a model of integrative psychotherapy that is grounded in a Christian view of persons. They begin with three major theological views of the *imago Dei* (image of God; see Gen 1:26). Functional views focus on humans being created as managers over creation, given responsibility to behave in particular ways in relation to themselves, other humans and nature. Structural views of the *imago Dei* emphasize that humans have substantive capacities that allow us to live differently than the rest of creation. Most often these structural capacities have been deemed to be rationality and morality, though many more capacities could be named. Relational views suggest that humans do not carry the image by themselves, but that God's image is evident in relationship. The language of Genesis 1:27 seems to connect God's nature as a triune being with humans being created male and female. Just as God is complete in communion between Father, Son and Spirit, so also humans are complete in relation to one another. Though some debate about which of the three views of the *imago Dei* is best, most theologians find value in each view. McMinn and Campbell build their theory of motivation and change on these three views of the *imago Dei,* noting the similarity between these three views and major paradigms in psychology: behavioral, cognitive and relational. The therapy they propose has three levels of intervention that can be applied in varying degrees depending on the client's needs and commitment to therapy: symptom-focused intervention, schema-focused intervention and relationship-focused intervention.

McMinn and Campbell's (2007) model is relatively new, empirically untested and built on a Christian view of persons that places it outside mainstream psychology. Thus, we need to turn our attention back to critiquing the mainstream cognitive therapies discussed throughout this chapter. But before we do it is worth noting that McMinn and Campbell emphasize that being made in God's image is a multifaceted phenomenon. A popular defense of psychodynamic theory offered by Christians is to pronounce that God is relational and so humanity—made in God's image—is also relational. This is partly right, but it is also partly wrong by limiting God's image to a single dimension. God is also rational and moral and functional (and much more), and so being made in God's image involves more than just being relational.

Thus, there is some compatibility between Christianity and any system that places a high premium on human rationality. Cognitive therapy would say that what we believe has tremendous implications for our personal well-being. This certainly resonates with biblical themes, such as the words of Paul in Philippians 4:8-9: "Whatever is true, whatever is noble, whatever is right, whatever is pure, whatever is lovely, . . . think about such things. . . . And the God of peace will be with you." According to cognitive therapy and the Bible, our thoughts are events over which we have control, and these thoughts have implications for the quality of our lives. A failure to believe the right things can lead to spiritual impoverishment, as we fail to appropriate God's resources. We see this especially in the area of suffering. When we view our temporal lives as primary and have as our highest goals comfort and prosperity, then suffering will be a misery-producing and faith-undermining experience. But if suffering is viewed as an opportunity for testimony for the gospel, as a means for fellowship with Christ in his sufferings, as preparation for eternal glory through learning to loosen our ties to this life, and as an opportunity to learn to better comfort others, suffering can be transformed into a meaningful path that one treads for the sake of God's love (Kreeft, 1986).

Some have drawn parallels between the Christian process of sanctification and the ways people change in cognitive therapy (Edwards, 1976; Pecheur, 1978). For example, Romans 8:5 reads, "Those who live according to the sinful nature have their minds set on what that nature desires; but those who live in accordance with the Spirit have their minds set on what the Spirit desires." This view of sanctification is one that fits well with many of the directive messages of Scripture that tend to be cognitive and behavioral in character; that is, they urge a dual emphasis on changing thoughts and actions (as Pecheur, 1978, ably points out). Further, this view meshes well with the methods advocated to promote spiritual growth by many conservative Christian groups, such as rigorous Bible study, Bible memorization, disciplined prayer and attention to good deeds.

We would agree that the processes and means for accomplishing sanctification are perhaps the most powerful parallel in the Scriptures to the therapeutic process of growth. We would not, however, assert a fundamental identity between sanctification and therapy generally or cognitive therapy particularly. Cognitive and behavioral change does not mesh well with the more charismatic understandings of spiritual growth, which emphasize direct experiences of God's grace, nor with the more socially oriented Anabaptist traditions, which emphasize corporate life, the dynamics of life together, and the imperative to pursue peace and justice as the route to growth (Foster, 1998; Propst, 1988; Dueck & Reimer, 2009).

Further, the emphasis on cognitive change does not thoroughly comport with a relational understanding of spirituality, wherein spiritual growth is more a function of an alive relationship with the personal God than anything else. As Tan (1987) says, "Cognitive-behavioral therapy may overemphasize the rational thinking dimension of human functioning and undermine the experiential, and even mystical aspects of the Christian life and faith" (p. 106; Tan cites 1 Cor 1:18-31; 2 Cor 2:12-16; 5:7 to support his contention). While the cognitive therapy emphasis on rationality is a positive, it cannot be made an absolute.

McMinn and Campbell (2007) note a number of limitations to cognitive therapy's optimistic views of rationality. First, cognitive therapists seem to assume that the fundamental human problem is irrationality, but such a view is not fully compatible with Christianity. The basic problem facing humanity is sin—both personal acts that cause damage to self and others and the state of brokenness in which our world languishes (Rom

8:20-25). Sin touches much more than our rationality; it reaches into every aspect of human nature (Berkouwer, 1971; McMinn, 2008). If sin is indeed the problem, then "the vision of calm reason is only ultimately possible with a faith in the providence of God" (Browning & Cooper, 2004, p. 233).

Second, cognitive therapists seem to assume that healthy people are basically rational, but a great deal of scientific and historical evidence demonstrates otherwise. Even the healthiest individuals have distorted perceptions of themselves and the world around them (Moroney, 2000).

Third, such an optimistic view of rationality does not account for human motivation. What causes a person to grow and change throughout life; is it really an urge to become more logical and rational? A Christian view of human motivation emphasizes one's yearning for restored relationship with God and others. McMinn and Campbell (2007) go on to suggest that many of the cognitive irrationalities that emerge in therapy are connected to strained or ruptured relationships in the person's past or present. Human rationality and irrationality is often motivated by an intrinsic desire for relationship. It is worth noting that cognitive scientists are also noting connections between thought processes and human relationships (Andersen & Chen, 2002).

Fourth, some approaches to cognitive therapy tend to elevate cognition to a place of preeminence while dismissing emotions as trivial or undesirable postcognitive phenomena. Woolfolk and Richardson (1984) make this same point, noting that in cognitive therapy emotion is often treated as an add-on, a nuisance variable that must be controlled, modified or explained. Emotion is not conceived as a human capacity that enriches life or as a source of knowledge and growth. Just as in many evangelical circles, emotion in cognitive therapy is treated as a nuisance, as in: "Get your beliefs and your actions straight, and the emotions will just fall in line." This is a demeaning view of emotion, and it is not consistent with a Christian perspective. All through Scripture we see that God experiences various emotions, including those we deem positive and those we deem negative. Jesus, the "image of the invisible God" (Col 1:15), certainly experienced and expressed a diverse array of emotions—joy, sadness, anger, dread, grief, to name a few—and so Christians ought to value emotions as an important part of God's image revealed in humanity.

Fifth, some cognitive therapists seem to prioritize the techniques of rational change above the therapeutic relationship, as if the change occurs only through cognitive awakening. Throughout Scripture we see the importance of both rationality and relationality in how people change, and the two are almost always intertwined. In Romans 12:1-2 Paul teaches his readers to renew their minds (rationality) so that they can present themselves in purity to God (relationality). In Ephesians 4:23 Paul again writes of renewing one's mind, and then gives a relational reason why Christians should do so: "Be imitators of God, therefore, as dearly loved children and live a life of love, just as Christ loved us and gave himself up for us as a fragrant offering and sacrifice to God" (Eph 5:1-2). We could go on and on with examples, but the point is clear: both rationality and relationality are important, and they are intertwined in the healthy life.

Sixth, cognitive therapy's emphasis on rationality can be quite insensitive to culture and context. What seems rational to a therapist of one culture and gender may seem less rational to a client of a different background. Although the Christian message contains universal truths for all people in all time, we also see examples in Scripture of Christ and his followers understanding and respecting the cultural context in which they lived and taught.

Perhaps the greatest danger in cognitive therapy is that of embracing a distorted standard of rationality. Since the goal of therapy is the eradication of pathological emotional reactions, the beliefs or cognitions of the client tend to be judged by their utility rather than by their truthfulness. (We introduced this problem earlier in this chapter when discussing the philosophical assumption of functional relativism.) For example, suppose that the continual recurrence of the thought *I am a sinner whose righteousness is as filthy rags before the Lord; I am wholly without merit before him* brought substantial distress to its thinker, including loss of sleep and loss of enjoyment of worldly success. With only a pragmatic standard to guide the therapist, the most expeditious course would be to attempt to undermine the belief by whatever means available with the goal of either eradicating or modifying the client's thought. Questions such as, What evidence is there that God exists or that God cares about your behavior at all? might be pursued by the secular therapist. The goal would be to eradicate the thought because it bothers the client. The religious counselor, on the

other hand, might judge the negative emotional reaction appropriate because of the validity of the thoughts themselves, and other explanations for
the emotional agitation possibly sought. A time of true repentance and
grieving over our sinfulness is a healthy part of the Christian life, and
might be a rational response under these conditions.

But it is also true that it does not seem to be God's wish that we all be
paralyzed by our grief over our sin, and there should come a time where
believers come to see their sinfulness in the context of the marvelous provision of salvation from God, and where our remorse becomes secondary
to our love for this marvelous redeeming God who desires us to worship
him and serve him, and to our celebration of his grace. So in the case of a
protracted and overly severe preoccupation with one's own sinfulness, the
Christian cognitive therapist would regard the thoughts as true but perhaps not in their proper context among other Christian beliefs, and hence
might see the emotional response as problematic. Thus the Christian
counselor would not be using the pragmatic standard for judging beliefs.
The therapist's method would not be to undermine the belief, but to put it
in proper perspective among other beliefs.

Another issue worth addressing is the underlying assumption that
humans are fundamentally motivated to enhance their own welfare. For
example, most cognitive and behavioral considerations of interpersonal
behavior use the organizing conception of competency to evaluate interpersonal action. This concept suggests that human behavior is primarily
directed at obtaining desired goods from the personal and impersonal
environment. Competent responses are most often defined as those that
are "effective" or "competent" at getting what we want or at accomplishing a specific task (see McFall, 1982). Behavioral theories and concepts
direct our attention inexorably to the functional value of any human
behavior; that is, *what it does for the organism*. This seems to be a hold-
over from the Skinnerian understanding that sees all significant behavior as operant—designed to operate on the environment to produce a
desired outcome.

This orientation manifests itself in the cognitive therapy understanding
of love and altruism. Cognitive therapists have been active in developing
clinical models of marriage therapy, typically beginning with the assumption that individuals are motivated to maximize rewards for themselves—

something Stuart (1980) has called the best bargain principle. Whereas this assumption is explicit for many behavioral therapists (e.g., Jacobson & Margolin, 1979), it is more subtle but equally pernicious in cognitive therapy. For example, Epstein and Baucom (2002) write, "We propose that adults seek to meet a variety of important human motives and needs, both communal and individual, within the context of their intimate relationships" (p. 15). Though this is a reasonable statement reflecting humans' desire for relationship, Epstein and Baucom are still assuming that each person in a relationship behaves based on motives to meet personal needs and desires. This assumption has its parallels in other social sciences as well, such as in rational choice theory in economics.

So even in the most giving of human relationships—marriage—persons are assumed to be attempting to maximize their own receipt of personal satisfactions. This is also true of cognitive therapy's view of altruism (doing good for another for no apparent reason). Kanfer (1979), for example, suggested that altruism is a form of behavior where one delays personal and immediate reinforcement for the sake of long-term outcomes: "[The] task, as in self-control, is to train persons to act for the benefits of another because it is in their own self-interest" (p. 237). They take for granted that people are basically out for themselves. People are seen as having their own welfare as their only ultimate concern.

In some ways Christian theology is similarly pessimistic about humanity. Seeing self-enhancement as a core motivation should not be a surprise for persons who believe in human depravity. But we are not just depraved, selfish beings; we are also all created in the image of God, the God of all love, the giving and self-sacrificing God. Thus it would seem that all humans have some capacity for transcending their human egocentrism and that Christians should have a special capacity for self-transcendence through God's grace, for compassion and self-sacrificing love. The love described in 1 Corinthians 13 is definitely not a self-interested love devoid of personal sacrifice. Love is a foundational human capacity created in us from the beginning, as when the first humans in the creation story were told to cleave to one another and that the two would become one flesh. Descriptively, the Christian Scriptures and tradition seem to take human selfishness into account, appealing, for example, to the rewards we will personally receive in heaven to motivate good behavior here on earth. But the Scriptures never stop at that point, going on to call persons to a life wherein our desires conform evermore to God's purposes without regard for our own welfare. With God's help, we are capable of such a transition.

Just as with behavior modification, cognitive therapists often emphasize competence and skill development. For example, the person with panic disorder can learn skills to escape the vicious cycle of rapid breathing and runaway thoughts. By learning calming self-talk the person regains control over breathing patterns and returns oxygen–carbon dioxide ratios to normal levels. Common competencies taught in cognitive therapy include self-efficacy, schema deactivation, assertive communication and countering automatic thoughts.

If we believe that the task of mastery is consistent with a biblical understanding of persons and that we are each to be about some dimension of a dominion work, then competence seems an important concept in human life. If self-efficacy (the idea that we are motivated by our beliefs in our own effectiveness) is equated with human pride, it will be viewed negatively by Christians, but it need not be viewed as such. Rather, our actions seem to have been meant by God to matter, to be effective. We are beings designed for meaningful work and effective interactions with our world. Christianity is not wedded to prescribing that each of us feel or perceive ourselves to be incompetent, as if the feeling of helplessness were a virtue. Propst (1988) correctly reminds us that Christianity is not merely a religion of the afterlife but one that endorses a certain spirituality of everyday life. As we submit our day-to-day lives to God, he redeems them and allows us to live to his glory. But we continue to live in this world and must have effective and righteous ways of dealing with it.

Thus it would seem that helping clients achieve meaningful mastery over their lives is a goal compatible with Christian faith. As Tan (1987) suggested, though, an overemphasis on self-efficacy can lead to pride. In our effectiveness we seem to have been meant to live in a dynamic tension of delight in our competencies and realization of our utter dependence on God. Perhaps the best summary of this dynamic is the statement of Paul in Philippians 4:13: "I can do everything through him who gives me strength."

A Christian view of will and self-control also has some broad compatibilities with the view expressed by cognitive therapy. The Christian view of will is that it is a capacity that can be developed, as opposed to it being an all-or-nothing, static personality trait. Hebrews 12, for instance, discusses at length the notion of discipline from God, noting that we are disciplined for our good (Heb 12:10; note the appeal to personally desirable consequences) and that discipline is often unpleasant. Hebrews 12:12-13 ("Strengthen your feeble arms and weak knees. 'Make level paths for your feet'") are especially interesting, in that they provide a practical agenda for strengthening weak spots in our personal discipline. The injunction to "make level paths for your feet" clearly means to choose a course that puts minimal stress on an area of personal weakness, as when a person consumed with envy might refrain from obtaining any knowledge about the performance and possessions of others in order not to open a window of opportunity for sin to occur. A voluntary refraining from opportunity for sin may give time for growth in strength to withstand sin.

Compare this view to that of cognitive therapy's view of self-regulation (as did Bufford, 1977). Self-regulation involves developing awareness of the external factors that are powerful determinants of one's behavior and altering them deliberately to produce desired change (for instance, avoiding temptation situations and surrounding oneself with encouraging, strengthening influences), and also developing effective internal or cognitive control capacities through more effective self-observation and administration of consequences to the self (e.g., naming God's commandments, instructing and exhorting oneself). In this view, will is developed as a skill, and thus growth in self-control is possible, rather than being an unalterable personality trait caused by toilet-training practices, as in classical psychoanalysis. In this area there are meaningful compatibilities between cognitive therapy and the biblical view of persons.

As with all the secular therapies, there is a danger in cognitive therapy that the therapist will focus only on psychological change without any spiritual emphasis at all. The focus of cognitive therapy is limited only to temporal aspects of personhood. Spiritual and religious matters have no intrinsic or integral part in the model. Reading a standard cognitive therapy work, one would think that religion only existed as one rather unusual category of belief that occasionally crops up with a client, or as a nuisance variable that affects what a client values. Despite some recent concessions that religion may not be as destructive as previously thought, religious beliefs—except perhaps for Buddhist beliefs in some third-wave approaches—are still not viewed as life-enhancing or intrinsically important in this approach.

One final positive attribute of this approach is its idiographic emphasis. Cognitive therapy embodies a high view of human uniqueness. Persons are not regarded as reducible to five scales on a personality inventory but are seen as individuals with unique abilities, interests, struggles and wounds. This idiographic method allows for some understanding of persons developmentally, and the current trends toward schema-based and constructivist cognitive therapies have made developmental exploration a legitimate part of cognitive therapy. Of course it is possible for a therapy to be too idiographic, making no use of common models for understanding human development, such as the psychosocial development model of Erikson. The extreme embrace of uniqueness can mean that no two persons' experience is comparable and that their development cannot be understood in common terms. This is perhaps a good example of how the idiographic tendencies can be a curse as well as a blessing. Historically, this extreme idiographic perspective has been a fault of cognitive therapy, but it appears to be changing. For example, Needleman (1999) demonstrates how Erickson's psychosocial stages correspond with various core beliefs contained in maladaptive cognitive schemas. Similarly, Young et al. (2003) have identified a taxonomy for early maladaptive schemas and a corresponding assessment device known as the Young Schema Questionnaire (www.schematherapy.com).

Model of Psychotherapy

Perhaps no other therapy approach so closely mirrors a biblical balance of cognitive and action orientation as cognitive therapy. Even a superficial reading of the pastoral exhortations of the New Testament epistles yields a clear theme of obedience in actions and in thoughts as the way to maturity. If one looks at Philippians 3–4 or Ephesians 4, one sees clearly an exhortation to think new thoughts and engage in new deeds to germinate the seed of faith into full spiritual maturity. Perhaps the reason why Adams's (1973) early versions of nouthetic counseling and Crabb's (1977) early model of biblical counseling have enjoyed some continuing popularity is that both embody a combined behavioral and cognitive emphasis that parallels the theme of direct change expressed in Scripture. The real issue is whether this is the exclusive or dominant theme of Scripture. In any case, cognitive therapy shares this focus.

One of Beck's earliest interventions for depression involved helping people plan daily goals and activities, to set goals and then experience the accomplishment of reaching those goals. Many other cognitive therapy techniques have been developed since Beck's early work, and a common theme is providing tools for clients to gain mastery over their thoughts and behaviors. To the extent that this represents a God-honoring development of the capacity to exercise better stewardship over the portion of creation God has placed us in, this can certainly be a worthwhile set of procedures for Christians to embrace. To live effectively, we must be able to order the practical challenges of daily life by managing time and setting goals as well as knowing how to pray, how to communicate our feelings to our spouses and so on. The cognitive approach assumes that many people experiencing problems of living lack one or more of these basic living skills and that therapy can help correct these deficits.

But just as we discussed with behavior modification, the *amorality* of cognitive therapy is problematic. Cognitive therapists seem content to have their clients' values dictate the course of therapy, as we noted earlier (Woolfolk & Richardson, 1984). To some extent it could be argued that all the modern psychotherapies are governed by clients' goals and values, but it is complicated in cognitive therapy because there is no clear theoretical vision for who a person should become. Because cognitive therapy has a less well-developed notion of the ideal human state than such theories as person-centered therapy, it is difficult for cognitive therapy to be a growth psychotherapy—there is no built-in compass pointing out the direction of growth.

From a Christian perspective the lack of prescriptive focus of cognitive therapy actually can allow for a more comfortable utilization of the system by the Christian than some other systems. The techniques of cognitive therapy seem less value-encrusted and thus the system might be more effectively adapted for use by the religious therapist. However, this requires intentional effort. Uncritical acceptance of prevailing cognitive therapy assumptions leads to shallow views of healing and growth. To read some cognitive therapy literature, one would get the constricted impression that growth means the absence of anxiety, depression and the major forms of discomfort; hence, to be fully human is to be without pain. This is a superficial and anemic view of human maturity. Cognitive therapists, consequently, seem proficient at eliminating suffering (about which clients have focused goals) but less capable at producing growth. But this raises the provocative question of whether psychotherapy should be properly limited to healing or problem solving, leaving promotion of growth to such traditional resources as the church.

Healing versus growth in psychotherapy is a topic of much discussion these days, illustrated by two opposing trends. The first is health care reimbursement, which has moved decisively toward symptom-reduction models of psychotherapy. It is more cost effective for an insurance company to pay for twelve sessions of therapy aimed at symptom alleviation than fifty sessions of growth-oriented therapy, even if the briefer therapy may make a person more prone to relapse. The second theme, much smaller in scope, is seen in the growing interest in spiritual direction and psychotherapy. Various Christian psychotherapists are looking back to ancient soul-care traditions and attempting to integrate healing and growth with spiritual and psychological methods (Benner, 2005).

There are risks with both of these trends, which call for caution and discernment. Though it makes sense from an economic perspective to prefer short-term symptom-focused therapy, for a Christian the goals of psychotherapy are inevitably more complex than helping a person feel better. As cognitive therapy models have evolved, they now offer clients ways to explore factors underlying their symptoms in order to gain a degree of self-understanding and to prevent the high rates of relapse associated with the symptom-based treatments. Cognitive therapy will never offer the depth of exploration evident in psychodynamic models, but it can still provide a degree of uncovering that encourages clients to confront their values and beliefs and to leave therapy having asked important questions about character issues, spiritual matters and the directions their lives are heading. It would be a loss for Christian therapists to be so influenced by economic forces that they fail to explore newer depth-oriented models of cognitive therapy.

But it is also worth considering risks of emphasizing spiritual growth as a primary goal for psychotherapists. Christian therapists attempting to blend psychotherapy and spiritual direction face a number of ethical challenges. For example, does the therapist bill the client's insurance company for psychotherapy if part or all of the session is used for spiritual direction? And there are questions of training. Is it legitimate to assume that an advanced degree in psychology, along with spiritual fervor and some experience with spiritual direction, sufficiently qualifies a person to provide spiritual direction services? Perhaps most important, what are the long-term consequences of removing spiritual direction from the authority of the church, where it has always been, and making it a privatized endeavor associated with psychotherapy? For these reasons and more, it seems important to be cautious about the extent that spiritual growth is an explicit goal in Christian versions of therapy.

Somewhere between the extremes of symptom-focused therapy and blending spiritual direction with therapy there is a balance where a Christian psychotherapist helps clients look beneath immediate symptoms to see their deeper wounds and questions about life, and yet the therapist does so in a way that remains within the bounds of training in psychotherapy.

Christian models of cognitive therapy have sometimes used imagery as a method to bring healing and promote spiritual growth. These range from approaches developed by scientifically grounded psychologists (Propst, 1988) to popularized Christian healing-of-memory approaches, such as theophostic ministry (Smith, 2002). It is beyond the scope of this book to critique theophostic ministry, though we recommend that those interested read the hard-hitting critiques that have been offered (e.g., Entwistle, 2004a, b). Our attention here will be limited to formal psychotherapy approaches, such as the model described by Propst (1988).

Propst rightly points out that often the cognitions troubling a client are not in verbal propositional form (such as a wrong doctrinal belief) but are better described as troublesome images, such as a sexually abused woman experiencing fragmentary memories of her childhood abuse as she interacts with men. Propst urges the explicit incorporation of religious imagery, specifically images of Christ. She discusses different imagery interventions, such as the use of the image of surrendering our thoughts, emotions and experiences to Christ. This example would seem acceptable to almost all Christians, in that such surrendering seems an implication of the concept of the lordship of Christ.

Propst (1988) then moves on to examples that may be more troublesome to some Christians, examples that involve the person imaging Christ doing or saying things judged to be therapeutic but which may or may not fit his real character. The imagery examples that Propst shares include the image of Christ telling a woman that it is okay to be scared of breast cancer, of Christ rescuing and comforting a client when as a child she was being abused, and of Christ expressing acceptance and encouraging a woman who had experienced gang rape to touch him. The problem here is that we are making the Christ of our image do what we want or expect him to do, to do what the therapist deems therapeutic, in situations where his (Jesus') response may not be clear.

We have talked with clients who on their own have used even more troubling images for comfort in situations where some Christians would believe that Christ would speak rebuke. For example, a man who had just left his wife because of his agony due to being "trapped" in a marriage with no love imagined Christ lovingly saying, "I understand. I have experienced unbearable agony too." In other words, he imagined Christ supporting his decision to desert his wife. Some would argue that in that situation Christ would really say, "Take up your cross and go back to your wife; follow me in obedience and I will sustain you." We risk twisting God into the shape we desire when we imagine specific responses on his part. At the same time, perhaps in many circumstances we can understand his character sufficiently to know with confidence what he would do. It will require real spiritual maturity and wisdom to understand when we are on firm ground in projecting the nature of his responses to us, and perhaps will require accountability to the church as well.

Finally, we turn to the question of effectiveness. In general, most psychotherapies have about equal effectiveness in reducing the symptoms assessed by outcome measures: approximately 80 percent of those receiving treatment do better than the average person who does not receive treatment (Asay & Lambert, 1999). As with other therapies, cognitive therapy is deemed to be effective with a variety of disorders. Butler and Beck (2001) reviewed fourteen meta-analyses in the scientific literature, involving over 300 studies and 9,000 clients, concluding that cognitive therapy is useful in treating depression and various anxiety disorders. Some studies have also shown cognitive therapy to be slightly more effective than other treatment approaches with particular disorders and populations (Ehlers & Clark, 2003; Barrowclough et al., 2001), though some of this may be due to the fact that cognitive therapy lends itself to research protocols better than some of the other approaches.

Only a few research studies have compared Christian versions of cognitive therapy with mainstream versions (Johnson, 1993b; McCullough, 1999), and all of these have focused on the treatment of depression. In general, no differences between the effectiveness of Christian and mainstream versions have been reported. Though Propst, Ostrom, Watkins, Dean and Mashburn (1992) found a religious form of cognitive therapy to be slightly better than a nonreligious form in helping religious clients recover from depression, interpreting their results is difficult because they found the most favorable outcome when nonreligious therapists delivered the religious form of therapy.

Various challenges face researchers interested in evaluating Christian forms of cognitive therapy. Most forms of cognitive therapy are relatively superficial adaptations of mainstream approaches, perhaps adding religious imagery or Scripture verses to a therapy that is otherwise unchanged. A more interesting project would be to develop and test a cognitive therapy based on a Christian view of persons. McMinn and Campbell (2007) have proposed such a model, but have not done empirical research to test its effectiveness. A related problem is how to measure outcome. Most researchers and cognitive therapists assume that symptom reduction is the primary outcome variable to consider, but Christians may have cause to question this. Perhaps some clients grow in depth of character and maturity through suffering even if they do not show dramatic decreases in symptom patterns. Conversely, some clients may show striking reductions in symptoms while avoiding the deeper issues of character development that need to be addressed. Finally, research demonstrating that a therapy works does not necessarily reveal how it works. One of the most provocative studies regarding cognitive therapy suggests that it may work because it emulates some of the same therapeutic processes that are used in psychodynamic therapy (Jones & Pulos, 1993). Though cognitive therapists tend to emphasize how to apply particular techniques to help people change, increasing attention is being given to the importance of the therapeutic relationship itself in promoting good outcomes (Lambert & Barley, 2002).

CONCLUSION

Cognitive therapy has at least the following strengths when evaluated from a Christian perspective: It posits limited freedom for the person, though the formal understanding of that freedom is incompatible with a Christian understanding of human responsibility. Cognitive therapy appreciates the embodied, human aspect of our existence and has a well-articulated understanding of at least some of the person variables and processes that seem foundational to human action. The ideographic assumptions seem respectful of human uniqueness. An appreciation of the influence of the environment on behavior (though not environmental determinism) seems appropriate from a Christian perspective. The humbling and broad understanding of human motivation as basically selfish but complex is a strength. Cognitive therapy's high view of rationality is a plus, though the standards of rationality must be modified for the Christian. The view of the centrality of habits of thought and action to making life adjustments seems realistic. The relatively shallow view of personality, as reflected in its amorality and lack of a vision of maturity, makes it a somewhat more adaptable tool for the Christian therapist than some other approaches to therapy. New adaptations of cognitive therapy are sensitive to childhood and cultural issues, yet without going as far toward developmental determinism as psychoanalysis. Finally, cognitive therapy emphasizes empirical accountability in all aspects of its practice, and, for Christians, this accords well with a commitment to good stewardship of time and energies, and with a commitment to honesty.

In spite of all these positives, one is left with a clear sense that there is much more to human beings than cognitive therapy would lead us to believe. Where is transcendence and spirituality? How do we understand self-deception or evil? Does this view really plumb the profound depths of relationships and the terrific impact we have on one another? Isn't emotion more than the output of cognitive habits? What about conflict within the person; isn't this inevitable and indeed helpful to our understanding what it means to be truly human? How are we to grow? Are there any important regularities to the way we develop as human beings? Cognitive therapy's silence on each of these questions is disconcerting.

It seems likely that we are what cognitive therapy depicts us as being: thinking and acting creatures who act on and are acted on by our environments for the purpose of obtaining that which we value. But it also seems clear to the Christian that we are more than this. Nevertheless, given its many strengths, cognitive therapy is likely to be one of the more fruitful models for Christians to explore for its integrative potentials.

FOR FURTHER READING

Barlow, D. H. (Ed.). (2001). *Clinical handbook of psychological disorders: A step-by-step treatment manual* (3rd ed.). New York, NY: Guilford Press.
An excellent reference book for contemporary cognitive and behavioral treatments.

Dobson, K. S. (Ed.). (2010). *Handbook of cognitive-behavioral therapies* (3rd ed.). New York, NY: Guilford Press.
An informative contemporary professional handbook for this approach.

McMinn, M. R., & Campbell, C. D. (2007). *Integrative psychotherapy: Toward a comprehensive Christian approach.* Downers Grove, IL: IVP Academic.
This is an attempt to provide a Christian foundation for cognitive therapy.

Young, J. E., Klosko, J. S., & Weishaar, M. E. (2003). *Schema therapy: A practitioner's guide.* New York, NY: Guilford Press.
A helpful introduction to schemas and how they relate to cognitive processes.

REFERENCES

Adams, J. (1973). *The Christian counselor's manual.* Grand Rapids, MI: Baker.

Andersen, S. M., & Chen, S. (2002). The relational self: An interpersonal social-cognitive theory. *Psychological Review, 109,* 619-645.

Asay, T. P., & Lambert, M. J. (1999). The empirical case for the common factors in therapy: Quantitative findings. In M. A. Hubble, B. L. Duncan & S. D. Miller (Eds.), *The heart and soul of change: What works in therapy.* Washington, DC: American Psychological Association.

Backus, W. (1985). *Telling the truth to troubled people.* Minneapolis, MN: Bethany.

Backus, W., & Chapian, M. (2000). *Telling yourself the truth: Finding your way out of depression, anxiety, fear, anger and other common problems by applying the principles of misbelieve therapy.* Minneapolis, MN: Bethany House.

Bandura, A. (1978). The self system in reciprocal determinism. *American Psychologist, 33,* 344-358.

Bandura, A. (1986). *Social foundations of thought and action.* Englewood Cliffs, NJ: Prentice-Hall.

Bandura, A. (1989). Human agency in social cognitive theory. *American Psychologist, 44,* 1175-1184.

Barrowclough, C., et al. (2001). A randomized trial of the effectiveness of cognitive-behavioral therapy and supportive counseling for anxiety symptoms in older adults. *Journal of Consulting and Clinical Psychology, 69,* 756-762.

Beck, A. T. (1976). *Cognitive therapy and the emotional disorders.* New York, NY: Meridian.

Beck, A. T. (1988). *Love is never enough.* New York, NY: Harper & Row.

Beck, A. T. (1993). Cognitive therapy: Past, present, and future. *Journal of Consulting and Clinical Psychology, 61,* 194-198.

Beck, A. T. (1996). Beyond belief: A theory of modes, personality, and psychopathology. In P. M. Sakovskis (Ed.), *Frontiers of cognitive therapy* (pp. 1-25). New York, NY: Guilford Press.

Beck, A. T., Emery, G., & Greenberg, R. L. (1985). *Anxiety disorders and phobias: A cognitive perspective.* New York, NY: Basic Books.

Beck, A. T., Freeman, A., & Associates. (1990). *Cognitive therapy of personality disorders.* New York, NY: Guilford Press.

Beck, A. T., Freeman, A., & Davis, D. D. (2003). *Cognitive therapy of personality disorders* (2nd ed.). New York, NY: Guilford Press.

Beck, A. T., Rush, A. J., Shaw, B. F., & Emery, G. (1979). *Cognitive therapy of depression.* New York, NY: Guilford Press.

Beck, A., Wright, F. D., Newman, C. F., & Liese, B. S. (1993). *Cognitive therapy of substance abuse.* New York, NY: Guilford Press.

Benner, D. G. (2005). Intensive soul care: Integrating psychotherapy and spiritual direction. In L. Sperry & E. P. Shafranske (Eds.), *Spiritually oriented psychotherapy* (pp. 287-306). Washington, DC: American Psychological Association.

Berkouwer, G. C. (1971). *Studies in dogmatics: Sin.* Grand Rapids, MI: Eerdmans.

Browning, D. S., & Cooper, T. D. (2004). *Religious thought and the modern psychologies* (2nd ed.). Minneapolis, MN: Fortress Press.

Bufford, R. (1977). *The human reflex: Behavioral psychology in biblical perspective.* San Francisco, CA: Harper & Row.

Butler, A. C., & Beck, J. S. (2001). Cognitive therapy outcomes: A review of meta-analyses. *Tidsskrift for Norsk Psykologforening, 38,* 698-706.

Chambless, D. L., & Hollon, S. D. (1998). Defining empirically supported therapies. *Journal of Consulting and Clinical Psychology, 66,* 7-18.

Cloud, H., & Townsend, J. (1995). *Twelve Christian beliefs that can drive you crazy: Relief from false assumptions.* Grand Rapids, MI: Zondervan.

Collins, F. S. (2006). *The language of God: A scientist presents evidence for belief.* New York, NY: Free Press.

Crabb, L. (1975). *Basic principles of biblical counseling.* Grand Rapids, MI: Zondervan.

Crabb, L. (1977). *Effective biblical counseling.* Grand Rapids, MI: Zondervan.

Crane, R. (2009). *Mindfulness-based cognitive therapy.* London: Routledge.

Craske, M. G., & Barlow, D. H. (2001). Panic disorder and agoraphobia. In D. H. Barlow (Ed.), *Clinical handbook of psychological disorders* (3rd ed., pp. 1-59). New York, NY: Guilford Press.

Dimeff, L. A., & Linehan, M. M. (2001). Dialectical behavior therapy in a nutshell. *The California Psychologist, 34,* 10-13.

Dobson, K. S. (Ed.). (2010). *Handbook of cognitive-behavioral therapies* (3rd ed.). New York, NY: Guilford Press.

Dueck, A., & Reimer, K. (2009). *A peaceable psychology: Christian therapy in a world of many cultures.* Grand Rapids, MI: Brazos.

Edwards, K. (1976). Effective counseling and psychotherapy: An integrative review of the research. *Journal of Psychology and Theology, 5,* 94-107.

Ehlers, A., & Clark, D. M. (2003). Early psychological interventions for adult survivors of trauma: A review. *Biological Psychiatry, 53,* 817-826.

Ellis, A. (1960). There is no place for the concept of sin in psychotherapy. *Journal of Counseling Psychology, 7,* 192.

Ellis, A. (1962). *Reason and emotion in psychotherapy.* New York, NY: Lyle Stuart.

Ellis, A. (1971). *The case against religion: A psychotherapist's view.* New York, NY: Institute for Rational Living.

Ellis, A. (1978). The theory of rational-emotive therapy. In A. Ellis & J. Whitely (Eds.), *Theoretical and empirical foundations of rational-emotive therapy* (pp. 33-60). Monterey, CA: Brooks/Cole.

Ellis, A. (1980). Psychotherapy and atheistic values: A response to A. E. Bergin's "Psychotherapy and religious values." *Journal of Consulting and Clinical Psychology, 48,* 635-639.

Ellis, A. (2000). Can Rational Emotive Behavior Therapy (REBT) be effectively used with people who have devout beliefs in God and religion? *Professional Psychology: Research and Practice, 31,* 29-33.

Entwistle, D. N. (2004a). Shedding light on theophostic ministry 1: Practice issues. *Journal of Psychology and Theology, 32,* 26-34.

Entwistle, D. N. (2004b). Shedding light on theophostic ministry 2: Practice issues. *Journal of Psychology and Theology, 32,* 35-42.

Epstein, N. B., & Baucom, D. H. (2002). *Enhanced cognitive-behavioral therapy for couples: A contextual approach.* Washington, DC: American Psychological Association.

Evans, C. (1986, January 17). The blessings of mental anguish. *Christianity Today,* pp. 26-30.

Evans, C. (1989). *Wisdom and humanness in psychology.* Grand Rapids, MI: Baker.

Foa, E. B., & Franklin, M. (2001). Obsessive-compulsive disorder. In D. H. Barlow (Ed.), *Clinical handbook of psychological disorders* (3rd ed., pp. 209-263). New York, NY: Guilford Press.

Foster, R. (1998). *Streams of living water: Celebrating the great traditions of the Christian faith.* San Francisco: HarperSanFrancisco.

Garfield, S. L. (1996). Some problems associated with "validated" forms of psychotherapy. *Clinical Psychology, 3*, 218-229.

Hathaway, W., & Tan, E. (2009). Religiously oriented mindfulness-based cognitive therapy. *Journal of Clinical Psychology: In Session, 65*, 158-171.

Hauck, P. A. (1972). *Reason in pastoral counseling.* Philadelphia, PA: Westminster Press.

Havik, O. E., & VandenBos, G. R. (1996). Limitations of manualized psychotherapy for everyday clinical practice. *Clinical Psychology, 3*, 264-267.

Hayes, S. C. (1993). Goals and varieties of scientific contextualism. In S. C. Hayes, L. J. Barnes, T. R. Sarbin & H. W. Reese (Eds.), *The varieties of scientific contextualism* (pp. 11-27). Reno, NV: Context Press.

Hayes, S. C. (2002). Buddhism and acceptance and commitment therapy. *Cognitive and Behavioral Practice, 9*, 58-66.

Hayes, S. C. (2004a). Acceptance and commitment therapy and the new behavior therapies: Mindfulness, acceptance, and relationship. In S. C. Hayes, V. M. Follette & M. M. Linehan (Eds.), *Mindfulness and acceptance: Expanding the cognitive-behavioral tradition* (pp. 1-29). New York, NY: Guilford Press.

Hayes, S. C. (2004b). Acceptance and commitment therapy, relational frame theory, and the third wave of behavior therapy. *Behavior Therapy, 35*, 639-665.

Hayes, S. C. (2005). *Get out of your mind and into life: The new acceptance and commitment therapy.* Oakland, CA: New Harbinger.

Hayes, S. C., & Strosahl, K. D. (Eds.). (2004). *A practical guide to acceptance and commitment therapy.* New York, NY: Springer.

Hayes, S. C., Strosahl, K. D., & Wilson, K. G. (1999). *Acceptance and commitment therapy: An experiential approach to behavior change.* New York, NY: Guilford Press.

Jacobson, N., & Margolin, G. (1979). *Marital therapy.* New York, NY: Brunner/Mazel.

Johnson, W. B. (1993a). Christian rational-emotive therapy: A treatment protocol. *Journal of Psychology and Christianity, 12*, 254-261.

Johnson, W. B. (1993b). Outcome research and religious psychotherapies: Where are we and where are we going? *Journal of Psychology and Theology, 21*, 297-308.

Johnson, W. B., & Ridley, C. R. (1992). Brief Christian and non-Christian rational-emotive therapy with depressed Christian clients: An exploratory study. *Counseling and Values, 36,* 220-229.

Jones, E. E., & Pulos, S. M. (1993). Comparing the process in psychodynamic and cognitive-behavioral therapies. *Journal of Consulting and Clinical Psychology, 61,* 306-316.

Kabat-Zinn, J. (1990). *Full catastrophe living: Using the wisdom of your body and mind to face stress, pain, and illness.* New York, NY: Dell Publishing.

Kanfer, F. (1979). Personal control, social control, and altruism: Can society survive the age of individualism? *American Psychologist, 34,* 231-239.

Koerner, K., & Dimeff, L. A. (2007). Overview of dialectical behavior therapy. In L. A. Dimeff & K. Koerner (Eds.), *Dialectical behavior therapy in clinical practice* (pp. 1-18). New York, NY: Guilford Press.

Kovacs, M. B., & Beck, A. T. (1978). Maladaptive cognitive structures in depression. *American Journal of Psychiatry, 135,* 525-533.

Kreeft, P. (1986). *Making sense out of suffering.* Ann Arbor, MI: Servant.

Lambert, M. J., & Barley, D. E. (2002). Research summary on the therapeutic relationship and psychotherapy outcome. In John C. Norcross (Ed.), *Psychotherapy relationships that work* (pp. 17-32). New York, NY: Oxford University Press.

Lazarus, A. (1980). Treatment of dyspareunia. In S. Leiblum and L. Pervin (Eds.), *Principles and practice of sex therapy* (pp. 147-166). New York, NY: Guilford Press.

Lieb, K., Zanarini, M. C., Schmahl, C., Linehan, M. M., & Bohus, M. (2004). Seminar section: Borderline personality disorder. *Lancet, 364,* 453-461.

Linehan, M. M. (1987). Dialectical behavior therapy: A cognitive behavioral approach to parasuicide. *Journal of Personality Disorders, 1,* 328-333.

Linehan, M. M. (1989). Cognitive and behavior therapy for borderline personality disorder. In A. Tasman, R. E. Hales & A. J. Frances (Eds.), *Review of psychiatry* (Vol. 8, pp. 84-102). Washington, DC: American Psychiatric Press.

Linehan, M. M. (1993a). *Cognitive-behavioral treatment of borderline personality disorder.* New York, NY: Guilford Press.

Linehan, M. M. (1993b). *Skills training manual for treating borderline personality disorder.* New York, NY: Guilford Press.

Mahoney, M. J. (1993). Introduction to special section: Theoretical developments in the cognitive psychotherapies. *Journal of Consulting and Clinical Psychology, 61,* 187-193.

Mahoney, M. J. (2003). *Constructive psychotherapy: A practical guide.* New York, NY: Guilford Press.

McCullough, M. E. (1999). Research on religion-accommodation counseling: Review and meta-analysis. *Journal of Counseling Psychology, 46*, 92-98.

McFall, R. (1982). A review and reformulation of the concept of social skills. *Behavioral Assessment, 4*, 1-33.

McMinn, M. R. (1991). *Cognitive therapy techniques in Christian counseling*. Waco, TX: Word.

McMinn, M. R. (2008). *Sin and grace in Christian counseling: An integrative paradigm*. Downers Grove, IL: IVP Academic.

McMinn, M. R., & Campbell, C. D. (2007). *Integrative psychotherapy: Toward a comprehensive Christian approach*. Downers Grove, IL: IVP Academic.

McRae, R. R., & Costa, P. T., Jr. (2003). *Personality in adulthood: A five-factor theory perspective*. New York, NY: Guilford Press.

Meichenbaum, D. (1977). *Cognitive-behavior modification*. New York, NY: Plenum.

Meichenbaum, D. (1985). *Stress inoculation training*. New York, NY: Pergamon.

Meichenbaum, D. (1993). Changing conceptions of cognitive behavior modification: Retrospect and prospect. *Journal of Consulting and Clinical Psychology, 61*, 202-204.

Messer, S. B. (2004). Evidence-based practice: Beyond empirically supported treatments. *Professional Psychology, 35*, 580-588.

Mischel, W. (1973). Toward a cognitive social learning reconceptualization of personality. *Psychological Review, 80*, 252-285.

Moroney, S. K. (2000). *The noetic effects of sin*. Lanham, MD: Lexington Books.

Needleman, L. D. (1999). *Cognitive case conceptualization: A guidebook for practitioners*. Mahwah, NJ: Erlbaum.

Newman, C. F., Leahy, R. L., Beck, A. T., Reilly-Harrington, N. A., & Gyulai, L. (2002). *Bipolar disorder: A cognitive therapy approach*. Washington, DC: American Psychological Association.

Nielsen, S. L., Johnson, W. B., & Ellis, A. (2001). *Counseling and psychotherapy with religious persons: A rational emotive behavior therapy approach*. Mahwah, NJ: Erlbaum.

Norcross, J. C., Hogan, T. P., & Koocher, G. P. (2008). *Clinician's guide to evidence-based practices: Mental health and the addictions*. New York, NY: Oxford University Press.

Öst, L-G. (2008). Efficacy of the third wave of behavioral therapies: A systematic review and meta-analysis. *Behaviour Research and Therapy, 46*, 296-321.

Pecheur, D. (1978). Cognitive theory/therapy and sanctification. *Journal of Psychology and Theology, 6*, 239-253.

Propst, R. (1988). *Psychotherapy in a religious framework: Spirituality in the emotional healing process*. New York, NY: Human Sciences Press.

Propst, L. R., Ostrom, R., Watkins, P., Dean, T., & Mashburn, D. (1992). Comparative efficacy of religious and nonreligious cognitive-behavioral therapy for the treatment of clinical depression in religious individuals. *Journal of Consulting and Clinical Psychology, 60,* 94-103.

Roberts, R. C. (2001). Outline of Pauline psychotherapy. In M. R. McMinn & T. R. Phillips (Eds.), *Care for the soul: Exploring the interface of psychology & theology* (pp. 134-163). Downers Grove, IL: InterVarsity Press.

Robins, C. J., & Chapman, A. L. (2004). Dialectical behavior therapy: Current status, recent developments, and future directions. *Journal of Personality Disorders, 18,* 73-89.

Robins, C. J., Schmidt, H., & Linehan, M. M. (2004). Dialectical behavior therapy: Synthesizing radical acceptance with skillful means. In S. C. Hayes, V. M. Follette & M. M. Linehan (Eds.), *Mindfulness and acceptance: Expanding the cognitive-behavioral tradition* (pp. 30-44). New York, NY: Guilford Press.

Robins, R. W., Gosling, S. D., & Craik, K. H. (1999). An empirical analysis of trends in psychology. *American Psychologist, 54,* 117-128.

Ryle, A. (1990). *Cognitive-analytic therapy: Active participation in change.* New York, NY: Wiley.

Safran, J. D. (1998). *Widening the scope of cognitive therapy: The therapeutic relationship, emotion, and the process of change.* Northvale, NJ: Aronson.

Safran, J. D., & Segal, Z. V. (1990). *Interpersonal process in cognitive therapy.* New York, NY: Basic Books.

Schmidt, J. (1983). *Do you hear what you're thinking?* Wheaton, IL: Victor Books.

Segal, Z. V., Williams, J. M. G., & Teasdale, J. D. (2002). *Mindfulness-based cognitive therapy for depression: A new approach to preventing relapse.* New York, NY: Guilford Press.

Shedler, J. (2010). The efficacy of psychodynamic psychotherapy. *American Psychologist, 65,* 98-109.

Silverman, W. H. (1996). Cookbooks, manuals, and paint-by-numbers: Psychotherapy in the 90s. *Psychotherapy, 33,* 207-215.

Smith, E. M. (2002). *Healing life's hurts through theophostic prayer.* Ventura, CA: Regal.

Sperry, R. (1980). Mind-brain interactionism: Mentalism, yes; dualism, no. *Neuroscience, 5,* 195-206.

Stuart, R. (1980). *Helping couples change.* New York, NY: Guilford Press.

Tan, S. (1987). Cognitive-behavior therapy: A biblical approach and critique. *Journal of Psychology and Theology, 15,* 103-112.

Thurman, C. (2003). *The lies we believe.* Nashville, TN: Thomas Nelson.

Wampold, B. E., & Bhati, K. S. (2004). Attending to the omissions: A historical examination of evidence-based practice movements. *Professional Psychology, 35,* 563-570.

Williams, J. M. G., Teasdale, J. D., Segal, Z. V., & Kabat-Zinn, J. (2007). *The mindful way through depression: Freeing yourself from chronic unhappiness.* New York, NY: Guilford Press.

Woolfolk, R., & Richardson, F. (1984). Behavior therapy and the ideology of modernity. *American Psychologist, 39,* 777-786.

Wren, T. (1982). Social learning theory, self-regulation, and morality. *Ethics, 92,* 409-424.

Young, J. E. (1990). *Cognitive therapy for personality disorders: A schema-focused approach.* Sarasota, FL: Professional Resource Press.

Young, J. E., Klosko, J. S., & Weishaar, M. E. (2003). *Schema therapy: A practitioner's guide.* New York, NY: Guilford Press.

Young, J. E., Weinberger, A. D., & Beck, A. T. (2001). Cognitive therapy for depression. In D. H. Barlow (Ed.), *Clinical handbook of psychological disorders* (3rd ed., pp. 264-308). New York, NY: Guilford Press.

7

PERSON-CENTERED THERAPY

Terri Watson, Stanton L. Jones and Richard E. Butman

*I*t is especially difficult to get beyond mere intuitive and emotional appeal when evaluating person-centered therapy. Indeed, a counselor in this tradition would strike many as a good model of what it means to be a wise and patient friend, a person with an enormous capacity to listen attentively and respectfully. In a culture like ours where interpersonal contact and intimacy can be lost to absorption in the tasks of everyday living, few would find these qualities unattractive. Perhaps one reason why Carl Rogers's theory and technique has been so warmly embraced within significant portions of the religious community is that it appears to give us valuable clues and guidance on how to respond to those in misery and distress, or how to concretely "love the brothers and sisters."

While only a small percentage of clinicians practice from a purely person-centered perspective, over one-third of "eclectic" therapists integrate Rogers's person-centered therapy and other experiential techniques with their orientation (Norcross & Prochaska, 1988, as cited in Bohart, 2003). During his career Rogers conceptualized what many believe to be the most comprehensive humanistic theory of personality (Bozarth, Zimring & Tausch, 2001). He is considered to be the father of psychotherapy outcome research (Bozarth et al., 2001), and his emphasis on the primary role of the therapeutic relationship in therapy outcomes has received wide support. Kirschenbaum and Henderson (1989) assert that Rogers is "the most influential psychologist in American History" (p. xi).

An ever-evolving approach since the early 1940s, humanistic and person-centered therapies have experienced a noticeable renewal of late as evidenced by the recent publication of two handbooks of humanistic therapy (Cain & Seeman, 2001; Schneider, Bugental & Pierson, 2001). The recent interest in empirically supported therapy relationships (Norcross, 2002), an attempt to counterbalance focus on empirically supported techniques (ESTs) in psychotherapy, had resulted in renewed interest in Rogers's original "necessary and sufficient conditions" for the therapeutic relationship, and compels the Christian student of psychology to take another look at this important historical figure.

DESCRIPTIVE SURVEY

Philosophical Assumptions

Probably no theory of counseling and psychotherapy more fully manifests the humanistic spirit in contemporary psychology than does person-centered therapy, and perhaps no single individual better embodied its essence than its founder, Carl Rogers. For that reason, an understanding of the philosophical assumptions of person-centered therapy must start with a deeper look at the person of Carl Rogers.

It is surprising to many Christians that Rogers grew up in a fundamentalist Christian home and was intent on pursuing full-time ministry during his college years. In fact, excerpts from Rogers's journal during his freshman year paint a picture of a young man fervently seeking God's will in his life:

> I'll try and keep my life in tune with God, so that He can guide me. I have plenty of ambition, in fact I sometimes think I'm too ambitions, but if I can only keep that terrible swelling force within me in the right path, I know all will be well. . . . Lord, I ask Thy guidance; I am seeking the kingdom of Heaven; and the door at which I knock Thou alone knowest beside myself. Lord help me to see in the right spirit that I may obtain. Amen. (Kirschenbaum, 1979, p. 20)

During a trip to China as a youth delegate to the World Christian Federation Conference, Rogers encountered liberal Christian thinking and rejected the faith of his parents in favor of liberal humanism (Van Belle,

1985b, p. 1016). Following his trip, Rogers wrote: "I have changed to the only logical viewpoint—that I want to know what is true, regardless of whether that leaves me a Christian or no" (Kirshenbaum, 1979, p. 25). Rogers pursued theological training at Union Theological Seminary, to the dismay of his parents who felt Union was one of the more liberal seminaries in the country. After attempting full-time ministry as the pastor of a church, Rogers decided to leave the ministry and pursue education in psychology at Teachers College at Columbia University. There, he was influenced by John Dewey, a humanist and pragmatist. Rogers spoke very little about spiritual and religious themes during his teaching and practice of psychology until the later years of his life, where he made increased reference to mystical experiences (Thorne, 2002).

It is quite clear that person-centered therapy is a reaction against what Rogers perceived as the dogmatism of "prescriptive" religion and the elitist and rationalistic tendencies of classical psychoanalysis. In stark contrast to the strongly biological and deterministic assumptions of the early Freudian model (chap. 3), Rogers stressed a highly personal, phenomenological and positive view of human experience. Person-centered therapy is often said to embody the permissive and pragmatic mindset of the contemporary North American milieu (Van Belle, 1980). Person-centered therapy emphasizes the primacy of the individual and is often criticized for contributing to modern narcissism and the erosion of any shared sense of meaning or value in contemporary society (Vitz, 1977).

The heritage of person-centered therapy is rooted in phenomenology. Edmund Husserl, often called the "father of phenomenology," strongly influenced this distinctive approach to philosophy. Phenomenology (as summarized by Carver & Scheier, 2004) contends that what we are and what we do is a reflection of our subjective experience of the world and ourselves. External reality can only be known through the inner reality of personal experience. All persons are viewed as unique and possessing a unique perspective or "frame of reference." Self-determinism, the ability to exercise free will in decision making, is also an important tenant of phenomenology that influenced Rogers's development of person-centered therapy. Finally, phenomenology maintains the optimistic perspective that human beings are moving toward health, perfection, goodness and self-sufficiency. Clear evidence of the influence of phenomenology is evident in Rogers's views of personality and human functioning.

As Van Belle (1985a) has observed, Rogers had a profound respect for the client's perception of reality since this inner reality was ultimately the means for promoting development and growth in the individual. Indeed, Rogers is dogmatic in asserting that experience is the ultimate authority in life: "It is to experience that I must return again and again; to discover a closer approximation to truth as it is in the process of becoming in me. Neither the Bible nor the prophets, neither Freud nor research, neither the revelations of God nor man, can take precedence over my own direct experience" (Rogers, 1961, pp. 23-24). Person-centered therapy boldly asserts that the client, not the therapist, should be at the heart of psychotherapy (and hence, it is person centered) since only the client has the resources by which to become more aware of and remove his or her obstacles to personal growth.

Rogers's philosophical assumptions were influenced by his historical and cultural milieu. North American values of individualism versus conformity, equality of all persons and rejection of the class system, aversion to authoritarianism, and the primacy of the individual and her freedom in society are all clearly reflected in Rogers's model of personality and health.

Model of Personality

Consistent with Rogers's pragmatic and phenomenological method of therapy, he developed his theory of therapy first, and then a theory of personality emerged from his clinical work.

Perhaps the core assertion of this personality theory is that there is but one motivational force for all humanity: the tendency toward self-actualization. All persons have an inherent tendency to develop their capacities to the fullest, in ways that will maintain or enhance their own well-being. Rogers believes this motivational force is present at birth. Inherent to all living things, Rogers suggests, is the tendency toward growth without any conscious effort. This growth is toward autonomy, away from dependence or control by external forces.

Detractors of person-centered therapy often equate self-actualization with selfishness, but this is not strictly true. Actualization is the realization of our potential, and our potential certainly includes the capacity to love. Thus, Rogers would believe that out of the fully actualized, fully functioning individual would come acts of charity and kindness that would be a free and loving expression of the person's true inner state. Profound narcissism would actually be one mark of a failure to actualize one's potential. Contemporary person-centered therapists view this self-actualizing tendency not as an indication that humans are basically "good," rather they suggest that we all possess an inherent capacity for growth and the ability to change, or a "self-righting tendency" (Bohart, 2003).

While this motivation produces our movement, the direction for the movement comes from the *organismic valuing process*—an inherent capacity to choose that which will enhance us and reject that which does not. The actualization drive creates in us an urge for fulfillment, and the organismic valuing process tells us what will provide that fulfillment. The organismic valuing process is presumed to be an infallible and instinctive compass or guide for choice and action.

Model of Health

What then is the ideal course for human development according to person-centered therapy? The child, blessed with a drive toward actualization and an inerrant organismic valuing process to guide her, still needs the acceptance and positive regard of her parents. If the parents provide this positive regard unconditionally, the child grows up always exquisitely aware of her natural urges and awareness (her self-experience). As consciousness of self emerges, the person will begin to define herself (develop her self-concept) in accord with her own experience of herself and not in terms of how others see her or expect her to be. Further, she has no aspirations to be other than what she is, and her *ideal* self, the perception of what she should be, then perfectly matches the self-concept, which in turn perfectly matches the self-experience.

As we develop and mature, our self-concept increasingly shapes and directs the organismic valuing process. Thus, a self-concept unpolluted by distortions caused by other persons' judgments of us allows the organismic valuing process to continue to operate as an infallible guide. Health, then, is seen as a congruence between what one wants to become, what one perceives one's self to be and what one actually experiences or is. To quote Rogers (1961) on the fully functioning person:

> He is more able to experience all of his feelings, and is less afraid of any of
> his feelings; he is his own sifter of evidence, and is more open to evidence

from all sources; he is completely engaged in the process of being and be-coming himself, and thus discovers that he is soundly and realistically so-cial; he lives more completely in this moment, but learns that this is the soundest living for all time. (p. 192)

The healthy person then is one who has an intact and functioning or-ganismic valuing process and who completely trusts the valuing process. That person is fully aware, honest, personally satisfied and spontaneous. Health reflects trust of self, openness to experiencing and existential liv-ing in the present. Ideally, person-centered therapy posits, this will lead to a new kind of freedom whereby the person chooses to direct his or her life from within rather than by the dictates of the external world. Such "cen-teredness" (in the sense of balance, not self-centeredness) will release enor-mous potential to further oneself even more. There will be no need to deny or distort the information that is received perceptually since a strong sense of self has emerged that is consistent with deeply internalized conditions of worth. The chief Rogerian virtues are to be fully alive to the moment, completely self-accepting and strongly committed to an ongoing process of personal growth. Rogers (1961), quoting Kierkegaard, suggests the goal of personhood is to "be that self which one truly is" (p. 166).

For contemporary person-centered therapists this includes "listening" to all of the different "voices" residing in the self, including thoughts, feel-ings and "including any internalized 'voices' from parents and society" (Bohart, 2003). While clients are encouraged to "listen" to their feelings, there is acknowledgment that feelings are not the best guide to decision making. "Person-centered theorists believe that fully functioning people use *all* their faculties. They use both their ability to think rationally and problem-solve with their ability to experientially sense what is personally meaningful to the self" (Bohart, 2003, p. 114).

Contemporary person-centered therapists recognize that Rogers's em-phasis on independence and autonomy as health is a reflection of mascu-line, North American cultural values, and thus limited (O'Hara, 1994; Bohart, 2003). They propose a view of self as developing in the context of relationships with fluid boundaries and influences from the environment. These contemporary theorists are sensitive to the cultural difference in the way people construct a sense of self, and suggest that it is necessary to work within the "perceptual universe" of individuals (O'Hara, 1994). This relational view of the self-in-context increases the cultural competency of person-centered therapists in working with disadvantaged people groups both within and outside of North America (Bohart, 2003).

Model of Abnormality

Unfortunately, few of us get through childhood so unscathed. Most of us are subjected to conditions of worth, are loved conditionally; that is, we are expected to act in accord with the expectations of parents or significant others rather than by our instincts in order to receive acceptance. Christian discipline and instruction would, for Rogers, be a prime example of disrespect for the child's self-directedness. The child is confronted with the need to deny certain aspects of his experience and act according to rules or judgments of authority figures (*God wants me to honor my parents; I guess I'm not really angry at Daddy*). He then develops an ideal self, dictated by parental wishes, which does not fit who he really is (*Good boys love their parents and don't get angry with them*) and develops a self-concept that is formed in part by what the child genuinely experiences of himself and partly of what the child feels he must be (*I'm a good boy who doesn't get angry at Mom and Dad*). The distorted self-concept quickly warps the organismic valuing process, resulting in impaired perceptions of himself and his world and of the choices he can make.

In person-centered therapy problems in living are seen primarily in terms of incongruence between different dimensions of the self. Psychopathology results when we become more externally oriented than internally oriented, trying to manufacture feelings or behavior that others demand we exhibit before we can be acceptable. The incongruence between what we really are and what we are trying to be creates psychological pain, rigidity and anxiety. The distortions in the self-concept warp the functioning of the organismic valuing process, so that the person makes more bad (incongruent) choices about what would further his or her personal actualization.

The symptoms of abnormality are seen as signs or symbols of ways that we prevent threatening experiences from becoming more accurately represented in our conscious and subjective awareness. As the symptoms become more pronounced, our informational and perceptual processes become increasingly inadequate and rigid. In short, psychopathology is a split or incongruence between self and experience.

Contemporary person-centered therapists also acknowledge the role of psychological problems stemming from real environmental stressors such as economic or physical hardship, dysfunctional relationships or situations that are beyond one's inherent problem-solving capacities (Bohart, 2003).

Model of Psychotherapy

If external conditions of worth result in the distortion of the self, what can be done about this condition formally in the context of counseling and psychotherapy, or more informally in the setting of everyday interactions? Person-centered therapy suggests that positive self-regard, and thus congruence between self-concept and the person's experience, can be encouraged by relating to the individual with *congruence, empathy* and *unconditional positive regard.*

This will, according to Rogers, encourage the person to more fully trust the organismic valuing process and move toward greater self-actualization. The major task of the therapist is to provide a climate of safety and trust, one that will encourage clients to reintegrate their self-actualizing and self-valuing processes. The therapist accomplishes this through encouraging the psychotherapeutic conditions (the "therapeutic triad") of accurate empathic understanding, congruence or genuineness, and unconditional positive regard, which are seen as the necessary and sufficient conditions for effective counseling (Bohart, 2003).

Empathy has received considerable attention in contemporary psychological literature and is so widely accepted as a key component of therapist effectiveness that nearly all approaches to psychotherapy explicitly value therapist empathy (Bohart, 2003). Empathy is not sympathy; rather, it is the therapist's capacity to experience with the client and accept the client's subjective inner world. It does not mean "agreeing with" the client's perspective; rather, it describes the ability to "intuit oneself inside the client's perceptual universe" (p.127). Some person-centered therapy proponents contend that empathy is *the* key therapist attitude and response to foster the therapeutic relationship (Bozarth, Zimring & Tausch, 2001).

Congruence or genuineness is the therapist's capacity to truthfully and accurately perceive her or his own inner experiencing in response to the client and to allow that inner experience to affect the counseling relationship in a healthy way; it is the capacity to be fully oneself while fully relating to the client. Person-centered therapists distinguish between congruence and transparency, which refers to open sharing of thoughts and feelings on the part of the therapist. In contrast, congruence refers to "attending inwardly to one's experience and working to sort out its meanings" (Bohart, 2003, p. 128). Person-centered therapists attend to their reactions to the client, but only share with the client what is in her or his best interest.

Unconditional positive regard is an unyielding acceptance of, respect for and prizing of the client's experience, actualizing tendencies and organismic valuing process. Each of these qualities are seen by Rogerians as being rooted in the personhood of the therapist, and not as mere techniques. They can be learned as practical skills (one can learn lists of empathic responses, genuine responses, etc.), but to be used effectively they must take root in the very being of the counselor. Person-centered therapy never involves advice giving, shaming, teaching, giving interpretations, manipulation or other ingenuine interactions. These, it is argued, are based on a fundamental disrespect of others; they foster dependency and thwart the development of any meaningful sense of autonomy.

Understandably, for the person-centered therapist, the therapeutic relationship is of utmost importance. Unlike other approaches that see therapy as the therapist "doing something to" the client, person-centered therapy is best understood by an analogy to gardening: It is the provision of the right interpersonal soil in which the client's hidden drive to grow and develop can finally be released. Only through the proper characteristics and competencies of the therapist can the client move toward greater congruence and release of his or her own innate capacities.

As coparticipants in a process of change and discovery, the client-therapist relationship is egalitarian, informal and nonauthoritarian. Formal assessment of the presenting concerns or underlying dynamics in the forms of psychological testing or psychiatric diagnosis are seen as inappropriate and unnecessary. Techniques, of which there are few in person-centered therapy, are secondary to the therapist's attitudes, sensitivities and skills. Active listening, clarification and reflection of feelings, personal presence and coparticipation are seen as the only necessary tools in the repertoire of the person-centered therapist, coupled with a profound respect for process and inner-directedness. It is assumed that the client will freely choose to translate the changes experienced in the intimate context of therapy to outside relationships with others.

Change occurs in person-centered therapy when new understandings of self and others emerge from the "creative process" of therapy. Described as "more of a process of creation than of repair" (Bohart, 2003, p. 131), person-centered therapy allows the client to creatively explore his or her thoughts, feelings and perceptions in a supportive, empathic relationship, and to "try on" new behaviors (Bohart, 2003).

While many person-centered therapists continue to be purists in their commitment to nondirectivity and trust in the client's growth direction, some person-centered therapists provide an empathic, genuine, egalitarian relationship, but utilize more directive techniques from other approaches to therapy (Bohart, 2003). Emotion-focused approaches to therapy, which will be reviewed in chapter eight, are examples of integrative therapies that incorporate person-centered therapy with contemporary research and practice.

CHRISTIAN CRITIQUE

The debate continues in contemporary Christian theological and psychological literature regarding Carl Rogers as a "friend" or "foe" in his influence on Judeo-Christian thought in the culture and in the church. Thorne (1998), a committed Anglican, emeritus professor and trained person-centered therapist, articulates the challenges of maintaining allegiance to both the church of England and the work of a Rogerian therapist as that of being branded a "liberal heretic doing Lucifer's work" by fellow Christians, and "loss of credibility at best and total rejection at worst" by the psychology community (p. x). Rogers's views of the person, in particular, have influenced the field of pastoral care, the church and the theological anthropology of many Christian thinkers (Browning & Cooper, 2004; Thorne, 1998). In this appraisal of person-centered theory we will draw from a diversity of Christian perspectives to evaluate the congruence of the theory and practice of person-centered therapy with Christian thought.

Philosophical Assumptions

Compared to some traditions, person-centered therapy is commendably explicit about its philosophical presuppositions. Many aspects of these assumptions can be appreciated. The insistence on seeing people holistically and as purposeful, the appreciation of other ways of knowing beyond rationality, and the profound respect of what it means to be a person are all positive in many ways. Rogers reminds us of the uniqueness and wonder of creation, the miracle of being created in the image of God. Thorne (2002), in fact, suggests the presence of a "covert spiritual thread in Rogers's work from the outset" (p. x) and proposes that person-centered sensibilities toward self and others prompt a great appreciation toward and connectedness with others and with creation, that "compassionate engagement with the suffering earth and identification with the beauty of creation become poignant areas for the person-centered therapist's spiritual agenda" as well as "an openness to be surprised by the resourcefulness and beauty of the human being" (p. 43).

For the Christian the philosophical presuppositions undergirding person-centered therapy ought also to raise a number of concerns. It would appear that Rogers developed his person-centered approach not only in reaction to the mainstream psychology of the day but also in reaction to (or against) his Christian upbringing and Judeo-Christian assumptions about authority, freedom and human nature. Thus, a reading of Rogers's thought seems oddly familiar, but also disturbing in his reformulation (or outright rejection) of many foundational components of a Christian theological anthropology.

Authority and the self. Person-centered therapy assumes that we are the ultimate force and the sole masters of our own destiny; in other words, all authority is within. We see this in Rogers's clear rejection of all other sources of authority. This is a paradigmatic humanistic approach to psychotherapy in the fullest sense of the word; humanity is the center. This rejection of all authority outside of the self to define truth is reflected in Rogers's life, and central to his decision to leave the ministry and the church to pursue training in psychology.

The self assumes a position of supreme importance in Rogers's person-centered therapy, a notion that can be traced back to the philosophy of idealism and romanticism in the nineteenth century. The strongly experiential, individualistic and relativistic "core assertions" of person-centered therapy unquestionably lead to inflated notions of the self (Vitz, 1977; Myers, 1981).

Certainly we are called as Christians to develop our identities as a matter of good stewardship, but we must also confront the realities of the created order, including the existence of evil both within us and without. Self is not all there is and should not be the center of what is. As Vitz (1977) has said, "To worship one's self (in self-realization) or to worship all humanity is, in Christian terms, simple idolatry operating from the usual motive of unconscious egotism" (p. 93). In the Christian tradition, to proclaim oneself to be in control of one's own existence is the ultimate act of rebellion. C. S. Lewis (1968) once remarked that a good functional definition of hell would be the kind of place where all acted as if they were the master of their own lives.

Phenomenology and the self. The emphasis on self is not only a problem for ontology but for epistemology as well. Person-centered therapy boldly states that when one's self-actualizing tendency is in tune with the organismic valuing process, trustworthy self-knowledge is fully obtainable and should take precedence over all else. But to boldly assert the complete trustworthiness of self-knowledge is certainly not within the mainstream of the Christian tradition (cf. Dodgen & McMinn, 1986). The organismic valuing process is not an inerrant guide! No aspect of human nature is untouched by sin and hence inerrant.

Thus the Christian must question Rogers's reliance on self-knowledge as the ultimate authority. The phenomenological approach places great value on subjective experience in discerning truth. Rogers is optimistic about one's experience as the basis of determining truth, but rather pessimistic about the value of culture, dogma, traditions and systems of morality (Roberts, 1993). In contrast, the Christian tradition has always had a high view of divine revelation and the authority of Scripture, as well as the role of the discerning community. Its regard for general revelation, including a deeper understanding of human nature through greater self-awareness and understanding, has been more hesitantly asserted (cf. Roberts, 1985).

Freedom and responsibility. Person-centered therapy is also implicitly a system of ethics. In person-centered therapy, one is ultimately responsible only to oneself. Personal wholeness assumes primacy; it becomes a moral imperative, often at the expense of a proper appreciation of our responsibilities to others. Browning and Cooper (2004) provide an excellent analysis of the moral implications of self-actualization and question the moral philosophy that would propose self-actualization as the objective of the human life and reliable guide for decision making. The authors suggest that humanistic theorists such as Rogers are practicing ethical egoism in their assumption that a pursuit of individual fulfillment, and encouragement of others to do the same, will naturally lead to harmony and altruism in society. In contrast, Browning and Cooper take the position that the individual pursuit of such aims should be in subordination to a social and interpersonal "ethic of justice" by basing moral behavior on what is best for the community. For the ethical egoist a belief in the harmony of nature results in a minimization of the need for individual moral behavior, "The only moral task to be concerned with is one's own growth" (p.80). Browning and Cooper point out important inconsistencies between the ethical egoist pursuit of self-actualization and the value of mutual and *agape* love in the Christian tradition. Mutual love, they argue, requires a significant degree of obligation and self-transcendence, rather than pursuit of one's own actualization and the assumption that this will harmonize with others who are doing the same.

Christians can appreciate the emphasis in person-centered therapy on individual freedom and responsibility. Individual choice and the capacity to change are affirmed in the Rogerian tradition. Initially, as Tisdale (1988) has noted, such an assessment of the human condition in the therapeutic context might seem harsh and insensitive since it centers responsibility on the client. It risks blaming clients for all their problems or regarding them as having more freedom than they actually possess. But this view also has reassuring implications. People are seen as having the potential to act and make decisions despite their situations, histories or limitations, as the Scriptures frequently assert.

On the other hand, the Christian tradition describes certain limitations on our freedom; we are portrayed as in bondage to evil, self-deception and sin. Person-centered therapy recognizes none of these limitations. Still, the emphasis on responsibility in person-centered therapy is a refreshing contrast to the more pessimistic tendencies of the deterministic models and the current infatuation with addiction models for all human problems. There is far too much externalization and projection of responsibility going on in contemporary American society.

Model of Personality

There is much in the Rogerian model of personality that is initially appealing to the Christian reader. The true self, according to Rogers, is potentially in an ever-changing process of "becoming a person," and this emphasis on unending growth is attractive. The true self is not a person who is fixed to any specific dispositions, roles or traits, and this respects our individuality. We would agree with Rogers that most of us are not now our true selves and that growth really does mean at some significant levels becoming one's true self. We are, after all, created in God's image, and each person has a unique calling from God to become the person he or she was meant to become.

The self's lack of form is troubling, for as Roberts (1993) has noted, the Rogerian self has no center or anchor, and if taken to an extreme, can turn into a formless entity defined only by its urges and sensing. According to the Christian tradition, true selves are not to be merely uncovered but are to be formed by acting in obedience to God's call (Evans, 1990; see chap. 11). Thus, we are not fundamentally good beings, as person-centered therapy asserts, but ones whose very selves need transformation. Certainly there is a sense in which we are troubled because we don't know ourselves, but it would be inaccurate to state that we "give birth to ourselves." In conversion we become more of a true self, but certainly not a complete self. For the Christian, God alone gives us birth—not the therapist, nor the increasingly congruent person. And with that profession of faith, new opportunities and responsibilities must be assumed, including a strong commitment to becoming manifestations of God's grace in this world in word and deed.

Becoming a self, in the Christian view, requires a willingness to face directly one's creatureliness as well as finiteness. In our uncorrupted state, we were the crown of creation, but we became estranged from our Creator. Inwardly depraved, we are incapable of returning to God apart from grace. The ultimate hope for our transformation is divine intervention as we confront our sinfulness. Christian maturity reaches its apex in terms of character formation when the Christian virtues are cultivated and expressed (Roberts, 1982). This truth, that human selves have to be transformed because we are not perfectly good, cannot be overemphasized. The Christian sees the need to balance a desire for self-fulfillment with a strong portion of self-discipline. We accept ourselves, but also yearn to become who and what God is calling us to be.

We would also argue that person-centered therapy errs in positing only one drive for human personality. Suggesting only one motivation toward growth requires attributing all human distress to forces external to the person. Thus, in this view, if we ever experience conflict, it cannot be due to a true struggle within ourselves, but rather is attributable to a pseudo-struggle between our true selves (all good) and some sort of false selves, which are presumed to have originated externally from how significant others have treated us. This is why Browning and Cooper (2004, p. 58) describe the person-centered therapy view as "instinctual utopianism"; it suggests perfect inner congruence at the deepest levels for the healthy person. Christianity, on the other hand, suggests that our good impulses and our bad impulses, our love for and rebellion against God, are both representative of our true selves. Conflict is real and goes on in the deepest dimensions of the person. Person-centered therapy thus has a trivial view of conflict within the person. Christianity views conflict as both internal and external, and evident at both the individual and corporate levels.

In person-centered therapy the true self is aware, through the organismic valuing process, of internal needs, but not necessarily of anything external like the needs and wants of others, at least until a high degree of personal congruence has been achieved. Such notions should trouble us as Christians. Person-centered therapy may appeal to our preexisting tendencies toward being overly individualistic. The true self in the Christian tradition is in part defined in terms of relationships—with God, with neighbor, with others and with God's absolutes. Our sense of identity is meant to be shaped by both organismic needs (which certainly play a role) and by a strong sense of belonging shaped by the Christian story and our place in the Christian community (cf. Gaede, 1985). A sense of meaning and personal contentment are potentially enriched and enlivened by a strong sense of heritage, history and tradition as children of the Creator God. The true self is the person who loves God with all of one's heart, seeks after righteousness and loves others as oneself. A more complete understanding of the true self goes beyond self-awareness and subjective experience to a keen awareness and knowledge of others (Roberts, 1993). In a very real sense we find our identity in being and doing.

It would be fair to say that there is a dimension of self-actualizing potential in all of us. But a more traditional Christian perspective would be that this is based on a potential for a gradual, painful process of recovering the original form of the *imago Dei* (image of God) that became distorted as a result of the Fall. A more balanced and theologically sensitive perspective on the forces that move us would contend that there are some less-than-noble drives within, and this is why we argued earlier that selves must be made and forged in the context of costly discipleship rather than merely being uncovered.

For the Christian an understanding of what it means to be fully human, created in the image of God, is found in Scripture and in the model of Jesus Christ. Reclaiming a Christian humanism that looks beyond self-actualization as the primary human need to address the spiritual, moral and historical dimensions of the person is the task of a Christian humanistic psychology (Olson, 2002). Clouse (1997), citing Packer and Howard (1985), proposes "sacred humanism" as a model for Christian anthropology, with "Jesus Christ as the standard of humanness" (p. 46). Only a "sacred humanism," Clouse proposes, can be embraced by pastors and counselors as compatible with Christian faith.

Model of Health

At first glance, there is much in these notions of health that is attractive to those who long for a more "honest Christianity" (cf. McLemore, 1984). It would be fair to state that Christians are, by and large, overly rational and often distrustful of feelings. We also put on our "happy faces" and play the roles of the conquering spiritual giants in our religious communities. It is no wonder that we feel alone in having problems among the Christians we know. If we are honest in our self-assessment, however, we are usually painfully aware of our tendencies to deny and distort reality, just as Rogers would suggest. We are called often in Scripture to be more truthful in our communications, especially with our Creator God (e.g., the frequent brutal honesty of the psalmists). Without such honesty, there can be no true repentance or confession, no true fidelity, no true reconciliation (cf. Tisdale, 1988, p.14).

Thus one of the greatest assets of the person-centered therapy is its strong emphasis on awareness of feelings. But this is also a liability. Awareness is an end in itself in this system; awareness is health. As Van Belle (1985a) has observed, greater awareness of emotional response might lead to a sense of emotional relief, freedom, improved self-awareness, personal autonomy and interpersonal competence. But there is no guarantee that "healthier," more emotionally "in-touch" persons will anchor themselves in any abiding structure outside themselves, because as we noted the self is formless in person-centered therapy theory.

For the Christian, the inward journey of awareness may be necessary, especially as the foundation for all true repentance, but it will be insufficient by itself for forming the true self. Greater self-actualization should serve a meaningful end, namely, that we submit ourselves to God, seek after righteousness and love others as ourselves. Freedom and autonomy ought not to be ends in themselves but rather vehicles by which we more fully achieve maturity in Christ.

The person-centered therapy ideal of health is the person without a past (we are always to live in the "now"), a person without any need to submit to authority (we are our own ultimate truth), a person without real dependence on anyone else (we contain all our resources within ourselves) and a person with no firm commitment to truth (all meanings are held tentatively and revised according to changing experiences). In contrast, Christianity paints humans as having pasts, presents and futures of fixed meanings determined by God. We are part of a community of faith that has a stable identity. We are not our own gods, but owe our submission to the rightful Lord of the universe.

Certainly there are absolutes in the Christian faith, but there are relatively few in person-centered therapy. External authority is seen as potentially obtrusive and often more as a vice than a virtue. Yet we are profoundly dependent on God (Col 1:9-20) and on others (e.g., "It is not good for the man to be alone" [Gen 2:18]). And we believe in a truth that is constant because it ultimately depends on a truth-speaking God who is "the same yesterday and today and forever" (Heb 13:8).

Rogers's concept of self has also been critiqued as characteristic of the Western cultural view of the self as independent, autonomous, separate and distinct, with the goal of becoming independent and separate from family and significant others. In contrast, many cultures view self as interdependent and place personal achievement and self-determination as secondary to the maintenance of harmonious relationships with others (Markus & Kitayama, 1991).

278 MODERN PSYCHOTHERAPIES

Model of Abnormality

There is a near consensus in the field of psychopathology that problems are typically multicausal and multimaintained. A whole host of biological, psychosocial and sociocultural variables are usually involved, even in what appears to be a "simple" problem. Rogerians prefer to concentrate on their unique experiential contribution to understanding the larger causal picture. Because of this exclusive focus, person-centered therapy may be most relevant to understanding the adjustment difficulties of relatively high-functioning persons, individuals struggling with problems of overcontrol or denial of their feelings.

But such an orientation runs the risk of trivializing or even ignoring the complex reality of serious psychopathology. Since careful assessment is seen as largely futile, according to this model (because of the emphasis on experiencing), important clinical symptoms can be missed or minimized. Person-centered therapy runs the risk of indifference to or ignorance about the full range of human misery and suffering. Its perspective on psychopathology is at best partial and seems to have less to add to our overall understanding of human psychopathology than any other mainline approach.

A fundamental flaw in the humanistic and relativistic philosophy behind person-centered therapy is what appears to be a lack of willingness to seriously confront the fundamental depravity of persons and the reality of sin. Rogers viewed the source of human incongruence, anxiety and maladaptive behavior as environmental. In contrast, as Christians, we recognize that no part of us is untouched by sin (total depravity), and we are unable to choose not to sin. In an excellent discussion of the relationship between anxiety, sin and self-understanding in Rogers's theories, Cooper (2003) proposes that Rogers's view of persons neglects the role of ontological anxiety as part of the human condition and a springboard for destructive and unhealthy behaviors. He writes, "Having self-esteem, then, will not end the sin problem. Even when we deeply value ourselves, the anxiety built into finitude will tempt us to find our source of security in some strategy rather than a trust in God" (p. 163). Rogers's optimistic view of persons cannot resonate fully with a Christian anthropology.

Perhaps person-centered therapy's most significant and enduring contribution is to examine the role of self-hate as a source of human suffering.

From a Rogerian perspective, even pride is thought to be a thin veneer for the more central problem of a lack of self-acceptance and self-love. Biblically, however, self-love is more fundamental to our human dilemma than is self-hate. The desire to love ourselves without reference to God could be argued to be the prime cause for the Fall. Perhaps we could even argue that the root of self-hate is the motive to make more of self than we ought due to our prideful and inflated expectations of self. Certainly self-love is as often a source of problems in living as is self-hate. As Cooper (2003) suggests, "there is an unexpected low self-esteem in pride, and unexpected pride in low self-esteem" (p. 165). Thus, person-centered therapy has a limited view of the problem of low self-esteem.

Model of Psychotherapy

The methods of change described in the person-centered therapy tradition—the therapeutic triad of empathy, genuineness and unconditional positive regard—have been enormously influential in contemporary psychology and the pastoral-care movement. A vast literature has emerged in the past three decades that has drawn out their implications for an amazingly diverse number of settings, populations and clinical concerns.

Let us first focus on the methods of change that have been the focal point for much of the discussion about person-centered therapy. The role of the therapist in the person-centered therapy is seen as that of a facilitator or catalyst, not that of a guide or teacher. The nature of this catalytic method is often summarized as love. In fact, Patterson (1985) explicitly equates the therapeutic triad with *agape* love.

Positively, it is hard to say enough about the redemptive power of divine love. Thielicke (1964) briefly discusses the power of God's *agape* love, which God lavishes upon us. Thielicke uses the analogy of photographic development, suggesting that God's love, experienced directly from God and more indirectly through God's people, could act as the developing chemicals, sharpening and bringing into focus the masked and dormant image of God within us. To whatever extent person-centered therapy encourages a human manifestation of *agape* love, it should claim our allegiance and profound respect.

A truly Christian approach to healing and helping will surely stress the primacy of warm, empathic and genuine relationships, thoroughly grounded in an understanding of *agape* love (Tan, 1987). Oden (1968), in his earlier analysis of person-centered therapy, went so far as to say that unconditional positive regard, mediated through a good psychotherapeutic relationship, was the secular translation of the Christian understanding of redemption. Ellens (1982) recognized and applauded the supreme emphasis placed on grace in the person-centered therapy tradition.

But it is a serious error for the Christian to equate unconditional positive regard, or even the whole triad, with Christian love (Oakland, 1974; Ortberg, 1981; Roberts, 1988). Christian love warmly embraces sinners, is gracious and unconditionally accepting, but does not cease to be firm and hold the self and others accountable. Certainly we need to be fed by deep affirmation and acceptance, but we also need to be pruned in the process of our growth by God's discipline and to be forgiven. Our Creator God disciplines because he loves us (Heb 12:7-10). In person-centered therapy there is no discipline, no firmness. The person-centered therapist is trained not to express disapproval or give instruction in any form or fashion (Ortberg, 1981).

As Christians we need to learn more about the importance of affirming persons deeply "as they are." Indeed, we are all too often preaching or talking when we should be attentively and respectfully listening. But divine acceptance and Christian love place certain demands and expectations on relationships. Discipline and struggle go hand in hand with accepting that we are of immense worth in the creational order. God's grace is a gift that is not merited but is given freely. It cannot be earned, and we should reject a works theology forthrightly. But that does not mean that there is no place for a proper understanding of discipline, moral accountability, judgment or repentance in the Christian life. And if these are present, therapy will certainly be more than the creation of a tolerant, accepting atmosphere in the counseling relationship. Unfortunately, we seem to know far more about preaching and exhorting than we do about listening and comforting. There is much we need to learn about love within limits and about caring and commitment (cf. Smedes, 1978).

Contemporary Christians have much to learn about what it means to "speak the truth in love." Richard Mouw (1992) exemplifies the balance of both civility and conviction, arguing that many of us err on the side of too much civility ("niceness") whereas others tend to focus, often to a fault, on conviction ("truth"). The risk of the former is a kind of permissive and tacit endorsement of relativism. The potential problem of the latter is dogmatism and rigidity, even pride. In our complex and multicultural communities, it is rare to find that delicate balance between grace and truth.

For counselors in training, an initial exposure to person-centered therapy—especially in a role-play situation—can lead to a one-sided acceptance that seems strikingly similar to Mouw's concerns about "grace without truth." Though we must have a high view of love as men and women of faith, we also must have the right view of love. We are concerned that less experienced therapists can seem unwilling to give honest and truthful feedback, as if they could hide behind a veil of aloof and disengaged involvement. McLemore (2002), in a similar vein, warns about the dangers of affiliation without assertion, the risk of being warm and expressive without ever being direct and frank. A skilled therapist knows that giving feedback requires great timing, tact and sensitivity, and that a real healing relationship must move beyond blandly affirming pseudo-intimacy, enmeshment or symbiosis. In a recent book, Hybels (2008) argues the risk of confusing compliance with integrity. She suggests that grace offered alone can lead to a kind of image management that is potentially lethal (i.e., warmth without assertion). It is hard for us to see how effective clinicians can foster the necessary and sufficient conditions for change without an appropriate combination of grace and truth, of affirmation and accountability.

Because of its one-sided embrace of love without discipline, person-centered therapy may support clients without challenging them. Client and therapist may hide behind empathic listening and reflecting without getting into the deeper issues that need to be confronted if growth and change are to occur. In all fairness, person-centered therapy has moved in the direction of "caring confrontation" (cf. Rogers, 1980), but there still seems to be an almost phobic avoidance of dealing with the inevitable differences of opinions or conflicts that occur in human relationships. In fact, descriptions and definitions of the therapeutic qualities are typically written in such a way that most confrontations that one might imagine flowing from Christian moral stances would be judged to be ingenuine, nonempathic or conditional, and hence to be avoided. Sometimes these concerns are well-taken; Christians probably engage in a fair amount of premature orthodoxy (i.e., jumping to conclusions). What we are concerned about, however, is a steadfast pattern of avoidance, which can only lead to a moral relativism or an ethic without any teeth. Truth-telling is full of risks and responsibilities, but so is the alternative.

Next we examine the motivation for love or positive regard of the counselee. For the person-centered therapist, we are to love because the other merits it, and it is congruent for us to do so. For the Christian there are a number of foundations for positive regard. First, love is rooted in the recognition of our common status as persons created in God's image; we are all part of one common family. We are also urged to love others because God first loved us, to love as an overflow of God's love of us (Roberts, 1988). We are urged to love as a reflection of God's character, of his presence in our lives. Finally, we are commanded to love others as ourselves because it is a deep expression of our understanding of our purpose on earth. *Agape* love is grounded in an objective reality outside the self, whereas positive regard is ultimately anchored within the individual.

What of the process by which therapy occurs, the type of experience the client is urged to have? Person-centered therapy appears to focus too much on inner subjective experience and present-centeredness. If problems in living are seen as rooted in aberrations in perception, then it makes sense to focus on the client's awareness of the here and now. Christian faith is not necessarily incompatible with a deep concern about individual inner experience, and there is a sense in which the Christian tradition values the immediacy of the present existential moment. After all, we were told to ask only for our "daily bread" and to live each moment fully "as unto the Lord."

But the Christian tradition values others as well. Even mystical contemplation is seen largely as a means to empower oneself for more focused and concentrated ministry rather than as an end in itself. And the Christian tradition is deeply rooted in a strong sense of God's working throughout redemptive history. Becoming centered "fully in the moment" runs the risk of leading to a limited sense of familial, historical, personal or spiritual identity. We need a personal and collective story or we will eventually have to face an overwhelming sense of emptiness (cf. Lasch, 1979; or Bellah, Madsen, Sullivan, Swindler & Tipton, 1985).

There are risks for the person-centered therapist as well. It is tempting for the therapist to mask his or her own identity and uniqueness by being constrained to relate to clients in a "person-centered" manner. The therapeutic triad of congruence, empathy and unconditional positive regard can all too easily degenerate into a bland, safe and ineffectual way of relating to persons in general. Further, these qualities should not be reduced to skills or sensitivities that can be turned on or off as the occasion demands. Indeed, this would be the epitome of incongruity.

Person-centered therapy has been assumed to be an effective approach for working with clients from a variety of cultural backgrounds due to its emphasis on respect for individual differences, understanding problems from the client's perspective and suspension of the therapist's own values. These tenants of person-centered therapy appear to be consistent with principles of multicultural competency (Ridley, 1995; Sue, 1998). However, the influence of Western humanism and the Enlightenment results in a view of the person that is incompatible with many people groups. Usher (1989) found that biases evident in person-centered therapy included individualism, neglect of personal history of the client, emphasis on autonomy and separateness from natural support systems.

Person-centered therapy has probably been the most widely adapted approach to people-helping that has ever been developed. Applications for the business, educational, familial, group, individual, marital and parental context abound in the literature (Corey, 2000). Person-centered therapy is also widely appreciated for the ways it has been adapted for the training of lay and paraprofessional counselors. It has helped mental health professionals to "give psychology away" to the people, with all the obvious risks and benefits that entails. No doubt person-centered therapy is the dominant method used in the initial phases of counselor training (cf. Meier, 2004)—perhaps because it has built-in safety features. Even eclectic, empirically based books on psychotherapy show a tremendous indebtedness to the person-centered therapy tradition (Norcross, 2002). An approach that stresses active listening, learning to respect the client's frame of reference, and minimizing advice and unsolicited interpretation has immediate and obvious appeal.

Carl Rogers is to be commended for his serious commitment to clinical research. Next to the cognitive and behavioral traditions, no approach has been as willing to state its formulations in terms of testable hypotheses and to commit itself to such extensive and collaborative research endeavors. Hardly a static system, person-centered therapy has gradually evolved over the past fifty years, due in part to its willingness to modify theory and technique in light of insights gained from research. Person-centered therapy has left an impressive legacy. After five decades of solid research, few clinicians or theoreticians would doubt that congruence, empathy and positive regard are essential building blocks for effective change. The debate is over whether they are sufficient conditions for change to occur. The issue of therapist directiveness is likely the most significant change in person-centered and humanistic therapies over the past fifty years as contemporary therapies have viewed the necessary and sufficient conditions as necessary, sometimes sufficient, but not always efficient (Cain, 2001).

DEMONSTRATED EFFECTIVENESS

As the father of psychotherapy research, perhaps Rogers's greatest contribution was his research on the process and outcome of psychotherapy. Ironically, contemporary psychotherapy research has provided strong support for Rogers's original emphasis on the primacy of the therapeutic relationship. Bozarth et al. (2001) writes, "The clear message of five decades of research identifies the relationship of the client and therapist in combination with the resources of the client (extratherapeutic variables) that respectively account for 30% to 40% of variance in successful psychotherapy" (p. 168).

A recent APA Division of Psychotherapy task force sought to provide balance to the field of psychotherapy's emphasis on promoting technique guidelines (empirically supported treatments, or ESTs) by developing research-based guidelines for the empirically supported (therapy) relationships (Norcross, 2002). In his excellent summary and evaluation of the "relationship factors" in therapy, Norcross analyzed over one hundred studies of therapy outcomes and concluded that the "common factors" account for approximately 30 percent of the improvement in psychotherapy, compared with technique (15 percent), expectancy (15 percent) and extratherapeutic factors (40 percent) (p. 18). Norcross's edited volume carefully summarizes psychotherapy outcome research over the past decade and finds strong support for Rogers's facilitative conditions of empathy, genuineness and positive regard. In addition, relational factors predictive of successful therapy outcomes are delineated, including client-therapist collaboration and consensus on treatment goals, accurate therapist feedback about client's functioning, capacity for repair of alliance ruptures, and accurate interpretations about relational dynamics (Norcross & Hill, 2004).

The largest and most recent meta-analysis of the effectiveness of the humanistic psychotherapies was conducted by Elliott (2002). His analysis of over one hundred treatment groups revealed that humanistic approaches in general are as effective as other therapies, including cognitive-behavioral therapy. Forty-four of the studies were of client-centered and nondirective therapies, and these yielded a moderate to large effect size of .80. This study also found that gains made in therapy were maintained in one-year follow-ups. The study concluded that humanistic therapies are effective for the treatment of "a wide range of problems, including depression, anxiety, 'mixed neurotic' problems, minor adjustment difficulties, and relationship difficulties" (p. 74), with the strongest findings for the treatment of depression and for difficulties in relationships. Certainly, psychotherapy outcome studies compel the responsible Christian clinician to pay serious attention to the centrality of the client-therapist relationship as predictive of successful psychotherapy.

CONCLUSION

Few models of people-helping have been as widely discussed in Christian circles as has person-centered therapy. We have already developed at length the most important criticisms of this model. As a purist humanistic theory there are too many inadequacies in person-centered therapy for it ever to serve as the foundation for a thoroughly Christian approach to personal healing. When integrated with a "Christian humanism" the relational values developed by Rogers and supported by psychotherapy research have much to offer the Christian clinician who seeks to offer the love of Christ to their clients.

Perhaps the enduring legacy of person-centered therapy for Christians will be the respect this tradition has for persons. Person-centered theorists and therapists have taught us much about what it means to deeply care for (and be cared for by) others. Although we must be careful to realign certain concepts so that they conform more closely to the truth of the revealed will of God, we can certainly be grateful that Rogers and his followers have deeply sensitized us to what it means to listen to someone (Jacobs, 1975). In the five decades of research that have followed Rogers's initial conceptualizations, the central role of the therapeutic relationship and the therapist's empathy, genuineness and positive regard remain unchallenged. It is likely that Rogers glimpsed something of truth about incarnational relationship in his years of psychotherapy research and practice.

As Bonhoeffer (1954) perceptively observed more than a half century before, "The first service one owes to others in the fellowship consists in listening to them. Just as love to God begins with listening to His Word, so the beginning of love for the brethren is learning to listen to them" (p. 97). All too often Christians are talking when we should be listening. Bonhoeffer warned, "It is little wonder that we are no longer capable of the greatest service of listening that God has committed to us, that of hearing our brother's confession, if we refuse to give ear to our brother on lesser subjects. . . . We should listen with the ears of God that we may speak the Word of God" (pp. 98-99).

A number of writers have observed that in the latter years of Rogers's work, he appeared to use increasingly mystical language in his understanding of the universal experiences and principles at the heart of all reality (Van Kalmthout, 1995; Thorne, 2002). Rogers himself acknowledged in his latter years that he had not paid enough attention to the spiritual dimension of his work and thought (Thorne, 2002). Although Rogers did not ever return to the Christian zeal of his early years, one must wonder if his honest questioning of his experience led him to once again seek the kingdom of heaven. Regardless, his legacy and impact on the field of psychotherapy endures.

FOR FURTHER READING

Cooper, T. D. (2003). *Sin, pride, and self-acceptance: The problem of identity in psychology and theology.* Downers Grove, IL: InterVarsity Press.

Offers theological insights on the human condition, comparing and contrasting humanistic psychology with Christian theology on issues of self-esteem, self-acceptance and self-actualization

Norcross, J. C. (Ed.). (2002). *Psychotherapy relationships that work.* New York, NY: Oxford University Press.

An excellent overview of research on characteristics of effective therapeutic relationships.

Oden, T. (1966). *Kerygma and counseling.* Philadelphia, PA: Westminster.

A widely referenced and influential initial study of person-centered therapy from a mainline Protestant perspective. The work reflects the initial enthusiasm about the application of person-centered therapy to the pastoral counseling setting.

Olson, R. P. (2002). Christian Humanism. In R. P. Olson (Ed.), *Religious theories of personality and psychotherapy: East meets west* (pp. 247-323). New York, NY: Hawthorn Press.

Develops Christian humanism as a Christ-centered alternative to humanistic psychology.

Rogers, C. (1961). *On becoming a person.* Boston, MA: Houghton Mifflin.

A widely read introduction to the values inherent in person-centered therapy. This is probably the most autobiographical of Rogers's many books and articles.

Thorne, Brian. (1998). *Person-centred counseling and Christian spirituality: The secular and the holy.* London: Whurr.

A depth-oriented exploration of the integration of Christian theology, pastoral care and person-centered therapy by an Anglican priest who is a practicing person-centered therapist.

Van Belle, H. (1980). *Basic intent and therapeutic approach of Carl R. Rogers.* Toronto: Wedge.

Perhaps the most comprehensive and intensive critique of person-centered therapy from a Christian perspective. Written specifically from a conservative Reformed viewpoint.

Vitz, P. (1977). *Psychology as religion: The cult of self-worship.* Grand Rapids, MI: Eerdmans.

A strong Christian critique of the "self-psychologies."

REFERENCES

Bellah, R., Madsen, R., Sullivan, W., Swindler, A., & Tipton, M. (1985). *Habits of the heart.* Berkeley, CA: University of California Press.

Bohart, A. C. (2003). Person-centered psychotherapy and related experiential approaches. In A. S. Gurman & S. B. Messer (Eds.), *Essential psychotherapies.* New York, NY: Guilford Press.

Bonhoeffer, D. (1954). *Life together.* New York, NY: Harper & Row.

Bozarth, J. D., Zimring, F. M., & Tausch, R. (2001). Client-centered therapy: The evolution of a revolution. In D. J. Cain & J. Seeman (Eds.), *Humanistic psychotherapies: Handbook of research and practice.* Washington, DC: American Psychological Association.

Boy, A., & Pine, G. (1982). *Client-centered counseling: A renewal.* Boston, MA: Allyn & Bacon.

Browning, D. S. & Cooper, T. D. (2004). *Religious thought and the modern psychologies* (2nd ed.). Minneapolis, MN: Fortress.

Cain, D. J., & Seeman, J. (Eds.). (2001). *Humanistic psychotherapies: Handbook of research and practice.* Washington, DC: American Psychological Association.

Carver, C. S., & Scheier, M. F. (2004). *Perspectives on Personality* (5th ed.). Boston, MA: Pearson Education.

Clouse, B. (1997). Can two walk together, except they be agreed? Psychology and theology—a journey together or paths apart? *Journal of Psychology and Theology, 25*(1), 38-48.

Cooper, T. D. (2003). *Sin, pride, and self-acceptance: The problem of identity in psychology and theology.* Downers Grove, IL: InterVarsity Press.

Corey, G. (2000). *Theory and practice of counseling and psychotherapy* (6th ed.). Belmont, CA: Wadsworth.

Dodgen, D., & McMinn, M. (1986). Humanistic psychology and Christian thought: A comparative analysis. *Journal of Psychology and Theology, 14,* 194-202.

Ellens, J. (1982). *God's grace and human health.* Nashville, TN: Abingdon.

Elliott, R. (2002). The effectiveness of humanistic therapies: A metaanalysis. In D. J. Cain & J. Seeman (Eds.), *Humanistic psychotherapies: Handbook of research and practice.* Washington, DC: American Psychological Association.

Evans, C. (1989). *Wisdom and humanness in psychology.* Grand Rapids, MI: Baker.

Evans, C. (1990). *Søren Kierkegaard's Christian psychology.* Grand Rapids, MI: Zondervan.

Farnsworth, K. (1985). *Whole-hearted integration.* Grand Rapids, MI: Baker.

Gaede, S. (1985). *Belonging.* Grand Rapids, MI: Zondervan.

Garfield, S. (1980). *Psychotherapy: An eclectic approach.* New York, NY: John Wiley.

Hybels, L. (2008). *Nice girls don't change the world.* Grand Rapids, MI: Zondervan.

Jacobs, J. (1975). A Christian client considers Carl Rogers. *Journal of Psychology and Theology, 3,* 25-30.

Kirschenbaum, C. (1979). *On becoming Carl Rogers.* New York, NY: Delta Books.

Kirschenbaum, H., & Henderson, V. M. (Eds.). (1989). *The Carl Rogers reader.* Boston, MA: Houghton Mifflin.

Kovel, J. (1976). *A complete guide to therapy.* New York, NY: Pantheon.

Lasch, J. (1979). *The culture of narcissism.* New York, NY: Warner Books.

Lewis, C. S. (1968). *A mind awake: An anthology of C. S. Lewis.* (C. Kilby, Ed.). New York, NY: Harcourt, Brace & World.

Markus, H. R., & Kitayama, S. (1991). Culture and the self: Implications for cognition, emotion, and motivation. *Psychological Review, 98,* 224-53.

McLemore, C. (1982). *The scandal of psychotherapy.* Wheaton, IL: Tyndale House.

McLemore, C. (1984). *Honest Christianity.* Philadelphia: Westminster.

McLemore, C. (2002). *Toxic relationships and how to change them.* Hoboken, NJ: Wiley.

Meier, S. (2004). *The elements of counseling.* Belmont, CA: Wadsworth.

Mouw, R. (1992). *Uncommon decency.* Downers Grove, IL: InterVarsity Press.

Myers, D. (1981). *The inflated self.* New York, NY: Seabury.

Norcross, J. C. (Ed.). (2002). *Psychotherapy relationships that work.* New York, NY: Oxford University Press.

Norcross, J. C., & Hill, C. (2004). Empirically supported (therapy) relationships: ESRs. *The Clinical Psychologist, 57.* Washington, DC: American Psychological Association.

Oakland, J. (1974). Self-actualization and sanctification. *Journal of Psychology and Theology, 2,* 202-209.

Oden, T. (1968). *Kerygma and counseling.* Philadelphia: Westminster Press.

O'Hara, M. (1994). Relational humanism: A psychology for a pluralistic world. In F. Wertz (Ed.), *The humanistic movement: Recovering the person in psychology.* Lake Worth, FL: Gardner Press.

Olson, R. P. (2002). Christian Humanism. In R. P. Olson (Ed.), *Religious theories of personality and psychotherapy: East meets west* (pp. 247-323). New York, NY: Hawthorn Press.

Ortberg, J. (1981). Accepting our acceptance: Some limitations of a Rogerian approach to the nature of grace. *Journal of Psychology and Christianity, 1,* 45-50.

Packer, J. I., & Howard, T. (1985). *Christianity: The true humanism.* Waco, TX: W Publishing.

Patterson, C. (1985). *The therapeutic relationship: Foundations for an eclectic psychotherapy.* Monterey, CA: Brooks/Cole.

Peck, S. (1983). *People of the lie.* New York, NY: Simon & Schuster.

Prochaska, J., & Norcross, J. C. (2006). *Systems of psychotherapy: A transtheoretical analysis* (4th ed.). Belmont, CA: Wadsworth.

Ridley, C. R. (1995). *Overcoming unintentional racism in counseling and therapy: A practitioner's guide to intentional intervention.* Thousand Oaks, CA: Sage.

Roberts, R. (1982). *Spirituality and human emotions.* Grand Rapids, MI: Eerdmans.

Roberts, R. (1985). Carl Rogers and the Christian virtues. *Journal of Psychology and Theology, 13,* 263-273.

Roberts, R. (1988). Unpublished class notes. Wheaton College Graduate School, Wheaton, IL.

Roberts, R. (1993). *Taking the word to heart: Self and others in an age of therapies.* Grand Rapids, MI: Eerdmans.

Rogers, C. (1961). *On becoming a person.* Boston, MA: Houghton Mifflin.

Rogers, C. (1980). *A way of being.* Boston, MA: Houghton Mifflin.

Rychlak, J. (1981). *Introduction to personality and psychotherapy* (2nd ed.). Boston, MA: Houghton Mifflin.

Schneider, K. J., & May, R. (1995). *The psychology of existence: An integrative, clinical perspective.* New York, NY: McGraw-Hill.

Schneider, K. J., Bugental, J. F. T., & Pierson, J. F. (Eds.). (2001). *The handbook of humanistic psychology: Leading edges in theory, research, and practice.* Thousand Oaks, CA: Sage.

Smedes, L. (1978). *Love within limits.* Grand Rapids, MI: Eerdmans.

Strupp, H., & Binder, G. (1986). *Psychotherapy in a new key.* New York, NY: Basic Books.

Sue, D. W., Carter, R. T., Casas, J. M., Fouad, N. A., Ivey, A. E., Jensen, M., LaFromboise, T., Manese, J. E., Ponterotto, J. G., & Vazquez-Nutall, E. (1998). *Multicultural counseling competencies: Individual and organizational development.* Thousand Oaks, CA: Sage.

Tan, S. (1987). Intrapersonal integration: The servant's spirituality. *Journal of Psychology and Christianity, 6*, 34-39.

Thielicke, H. (1964). *The ethics of sex.* (T. Doberstein, Trans.). New York, NY: Harper & Row.

Thorne, B. (1998). *Person-centred counselling and Christian spirituality.* London: Whurr.

Thorne, B. (2002). *The mystical power of person-centred therapy.* London: Whurr.

Tisdale, J. (1988, October). Humanistic psychotherapy assumptions and Christian counseling. Paper presented at the International Conference on Christian Counseling, Atlanta, Georgia.

Usher, C. H. (1989). Recognizing cultural bias in counseling theory and practice: The case of Rogers. *Multicultural Counseling and Development, 17*, 62-70.

Van Belle, H. (1980). *Basic intent and therapeutic approach of Carl R. Rogers.* Toronto: Wedge.

Van Belle, H. (1985a). Person-centered therapy. In D. Benner (Ed.), *Baker encyclopedia of psychology* (pp. 822-825). Grand Rapids, MI: Baker.

Van Belle, H. (1985b). Rogers, Carl Ransom. In D. Benner (Ed.), *Baker encyclopedia of psychology* (pp. 1016-1017). Grand Rapids, MI: Baker.

Van Kalmthout, M. A. (1995). The religious dimension of Rogers' work. *Journal of Humanistic Psychology, 35*, 23-39.

Van Leeuwen, M. (1985). *The person in psychology: A contemporary Christian appraisal.* Grand Rapids, MI: Eerdmans.

Vitz, P. (1977). *Psychology as religion: The cult of self-worship.* Grand Rapids, MI: Eerdmans.

Wagner, M. (1975). *The sensation of being somebody.* Grand Rapids, MI: Zondervan.

Wohl, J. (1982). Eclecticism and Asian counseling: Critique and application. *International Journal for the Advancement of Counseling, 5*, 215-222.

8

EXPERIENTIAL THERAPIES

Terri Watson, Tracey Lee, Stanton L. Jones and Richard E. Butman

*E*xperiential psychotherapies" commonly refers to the humanistic approaches to counseling that prioritize the necessity of a genuine, empathic therapeutic relationship and emphasize facilitation of in-session client experience as the primary task of treatment (Greenberg, Watson & Lietaer, 1998). Although only about 10 percent of psychotherapists in North America classify themselves as "humanistic" in their primary orientation (Cain & Seeman, 2001), experiential psychotherapies are widely utilized by clinicians, particularly to help clients with emotions in therapy. In fact, over a third of the therapists who identify themselves as "eclectic" integrate humanistic-experiential approaches with an additional orientation (Norcross & Prochaska, 1988, as cited in Bohart, 2003). Contemporary experiential therapies include *experiential* (Mahrer, 1996), *emotionally focused* (Greenberg, Rice & Elliott, 1993), *existential* (Yalom, 1980; Bugental, 1999; Schneider & May, 1995), *focusing-oriented* (Gendlin, 1996), and *gestalt* (Perls, Hefferline & Goodman, 1951; Yontef, 1993; Polster & Polster, 1973; Woldt & Toman, 2005; Brownell, 2008). Important contributions have been made by humanistic-experiential therapists (adapted from Cain, 2001) to child play therapy (Axeline, 1947; Moustakas, 1975; Oaklander, 1988; Bratton & Ray, 2001), psychotherapy with adolescents (Wheeler & McConville, 2001), parent training (Gordon, 2000), couple treatment (Johnson & Greenberg, 1994; Wheeler & Backman, 1997;

Johnson, 2004), and family therapy (Satir, 1983).

Historically, experiential psychotherapies have their roots in the "third force" humanistic psychologies influential in providing a more positive and holistic view of persons. In a similar way, contemporary experiential therapy proponents view themselves as providing an important corrective to the reductionist, medical-model approaches to psychotherapy that currently dominate the field and reduce clinical practice to a focus on psychopathology and manual-based treatments. In contrast, experiential psychotherapists emphasize the uniqueness and holistic views of the person, the importance of empathy and the therapeutic relationship, and client-directed treatments (Cain, 2001). Experiential psychologists see themselves as playing an important role in the continued "humanizing" of psychology and encouraging the discipline to broaden research methodology to include phenomenological approaches (Mahoney & Mahoney, 2001).

The beginning of the twenty-first century saw a resurgence of interest in the humanistic-experiential therapies. In 2001, two major handbooks of humanistic psychology were published (Cain & Seeman, 2001; Schneider, Bugental & Pierson, 2001). Emerging research on the effectiveness of the experiential therapies concludes that they are at least as effective as cognitive-behavioral therapy (Elliott, 2001) and propose that process-directive approaches such as emotion-focused, gestalt, and focusing-oriented approaches are particularly effective. Greenberg and his colleagues' research on emotion-focused therapy in particular has made a key contribution to renewed interest in the role of emotions in psychotherapy (Bohart, 2003). Contemporary experiential approaches have utilized findings from the science of emotion and cognition to develop approaches highly effective in treatment of a variety of client problems (Greenberg, Watson & Lietaer, 1998).

Christian mental health professionals are cautious in their use of the experiential psychotherapies. Humanistic psychotherapies are often associated with the self-help movement of the 1960s and 1970s, where unquestioning acceptance of humanistic approaches to healing contributed to the decline of Judeo-Christian values in North American culture (Vitz, 1977; Van Leeuwen, 1985; Browning & Cooper, 2004). Christian appraisals of humanistic therapies have found the individualistic, self-focused, subjective nature of this approach to be incompatible with Christian values

(Jones & Butman, 1991; Browning & Cooper, 2004) Yet many Christian clients demonstrate significant difficulties recognizing, regulating and understanding their emotions, and could therefore benefit from a more emotion-focused approach to psychotherapy that would help integrate their head with their heart.

Unfortunately, we have given minimal consideration to contemporary humanistic-experiential therapies in our Christian integrative efforts. In doing so we have overlooked a number of well-researched, clinically so-phisticated approaches to helping clients make sense of their emotional experience, which may be less antithetical to a Christian worldview than their historical counterparts. We propose that careful, reflective use of contemporary experiential approaches to psychotherapy can be beneficial for many Christian clients to assist them in improving their emotional intelligence, an undisputedly integral component of personal, spiritual and relational health. This chapter will provide an introduction and Christian appraisal of three of the more widely utilized experiential psy-chotherapies: contemporary existential therapy, emotionally focused therapy and gestalt therapy.

Descriptive Summary/Overview

Existential therapy. Existential therapy has been defined as "a dynamic ap-proach to therapy which focuses on concerns that are rooted in the indi-vidual's existence" (Yalom, 1980, p. 5). The word *existential* comes from the Latin *ex sistre*, meaning literally "to emerge or to stand out" (Finch & Van Dragt, 1985). Perhaps most accurately described as a diverse group of attitudes and philosophical approaches to psychotherapeutic practice, ex-istential therapy is generally not seen as a separate school of psychotherapy, like behaviorism or psychoanalysis. Nor does existential therapy seem to lend itself to neatly defined models of personality, psychopathology or psychotherapy. Yet the attitudes and values that undergird existential ther-apy have been incorporated into many systems of counseling and psycho-therapy; so that existentialism has become a "strange but oddly familiar" orientation for therapists of all persuasions irrespective of their control be-liefs and worldviews (Yalom, 1980).

Emotionally focused therapy. Emotionally focused therapy (EFT) is an integrative, experiential approach to individual and couples treatment pri-oritizing the role of emotions in psychotherapy (Elliott, Watson, Goldman & Greenberg, 2004). Psychotherapy is "emotionally focused" as the therapist helps clients attend to their moment-by-moment emotional experience. These experiential therapies offer the clinician sound theoretical and research-based models, as well as specific, practical techniques to facilitate in-session change. A recent meta-analysis of outcome studies of emotionally focused therapy found an effect size comparable to similar analyses of cognitive-behavioral therapies (Elliott, Greenberg & Lietaer, 2003). The process-experiential approach of Leslie Greenberg and the emotion-focused couples therapy approach of Sue Johnson, both Canadian psychologists, are the most widely researched and utilized EFTs.

Emotionally focused therapy, a process-experiential approach, has made a significant contribution to the understanding of emotions and cognition in psychotherapy (Greenberg, Rice & Elliot, 1993). The writings of Greenberg and colleagues integrate contemporary theories in the science of cognition and emotion with person-centered, gestalt, object relations and cognitive-behavioral psychology. This convergence of theory provides a sophisticated understanding of the centrality of emotions in the development of one's view of self, others and the world. Process-experiential therapy has been gaining wide attention in the field of psychology, as illustrated by its inclusion in the APA Psychotherapy Videotape Series "Handbook of Psychotherapy and Behavior Change" (Bergin & Garfield, 1994), and "Handbook of Psychotherapy Case Formulation" (Eels, 1997).

Susan Johnson, a graduate student of Greenberg in the 1970s, applied EFT to work with couples. Emotionally focused couples' therapy integrates experiential approaches with systems theory and attachment theory, and focuses on tracking couples' emotional responses to explore attachment injuries, needs and fears. By increasing emotional responsiveness, couples can become more securely attached and find a way out of their problematic patterns. EFT is one of the most effective contemporary couples' therapies as evidenced by promising outcome research (Johnson & Greenberg, 1994; Elliott et al., 2004).

Gestalt therapy. Gestalt therapy is perhaps the most phenomenological and pragmatic of the humanistic approaches to people-helping. The exclusive focus in gestalt therapy is on the here and now of immediate experience and the integration of fragmented parts of the personality. Gestalt therapists agree that emphasizing the *why* of behavior (i.e., insight and explanations) or analyzing past events is far less therapeutically useful than stressing the more overt *what* and *how* of present behavior, or the specific ways that unfinished business from the past intrudes on current functioning. Gestalt therapy appeals to those who value honesty, depth and wholeness in their experiences of self and others.

The founder of gestalt therapy, "Fritz" Perls, was trained as a psychoanalyst in Germany between the wars (as he discusses in his autobiography, 1969b). Gestalt therapy reflects certain emphases of the psychoanalytic tradition, especially the role of the defense mechanisms in the development of symptoms. The academic gestalt psychology tradition in Europe, which researched sensation and perception, also influenced Perls. The major characteristics of perception that these researchers stressed are summarized in such maxims as "The whole is more than the sum of the parts." Laura Posner Perls, Fritz's wife and a cofounder of gestalt therapy, is credited with the incorporation of existential philosophy and phenomenology into gestalt therapy practices, which resulted in a strong emphasis on the importance of the client-therapist relationship (Cain, 2001). Together with writer and philosopher Paul Goodman, the Perlses forged gestalt therapy as a creative merger of concepts from existential philosophy, phenomenology, psychoanalytic and gestalt psychology, and techniques developed in the creative or expressive arts (e.g., psychodrama). Before his death in 1970, Perls made considerable use of ideas from Zen Buddhism, Taoism and the human-potential movement. For years he was a resident "guru" in workshop and retreat centers across North America. A strong and forceful personality, Perls utilized a highly confrontational, controlling, dramatic and often insensitive approach, which became for many a model of the gestalt therapist (Cain, 2001).

Contemporary gestalt therapy has softened significantly from the antiintellectual, confrontational and cathartic "California model" to an emphasis on a supportive, collaborative approach (Yontef, 1998). Gestalt therapy has made great strides in articulating a more comprehensive theory of personality, psychotherapy (Woldt & Toman, 2005; Brownell, 2008), and in researching the effectiveness of this approach for different client problems (Strümpfel & Goldman, 2001). This clinical tradition of gestalt therapists clearly differentiate themselves from the "guru models" by focusing on professionalism, research, formal diagnosis and longer-term treatment (Strümpfel & Goldman, 2001). Although only a small percentage of clinicians in North America today would describe themselves as gestalt therapy purists, philosophically or methodologically, gestalt therapy is growing in popularity around the world (Brownell, 2010). In addition, many of the techniques of gestalt therapy have been widely adapted by other approaches to psychotherapy, including EFT, as this chapter will illustrate.

Philosophical Assumptions

Cain (2001) suggests that humanistic psychotherapies share several defining philosophical assumptions. First, people are viewed as self-actualizing, unique, self-aware, free to choose, responsible and holistic social beings. Second, humanistic-experiential therapists hold a pluralistic and constructivist view of reality in that people construct or create their own meanings. Third, phenomenology is held as the primary method in both therapeutic exploration and scientific inquiry. We will now explore the specific philosophical assumptions of existential, emotionally focused and gestalt psychotherapies.

Existential therapy. The philosophical assumptions behind existentialist psychology can be traced back to a nineteenth-century Danish Christian theologian and philosopher, Søren Kierkegaard (1813-1855), who is often regarded as the father of existentialism. He began his writings in a reaction against Hegel's idealism. In contrast to Hegel, who emphasized the objective and sought to systematically describe all of reality from this viewpoint, Kierkegaard contended that no philosophical system could adequately portray the human condition. Rather, he advocated a more balanced approach that focused more on subjectivity and human experience, but not to the neglect of objective experience. "Neither objectivism, with its emphasis on the publicly measurable and verifiable, nor subjectivism, with its accent on the private and emotional, can, in isolation, provide us with a complete picture of human functioning. Only taken together can they help us to understand our condition" (Schneider & May, 1995, p. 57). This shift in thinking laid the foundation for existentialist thought and ultimately existentialist psychology.

Kierkegaard also wrote on personality and selfhood. As cited by Schneider and May (1995, p. 57), famous quotes on this topic include "Personhood is a synthesis of possibility and necessity" and "The more consciousness, the more self." He talked about persons in their ability to limit ("finitize") and extend ("infinitize"), and believed that objectivists focused too much on the finite, while subjectivists focused too much on the infinite. Being too far to one side of the polarity or the other could cause psychopathology. In contrast, the psychologically healthy person is able to resolve seeming contradictions and synthesize both perspectives.

A generation later Friedrich Nietzsche (1844-1900), a German philosopher, built on the ideas of Kierkegaard to further extend the perceived autonomy, power and value of persons. He criticized Western civilization, and in particular the church, for its degradation and devaluation of the human person. In one of his later and most famous writings, *Thus Spoke Zarathustra*, he proposed a way of being he termed "superhuman" (*ubermenschlich*), advocating that this mode was more psychologically healthy and beyond what is typically attained by humans. He argued that a person seeking this mode of being must reject everything that is traditional and seek to live more authentically.

Although Kierkegaard and Nietzsche built the foundation for existentialist thought, it was Jean Paul Sartre (1905-1980), a French philosopher, who first used the term *existential*. In his most influential work, *Being and Nothingness* (1943/1965), he challenged the worldview of the time that he believed embraced an oppressive, spiritually destructive conformity (*mauvaise foi*, literally, "bad faith"). In contrast, he endorsed striving toward an "authentic" state of being.

Other key figures include Edmund Husserl (1859-1938), a Moravian Jewish philosopher and mathematician, who came to be known as the father of phenomenology, the systematic study of the phenomena that we experience. Husserl emphasized intentionality of human mental activity and sought to apprehend human experience in its living reality, including its full subjective and intersubjective context. Martin Heidegger (1889-1976), another important person in the history of existentialism, was a German philosopher who studied with Husserl. In his famous work *Being and Time*, he provided a method and foundation to examine the ontological structure of "being," which he termed *Dasein* (translated "there-being"). He also described the "existential," that is, the essential structures of human existence. Expanding on Kierkegaard's emphasis on the subjective, he contended that our Western tradition of separating the objective from subjecting was misleading because they are not distinct entities. Humans are both subjective and related to the external world.

At the same time that these philosophical forerunners were building a foundation for existentialist thought, behaviorism was taking root in the world of psychology. John Watson (1878-1958), an American psychologist, believed that that psychology would only advance by the study of observable behavior. He rejected introspection and theories related to the unconscious mind. In contrast, he believed that human behavior should be studied in terms of physiological responses to stimuli. Later known as behaviorism, this school of thought was criticized for being overly deterministic, mechanistic and reductionistic, opening the way for a new approach to therapy that considered the whole person and valued their subjective experience.

Based on the early philosophies of existentialism, combined with a reaction in the psychological world against the overly reductionistic approaches of the behaviorists, the first generation of existential therapists arose in Europe: Ludwig Binswanger (1881-1966), Medard Boss (1903-1990) and Viktor Frankl (1905-1997). Binswanger, a Swiss psychiatrist, was likely the first person to practice existentialism within a therapy context. In the 1930s he pioneered this new approach with his patients at the Kreuzlinger sanatorium. His writings were translated during the 1940s and 1950s, spreading his ideas among other psychiatrists and therapists in Europe and America. Boss, a Swiss psychotherapist and physician, built on Heidegger's term *Dasein* to coin a new term for this paradigm shift in psychology, *Daseinalysis*. This new approach sought to humanize medicine and psychiatry by utilizing existential principles in everyday practice, and ultimately, bringing greater justice and value to the patient.

Viktor Frankl, an Austrian psychoanalyst who was imprisoned in a Nazi concentration camp during World War II, is most known for his approach termed *logotherapy*. In his famous *Man's Search for Meaning* (1959/1984), he discussed the formative impact of his personal experiences in the concentration camps and later outlined the essentials of logotherapy, a type of existential therapy. Based on his concentration-camp experiences, he asserted that persons who have a purpose or meaning for what they are experiencing can endure and grow even in the most devastating of circumstances, while those without meaning will wither and languish, and, in a prison-camp setting, might actually die, all as a direct result of their apathy and despair. From this, Frankl came to believe that there is a fundamental drive to have a meaning or meanings to live by, what he called the "will to meaning."

In the United States, Rollo May (1909-1994) is the best-known existential psychologist. Suffering with tuberculosis for three years in a sanatorium, he studied the works of Kierkegaard and was drawn to existentialist psychology. With his writing of *Existence* (1958), the existentialist movement was launched in American psychology. More recently, Bugental, Yalom and Schneider have had a significant impact on shaping the character of the movement through their more clinically oriented efforts. Bugental is credited for an integrated version of existentialist psychology he calls an "existential humanistic" psychotherapy. Moreover, he has created a series of videotapes that demonstrate this method. Yalom's largest contribution to existentialist psychology was his landmark publication *Existential Psychotherapy* (1980), which provided an organization and structure to a field that had been criticized for lack of cohesiveness. Kirk Schneider has provided a detailed model for an "existential integrative" approach. This model includes psychiatric symptoms and underlying existential fears as well as a developmental model for working with clients in different stages of therapy (Schneider & May, 1995).

Although diversity is quite apparent between the various existentialist models of psychotherapy, commonalities are also evident in the philosophical underpinnings. First there is more of an emphasis on the subjective or the importance of a balanced approach that includes both the subjective and objective. Second, similar to all humanistic therapies, existential psychology emphasizes the value of persons and the capacity for self-actualization. Third, existential psychology assumes that all persons are free to make choices and decisions that will lead them to a more "authentic" way of "being."

Emotionally focused therapy. Process-experiential (PE) theory is impressive in its clear articulation of philosophical underpinnings. Theorists identify neo-humanism as the philosophical tradition that has provided the soil for the guiding values of this particular approach. Neo-humanism is described as a reformulation of traditional humanistic position, which places a high value on growth and self-determinism without adopting the more radically pure phenomenological and subjectivist positions of some humanists (Elliott, Watson, Goldman & Greenberg, 2004). Process-experiential theorists seek to steer a middle course between more radical constructivist and postmodern positions by adopting dialectical constructivism as the philosophical perspective on self and reality. Dialectical constructivists acknowledge the constraints of reality that impact an individual's freedom to construct meaning, and believe that "not all constructions fit the data equally well, although . . . several different accounts (or versions) might end up being plausible or valid" (Elliott, Watson, Goldman & Greenberg, 2004, p. 37).

Dialectical constructivism holds that people are "holistic, organismic beings, in whom affect, cognition, motivation, and action are continually integrated in everything they do" (Greenberg, Rice & Elliott, 1993, p. 5). Individuals create meaning moment by moment through the dialectical synthesis of emotional experience and cognitive processes. Thus PE therapists believe that people use "emotional intelligence" to understand themselves and the world around them by actively processing their experiences on both an emotional and cognitive level.

PE therapists drew from contemporary theory of emotion and cognition in this neo-humanistic formulation. Linking contemporary neuroscience with clinical practice, the authors utilize findings from the science of emotions and cognitions to demonstrate that human emotional experience is an important aspect of the way people organize, adapt and solve problems. In contrast to the widely held notion that emotions are related to intense physiological arousal and expression, which tends to relegate emotions to a phenomenon of little real importance, the authors define emotions as an "organized, meaningful, and generally adaptive action system" for the purpose of "providing feedback about reactions to situations to aid adaptation and problem solving" (Greenberg, Rice & Elliott, 1993, p. viii). Emotion serves the adaptive functions of providing meaning and salience to experience, providing motivation for goal setting, and enhancing interactions with others through communication and empathy. Maladaptive emotional regulation, on the other hand, is characterized by either emotional overarousal or emotional suppression and avoidance, and can contribute to a variety of conditions, including mood disorders, substance abuse, posttraumatic stress reactions or acting out behaviors.

The authors acknowledge that emotions are viewed negatively in contemporary North American culture, and emotional individuals are often perceived as immature and impulsive. Greenberg (2002) suggests, in actuality, the modernist position of overreliance on cognition is problematic and limiting:

> The tradition of believing that reason is the best way to guide life has short-changed the complexity of human experience. This view has led to an over-simplification of how emotions should be handled: that emotions either should be controlled—the mind-over-mood view—or they should be vented so that one can get rid of feelings—the polarized view. To deal effectively with emotions, people instead need to be able to identify on each occasion what type of emotion is being experienced and to determine the best way of dealing with this emotion in this situation. As Aristotle offered, being angry is easy: It is knowing when, where, how, in what intensity, and with whom to be angry that takes intelligence. (p. 40)

Thus, PE therapy becomes emotionally focused in its emphasis on trusting the client's emotions as a "therapeutic compass" that can direct the client's and therapist's attention to the important and primary needs, wishes, thoughts and feelings that can lead to effective emotional processing and good decision making (Elliott, Watson, Goldman & Greenberg, 2004).

PE psychotherapists identify themselves as "clinical humanists" who oppose attempts to reduce the practice of psychotherapy to standardized, manual-based treatments or psychopharmacological interventions alone. Instead, they advocate a process-oriented approach to psychotherapy that emphasizes the client-therapist relationship. They describe six important principles reflective of clinical humanism: (1) a primary focus on "experiencing" and immediacy as foundational to human experience, (2) client agency and self determination, (3) wholeness/interconnectedness of the different parts of persons, (4) cultural, personal and methodological pluralism and equality, (5) psychological presence and authenticity as key facilitative conditions of therapy, and 6) growth-oriented nature of persons based on "biologically adaptive internal processes that evaluate what is significant for well being" (Elliott et al., 2004, p. 22).

Gestalt therapy. Foundational to contemporary gestalt therapy are four philosophical and theoretical cornerstones: field theory, phenomenology, client-therapist dialogue (Strümpfel & Goldman, 2001; Yontef, 1998), and experiment (Roubal, 2009; Brownell, 2010). Field theory is a view of reality, developed by quantum physicists and applied to the social sciences by Lewin (1943), proposing the interconnectedness and interdependence of all phenomena. In gestalt therapy a person is always viewed in the context of her "field," which is in perpetual movement as she continually shifts and constructs her views of self and others. Interconnection between environment, experiences and personal characteristics help the client understand important patterns that are considered parts of the wholes. As the therapist engages with a client, he or she also becomes part of the client's "field."

The *phenomenological* foundations of gestalt therapy can be seen in the primacy of the client's here-and-now perceptions and experiences as the focus of psychotherapy. In essence the aim of gestalt therapy is to increase the client's *awareness* of his current experience of self, others and the environment so that client can make contact with parts of himself that have been split off and need to be integrated toward a holistic experience of self (Cain, 2001).

The influence of existential philosophy on gestalt therapy is evident in several key areas. *Client-therapist dialogue* is central to the therapeutic process and is defined as the establishment of a genuine, collaborative, authentic relationship with clients. Clients consider "ultimate concerns" as part of their ongoing experience, and are encouraged to take full responsibility for their thoughts, feelings and needs. These existential themes reflect the influence of existential theologians Martin Buber and Paul Tillich on Laura Perls (Cain, 2001). The history of gestalt therapy suggests that the founders of gestalt therapy chose to incorporate the more positive, relational existential philosophy of Kierkegaard, Buber and Tillich, versus the nihilistic existential philosophy associated with Sartre (Rosenfeld, 1977).

Integral to the phenomenological approach to psychotherapy is the role of *experiment* in the therapeutic process. A gestalt therapist might suggest to a client that she express her feelings or thoughts in a certain way to facilitate greater awareness and understanding. Examples include the empty chair technique, the two-chair dialogue or two-chair enactment (Elliott et al., 2004). Roubal (2009) describes experiments as "process oriented" where the "basic procedure is learning through doing" (p. 264). Different from therapist-directed techniques, experiments are "creative adventure(s) co-created by both therapist and client" (p. 263). Experiments allow the "figure" of the client to arise from the "field" of the client-therapist relationship and lead to greater awareness and understanding.

Personality Theory

Contemporary humanistic-experiential psychotherapies draw heavily from the personality theory of Carl Rogers's client-centered therapy. Common characteristics shared by most experiential psychotherapies include a view of the person as self-actualizing, unique, self-aware, responsible, free social beings (Cain & Seeman, 2001). "Personality as a process" is a view shared by person-centered, experiential and gestalt psychologies, and emphasizes the capacity of the individual to be present, available and open to all sources of information (Bohart, 2003). We'll now explore the specific personality theories espoused by existential, emotion-focused and gestalt psychotherapies.

Existential therapy. In existential psychology, personality theory is difficult to describe since "one does not experience a personality; one lives an experience" (Schneider, 2005, p. 151). Existential psychologists tend to believe that personality theory reduces human complexity to fundamental rules and universal laws. Rather than personality, existential psychologists tend to talk about persons in general or the human condition and the importance of becoming authentic. Persons are radically free and responsible for the quality of their existence and the choices they make. When existentialists describe persons, they stress the uniqueness of each person and emphasize that persons are always becoming. The nature of humanity is fluid, being defined and bounded only by the choices we make. We are all in a continual, ongoing process of becoming, according to existential theorists, trying to discover and make sense of our existence, with the goal of ultimately being authentic.

At the foundation of an existential understanding of persons is the delineation of the three levels of human existence, originally established by Binswanger (1946/1963). These are referred to as *umwelt, mitwelt* and *eigenwelt. Umwelt* refers to the physical or biological dimension of existence. *Mitwelt* is the relational aspect of existence. And *eigenwelt* is the personal, existential world of meaning (i.e., the reality that Kierkegaard termed *spirit*, the most important concept in an existential understanding of human nature). Because we are capable of self-awareness, we can reflect and make choices in all aspects of being, thereby increasing our possibilities for freedom.

Though individual existential therapists may vary in their specific personality theories, core assertions concerning the existential view of persons are summarized as follows and explained in more detail in the sections of abnormality and health (May & Yalom, 1984): (1) human beings are free and have to make a choice of whether or not to be authentic—we create ourselves through our choices; (2) we must make choices in a world without fixed meanings; (3) we are deeply related to others and to the world, but ultimately we are alone in the universe; (4) existence inescapably implies nonexistence or death, which is the source of much of our anxiety; (5) we grow through encounter with the abyss, our personal and private "dark night of the soul" (Van Dragt, 1985); (6) modern humans feel alienated, resulting in an "existential vacuum"; (7) psychological symptoms are symbols and signs of our despair, the meanings of which need to be explored; and (8) we tend to become dependent persons who want other persons, places and things to be "good to us on our terms" (cf. Finch, 1982).

Emotionally focused therapy. While humanistic-experiential techniques have historically focused on self-actualization as the primary human motivation, the process-experiential theory of personality integrates object relations, attachment theory and evolutionary psychology to suggest a relational component to the "growth tendency" that all human beings possess. Process-experiential therapy proposes that the primary motivations for individuals include the drive toward attachment to others and the drive toward mastery and exploration of the environment. The "developmental growth edge" is viewed as the self's healthy expression of needs and feelings, and is a trustworthy guide in life (Elliott et al., 2004, p. 227).

Process-experiential therapy places a strong emphasis on the role of emotional functioning in human personality development and behavior. The authors suggest that emotions provide a primary means of organizing one's experience through "emotion schemes," the internal synthesizing processes that integrate thinking and motivation with feelings and actions. Out of this synthesis, we develop "emotion beliefs" or "schemes" that are foundational for how we view the world. Emotion schemes, like grids, lodge in the unconscious through early experiences in the world and come into play in similar situations later in life. Each individual possesses a variety of related and possibly conflicting emotion schemes, which form the self structure. Elliott et al. (2004) suggest that a chorus of voices is a useful metaphor for the multiplicity of emotional schemes that operate on one's experience of the world. The process of knowing is conceptualized as an integration of emotions, beliefs and cognitions.

When a person pays attention to the information provided by emotional schemes, their ways of understanding and taking action in the world are brought into awareness. By attending to one's experience and cognitions, faulty emotion schemes can be brought into awareness and reorganized, resulting in greater understanding and integration. This process sounds similar to the cognitive-behavioral technique involving the identification of problematic "schemas." The major difference is that in PE our emotional experience, rather than cognition, is viewed as providing the client better access to primary needs, thoughts and emotions. Priority is given to helping clients become aware of the more negative or critical voices that contribute to faulty emotional schemes and restricted emotional experience, while at the same time supporting and enhancing the growth-oriented schemes (Elliott et al., 2004).

Gestalt therapy. Gestalt therapy posits a view of self that is distinctly relational, holistic and dynamic. As described by Strümpfel and Goldman (2001), a subjective sense of self emerges as the individual seeks to meet needs and wishes, and makes contact with boundaries in the environment. The self as subject can recognize itself as a part of the dynamic, ever-changing field of current experiences, relationships and environmental issues, and the experience of self is always understood at the point of contact. Thus, there is no understanding of self apart from contact with others. Individuals subjectively construct their personality on an ongoing basis as expressed needs make contact with boundaries, and the experiences are integrated into a holistic sense of self.

Theory of Abnormality

Existential therapy. All psychological symptoms, according to existential therapy, result at some level from decisions to be inauthentic. We too often prefer the illusory safety and security of superficial self-protectiveness over and against the more meaningful and significant life of the self.

We make a conscious and deliberate choice to live in a "state of forgetful-ness of being" (after Heidegger, 1962). We allow ourselves to become trapped in a web of self-deceit. Rather than directly confronting and dealing with the anxiety, we tend to lie to ourselves and others about the nature of our predicament and attempt to coerce or manipulate others into supporting this deception.

Living in the awareness of one's being produces authenticity, but this process is also full of anxiety. As we go through life, we confront impor-tant issues such as death, freedom, isolation and meaninglessness. Our responses to these issues could lead to psychopathology or well-being. Psy-chological symptoms such as depression or anxiety attacks are then seen as means of self-protection or avoiding existential anxiety and guilt, as when a person avoids confronting fears about one's own competence, meaningfulness and adequacy by being too anxious to ask for a promotion at work.

Furthermore, we must live responsibly in all of the levels of existence (*umwelt*, *mitwelt*, *eigenwelt*). All too often we adopt defenses and strategies that are inauthentic and self-deceptive, in that they evade freedom and responsibility (i.e., we lie to ourselves or others). This is especially evident when we are afraid to stand on our own two feet and are intimidated by the possibility of self-transcendence. We tend to lose touch with our own vital center, our capacity to be a self, and thereby commit ourselves to an inadequate philosophy of life that inevitably gives rise to symptoms. If we do not embrace both the freedom and responsibility of being a true self, we are choosing to stagnate or regress toward a more inauthentic and imma-ture life stance. It is not surprising, considering the enormity of this task, that so many in our confused society choose to become externally directed beings only, resulting in an inward sense of emptiness and hollowness, and a lack of any clear sense of identity or worth.

Emotionally focused therapy. Process-experiential therapists focus on three areas of emotional health and dysfunction in their conceptualization of personality (Elliott, Watson, Goldman & Greenberg, 2004). First, dys-function can occur as a result of maladaptive emotional schemes that in-hibit emotional processing of experience and lead to constricted emotional responses and incomplete views of self and others. For example, the trau-matized client may be unable to fully access more emotional or experiential aspects of their experience and become stuck in purely intellectual appraisals of self and others (Elliott et al., 2004). Second, dysfunction can also occur when a secondary emotion, such as anger, masks a more primary emotion, such as fear, resulting in decision making and actions that are maladaptive. Third, problems in emotional regulation occur when clients are unable to access, experience and use their emotions effectively in their lives. Individuals may be unable or fearful of accessing their emotions, or may feel besieged by painful and overwhelming emotional experiences. Problems in both overarousal and underarousal lead to faulty emotional processing and ineffective coping. Paradoxically, helping clients better access their emotion experience in therapy leads to better emotional regulation (Elliot et al., 2004).

Another aspect of dysfunction in process-experiential therapy involves problems in the dialectically constructed view of self. Normally, individuals experience numerous and sometimes paradoxical aspects of the self. However, when these conflicting parts of self are critical or hostile toward one another, clients become stuck in their problem solving or may experience painful, conflictual feelings. Attempts to suppress or silence one side of the conflicted "voices" is also dysfunctional and can lead to an incomplete understanding of the emotional schemes necessary for successful resolution (Elliott et al., 2004). The process of therapy brings both sides of this conflict into dialogue, leading to new information necessary for effective problem solving.

Process-experiential therapy delineates a number of common problems in emotional processing that occur. Problems include confusion or overreaction to a situation, unfinished business about a significant other, self-criticism, feelings of being "torn," blocked feelings and the occurrence of life events that violate a cherished belief. In therapy the clinician looks for the specific marker that signifies an emotional processing difficulty and makes a process diagnosis. Specific interventions are utilized to help the client reprocess their experience in a way that leads to new understandings and changed behavior.

Gestalt therapy. For the contemporary gestalt therapist, dysfunction occurs when a person is not sufficiently "in contact" with themselves and the situation in the present moment. As a result, they are unable to access all sources of information and make intelligent decisions (Bohart, 2003).

Dysfunction also can occur when boundaries are blurred, resulting in a disturbance in the healthy contact cycle. Examples of boundary disturbances include *projection,* where the client attributes their own unacceptable feelings to another; *introjection,* where the client uncritically accepts taboos or expectations that interfere and inhibit their experience; *retroflection,* where a client turns feelings toward another onto oneself in a hurtful manner; and *confluence,* which describes the process of ignoring or minimizing the way others are different than oneself (Strümpfel & Goldman, 2001; Cain, 2001). As with process-experiential therapy, gestalt therapists also make a process diagnosis to identify where clients are stuck in the contact cycle.

In short, psychopathology in gestalt therapy is the failure to take the risk of being a truly alive and responsible person. We surround our core being with multiple layers of deception. Our defense mechanisms are used extensively and rigidly to distort reality so that we lose any real sense of who we are or who we could become.

Theory of Health

Existential therapy. Although different existentialists may emphasize diverse existential domains, the importance of a person's response to significant life questions is at the heart of existential psychology's view of health. According to Yalom (1980), the quality of a person's life is determined by how one interacts with the four givens of human existence: death, freedom, isolation and meaninglessness. Overcoming anxiety related to death, for example, is a chief developmental task of childhood. Freedom is the absence of external structure. Although various existentialists disagree on the amount of true freedom, Yalom asserts that "the individual is entirely responsible for—that is, is the author of—his or her own world, life design, choices, and actions" (p. 9). Isolation, according to Yalom, occurs in three different forms: interpersonal, intrapersonal and existential. Interpersonal isolation is similar to loneliness, whereas intrapersonal isolation is detachment from parts of one's self. Yalom believed that existential isolation was the most basic form of isolation and referred to "an unbridgeable gulf between oneself and any other being" (p. 355). Finally, Yalom draws on the work of Salvatore Maddi to describe meaninglessness: "a chronic inability to believe in the true, importance, usefulness or interest value of any of the things one is engaged in or can imagine doing" (Yalom, 1980, p. 421). It is a person's response to these four ultimate concerns, according to Yalom, that can bring psychological well-being or anxiety and its maladaptive consequences.

In contrast to Yalom, more recent existential psychologists Schneider amd May (1995) assert that "the existential-humanist understanding of functionality rests on three interdependent dimensions: freedom, experiential reflection, and responsibility" (p. 150). Building off the work of May (1981), they contend that "it is only through struggle that freedom and destiny—capabilities and limits—can be illuminated in their fullness, substantively explored, and meaningfully transformed" (p. 152). By freedom they mean "the capacity to choose with the natural and self-imposed limits of living" (p. 151). Experiential reflection can be used to facilitate the process of being conscious of one's freedom and making appropriate choices. Responsibility is being accountable for one's choices or being "aware of creating one's own self, destiny, life predicament, feelings, and if such be the case, one's own suffering" (Yalom, 1980, p. 218).

In summary, existentialist psychology views persons as autonomous agents capable of freely making choices that may lead to a meaningful life or psychopathology. The mature person uses reflection to be conscious of their choices and take accountability for their decisions. As we develop a clear sense of identity, we have an increasing ability to make conscious and deliberate choices about whether we will be a self in truth and achieve the goal of authenticity. The healthy adult has a clear commitment to becoming authentic, which includes having a well-formulated philosophy of life that will guide current and future actions.

Emotionally focused therapy. Emotional intelligence is defined as "The ability to access, make use of, and regulate emotions" (Elliott, Watson, Goldman & Greenberg, 2004, p. 19). Healthy emotional regulation occurs when individuals are able to access and process their moment-by-moment emotional experience. Adaptive emotional regulation indicates that an individual can "use emotions adaptively to regulate distress and to promote needs and goals" (p. 32). Healthy individuals can experience a direct emotional response that matches the situation, and then determine the necessary and appropriate action (p. 28). The authors suggest that such adaptive emotional responses have ensured survival of our species, and continue to be important "internal guides" today.

Healthy emotional schemes lead to flexible self-organization and the ability of the person to be "a complex, ever-changing, organized collection of various part aspects of self" (Elliott et al., 2004, p. 37). The healthy self "continually constructs itself" (p. 37), thus, it is not viewed as a fixed or permanent structure. From a dialectical constructivist perspective, the healthy self contains a multiplicity of parts that can be metaphorically understood as "different voices" that can be organized cohesively both in the moment and across time. The authors indicate that the "music" of the voices of the self is much more akin to the improvisational style of a jazz piece than the structural composition of traditional, classical music.

Gestalt therapy. Gestalt therapists propose a "contact process" or "need cycle" to describe healthy development of the self-concept. First, needs and impulses emerge and are expressed in emotions, which guide intentions and actions. Second, contacting occurs when particular needs and feelings are attended to, selected and transformed into action. Third, full contact occurs and gratification is achieved. Finally, the full awareness of the experience is incorporated and a subjective sense of self is constructed (Strümpfel & Goldman, 2001).

Individuals who are fully present in the moment and aware of their experience of self, others and the environment are said to be "in contact." Being in contact also involves a good sense of boundaries between parts of self, self and others, and people and objects in the environment. The healthy self in contact feels acceptable, worthy and cohesive (Yontef, 1998)

Psychotherapeutic methods

Experiential psychotherapies share in common the use of phenomenology as the primary method for understanding the person in psychotherapy (Cain, 2001). In addition, empathy and the therapeutic relationship are viewed as necessary conditions to effective psychotherapy. Unlike Rogers, however, experiential psychotherapists tend to be more active and directive in facilitating in-session experiencing with a focus on the emotional processing of therapeutic material. Freedom, choice and responsibility are key themes in the therapeutic process; thus, experiential therapists view themselves as partners with their clients rather than experts (Cain, 2001).

Existential therapy. Existential therapy is difficult to describe since it is less a coherent and consistent set of theories and techniques and more of an approach or attitude about how best to help others grow. The core goals in existential therapy are to enable clients to realize that they are free to make choices about the direction of their lives and to help them make commitments that hopefully will assist them in becoming more authentic in their existence. This is done not through mechanistic techniques, but through the highly personal encounter between therapist and client.

Existential therapists are very concerned about the risk of objectifying (making objects of) clients. Schneider and May (1995) describe the first task of the existential therapist as cultivating a "therapeutic presence" that serves as "ground" for the client. They contrast the type of therapist who serves as a "problem solving doctor" with that of a "healer who is available for inter- and intrapersonal connection" (p. 157). The latter is the role of the existential therapist. From here, the therapist "activates" the client's growth process by listening, guiding, instructing and requiring. Drawing from the work of Bugental (1987), Schneider and May describe the process of listening as drawing clients out, encouraging them to keep talking and obtaining their stories without contamination from the therapist. In *guiding*, the therapist "gives directions and support to clients' speech, keeps it on track, and brings out other aspects" (p. 157). *Instructing* means to give information that has objective or rational support. Finally, *requiring* provokes the client to change by bringing in the therapist's personal and emotional perspectives.

In the process of existential therapy clients will become more aware of issues that have blocked them from experiencing authenticity in the past. As they become more confident in their own identity and purposes, it is the therapist's job to assist and guide the client to synthesize their sense of personal meaning for the life that they are deliberately choosing to pursue. In this process, they will become more intentional about living according to their own values and goals.

It should also be noted that existential therapy is not well suited for every person or every psychological issue. Rather, existential therapy appears to be particularly well suited for individuals who must confront developmental and personal crises. "Existential concerns" are widespread in our culture, and many struggle with issues like making choices, dealing with freedom and responsibility, coping with anxiety and guilt, or finding a sense of direction in life.

Emotionally focused therapy. The theory and techniques of the process-experiential approach were developed in response to the authors' observations of hundreds of hours of taped psychotherapy sessions, an approach to theory development that is reminiscent of Carl Rogers's phenomenological method. The theorists observed that there seemed to be certain key moments in psychotherapy where significant shifts in feeling, thinking and action occurred for the client. The theorists set out to identify how these change events occurred. They identified common problems that occurred in session where clients became stuck in their ability to process emotions. Therapeutic tasks were developed to address these problems utilizing commonly practiced gestalt techniques. The role of the clinician, then, is to identify the client "marker" that is suggestive of a particular processing problem occurring, then to direct the therapeutic task in a way that promotes a shift or new understanding of the current difficulties. For example, the marker for "unfinished business" would prompt the clinician to implement the empty chair technique to assist in exploration of problematic emotional schemes and facilitate a more adaptive integration of memories, thoughts and emotions.

In emotion-focused therapy, clients are encouraged to process previously denied and disallowed emotions in session to reorganize their understanding of self and the world, taking into account the important internal resource of their emotions. A key assumption is that "changing emotion requires experiencing it" (Greenberg, 2002, p. 7). The goal of the emotion-focused therapy is not to encourage the client to act on impulse or to just do what feels right. Rather, clients engage in a dialectical process of integrating emotions with thoughts, beliefs, needs and values.

> Reason is best integrated with emotion, to help guide it once it is aroused. Then people are not working against their emotions, trying not to have them; instead, they are working with their emotions, trying to guide them by integrating their social and cultural knowledge and their personal values and goals with their body-based emotional knowledge. (Greenberg, 2002, p. 35)

Process-experiential therapy involves both "relationship principles" and "task principles," and seeks to balance an emphasis on both the development of a genuine, empathic relationship and the tasks or techniques of therapy. The clinician's role is to create a safe environment through empathic attunement to the client. The clinician identifies where the client is stuck in their emotional processing of experience and makes a process diagnosis. The identification of a marker of a specific emotional processing problem is key in guiding the therapist to implement a specific in-session task. The therapist directs the client's cognitive and affective processing to the areas that are previously avoided. The client is able to process experiences in a new way, construct new emotional schemes, and eventually make changes in their perceptions of self and others. The reorganization of schemes leads to new understandings, problem-solving abilities and interpersonal changes.

The two-chair dialogue for "splits" is an example of a type of in-session integration where the client is directed to utilize emotions constructively in psychotherapy while still integrating beliefs and values into the process of decision making and change. Specifically, this technique utilizes the gestalt two-chair technique for helping clients deal with conflicts between "shoulds" and "wants." The therapist, directing the process, helps the person experientially express each side of the conflict and negotiate compromise.

The processing difficulty involves the internal split between the emotions and needs of the individual and their beliefs/values/expectations. Two sides of the self, or schemes, are in conflict. The needs/wants/feelings of the person are at odds with the cognitions, values and perceived expectations. Clients experiencing this processing difficulty will exhibit a marker involving self-evaluative split, such as self-criticism and feelings of being "torn." Two aspects of the self are in conflict. The individual is caught between the "internal critic" and the "experiencing self." The PE therapist presumes that what prevents the client from moving forward is a failure to fully experience all dimensions (that is, both sides) of their current reality.

The client fully explores his or her needs, feelings and emotions, and conflicting expectations, values and beliefs by use of two chairs, one to represent each side of the split. Typically, clients are much more able to articulate one side of the response than the other, and so the therapist may start with the easier-to-express side. Specific, prescribed strategies may be used in the session to draw out the suppressed side of the experience. As the schemas of both sides are fully explored, the therapist encourages dialogue between them, which eventually results in a softening of the critical side while still maintaining important beliefs and values. The goal is the development of an "integrative solution," which may involve giving greater weight to needs and feelings in decision making, or consciously setting aside these needs and feelings for the sake of the guiding values and beliefs. Problem solving is enhanced by full exploration of feelings and needs as well as cognitions and values, leading to solutions that integrate the head and the heart. The client acknowledges previously disowned feelings and needs while still maintaining integrity and values. Emotions and beliefs are brought into harmony.

Gestalt therapy. The gestalt therapy treatment process can be described as follows. First, the therapist provides an empathic, genuine "presence" in attempts to "make contact" with clients and "start where they are." Second, clients and therapist utilize the phenomenological method by exploring here-and-now experiences through use of various "experiments" or techniques that help the clients access their feelings and thoughts in an immediate way. Clients integrate fragmented parts of their personality by focusing on the direct experience of the here and now. Working primarily through the observable nonverbal and bodily clues, the therapist works toward the goal of assisting the clients in seeking fewer environmental or external supports and toward greater integrity and personal responsibility. By focusing exclusively on the here and now of immediate experiencing, clients develop greater self-initiative and risk-taking. Biological needs are then met in more adaptive and constructive ways. The ultimate goals of gestalt therapy are (1) growth into self-support, (2) personal integration of the fragmented experience of self, and (3) greater integrity and responsibility with reference to self (Yontef, 1998).

Gestalt psychotherapy is perhaps best known for the creative psychotherapeutic techniques its practitioners have developed to facilitate in-session awareness of immediate experience. Contemporary gestalt therapists utilize two general types of interventions to focus clients' awareness on their feelings and experiences. "Microtechniques" are the therapist's moment-by-moment interventions with the client utilized to facilitate greater awareness. Examples of microtechniques include *repetition*, where a client is instructed to repeat a word or gesture several times (as when a passive client who demonstrated mild resistance to the therapist is told "shake your head again"). *Exaggeration* is utilized by asking the client to repeat a statement or behavior and intensify it (as when a client who denies experiencing anger is told "do that gesture again; what is going on for you when you hit your fist in your hand?"). *Identification* involves asking clients to direct their attention toward a bodily sensation and describe the experience ("what is that tension in your stomach saying to you now?"). *Representing* involves the use of drama to allow clients to express their perceptions of significant others in their lives. *Psychodrama* is an example of this type of dramatic enactment and is often utilized in group settings (adapted from Strümpfel & Goldman, 2001).

Macrotechniques refer to the use of interventions to promote in-session experiencing. Gestalt "chair work" is the most widely utilized example of this. The two-chair technique involves directing clients to act out different "splits" or polarities within their personalities by imagining parts of themselves on an empty chair. The empty chair technique is utilized to facilitate awareness of "unfinished business" as clients imagine a significant other on the empty chair and engages in dialogue with him or her. Dream analysis is also a widely used gestalt technique. Clients may act out parts of their dreams, or are asked to identify themselves with a particular character in the dream and narrate the dream from that perspective (Strümpfel & Goldman, 2001).

Gestalt therapists propose that therapy is "dialogic" in focusing on various "polarities" of experience. For example, therapy focuses on both the therapeutic relationship and therapeutic techniques simultaneously. Likewise, for the gestalt therapy client, change occurs naturally depending on the quality of contact made in the client-therapist relationship, and the quality of the "awareness work" (Yontef, 1998).

Clients are encouraged to experiment between sessions with various techniques and exercises, called "actively guided phenomenological experiments," for increasing their awareness and contact (Yontef, 1998, p. 92). Homework can involve encouraging clients to experiment with new behaviors, then pay attention to their resulting thoughts and feelings. Clients are also encouraged to "stay with" certain emotions or reactions during the week as a means of increasing the client's awareness between sessions.

Christian Appraisal

Philosophical assumptions. Since the humanistic-experiential-existential therapies share many of the same philosophical foundations, we will start our critique by focusing on the three defining characteristics underlying these approaches as suggested by Cain and Seeman (2001): humans as self-actualizing, the constructivist view of self and the phenomenological method.

Critique of self-actualization. Browning and Cooper (2004) propose important philosophical critiques of the humanistic conceptualizations of self-actualization from a Judeo-Christian perspective. They propose that humanistic theorists made a significant error in elevating self-actualization from a descriptive term to the level of an ethical norm and moral imperative for human beings. Consequently, experiential therapies assume that: "self-actualization can serve as an ethical norm, that what promotes it is 'good' and what blocks it is 'bad,' that humans should be exhorted to self-actualization, and that self-actualization provides a single fundamental goal for all human beings" (p. 66). The concept of self-actualization may be useful in describing a "growth orientation" that may be part of what it means to be created in the image of God, but it clearly falls short of providing an ethic for Christian living.

Browning and Cooper (2004) also question the moral philosophy that would suggest that self-actualization is the objective of the human life and is a reliable guide for decision making. The authors suggest that humanist theorists are practicing ethical egoism: "Self-actualization is the nonmoral good that all humans should pursue to the degree that it is possible" (p. 67). The broader issue in their analysis is that psychotherapy systems often take somewhat legitimate descriptions of "nonmoral goods," such as feelings, needs, awareness and so forth, and then arrange them in contrasting priority with other facets of human experience. In so doing, the psychological system becomes a moral system, because a moral system is, at least in part, a comparative ranking of the "goods" and "not goods" that we face. For example, humanistic-experiential therapies take a nonmoral good, such as emotional awareness, and transform this experience into a moral imperative by proposing that emotional awareness should take precedence over other human experiences as a source of wisdom. Experiential therapy arranges needs into a quasi-moral system by prizing experiencing above all else. This is clearly in contrast to a Christian moral system where loving God and loving others provides the moral imperative for the Christian life. Our ethical lives are just not that simple; no dimension of human life has escaped the Fall.

Browning and Cooper (2004) suggest that a final problem with this ethical egoist position of humanist theorists is that it assumes an inherent harmony in reality. The authors write: "This view postulates that the actualization of all potentialities is basically complementary, that differing potentialities can never really conflict, and that, for this reason, all people can pursue their own interests without fear that they will conflict with or be extinguished by the interests of other people" (p. 69). This view of the harmony of nature leads to a minimization of the need for moral reflection, decision and behavior, and of an ethic of care for others; in this simplistic system, "The only moral task to be concerned with is one's own growth" (p. 80).

Again, this is just too simplistic. The authors make the important point that this assumption of "pre-established harmony" as justifying the pursuit of one's own gain is akin to the values of a capitalistic society: "One could argue that humanistic psychology is the psychology most compatible with the values and worldview of capitalism" (p. 77). Experiential therapies optimistically assume that all human needs will ultimately harmonize, with the result that if everyone were truly doing what was best in his or her own eyes, we would be doing what was best for everyone else. In short, experiential therapies are far less clear on how greater self-awareness in the present moment will translate into a responsible and well-formulated interpersonal ethic. The assumption appears to be that individual integrity and wholeness are the necessary and sufficient conditions for producing corporate change and instilling responsibility. This is an incomplete ethic at best (cf. Prov 14:12).

Olson (2002) suggests that a Christian humanistic psychology must look beyond self-actualization as a primary human need. Olson suggests that the "reconciled life" is the goal for the Christian, rather than the "actualized life." He writes, "In Christian humanism, the need for reconciling life with God, self, and others constitutes the overarching need and the primary purpose by which all other motives are ordered" (p. 255). He suggests that the Christian humanist include spiritual, moral and historical dimensions for primary human needs and motivations:

> In the spiritual dimension are the needs for transcendence and meaning, authenticity and love. In the moral dimension are the needs for integrity of character, the need to abide by one's conscience, to fulfill one's sense of

duty, to be virtuous, and to act ethically. In the historical dimension are the needs to remember one's collective heritage and personal past, and to anticipate a meaningful future while living fully in the present. (p. 255)

Olson (2002) suggests "the goal is a person (body-mind-spirit) who is reconciled with God, who emulates the life of Christ, and whose spirit is guided and sustained by the Spirit" (p. 262).

Browning and Cooper (2004) also point out important inconsistencies between the ethical egoist pursuit of self-actualization and the value of mutual and *agape* love in the Christian tradition. Mutual love, they argue, requires a significant degree of obligation and self-transcendence, rather than pursuit of one's own actualization and the assumption that this will harmonize with others who are doing the same.

Feminist critics within humanistic psychology have offered similar critiques of the individualistic, autonomous self that has been the traditional goal or outcome of the self-actualization process. They propose "relational humanism" as a necessary postmodern corrective to this very Western and egocentric conceptualization of personhood (O'Hara, 1994). O'Hara describes a new relational humanism as one that "understands selves as contextual and relational, that will acknowledge individual subjectivity in all its glorious diversity, that will establish and value relational norms of mutuality, civility, responsibility, and accountability" (p. 329). Relational humanists views environmental and contextual factors not as a "hindrance" to growth and development, but rather "the very source of who we are and of who we might possibly become" (p. 328).

Critique of constructivist views of self. From a Christian worldview, contemporary humanistic psychotherapy is most in danger of extreme subjectivity leading to relativism or pluralism. In subjectivism the person's conscious experience is at the center of determining reality and truth. Although there is certainly room for the subjective in the Christian life, the main problem with the experiential therapies, from a Christian view, is the perceived overemphasis on the subjectivity of our inner experience to the neglect of any acknowledgment of external moral standards, potentially leading to relativism. In relativism there is no room for external standards or an omnipotent God who has lovingly designed creation and provided meaning for his creation. Instead, truth is determined by each individual. Having no anchor from which to explore life's difficult questions could be unsettling in times of crisis. For example, when coming to terms with death, the person who does not have knowledge of God's grace or eternal life risks significant distress. For them, purpose, meaning and hope are limited to this life. In contrast, the Christian has a frame of objective truth from which to stand in life's difficulties. Moreover, if we limit our understanding of morality to our own inner experience, we lose the concept of sin, which provides a rich foundation for grace and forgiveness in the Christian life.

Critique of phenomenological method. Certain emphases in the experiential therapies on the importance of the phenomenal world can be appreciated. Indeed, much of Anglo-American psychology is probably overly objective, deterministic or detached from the "subject" (Van Leeuwen, 1985). But experiential therapies run the risk of overstating the case for conscious and contemporary experience (Korchin, 1976). There is a clear ahistorical bias in the experiential therapies that risks ignoring the fact that who we are at any moment in our development surely reflects where we have come from. Our capacities to deal with the demands of everyday living can surely be increased by a deeper recognition of how we have coped in the past and what skills and sensitivities we need currently to adapt even more effectively. This ahistorical bias in the phenomenological method has also been critiqued as a cultural bias in the humanistic psychotherapies toward cultures that value a strong sense of connection with their ancestry, such as American Indian culture (Usher, 1989). Thus, this exclusive focus on one's experience in the moment is inconsistent with a Judeo-Christian perspective and the perspectives of many ethnic groups.

Another problem with the experiential therapy understanding of human nature is the tendency to give the subjective psychological perspective on any phenomenon preeminence over other valid perspectives, or the tendency to assume that the psychological perspective is the most basic perspective (Vande Kemp, 1986). In the experiential therapies the problem is the extreme emphasis on the subjectivity of our inner experience. By understanding the reality "out there" only through the reality "in here," we run the risk of becoming almost reductionistic ourselves. The radical openness to experience so deeply valued in the experiential therapies can all too easily degenerate into an almost excessive emotionalism. Since a true understanding of our self depends on a deep appreciation of a reality external to ourselves (i.e., God), we must become fully cognizant of how we limit our full awareness of the nature of personhood when we adopt an epistemological stance of extreme relativism and subjectivity. We must understand the limits of our capacities to know or to be known.

Our identity as Christians is deeply rooted in a growing sense of our place in the march of redemptive history, nurtured in the context of Christian community. We feel strongly that it is a decided risk in experiential therapy that one can be so "fully alive to the moment" that one loses all sense of a proper respect for the past or appropriate concern about the future. The potential distrust of "right thinking" (i.e., orthodoxy) can result in such extreme detachment from external reality and transcendent absolutes that there is little engagement in the demands of everyday living beyond the personal realm. Although it may be argued that we exaggerate the risks involved, from an eternal perspective, we should not take these concerns lightly. We fear that one of the main virtues of experiential therapy, self-understanding, might potentially lead to the pride inherent in a growing sense of self-sufficiency rather than self-support.

Christian Appraisal: Model of Personality

Existential therapy. Before critiquing the assumptions behind existentialist psychology theory of personality, it is important to point out that existentialist philosophers range dramatically in terms of their beliefs regarding the supernatural. For example, Nietzsche denied the supernatural and therefore inherently believed that there was no higher calling than to improve the human condition. In contrast, there are also Christian existentialist philosophers such as Kierkegaard who have grounded their work in the Christian faith and therefore have already integrated their Christian beliefs with existentialism. Since the writings of Christian existentialists are inherently compatible with the Christian faith, their writings will not be critiqued in this section. In contrast, this section will critique the more general principles of existentialist psychology that are common to writers of every theological and philosophical background.

What does Christianity have to say about existential psychology's approach to understanding the nature of human beings and personality structure? First we will examine existential psychology's view concerning the status of human beings. In contrast to behaviorism, which reduces persons to the study of observable behavior based on physiological responses to external stimuli, existentialist psychology emphasizes a whole person who has the capacity to think, imagine, introspect and develop a sense of meaning in life. One could argue that this latter position is more consistent with the Christian faith, which also construes humans as more than animals that can be trained to achieve certain behavior patterns. In fact, the Christian faith asserts that humans are created in the image of God, with purpose and dignity. When the Bible talks about humans, it talks about them as having bodies, minds, spirits and souls. In contrast, animals do not have spirits or souls in the biblical texts. Similarly, Olson (2002) argues that the existential view of persons as "motivated beings in the process of becoming" is more consistent with a Christian viewpoint than the perspective of behavioral psychology which does not tend to differentiate human beings from animals.

> A behavioral theory that attempts to explain motivation in terms of eliciting, discriminative, and reinforcing stimuli originating externally in one's environment is not compatible with Jesus' emphasis upon inner intentions and human motives. He rejected particularly a moralistic meritocracy in which motivation is understood in terms of earned rewards or deserved punishments. Moreover, Jesus was critical of behavioral conformity to religious and moral commands based upon formal obedience, that is, performing only because it is commanded. That is the error of legalism expressed religiously in one's question for holiness as a form of works righteousness and self-justification. In the entire New Testament, the most common motivational terms are cognates of will, want, desire, need, choose, and wish. Three primary terms—want, will, and desire—appear about 255 times in the New Testament, and more than all other motivational terms combined. These terms suggest that persons are motivated beings in the process of becoming. Consequently, to comprehend human behavior we must understand what a person wants and intends to do. (p. 253)

Similarly, Moss (2001) points out that Christian writers such as Kierkegaard viewed Christ "as symbolizing that the divine principle entered the human, elevating and glorifying the human" (p. 9). He bases this notion on Paul's letter to the Romans that discusses creation "giving birth to a new glorified human, liberated from enslavement to the law and made perfect in Christ (Roman 8)." He continues his point by citing Irenaeus, an early Christian writer who wrote that the glory of God was made known when Christ became human. According to Moss, Irenaeus taught "that the essence of being human is the potential and destiny to actualize the full-orbed self in its material and spiritual, mundane and transcendent dimensions. Thus he laid the foundation stone for what has come to be known as humanistic psychology" (p. 9).

In contrast, one could argue that the elevation of humans in existentialist psychology may have gone too far. When Nietzsche talks about the "superhuman," he assumes that this ultimate level of transcendence can actually be achieved in this life. In contrast, the Christian faith teaches that in this life, we have been tainted with sin (Rom 3:23; 1 Jn 1:8) and can not reach the "superhuman" status on our own (Eph 2:8-9). The Christian faith is clear that Jesus was the only "superhuman" who was able to live a perfect life, free from sin (Heb 4:15). Moreover, the mechanism for growth in existentialist thought is only partially compatible with the Christian faith. As the Bible clearly states, it is God who has redeemed the human (Jn 3:16, Eph 2:8-9) and continues to work within the human person (Phil 1:6). As pointed out by Moss (2001), the Christian faith clearly teaches that only through Jesus can persons come to their full potential.

When talking about human nature from an existentialist point of view, it is also important to comment on freedom. Existentialism emphasizes humans as free autonomous agents, but what does the Christian faith teach about our freedom? Are we radically free to make choices and take responsibility for our actions as proposed in existentialist philosophy? Historically, there has been an animated debate concerning human "free will" stemming back to the fifth century when Pelagius, a British monk, raised the question of whether God's grace is necessary to obey God's commands. According to Pelagius, there was no original sin, and therefore, humans have free will to behave morally and seek God of their own accord. After much debate between Augustine and other theologians at the time, these ideas were condemned by the church at the third ecumenical council in Ephesus (A.D. 431), which stated that humans did not have such free will, but rather, required the grace of God for redemption and justification.

Nevertheless, similar debates occurred in following centuries. In the sixteenth century Luther argued a similar point with Erasmus. The debate continued between Calvin and Arminius at the Synod of Dort. Although the church has consistently condemned free will and endorsed a position that requires the grace of God, freedom is still an important topic in Christianity. The question remains: From what have we been set free? Romans 6:6-19 explains that a person can have "freedom in Christ" so that once a person is "saved" they are no longer under the power of sin and have been set free to do good works (Rom 6:6-19). In contrast, the person who is without Christ is not free and remains a slave to sin (Rom 6:20). As existentialist psychology does not use the language of sin, it is difficult to compare and contrast the existentialist and Christian notions of freedom. Clearly, human beings make choices every day; however, the extent to which these are directed by a sovereign God or the function of human decision remains a debatable topic between Christians. On one thing we can all agree, that a righteous God holds all human beings morally culpable to some significant degree for our actions, in spite of the fact that none of us made the choice to be born with a sin nature and that many of the circumstances and events that shape us are largely beyond our control.

Emotionally focused therapy. The authors of process-experiential therapy clearly identify themselves within the discipline of humanistic/experiential psychology, and the critiques outlined previously also apply to a Christian appraisal of emotion-focused therapy. However, several factors suggest that the process-experiential model of personality may be more appropriate for Christian clients than other experiential approaches. Emotion-focused therapy makes room for cognition and belief as a part of the dialectical synthesis. The internalized values of the religious client are brought to bear on the way they process experiences and construe meaning. Greenberg (2002) writes that emotions have an important role in healthy living but are not the only guide to living; rather, emotion moves us and gives us passion for life, while reason guides us. Process-experiential therapy proposes that both are necessary to healthy living.

In contrast to the early humanistic/experiential therapists who gave emotions free reign, the process-experiential psychotherapists utilize contemporary neuroscience to provide the client with the means of bringing together reason and emotion in decision making. This holistic view of persons is an attractive contrast to other psychological approaches that tend to focus primarily on either cognition or emotion. In addition, the dialectical constructivist view of personality provides the opportunity for greater prioritization of values, goals and beliefs in decision making, certainly more attractive to the Christian client and therapist.

Humanistic/experiential techniques have historically focused on self-actualization as the primary human motivation. This individualistic perspective has been heavily critiqued by both postmodern and Christian writers. Process-experiential therapy, on the other hand, integrates object relations and attachment theory to suggest individuals are also motivated by the need for attachment to others and mastery and exploration of the environment. With this theory of motivation in mind, emotion-focused therapy gives relationships a more primary role in views of health. Certainly, this is more consistent with a Christian worldview that places loving God and others at the center of the Christian life and experience.

Gestalt therapy. Christian mental health professionals interested in the theory and practice of gestalt therapy should familiarize themselves with the writing of Philip Brownell, an active contributor to the contemporary gestalt therapy literature who works from a theistic worldview. Our Christian appraisal of the theory and practice of gestalt therapy will introduce Brownell's integration of Christian spirituality and gestalt therapy.

Brownell (2011) identifies themes of both Eastern and Western spirituality in the development of gestalt therapy, and proposes that gestalt therapy has not sufficiently integrated Western theistic relational perspectives into theory and praxis. To be truly holistic, Brownell insists, gestalt therapy needs to include the spiritual experiences of the client and move beyond a purely naturalistic view of experience to also incorporate spiritual beliefs and attitudes. He proposes the term *pneumenal field* to signify a spiritual attitude or approach that incorporates the client's experience of a real relationship with an imminent God (Brownell, 2011). Brownell (2010) writes:

> God does not shout, stamp His feet, and demand to be heard. A human being must attune to God, just as he or she must learn to attune to another human being. If you race past Him and blot out His gentle voice with noise of various kinds, you will not have a chance to harden your hearts, because you will not even be aware that you have heard from God. Thus, a heart made ready to hear from God is a soft heart, often arising from a broken and contrite spirit. When God wants to get someone's attention, He often breaks that person down enough so that he or she is ready to hear. To be

ready to hear from God can be understood as being in a dialogical attitude on the part of a person attempting to integrate theistic spiritual process into the practice of gestalt therapy. (p. 194)

Healthy development of the self, therefore, occurs through contact with one's own feelings and attitudes, contact with others, *and* contact with God in a real relationship.

Brownell (2010) suggests that integrating a relational, theistic spirituality with gestalt therapy is one of the growing edges of contemporary gestalt practice.

Christian Appraisal: Model of Abnormality

Existential therapy. We appreciate that in existential therapy choice and responsibility are taken seriously. The Christian gospel clearly asserts that to be human is to evade responsibilities (cf. the story of Adam and Eve; Gen 3). There are striking parallels between the existential therapy account of pathology and the Romans 1 drama depicting humans "who suppress the truth by their wickedness" (v. 18); this suppression is both the result of their failure to acknowledge the truth they know (self-deception) and a defense that allows them to sustain their self-deception.

Nevertheless, we are convinced (as with all therapies that try to describe human behavior outside the context of their Creator) that the existential understanding of psychopathology is incomplete. First, it looks at guilt only existentially as a manifestation of inauthenticity, and not as the result of moral violation (Tweedie, 1961, p. 167). As with other humanistic approaches, existential therapy also seems to ignore or minimize the importance of the creaturely aspects of our existence; particularly few biological or sociocultural factors are discussed by existential psychologists. Although Schneider and May (1995) do include these factors in their model of existential integrative therapy, many other existential writers leave these out. Because these factors can play such an important role in the causation or maintenance of psychopathology, this omission could lead individuals to blame themselves for having psychological symptoms that are truly outside of their control.

On the other hand, it is all too common for persons who have great capacities to change to hide behind their symptoms. Existential therapy correctly states that anxiety and guilt are all too quickly interpreted as negative symptoms to be eliminated, rather than signs or symbols of the specific manner we haven't listened to our awareness. Indeed, existential therapy seems to be a much needed corrective for those of us who become content in our current situations, unwilling to discipline ourselves to "become a self in truth, relentlessly" (cf. Malony, 1980). We are far too easily pleased and content with the preservation of homeostasis or stability in our lives, often at great expense to our personal development.

Existentialism tends to assume that there are enormous resources for choice to draw on within all individuals. Existential therapy should be appreciated for the contribution it has made to our understanding of how high-functioning persons struggle in the quest for meaning and significance in their lives, but there are probably different degrees of capacities for choice and responsibility in the broad spectrum of humanity. People struggle with such a diverse range of problems in living that it seems likely that some are pure "choice" issues (e.g., to be authentic or inauthentic) while others may involve lesser degrees of choice (e.g., a biologically based mania or the residual struggles of a person severely abused as a child). Thus the expectations for responsibility of the existential therapy tradition are highly appropriate for many, but they could become inappropriate or unrealistic for others. We thus must be careful about the potential arrogance or pride of applying such an interpretation of competence in a condescending or patronizing manner.

One can only wonder whether or not these keen assertions about psychopathology are generalizable outside the context of Anglo-American psychology. Although this could be said of nearly all major psychotherapies, we often are not aware of the ways that fundamental assumptions might be limited beyond a particular sociocultural context. While choice and the ability to shape our self through reflection would clearly seem to be universal human capacities, is existential therapy's way of understanding these choices peculiar to our highly individualistic and selfish culture? Do persons in more communal and less pluralistic cultures look at these choices differently? Persons in societies with less leisure time and material prosperity may not have the luxury of reflecting on issues of meaning to such a length as to cause problems in living as they might in our culture.

Emotionally focused therapy. Similar to other humanistic-experiential therapies, emotion-focused therapy places a great degree of trust on the "organism" and one's natural urges toward mastery and attachment. Problems in living are viewed as a result of faulty emotional schemes developed from interactions with the environment.

In contrast, Browning and Cooper (2004) point out that Christian anthropology, particularly as articulated by Kierkegaard, Niebuhr and Augustine, view anxiety and strife as an inherent part of human existence. Unlike the humanists, who view anxiety as a byproduct of environmental expectations and pressures on the person, a Christian view sees anxiety as endemic to the Fall: "This anxiety is intrinsic to the human condition and cannot be overcome no matter how sweetly parents treat their infants" (p. 78).

Olson (2002) emphasizes that a Christian psychology must look beyond the secular nomenclature of the DSM to also identify spiritual, moral and historical sources of suffering and alienation: "The fundamental human problem is the pretense to divinity, expressed in one's turning away from God (unbelief) toward a life centered in self (hubris), and resulting in ambiguity and suffering" (p. 261).

While we see a greater respect for the individual values and a holistic, nonpathologizing view of the client in contemporary experiential therapies, the Christian clinician and PE clinician differ on how client beliefs and values are "deconstructed." Specifically, the Christian worldview parts company with process-experiential therapy in the evaluation of emotions and beliefs. Greenberg (2002) adopts a pragmatic approach to working with negative beliefs: "beliefs are maladaptive if they make people feel bad" (p. 185). Certainly, believers and nonbelievers alike are subject to false beliefs. However, the Christian clinician will also value the role of healthy remorse, guilt and conviction in the life of the client. Sometimes our sin makes us feel bad. As Christians, we place our highest regard on the role of values and beliefs as set forth in Scripture for guidance, rather than guiding our lives based on what is most adaptive for the self.

In reading the process-experiential therapy transcripts, in particular, one can still see the bias against the subjectively experienced "critical voice" as the oppressor of growth and self-enhancement (cf. Elliott, Watson, Goldman & Greenberg, 2004; Greenberg, 2002; Greenberg, Rice & Elliott, 1993), reflective of the gestalt therapy influence on this approach. In contrast, the Christian values the role of conviction and healthy guilt in a life committed to Christ. As Christians, we part company with the experiential therapists in the view that "critical" aspects of self are bad and should be disavowed.

Gestalt therapy. In gestalt therapy psychopathology is viewed as "boundary disturbance," evidenced by interruptions in the person's capacity to make contact with self and others in the present moment. In addition to the classic gestalt boundary disturbances discussed previously, Brownell (2010) adds an additional classification to describe an interruption in a person's ability to experience God. "Hardening [is] the resistance of unbelief and the determination to minimize, discount, deny or otherwise turn a deaf ear to the voice of God. The psalmist and the writer to the Hebrew Christians both referred to it when they said, 'today if you would hear His voice, do not harden you hearts' (Psalm 95:7-8; Hebrews 3:7-19)" (p. 193). A theistic, relational approach to gestalt therapy, therefore, attends to disruptions in the client's real relationship with an imminent God.

Christian Appraisal: Health

Existential therapy. Turning now to the model of health in existential psychology, what is the goal or to what are we striving? In existential psychology the person is headed toward the goal of improving his or her human condition by becoming more authentic. In existentialist language this means that one takes responsibility for one's own life and choices rather than being manipulated by the social world one lives in. In summary of Heidegger's view of authenticity, Guignon (2000) writes, "Authenticity is a matter of 'choosing to choose,' that is, of making one's choices one's own and so being 'answerable' or responsible for one's life" (p. 71). One must ask how this goal fits in with a Christian worldview. Certainly, the Christian faith teaches that we are morally responsible for our actions (2 Cor 5:10). We are not only responsible for our individual actions but are also held responsible by God for the original sin of Adam and Eve in creation (Rom 5:12). Moreover, we are also held accountable for our inner motives and thoughts (Rom 8:27; 1 Cor 4:5; 1 Thess 2:4). The difference here seems to be our answer to the question, To whom is the human accountable? In existential psychology it is to the self; whereas in the Christian faith the human being is ultimately accountable to God.

Now, exploring the second part of existential psychology's definition of authenticity, how does the Christian respond to the pulls of the social world around him or her? Certainly, the Christian faith does not teach that Christians should mindlessly conform to the agendas of others or the culture in which they are enveloped. In fact, the Bible even tells us directly not to conform to the patterns of the world (Rom 12:2; Col 2:20). In this manner the existential call for authenticity appears in line with the Christian faith. However, it is also not intended that the Christian live outside the context of community or make decisions without taking the church or biblical teachings into consideration. In fact, the Christian is actually instructed to submit to the authority of the government (Rom 13:1-7; Heb 13:16-18) and follow the instructions of church leaders (1 Cor 10:33; 2 Cor 10:13; 2 Thess 3:4, 14). Moreover, Christians are called to obey the commands of God (1 Jn 2:3), seek to please God rather than themselves (2 Cor 5:15; 1 Jn 3:22, 24) and ultimately conform their lives to that of Jesus Christ (Eph 5:1-20).

Although existential psychology does not assert that one should only live for oneself, outside the context of morality or care of others there is no moral absolute in existential psychology that provides structure for seeking "authenticity." Rather, the person finds this guide within him- or herself. The tension for the Christian, therefore, is to form one's own opinions and values, but not to become excessively individualistic. Rather, the Christian humanist should study the Bible and be involved with a church, while deliberately living according to one's personal synthesis of Christian principles and church teachings. In summary, "the Christian humanist values culture but confesses that man is fully developed only as he comes into a right relationship with Christ. When this happens, a person can begin to experience growth in all areas of life as the new creation of revelation (II Corinthians 5:17, Galatians 6:15)" (Clouse, 1984, p. 536).

Emotionally focused therapy. The role of "emotional intelligence" and appropriate emotional regulation in psychological health is a worthy goal and a much-needed perspective for holistic Christian living. Few areas cause Christian clients greater distress, confusion, shame and helplessness than determining the role emotions should play in the life of the believer. Many Christians seek psychotherapy for assistance with emotional difficulties such as depression, anxiety, loss and anger, yet much of the theological teaching they have received on the subject has led them to believe that they are a spiritual and moral failure for their inability to control this area of their lives. In essence they are taught from the pulpit to suppress or deny their emotional reactions. Many believers attempt to use prayer, Scripture and reason to tightly control all of their emotional experiences with limited success, often resulting in personal and spiritual lives devoid of joy and a daily experience of God's presence.

Church teaching varies widely in the role emotions should be given in the life of the believer. Because many Christians seek mental health services due to difficulties in their emotional life, the Christian client and therapist are often challenged to find a method by which emotions can be utilized in therapy that is consistent with a Christian worldview. Christian clients often feel confused about the morality and validity of their feelings, resulting in a tendency to ignore, deny or avoid feelings that are viewed as negative. Regardless of one's theoretical orientation, most clinicians agree that an inability to identify, express and regulate emotions will have a detrimental impact on the individual and can result in a variety of symptoms, including somatic concerns, acting out behaviors and rigidity. Moreover, neglecting emotions results in loss of a critical resource for the fruitful and well-lived Christian life, because emotions are often what fuels our passions, our convictions and our worship, and allows us to experience God moment by moment. The socialization of most believers, however, results in the belief that emotions must always take the back seat to fact and faith, and that they are not to be trusted. Christians often fear that encouraging expression of affect will lead to unrestrained catharsis and impulsive behaviors.

One of the unfortunate effects of modernism has been this split between the antithetical assertions that "thinking is good" and that "emotions are bad." By emphasizing one over the other, we risk the heresy of gnosticism—viewing the body and its urges, moods and intuitions as sinful, and the mind as sinless. In contrast, the doctrine of total depravity reminds us that sin affects all parts of all persons—the head is no less vulnerable than the heart. Integrating emotions with a solid biblical belief system provides the opportunity to mend this split and provides an important corrective to pietistic notions that have subtly influenced the church and Christian applications of psychology.

Helping clients attend to both their head and their heart in a way that facilitates spiritual and emotional health is an important and often challenging task for the clinician. Emotions and beliefs are powerful and often conflicting forces in our lives. Process-experiential therapy's incorporation of the advances in contemporary neuroscience have led to a more sophisticated, less dualistic perspective on the role of thought and emotion. The dialectical constructivist theory of personality suggests that thought, belief, emotion and action are closely intertwined. Our emotions affect our thoughts and beliefs much more than we would like to think. As good scientist-practitioner consumers of the science of psychology, paying attention to this growing wealth of knowledge can help us serve our clients more effectively as we help them integrate mind and heart.

Although it is beyond the scope of this current appraisal, several Christian writers have also sought to dispel the false dichotomy between emotions and beliefs, and focused on the importance of reclaiming Christian "affections" (Saliers, 1991; Roberts, 1986). By immersing oneself in the Christian story and in prayer, believers are able to conceptually link their emotional experience with their belief system. Worship, prayer and liturgy are all moments of true integration of belief and emotion. Reclaiming truly Christian affections, such as gratitude, holy fear and repentance, grief over one's sins, and joy, are examples of such emotions (Salier, 1991).

Gestalt therapy. The gestalt therapy picture of health is the person who is able to be fully present in the moment and incorporate an experiential understanding of self, others and environment into their decision making and actions, and thus live responsibly and authentically. As discussed previously, a Christian appraisal questions whether this view of the self runs the risk of extreme subjectivism and a devaluing of external moral standards.

However, the gestalt psychotherapy view of health is an important reminder to Christians of the need to be fully present and aware moment by moment, not only of one's self and others, but of God's active presence. Author Ronald Rolheiser, in his book *The Shattered Lantern* (2001), suggests that one of the greatest problems professed by contemporary Christians is the lack of a "felt presence" of God in their day-to-day lives. Rolheiser attributes this problem in part to contemporary cultural values of narcissism, pragmatism and unbridled restlessness, which make it difficult for the Christian to develop the mental software to pay attention to God's presence. He writes, "God is always present, but we are not always present to God" (p. 21). The solution, according to Rolheiser, is to rediscover the ancient Christian practice of contemplation. "Contemplation is about waking up. Simply defined, to be contemplative is to experience an event fully, in all its aspects. Biblically, this is expressed as knowing 'face to face'" (p. 23). Christian contemplative practices, such as meditation on God's Word, centering prayer and lectio divina, can help the Christian develop a deeper capacity to experience God's active presence, which is an important component of overall spiritual health.

Christian Appraisal: Therapy

Existential therapy. In many ways, existential psychology encourages individuals to explore the very aspects of existence that Christians find to be most significant. Compared to the bulk of mainline psychology, which is preoccupied with what seem at times to be comparatively trivial slices of life, existential therapy distinguishes itself by grappling with death, aloneness, choice, meaning, growth, responsibility, guilt and so forth (Tweedie, 1961, p. 163). No approach to psychology mirrors the concerns of the faith as well as does existential therapy. The book of Ecclesiastes demonstrates the Christian struggle to find meaning in life. The writer begins by asserting, "Utterly meaningless! / Everything is meaningless" (Eccles 1:2). The writer then proceeds to painstakingly question the purpose of life. He considers wealth, wisdom, popularity and pleasure, and finally concludes that fearing the Lord is the highest goal to seek. In other passages we are also taught to seek insight and understanding (Prov 1:1-3), examine ourselves to see if our faith is genuine (2 Cor 13:5-6), and live for purposes beyond those humans are often drawn to. This pattern of self-examination and living beyond the superficial is at the core of existential therapy. In this manner, existential therapy comports well with the Christian faith.

The role of the therapist and the process of self-examination in existential therapy is another way this approach is compatible with the Christian faith, and even offers the opportunity for the client to experience God's love and grace. As discussed previously, existential therapists are required to explore their own weaknesses and shortcomings, and from this position, offer a grounding presence from which the client is able to explore themselves and the depths of their suffering. Bretherton (2006) reflects on existential therapy from a Christian perspective and asserts that Christian existential therapists who are aware of their own sin, as well as God's grace, have the potential to be even more honest with themselves. They don't need to be afraid of looking deeper because they don't have to fear guilt or worry about God's disapproval. They know that they are totally acceptable to God. He explains,

> From a Christian perspective, the life, death, and resurrection of Jesus Christ justify human existence and provide evidence of God's love. Acceptance of this can allow the Christian psychotherapist to be cognizant of potential shortcomings and thereby experience a strong identification with the challenges of living presented by the client. This can enable a positive and non-pathologizing relationship with clients of any religious or ideological persuasion. (p. 265)

Additionally, just as existential therapists also take an active role with their clients in the processes of "instructing" and "requiring," Christian existential therapists have the opportunity to provide objective information to the client and share their own personal and emotional perspectives. In this way Christian existential therapists may share information with clients concerning God's love and grace, as well as their personal experiences of failure and forgiveness.

Even if the existential therapist were not a Christian, the process of joining with the client in their weakness and suffering mirrors the type of nonjudging relationship that is likely to foster honest self-reflection rather than an avoidance or denial of sin. In this process the client has the opportunity to long for the gospel of Christ, which provides ultimate freedom and security.

On the negative side, existential therapy in the context of atheism falls short. From this perspective life really ends with death, and hope for the future is much less secure. The best one can do is to improve one's own human condition and meaning, which is limited to this world. Exploring life's difficult questions from this perspective could hypothetically foster depression and anxiety rather than wholeness and healing.

Emotionally focused therapy. Emotion-focused therapy techniques can help Christian clients utilize emotions constructively in psychotherapy while still integrating their beliefs and values into the process of decision making and change. Unfortunately, process-experiential therapy has received little attention from the Christian psychological community. Searches of the Christian integrative literature revealed only a few published critiques (Hurst, 2003; Versaveldt, 2006).

Process-experiential theory and techniques are different from many experiential approaches in that clients are encouraged to identify core values and guiding principles that influence decision making. Clients are encouraged to identify and take responsibility for their values and ideals, and distinguish them from familial and societal expectations that are not consistent with the individual. The authors affirm that at times clients will choose to let go of certain needs in favor of allowing values or ideals to guide behaviors. This recognition of the importance of values and beliefs is unique among experiential therapies and may be more effective with religious clients.

Clients are encouraged to live beyond the moment and consider consequences of their choices in emotion-focused therapy. As Greenberg (2002) states,

> People thus always need to integrate their emotionally based biological knowledge with their more learned personal and cultural knowledge. Doing something because it feels good, as we know, is not always the best guide to action. People need to take their social context and future into account before acting. . . . Thus, present feelings must be integrated with awareness of future consequences and informed by past living. Living only for the present and ignoring consequences is not wise: What one did today will affect what happens tomorrow. (pp. 17-18)

A Christian appraisal also looks favorably on the relational emphasis of process-experiential therapy. Drawing from the theories of Carl Rogers and person-centered therapy, emotion-focused therapy places primary emphasis on the client-therapist relationship and acknowledges that the relationship must always take precedence over the application of technique. However, the authors suggest that the necessary and sufficient conditions for change proposed by Rogers are necessary, sufficient, but not always efficient. They suggest that the therapist take an active role in facilitating the process of therapy while the content of sessions is left up to the client. "Direct process, not content" is the guiding principal of emotion-focused therapy (Elliott et al., 2004). Clinicians who find themselves drawn to the relational emphasis of person-centered therapy but frustrated with the nondirective style will find emotion-focused therapy compelling.

Even more compelling, this approach provides a specific rationale and technique for facilitating the process of integration within clients them-selves, as the two-chair dialogue illustrates. Helping individuals live more fully integrated lives where all aspects of self, including emotions, cognitions and values, are brought together is certainly an important task for the Christian clinician.

Greenberg's (2002) emphasis on the role of emotion in this process provides an important corrective to modern psychologies and offers possibilities for a more experiential integration consistent with a value-driven approach to life. Specific techniques are utilized to help the client's reason and emotion engage in dialogue, uncovering emotional schemes and providing opportunities to modify. At least on paper this approach gives maximum freedom and respect for the Christian client to actively integrate values and belief systems, rather than receive an imposed diagnosis and formulation dependent on the clinician's perceptions and biases. The Christian client and therapist, with the guidance of the Holy Spirit, seek to discern truth by integrating beliefs, emotions and actions.

Utilizing this approach with Christian clients requires consideration of several important issues. First, for the Christian, empowerment and freedom of the self are not the ultimate goals of therapy. True Christian freedom and responsibility also involve accountability to the body of Christ. Thus, the Christian client might be encouraged to seek the wise counsel of their church or pastor for spiritual guidance in their decision-making process rather than relying solely on their internal processes. Second, this approach may be most appropriate with more spiritually mature clients who have internalized the beliefs and values of the Christian faith versus experiencing their faith as an external pressure or expectation. Such clients can benefit from emotion-focused techniques that help them distinguish between self-critical tendencies based on unhealthy perfectionism and internalized core Christian values and beliefs.

Finally, the Christian client and therapist will value character development as evidenced by love of God and others as an ultimate goal of true healing. Olson (2002) asserts that a Christian humanistic approach to psychotherapy will facilitate change of character, conduct, conscience, cognition and, most of all, conformity to God's will. He reminds the Christian clinician that this is accomplished not by one's own power but by the grace of God and through his empowerment.

Gestalt therapy. Similarly, in utilizing gestalt therapy with the Christian client, the Christian clinician would view core Christian beliefs and practices and accountability to the body of Christ as part of the "field." According to Brownell (2010), a theistic, relational and spiritual attitude in gestalt therapy will help the client (and therapist) be aware of God's active presence in the pneumenal field and "experience(s) oneself as a valued child of God" (p. 200). Brownell provides the following picture of what this might look like:

> A person can track, using gestalt phenomenological inquiry, the way it actually is and what is actually going on between oneself and God. Sin, for instance, becomes a normal part of life and something to be picked through in order to understand its power and dynamic. One might practice a way filled with disciplines that shape a relationship with God. One might learn to dialogue in the three-person field convened by God (therapist-client-God), and one might appreciate the wider and more complex situation resident in the pneumenal field. (2010, p. 201)

Brownell (2011) gives other specific examples of bringing the client's theistic beliefs and practices into therapy, such as including questions about the client's spiritual history in treatment, suggesting in-session experiments that involve listening to God or speaking to God, or praying to God for help and guidance in the therapist's work with a client.

Effectiveness

Existential therapy. As discussed by Schneider (2005), the effectiveness of existential psychotherapy remains somewhat in question because the number of systematic outcome studies is limited. Furthermore, those studies that have been completed do not always employ standardized experimental procedures or quantitative analysis. In fact, as existential therapy inherently assumes that each client is unique and tailors the approach to each new client, precise systematization of procedures is dubious. Nevertheless, there is some evidence suggesting that this type of treatment is effective. For example, in a pre- and post-test waitlist-controlled design, Van der Pompe, Duivenvoorden, Antoni & Visser (1997) demonstrated improved endocrine and immune functioning in breast cancer patients treated in thirteen-week experiential existential group psychotherapy.

Outcome research with couples has also yielded some modest support for existential therapy. In a ten-year longitudinal study with twenty-four couples, Lantz and Gregoire (2003) demonstrated that existential therapy can be useful in combination with medical services for patients who have suffered a myocardial infarction. Similarly, another study involving Vietnam combat veterans (Lantz & Gregoire, 2000) suggests modest improvements on self-report and marital-adjustment measures for fifty-three couples. Nevertheless, results of this study should be interpreted with caution because of significant limitations with the study (e.g., no control group, no pretest measurement of symptoms, and only descriptive statistics were provided).

Additionally, research suggests that various components of existential therapy demonstrate better outcomes than other types of therapies. For instance, Wampold (2001) indicates that relationships as opposed to technical factors are the most important components to the therapy process. As cited by Schneider (2005), "therapeutic alliance (Hovarth, 1995), empathy (Bohart & Greenberg, 1997), genuineness and positive regard (Orlinsky, Grawe & Parks, 1994), and clients' capacity for self-healing (Bohart & Tallman, 1999)" also appear important to the psychotherapeutic process. Finally, Schneider (1985) has also shown that the personal involvement of the therapist is more important than specific therapeutic techniques.

Emotionally focused therapy. Greenberg and his colleagues have been quite active with psychotherapy outcome research. Unlike most of the experiential therapies, emotion-focused therapy has been supported by a growing body of outcome studies (Elliott, Greenberg & Lietaer, 2003; Elliot, 2002; and Greenberg, Elliot & Lietaer, 1994), including several controlled studies comparing clients receiving process-experiential treatment to control groups. A meta-analysis of eighteen outcome studies of process-experiential therapy conducted by Elliott et al. (2003) found that the average client receiving process-experiential therapy experienced an improvement larger than a standard deviation in therapeutic effect (an effect size of 1.26), providing strong support for the effectiveness of this approach. In addition, gains made in therapy are stable in short-term and long-term follow-up studies. Process-experiential therapies have demonstrated effectiveness with a variety of presenting problems, including depression, resolution of abuse and trauma, decisional conflicts, and unresolved relationship issues. Emotionally focused therapy for couples has also received strong empirical support as well (Johnson & Greenberg, 1985). Findings indicate that humanistic-experiential therapies in general are as effective as cognitive-behavioral therapy and other approaches. Elliott et al. (2004) conclude from their meta-analysis that the process-directive approaches of process-experiential, emotionally focused therapy for couples, and gestalt appear to be particularly promising based on the outcome research.

Such empirical support is intriguing and compels the responsible Christian clinician to look closer at this approach to determine the benefits and risks of integration of process-experiential therapy with an explicitly Christian worldview.

Gestalt therapy. Strümpfel and Goldman's (2001) review of sixty studies evaluating the effectiveness of gestalt therapy with a variety of clinical syndromes indicates that gestalt therapy is as effective or more effective than other approaches to therapy. Effects of gestalt therapy also appear to continue to be apparent one to three years following termination. Findings support the use of gestalt therapy with mood disorders, personality distur-bances, psychosomatic disorders and addictions (p. 212). Strümpfel and Goldman's review of the research on the effectiveness of specific gestalt techniques indicates that the two-chair technique and the empty-chair method have been found to effectively lead to deeper client experiencing, significant improvements in awareness and client resolution of conflicts when compared with other techniques such as empathic mirroring alone.

CONCLUSION

Christians utilizing existential, emotion-focused or gestalt psychotherapy should keep in mind three areas of incompatibility between the humanistic-experiential therapies and a Christian worldview: *authority, authenticity* and *anxiety.* The reliance on the phenomenological method in the experi-ential therapies results in a mistrust of sources of authority outside of one's own experience, and external sources of authority are often dismissed as "critical voices." In contrast, a Christian worldview places high value on the Word of God as a primary source of authority and on accountability to other believers. Authenticity and honest expression of needs and feelings is given highest priority in the experiential therapies to the point of be-coming an ethic for living (Browning & Cooper, 2004). A Christian worldview prioritizes love of God with love for others. Thus, authentic expression of needs and feelings, for the Christian, must be tempered with charity. And finally, psychopathology in the experiential therapies is often related to the experience of anxiety: emotional schemes and beliefs are maladaptive if they feel bad. For the Christian, anxiety, pain and suffering are viewed as an inevitable result of living in a fallen world as sinful beings. Indeed, anxiety and tension often direct our attention to areas of sin in our lives. A sensitive, Spirit-led clinician can help clients discern the difference between the "critical voice" that may lead to healthy spiritual conviction, recognition of sin and confession, and those "critical voices" that are related to false guilt, shame and spiritual oppression.

Keeping in mind issues of authority, authenticity and anxiety, we propose that careful, reflective use of experiential therapies, when integrated with the Christian client's core beliefs, can be beneficial for the Christian client to help integrate head and heart. Compared to the humanistic approaches of the past, contemporary experiential therapies demonstrate a more relational and contextual view of the self, with a higher respect and valuing of the whole person. Solid outcome research concludes that existential, emotion-focused and gestalt psychotherapies demonstrate effectiveness with a variety of client populations. Advances in neuroscience provide a rich understanding of cognition and emotion that move us beyond dualism to exciting clinical ideas for integration of belief, emotions and behavior. Experiential therapies with individuals and couples can provide a clinically effective, well-researched, systematic approach for working with client emotional experience in a way that leads to in-session change, while still respecting and incorporating client values and beliefs. It is time for Christian clinicians to take another look at what the experiential therapies have to offer.

FOR FURTHER READING

Brownell, P. (2010). *Gestalt therapy: A guide to contemporary practice.* New York, NY: Springer.

A good introduction to contemporary gestalt therapy with frequent references to the author's Christian worldview.

Brownell, P. (in press, 2011). Spirituality in gestalt therapy. In T. L. Bar-Yoseph (Ed.), *Gestalt therapy: Advances in theory and practice.* New York, NY: Routledge.

Brownell traces the history of Eastern and Western spirituality in gestalt therapy and introduces the integration of a theistic, relational worldview with gestalt therapy.

Greenberg, L. S. (2002). *Emotion-focused therapy: Coaching clients to work through their feelings.* Washington, DC: American Psychological Association.
The introductory text to process-experiential therapy.

Johnson, Susan (2004). *The practice of emotionally focused couples therapy: Creating connections* (2nd ed.). New York, NY: Brunner-Routledge.
Excellent overview of the theory and practice of emotionally focused couple's therapy.

Yalom, I. D. (1980). *Existential psychotherapy.* New York, NY: Basic Books.
The classic existential therapy introductory text.

REFERENCES

Axeline, V. M. (1947). *Play therapy.* New York, NY: Houghton Mifflin.

Bergin, A. E., & Garfield, S. L. (1994). *Handbook of psychotherapy and behavior change* (4th ed.). New York, NY: Wiley.

Binswanger, L. (1963). *Being-in-the-world: Selected papers of Ludwig Binswanger* (J. Needleman, Trans.). Ludwig, NY: Basic Books. (Original work published 1946).

Bohart, A. C. (2003). Person-centered psychotherapy and related experiential approaches. In A. S. Gurman & S. B. Messer (Eds.), *Essential psychotherapies: Theory and practice* (2nd ed.). New York, NY: Guilford.

Bohart, A. C., & Greenberg, L. S. (Eds.). (1997). *Empathy reconsidered: New directions in psychotherapy.* Washington, DC: American Psychological Association.

Bohart, A. C., & Tallman, K. (1999). *How clients make therapy work: The process of active self-healing.* Washington, DC: American Psychological Association.

Bratton, S. C., & Ray, D. (2001). Humanistic play therapy. In D. J. Cain & J. Seeman (Eds.), *Humanistic psychotherapies: Handbook of research and practice.* Washington, DC: American Psychological Association.

Bretherton, R. (2006). Can existential psychotherapy be good news? Reflections on existential psychotherapy from a Christian perspective. *Mental Health, Religion & Culture, 9*(3), 265-275.

Brownell, P. (Ed.). (2008). *Handbook of theory, research, and practice in gestalt therapy.* Newcastle, UK: Cambridge Scholars.

Brownell, P. (2010). Spirituality in the praxis of gestalt therapy. In J. H. Ellens (Ed.), *The healing power of spirituality: How religion helps humans thrive, vol. 3. The psychodynamics of healing spirituality and religion* (pp. 102-125). Westport, CT: Praeger/ABC-CLIO.

Brownell, P. (in press, 2011). Spirituality in gestalt therapy. In T. Levine Bar-Yoseph (Ed.), *Gestalt therapy: Advances in theory and practice.* New York, NY: Routledge.

Browning, D. S., & Cooper, T. D. (2004). *Religious thought and the modern psychologies* (2nd ed.). Minneapolis, MN: Fortress.

Bugental, J. F. (1999). *Psychotherapy isn't what you think*. Phoenix, AZ: Zeig, Tucker.

Bugental, J. F. T. (1978). *Psychotherapy and process: The fundamentals of an existential-humanistic approach*. Reading, MA: Addison-Wesley.

Bugental, J. F. T. (1987). *The art of the psychotherapist*. New York, NY: Norton.

Cain, D. J. (2001). Defining characteristics, history, and evolution of humanistic psychotherapies. In D. J. Cain & J. Seeman (Eds.), *Humanistic psychotherapies: Handbook of research and practice*. Washington, DC: American Psychological Association.

Cain, D. J., & Seeman, J. (Eds.). (2001). *Humanistic psychotherapies: Handbook of research and practice*. Washington, DC: American Psychological Association.

Clouse, R. G. (1984). Humanism, Christian. In W. A. Elwell (Ed.), *Evangelical dictionary of theology* (p. 536). Grand Rapids, MI: Baker.

Dodgen, D. J., & McMinn, M. R. (1986). Humanistic psychology and Christian thought: A comparative analysis. *Journal of Psychology and Theology, 14*(3), 194-202.

Eels, T. (1997). *Handbook of psychotherapy case formulation*. Washington, DC: American Psychological Association.

Ellens, J. H., & Sloat, D. E. (1999). Christian humanistic psychology. In D. Moss (Ed.), *Humanistic and transpersonal psychology* (pp. 167-191). Westport, CT: Greenwood Press.

Elliott, R. (2002). The effectiveness of humanistic therapies: A meta-analysis. In D. J. Cain & J. Seeman (Eds.), *Humanistic psychotherapies: Handbook of research and practice* (pp. 55-82). Washington, DC: American Psychological Association.

Elliott, R., Greenberg, L., & Lietaer, G. (2003). Research on experiential psychotherapies. In M. J. Lambert, A. E. Bergin & S. L. Garfield (Eds.), *Handbook of psychotherapy and behavior change* (5th ed., pp. 493-539). New York, NY: Wiley.

Elliott, R., Watson, J., Goldman, R., & Greenberg, L. (2004). *Learning emotion-focused therapy*. Washington, DC: American Psychological Association.

Finch, J. (1982). *Nishkamakarma*. Pasadena, CA: Integration Press.

Finch, J., & Van Dragt, B. (1985). Existential psychology and psychotherapy. In D. Benner (Ed.), *Baker encyclopedia of psychology* (pp. 372-377). Grand Rapids, MI: Baker.

Frankl, V. E. (1984). *Man's search for meaning*. New York, NY: Pocket Books. (Original work published 1959).

Gassin, E. A., & Enright, R. D. (1995). The will to meaning in the process of forgiveness. *Journal of Psychology and Christianity, 14*(1), 38-49.

Gendlin, E. T. (1996). *Focusing-oriented psychotherapy*. New York, NY: Guilford Press.

Gordon, T. (2000). *PET: Parent effectiveness training*. New York, NY: Three Rivers Press.

Greenberg, L., Elliott, R., & Lietaer, G. (1994). Research on experiential psychotherapies. In A. Bergin & S. Garfield. *Handbook of psychotherapy and behavior change* (4th ed., pp. 509-539). New York, NY: John Wiley.

Greenberg, L., & Paivio, S. (1997). *The process of change in emotionally focused therapy*. New York, NY: Guilford Press.

Greenberg, L., Rice, L., & Elliott, R. (1993). *Facilitating emotional change: The moment by moment process*. New York, NY: Guilford Press.

Greenberg, L., & Safran, J. (1989). Emotion in psychotherapy. *American Psychologist, 44*, 19-29.

Greenberg, L. S. (2002). *Emotion-focused therapy: Coaching clients to work through their feelings*. Washington, DC: American Psychological Association.

Greenberg, L. S., & Johnson, S. M. (1988). *Emotionally focused therapy for couples*. New York, NY: Guilford Press.

Greenberg, L. S., Watson, J. C., & Lietaer, G. (Eds.). (1998). *Handbook of experiential psychotherapy*. New York, NY: Guilford Press.

Guignon, C. (2000). Authenticity and integrity: A Heideggerian perspective. In P. Young-Eisendrath & M. E. Miller (Eds.), *The psychology of mature spirituality: Integrity, wisdom, transcendence* (pp. 62-74). London: Routledge.

Heidegger, M. (1962). *Being and time* (J. Macquarrie & E. Robinson, Trans.). New York, NY: Harper & Row.

Hovarth, A. O. (1995). The therapeutic relationship: From transference to alliance. *In Session, 1*, 7-17.

Hurst, L. (2003). Review of EFT: Coaching clients to work through their feelings. *Journal of Psychology and Christianity, 22*(3), 274-275.

Johnson, S. M. (2004). *The practice of emotionally focused marital therapy: Creating connections* (2nd ed.). New York, NY: Brunner/Routledge.

Johnson, S., & Greenberg, L. (1985). Emotionally focused marital therapy: An outcome study. *Journal of Marital and Family Therapy, 11*, 313-317.

Johnson, S. M., & Greenberg, L. S. (Eds.). (1994). *The heart of the matter: Perspectives on emotion in marital therapy*. New York, NY: Brunner Mazel.

Jones, S., & Butman, R. (1991). *Modern psychotherapies: A Christian appraisal* (1st ed.). Downers Grove, IL: InterVarsity Press.

Kirby, S. (2004). Choice or discovery: An exploration of Kierkegaard's theory of the self. *Existential Analysis, 15*(2), 256-263.

Korchin, S. (1976). *Modern clinical psychology*. New York, NY: Basic Books.

Lantz, J., & Gregoire, T. (2000). Existential psychotherapy with Vietnam veteran couples: A twenty-five year report. *Family Therapy: An International Journal, 22*(1), 19-37.

Lantz, J., & Gregoire, T. (2003). Couples, existential psychotherapy, and myocardial infarction: A ten year evaluation study. *Contemporary Family Therapy: An International Journal, 25*(4), 367-379.

Lewin, K. (1943). Defining the "Field at a Given Time." *Psychological Review, 50,* 292-310. Republished in K. Lewin (1997), *Resolving social conflicts & field theory in social science,* Washington, DC: American Psychological Association.

Mahoney, M. J., & Mahoney, S. (2001). Living within essential tensions: Dialectics and future development. In K. J. Schneider, J. F. T. Bugental & J. F. Pierson (Eds.), *The handbook of humanistic psychology: Leading edges in theory, research, and practice.* Thousand Oaks, CA: Sage.

Mahrer, A. R. (1996). *A complete guide to experiential psychotherapy.* New York, NY: Wiley.

Maloney, H. (Ed.). (1980). *A Christian existential psychology: The contribution of John G. Finch.* Washington, DC: University Press of America.

May, R. (1981). *Freedom and destiny.* New York, NY: Norton.

May, R., & Yalom, I. (1984). Existential psychotherapy. In R. Corsini (Ed.), *Current psychotherapies* (3rd ed.). Itasca, IL: Peacock Publishers.

May, R., Angel, E., & Ellenberger, H. (Eds.). (1958). *Existence: A new dimension in psychiatry and psychology.* New York: Basic Books.

McMinn, M. R. (1996). *Why sin matters: The surprising relationship between our sin and God's grace.* Wheaton, IL: Tyndale House.

Moss, D. (2001). The roots and genealogy of humanistic psychology. In K. J. Schneider, J. F. T. Bugental & J. F. Pierson (Eds.), *The handbook of humanistic psychology* (pp. 5-20). Thousand Oaks, CA: Sage.

Moustakas, C. E. (1975). *Who will listen? Children and parents in play therapy.* New York, NY: Ballantine Books.

Moustakas, C. E. (1997). *Relationship play therapy.* Northvale, NJ: Jason Aronson.

Nietzsche, F. (1933). *Thus spoke Zarathustra* (A. Tille, Trans.). London: J. M. Dent & Sons.

Oaklander, V. (1988). *Windows to our children: A gestalt therapy approach to children and adolescents.* Highland, NY: Gestalt Journal.

O'Hara, M. (1994). Relational humanism: A psychology for a pluralistic world. In F. Wertz (Ed.), *The humanistic movement: Recovering the person in psychology.* Lake Worth, FL: Gardner Press.

Olson, R. P. (2001). *The reconciled life: A critical theory of counseling.* Peabody, MA: Hendrickson.

Olson, R. P. (2002). Christian humanism. In R. P. Olson (Ed.), *Religious theories of personality and psychotherapy: East meets west* (pp. 247-323). New York, NY: Hawthorn Press.

Orlinsky, D. E., Grawe, K., & Parks, B. K. (1994). Process and outcome in psychotherapy. In A. E. Bergin & S. L. Garfield (Eds.), *Handbook of psychotherapy and behavior change* (4th ed., pp. 270-376). Oxford: John Wiley.

Perls, F. (1969a). *Gestalt therapy verbatim.* Moab, UT: Real People Press.

Perls, F. (1969b). *In and out of the garbage pail.* Moab, UT: Real People Press.

Perls, F., & Shostrum, E. (1965). *Three approaches to psychotherapy: part 2, Fredrick Perls.* Corona Del Mar, CA: Psychological and Educational Films.

Perls, F. S., Hefferline, R. F., & Goodman, P. (1951). *Gestalt therapy: Excitement and growth in the human personality.* New York, NY: Julian Press.

Polster, E., & Polster, M. (1973). *Gestalt therapy integrated: Contours of theory and practice.* New York, NY: Brunner/Mazel.

Roberts, R. (1986). Emotion and the fruit of the spirit. In S. L. Jones (Ed.), *Psychology and the Christian faith: An introductory reader.* Grand Rapids, MI: Baker.

Rolheiser, R. (2001). *The shattered lantern: Rediscovering a felt presence of God* (Rev. ed.). New York, NY: Crossroad.

Rosenfeld, E. (1977). *An oral history of gestalt therapy: part one, A conversation with Laura Perls.* www.gestalt.org/perlsint.htm.

Roubal, J. (2009). Experiment: A creative phenomenon of the field. *Gestalt Review, 13*(3), 263-276.

Saliers, D. E. (1991). *The Soul in paraphrase: Prayer and the religious affections* (2nd ed.). Cleveland, OH: Order of St. Luke Publishers.

Sartre, J. P. (1965). *Being and nothingness* (H. E. Barnes, Trans.). New York, NY: Citadel Press. (Original work published 1943).

Satir, V. (1983). *Conjoint family therapy* (3rd ed.). Palo Alto, CA: Science & Behavior.

Schneider, K. J. (1985). Clients' perceptions of the positive and negative characteristics of their counselors. *Dissertation Abstracts International, 45*(10), 3345b.

Schneider, K. J. (1998). Existential processes. In L. S. Greenberg, J. C. Watson & G. Lietaer (Eds.), *Handbook of experiential psychotherapy* (pp. 103-120). New York, NY: Guilford Press.

Schneider, K. J. (2005). Existential-humanistic psychotherapy. In A. S. Gurman & S. B. Messer (Eds.), *Essential psychotherapies: Theory and practice* (pp. 149-181). New York, NY: Guilford Press.

Schneider, K. J., & May, R. (1995). *The psychology of existence: An integrative, clinical perspective.* New York, NY: McGraw-Hill.

Schneider, K. J., Bugental, J. F. T., & Pierson, J. F. (2001). *The handbook of humanistic psychology: Leading edges in theory, research, and practice.* Thousand Oaks, CA: Sage.

Strümpfel, U., & Goldman, R. (2001). Contacting gestalt therapy. In D. J. Cain & J. Seeman (Eds.), *Humanistic psychotherapies: Handbook of research and practice*. Washington, DC: American Psychological Association.

Tweedie, D. F. (1961). *Logotherapy and the Christian faith: An evaluation of Frankl's existential approach to psychotherapy*. Grand Rapids, MI: Baker.

Usher, C. H. (1989). Recognizing cultural bias in counseling theory and practice: The case of Rogers. *Multicultural Counseling and Development, 17,* 62-70.

Van der Pompe, G., Duivenvoorden, H. J., Antoni, M. H., & Visser, A. (1997). Effectiveness of a short-term group psychotherapy program on endocrine and immune function in breast cancer patients: An exploratory study. *Journal of Psychosomatic Research, 42*(5), 453-466.

Van Dragt, B. (1985). A peace that passes understanding: An existential view of the "Dark Night." *Journal of Psychology and Christianity, 4*(2), 15-18.

Vande Kemp, H. (1986). Dangers of psychologism: The place of God in psychology. *Journal of Psychology and Theology, 14,* 97-109.

Van Leeuwen, M. (1985). *The person in psychology: A contemporary Christian appraisal.* Grand Rapids, MI: Eerdmans.

Versaveldt, J. (2006). Emotionally-focused couples therapy: An examination using Browning's (1987) model. *Journal of Psychology and Theology, 23*(3), 216-225.

Vitz, P. (1977). *Psychology as religion: The cult of self-worship.* Grand Rapids, MI: Eerdmans.

Wampold, B. E. (2001). *The great psychotherapy debate: Models, methods, and findings.* Mahwah, NJ: L. Erlbaum.

Wheeler, G., & Backman, S. (1997). *On intimate ground: A gestalt approach to working with couples.* Cambridge, MA: Gestalt Press.

Wheeler, G., & McConville, M. (Eds.). (2001). *The heart of development: Gestalt approaches to working with children, adolescents and their worlds, volume 2: Adolescence.* Cambridge, MA: Gestalt Press.

Woldt, A., & Toman, S. (Eds.). (2005). *Gestalt therapy: History, theory, and practice.* London: Sage.

Yalom, I. D. (1980). *Existential psychotherapy.* New York, NY: Basic Books.

Yankelovich, D. (1982). *New rules: Searching for self-fulfillment in a world turned upside down.* New York, NY: Bantam Books.

Yontef, G. (1993). *Awareness, dialogue and process: Essays on gestalt therapy.* Highland, NY: Gestalt Journal Press.

Yontef, G. (1998). Dialogic gestalt therapy. In L. S. Greenberg, J. C. Watson & G. Lietaer (Eds.), *Handbook of experiential psychotherapy* (pp. 103-120). New York, NY: Guilford Press.

9

FAMILY SYSTEMS
THEORY AND THERAPY

David Van Dyke, Stanton L. Jones and Richard E. Butman

*F*amily systems theory provides a cohesive framework for numerous therapeutic approaches that assist individuals, couples, families and groups. Family systems theory (or systemic thought) arose in the late 1940s. Practical work with families predated the development of theory. During the first half of the twentieth century the primary approach to treatment was long-term therapy provided by psychoanalytically trained psychiatrists and therapists. Freud's perspective was that internal psychological structure of an individual forms through early childhood attachment and provides the means of sating libidinal and thanatos drives. Pathology and change resided within the individual. For the psychoanalytically oriented, working with the family was seen as chaotic and often counterproductive. Better to see a client individually to work on relationship issues in the controlled environment of the client-therapist transference relationship than to see the family and have reinjury occurring in the therapeutic space meant for safety and protection. Therefore, it was uncommon to hear about clinicians working with anyone other than the individual.

Some were frustrated with the slow rate of improvement in psychoanalysis and were looking for alternative modes of treatment. Family therapy was considered countercultural in that it moved the attention from the internal workings of the mind (psyche) to the external domains of relationships. Proponents stressed that if not enough attention was paid to the family, then the "identified patient" would continue to maintain the problematic symptoms for the family. The first credited publication in family therapy was by attachment theorist and child psychiatrist John Bowlby in 1949. Bowlby, working as the head of the Children's Department at Tavistock Clinic, which he ultimately renamed the Department for Children and Parents, was treating an adolescent individually for over two years with minimal progress and spotty attendance. He decided to pull in the mother and father for a family interview. It was a two-hour session that involved Bowlby making interpretations on how all members and their interactions contributed to the problem. This was the turning point in his individual therapy with this adolescent. He credited Bion and colleagues at the Tavistock Institute of Human Relations for his formation of the "joint interview technique." Bowlby stated that he was apprehensive about seeing the family together because of the potential for chaos and conflict, but he felt this type of interview was beneficial in child guidance settings (Bowlby, 1949). Bowlby's intent was not to start doing family therapy, and in fact he continued to work individually with the adolescent. However, he did want a greater emphasis on the family interaction patterns with the individual.

John Bell, a psychologist, was possibly the first family therapist. He began working with families in the early 1950s, but he did not publish his work until the 1960s. He had worked at the Tavistock Clinic for a brief time. He learned that Bowlby was working with families while applying group techniques. Bell worked individually with children, then individually with parents, then brought the family together to facilitate new conversation patterns. This family-interview intervention by Bowlby opened the door for others who were trained in psychiatry and psychoanalysis to consider working with families. Nathan Ackerman, a psychoanalytically trained psychiatrist working for the Child Guidance Clinic at Menninger Clinic in Topeka, Kansas, began seeing mother and child dyads instead of splitting them into two individual sessions. He focused his work on the importance of role relations within the family as it contributed to individual pathology.

Family therapy theory developed embedded in the context of the research and cultural concerns of the day. Systems theory emerged out of several different scientific fields of the 1930s and 1940s, but was first applied to family units in the 1950s. The 1930s were dominated by economic hardships of the Great Depression. Community became important during this time as a function of survival and reliance on others. Structure in the form of government (like the New Deal) became critical to people's sense of survival. The 1940s were marked by global uncertainty, struggle and transitions. The First and Second World Wars created unprecedented disequilibrium at national and cultural levels, and the responsibility of establishing new forms of order as exemplified by the Marshall Plan, which directed reconstruction in western Europe. The huge demand for men to serve in the militaries across the world changed family patterns and work patterns (with women carrying vocational workloads in many countries) and resulted in the renegotiating of family roles in postwar society. It was during these transitional times of disequilibrium for families and societies that family therapy emerged on both sides of the Atlantic.

Warren McCulloch and the Josiah Macy Jr. Foundation began the Macy Conferences in 1946, following the end of World War II. The Macy Conferences fostered interdisciplinary scholarship with the purpose of laying the foundation for a general science regarding the workings of the mind (American Society for Cybernetics, 2010). The fields represented were anthropology (Gregory Bateson, Margaret Mead), psychology (Kurt Lewin, Lawrence Kubie, Erik Erikson), mathematics (Norbert Wiener), biology (Ludwig von Bertalanffy) and others. From these conferences emerged general systems theory and cybernetics, with multiple applications to various disciplines. These products have provided the overarching epistemologies for all the family therapy approaches.

HISTORY AND PHILOSOPHICAL ASSUMPTIONS

The overarching philosophy for family therapy approaches are grounded in general systems theory and cybernetics. Systemic thinkers are like good improvisational artists. They emphasize "yes-and" comments instead of "yes-but" comments. Good improv does not negate the previous actor's contribution but instead builds on the previous action or statement. The skit becomes an evolving entity that is produced by each actor and all of the actors simultaneously. The individual actor has agency, while simultaneously being part of something bigger (the whole). Each improv skit has new topics (content) and different responses (interactions), and the actors never know what the outcome will be (indeterminacy). The same actors may be hilarious one moment yet fall painfully flat in the next. The focus in improv is *how* the actors interact, respond and participate. Likewise, family therapy involves rules about what to attend to, how to respond, and what to do with the concept of "knowing." The next section addresses some of these epistemological foundations for systemic thinkers.

GENERAL SYSTEMS THEORY

Ludwig von Bertalanffy (1968) was fascinated with the systems found in the world. He looked for a "theory of everything" and believed general systems thinking could encompass the idea of a unified science. He believed that there were structural similarities or isomorphs that could be seen in various disciplines of science (e.g., biology, physics, anthropology, mathematics, business, engineering and psychology). He defined systems as consisting of independent yet interacting parts. These parts interact to create a balance for both the individual and the entire system. Von Bertalanffy saw the world as empirically knowable, observable and anchored in behavior. He was a neopositivist who was influenced by Spengler's (1991) historical relativism; an argument for a circular rather than linear view of history. History involves an object (event) and an observer. Both the object and the observer affect each other and are affected by each other, creating a recursive trajectory rather than a linear trajectory from the past to today. Von Bertalanffy began his exploration of circular causality and homeostatic-systems thinking in the 1920s and proposed general systems theory in 1928. Von Bertalanffy did not believe that a system's individual components could be evaluated as independent entities, or the individual components assembled in a linear fashion to encompass the totality of the system. He proposed the definition of a system as characterized by the interactions of its parts and the nonlinearity of their interactions (von Bertalanffy, 1968). Concepts of wholeness and recursion were privileged over reductionism and linear causal models.

This approach was a reaction to the reductionist movement in science. Modernist thought emphasized that one could reduce elements (physics, biology, psyche) to their smallest units and investigate them independently. Von Bertalanffy thought it logical instead to investigate systems by focusing on wholeness while assuming that the whole is greater than the sum of the individual parts. In general systems theory (von Bertalanffy, 1968) a system consists of four constructs: object, attributes, mutually influencing relationships among objects, and an environment. Therefore, a system is a set of objects (individuals) that affect one another within an environment and form a greater pattern that is different from and more than its separate parts.

How this system interacts with the environment determines whether it is a closed system or an open system. Open systems are responsive to their environment, which increases its likelihood of adaptation, survival and prosperity. Closed systems do not take in information, do not interact with their environments, and trend more toward atrophy. For von Bertalanffy, human systems contain a unique attribute of self-reflexivity; that is, they have the ability to make themselves and their behavior the object of examination and target of explanation. Open systems concepts that were applied to family therapy included subsystems, hierarchy, power, self-regulation and control, homeostasis, change and adaptability, and equifinality. General systems theory formed half of the foundation for the family therapies; the other half of the foundation is first-, second- and third-order cybernetics.

CYBERNETICS

Norbert Wiener conceptualized cybernetics during World War II. Wiener was working on naval anti-aircraft defense, specifically the question of how to accurately target incoming aircraft with guns on rolling ships at sea. This mathematical challenge gave rise to cybernetics. He created the word based on the Greek *kybernetike*, literally meaning "the art of the steersman." Cybernetics can also be thought of as self-governing (self-steering). This self-governing involves regulation and signal transmission within the system. Wiener talked about the necessity of a system to transmit information and the system itself being altered by the feedback that it receives. Wiener formalized this notion of feedback loops (causal pathways that lead signals to modifications of an event) with focus on negative and positive feedback loops. Negative feedback loops restore or maintain previous homeostasis and reduce the deviation from the system, in essence keeping things at the status quo. The classic example of a negative feedback loop is a thermostat that responds to deviations from a designated temperature in a room by turning on a heater (or air conditioner) to return the temperature to the designated status quo. A human example from the film *The Godfather* is Michael Corleone's efforts to stay out of the family business. He receives multiple messages (negative feedback loops) that lead him to say, "I try to get out [which would be a deviation from the family homeostasis], but they keep pulling me back in [maintain the status quo]." Positive feedback loops, in contrast, are messages that promote or amplify deviation from the system's homeostasis, thus altering or destroying the status quo.

Gregory Bateson was a participant at the Macy Conferences and became excited about the possibilities for cybernetics in relational systems. He was exposed to von Bertalanffy's general system theory and to Wiener's cybernetics. As an anthropologist Bateson was interested in social communication. Bateson's contribution to family system theory was in the realm of epistemology. He translated the concepts of cybernetics from engineering and mathematics into behavioral science. His first publication with the Mental Research Institute (MRI) in Palo Alto, California, was "Toward a Theory of Schizophrenia" (Bateson, Jackson, Haley & Weakland, 1956). Batson wrote about the "economics of flexibility," where environmental stress can produce physical/structural changes in the organism over time. He theorized that the environment and the body have mutual influencing effects that over time may change the very genetic contribution in a family line (his hypothesis is not unrelated to current work on the human genome project looking at how epigenetic changes manifest themselves in our biology and behavior; Hall, 2010). This hypothesis was applied to clinicians' work with schizophrenic families. The MRI group realized that there were physical structures that were associated with schizophrenia, but believed that the interaction of person and environment, over generations, could produce not only the symptoms, but also physical changes in brain functioning within the identified patient.

Bateson's theory involved the "double bind," a paradoxical communication process within the family. There are four axioms for the double-bind theory (Bateson, 2000):

1. A person receives a primary injunction (e.g., a child is encouraged to demonstrate emotions, and threatened that failure to do so will lead to punishment).

2. A secondary injunction is subtly communicated that is at odds with the primary injunction (e.g., if you show emotions you will be punished).

3. A tertiary injunction is that there is no metacommunication about the conflicting messages allowed (e.g., the child will be punished if he or she points out the contradiction or seeks clarification).

4. The individual is unable to escape the field (e.g., no matter what the child does, he or she is punished).

Bateson (2000) argued that they noted this type of communication was found in schizophrenic families over multiple generations. They believed that this double-bind condition, in addition to biological predispositions of the individual, leads to psychiatric symptoms.

This work by Bateson is an example of systemic thought, of how recursive interactions between person, environment and behavior create trajectories that may at one point in time or in other contexts have utility, but with changes in context these balances (homeostases) contribute to stuckness (pathology). Later Bateson's works were collected into an anthology that provided the epistemological foundation for clinical development from the various orders of cybernetics.

Over time there developed more complex orders of cybernetics: second-order cybernetics, or the self-governance of self-governance; and third-order cybernetics, or how language constructs the observer-observed system. The difference between first-, second- and third-order cybernetics is about where the punctuation of the system occurs. In first-order cybernetics (the original version), the family system is the self-contained, observed system. Therapists are outside the influence of the family as observers and can affect the system. The role of the therapist in therapeutic approaches grounded in a first-order perspective is that of the expert that changes the family structure and fosters a new outcome. Family therapy approaches (and their primary proponents) emerging from first-order cybernetics would include structural family therapy (Salvador Minuchin), strategic (Jay Haley) and Bowenian family therapy (Murray Bowen). Second-order cybernetics sees the system as a combination of the family system (observed) and the therapist (who moves from the role of the observer who is not a part of the system, to the role of the observer who is a part of the system). Both affect and are affected by the other, with boundaries, rules and feedback loops that establish their own homeostasis. The therapist then moves from the expert position of "doing something to the family" to a position of consultant-participant. How the therapist relates with the family becomes an integral intervention. Family therapy approaches emerging from second-order cybernetics include the solution-focused approaches (Insoo Kim Berg, Steve de Shazer). Third-order cybernetics is about the language that society, the family and the therapist use to create and maintain all the components, including the observed system, observer and the observed-observer system. From this perspective the therapist is a cocreator with the family. The goal is to create through the discursive process something new that shifts relationships to a new trajectory. Family-therapy approaches based on this model of cybernetics include narrative therapy (Michael White, David Epston).

The early pioneers in various fields shifted the focus from pathology residing within the individual to treatment of "problem families." They did not presume that things were determined solely by the environment, nor by the individual, but rather that it is their mutual contribution, and the interaction between them, that together provide a trajectory. Individual agency is still a part of the process, albeit a significantly reduced part. These theories contain common philosophical assumptions that family system theories hold regarding personhood, brokenness, healing and the methods to obtain change.

MODEL OF PERSONHOOD (PERSONALITY)

Some family therapy approaches focus in part on the internal emotional system and cognitive reactivity of the individual. Johnson's emotionally focused therapy (EFT) focuses on the individual's attachment needs and emotions as a driving force in the establishment of the relational system. Bowen looks to the biological functioning of the brain and the communication process between the amygdala and the cerebrum through the prefrontal cortex (intentionality versus reactivity). Slipp and Scharff explore the effects of psychological representations of early childhood systems ("introjected families") as maintaining and creating current family systems. But the internal psychic structure of an individual is rarely the sole or main focus of family system theory. With all of these approaches, and systems theory in general, there are assumptions about personhood best understood through six important considerations: nature of reality, unit of analysis, causality, indeterminacy, self-reflexivity and self-governing (cybernetics).

Nature of Reality

Working with families involves hearing many different "truths" in the perspectives of the members. The big question is whether there is one Truth somewhere in all the different perspectives. Traditional, individual-focused psychological approaches involve a bit of modernist (Lockean) thinking, namely, the reductionistic perspective of "if we could just get to the (solitary) root cause we could alleviate the symptom." The cognitive-behavioral therapist focusing on cognitive distortions operates from the implied belief that there can be rational, true cognitive process that maps on to a Truth (see chap. 6). Likewise, the psychoanalytically oriented clinician may believe that once the individual has insight into the unconscious drives, reactions and defenses that this will reduce/alleviate the symptoms (see chap. 3). However, working with families muddles the situations because of the numerous "realities" present in the room. The father/husband has a perspective on the nature of the problem, the mother/wife has another, and somehow the adolescent sees it completely differently than both parents. How is this possible? We might naively assume that the Truth must be here somewhere. Which reporter in the family is telling the Truth? The philosophical foundation for a systemic thinker questions this presumption. Instead, the emphasis is that Truth does exist, but we can only approximate it. In fact, Maturana (1980) states that we are biologically wired and limited to perceive only in ways we can perceive. There remains the possibility for richness in our immediate context that we cannot access, yet which remains very real. Kant wrote about the knowable (phenomena) and the reality beyond the knowable (noumena). We can only approximate the noumena through what we experience. The truth of the situation for the systemic thinker isn't the noise of the story and why things are happening (or symptoms occurring). If anything, the emphasis of the family therapist is not on any of the singular "realities" of the members of the family but on the bigger reality of the family system composed of the relationships of its members. The emphasis is on how the system (with all the many beliefs of its members) is maintaining its homeostasis. For example, the systemic thinker may not care about why someone is struggling but may be more interested in the perspective of each family member on those struggles for the utility it has in the given context. The assumption is that it is the whole, not the parts, that really matters, and the resulting focus is on *how* the interactions shift, resulting in the shift of the whole of the situation.

Unit of Analysis

Traditional individual approaches to psychotherapy view the individual as the unit of analysis. Even when considering context, the emphasis remains on the individual in a given context, as when behavioral therapists look at the impact of environmental contexts on individual behavior. Systemic thought shifts the focus from the individual to the *relationship* as the unit of analysis. The individual exists and has autonomy, yet cannot be defined apart from a relational context. Consider a river analogy. What makes a river a river? Is it a body of water? Is it about the flow of that water? Is it about the bank framing the water? It is about the interaction of all these parts: water, flow, bank. They each define the other and create an understandable whole. A systemic clinician, even when working with an individual, is treating relationships. The relationship (between individuals, between subsystems within the family, between the family and the environment) are the focal point. Individuals only take on definition when considered in relationship. Psychoanalytic approaches look at the effects of early relationships on the individuals. Systemic approaches look at the relationship as containing, maintaining and creating the trajectories of the individual.

Causality

If the family theorist's focus is on the contribution of relationships between people, how do they conceptualize causation? The education system in the United States teaches the scientific method to understand causes, focusing on linear, cause-and-effect thinking ("A affects B, which affects C," as in a series of billiard ball collisions). Systemic thinkers see causal paths as recursive or circular. Von Foerster and colleagues (1952) at the Macy Conference argued that "a state reproducing itself, like an organism, or a social system in equilibrium, or a physiochemical aggregate in a steady state, defied analysis until the simple notion of a one-dimensional cause-and-effect chain was replaced by the two-dimensional notion of a circular process" (p. xiv). The concept of circular causality acknowledges that the interaction of all the parts is crucial, and, unlike a linear model, provides a clear approximation of a given event. This type of causality can be thought of as "A affects and is affected by B, and B affects and is affected by C, which affects and is affected by A." The multidirectional interaction and effects of A, B and C creates a balance (homeostasis) and possible trajectory of behavior. The interactions are the causal focus.

Thus, in family therapy the clinician focuses on how the family members interact to create the balance and trajectory they are on, instead of focusing on one person's right or wrong, adaptive or maladaptive behavior. The causal path is a collaborative one in which multiple members affect the outcome and are affected by the outcome. Examples of this can be seen in the hospitalization of adolescents for behavioral issues. The adolescent, while in the hospital, improves in his choices and attains reduction in symptoms. The adolescent is then discharged back to his original environment and the symptoms/behaviors return with a vengeance. Rather than simply blame the parents, the family therapist's focus is on how the individual symptoms (within the individual) serve a great function for the whole of the family system comprised of the parents and the adolescent.

Indeterminacy

Given the idea of circular causality and the multiple influences that occur in forming the balance/trajectory, systems thinkers apply the perspective of indeterminacy to the family system. Heisenberg's principle of indeterminacy refers to the impossibility of absolutely precise measurements, and the impact that observation has on the observed system. Social scientists encounter this difficulty when researching individuals and families. There are so many variables unaccounted for and impossible to measure precisely that outcome prediction is difficult. This is the case in family therapy. We can appreciate the circular causal path that has led to the current balance (and symptoms); however, as we change the system there is no way to know the outcome. The clinician becomes an agitating agent in the equation, perturbing the system and preventing previous interaction cycles. This allows for something new to occur, a new if unpredictable homeostasis.

Self-Reflexivity and Self-Governing

Individuals in relationship have the ability to examine themselves and their behavior. This ability to step back and take a broader metaperspective on the self-governance of the system is important to the therapeutic process. Thermostats are great self-governing systems. They have operating parameters, sensors assessing the environment, feedback mechanisms and the ability to influence the environment. We all set the thermostats in our places of residence to determine the acceptable temperature range, and the system works to keep the environment within those operating parameters. Families work the same way. We have a set of operating parameters that have been established either intentionally or reactively. Anytime an individual in the system works outside of those parameters, the environment changes and the system works to return the system to acceptable operating parameters. As individuals, families and therapists we have the ability to reflect on the rules of the system and the operating parameters. We can be aware of how we respond and create something new that hasn't occurred before. This creativity is possible, yet some contexts make the exercise of such creativity very challenging. The positing of this self-reflexivity is a tacit acknowledgment that there is something unique about the individual that puts each of us on standing at least equal to that of the system.

THEORY OF PATHOLOGY

The field of psychology on some level is defined by pathology. Insurance companies reimburse clinicians based on the psychiatric diagnostic manual. Clinicians are taught to assess for pathology that resides in the individual. Systems thinking conceptualizes that pathology resides not in individuals but in relational systems. Families that lack a means for modifying rules and structures that are outdated or no longer relevant are at risk for becoming stuck, unable to adapt. In biology an organism that is unable to adapt to changing environments will languish or die. The core understanding of pathology from a family systems perspective is behavior reflecting this stuck, stagnating systemic response.

A simple family example might be a couple with a misbehaving, rebellious adolescent. A common parental reaction to childhood misbehavior is putting a four-year-old in time-out for an infraction. This tends to be an effective negative feedback loop for the system at that age in childhood development. Fastforward to the same couple with a fourteen-year-old. The teen misbehaves and the couple puts him in time-out. This would be a feedback loop, but most probably a positive feedback loop that would maintain and encourage the rebellious behavior in a subsequent accelerating cycle of outrage. Developmental change has created a context where the once adaptive behavior is no longer functioning. It is the failure of the system to change, rather than the pathology of any individual, that is the problem. The adolescent behavior remains a volitional act, however, that act serves both an individual function and a larger systemic function.

Individual behavior occurs and is maintained in the context of family or other relational systems. The early models of family therapy postulated that problems should not be attributed to the individual symptom bearer (the identified patient), but instead, were assumed to be a signal that the system was in trouble. The disobedient child, the rebellious adolescent, the depressed wife, the abusive father—all are people whose behavioral choices serve a function in a family system, and hence *both* the individual choices and the systems need to change. The behavior of each individual is communicating or signaling a systemic problem, and represents an attempt to regulate a broken or dysfunctional system. If the system problem is corrected, the symptom (problem) will no longer be needed and may decrease. A more serious example would be the child of feuding parents who gets in trouble at school, which brings the parents together to discipline the child. Once the situation is handled the couple returns to conflictual interactions. The family gets stuck when the child's acting out serves the function of reducing couple conflict and thus is maintained in the system.

THEORY OF HEALTH

There is no template of a healthy family. Health is about goodness of fit between person, family and behavior. Family systems therapists would not say any certain family is healthy or would privilege a certain way of relating. Rather the focus is on how responsive and flexible the system is to the individuals and the environment. A pragmatic definition of health is a functional system—does the system work? Therapists are expected to refrain from predetermining the nature of a good outcome for the family, other than helping the family carry out its required tasks without reporting symptoms or problems. Therapists have theory-specific criteria for evaluating effective family functioning: the structure of the family, how individuals and family deal with anxiety, the language that members use, family adaptability to developmental changes, and the capacity to monitor and self-regulate. These criteria focus on the ability of the system to do its job, rather than on individuals' behavior within the system. Presumably, the therapist does not impose his or her idea of an "ideal" system on the family. The therapist does not presume that all families must follow the same format for achieving this goal. The only expectation is that the family can successfully regulate and balance the system's functioning. The assumption is that if the system is functioning in a healthy way, then the components within the system are most likely functioning well.

SYSTEMIC METHODS

There are a multitude of systemic approaches to therapy, such as object-relations family therapy, behavioral family therapy, functional family therapy and contextual family therapy (Piercy, Sprenkle, Wetchler & Associates, 1996). Providing an explanation and examples of each family therapy approach is beyond the scope of this chapter. Instead we will summarize the major conceptual movements of family therapy with an example or two from each. The American Association for Marriage and Family Therapy's *Family Therapy* magazine (September-October, 2008) provided a retrospective on the academic genogram (a sketch of the ancestry) of each of the major approaches to family therapy. The time line was by decades and philosophy (on a continuum from structural/functionalism to postpositivists to postmodern and contemporary empirically based models); this is a helpful summary of the family relationships among the various family therapies.

STRUCTURAL/FUNCTIONALISM MOVEMENT

The theorists and approaches in the table represent, to varying degrees, the first-order cybernetic family therapies. These approaches are primarily concerned with the function of the system. Meaning and insight on the part of the clients are not necessary for change and are not emphasized. The functional goal of the therapist is to extinguish the symptom/problem through changing the system. The therapist tends to be the agent of change and is working from the outside to facilitate different interactions. The therapist's stance is one of the expert (even if only expert on the process) who stands outside the family with certain power to manipulate the interactions of members in the room. Most of these modalities use a technique called "reframing," such as displaying a photo to depict the meaning we want by highlighting certain aspects of the photo. For example, if parents come for family therapy to address the defiant behavior of their adolescent, it is clear they are defining his behavior as a problem by labeling it as "defiant." The methods they have used to eliminate the defiance may have been ineffective. To get the family to try something different (change), the therapist may reframe the problem as a child who, like the parents, values independence but may be having a hard time telling the difference between independence and defiance. If parents accept this reframe, they are suddenly free to try a different response to his behavior since they see the problem as a struggle for age-appropriate independence (which the family values) that needs some regulation but not elimination.

Techniques used in these orientations tend to focus on the here and now. They also focus on the homeostatic value of symptoms. The first-order family therapy approaches assume that the family wants to change and gives directives to move the family to new interactions. If the family resists these requests for change, the techniques may become more paradoxical so that the therapist can use the resistance of the family to force it to change. Thus, by such techniques as "prescribing the symptom," the therapist tells the resistant family to stay the same. To resist the therapist, the family does not comply with the request to maintain the symptom but rather defies the therapist by eliminating the symptom. The goal is to achieve change *whether the family complies or not*. If the family rebels against the therapist's directive and changes the behavior, therapy has been successful, but if the family accommodates to the therapist's directive and maintains the problem state, they demonstrate that they are in fact in control and have been all along, thus taking responsibility for the "pathology." The techniques are designed to overcome lack of compliance and push the family into changing despite their resistance (Haley, MRI, Milan). The more analytic in this grouping (Ackerman, Bowen, Nagy, Lidz) still use the expert role, though they are more interested in the historical patterns and insight of the family. To exemplify this general movement, the following section will give brief overviews of structural family therapy and Bowenian family therapy.

Table 9.1. Structural/Functional Therapy Orientations

Theorist(s)	Therapeutic Orientation
Nathan Ackerman	psychoanalytic family therapy (NY)
Murray Bowen	multigenerational (Bowen) family therapy
Ivan Boszormenyi-Nagy, James Framo	contextual family therapy
Gregory Bateson, Jay Haley, Virginia Satir, Don Jackson, John Weakland, Paul Watzlewick	brief strategic (MRI Group, Palo Alto, CA)
Theodore Lidz	psychoanalytic family therapy (CT)
Carl Whitaker, Augustus Napier	experiential family therapy
Mara Selvini Palazzoli, Guiliana Prata, Luigi Boscolo, Gianfranco Cecchin	strategic (Milan Group, Italy)
Salvador Minuchin	structural family therapy

Structural Family Therapy

Structural family therapy is a first-order cybernetic perspective most closely affiliated with the work of Salvador Minuchin at the Philadelphia Child Guidance Clinic. Minuchin (1974) and his colleagues focused on a fundamental premise of systems theory that all systems require organization and structure to enable them to carry out tasks and function effectively. Complex systems like families require that tasks be assigned to designated subsystems responsible for ensuring that those specific tasks/functions are carried out, much like the human biological system that requires multiple subsystems to ensure its survival (cardiovascular system, digestive system, nervous system, immune system, etc.).

Three of the core *subsystems* identified by structural family therapy as essential for the survival and success of a family system are the spousal subsystem (provides executive oversight), the parental subsystem (oversees care of children) and the sibling subsystem (fosters peer relationship skills). Each of these subsystems performs specific tasks that contribute to the overall functioning of the family system. In addition to subsystems, the structural family therapist evaluates the clarity of *boundaries* between individuals, the various subsystems, and the family as a whole with its environment. Also of concern is how *hierarchy* and *power* are distributed through the system. If these structural elements are missing or are not functioning well, the family system will be at risk for developing problems. When there is an identified "problem" family member, structural family therapists assume that this symptomatic person is alerting the system to a breakdown in some aspect of its organization and structure, and possible intrusion across subsystems and boundaries (Minuchin & Nichols, 1993).

If the structure is unable to adapt to changing demands (e.g., by failing to realign responsibilities when a new baby is born, or by failing to modify expectations when a young child moves into adolescence), the system becomes rigid and stuck in dysfunctional patterns. The goal of structural family therapy is to help the family restructure in ways that allow for an effective balance between the competing demands to maintain stability in functioning (subsystems, boundaries, hierarchy) and to adapt to change (modify the structure to adapt to developmental and situational challenges). The focus is on the here and now with little emphasis on how problems developed. In application in a therapeutic session Minuchin would say that therapy is action. Some of the techniques associated with structural family therapy include *joining* (therapist enters family system without disrupting the pattern so as to accurately observe how the family actually functions as a system), *enactments* (therapist asks clients to carry out a task within the session so the therapist can understand how the system's structure is broken), *boundary making* and *unbalancing* (therapist actively uses session to establish generational and subsystem boundaries, realign inappropriate power/competence differentials), and *reframing* (therapist redefines the problem in such a way that the family is pushed to respond differently). The goal of all of these techniques is to enable the therapist to restructure the system to function more effectively (Minuchin & Fishman, 2004).

Bowenian/Intergenerational Therapy

Bowenian approaches to family problems differ from structural family therapy in two significant ways. First, the therapist is an expert coach who comes alongside and prompts change for the purpose of differentiation of self, of the individual being able to better negotiate togetherness and separateness in relationship. This negotiation requires an intentional and nonreactive response to anxiety that may arise in relationships. The therapist coach models this in session and creates moments for family members to be intentional when perceiving emotional threats. This focus on individual development to complement the attention to family structures is a distinct contrast to the structural approach. The second difference in Bowen's theory is the claim that intergenerational patterns are important in understanding the transmission of anxiety and low differentiation of self. Murray Bowen was a psychiatrist working with schizophrenic patients and their families at the National Institute of Health and later at Georgetown Medical School in Washington, D.C. Bowen was heavily influenced by psychodynamic theory, but sought a different explanation for what drives interpersonal interactions. Bowen was interested in the underlying emotional system that *drives* behavior. In particular, Bowen noticed that emotional intensity seemed to have a negative impact on patients' recovery. Highly emotionally charged visits with family members seemed characteristic of the schizophrenic patients he was treating.

Bowen turned to evolutionary biology to understand the more "primitive" emotionality in dysfunctional families. Evolutionary biological theory argues that the development of the brain in different species reflects a hierarchy, from the primitive brain of lower animals to the highly developed brain of humans. The unique characteristic of the highly developed human brain is the presence of the frontal cortex. Bowen argued that it is the "thinking" capacity of the cortex that creates the possibility for humans to override the emotionality that governs the primitive brain (fight-or-flight response to a threat) with a more rational and thoughtful response to a perceived threat. Family systems also reflect this evolutionary hierarchy, so that "primitive" family systems are highly emotionally reactive (high levels of fusion or cutoff), whereas more highly developed family systems have the capacity to modulate emotion by overriding the primitive reaction with a more rational/reasoned response. He called this capacity to distinguish between feeling (emotionality) and thinking (reason) "differentiation." He noted that the more highly differentiated the family emotional system was, the lower the level of dysfunction in the system (Sagar, 2006).

The family emotional system's function is to regulate competing demands for autonomy and relationship within the system. Bowen noted that the fundamental paradox in intimate relationships is the need to find a balance between the competing needs to both belong and to be separate. These opposing demands can place huge emotional stress on individuals and the family system, which must find a way to balance the conflicting needs of its members. Chronic anxiety is the consequence of this ongoing struggle for balance. For some, the anxiety is related to the fear of being rejected, of not belonging. These individuals will subjugate their own self in order to be accepted or belong (fusion/enmeshment). For others, the anxiety is related to the fear of losing the self by becoming too connected to others. These individuals will distance themselves from relationships and avoid commitment in order to preserve or protect the self (distancing, emotional cutoff). Neither fusion nor cutoff is representative of differentiation. The mature, differentiated individual can care about and connect with others without losing the genuine self. Bowen argued that when the system experiences emotional threat, anxiety intensifies and differentiation decreases. Family dysfunction and individual relationship problems are directly related to the degree of unresolved emotional attachments in the family of origin. The level of differentiation in a family system is handed down from generation to generation in that individuals tend to marry someone at the same level of differentiation as themselves and then pass this along to their own children.

The goal of this approach to therapy is to help individual clients understand the emotional processes operating within their own family of origin. The assumption is that one must have awareness of the emotional pressures being exerted in the system in order to avoid simply reacting (fight or flight) and instead make principled/rational choices in relationships. Bowen family system therapists assume that insight creates the possibility for the person to change how they interact with the family emotional system. The therapist's role is not to change the system but rather to help the client gain awareness of their family's emotional dynamics and to increase their capacity and potential to behave in a more differentiated way and to thus change the system.

The major technique developed to help the therapist increase the client's level of awareness and differentiation is the *genogram*, a diagram depicting all family members for three generations of the extended family, much like a family genealogy. The construction of the multigenerational genogram allows the client and therapist to observe the family system from an objective perspective. Emotional relationships are noted and diagrammed onto the genogram so that the client can see what patterns emerge. For example, in a family in which there are many divorces, the client can begin to recognize that cutoff is the preferred family response to emotional threat/anxiety. The assumption is that this family pattern will be repeated by the individual and will influence all their intimate relationships, even those outside the family of origin. By recognizing the tendency toward cutoff in stressful relationships, the client can begin to make other choices rather than simply following the old patterns.

FEMINIST CRITIQUE OF THE STRUCTURAL/FUNCTIONALISM MOVEMENT (PIERCY ET AL., 1996)

In the 1970s and 1980s family therapy received its fair share of criticism. Feminists from within family therapy began questioning the theory. The field's responses to these critiques led to the development of second- and third-order cybernetic family therapy approaches. The first criticism was that family therapy had embraced an arbitrary boundary with its exclusive focus on the nuclear family. Critics suggested taking the theory to its logical conclusion by focusing on a more diverse and larger array of systems (religion, government, schools, communities, police, etc.) that were constraining and maintaining families' functioning, whether adaptive or not. Power in a system constituted a privileged base in the larger systems, and often these norms were reinforced by expert therapists. McGoldrick (1988) pointed out the American and Eurocentric privilege, which focuses on fostering differentiation, hierarchy, nuclear family and independence. The question was asked, Can a family be functional if it is extended (multiple generations living in the home), matriarchal, or focused on interdependence instead of autonomy and differentiation?

Another criticism from feminists focused on the assumption that each party contributed and shared equally in dysfunctional responses in the family (e.g., cases of rape, incest and battery). The assumption that all shared responsibility for pathology in the family risked blaming the victim in cases of severe pathology (so that the abused wife, for instance, must at some level be contributing to creating her own reality). Concepts like circularity are problematic because it is impossible to think about cause separate from interaction. The feminist response focused on moving from presuming equal contribution to emphasizing the constructed meaning and use of power within embedded systems. Hoffman (1985) argued that therapists cannot consider themselves separate from the family system, but must consider the larger therapeutic system in which they function. No longer were therapists experts working from the outside through the use of power, but now were conceptualized as participant-observers. Training changed. Therapists were not trained as "knowers" but as collaborators with the family on the journey, learning together the best balance and meaning that they could create in the multiple contexts in which they all reside. The resulting transformation in the field led to the poststructural, constructivist approaches. Therapists were encouraged to disclose biases, include attention to diversity in the therapeutic conversation and change to a solution-saturated orientation.

CONSTRUCTIVISTS AND POSTSTRUCTURAL MOVEMENTS

Family therapy, from second-order cybernetics, understands the outside observer of the system to comprise a secondary self-governing system. The family has its own self-governance and homeostasis. The first-order thinkers believed that they could observe the family and perceive its balance. The dilemma is that by the very act of observing and knowing, the therapist is also being observed, creating new rules and a new balance. This

Table 9.2. Constructivists and Poststructural Therapy Orientations

Theorist(s)	Therapeutic Orientation
Tom Anderson	reflecting team (Norway)
Lyn Hoffman	multifaceted collaboration
Monica McGoldrick	multiculturalism international
Peggy Papp	collaborative questions
Nancy Boyd-Franklin	multiculturalism
Steve de Shazer, Insoo Kim Berg	solution-focused
Bill O'Hanlon, Michelle Weiner-Davis	solution-oriented
Marianne Walters, Betty Carter, Peggy Papp, Olga Silverstein	"The Women's Project"

second-order thinking highlighted the concept of constructivism. Maturana and Varela (1984) argue that what we "know" is determined by our biology, our innate mental and sensory structures. A dog would experience a therapy room differently than a human would because of our olfactory differences. This doesn't make the room any less real, but the perceptions differ as does the approximation of what is real. Therapists in the post-structural approaches no longer conceptualized themselves as outside experts but rather as a collaborative agents whose own personal journeys and theoretical frameworks are part of the process and observation.

Solution-Focused Family Therapy

The solution-focused approach to family therapy has its origins from Milton Erickson's persuasive and hypnotherapy approach, and in the MRI group's brief strategic family therapy model. Instead of having the family focus on the problem (symptom) and how they have tried to solve it, the family is encouraged to envision how things would be different if the problem were no longer a problem. The goal is to look for the positive exceptions to the rule and to act to increase the likelihood of such exceptional moments. The premise is that families tend to get stuck focusing on their unsolvable problems and, therefore, lose their ability to envision life without it. The shift in focus from the family's behavioral response to a problem, on the one hand, to their expectations or beliefs about how life would be different without the problem, reflects the influence of cognitive theory and a constructionist perspective.

The basic assumption of the solution-focused approach is that people are constrained by narrow views of their problems, which in turn lead to narrow and rigid patterns or solutions. The family, by changing the emphasis from their problems, frees themselves to try different solutions. De Shazer (1991) states, "therapists and clients jointly assign meaning to aspects of clients' lives and justify actions intended to develop a solution" (p. 74). The most well-known technique developed by proponents of this model is "the miracle question": "Suppose one night, while you were asleep, there was a miracle and this problem was solved. How would you know? What would be different?" For example, if a wife complains that the problem is her "unromantic husband," the miracle question will ask her to identify specific things her husband would be doing that let her know he is becoming more "romantic" (such as "he brings me flowers, kisses me when he comes home at night, tells me he loves me, takes me out for a date," etc.).

SOCIAL CONSTRUCTIONIST MOVEMENT

Another large shift came in the 1990s, resulting in a new focus on creativity through language in the system. The big idea in social constructionism is that reality is not only not approximated, it isn't even out there (Foucault, 1975). Reality is instead constructed by individuals in the relational process. The focus of structure shifted to the meaning making that creates the possibilities and the structure. Harlene Anderson describes her and Goolishian's work as expanding and uncovering meanings for the individual in the system. The therapist, no longer an expert, is the participant-manager in constructing a conversation that emphasizes, embellishes and elaborates on themes in a collaborative manner. The system that the therapist attends to becomes language itself rather than the interactional patterns of the family per se. In fact, clinicians from this approach believe the metaphor of family as a system is limiting and often ineffective. The clinical skills developed from this movement explore how language is shaping and constraining interactions. What happens when the family talks about the child, previously labeled as defiant, as passionate instead? How do the family story and interactions change, grow and morph as their language and meanings changes?

Table 9.3. Social Constructionist Therapy Orientations

Theorist(s)	Therapeutic Orientation
Harry Goolishian, Harlene Anderson	collaborative language systems
Michael White, David Epston	narrative (Australia)
Ken Hardy	multiculturalism
Richard Schwartz	internal family systems
Neil Jacobson	integrative couples therapy

Narrative Therapy

White and Epston (White & Epston, 1990; Epston & White, 1992) look at societal, familial and individual stories, called narratives, which privilege certain stories and relegate others to mere whispers. They presume

that the stories that families emphasize and repeat create a linguistic structure of self-understanding for the family, one that is determinative of their
functioning. The philosophical underpinnings are based on Michael Foucault's philosophy (1975) that reality exists only in agreed-upon reality
created between people. These epistemological approaches would state
there are no techniques or methods to the therapy process. Narrative therapy is the creative aspect of telling the story, deconstructing it and retelling
it with new possibilities. The therapeutic stance is one of respect and non-
blaming, a collaborative approach. While first-order approaches see the
therapist as expert, the narrative approach sees the individuals and families as experts about their own lives. The therapist assists in the telling of
their story and reduces the influence of problem-saturated stories. Morgan
(2000) states that most narrative therapists encompass two primary ways
of being: always curious, and always asking questions they really don't
know the answers to. The process of asking questions is about possibilities
and journeys. The questions therapists ask are a step on the journey, but
grounded in the assumption that there is no "right" way to go. The therapists always take positions that they can retreat from. The conversation is
collaborative and assumes that the individual and family will find and create the path that fits best.

An example would be a young man who was brought to therapy because
of anger issues. He was throwing his football helmet after unsuccessful
efforts on the field. These expressions of anger began finding their way to
home and to school as well. The family went to a narrative-oriented family
therapist, who listened to the family's story and asked the boy to describe
his anger. The boy immediately labeled the anger "Mrs. RSD." At these
words the mother started crying. Her husband explained, "She has reflex
sympathetic dystrophy (RSD), a chronic, painful, and degenerative disorder. She is in pain most days, but some are worse than others. As a result,
she will yell, be cross, but we all understand that it is the disease." The
therapist spent time understanding the family's story. The mother felt as if
she were destroying the family because of the disease and her response to
it. The therapist asked, using the previous externalization the boy created,
"When does Mrs. RSD egg you on? Who helps Mrs. RSD grow bigger
and stronger? How do each of you manage to ignore Mrs. RSD? What is
mom's relationship with Mrs. RSD?" The objective of the process is to

promote an alternative story that might relate to strength-based behaviors and experiences. There might be discussion of the strength the teacher notices when the boy banishes Mrs. RSD from the classroom. The story might shift for the boy from anger to encouraging elements that serve to bolster the emerging self. The story might shift for the mom from being the cause of the anger, to everyone having a relationship with Mrs. RSD.

Emerging Movements: Moving into the Twenty-First Century

The current trend in psychology is one of empirically validated approaches. There are now textbooks for graduate students emphasizing the science-based interventions (Liddle, Santisteban, Levant & Bray, 2010) and common factors that foster change across theories (Sprenkle, Davis & Lebow, 2009). The focus of the field has moved from theoretical conceptualization (often seen as seeking a knowing position) to a more scientific/practical approach (what works?). The movement has focused on meta-analytic issues like, Who is responsible for change? How do we all get motivated for change? How important is the therapeutic alliance?

These questions have moved family therapists from theory to praxis. The conflicts regarding philosophy are now about how we measure what we really "know" is effective. Should the evidence be from within the family (individuals)? Outside reporters (therapists)? Behaviorally anchored? There are many complex questions, and the field is experiencing growing pains as therapists merge empiricism with the various levels of cybernetics that have led them to this point. The table 9.4 documents some approaches that have received empirical support. Some, like Szapocznik's brief strategic family therapy, have been supported by numerous federal, state and local governments as the primary means of dealing with adolescent substance use.

One criticism of this movement is that each "validated" approach, due to the nature of empiricism, is targeted to a small, specific group or problem issue. This does provide new avenues into specializations like medical family therapy and work with military families. The common factors currently being researched and taught in marriage and family therapy programs are client/extratherapeutic factors (relationship, model/technique, hope/expectancy) and unique common factors (relational conceptualization, expanded direct treatment system, expanded therapeutic alliance, behavioral/cognitive/affective common factors, and privileging of the clients' experiences; Blow & Sprenkle, 2001). The next generation of family therapies will require more in-depth and pervasive outcome research than what developed over the past sixty years.

Table 9.4. Empirical Support for Emerging Movements

Therapeutic Orientation	Empirical Evidence
Emotion-focused couples therapy	Johnson & Greenberg (1985)
Brief strategic family therapy	Szapocznik et al. (1989) Santisteban et al. (1994) Santisteban et al. (2003)
Behavioral marital therapy	Azrin et al. (1980) Jacobson & Follette (1985)
Insight-oriented marital therapy	Snyder et al. (1989, 1991)
Family anxiety management training for anxiety disorders	Barrett et al. (1996)
Parent training programs for children with oppositional behavior	Wells & Egan (1988)
Multiple systems therapy	Henggeler et al. (1998) Kazdin & Weisz (1998) NMHA (2004)

Emotion-focused couples therapy. Leslie Greenberg began developing EFT in the early 1980s. He and his colleague, Susan Johnson, emphasized the emotional connection that shapes the structure of human interaction. Susan Johnson focused the theory on working with couples. Currently, there is a growing database of empirical studies supporting the effectiveness of EFT in symptom reduction, as well as enhancing sexual and marital satisfaction (Greenberg & Johnson, 1989; Goldman & Greenberg, 1992; Sherma, 2007; Honarparvaran et al., 2010). Emotion-focused therapy for couples (EFT-C) is an integrative theory that combines three distinct theories: structural family therapy, attachment theory, and humanistic theory. Consistent with the focus on empirical support for therapy approaches, EFT treatment has robust supportive data. Woolley and Johnson (2006) demonstrated in a meta-analysis that just under 90 percent of couples reported improved compared to the control group. This improved percentage declines only slightly at the two-year follow-up (with 80 percent reporting stability maintained from change since therapy).

EFT consists of nine steps, which a clinician will navigate with a couple. There are three foundational assumptions: (1) people, given the opportunity, will seek relational connection, (2) secure attachment provides a safe and secure base from which to develop these relationships, and (3) people will create balances and structures to optimally secure these attachments. It is interesting that John Bowlby's (the "first" family therapist) concepts of attachment are being revisioned in the twenty-first century. Symptoms and problems for couples are a consequence of repetitive cycles of behavior that do not fully satisfy attachment needs. EFT seeks to interrupt these repetitive cycles through changing physical boundaries, emphasizing the exceptions and enacting new behaviors. The content of these systemic shifts are always focused on the emotional and attachment needs of both partners. Johnson talks about the structure of the therapeutic relationship being like a dance, with the role of music served by the emotions. EFT is a brief treatment (8-20 sessions) that aligns with John Gottman's research (1999) suggesting the importance of increasing the number of positive/soothing interactions, and which also emphasizes (as a response to the feminist critique) interdependence, depathologizes the couple/individuals, embraces a collaborative therapeutic relationship, and privileges emotions/attachments.

A common "stuck" way of interacting understood well by the EFT approach is the circular pattern of withdraw-attack. The emotional need is one of connection. The attacker might feel as if the other partner doesn't see his or her need and thus pursues, demanding an emotionally satisfying response. The partner might feel overwhelmed and retreat. Thus the response of both is perceived as an attachment injury, providing positive feedback for more of the same interaction. This is a vicious homeostasis of a wounded couple. Changing the pattern in a safe context allows the needs to be acknowledged and the dance to occur in new ways. The following interventions emerge from this key principle: couples need new emotional interactions and secure attachments in a "positive holding" environment of the couples relationship (i.e., relational dance). Only in a "safe" relationship can we express our needs and respond to the other's needs.

The process of EFT-C involves three stages of therapy: (1) cycle deescalation, (2) changing the interactional positions, and (3) consolidation and integration. Within the first stage of *cycle deescalation,* the therapist goes through the following steps: (1) identifies the relational conflict, (2) identifies the negative interaction cycle, (3) accesses the unacknowledged emotions underlying each partner's position, and (4) reframes the problem in terms of the cycle while focusing on the primary emotions and attachment needs. Often the privileged (secondary) emotion for couples is anger. The therapist will want to deconstruct such reactive secondary emotions (anger) and expand the person's view to the marginalized, unattended to primary emotions (fear, abandonment, rejection, helplessness, incompetence, vulnerability, etc). Interventions during stage one involve alliance building to provide a secure base, facilitating expression of emotions and restructuring the interactions. At the conclusion of this stage the therapist and couple are able to see the patterns of relating, each of their respective underlying needs and how the process of protecting and meeting these needs is maintaining the pain (dance) in the relationship.

This insight leads to the second stage: *changing interactional patterns.* New patterns of relating need to be created and reinforced. Step five in EFT involves promoting each partner's appreciation of their own attachment needs. Often the couple will still focus on what the other is doing or not doing. The emphasis here is to reach a level of vulnerability and acknowledge their need. Once both are able to recognize their primary emotions and legitimate attachment needs, step six involves accepting and validating each partner's experience and needs. Couples will seek to negate their partner's perspective or feeling at this point. The therapist seeks only an understanding and acceptance of the other's perspective. At step seven the therapist encourages the partners to reach out and express their needs to each other. This is a pivotal time in the therapy process in which new interaction sequences are being established. If at any time the therapist gets stuck, or the couple reverts back to old patterns, the therapist can move back in the steps. Sentences from the various steps might go something like this: Step five: "This is what I need, this is a part of me that I have neglected." Step six: "I see you in a new way." Step seven: "When I hear criticism I feel like this little boy that is never enough. What I would like from you in those moments is encouragement. It could be words, a hug, something." A lot of previous work must be done before bringing a couple to step seven and having them reach out. Johnson talks about softening the partners to decrease blame and focus on acknowledgment and support of legitimate expressed needs.

The final stage, *consolidation and integration*, is about repetitions of the supportive new pattern. Step eight promotes new solutions to the couple's old problems. Step nine reinforces the new cycle of behavior. EFT sees the relationship as the client. The relationship is stuck. Each partner has legitimate needs. The therapist helps both partners to acknowledge those needs and to ask the other to meet with them in those needs, thus consolidating a new dance with the couple.

In addition to empirical evidence the field of family therapy is moving from a theory-driven focus to one on effective common factors. Nelson and colleagues (2007) have developed the common factors within EFT that promote change and healing. Theories will need to be able to demonstrate their effectiveness, and by doing so will contribute to the constructs that are common across theories that lead to change. Common factors and core competencies have returned therapists to their roots of looking for the "unified system" that promotes health, well-being and growth.

CHRISTIAN CRITIQUE

We applaud the emphasis the family therapy tradition places on the family as the primary context in which people can grow. For the Christian the normative structure and essential functions of the family are a crucial part of the creational order. Indeed, an important part of our identity as Christians has to do with our place in both our biological families and in the church as our new family of God. Evangelical Christianity is often noted for its individualism, a characteristic that is treated both as a strength and weakness. At the extreme, some can lose touch with the reality that God clearly seems concerned with more than just individuals; we see in the biblical record that he has dealt with his people as individuals, but also as families, as a tribe and as a body. Through Christ we are connected to each other by grace and by a covenant of love in which we are all brothers and sisters—a family in a very deep sense (cf. Anderson & Guernsey, 1985).

Interest in family therapy has certainly been fueled by the many cultural shifts relating to marriage and family that have permeated the Christian church. Divorces rate hover around 50 percent, with some statistics showing higher rates of divorce for Christians (Barlow, 1999). Researchers (and pastors) have found that premarital counseling is an effective strategy to reduce likelihood of divorce and support healthy relationships (Carroll & Doherty, 2003). Professional organizations like Smart Marriages: The Coalition for Marriage, Family, and Couples Education (www.smart marriages.com) and their religious counterparts emphasize building strong foundations before the need to mend broken marriages. Some states and churches have offered incentives of reduced fees (license fees and ceremony fees) to encourage premarital counseling. Churches are offering an increasing number of Sunday morning education classes on marriage, parenting and family relationships, and such offerings constitute a wonderful opportunity for churches to collaborate with marriage and family professionals around fostering healthy, God-honoring relationships.

Alan Dueck (1991) began writing about integration of family therapy and Christianity around the concept of the reign of God. He wrote that

> the reign of God, with the church as a sign of its presence, is the normative context of the family. The church is then the family's new home. Not simply a collection of individuals or of families, the church is called to be a community in which individuals and families obtain their nourishment and identity. The church is a community that provides to the family an alternative context to the one provided by fragmented modern society. (p. 200)

Dueck's initial attempt was at integrating his Anabaptist-Mennonite perspective with the second-order cybernetic approach of Boszormenyi-Nagy's emphasis on family work around justice issue. The integration of family therapy and Christianity is in its elementary phase. There needs to be more scholarship at the epistemological level as well as individual theoretical approach. The research in support of marriage and family therapy has radically expanded, as evidenced by the increasing empirically based systemic interventions and process research being published in such professional journals dedicated to the field as the *Journal of Marriage and Family Therapy; Journal of Systemic Therapies; Family Process; International Journal of Family Therapy; Contemporary Family Therapy; Journal of Family Psychotherapy; Journal of Feminist Family Therapy; Family, Systems, & Health;* and *The Family Psychologist.* However, within the Christian academic community, integration research and publications have been slim. Yarhouse and Sells (2008) have offered a strong perspective providing a map of the territory in family therapy and a beginning integration of theory, philosophy and content areas that clinicians will encounter. Cook and Alexander (2008) have made an effort to integrate Christianity and narrative therapy, one seeking to bridge the postmodern philosophy of our current culture and the foundational beliefs of Christianity as a means of coming alongside families and churches that are suffering and stuck in destructive patterns. There are also scholars working on content/theme-specific integration models like hope-focused marriage counseling (Worthington, 2005).

The following reflections will hopefully provide an initial orientation to some of the integrated issues with which Christians have dealt in this field.

Philosophical Assumptions

The core philosophical assumptions of systems theory and the therapeutic approaches provide mechanisms for meaning making about personhood, brokenness and the means to achieve healing. There is fertile soil for integration with a Christian worldview, and some rocky patches of soil as well. The Old Testament is a relational story emphasizing God's connection with Israel and the covenants (operating parameters) he established with them. The New Testament is a relational story of God's redemptive act to restore relationship with him. Two core philosophical issues embedded in the family-therapy movement demand our careful attention: the nature of truth and the nature of personhood; the concepts of both truth and personhood are crucial to how we understand the very nature of relationship.

Truth. A significant criticism of systems theory, and possibly the first rocky patch of soil, revolves around the concept of reality and truth. If one approaches reality from the perspective of first-order cybernetics, reality is knowable and observable, and there is the possibility of knowing objective truth. When we begin to look at reality from a second- or third-order cybernetics, things tend to be more complicated. These higher order cybernetic conceptualizations embrace postmodern, relativistic perspectives. On first blush we would assume that this would place this theory in conflict with Christianity's position on truth, but some possible compatibilities are worth examination.

Second- and third-order cybernetics suggest there are "multiple truths" or "co-constructed truths" representing the multiple perspectives of the individual parts within the system. Let's consider second- and third-order cybernetics separately. Clearly, Christians hold to the core assumption that "God is truth" and that objective truth exists and matters. A second-order cybernetic position could accept the idea that "God is truth," though this position would also emphasize that due to our biological limitations (to which Christians would add both our finiteness and our sinful separation from God) we are only ever able to approximate God and his truth. Such a position at least resembles a position of Christian humility as discussed in chapter two. Second-order cybernetic thinkers who are Christians would believe that Scripture provides a glimpse of God and that he is more than our individual conceptualizations. This idea that Scripture is necessary to understand God, yet not sufficient to encapsulate all of who God is can be seen in J. B. Phillips's (1997) discussion of how we conceptualize God and thereby, by definition, limit the omnipotent, omnipresent, omniscient aspects of God. We do "see through a glass darkly" and consequently must maintain humility in claiming that we can know what is true in a given situation. At the same time, we take encouragement in the process of knowing by the very fact that God chooses to communicate with us at all; such action on God's part clearly is communication and while our knowing may be in part it is nevertheless trustworthy at some level. Such a balance of humility and confidence seems to accord well with a second-order cybernetic approach.

Third-order cybernetic approaches present more challenges on the core issue of truth, however, because of their full embrace of constructionism, which argues that truth is only a human creation of our interactions. Even so, there are possibilities for constructive engagement with third-order cybernetic assumptions. We are created in the image of God, having the gift of relationship and creativity, and thus we are at some level empowered as cocreators with God. There are two philosophical challenges: first, the question of whether we create equally with God, and second, the question of whether God exists merely as a statement that is true because of community agreement.

For the first challenge we can quickly respond that we are not equal with God, but that nevertheless he invites us to coauthor our lives with him. The fact that we are not God's equal does not mean that our role as cocreators is insignificant. He provides the structure and major themes (his narrative, as demonstrated in Scripture) and asks that we interact and write our lives with him. We see this collaborative storytelling throughout the life of Christ. Through repentance and forgiveness a new truth emerged for the first-century Hebrew, a truth grounded in a revolutionary Messiah, not one offering militaristic or political change, but spiritual and eternal change. We are now able to accept connection through Christ and start telling a new story of ourselves with him (old self-story, new self-story). The goal in narrative family therapy, a third-order cybernetic approach, is to coconstruct a story that represents the family's subjective truth about itself. This subjective truth is constructed from the multiple minitruths (perspectives) that are available. As a Christian, and using a second-order cybernetic solution, we would say that Christians do creatively coauthor our lives (and subjective truth) with Christ. However, we do so with truths rooted in Scripture, the Holy Spirit and the church community (historical and local).

An example of this writing of a life can be seen with Dietrich Bonhoeffer (Bethge & Barnett, 2000). Bonhoeffer, while in prison, was asked by a German guard to perform the Eucharist. Bonhoeffer paused, then said he would need permission from his Russian atheist friend. The guard was perplexed, wondering why an atheist should determine whether a pastor would perform the Eucharist. Bonhoeffer told the guard that his relationship with the atheist was as sacramental as the Eucharist and cited "where two or three are gathered, there am I in their midst" as support. Bonhoeffer believed that the indwelling of the Holy Spirit and our dialectic/relational nature created a system in which God was present. He believed that how humans relate and tell their stories creates "set apart" moments. Truth and reality exist regardless of the observer/participant (us). God has created us in such a way, in his image, that allows for contribution and creativity.

Addressing the second challenge of third-order cybernetics, the denial of objective truth, is more difficult. This assumption that truth is only created is foundational to third-order cybernetics. For Christians, however, objective truth is a reality that exists and that matters. In fact, saying God exists outside of our concepts and creations over time nullifies the central philosophical foundation of constructionism. Due to the agency granted and basic to our humanity, we can either cocreate within or outside of God's narrative, and in an absolutely fundamental sense cocreation within

God's narrative has an opportunity to be true (or a close approximation thereof), and cocreation outside of God's narrative will necessarily be false. Either way, God's narrative remains.

Personhood. There are epistemological questions that have not been addressed in the literature regarding family systems and Christianity. This is especially true in dealing with the nature of personhood. Richardson (1996), working on integrating church leadership and Bowenian theory, discusses the nature of personhood: "two deep and basic life forces are built into the biology of each human being and at work in each human emotional system or community. These are the life forces for togetherness and for individuality" (p. 56). His work emphasizes the recursive nature of systemic thought.

Personhood is *both* individualistic and contextual; humanity embodies the attributes of God's image in creativity, rationality and relationality. This recursive process suggests that Christians are both responsible for their choices (which shape their contexts like church and family) and can be constrained by the contexts they live in (some choices are easier or more difficult based on family, church, societal structures). These are second- and third-order perspectives on personhood. The first-order assumptions were addressed twenty years ago by Jones and Butman (1991) in forging a critique of family therapy, focusing largely on Jay Haley's strategic and Minuchin's structural assumptions about personhood and change. The emphasis of these two early family models discounted insight, emphasizing "the system" as the main mechanism for change and growth. Personhood was minimized as "the system" drove behavior. Jones and Butman (1991) were concerned about the difference between studying *both* the family *and* the individual, versus focusing on the family system *rather* than the individual. Structural and strategic versions of family therapy seem to implicitly or explicitly embrace what might be called a "collectivist" view of persons, which sees persons as largely or exclusively a product of social interaction. More specifically, it contends that our core identity is best seen as being part of a system, a collective of people, whether that be a class, familial or societal grouping. Individual personality is deemed trivial or insignificant. Because who we are and how we behave is a function of the interpersonal systems we exist in, what matters is the character and functioning of the system, not the person.

The fear is that in a collectivist perspective, individuality largely disappears. With this largely exclusive focus on structured relationships in family systems, a respect for internal processes and developmental histories vanishes. These concerns are similar to those expressed about a much more strident and extreme collectivist approach to persons, that of doctrinaire Marxism, where individuality evaporates into the collective of the social class. Jones and Butman (1991) drew some valid critique of these first-order cybernetic approaches from one critique of Marxism. In making this argument, please note that they were not equating family therapy with Marxism, nor were they saying that family therapy is Marxist; rather, the arguments that emerge from this critique have applicability.

Pannenberg's (1989) critique of Marxism states that a collectivist view of persons is "sharply opposed to Christian personalism, because in a Christian perspective the individual person is constituted by his or her immediate relation to God. Therefore in a Christian view the person cannot be considered to be thoroughly dependent on the social context" (p. 217). Note that in this argument Pannenberg assumes that relationship, specifically between person and God, is vital. However, the disappearance of the individual within other social contexts is the concern. Any conception of persons that minimizes or obliterates the individual on behalf of the family runs the risk of seriously degrading a Christian understanding of personhood. A healthy family is one that fully appreciates the richness and strength of diversity, and encourages individuation; it does not stress homogeneity to the neglect of heterogeneity.

Should not a healthy family-therapy theory also respect appropriate individualism? To their credit, a number of the family therapy approaches discussed in the first half of the chapter do support such an understanding of the individual in the family. There is a need for more scholarship on the complexity of an autonomous self while existing in contexts (family, church, society) that constrict, constrain and promote certain expressions of that individuality.

Further, in Marxism alienation from the collective, which occurs in the form of individualism in various forms, is considered to be the fundamental problem of human experience. But "in a Christian perspective, of course, it is the Marxist reductionism, the reductionism of the person to a function of social interaction, that produces the alienation of the human person from the constitutive center of his or her human life, i.e., from God" (Pannenberg, 1989, p. 217). We cannot be truly human when our understanding of ourselves and our condition uproots a fundamental sense of ourselves as individuals, though grounded in our relationships with God, family and others. Such a view would cause, not alleviate, true alienation.

A significant problem within system approaches is that the *content* of the relationships are considered noise and often deemed irrelevant. This lack of content reduces relationships to mere behaviors. Pannenberg (1989, p. 218) argues a similar point regarding content of relationships; specifically, that atheism is not accidental or incidental to Marxism, but interwoven throughout the system. It is central to Marxism to argue that human systems create persons, while Christianity, on the other hand, argues that we are creatures of God. The central content to relationship is God. Thus, in the Christian view, people must transcend the social context and be ultimately grounded in relationship to God to be a self. Unless humans are, they run the risk of asserting that they create their own identities primarily by the way they relate to others. Consequently, they have little use for a transcendent reality like God. Family theory can, in like fashion, see the individual as purely a product of family processes and hence judge God to be irrelevant. A more balanced perspective on personhood would stress dimensions of community, family and individuality as bases for our identity, but anchor our understanding of them in the context of a personal relationship with a Creator God. In other words, understanding personhood only in horizontal relationships in the social context is inadequate without the vertical dimension as well.

Jones and Butman (1991) thus object to the loss of respect for individuality evident in the more strategic and structural models of family therapy. The most striking and salient characteristics of an individual are at risk of being replaced by the global and sometimes generic characteristics of family systems. They themselves noted that it might seem ironic to make this criticism, in that they have roundly criticized many other therapeutic approaches for their rank individualism, however the main argument was that personhood is individual, contextual and the interaction of the two. Christians have always had a high view of the person and the family. Persons are created in the image and likeness of their Creator God (i.e., the doctrine of the *imago Dei*), and the family has certain God-ordained functions (e.g., procreation, socialization and support, mediating between the individual and society, etc.). Systemic thinking, although it is a refreshing alternative paradigm for creative working models of personality, psychopathology and psychotherapy, tends to blur those qualities that make us most distinctive (i.e., our potential to be active agents engaged in a quest for meaning and significance). Responsible persons who make choices are surely more than the sum product of external social forces.

In summary, a fully developed and comprehensive Christian view of persons will balance an emphasis on individualism that treasures the individual person's relationship with a God who loves him or her as an individual with a broader realization that individuals do indeed exist as parts of systems. We are part of and defined by our families, our friendships, the organizations we give ourselves to, and the cultures we are a part of. From a spiritual perspective, we are part of the body of Christ; we are branches grafted into a single line; we are brothers and sisters adopted into a single family. The church is present as the body of Christ (e.g., Rom 12; 1 Cor 12) working together and relating to the world as Christ. The church also provides a safe family context for many. Paul provides an example of systemic thinking in his letter to the church in Philippi, as he is encouraging and emphasizing right relationship with God, unity within the community, negotiating conflict and being intentional in relationship instead of reactive.

It must also be noted that as systemic theory and approaches continued to develop over the ensuing twenty years, this critique has less relevance to the second- and third-order cybernetics. There remains a need for conceptualization of personhood from a Christian systemic perspective. Some examples of pivotal personhood questions focused on human agency include: Is sin mutual, individual and contextual? Philosophically (and theologically) is all of creation, including institutions, sinful (sinning, tainted by sin)? Or is it the individual's sin and its consequence that affects all of creation? What does mutuality and recursion mean regarding individual responsibility?

Determinism. At least at a covert level the strategic approaches assume that family members often have very limited resources to directly and responsibly confront their issues or really control their lives. The therapist is seen as an expert that does something to the family system, which produces a new product. If that product is functional, the therapy is successful.

Certainly we do not want to minimize the reality of the fears and failures of many family systems, especially in a time of social upheaval and transition in contemporary American society. First-order family therapists, especially, assume an extreme utilitarian stance toward family dynamics, assisting members in adjusting to each other, but not really providing them insight into their potential as responsible agents. One concrete manifestation of this is how rarely it is in strategic versions of family therapy for clients to be encouraged to understand the interventions offered by the therapist or to develop insight about the changes they have been through. Restructuring is often deemed more important (or curative) than awareness and understanding. Free will and the personal dimensions of causation need to be taken more seriously in systemic thinking. More recent family approaches, however, have shifted from viewing the therapist as an expert (first order) to more collaborative approaches that emphasize the strengths of the family members, as seen in the emphasis of Froma Walsh's (1998) book *Strengthening Family Resilience.*

NATURE OF PERSONHOOD/PERSONALITY THEORY

Rather than looking at personhood from each family therapy approach, we will look at the systemic epistemology (specifically first- and second-order orientations) and how it is congruent with and divergent from Christianity. Systems theory implicitly acknowledges the individual and makes assumptions about the individual. However, the most important aspect of individuals is that they are relational, make meaning, affect and are affected by the other, and have the capacity for self-reflection.

Ray Anderson (1991) wrote about the meaning of humanity being made in the *imago Dei* (image of God) as, at the core, our relationality (this same theme was developed in chap. 2). Genesis 1:26 says, "Then God said, 'Let us make humankind in our image, according to our likeness'" (NRSV). God addresses humanity in relationship (male and female). This concept of relationship exists on three levels within the creation story. Relationship is seen in the mystery of the recursive nature (same essence yet distinct) within the Godhead (*our* image, let *us*), between God

and humanity, and within humanity (male and female). These relationships are seen from the creation story in Genesis to the apocalyptic writing of John in Revelation.

A primary assumption about individual behavior in systems thinking is
that individuals do not behave in a vacuum but rather in the context of
social and emotional systems. The desire and capacity for being in relationship with others is assumed to be biologically wired into humanity.
The social networks formed by these relational ties create the larger systems in which all people function. These relational systems follow the
same rules as any other system. While this assertion might initially offend
some Christian sensibilities, it is not incompatible with our understanding
of community as part of the created order. Humans are subject to the laws
of physics and chemistry; might we also be subject to broader patterns that
characterize created systems?

Systems that function well benefit all individuals within the system.
Systems that are dysfunctional are not responsive to environmental
changes, do not have the flexibility to adapt and negatively impact the
individuals within the system. Some argue that individualism is neglected
at best and destroyed at worst from a systems perspective. This is not necessarily the case. Individual agency remains important, however, it is understood as operating only in the contexts it occurs in. This contextual
focus is not deterministic, rather it provides an understanding of the plas-
ticity of development and individual choice as a function of the trajectory
of individual-relational-contextual dance or interrelationship. Systemic
thinking provides solid arguments for Christians to be active in a community of faith. Since we are relational, and how we do this relationship
provides the structure for our thoughts, emotions and behavior, being involved in a community will allow opportunities to seek truth together and
experience grace in a secure-attachment environment. Local communities
(churches) can be informed by systemic thought in establishing their structure and how they live out their mission. The body of Christ is a great
systemic metaphor because it emphasizes the necessary uniqueness within
community and the concept of wholeness/unity of the church. Paul describes this relational dance of individual-relationship as a metaphor of the
body (the body of Christ) to emphasize the interrelationships among the
individual believers who make up the church:

The body is a unit, though it is made up of many parts; and though all its parts are many, they form one body. So it is with Christ. For we were all baptized by one Spirit into one body. . . .

Now the body is not made up of one part but of many. . . . If one part suffers, every part suffers with it; if one part is honored, every part rejoices with it. (1 Cor 12:12-14, 26)

This analogy of the church as a body evokes the essential assumption of systems theory, namely, that a system consists of different parts (individuals) that must function together for the good of the whole system. Scripture reports many instances when God has used systems to accomplish his purposes (e.g., Abraham's family, the nation of Israel, the church). Systemic thinking can help in establishing how the church lives out relationships internally and within its context. Ask the following questions: Who would notice if the church closed its doors and didn't meet anymore? What needs would not be met if we weren't in this community? How would the neighborhood, local government, schools and businesses be affected by the church's absence? How are these contexts (see previous question) affecting and being affected by the body of Christ of this congregation? The systemic assumption is that we are relational and that there is mutual influencing between self (church) and others (community). How intentional has the body of Christ been in living out relationships with each other and with the neighborhood and world? Is the church relevant or is it stuck in a structure that was helpful twenty, fifty or one hundred years ago, but hasn't adapted to current cultural, global and technological changes?

A final assumption about personhood from a systems perspective is that humans have the capacity to monitor and regulate their own and the system's functioning, and that this capacity is fundamental if they are to achieve their purposes. Individuals and families need to have internal mechanisms for monitoring function and repairing perceived imbalance. The expectation that individuals should be self-regulating and self-correcting seems consistent with a Christian perspective. For example, in Romans 8 Paul talks about why he does what he doesn't want to do. This is an example of the awareness he has about his limited ability to choose righteousness and the pressures of the system to direct (not determine) to certain behaviors. The context shapes Paul's choices. The ultimate context is that we are separated from God and can try to do something (but to no avail) on our own power to restore that relationship. The law was given to demonstrate what needs to be done to live a holy life: "Therefore no one will be declared righteous in [God's] sight by observing the law; rather, through the law we become conscious of sin" (Rom 3:20). None have been able to live in holiness, let alone restore a right relationship with God. There is an awareness of this, and yet a stuckness in that we can do no other. The only mechanism for renewed relationship is the redemptive work of Christ. Through God's work in changing the system, becoming flesh himself and sacrificing for us, we are able to enter relationship with him anew. It is a both/and situation. We need God's systemic change, and we need to respond.

Personhood is best experienced in tension between being aware of our situation, being relational by nature (ontic); being bound by the biological, social and spiritual system; and being able to choose to respond to a new context. During the past thirty years the cultural context in the United States has been consumerism. The emphasis is on business and consumption. The church, being connected with the culture, has found a balance by becoming more like businesses. Pastoral staffs have a corporate structure. The entry-level jobs are youth pastors, while the senior pastor is like the CEO. As a church we have to be intentional about how we respond to (influence and are influenced by) the current culture. The relational emphasis in personhood allows the church to be the location for change. Bonhoeffer (1991) talked about two theologies: theology of sociality and theology of forgiveness. Relational personhood, and thus the church, is central to both. Theology of sociality emphasizes the isomorphic process in relationship. We are free to rule and act in creation, and with that freedom we are also free to obey. Christ's redemptive act empowers us, through our relationship with him, to be in right relationship with God. It also requires us to be in right relationship with each other.

This leads to the theology of forgiveness. It is only through relationship that we have forgiveness. Through Christ we are to be not only sanctified and justified individuals, but we are called to be a living community, supporting and challenging each other. We believe this deeply because it is congruent with both our faith and systemic thinking, and yet when we encounter this type of community it is painful. Culturally, we are individualists. We value our ability to choose, create and act. We are less comfortable with the freedom to obey (to submit to authority, to make a sacrificial commitment to community, to obey Christ). We don't like others pointing out what we need to do, or how our response affects them. We are comfortable being consumers, because that is the culture we live in. Yet this is what the church, and systemic change, is about: creating a space for change, growth and healing that is not only influenced by the culture but can also influence the cultural context. Family therapy focuses on changing relationships. The church focuses on changing relationship with God. Family therapy focuses on finding a process that promotes growth for each family member in their current context. We believe that family therapy is moving communities into thinking about relationships and that the church can be a family that fosters healthy relationship (in both redemptive and preventative processes) in how it serves its members and its neighborhoods.

Despite the utility and importance of the foregoing, it must be said that family therapy does not give us a personality theory. The fundamental characteristics of a "functional" system remain obscure. The Bible provides numerous injunctions about the specific shape of virtue and of the qualities we are to manifest as the fruit of the Spirit. Yet our understanding of these biblical imperatives will always be interpreted within the context of our personal problems, failings and inevitable distortions due to our humanness, fallenness and finiteness. All too easily our family relationships can become distorted, fixated or stagnated—grace can turn into law, empowerment can lead to a sense of possessive power, covenant can be replaced by contract, and personal aloofness can substitute for a real sense of intimacy (cf. Balswick & Balswick, 2007). Once again, it is imperative that we draw from the resources of our faith and the local discerning community of believers. This presupposes that we are connected in the kind of support system that is characterized by a healthy balance between affirmation and accountability, and by a strong commitment to "being the church" in word and deed (Anderson & Guernsey, 1985).

In summary, then, we see much in the family therapy understanding of families that has exciting integrative possibilities for the Christian concerned about helping people grow. The importance of roles and structures, and firm but flexible boundaries, has been consistently emphasized. A key

difference between much of family therapy and the Christian view appears
to be the ultimate basis for such characteristics: the former based in a pragmatic and utilitarian mindset (i.e., because it "works"), but the latter rooted
in the command to manifest these qualities as an expression of our covenantal and grace relationship with the Creator God (i.e., we love because
God first loved us).

NATURE OF BROKENNESS/THEORY OF ABNORMALITY

The systemic perspective on abnormality is that it is relational, is contextual, has consequences for the individual and the system, and is about
being stuck with no way for the system to adapt to the situation. Scripture makes it clear that individuals are at some level accountable for their
choices and the behaviors they engage in. Humans are individually responsible for the moral failures, the injustices, the sins that they commit.
But our brokenness also reflects a system failure or flaw, as all of creation
has been affected by sin, which affects us with its brokenness (sinful
stain). Sin is both an individual sin and a community/system problem
(see chap. 2).

Sin is a relational endeavor. The Genesis story provides the initial template that relational violation creates a system separate from God. Every
sinful act is relational. Despite being an individual act, it affects and is affected by the multiple embedded systems. The systemic perspective that
Adam and Eve's relational violation continues to ripple through our world
and lives is a testimony to the relational nature of sin. The context in
which we develop affects us (the sins of the father passed down to the third
or fourth generations [Deut 5:9]). We can only do what we know to do,
and what we know to do is largely a function of the self-governing system(s)
we reside in. We are affected by a sinful system that we also contribute to,
whether our very biology is such that from conception we are affected by
sin, or at the moment of birth we have the potential for holiness but are
unable to do anything but sin because of our context. This recursive process keeps us separate from God. God reminds us of this, "All have sinned
and fall short of the glory of God" (Rom 3:23).

Individuals with agency or free will can choose behavior, but it is nevertheless the case that the choices available, constrained by systemic influences, present limited opportunities for righteousness and create a greater

likelihood of a sinful trajectory. Because of the system (sinful nature) we are constrained or bound by our sin. It takes a focus from outside the system (Christ) to provide flexibility (freedom) for a new response. Our bonds are broken and we are set free through the death and resurrection of Christ. This is a systemic change that allows new things (and us as new creatures). How we think about pathology and sin will directly affect how we think about healing. Sin and pathology are complicated. There are the situations that we choose, albeit affected by our context. There are the situations that happen to us due to conflict in a larger system and regarding which we don't have any direct causal involvement (such as those presented in the book of Job). Most often it is a combination of individual choice and context interacting to create a sinful trajectory. Since the context affects us, there is a strong argument that being involved in church community can become a healing context that fosters a holy trajectory.

NATURE OF HEALING/THEORY OF HEALTH

Health is a function of how well the system balances within its environment as well as how information flows in and out of the system. Systems need structure, flexibility, responsiveness and emotional presence. None of these characteristics are in tension with Scripture. In fact, Scripture provides many examples and admonitions regarding the need to establish clear lines of responsibility and authority in different kinds of systems (e.g., Ex 18:17-23; Eph). Minuchin and others emphasize that the executive subsystem needs to provide the structure and frame for the family. This provides clear boundaries, communication and sense of security.

However, the family systems approach is pragmatic in its concept of health: whatever works is regarded as healthy. There are tacit ideas of what works for many of the specific approaches, such as vulnerability, flexibility and openness. But these concepts of health are about adaptability; there is no moral sense of health from a systems perspective. This is in tension with Christianity. Scripture provides templates for what is considered healthy and holy, though Christians may debate the contextual nature of biblical guidelines about gender roles, authority, behaviors, money, language and so on. There are times when the pragmatism of systems theory collides with a Christian's sense of right and wrong.

Healing from our brokenness involves not only structure, flexibility and responsiveness of an individual and system; it also requires meeting emotional needs. Johnson's EFT approach demonstrates the power and effectiveness of acknowledging our own and the other's needs. Not only do we acknowledge these, we are active in meeting these needs in new ways. Often the sins we commit originate from legitimate needs or feelings that we meet in unhealthy or ungodly ways. These misdirected ways of meeting our needs could be conceptualized as the stuck emotional dance we do (Johnson & Greenberg, 1985). Christians might conceptualize the stuck dance as the repetitive ways we violate what God designed for us and commands of us. We find a balance either from the feedback we are receiving or the family patterns we learned. The challenge is doing these dances in new ways. The freedom we have in Christ is the freedom to be in relationship with him. The freedom we have is to be vulnerable and present, and to receive grace when we deviate from his path. Thus, how do we as Christ followers and as systemic thinkers facilitate a relational dance that fosters emotional presence?

> Do to others as you would have them do to you. If you love those who love you, what credit is that to you? Even sinners love those who love them. And if you do good to those who are good to you, what credit is that to you? Even sinners do that. And if you lend to those from whom you expect repayment, what credit is that to you? Even sinners lend to sinners, expecting to be repaid in full. But love your enemies, do good to them, and lend to them without expecting to get anything back. . . . Be merciful, just as your Father is merciful. (Lk 6:31-36)

This passage calls us to live out the relationship we have with God. The old system is a self-serving one. Christ's redemptive work in our lives provides an alternative positive feedback loop that will foster more of this merciful, Christlike relationship. Our relational system is strikingly compatible with a Christological theology of relationships. The systems theory of health is an empty frame that emphasizes the structure of interacting and healing. This opens creative possibilities for the Christian practitioner to lead and shape families in ways consistent with God's desires for that family. There are dangers in cocreation, depending on the clinician, that could lead others, as they cocreate a new balance, away from Christ. This leads to an important anchor for the Christian clinician (God's Word as the ultimate author): The content of the system is as vital as the process of experiencing and expressing it. Christian theology expects the redemptive work of Christ in the life of the believer to be what makes change possible; systems approaches are often saying that it isn't the content of the system but the process itself that heals. But can the process ever be completely separated from the content? Powerful results are possible when the message, method and person are complementary. The challenge then is for Christians and churches to take the message of Christ and the method of doing church, relationship and community equally important.

CONCLUSION

The field of family therapy continues to develop from its cybernetic heritage and the cultural and historical contexts it is embedded in. The variety of models makes it difficult to develop a single Christian critique of family therapy. Rather, the critique must, on the one hand, focus at a very high level of abstraction on shared common principles across the diverse array of family therapies (which is the emphasis in this brief treatment), but on the other hand, be less universal and focused more on evaluating the varying assumptions, goals and techniques of each different model. In addition, the field is moving to a focus on treatment efficacy and common factors with emphasis on the product of the therapy and system. When a family asks for "family therapy," which model of treatment will the family actually receive? The common factors (Sprenkle et al., 2009) movement will hopefully engender greater consistency in delivery of systemic treatment. However, consumers should be thoughtful in the selection of family therapists. The lack of a common model of treatment similar to psychodynamic or cognitive-behavioral approaches is a significant concern that will hopefully be addressed by current research that is asking which models are most effective for what kind of problems with which families.

There is solid empirical research supporting systemic work with couples (EFT), health issues, delinquency and child issues. Evidence-based research continues to be the focus of graduate programs and the professional organizations within family therapy (American Association for Family Therapy, International Family Therapy Association, and Division 43: Family Psychology of the American Psychology Association). Understanding the foundational assumptions will help Christians select "goodness of fit" clinicians.

Family therapy provides an alternative to the highly individualistic approaches of many other models of psychotherapy. Based on its contextual focus, it highly values the diversity found in families today. The approach embodies an appreciation for the contributions (growth promoting and stagnating) of cultural, religious and other contexts. From a theological perspective its strengths are reflected in the high value it places on helping families carry out their functions and the emphasis on understanding individual functioning in the broader context of personal relationship systems. Many current models have spotlighted and challenged the unjust constraints placed on families by oppressive systems that affect their functioning. Certainly, this is a stance that Christian theology supports. Care for the marginalized and oppressed should be a hallmark of the believer.

In summary, both practitioners and clients who want to work and be treated from a theologically appropriate model of family systems will be challenged to understand which aspects of the different models are most consistent with a Christian worldview. How does a Christian worldview of reality, sin and healing overlap or diverge from a systems perspective in general? And what of each specific family therapy approach (e.g., Bowen, EFT, solution focus, narrative)? The encouraging news is that many of the assumptions and techniques of family therapy models are compatible with a biblical perspective. In particular, family therapy reinforces the Christian values of principled interpersonal relationships, concern for social justice for the marginalized, resources found in community and support for families to help them accomplish their functions and purposes.

FOR FURTHER READING

Anderson, H., & Gehart, D. (2006). *Collaborative therapy: Relationships and conversations that make a difference.* New York, NY: Brunner Routledge.

Balswick, J. O., & Balswick, J. K. (2007). *The family: A Christian perspective on the contemporary home.* Grand Rapids, MI: Baker Academic.

Bateson, G. (2000). *Steps to an ecology of mind: Collected essays in anthropology, psychiatry, evolution, and epistemology.* Chicago, IL: University of Chicago Press.

Cook, R., & Alexander, I. (2008). *Interweavings: Conversations between narrative therapy and Christian faith.* North Charleston, SC: CreateSpace.

Furrow, J. L., Johnson, S. M., & Bradley, B. A. (2011). *The emotionally focused casebook: New directions in treating couples.* New York, NY: Brunner Routledge.

Johnson, S. M. (2004). *The practice of emotionally focused couple therapy: Creating connections* (Basic Principles into Practice series). New York, NY: Guilford Press.

Lebow, J. L. (2005). *Handbook of clinical family therapy.* New Jersey: Wiley.

McGoldrick, M., Giordano, J., & Garcia-Preto, N. (2005). *Ethnicity and family therapy.* New York, NY: Guilford Press.

Minuchin, S., & Fishman, C. (2002). *Family therapy and techniques.* Cambridge, MA: Harvard University Press.

Selekman, M. D. (2010). *Collaborative brief therapy with children.* New York, NY: Guilford Press.

Sprenkle, D., Davis, S., & Lebow, J. (2009). *Common factors in couple and family therapy: The overlooked foundation for effective practice.* New York, NY: Guilford Press.

Von Bertalanffy, L. (1969). *General systems theory: Foundations, development, applications.* New York, NY: Braziller.

Yarhouse, M. A., & Sells, J. N. (2008). *Family therapies: A comprehensive Christian appaisal.* Downers Grove, IL: IVP Academic.

REFERENCES

AAMFT. (2008, September-October). Family therapy pioneers: A directory. *Family Therapy, 23*-49.

American Society for Cybernetics. (2010). *Foundations: Coalescence of cybernetics.* Retrieved 11, October, 2010. www.asc-cybernetics.org/foundations/history2.htm.

Anderson, H. (1997). *Conversation, language, and possibilities: A postmodern approach to therapy.* New York, NY: Basic Books.

Anderson, H., & Goolishian, H. (1988). Human systems as linguistic systems. *Family Process, 27,* 371–393.

Anderson, H., & Goolishian, H. (1992). The client as the expert: A not knowing approach to therapy. In S. McNee & K. Gergen (Eds.), *Therapy as a Social Construction* (pp. 25-39). London: Sage.

Anderson, R. (1991). *On being human: Essays in theological anthropology.* Pasadena, CA: Fuller Seminary Press.

Anderson, R., & Guernsey, D. (1985). *On becoming family.* Grand Rapids, MI: Eerdmans.

Azrin, N. H., Bersalel, A., Bechtel, R., Michalicek, A., Mancera, M., Carroll, D., Shuford, D., & Cox, J. (1980). Comparison of reciprocity and discussion-type counseling for marital problems. *American Journal of Family Therapy, 8,* 21-28.

Balswick, J. O., & Balswick, J. K. (2007). *The family: A Christian perspective on the contemporary home.* Grand Rapids, MI: Baker Academic.

Barlow, J. L. (1999). A new model for premarital counseling within the church. *Pastoral Psychology, 48*(1), pp. 3-9.

Barrett, P. M., Dadds, M. R., Rapee, R. M., & Ryan, S. M. (1996). Family intervention for childhood anxiety: A controlled trial. *Journal of Consulting and Clinical Psychology, 64*(2), 333-42.

Bateson, G. (2000). *Steps to an ecology of mind: Collected essays in anthropology, psychiatry, evolution, and epistemology.* Chicago, IL: University of Chicago Press.

Bateson, G., Jackson, D. D., Haley, J., & Weakland, J. (1956). Toward a theory of schizophrenia. *Behavioral Science, 1,* 251-264.

Bethge, E., & Barnett, V. (2000). *Dietrich Bonhoeffer: A biology.* Minneapolis, MN: Augsburg Fortress Publishers.

Blow, A., & Sprenkle, D. (2001). Common factors across theories of marriage and family therapy: A modified delphi study. *Journal of Marital and Family Therapy, 27*(3), 385-401.

Bonhoeffer, D. (1991). *Dietrich Bonhoeffer: Witness to Jesus Christ* (Making of Modern Theology). Minneapolis, MN: Augsburg Fortress Publishers.

Bowlby, J. (1949). The study and reduction of group tensions in the family. *Human Relations, 2,* 123-128.

Carroll, J. S., & Doherty, W. J. (2003). Evaluating the effectiveness of premarital prevention programs: A meta-analytic review of outcome research. *Family Relations, 52*(2), 105-118.

Cook, R., & Alexander, I. (2008). *Interweavings: Conversations between narrative therapy and Christian faith.* North Charleston, SC: CreateSpace.

De Shazer, S. (1991). *Putting difference to work.* New York, NY: Norton.

Dueck, A. (1991). Metaphors, models, paradigms and stories in family therapy. In H. Vande Kemp (Ed.), *Family therapy: Christian perspectives* (pp. 175-207). Grand Rapids, MI: Baker.

Epston, D., & White, M. (1992). *Experience, contradiction, narrative and imagination.* Adelaide, Australia: Dulwich Centre Publications.

Foucault, M. (1975). *The archaeology of knowledge.* London: Tavistock.

Goldman, A., & Greenberg, L. (1992). A comparison of systemic and emotionally focuses outcome studies. *Journal of Marriage and Family, 5,* 21- 28.

Gottman, J. M. (1999). *The marriage clinic: A scientifically based marital therapy.* New York, NY: W. W. Norton & Company.

Greenberg, L. S., & Johnson, S. M. (1989). Different effects of experiential and problem-solving interventions in resolving marital conflict. *Journal of Clinical and Consulting Psychology, 63,* 67-79.

Hall, S. S. (2010, October). Revolution postponed. *Scientific American,* 60-67.

Henggeler, S. W., Schoenwald, S. K., Borduin, C. M., Rowland, M. D., & Cunningham, P. B. (1998). *Multisystemic treatment of antisocial behavior in children and adolescents*. New York, NY: Guilford Press.

Hoffman, L. (1985). Beyond power and control: Toward a "second-order" family systems therapy. *Family Systems Medicine, 3*, 381-396.

Honarparvaran, N., Tabrizy, M., Navabinejad, S., & Shafiabady, A. (2010). The efficacy of emotionally focused couple therapy (EFT-C) training with regard to reducing sexual dissatisfaction among couples. *European Journal of Scientific Research, 43*, 538-545.

Jacobson, N. S., & Follette, W. C. (1985). Clinical significance of improvement resulting from two behavioral marital therapy components. *Behavior Therapy, 16*, 249-262.

Johnson, S. M., & Greenberg, L. S. (1985). Differential effects of experiential and problem-solving interventions in resolving marital conflict. *Journal of Consulting and Clinical Psychology, 53*, 175-184.

Jones, S., & Butman, R. (1991). *Modern psychotherapies* (1st ed.). Downers Grove, IL: InterVarsity Press.

Kazdin, A. E., & Weisz, J. R. (1998). Identifying and developing empirically supported child and adolescent treatments. *Journal of Consulting and Clinical Psychology, 66*, 19-36.

Liddle, H., Santisteban, D., Levant, R., & Bray, J. (2010). *Family psychology: Science-based interventions (decade of behavior)*. Washington, DC: American Psychological Association.

Maturana, H. (1980). *Biology of cognition*. In H. Maturana & F. J. Varela (Eds.), *Auteoporesis and cognition: The realization of the living* (Boston Studies in the Philosophy of Science, vol. 42., pp. 5-58). Boston, MA: D. Reidel Publishing.

Maturana, H., & Varela, F. (1984). *The tree of knowledge: Biological roots of human understanding*. London: Shambhala.

McGoldrick, M. (1988). Ethnicity and the family life cycle. In B. Carter & M. McGoldrick (Eds.), *The changing family life cycle: A framework for family therapy* (2nd ed.). New York, NY: Gardner Press.

Minuchin, S. (1974). *Families and family therapy*. Cambridge, MA: Harvard University Press.

Minuchin, S., & Fishman, H. C. (2004). *Family therapy techniques*. Cambridge, MA: Harvard University Press.

Minuchin, S., & Nichols, M. P. (1993). *Family healing: Strategies for hope and understanding*. New York, NY: Free Press.

Morgan, A. (2000). *What is narrative therapy? An easy-to-read introduction*. Adelaide, Australia: Dulwich Centre Publications.

National Mental Health Association. (2004). *Mental health treatment for youth in the juvenile justice system: A compendium of promising practices.* Alexandria, VA: National Mental Health Association.

Nelson, T., Chenail, R. J., Alexander, J., Craine, D. R., Johnson, S. M., & Schwallie, L. (2007). The development of core competencies for the practice of marriage and family therapy. *Journal of Marital and Family Therapy, 33*(4): 417-438.

Pannenberg, W. (1989). Christianity, Marxism, and liberation theology. *Christian Scholar's Review, 18*(3), 215-226.

Phillips, J. B. (1997). *Your god is too small.* Woodland Park, CO: Touchstone.

Piercy, F., Sprenkle, D., Wetchler, J., & Associates. (1996). *Family therapy sourcebook* (2nd ed.). New York, NY: Guilford Press.

Richardson, R. W. (1996). *Creating a healthier church: Family systems theory, leadership, and congregational life.* Minneapolis, MN: Augsburg Fortress.

Sagar, R. R. (2006). *Bowen: Theory and practice.* Washington, DC: Georgetown Family Center.

Santisteban, D. A., et al. (2003). The efficacy of brief strategic family therapy in modifying Hispanic adolescent behavior problems and substance use. *Journal of Family Psychology, 17*(1), 121-133.

Santisteban, D. A., Szapocznik, J., & Kurtines, W. M. (1994). Behavior problems among Hispanic youths: The family as moderator of adjustment. In J. Szapocznik (Ed.), *A Hispanic/Latino family approach to substance abuse prevention* (pp. 19-40). OSAP Prevention Monograph No. 8. DHHS Pub. No. 91-1725. Rockville, MD: Center for Substance Abuse Prevention.

Sherma, R. (2007). *A task analytic examination of dominance in emotion-focused couple therapy.* Doctoral thesis. York University, Toronto.

Snyder, D. K., & Wills, R. M. (1989). Behavioral versus insight-oriented marital therapy: Effects on individual and interspousal functioning. *Journal of Consulting and Clinical Psychology, 57,* 39-46.

Snyder, D. K., Wills, R. M., & Grady-Fletcher, A. (1991). Long-term effectiveness of behavioral versus insight-oriented marital therapy: A four-year follow-up study. *Journal of Consulting and Clinical Psychology, 59,* 138-141.

Spengler, O. (1991). *The decline of the west.* (A. Helps & H. Werner, Ed., C. F. Atkinson, Trans.). New York, NY: Oxford University Press.

Sprenkle, D., Davis., S., & Lebow, J. (2009). *Common factors in couple and family therapy: The overlooked foundation for effective practice.* New York, NY: Guilford Press.

Szapocznik, J., Perez-Vidal, A., Hervis, O. E., Brickman, A. L., & Kurtines, W. M. (1989). Innovations in family therapy: Strategies for overcoming resistance to treatment. In R. A. Wells & V. J. Giannetti (Eds.), *Handbook of the brief psychotherapies* (pp. 93-114). New York, NY: Plenum.

Von Bertalanffy, L. (1968). *General systems theory.* New York, NY: Braziller.

Von Foerster, H., Mead, M., & Teuber, H. L. (1952). *Cybernetics: Circular causal and feedback mechanisms in biological and social systems.* New York, NY: Josiah Macy Jr. Foundation.

Walsh, F. (1998). *Strengthening family resilience* (2nd ed.). New York, NY: Guilford Press.

Wells, K. C., & Egan, J. (1988). Social learning and systems family therapy for childhood oppositional disorder: Comparative treatment outcome. *Comprehensive Psychiatry, 29,* 138-146.

White, M., & Epston, D. (1990). *Narrative means to therapeutic ends.* New York, NY: Norton.

Wiener, N. (1948). *Cybernetics or control and communication in the animal and the machine.* Cambridge, MA: MIT Press; New York, NY: Wiley.

Woolley, S., & Johnson, S. M. (2006). Emotionally focused couples therapy: An empirically validated intervention. *Addiction & the Family, 22,* 329-346.

Worthington, E. L. (2005). *Hope-focused marriage counseling: A guide to brief therapy.* Downers Grove, IL: IVP Academic.

Yarhouse, M. A., & Sells, J. N. (2008). *Family therapies: A comprehensive Christian appraisal.* Downers Grove, IL: IVP Academic.

10

COMMUNITY PSYCHOLOGY
AND PREVENTATIVE
INTERVENTION STRATEGIES

Sally Schwer Canning

This chapter represents somewhat of a departure from the rest of the treatment approaches in this volume. Community and preventive strategies are not typically classified as psychotherapies by either their proponents or critics. We include them here because these interventions rely on assumptions and methods that differ in significant ways from psychotherapeutic approaches. Psychotherapeutic perspectives have shaped many forms of helping within the church and across the broader culture over the last decades. Community and preventive approaches stand in contrast with, and provide some correction to, a number of features of psychotherapeutic approaches to helping. Thus, they provide a helpful "lens" through which to see the counseling enterprise, as well as constituting an important alternative approach to traditional forms of intervention.

BRIEF DESCRIPTIVE SUMMARY
Community psychology and prevention are separate but related entities. Both refer to models of understanding and intervening in the human condition. Concerned with the connections between individuals and the contexts in which they live, community psychology "seeks to understand and

enhance quality of life for individuals, communities and societies" (Dalton, Elias & Wandersman, 2007, p. 15). The mission of community psychology as articulated by the group's representative body, the Society for Community Research and Action (Division 27 of the American Psychological Association) is "advancing theory, research, and social action . . . promoting health and empowerment and . . . preventing problems in communities, groups, and individuals" (www.scra27.org).

Community psychology's emergence as a discipline is typically traced to a 1965 meeting of clinical psychologists in Swampscott, Massachusetts, although this account has been criticized as U.S.-centric (Fryer, 2008). Concerned about social problems such as poverty and racism, and struggling with the limitations of their clinical discipline, these psychologists agreed to focus on advancing our understanding of social processes and on planning for social change. The emergence of community psychology in Latin America occurred around the same time through a variety of social and political influences and change agents such as Brazilian educator Paulo Freire and Colombian sociologist Orlando Fals Borda, as well as others in many countries (Montero, 2008). Graduate programs offering degrees in community as well as clinical-community psychology may now be found in the United States, Latin America and elsewhere. Community psychologists are found in a variety of community and academic settings, and they focus their attention on an astonishingly wide array of concerns within healthcare, education, law, social and human services, and organizations in many nations.

Prevention is one of the core values and activities of community psychologists, but prevention is also the focus of a large, relatively unsystematized movement across multiple disciplines. Simply put, prevention seeks to keep an illness or problem from ever occurring in the first place or to minimize the severity or duration of the problem. Preventive strategies were first used to combat public health concerns, such as malaria (by draining swamp land) and tooth decay (by increasing brushing and adding fluoride to water systems), and appeared in application to mental health problems around the same time as the emergence of community psychology.

The classification of prevention interventions by the Institute of Medicine (1994) has gained widespread acceptance; this scheme classifies programs according to how wide or narrow the intended target audience is.

Universal prevention programs are offered to everyone, regardless of risk status, and include such examples as a social competence promotion program offered in the regular curriculum to all students in an elementary school. *Selective* prevention strategies are aimed toward those at above-average risk for a particular problem because of environmental or individual characteristics, or both. A depression prevention program offered to children of parents with a mood disorder illustrates the selective approach. Finally, *indicated* prevention efforts target individuals at high risk or those who are already exhibiting symptoms of an illness, such as intravenous drug users in an HIV/AIDS screening and prevention program. Effective prevention programs depend on an accurate understanding of the levels of risk and protective capacity present within particular individuals and groups.

PHILOSOPHICAL ASSUMPTIONS

Community psychologists have been rather explicit in identifying the foundations of their work, and enough agreement exists to allow for a coherent introduction to some core values and assumptions embedded within this approach. Assumptions widely acknowledged by community psychologists include (1) that people are best understood ecologically, that is, as people in context, over time; (2) that human behavior and the functioning of human systems are best understood as a series of transactional adaptations by the person to resources and stressors within particular sets of circumstances; (3) that individuals' and communities' strengths, competencies and well-being (i.e., positive or health factors) deserve at least as much attention and emphasis as psychopathology and illness have received; (4) that preventing problems and illness, rather than waiting to intervene until they are full-blown, is not only feasible, but morally and ethically responsible as well as potentially cost effective; (5) that social change is best brought about collaboratively through processes that engage and empower community members rather than fostering dependence on experts; and (6) that the responsibility and complexity inherent in social change efforts commit the community psychologist to a combined emphasis on social action and rigorous research related to that action. Other, oft-cited foundational values include (7) respect for the dignity of all persons and the need to honor and engage diversity in the methods of the discipline; and

(8) rejection of injustice and oppression of marginalized individuals and groups, in favor of a commitment to individual and community justice and well-being through collaborative, empowering social change efforts.

VIEWS OF PERSONS

Community and preventive strategies emphasize understanding persons within their social contexts. Without denying the existence of personality, they look beyond the person to the powerful role of settings and events. Individuals are understood in an *ecological perspective* in which both people and contexts mutually influence each other in a dynamic process over time. Following this approach to problem formulation, interventions are often crafted from an ecological framework (see, for example, Baber & Bean's [2009] community-based suicide prevention program). Community psychology provides ecologically based models for understanding and intervening in smaller social systems like classrooms, organizations like workplaces or congregations, larger settings like neighborhoods, and even the largest units of society and culture. Because of this nested, multitiered approach, presenting a concise community psychology view of persons is a challenge.

The ecological perspective, borrowed from the natural sciences, emphasizes four principles for describing transactions among persons and their environment: interdependence, cycling of resources, adaptation and succession (see Vincent & Trickett, 1983, for a complete discussion). Systems are *interdependent* in that the components of systems are in dynamic interaction. Changes in one part of the system will impact other parts of the system. The classroom teacher who spends large amounts of time preparing her students for a standardized test may be responding less to her personal values and more to administrative pressures or state and federal mandates that determine how her effectiveness will be measured.

Cycling of resources refers to the way in which resources are identified, fostered and distributed within a given context, both in naturally occurring patterns and as interventionists try to alter those patterns. Interventionists conclude that latent resources are being underutilized and seek to instigate better use of those resources to contribute to the health and functioning of the system (as when development of a church lay counseling training program may serve more hurting individuals and enhance the competencies and well-being of all congregation members compared to a professional counseling program that is comparatively expensive and serves few parishioners).

Adaptation conveys "a continual process of accommodation between persons and their environment as individuals revise their coping behavior in response to environmental constraints and opportunities" (Vincent & Trickett, 1983, p. 71). Adaptation focuses on how individuals respond to the dynamic conditions of their setting, but also "how norms, values, and demand characteristics of the social setting constrain and promote certain behaviors" (Vincent & Trickett, 1983, p. 71). A practitioner in a farming community experiencing high numbers of farm foreclosures, for example, must attend to the implicit and explicit norms of the community related to work, help-seeking, and expression of emotions, as these provide information helpful to crafting interventions for community members that will be acceptable, as well as effective. Applying this lens has lead to some strikingly alternative interpretations of social phenomenon, such as Swisher and Latzman's (2008) formulation of youth violence as adaptation in difficult environments.

Finally, *succession* captures the historical, developmental nature of systems by noting that current and future policies are built in the context of past events, traditions and structures. Returning to an earlier example, imagine the land mine awaiting a consultant charged with launching a lay counseling program if he is unaware of the dismissal of a church leader a year earlier for sexual misconduct in the context of counseling a congregation member.

An ecological perspective requires a language for the expanding levels of our social systems. Urie Bronfenbrenner (1979) begins with the *microsystems* that a person directly takes part in, such as the family or workplace, which in turn are embedded in *exosystems* she is influenced by (such as a neighborhood or local school district), to the very broadest units of society or culture, *macrosystems. Mesosystems* demonstrate how systems interrelate, such as the tensions that can arise when the demands of a parent's workplace increase at the same time as their child's school increases expectations for parental involvement.

Two other concepts bear mentioning. *Social climate* refers to an environment's levels of supportiveness and cohesion, the degree to which it facilitates the personal development of participants, the extent of order and clarity in rules and expectations, as well as the relative stability or changeableness of the system (Moos, 1994, for example). Interventions aimed at improving social climate have been designed, often in school settings (Rhodes, Camic, Milburn & Lowe, 2009, provide a good example). Similarly, the concept of *psychological sense of community* includes the less tangible contours of relationship, affect and ideation. McMillan and Chavis's (1986) influential research identified essential elements to sense of community as membership, influence, integration and fulfillment of needs, and shared emotional connection, later revised by McMillan (1996) as spirit, trade, trust and art.

THEORY OF HEALTH

The dominant emphasis on psychopathology within clinical psychology yields a view of health understood predominantly as the reduction of symptoms and as the absence of disease. In contrast, community theorists and practitioners have worked at developing richer and interrelated notions of wellness, competence and resilience to envision health at both individual and community levels. We might imagine an analogy to physical health: Are individuals healthy merely because they are not currently diagnosed with a disease? Or are they healthy when they are disease-free, energetic, strong, happy, socially connected and have a sense that their life is meaningful?

At the individual level, Cowen's (1991) influential formulation of *wellness* incorporates "'earthy indicators' like eating well, sleeping well and doing one's mandated life tasks well" along with "life satisfaction indicators, such as purposefulness, belongingness, sense of control over one's fate, basic satisfaction with oneself and one's existence" (p. 404). But it is not enough that individuals experience wellness; broader systems and communities of persons must also. In assets-based approaches, the practitioner identifies and then seeks to enhance assets of all kinds to further the objectives of community members. Community assets may be tangible in nature, such as accessible, high-quality grocery stores or healthcare, or refer to less observable characteristics such as a strong sense of connectedness among stable, long-term residents.

Competence refers to particular abilities or sets of abilities that contribute to overall wellness. At least one competence-based taxonomy has been developed as an alternative to the pathology-based DSM categorization. Strayhorn (1983) proposed a set of fifty-nine individual abilities under the general categories of forming and managing social bonds, dealing with stresses and taking pleasure, working and playing, the influence of thought on action, and assigning meaning and purpose. Systemic competencies may also be conceived. Combining the work of a variety of scholars, Dalton, Elias and Wandersman (2007) include commitment, self-other awareness, articulateness, communication, conflict containment and accommodation, and participation in decision making in their characterization of a competent community.

Resilience adds another dimension to community and preventive perspectives on health. Cowen's (1991) simple, but brilliant, definition of resilience is the ability of a person to "swim well, when all known predictors say they should sink" (p. 407). Here we have in view the individual whose ability to cope with stressors exceeds, even defies, expectations, enabling them to thrive despite life challenges. In 1960, one of four young, African American girls in New Orleans exemplified resilience while being taunted with hate speech and death threats by mobs trying to prevent her from attending a so-called white school. Psychiatrist Robert Coles (1996) describes this experience of Ruby Bridge's undeterred, self-possessed and forgiving response to her ordeal and to the people inflicting it on her in his essay "The Inexplicable Prayers of Ruby Bridges," conveying some of the baffling quality of resiliency in his choice of title. Studies within this fascinating body of research have identified a variety of individual, familial and contextual variables that appear to buoy individuals above the waves of poverty, violence, and other traumas and deprivations. Religious participation and the presence of a supportive adult in the life of a child are two such contributors to resilience.

The recent emergence of *positive psychology* is consistent with community psychology's emphasis on wellness, competence and resilience. Researchers within this movement share a commitment to understanding and employing strengths with community psychologists, but differ in their attention to settings and systems. While positive psychologists articulate a concern for "positive institutions" (Penn Positive Psychology Center, 2010) their attentions, thus far, have been given to individual virtues and strengths such as hope, courage and leadership. The two disciplines also differ in their emphases on happiness (positive psychology) versus justice (community psychology) at the heart of their formulations of human thriving (Schueller, 2009).

THEORY OF ABNORMALITY

In ecological perspective, problems and illness always develop and are maintained within systems. Problems are formulated through ecological lenses, allowing contributing factors outside the individual to be detected (see Emory, Caughy, Harris & Franzini, 2008; Vega, Ang, Rodriguez & Finch, 2010, for examples of literature on the effects of neighborhoods on child development.) The problem-solving (i.e., adaptive) capacity of the social setting may be blocked (Levine, 1969). Individuals and systems are in an ongoing process of dynamic adaptation. Adaptation is affected by the particular risks, vulnerabilities and resources available to the individual or the system as coping with environmental demands, opportunities and stressors proceeds. Stressors may come in the form of major life events such as the death of a spouse; life transitions such as entry into kindergarten or marriage; daily hassles like money concerns or long commutes to work; chronic or ambient stressors such as noise, overcrowding and the threat to violence in a high density, low-income urban neighborhood; or vicious spirals (Hobfoll, 1998), the pernicious tendency for one stress to set off others, especially for individuals or settings with limited resources. Resources, on the other hand, may be material (money), social (easy access to professional support), personal (supportive friendships), psychosocial (well-developed problem-solving ability) or spiritual (belief in a benevolent god).

Albee (1982) and Elias (1987) conceptualized the emergence of disorders as the results of a ratio of resources to stresses: when stressors exceed resources, the individual's coping capacity is inadequate, rendering the person vulnerable to illness. Dowhrenrind (1978) argued for a more complex model that included both situational and psychological mediators. Beyond the objective features of stressors or resources themselves, the individual's *appraisal* of those stressors and resources substantially affects outcomes. Two people who lose their homes in a fire, for example, experience the same stressor but may utilize different cognitive appraisals in response to the event and to utilizing their remaining resources. One victim may focus on her overriding gratitude for the safety of unharmed family members and the hospitality of family members offering a place to stay; the second may focus on his catastrophic loss of property and be repulsed at the prospect of dependence on his family's hospitality. The first psychological appraisal will likely contribute to better coping and lower risk of succumbing to illness than her unfortunate counterpart.

Coping refers to the cognitive, affective and behavioral responses to a stressor or circumstance by an individual or system. Coping strategies can be more or less effective, depending on the type of stressors or situation faced (Dalton, Elias & Wandersman, 2007). For example, problem-focused coping strategies, such as seeking information about an illness or recruiting someone to help study for an exam, are more likely to be helpful if the stressor is relatively controllable. In contrast, emotion-focused coping, such as prayer or seeking emotional support from a friend, may be more desirable when a stressor is relatively uncontrollable. Certain emotion-focused strategies are generally unhelpful regardless of stressor type, such as ruminating on the problem, blaming others or using harmful drugs.

Social support has emerged in the research as having a robust relationship to both physical and mental health. The type and timing of such support is important. Research on a program designed to prevent complications in the bereavement process of widows determined that practical assistance, such as help with burial and financial arrangements, was important in the earliest portion of the bereavement process, but later that emotional support became increasingly important as the impact of the loss continued to unfold and the widow's previous social roles unraveled and required redefinition. (See Silverman in Price, Cowen, Lorion & Ramos-McKay, 1988, for a description of the Widow-to-Widow program.)

INTERVENTION METHODS

The diversity of perspectives, settings, targets and objectives developed by community and preventive practitioners yields a correspondingly varied set of intervention methods. We focus our discussion on six features of community and preventive intervention strategies. The first four have already been explained: (1) the point in the disease process at which intervention takes place (prevention); (2) the unit of analysis at which interventions are targeted (the ecological perspective); (3) the tendency to build health rather than fight disease (understood as building wellness, competency or resilience (Cowen, 1991); and (4) the emphasis on coping and adaptation as the dominant means of growth and change. The remaining concepts are (5) the role of the practitioner and the structure and quality of the helping relationship (understanding the helper's role not as expert or therapist but as consultant and contributor to collaboration, empowerment and citizen participation); and (6) the (ideally) inextricable relationship between research and action.

In exploring *helping relationships*, community psychologists eschew the hierarchical, expert-driven, medical model in favor of a more collaborative, empowering relationship among community and professional partners. Levine (1969) describes three of the ways interventions should reflect collaboration and empowerment with the community: (1) help has to be located strategically in relation to the manifestation of the problem; (2) the goals and values of the helping agent or service must be consistent with the goals and values of the setting; and (3) the helpful intervention should have potential for being established on a systematic basis, using the natural resources of the setting and having the potential to become institutionalized as part of the setting.

Within this approach the role of community members is elevated and that of "the professional" diminished. Existing individuals, groups and organizations such as lay helpers, self-help groups and grass-roots organizations, represent vital resources for the health of communities, and they partner as equals with the professional. Nonprofessionals may have integral roles in all phases and aspects of an intervention, such as acting as key informants identifying community strengths and needs as well as the methodologies that will be acceptable and effective. The professional is less the therapist and rather becomes the consultant, program developer, evaluator or advocate. The consultation process is a complex and challenging one that involves entry into a context, identification of a mutually agreed-upon set of methods and goals for the consultation, implementation of the project, feedback and (typically) disengagement from the context. While the perspectives, values, needs and resources of the community are meant to significantly shape the aims and methods used in these efforts, community strategists vary in their conclusions regarding how effectively this ideal is met. Still, in the ideal, community psychologists are sensitive to differences in power within society generally, and within the helping relationship specifically, and seek to minimize their power status as professionals in favor of honoring the resources and strengths within communities.

Finally, community interventions embody a combined commitment to both research and action, to the practice of combining intervention with evaluation. Community and preventive strategists utilize varied methodologies to assess the impact of their interventions, including quantitative and qualitative approaches. Participatory action research is widely used, similarly reflecting the commitment to collaboration and empowerment seen in interventions. This approach makes room for the unique perspective and contributions of community stakeholders, even those who have traditionally been "subjects" of research rather than active participants. Langhout and Thomas's (2010) recent special issue of the *American Journal of Community Psychology* on research in collaboration with children provides striking examples. A review of community and preventive interventions in journals such as *Journal of Community Psychology, the American Journal of Community Psychology, Journal of Primary Prevention* or *Journal of Prevention and Intervention in the Community* reveals considerable variation in the methods of intervention and assessment used in this dynamic field.

DEMONSTRATED EFFECTIVENESS

Initially, prevention advocates were criticized for the lack of any evidence supporting effectiveness. Reviews of primary general prevention programs (Institute of Medicine, 1994) and of primary prevention efforts targeting children and adolescents (Durlak & Wells, 1997) began to establish that preventive efforts could "produce outcomes similar to or higher in magnitude than those obtained by many other established preventive and treatment interventions in the social sciences and medicine" (p. 115). Durlak and Wells's meta-analysis showed the average prevention participant outperforming 59-82 percent of nonparticipants. By reducing risk factors or enhancing protective factors, a wide array of interventions have yielded reductions in a variety of problem behaviors in youth, such as delinquency and drug use (Fagan, Hanson, Hawkins & Arthur, 2009). Research methodology has become more rigorous over time, including randomized trials.

More recently, prevention- and community-based researchers have turned their attention to the need for improving technologies for effective dissemination and implementation of evidence-based practices in the community (Fagan, Hanson, Hawkins & Arthur, 2009). Failures in community stakeholders' awareness, selection or implementation of evidence-based prevention programs have led to these efforts. "Translational research" and capacity-building interventions aim to facilitate their use more widely. Progress is being made, and a recent model, the Interactive Systems Framework (Wandersman et al., 2008), shows promise.

CHRISTIAN CRITIQUE

At the end of the first edition of this text, Jones and Butman (1991) challenged Christian practitioners to image God in their work—to labor at expressing his roles, character and concerns. Asking ourselves who God is, what he is doing and what he cares about raises a set of stimulating questions, the answers to which may serve as orienting points for integrative analysis. Here these questions serve as a sort of filter for critical consideration of community and preventive approaches from a Christian perspective. The explicit identification of the underlying values and assumptions within community psychology facilitates a critique of its approach.

PHILOSOPHICAL ASSUMPTIONS

Earlier, we identified eight assumptions embedded within community and preventive strategies: (1) the ecological perspective as a lens for viewing human behavior, (2) adaptation as the prominent means of development and change, (3) wellness and strengths as a focus over psychopathology, (4) prevention and promotion over treatment, (5) collaborative, empowering helping relationships, (6) the importance of joining action and research, (7) a high value on diversity, and (8) the rejection of injustice and oppression and a commitment to justice through social change. Many of these assumptions will be dealt with in the sections on views of persons, health, illness and intervention; we discuss the last two here.

Justice and Social Change

In chapter twelve, Jones and Butman suggested that Christian thinkers must ask, "What are God's concerns? What does he care about deeply and passionately?" We ask these questions in order to align our concerns with God's concerns. In my (Canning's) own development as a believer and psychologist, I have come to believe that one of these deep passions of God is his tender and zealous concern to bring about justice and human flourishing for those who are poor, oppressed and at the margins of our society. The poor, the widow, the orphan and the alien are repeatedly named in Scripture as the focus of God's concern. More than any other approach to intervention, community psychology has unabashedly aligned itself with these individuals and their communities. Both in practice and in scholarship, community psychologists aim to reform systems that foster injustice in all its dehumanizing forms, including poverty, racism, social fragmentation and isolation. But community psychology itself has not provided a sufficiently compelling rationale for why these values should be preeminent.

Evangelical Christians have struggled with God's concern for justice for the poor and oppressed. Aspects of the church emphasizing the social dimensions of the gospel, such as in liberation theology and the social gospel movement in nineteenth-century North America, have tended to be alienated from those emphasizing the personal and spiritual dimensions of the gospel (Sugden, 1995). Evangelicals have wisely sought to avoid the errors present in theologies that reduce Jesus' salvific action to political, economic and cultural outcomes alone. Views that reduce salvation merely to the alleviation of temporal suffering and promotion of health and happiness are rightly to be avoided. On the other hand, overly individualistic or spiritualized views that emphasize a disembodied, decontextualized "salvation of souls" but ignore the implications of salvation for human suffering and injustice have obscured the social dimensions of the kingdom and of God's redemptive and reconciling work.

There have always been exceptions to this historic dichotomization. Wolterstorff (1995) provides one such example. In his view, a concern for justice must be rooted in three truths: that God loves justice, that God carries out works of justice, and finally that he enjoins us to do so as well. In contrast to community and preventive views, then, a Christian devotion to justice is rooted much deeper than in a humanistic concern for all people. It finds its source in a God who loves those who experience injustice, who longs for them to flourish and who sorrows when they do not. If we are to do justice,

> we are also to see God's invitation to image God as lying behind it. . . . We are to be icons of God, imaging God's justice in our justice. . . . More prominent in the Scriptures themselves than the theme of doing justice as a *manifestation of our respect for* the image of God in persons is the theme of doing justice as *constituting (part of) our imaging* of God. (Wolterstorff, 1995, pp. 17-18)

What sort of justice? Biblical justice is best understood in the context of the larger concept of shalom. Shalom is the person dwelling peaceably with God, self, others and nature (Wolterstorff, 1983). Justice is an essential feature of the peace that is to be found in these relationships, because in these relationships people must receive what they are due. "If individuals are not granted what is due them, if their claim on others is not acknowledged by those others, if others do not carry out their obligations to them, then shalom is wounded" (Wolterstorff, 1983, p. 71). Beyond merely granting what is due, Wolterstorff reminds us that shalom is truly present only when these relationships are characterized by the radical notion of delight. Modern ears must not misunderstand the context to be solely personal or interpersonal; it is communal as well. The fabric of Jewish and early Jewish Christian communities illustrates this quality:

> It embraced Judaism's sense of a covenant relationship with the one God, who had heard the cries of the Israelites in slavery and responded to their suffering. And it embraced the imperatives of Israel's community practices first fashioned in Sinai. These were imperatives to redress social inequities, protect the vulnerable, keep the power of privilege in check and under critique, steward the gifts of earth as a God-given trust held in common, extend hospitality to the stranger and sojourner, and consider the enemy's welfare on the same terms as one's own. (Rasmussen, 1997, p. 125)

In contrast to a Christian understanding of justice, social change in community and preventive models is typically supported on evolutionary/ sociobiological, humanistic or utilitarian grounds. Evolutionary rationales claim the communal and altruistic behaviors displayed by humans are hardwired because they aid in our individual and species survival (Lawler, 2006). Humanistic approaches attribute such concerns to our self-evident worth as human beings and as autonomous, self-determining actors. Utilitarian approaches attempt rational cost-benefit analyses to justify investing in prevention programs. As we have just developed, Christians, in contrast, ground their thirst for justice in God's character and concerns, and in our desire to participate in his good work in the world.

What kinds of social change ought we to seek? In what contexts? To what extent? Under which conditions? Underlying these questions is the question of authority: Who decides the answers to these questions? Intervention outcomes that seem self-evidentially beneficial (e.g., reductions in depression rates, smoking-related diseases or teenage pregnancies) can appear to make these questions moot. But the sinister aura of such terms as *social engineering* or *environmental manipulation* reminds us that the authority question is anything but moot. Levine, Perkins and Perkins (2005) put it simply: "'Who asked you?' By what authority does a community psychologist or any other social scientist try to influence other people's lives?" (p. 464).

Community and preventive strategies address these concerns by placing a high value on collaboration, citizen participation and empowerment, as well as their commitment to closely evaluating outcomes. Power to make decisions about interventions is to be distributed in such a way as to minimize these threats and be consistent with high values for diversity and justice. However, while commitment to the interests of all parties is firmly articulated by adherents to this perspective, in practice differences in power, values and perspective among partners are often significant, complex and challenging to juggle.

While Christians have an authoritative ground in God's character and purposes for their commitment to justice, this does not answer all our questions for us. We still face hard questions about the kinds of social change we ought to seek. The goals of any social change effort are value-laden. Some goals will be in harmony with particular Christians' values and ethics (e.g., aiming to decrease adolescent drug abuse) while other goals could clash sharply (e.g., increasing adolescent condom use to prevent HIV/AIDS). Choices of goals and methods are often more complex than we might anticipate, and even Christians who agree on fundamental values might disagree profoundly on methods (e.g., income redistribution, needle exchange programs). The community psychology valuing of collaboration resonates with a Christian respect for all persons as created equal in the eyes of God, but does not capture the added complexity of a Christian understanding that, owing to our sin nature, groups of persons are no more likely to perceive or achieve justice than the individual. If groups are formed of sinful individuals, then groups can be as distorted as any individual in their views of what constitutes justice or how we should seek to attain it.

Diversity

Community psychology stands out for its valuing of the worth, dignity and particularity of all individuals and communities, with special attention to those who have been oppressed or marginalized. This value affects what community psychologists attend to, what they do and how they do it (Dionne, Davis, Sheeber & Madrigal, 2009; Mankowski, Galvez & Glass 2010). Many psychotherapy approaches are to be commended for their recent attention to such factors as the role of culture, ethnicity and stage of life in human identity and functioning. In many cases, though, these are recent developments and reflect changes that maintain the basic structure of existing forms of helping. In contrast, this focus was foundational to the emergence of community psychology as a qualitatively different approach to human problems, one in direct response to the social conditions of individuals, groups and communities that had previously received little attention from our discipline. Indeed, some within community psychology continue to push for a more complete expression of this value in the discipline (Cruz & Sonn, 2010).

At the same time, community psychology theorists have not provided an adequate rationale for caring and investing in people and communities other than our own, nor an adequate answer to the question, Why value diversity? The lack of a sufficient base for valuing diversity is mirrored in the larger culture as well. Acceptance and enthusiasm for diversity has grown, but it is a shallow growth that may wither under the cultural, political and economic heat to come.

A firmer foundation from which to understand and respond to diversity in our society may be found in biblical truth (McNeil, 2005). "Unity in diversity" is a phrase used to summarize Paul's treatment of this issue in the New Testament. "Paul's thinking does not begin with the differences that divide people from one another but with the differences that divide all people from God" (Banks, 1994, p. 110). "God does not show favoritism" (Rom 2:11) when it comes to salvation. National identity, race, social status, gender—none of these qualify for special status. Membership in the community of faith is initiated and established by the work of God through the Messiah, not in any qualifications of its members.

At the same time, particularities in people are not ignored or erased. Paul

> does not deny the continuing legitimacy of national, social and gender differences—Paul is no advocate of a universal, classless and unisex society— he merely affirms that these differences do not affect one's relationship with Christ and membership in the community. There is an egalitarian strain in Paul's pronouncement, but it is secondary. He is more interested in the unity the gospel brings than in its equality, and in this unity diversity is preserved rather than uniformity imposed. (Banks, 1994, p. 114)

Notice how this picture contrasts with the "melting pot" metaphor in which all distinctions dissolve away into a larger, amorphous substance that renders its constituent ingredients indistinguishable. In the believing community, such particularities as culture, experience, gifting and resources are to be employed in service to the community and larger world.

One of the great failures of the church in America is that we often embody "coexistence via segregation" rather than "unity in diversity." Not only does this condition reveal a failure to love our own brothers and sisters, it also diminishes and distorts our experience of God and his kingdom by our socioeconomic and ethnic isolation (mirroring that of much of our society). Our understanding of God is meant to be enlarged and enriched by our communion with his whole body. True unity in diversity more fully images the Christ whose body on earth is formed of people of every tribe and tongue and nation.

Relativism in the broader culture unreflectively considers differences as inherently good. Biblical formulations must be more complex, accepting that all persons and groups reflect both God's image and the effects of the Fall; we all are vulnerable to error as well as capable of grasping truth, and so not all differences are good. Movement toward unity in diversity in communities will include interactions whereby we are sharpened by one another and by God. Love and truth—rather than power, self-interest and fear—characterize the sharpening process. The purpose of our unity in diversity—to image a magnificent, triune, loving God—provides a fixed point on the horizon to travel toward and against which to evaluate our progress as an imaging community. The process is an inherently relational one, not simply an intellectual exercise in adjudicating diverse beliefs and practices. Therefore, we must be concerned about fidelity to the truth, while at the same time not using this concern to hide from the challenging aspects of respectfully and lovingly engaging in diverse community.

VIEWS OF PERSONS

Views of the Individual

There is no one coherent view of persons in this community/ecological view. The major concern with the ecological view of "the person in context" is its potential for negating or submerging the worth and responsibility of individuals. This is a real danger; Christians emphasize our belief in a personal God who both loves and holds accountable his people as individuals. In response we must be clear both about community psychology and biblical truth. We have discussed biblical perspectives on the valuing of individuals and groups/communities in the previous sections on social justice and diversity, as well as in chapter nine on family therapy. Still, this danger should not be overstated. Community psychology does not just value collectives of people; its valuing of social justice and diversity claim a high place for the worth of the individual, group and community.

The individual is not negated or discounted by adding attention to collectives of persons. Community psychology may be helpfully understood as a corrective to the hyperindividualistic views predominant in clinical psychology, especially at the time the subfield began. This ecological view adds a useful perspective to more individualistic views of persons; it expands our understanding of the human condition. Just as we might study wheat by viewing individual cells under a microscope, a single stalk with the human eye and hand, or a whole field from the cockpit of a twin-engine plane, so also each method is both valuable and limited—each one reveals and obscures aspects of our subject.

In their brilliant analysis of the role of religion in white and black Americans' views on race, sociologists Michael Emerson and Christian

Smith (2000) identify a set of "cultural tools" employed by white evangelicals, a set of ideas, habits, skills and styles that help people make sense of their experiences in the world. The three tools of *accountable freewill individualism, relationalism* and *antistructuralism* create a mindset that is discordant with community psychology views in some important ways.

An emphasis on accountable freewill individualism leads us to believe that people are

> independent of structures and institutions, have freewill, and are individually accountable for their own actions. . . . Although the larger American culture is itself highly individualistic, the close connection between faith and freewill individualism to the exclusion of progressive thought renders white evangelicals even more individualistic than other white Americans. (Emerson & Smith, 2000, p. 77)

The relational component connects persons to others, but only through a series of dyadic relationships: person A with God, A with B, A with C, and so on. Because of this focus on dyadic relationships, the roots of social problems tend to be traced to individual sin expressing itself through poor relationships, rarely including larger or more complex levels of society in the formulation. Antistructuralism arises as structural understandings of social problems are not only overlooked but are seen as

> irrelevant or even wrongheaded. . . . Although much in Christian scripture and tradition points to the influence of social structures on individuals, the stress on individualism has been so complete for such a long time in white American evangelical culture that such tools are nearly unavailable. What is more, white conservative Protestants believe that sinful humans typically deny their own personal sin by shifting blame somewhere else, such as on "the system." Evangelicals are thus also antistructural because they believe that invoking social structures shifts guilt away from its root source—the accountable individual. However, evangelicals are selectively aware of social institutions—they see those that both impact them in their own social location and tend to undermine accountable freewill individualism. (Emerson & Smith, 2000, pp. 78-79)

Reliance on these cultural tools links to the pervasive socioeconomic and ethnic divisions and isolation that are deeply entrenched in American society. The combination is likely to mean that systemic perspectives on social problems—perspectives that complement rather than negate individualistic perspective—will be difficult for evangelicals to recognize and accept. Those who do will find a rich set of conceptual and applied tools in community psychology with which to understand and engage those systems.

Views of Community

The emphasis on community within this approach is a significant contribution. The hyper-individualistic nature of modern Western culture obscures the communal, interdependent nature of persons portrayed in the Scriptures. Foundationally, the very nature of God himself is portrayed as both a unity *and* as communal or triune. In accounts of creation, communities are prominent. In the Old Testament, God calls a nation, a people, into covenantal relationship, even as he enacts his covenant through the lives of individuals like Abraham and Sarah. In the New Testament, Paul's writings emphasize the communal nature of persons. In his review of Paul's teachings, Banks (1994) shows

> how closely Paul's understanding of freedom, or salvation, is bound up with his idea of community. He does not view salvation as simply a transaction between the individual and God. Prior to their encounter with Christ people belong to a community, however much their actions incline them to pursue their own (or their immediate circle's) self-interest. And it is into a new community that their reconciliation with God in Christ brings them, however much they experience that event as an individual affair. Correlatively, the salvation effected by Christ follows from his being not just an individual but a corporate personality, the "second" and "last" Adam. (p. 17)

Both Jesus' and Paul's teachings, as well as what we know about the early Jewish-Christian community, portray an "upside down kingdom" in which new community values often stand out in stark contrast against those of the larger society and status distinctions are transformed.

> The Gospel materials reflect practices that display this Jewish heritage as Jesus and his movement embodied it. Discipleship (joining the way of Jesus) is decidedly egalitarian. People who are routinely excluded elsewhere are included here. Pride of rank is rejected and has no place. Followers are to teach all they have learned to all who will hear, but no particular deference is given scribes as teachers. Rather than being offered front-row seats at Jesus' gatherings, disciples are invited to enter more resolutely the way of service, even suffering. (Rasmussen, 1997, pp. 125-126)

THEORY OF HEALTH

View of health

A few community models include a kind of transcendent aspect, such as McMillan's (1996) proposal that the elements of community include "Spirit." Most community conceptualizations of wellness, however, do not include spiritual or supernatural perspectives in any form. At the same time, in practice, community and preventive research embraces empirical findings from psychology of religion that robustly relate religious and spiritual variables to coping and both physical and spiritual health. While some of this literature treats religious and spiritual phenomena in reductionistic terms, not all of it does (see for example Ellison, Finch, Ryan & Salinas, 2009). Dalton, Elias and Wandersman (2007) acknowledge the value of religious and spiritual resources as well as the fact that they cannot be reduced simply to their value in coping (see also Pargament, 1997).

Christian understandings of wellness construe our relatedness to the living God as the foundation of human health. Again we return to the concept of shalom, probably the most compelling biblical image of human wellness. Williams (1997) describes shalom as social as well as personal:

> [Shalom includes] completeness, soundness, well-being, and prosperity, and includes every aspect of life: personal, relational, and national. Because shalom entails living in covenantal relationship with God and others, holiness and righteousness are inherent in it. This view of shalom is reflected in the New Testament, where healing consistently involves not only physical recovery from sickness but the renewal of relationships with God and others. . . . Therefore, from a Christian perspective, the aim of healing is the complete well-being of the person. It entails being in right relation to God, oneself, others, and the rest of creation. (p. 100)

Christians believe that health or shalom is unattainable in any complete sense apart from a right relationship with God. Though this understanding is lacking in community and preventive conceptions of health, these views do help us better see the holistic and unambiguously social dimensions of health. Although approaches to psychotherapy are increasingly incorporating relational and social elements into their views of health, they do so to lesser degrees than either community or biblical conceptions of wellness.

Emphasis on Health

Beyond the particular vision of health being propounded, what do we make of the primary emphasis placed by community psychology on health over pathology? Let's dispense with two superficial objections to an emphasis on health and prevention. First, community and preventive approaches do not require ignoring or denying the existence of problems or pathology; after all, community and preventive interventions are occasioned by deep concern over the impact of problems and illness on individuals and society. Second, valuing and prioritizing wellness and prevention does not mean that we ignore existing suffering. Even the most ardent advocates of prevention do not dismiss the benefits of treatment for those who are already ill (see Albee, 1990, for example).

The thorny question is how resources should be allocated. Our health care system's attention has historically been disproportionately toward treatment over prevention. This emphasis has left many individuals and groups systematically underserved and has done little to prevent problems (and suffering) before they occur (Canning, Case & Kruse, 2001). The enormous difficulty of these choices is immediately evident if we consider even one example: if you have to choose how to allocate limited funds, should $500,000 be spent on a heart transplant to extend one life, or distributed to implement a program to prevent future heart disease in multiple individuals?

Now we move to a more substantive challenge. Can Christian practitioners with a firm conviction of the reality of sin embrace a predominantly wellness-based approach to their work? If we turn our attention in the direction of strengths rather than pathology, are we tacitly denying the reality of sin? We contend that it is possible to apply this emphasis at both conceptual and applied levels without succumbing to a denial of the Fall, espousing a view of persons as ontologically and essentially good, or holding out an idealized vision of achieving perfection in individuals or utopia in community. The Fall is not the only or first reality about human nature; creational goodness came first, and God's redemption comes after. Identifying, engaging and fostering human strengths, competencies, virtues and resources that reflect the image of God and may be present through the common grace extended to all human beings or have emerged by the transforming power of the Holy Spirit must be options for the Christian practitioner.

It is important to keep in mind as well that the commitment of this field is to individuals and communities who are disproportionately vulnerable to health risks, stressors and diseases. These persons have disproportionately fewer resources to cope with those factors and are mired in a larger cultural, economic and historical context that tends to ignore, minimize, marginalize, stigmatize or actively exclude their strengths, contributions and worth. An emphasis on strengths, assets, competencies and human flourishing in this context provides a corrective to the orientation of the broader culture (see Wexler, 2010 for an example in a Native American context). In this way it reflects the upside-down quality of Jesus' and Paul's actions and teachings with respect to the believing community (see, e.g., Mk 12:38-44; 1 Cor 12:22-26; Jas 2:1-9).

Extent to Which Wellness Is Achievable

Students studying community and preventive models often inquire whether adherents are actually pursuing utopian ends. Is the field premised on human perfectibility, and is prevention worth pursuing if sinful imperfection is our human condition? In practice, community and preventive efforts in the mental health arena do not appear to be built on utopian hopes for a world entirely free of illness, dysfunction or oppression. Community and preventive strategists' keen understanding and appreciation for the complexity and intractability of human problems likely temper their zeal.

The pursuit of wellness is not necessarily utopian. Wolterstorff (1983) characterizes shalom in *now* and *not-yet* terms. Shalom is only partially attainable in this life. Still, "shalom is both God's cause in the world and our human calling," and "it is shalom that we are to work and struggle for. We are not to stand around, hands folded, waiting for shalom to arrive. We are workers in God's cause, his peace-workers. The *missio Dei* is *our* mission" (p. 72). We avoid a pursuit of "the spiritual, psychological or social salvation of people as a result of extensive human efforts; [we avoid thinking we are accomplishing] the salvation of humans by humans. . . . A form of 'Christian Humanism,' where we trust our goodness to overcome evil" (Canning, Pozzi, McNeil & McMinn, 2000). But we also avoid passivity or disengagement from the problems and ills around us, the kind of passivity engendered by fixing our eyes only on the healing and health to come in another life. We fix our eyes on what we can fruitfully achieve here and now. We do so noting that Christians disagree among themselves about the degree to which healing is available from God in this life. Williams (1997), for example, surveys different traditions within African American churches on how and how much God's healing in this life can be experienced among God's people.

THEORY OF ABNORMALITY

Although we use the concept *abnormality* to organize our discussions across this volume, a great many other terms are used to describe what is wrong with people, including psychopathology, disease, illness, problems in living and, that favorite of therapists, "issues." Within the community perspective, variations in views of abnormality exist. Some preventive and community strategies embrace the concepts of disease and psychopathology; this tends to suit those at the more empirical, individual end of the spectrum. Others featuring the social, ecological and strengths-based emphases within the model tend to use the term *problems in living.* Williams (1997) points out the connection between our conception of what's wrong and our conception of what helps. How we think about the problems determines what we propose to address those problems.

Ecological Perspective

The ecological perspective contributes a systemic lens that can increase our ability to identify and explain important phenomena and, potentially, to bring about positive changes. The individualistic therapist to whom a child with academic difficulties is referred may discover problems with homework completion and accuracy, and attribute those problems to individualistic concerns of the child such as intellectual and emotional factors. Such a focus risks missing systemic factors such as the child's home lacking a quiet, regular place and time conducive to homework completion, or missing an adult available to encourage and supervise him until shortly before bedtime. Even more broadly, she might miss the source of anxiety that disrupts the child's concentration, this anxiety caused by exposure to high rates of violence in his neighborhood.

Acute awareness of larger societal forces such as racism, poverty and health care disparities that influence human functioning, especially for those on the margins of society, is thus a key contribution of this perspective. Community psychology locates problems and pathology within and across systems, and in interactions among individuals, groups and systems, in addition to the individuals. If we accept the notion of sin being manifested at systemic and societal levels (Emerson & Smith, 2000), and also accept a Christian understanding of social justice and action, the Christian psychologist will see much of value in the ecological paradigm.

Adaptation and Coping

Within this perspective people and groups are seen in an ongoing process of adaptation with the complex social, physical, cultural systems and situations around them. It seems possible to embrace an appreciation for the process of adaptation within the environment without swallowing the complete originating Darwinian or sociobiological perspectives whole. One does not have to accept a naturalistic, evolutionary explanation of origins in order to accept that human beings are set in a larger living context with which they dynamically interrelate and adapt.

Individualistic American Christians tend to be especially inattentive to transactions between us and our social and physical environment; our attention is focused inwardly, subjectively, emotionally. Community practitioners have been trained to discern and employ these exchanges. A fully Christian view can encompass the complexity of interrelatedness in multileveled creation, anticipating that the processes of adaptation can be observed within these interrelationships that will bear the marks of creation (goodness) and Fall (sin and death) as well as redemption (new life). Rather than the morally bankrupt vision of adaptation for survival, actions in the world have ethical, moral and spiritual meaning and consequences. Likewise we may characterize the process of adaptation from a biblical perspective as one of interrelatedness and interdependence, rather than competition. In our interactions with creation we may come to some knowledge of God (Rom 1:19-20; Col 1:23) and may glorify him in our actions (Gen 1:24-28; 1 Jn 4:7). If governed by the concept of shalom, adaptation may be oriented toward the glory of God and toward human flourishing in relationship with him and with all creation, rather than oriented solely toward self-preservation.

Social Support

Social support holds an elevated place in the views of preventive and community psychology researchers and practitioners because of its strong empirical link to positive health outcomes. Social support is usually valued, studied and fostered for utilitarian reasons: social support benefits human beings. Social support appears to be typically explained by employing a sociobiological frame of understanding.

This account will strike most Christians as flat at best. Above all, social support appears to be a secularized, shrunken version of love, one left lifeless and pragmatic in its construction. Biblical accounts of God and human nature feature love as the central reality of and central virtue to be manifested in relationship. Love is both characteristic of God and his actions in the world and a fruit of the Spirit that his creation is commanded and empowered to express back to him and to our fellows through the Holy Spirit. We are interdependent as human beings and as a body of believers. Our willingness, in love, to put the other before ourselves is an act of submission and obedience to God, and love calls for our mutual participation in God's provision for all his creation. Love is also linked to joy—joy in gathering together to share, testify, worship and encounter Christ in one another. Social support is a part of, or an outcome of, love, grounded in our nature as created, interdependent beings. We support and need support not only because it aids our survival but because we are created with those capacities, we are buoyed up by them in a fallen world, and we are being restored to image our loving, triune Creator with greater fidelity.

INTERVENTION METHODS

Timing of Help

Each year, my clinical students wrestle with the idea of prevention. Filled with the desire to help the hurting, they often respond initially to the idea of prevention as if it were a less compassionate response to human suffering than treatment. To invest in prevention seems to require turning their backs on suffering individuals. Their concern must not be dismissed. The infinite value of the suffering individual to our loving God is reflected in the parable of the shepherd who leaves ninety-nine sheep to restore the one in distress. But the matter is more complex than this.

First, proponents of psychotherapy are not always attentive to the reality that psychotherapy insufficiently meets the needs of suffering individuals. Economic, geographical, cultural and political barriers to health care

access means that effective, acceptable psychotherapy resources are woe-
fully inadequate to the needs that exist. This unhappy reality must also be
kept in view as we consider how to allocate personal and societal time,
talents and energies to both treatment and prevention.

Second, it is misguided to view psychotherapy as necessarily more compassionate than prevention. A story often repeated in different forms by
prevention proponents conveys this point. Two people come upon horribly
injured people at the site of a terrible automobile accident. As in the parable of the good Samaritan (Lk 10:30-35), the compassionate travelers
interrupt their own journey to care for the victims. As they do, another
accident happens, and then another, resulting in more and more casualties.
Overwhelmed, one caregiver stays to care for the victims while the second
leaves to get more help, and only then discovers the road condition causing
the crashes. The second Samaritan, by addressing the cause of the acci-
dents, prevents additional crashes from occurring. Is the second helper less
compassionate or helpful than the first? Is preventing further harm less
caring or useful than ministering to the wounds or holding the hands of
the dying? Most see the value in both responses. Some attribute greater
worth to the actions of the second.

As with views of health, justice and social action, preventive efforts
must be grounded in the larger themes of creation, Fall and redemption.
Referring to preventive measures individuals can take, Williams (1997)
observes

> practitioners could connect prevention efforts with God's activity of pre-
> serving and sustaining creation, and associate support groups with God's
> redemptive and restorative activity. In like manner, practitioners might
> draw closer ties between creation and stewardship of the body, with the
> result that caring for one's body is understood as a concrete response to re-
> ceiving it as a gift from God. (pp. 118-119)

Helping Context

Community psychology has been willing to reenvision contexts of helping. Rather than requiring community members to come to the offices of
professionals, community professionals go out to the community. Community and preventive interventionists have also broken the mold of traditional forms for intervention (e.g., counseling) in favor of new forms

such as consultation, prevention, policy making and grassroots organizing that are more acceptable and effective for some groups. This willingness to shape one's way of doing things to better fit the needs of others can demonstrate respect for the perspectives, values and constraints of those we desire to serve. My own experience working from this approach has shown how trust and engagement is facilitated when people feel cared about and honored enough to have us meet them on their turf, engage in their experience, and respect their style and values. In a very limited and imperfect sense, this approach follows the method of Jesus, who went to those in need.

Christians will appreciate how community-based approaches and interventions could be effective in congregations. Congregations are central for people from every walk of life, across the life span and during crucial transitions of birth, marriage and death. They contain rich resources of many kinds. Congregations and other faith-based organizations would appear to be of utmost relevance and value to community and preventive strategists. Sadly, despite acknowledging their importance and the rich opportunities they represent (Kloos & Moore, 2000; Pargament & Maton, 2000), community psychologists have given such contexts little attention compared to other community settings such as schools. Christian psychologists have too often seen congregations only as settings in which to offer traditional counseling. Much opportunity exists for applying community approaches in faith-based settings (Uomoto, 1982; Bufford & Buckler, 1987; Prater, 1987; Canning, 2003; Kramer, 2010).

Helping Relationship

The structure of the community-psychology helping relationship differs from the structure of psychotherapy. The professional-treats-patient hierarchy built into the medical model is reconfigured as a collaboration of professional and community members. Community interventions are designed to foster citizen participation, collaboration, self-determination and empowerment.

Community psychologists have pointed out the humility a collaboration model requires of professionals. Interestingly, Christian discussions of humility in psychological practice have typically envisioned its expression through the psychotherapist's attitudes, words and actions toward the client, but have failed to note that structurally, a therapist-client relationship by its very nature protects the professional power of the therapist. Perhaps we have not allowed humility to lead us far enough—to examine the extent to which our very helping structures demonstrate respect for the other and to consider how the forms of assessment and treatment we are accustomed to using may likewise not hold the answers for everyone. At this level, humility may mean seeking the input of community members to identify desired services rather than simply setting up shop offering our preferred therapy approach. Or it may mean being willing to act as consultant or support person to a parent-run parenting group, rather than running it ourselves.

Helping Perspective

Interventions from this approach employ a strength-based versus deficit-based perspective. Rudkin (2003) discusses how causal attributions about problems or disease that focus on deficits within people or situations can lead to blaming and distancing that minimizes identification with the other and interferes with empathy. By distancing ourselves, we reduce threats to our sense of safety and control, which helps protect us from feeling overwhelmed and helpless in the face of suffering. It can also enable the helper to experience herself as both better off and as compassionate, thereby elevating her self-esteem. We are warned that the wounded healer

> finds an almost wholly satisfying refuge in the profession of psychotherapy, where he is admired and seemingly loved and can enjoy intimacy without the risks of involvement, where he learns techniques to deflect criticism and justify himself, and where he is engaged in an unquestionably valuable profession. (Maeder, cited in Rudkin, 2003, p. 195)

Readers familiar with Henri Nouwen's (1979) more redemptive characterization of the wounded healer may bristle at Rudkin's use of the image. Nouwen adeptly describes how the wounds we have experienced may serve to humble us and increase our empathy and compassion for those we seek to help. Even so, community perspectives challenge us to evaluate the unwitting ways we may actually perpetuate a demeaning and disempowering deficit-orientation toward those we seek to help.

Hospitality

Old Testament Jewish and early Christian hospitality practices are part of our heritage and are worth considering for their relevance to the aims, methods and contexts of providing care (Yangarber-Hicks et al., 2006). Judeo-Christian hospitality to travelers and guests, like that of surrounding cultures, was extended in the home, around the table, directed at the whole person, and supported by a web of cultural and communal expectations (see Pohl, 1999 for an extended discussion of this historical practice). Distinct from these cultural expectations, however, was the emphasis on welcoming individuals who were outsiders (aliens) and those most disadvantaged in society who could not hope to repay their host for the sustenance and shelter provided (the orphan, the widow). Discordant with other cultural traditions was the rationale for providing hospitality, one that was deeply rooted in the history of God's hospitality toward his people. Biblical accounts of hospitality were also unique for their inclusion of needy (widow of Zarephath) or socially stigmatized (Rahab) hosts and for the ways in which hosts were blessed by extending themselves to those who would not be expected to have anything to give back.

Though home-based hospitality to the poor gave way to institutional care over the centuries, modern healthcare practices have roots in these ancient practices. The responsibility for caring for widows, orphans and strangers moved from community members to professional experts. While professional disciplines and systems of care have made extraordinary contributions to the well-being of individuals and communities, there is much that is lacking within contemporary healthcare that money alone cannot fix. A serious consideration of a biblical model of hospitality may be fruitful as we consider why, how, where and to whom we provide care. The value placed on respect, reciprocity and humility in the helping relationship, and the emphases on mutuality, accessibility and destigmatization in the helping context found in community psychology perspectives and approaches are valuable resources for those who wish to consider how psychological care may be hospitably provided.

Research and Action

The emphasis placed by community psychologists on action reflects their commitments to justice, social action and respect for persons. Community and preventive strategies reflect boldness, some would say hubris, in their attempts to effect social change. At the same time, the emphasis on research demonstrates respect for the complexity of social phenomena, humility regarding their methods, and concern over the effects of their interventions on people. When carried out in ways consistent with the kind of community psychology values we have identified previously, it is possible to see the enterprise as compatible with Christian concerns for stewardship of both human and material resources.

Here we can see an alternative to ivory-tower research that objectifies its "subject," one Christians may believe to embody proper connections between gathering knowledge and an action-oriented response to the needs of the world about which we seek knowledge. Wolterstorff (1983) similarly calls for theorizing that "place(s) itself in the service of the cause of struggling for justice" (p. 164). In praxis-oriented scholarship "Christian conviction shapes the *direction* in which scholars turn their inquiries; it determines the *governing interest* of their theorizing" (p. 166). The many decisions and commitments made in the research process are to be made "in the light of the deprivations and oppressions to be found in the social order as it stands" (p. 172).

CONCLUSION

Community psychology and preventative frameworks offer rich alternatives for understanding people-helping. The distinctives and emphases outlined in this chapter raise new and provocative questions in understanding the very nature of counseling and psychotherapy. The intersections of these schools of thought with Christian beliefs and teaching expand our understanding of what it means to enhance human well-being and flourishing. Those who have an interest in the practice of counseling and psychotherapy would do well to consider whether the field of community psychology provides compelling and sometimes alternative models and interventions in which compassion and care can be professionally exercised.

FOR FURTHER READING

Conyne, R. K. (2010). *Prevention program development and evaluation: An incidence reduction, culturally relevant approach.* Thousand Oaks, CA: Sage.

A practical and very accessible introduction to developing and evaluating community-based prevention programs.

Dalton, J. H., Elias, M. J., & Wandersman, A. (2006). *Community psychology:*

Linking individuals and communities (2nd ed.). Belmont, CA: Wadsworth/ Thomson Learning.

Written for advanced undergraduates and graduate students, this textbook provides a thorough introduction to the discipline, including many examples of interventions and additional resources.

Kenny, M. E., Horne, A. M., Orpinas, P., & Reese, L. E. (2009). *Realizing social justice: The challenge of preventive interventions.* Washington, DC: American Psychological Association.

This volume puts social justice at the heart of both a rationale and aim for preventive efforts. Prevention history, theory, core concepts and practices, and ethical matters are covered including featured interventions linking social justice and prevention across a variety of contexts.

Wolterstorff, N. (1983). *Until justice and peace embrace.* Grand Rapids, MI: Eerdmans.

A collection of Wolterstorff's Kuyper lectures given at the Free University of Amsterdam in which he discusses his views of the Christian's relationship to the social order. The following chapters are particularly relevant to community psychology: For Justice in Shalom, The Rich and the Poor, A City of Delight.

For those who want to explore Wolterstorff's theory of justice further, I also recommend:

Wolterstorff, N. (2008). *Justice: Rights and wrongs.* Princeton, NJ: Princeton University Press.

This is a serious work of moral philosophy and Christian ethics in which Wolterstorff develops a theistic theory of justice based upon rights that are located in the worth of the person, tracing back to Hebrew and Christian Scriptures.

REFERENCES

Albee, G. W. (1982). Preventing psychopathology and promoting human potential. *American psychologist, 37*(9), 1043-1050.

Albee, G. A. (1990). The futility of psychotherapy. *The Journal of Mind and Behavior, 11*(3, 4), 369-384.

Baber, K., & Bean, G. (2009). Frameworks: A community-based approach to preventing youth suicide. *Journal of Community Psychology, 37*(6), 684-696.

Banks, R. (1994). *Paul's idea of community* (Rev. ed.). Peabody, MA: Hendrickson Publishers.

Bronfenbrenner, U. (1979). *The ecology of human development: Experiments by nature and design.* Cambridge, MA: Harvard University Press.

Bufford, R. K., & Buckler, R. E. (1987). Counseling in the church: A proposed strategy for ministering to mental health needs in the church. *Journal of Psychology and Christianity, 6*(2), 22-29.

Canning, S. S. (2003). Psychological resources in faith-based community settings: Applications, adaptations, and innovations. *Journal of Psychology and Christianity, 22*(4), 348-352.

Canning, S. S., Case, P. W., & Kruse, S. L. (2001). Contemporary Christian psychological scholarship and 'The least of these': An empirical review. *Journal of Psychology and Christianity, 20,* 205-223.

Canning, S. S., Pozzi, C. F., McNeil, J. D., & McMinn, M. R. (2000). Integration as service: Implications of faith-praxis integration for training. *Journal of Psychology & Theology, 28*(3), 201-211.

Coles, R. (1996). The inexplicable prayers of Ruby Bridges. In K. Monroe (Ed.), *Finding God at Harvard: Spiritual journeys of thinking Christians* (pp. 33-40). Grand Rapids, MI: Zondervan.

Cowen, E. L. (1991). In pursuit of wellness. *American Psychologist, 46*(4), 404-408.

Cruz, M. R., & Sonn, C. C. (2010). (De)colonizing culture in community psychology: Reflections from critical social science. *American Journal of Community Psychology, 47*(1), 203-214. DOI 10.1007/s10464-010-9378-x.

Dalton, J. H., Elias, M. J., & Wandersman, A. (2007). *Community psychology: Linking individuals and communities* (2nd ed.). Belmont, CA: Wadsworth/ Thomson Learning.

Dionne, R., Davis, B., Sheeber, L., & Madrigal, L. (2009). *Journal of Community Psychology, 37*(7), 911-921.

Dowhrenrind, B. S. (1978). Social stress and community psychology. *American Journal of Community Psychology, 6,* 1-14.

Duffy, K. G., & Wong, F. Y. (2003). *Community psychology* (3rd ed.). Boston, MA: Allyn & Bacon.

Durlak, J. A., & Wells, A. M. (1997). Primary prevention mental health programs for children and adolescents: A meta-analytic review. *American Journal of Community Psychology, 25*(2), 115-152.

Elias, M. J. (1987). Establishing enduring prevention programs: Advancing the legacy of Swampscott. *American Journal of Community Psychology, 15,* 539-553.

Ellison, C. G., Finch, B. K., Ryan, D. N., & Salinas, J. J. (2009). Religious involvement and depressive symptoms among Mexican-origin adults in California. *Journal of Community Psychology, 37*(2), 171-193.

Emerson, M. O., & Smith, C. (2000). *Divided by faith: Evangelical religion and the problem of race in America.* New York, NY: Oxford University Press.

Emory, R., Caughy, M., Harris, T. R., & Franzini, L. (2008). Neighborhood social processes and academic achievement in elementary school. *Journal of Community Psychology, 36*(7), 885-898.

Fagan, A. A., Hanson, K., Hawkins, J. D., & Arthur, M. W. (2009). Translational research in action: Implementation of the communities that care prevention system in 12 communities. *Journal of Community Psychology, 37*(7), 809-829.

Fryer, D. (2008). Some questions about "the history of community psychology." *Journal of Community Psychology, 36*(5), 572-586.

Hobfoll, S. (1998). *Stress, culture, and the community: The psychology and philosophy of stress.* New York, NY: Plenum.

Institute of Medicine. (1994). *Reducing risks for mental disorder: Summary.* Washington, DC: National Academy Press.

Jones, S. L., & Butman, R. E. (1991). *Modern psychotherapies: A comprehensive Christian appraisal* (1st ed.). Downers Grove, IL: InterVarsity Press.

Kloos, B., & Moore, T. (2000). The prospect and purpose of locating community research and action in religious settings. *Journal of Community Psychology, 28*(2), 119-137.

Kramer, F. D. (2010). The role for public funding of faith-based organizations delivering behavioral health services: Guideposts for monitoring and evaluation. *American Journal of Community Psychology, 46*, 342-360.

Langhout, R. D., & Thomas, E. (2010). Imagining participatory action research in collaboration with children: An introduction. *American Journal of Community Psychology, 46*(1-2), 60-66.

Lawler, P. A. (2006). Stuck with virtue. *Mars Hill Audio Journal 79.* Charlottesville, VA: Mars Hill Audio.

Levine, M. (1969). Some postulates of community psychology practice. In F. Kaplan & S. B. Sarason (Eds.), *The psycho-educational clinic papers and research studies.* Springfield, MA: Department of Mental Health.

Levine, M., Perkins, D. D., & Perkins, D. V. (2005). *Principles of community psychology: Perspectives and applications* (3rd ed.). New York, NY: Oxford University Press.

Lopez, S. J., & Snyder, C. R. (2003). *Positive psychological assessment: A handbook of models and measures.* Washington, DC: American Psychological Association.

Mankowski, E. S., Galvez, G., & Glass, N. (2010). Interdisciplinary linkage of community psychology and cross-cultural psychology: History, values, and an illustrative research and action project on intimate partner violence. *American Journal of Community Psychology,* published online October 30, 2010. DOI 10.1007/s10464-010-9377-y. www.springerlink.com/content/q552u341u1534654/.

McMillan, D. W. (1996). Sense of community. *Journal of Community Psychology, 24*(4), 315-325.

McMillan, D. W., & Chavis, D. M. (1986). Sense of community: A definition and theory. *Journal of Community Psychology, 14*, 6-23.

McNeil, J. D. (2005). Unequally yoked? The role of culture in the relationship between theology and psychology. In A. Dueck & C. Lee (Eds.), *Why psychology needs theology* (pp. 140-160). Grand Rapids, MI: Eerdmans.

Montero, M. (2008). An insider's look at the development and current state of community psychology in Latin America. *Journal of Community Psychology, 36*(5), 661-674.

Moos, R. (1994). *The social climate scales: A user's guide* (2nd ed.). Palo Alto, CA: Consulting Psychologists Press.

Nouwen, H. J. M. (1979). *The wounded healer.* New York, NY: Doubleday.

Pargament, K. I. (1997). *The psychology of religion and coping.* New York, NY: Guilford.

Pargament, K. I., & Maton, K. (2000). Religion in American life: A community psychology perspective. In J. Rappaport & E. Seidman (Eds.), *Handbook of Community Psychology* (pp. 495-522). New York, NY: Kluwer Academic/Plenum.

Penn Positive Psychology Center. (2010). Positive Psychology Center. Retrieved from: www.ppc.sas.upenn.edu.

Pohl, C. D. (1999). *Making room: Recovering hospitality as a Christian tradition.* Grand Rapids, MI: Eerdmans.

Prater, J. S. (1987). Training Christian lay counselors in techniques of prevention and outreach. *Journal of Psychology and Christianity, 6*(2), 30-34.

Rasmussen, L. (1997). Shaping communities. In D. C. Bass (Ed.), *Practicing our faith: A way of life for a searching people* (pp. 119-132). San Francisco: Jossey-Bass.

Reyes, M. C., & Sonn, C. C. (2010). (De)colonizing culture in community psychology: Reflections from critical social science. *American Journal of Community Psychology,* published online October 30, 2010. DOI 10.1007/s10464-010-9378-x. www.springerlink.com/content/t5782784m217570l/.

Rhodes, J. E., Camic, P. M., Milburn, M., & Lowe, S. R. (2009). Improving middle school climate through teacher-centered change. *Journal of Community Psychology, 37*(6), 711-724.

Rudkin, J. K. (2003). *Community psychology: Guiding principles and orienting concepts.* Upper Saddle River, NJ: Prentice Hall.

Schueller, S. M. (2009). Promoting wellness: Integrating community and positive psychology. *Journal of Community Psychology, 37*(7), 922-937.

Silverman, P. R. (1988). Widow-to-widow: A mutual help program for the widowed. In R. H. Price, E. L. Cowen, R. P. Lorion & J. Ramos-McKay (Eds.), *14 ounces of prevention: A casebook for practitioners* (pp. 175-186). Washington, DC: American Psychological Association.

Society for Community Research and Action (2011). *Society for community research and action: The mission,* published online June 14, 2011, www.scra27.org/documents/practicecouncildocuments/scravisionmissionvaluesdoc.

Strayhorn, J. M. (1983). A diagnostic axis relevant to psychotherapy and preventive mental health. *American Journal of Orthopsychiatry, 53*(4), 677-696.

Sugden, C. M. N. (1995). Social gospel. In D. Atkinson, D. Field, A. Holmes & O. O'Donovan (Eds.), *New dictionary of Christian ethics & pastoral theology* (pp. 799-800). Downers Grove, IL: InterVarsity Press.

Swisher, R. R., & Latzman, R. D. (2008). Youth violence as adaptation? Introduction to the special issue. *Journal of Community Psychology, 36*(8), 959-968.

University of Pennsylvania. (2007). Penn Positive Psychology Center, http://www.ppc.sas.upenn.edu.

Uomoto, J. M. (1982). Preventive intervention: A convergence of the church and community psychology. *Journal of Psychology and Christianity, 1*(3), 12-22.

Vega, W. A., Ang, A., Rodriguez, M. A., & Finch, B. K. (2010). Neighborhood protective effects on depression in Latinos. *American Journal of Community Psychology*, published online October 30, 2010. DOI 10.1007/s10464-010-9370-5. www.springerlink.com/content/08158u3215520178/.

Vincent, T. A., & Trickett, E. J. (1983). Preventive interventions and the human context: Ecological approaches to environmental assessment and change. In R. D. Felner, L. A. Jason, J. N. Moritsugu & S. S. Farber (Eds.), *Preventive psychology: Theory, research and practice* (pp. 67-86). New York, NY: Pergamon Press.

Volf, M. (2002). Theology for a way of life. In M. Volf & E. Bass, *Practicing theology: Beliefs and practices in Christian life* (pp. 245-263). Grand Rapids, MI: Eerdmans.

Wandersman, A. et al. (2008). Bridging the gap between prevention research and practice: The interactive systems framework for dissemination and implementation. *American Journal of Community Psychology, 41*, 171-181.

Wexler, L. (2010). Behavioral health services "don't work for us": Cultural incongruities in human service systems for Alaska native communities. *American Journal of Community Psychology*, published online October 30, 2010. DOI 10.1007/s10464-010-9380-3. www.springerlink.com/content/271175862p6q1131/.

Williams, T. R. (1997). Is there a doctor in the house? Reflections on the practice of healing in African American churches. In D. C. Bass (Ed.), *Practicing our faith: A way of life for a searching people* (pp. 94-120). San Francisco, CA: Jossey-Bass.

Wolterstorff, N. (1983). *Until justice and peace embrace*. Grand Rapids, MI: Eerdmans.

Wolterstorff, N. (1995). Justice and peace. In D. J. Atkinson, D. H. Field, A. F. Holmes & O. O'Donovan (Eds.), *New dictionary of Christian ethics and pastoral theology* (pp. 15-21). Downers Grove, IL: InterVarsity Press.

Yangarber-Hicks, N., Behensky, C., Canning, S. S., Flanagan, K. S., Gibson, N. J. S., Hicks, M. W., & Porter, S. L. (2006). Invitation to the table conversation: A few diverse perspectives on integration. *Journal of Psychology and Christianity, 25*(4), 338-353.

11

RESPONSIBLE ECLECTICISM
AND THE CHALLENGES OF
CONTEMPORARY PRACTICE

Richard E. Butman and Stanton L. Jones

At the broadest possible levels, what have we claimed so far in this book? It is legitimate and necessary for the dedicated Christian to stand on the fundamentals of the faith. We must let those beliefs, values, attitudes and commitments have their proper sway in all that we think, do and feel. This is what integration of faith and understanding means at the most basic level as applied to all areas of life. We have argued that the Christian faith has a great deal to say about personhood, though it does not propose a specific psychology as we understand it today. But the Christian faith should deeply inform our notions of what it means to be a person, of key dimensions of the core nature and identity of persons, of our understandings of health and happiness as well as of brokenness and pathology, and shape our vision of what it means to change. Thus, we are arguing that the Christian faith should inform and shape our psychology even if it does not propose a specific psychological approach.

Further, we need a psychology, a comprehensive and explicit understanding of persons, if we are to be of optimal assistance in helping hurting people achieve healing and growth. In our analysis of the main psychotherapy theories, we hope we have documented two main points. First, that each of the models has several compatibilities with the faith, as well as many insights, strengths, uses and points of attractiveness. Second, that each model has both incompatibilities with biblical faith and other flaws, inconsistencies, weaknesses and problems. None of the theories can be rejected out of hand, but none can be wholeheartedly endorsed by the Christian counselor. Some models hold more promise than others, because they are more fully developed, have more evidence supporting their effectiveness or have more pervasive commonalities with Christian belief and practice. Thus, in addition to drawing with confidence on biblical truth, we also have helpful tools at hand from among the findings of psychological theory, science and practice that can contribute to forming an effective approach to people-helping. While we can approach this task with confidence and enthusiasm, we would also be wise to adopt a respectful and thoughtful stance of epistemic humility (cf. McMinn & Campbell, 2007). There is much work that still needs to be done before more integrative and comprehensive models can be offered.

We do not have a definitive model to propose in place of the many theories we have examined. In fact, we do not believe that a definitive model exists and think it unlikely that it will ever exist. If after two millennia Christians cannot agree about some of the most fundamental points of theology (as documented by the diversity of denominations and theological "schools"), how can we expect congruence on a "Christian" psychology? Similarly, in the field of counseling, we have no clear consensus on how best to ascertain truth, what goals should be pursued, how treatment effects can best be measured, and how to incorporate spirituality and religion into psychotherapy (cf. various perspectives of Gonsiorek, Pargament, Richards & McMinn, 2009).

So how then should we proceed? Can counselors achieve some order in their understanding of people so as not to be paralyzed with indecision and confusion when confronted with a hurting person? We would argue that it is reasonable at this point in history for Christian counselors to be eclectic or pluralistic in their approach, drawing first on the faith for the foundations of a view of persons and then elaborating on that view with conceptions taken from secular psychology or the writings of the Christian counselors of the past and the present. And lest the result of this process of appropriation and synthesis be a sloppy, unsystematic hodgepodge of ideas, we will survey ways that this eclecticism might be conducted.

As we start out, we would argue again, as we did in chapter two, that the Bible does not teach a personality theory, though it does teach us much about persons. Van Leeuwen (1987), working within the framework of personality theorist Salvatore Maddi, suggests that it is vital to distinguish between suppositions of core personality tendencies and characteristics (about which the Bible and the faith has much, though not everything, to say) and their more peripheral statements about personality types, modes of human development and the like. She argues that it is at this abstract level that the clearest engagement with scriptural truth must occur, and we concur with this argument. We must remember that the intent of the Bible is first and foremost to offer a record of redemption history and present a plan of salvation—not to satisfy our desire for a clear and comprehensive model of personality (cf. chap. 2 in this volume for greater clarification).

For example, the concept of sin is central to the faith, but that concept, with all its meaning, does not tell us why one person sins by committing adultery while another sins with a prideful, arrogant attitude or by a lack of compassion for the poor (cf. chap. 4 in Yarhouse, Butman & McRay, 2005). The faith tells us that God did not intend for us to be riddled with anxiety, but it does not tell us how to deal with a person who is phobicly afraid of social situations, nor does it tell us why some avoid feared objects while others overcompensate for their fear with an exaggerated bravado. Our faith tells us the ultimate meaning of life, but it does not tell us why so many conversions to saving faith occur in adolescence rather than in late adulthood. It is our psychologies that address these complex and intricate issues. Men and women of faith have always struggled with problems of anxiety, and we would be wise to look closely to the rich traditions of pastoral care and spiritual formation for some helpful perspectives about what it means to care for struggling persons (cf. chap. 1 in Yarhouse, Butman & McRay, 2005).

Several authors have noted that the theoretical allegiances of counselors to different counseling approaches tend to change over time (cf. Corey & Corey, 2011). While there is limited empirical research to back up these claims, they are intuitively appealing. A generation ago Halgin (1985) suggested that there are a number of pressures that encourage students of counseling to make identifications with particular approaches even before they have received substantive training in these approaches. This may be due to student-perceived congruences between a model and that student's personal life philosophy, identification with a professor or teacher who emulates a certain approach, or pressure exerted by graduate admission processes that encourage early identification of a preferred model. In the graduate training environment student allegiances to a model are dramatically affected by socialization pressures exerted in graduate training programs, as well as the nature of the clinical training opportunities available to the trainee, both in terms of courses and practicum experiences and personal experiences with therapy. Training programs often are strong in one approach to the detriment of others. Those educating students in therapy also seem more likely to be theoretical purists than community practitioners because such theoretical purity makes classroom communication easier and may facilitate research productivity (e.g., "If I can't measure it, it does not exist."). Students today tell us that they feel these pressures even more acutely, especially in highly competitive and stressful educational and training settings. The implicit or explicit messages they so often hear are that they need to please the often competing demands of clients, supervisors and professors to demonstrate "effectiveness" in all that they do (cf. excellent discussion in Swift & Callahan, 2010).

In practicing therapy (following Corey & Corey, 2011; Halgin, 1985; Meier, 2008; and Norcross, 1985) the clinician inevitably confronts the limits of his or her model. This may be minimized for those who work in settings where they are exposed only to a homogeneous population needing help, as in the case of the behavior modifier working only with the mildly developmentally disabled (retarded), the graduate student working with a highly selective and homogeneous population exhibiting a narrow range of psychological symptoms pursuant to the purposes of a particular grant-funded study, or the existential therapist only working with high-functioning, verbal and intelligent persons experiencing milder dissatisfactions with life. For most, though, confrontations with the limits of one's model occur quite soon in practice; we run into counseling problems that either stretch our working model to the limits or clearly fall beyond the bounds of our model. One only has to look at the bewildering variety of psychopathologies in our current psychiatric classification manual (the

DSM-IV-TR) to realize that no one approach can possibly be effective with all problems in living.

We also encounter cases where it seems that our model should have worked if the approach is true, and we must confront the fact that it did *not* work. Psychotherapy outcomes reflect a synergistic combination of *at least* four distinct variables: (1) hope and expectancy effects, (2) techniques utilized, (3) therapist-client interactions, and (4) contextual, developmental and situational variables (after McMinn & Campbell, 2007). And, it seems, there probably should be always understood to be a fifth variable in play: (5) "error variance" or the influence of the unknown. Success—or lack thereof—is not always an easy determination. These experiences are akin to the psychological challenges we face in our own personal development when our status quo is shaken and the resulting disequilibrium forces us to grow a bit more (cf. Garber, 1996). Without such crises we would be unlikely to ever grow.

Our reaction to such challenges may be rigidly to claim the exclusive correctness of our model and to deny its limitations (a response not in the best interest of therapist or client). Some will acknowledge the limitations but confidently believe that it is only a matter of time until the essential correctness of their approach is borne out. Some may lapse into a relativism that results in the kind of "supermarket" (Nelson-Jones, 1985) or chaotic eclecticism we will describe later in this chapter. But the healthiest response is to make a commitment to growing in effectiveness through knowing the limits of our approach and understanding how other models might complement and make up for the weaknesses of our own (McMinn & Campbell, 2007). And we suspect that such growth might occur best in the context of mutually respectful and truly collaborative conversations about our core assumptions and convictions with wise peers and mentors.

It should be noted at the outset that there has been a virtual explosion of research on treatments that work (i.e., outcome-based treatment strategies) in the past two decades (e.g., Nathan & Gorman, 2002; Norcross, 2002; Kronenberger & Meyer, 2001; Meyer & Weaver, 2007; and Jongsma & Peterson, 2003). Careful reviews of the available and theoretical literatures have suggested that our knowledge of what strategies work best with what populations and problems has increased substantially. This has sparked fierce debates between practitioners and researchers, and between insurance companies and providers of mental health services. Accreditation agencies are now insisting that approaches that have been shown empirically to be demonstrably effective or superior to other alternatives be taught in all interventions courses in graduate and professional training settings. The critics of this movement contend that counseling and psychotherapy runs the risk of becoming formulaic (i.e., extremely pragmatic), and that mental health professionals run the risk of minimizing the importance of the personhood of both the therapist and client in the healing and helping process (cf. Yarhouse, Butman & McRay, 2005; or McMinn & Campbell, 2007). In our contemporary debates about health care reform, economic and political forces seem to be increasingly dictating the agenda, often leaving thoughtful practitioners "in the dust." Those of us charged with training the next generation of mental health professionals have often come to lament the decreased desire to do the kind of deep, disciplined and reflective thinking that ought to characterize effective agents of change and healing (Garber, 1996).

If the responsible Christian counselor were to systematically explore the available literature on outcome-based therapy, she or he would immediately be deluged with hundreds of articles, books or chapters on the complex and multifaceted topic. There has been a virtual explosion of work in the interface between theory, research and practice (cf. Corey, 2009; or Corsini, 2008). The broad question two decades ago may have been, Is therapy generally effective? The accumulative evidence using such powerful statistical techniques as meta-analysis has certainly answered that question in the affirmative (Comer, 2007).

The questions being raised more recently are not nearly as broad or global—they are far more concrete and specific (e.g., What *particular* therapies work best with what types of *problems* and with what types of *populations?*). Further, there is intense interest in whether or not these interventions produce lasting changes—either personally or systemically (cf. Dueck & Reimer, 2009). It appears that our intervention methods will have to become more sophisticated as our understanding of the causation of psychological disorders grows exponentially. Major paradigm shifts have occurred in the past two decades, especially in the growing recognition of the importance of both biological and sociocultural factors that are significant in the etiology and maintenance of mental illness (e.g., First &

Tasman, 2004; Pliszka, 2003; or Sue & Sue, 2008). A companion text to this current volume, *Modern Psychopathologies: A Comprehensive Christian Appraisal* (Yarhouse, Butman & McRay, 2005), has attempted to address this and related concerns directly.

We sense there has been a rapprochement movement of sorts between theoreticians, researchers and clinicians, a movement that effectively points in two different directions. On the one hand, there seems to be a concerted effort to try to identify a set of common strategies that may run through the work of all effective psychotherapists, regardless of their stated theoretical orientation (Norcross & Beutler, 2008). This movement focuses on the question of what characterizes all effective psychotherapists, what is often called the search for "common factors." There is also a balancing movement that drives us toward greater specificity and focus as it asks the discerning question, What *specific* treatment, offered by *whom*, is most effective for this *individual* with these *specific problems*, and under which set of *circumstances*, and for how *long*? Indeed, the two most cited resources (Nathan & Gorman, 2002; Norcross, 2002) appear to approach the topic from this latter, more pragmatic mindset. The fruits of these debates can be of great assistance to us as we seek a psychological model that fits for us, with the answers often organized around a theoretical orientation, an identified clinical concern, a preferred research methodology, a favored classification system or even worldview (Plate, 2005). We will try to sample from these far-reaching emphases.

Persons who favor a strong cognitive-behavioral approach (e.g., Barlow, 2008) have contributed much to our understanding of how best to treat problems of anxiety and mood. This has been especially evident in much of the important work that has been done with children and adolescents in the past two decades (e.g., Christophersen & Mortweet, 2001; Fonagy, Target, Cottrel, Phillips & Kurtz, 2002). Those who have a strong allegiance to more interpersonal approaches have likewise been remarkably productive with these types of problems (e.g., McLemore, 2003; Norcross, 2002; Schultheis, 1998; Shedler, 2010). With reference to specific diagnosable disorders, the important work of Nathan and Gorman (2002) is widely cited and appears to be greatly favored by those who often pay for mental health services (i.e., insurance companies). Ongoing debates between the current classification system (American Psychiatric Association, 2000) or its major alternative (PDM Task Force, 2006) no doubt complicate the basic definitional issues (e.g., How do we best understand the presenting concerns of the client?). Those with a strong commitment to empirical research (e.g., Meyer & Weaver, 2007; Kronenberger & Meyer, 2001) offer clear direction on how best to proceed, but there are nevertheless those who still prefer a more qualitative approach (narrative) toward understanding the "calamities of the soul" over the highly defined, manualized approaches (e.g., Dueck & Reimer, 2009; Frattaroli, 2001). Finally, we find it most encouraging that some of our colleagues have made important contributions to the conversation as well from a distinctly Christian perspective (e.g., McMinn & Campbell, 2007; Tan, 2011).

Another clear trend that is emerging is that extremely complex problems in living often respond best to combined strategies (e.g., CBT, interpersonal therapy and psychopharmacology) rather than a single, specific, pure strategy (cf. Yarhouse, Butman & McRay, 2005). This seems consistent with the evidence that the vast majority of psychological disorders are the result of a complex interaction of biological, psychosocial and sociocultural factors. It logically follows that the appropriate professional response would reflect an appreciation for the complexity of etiology and maintenance. Sensitive and skilled psychotherapists have come to appreciate the need to do careful and comprehensive case formulation before developing a treatment plan (cf. Schwartzberg, 2000). Hopefully, knowledge of how particular therapies work with particular disorders can help therapists and clients alike make more informed decisions of how best to proceed in this process of mutual discernment and responsible stewardship in light of the increasingly limited resources and seemingly endless demands for services (cf. Yarhouse, Butman & McRay, 2005).

In the first edition of our book we suggested that the best way to proceed was to carefully examine the assumptions that undergird our working models of personality, psychopathology and psychotherapy. In every approach we found values that were compatible with a Christian worldview, and others that were certainly in conflict. Four options for responsible eclecticism were explored, with a clear preference for theoretical integrationism emerging (cf. chap. 15 in Jones & Butman, 1991). Twenty years later we have noticed that the language appears to be changing in some interesting and intriguing ways.

It seems use of the word *eclecticism* is waning in preference for the word *integration* (after Corsini, 2008; Norcross & Beutler, 2008). Those whose approach we described as "technical eclecticism" would today state that they are merely pragmatists who make an intentional effort to find the best treatment techniques for each problem identified with each client (cf. Cohen-Possey, 2000). This appears to be the major emphasis of the massive tome now in its third edition, *Treatments That Work* (Nathan & Gorman, 2002), and its popularity testifies to the strength of this tradition.

The approach to eclecticism which we advocated previously was "theoretical integrationism" (Jones & Butman, 1991), wherein an attempt is made to blend ideas at a conceptual or theoretical level. We believe this is the approach that McMinn and Campbell (2007) used when they tried to blend the best of CBT and interpersonal therapies with the parameters of a Christian worldview. We applaud their efforts, and continue to regard this approach as a strong alternative. We will return to this approach in our later discussion of metatheoretical perspectives.

A third approach, according to Norcross and Beutler (2008) has been called "common factors integration." There is a compelling dimension to this approach in light of some of the important and indisputable empirical findings about the heart and soul of change (cf. Hubble, Duncan & Miller, 1999). McMinn and Campbell (2007) have us imagine a pie chart, based on the best meta-analytic empirical research, wherein specific psychotherapeutic techniques (the clearest points of difference between different therapy approaches) account for about 15 percent of the total potential for change, expectancy effects (the degree of hopefulness and optimism versus pessimism of the client) account for another 15 percent of the potential for change, relationship factors between the counselor and client for 30 percent, and contextual or situational variables for the greatest proportion—40 percent. If their appraisal of the meta-analytic evidence is indeed accurate, then this places a tremendous premium on our recognition of what goes on between the therapist and client, how hope is communicated in word and deed, and a renewed appreciation for the world in which the client actually lives. Notably, these three variables of relationship, expectancy and context are generic across therapy approaches regardless of how distinctive and unique their theoretical conceptualizations and the specific techniques that flow from them are.

Thus, the common-factors approach is one that does not place the primary emphasis on the "technique." It is for this reason that the approach stands in stark contrast to more formulaic or pragmatic emphases in the contemporary literature (e.g., Jongsma & Peterson, 2003).

The final approach to integration would be "assimilative integration," an approach that is rooted primarily in one specific approach to psychotherapy but with an openness to the supportive and helpful but minor contributions from other approaches (cf. Norcross, Karpiak & Liser, 2008; Norcross, Karpiak & Santoro, 2005). Such an approach might be exemplified by the psychodynamic practitioner who nevertheless utilizes a short-term behavioral intervention to help a client in acute distress. We suspect that this approach is still quite widely adopted today.

Indeed, Norcross and Beutler (2008) have suggested that theoretical integration, common-factors integration and assimilative integration are widely endorsed by practicing clinicians, in almost equal proportions (28%, 28% and 26%). In contrast, technical eclecticism is practiced by a relatively small minority (less than 20%). Frankly, we are encouraged by these trends. Contemporary clinicians appear to be responding to findings of evidenced-based therapy, as noted by Corey and Corey (2011) and Gurman and Messer (2003). It is an unquestionably good thing that practitioners appear to be more and more influenced by the empirical findings regarding therapeutic effectiveness. We would like to believe that these same individuals are simultaneously striving to be more coherent conceptually, to be more intentional and clear about their core assumptions and beliefs—but we are not always so sure.

We are convinced, however, that it is important for Christians to be even more actively involved in this conversation about eclecticism or psychotherapy integration. Excellent work has been done recently to explore ways that specific religious beliefs and practices can be more directly incorporated into contemporary clinical practices without compromising our integrity or professionalism (e.g., Post & Wade, 2009). Not only is this important in terms of the religious and theological integrity of practitioners, but it also is vitally important from the perspective of the client, the consumer of psychological services. While the vast majority of mental health professionals are nonreligious or nontraditionally religious, the vast majority of the general population in the United States is deeply and conservatively religious. Practitioners ignore the religion of their clients, and the resources that the religious community offers to their clients, to their detriment. Several decades of research—often from a faith-based perspective—has made a strong case for taking seriously a person's faith commitments (e.g., Hood, Hill & Spilka, 2009; Paloutzian & Parks, 2005).

Religion has been shown to be correlated with dimensions of health, psychopathology and coping. This should not be surprising since there has been a centuries-old tradition of effective pastoral care (cf. chap. 1 in *Modern Psychopathologies* by Yarhouse, Butman & McRay, 2005). For example, it has been clearly demonstrated that persons with strong social support systems, a sense of efficacy, and clear sense of meaning and purpose in life cope much more effectively with the demands of everyday living than those with fewer resources in these areas. As was noted in chapter ten on community psychology and prevention, it makes clear sense to think not only about an individual's liabilities but his or her assets as well. The meta-analytic findings regarding common factors from psychotherapy outcome research clearly indicate the wisdom of considering the contextual and situational variables that can so deeply impact the etiology and maintenance of psychopathology.

It also becomes more than defensible to talk about hope and expectancy effects—or what really gives a person a sense of meaning and purpose in life (cf. Bilezikian, 1993, 1997). Simply put, so many of our problems in living have to do with our sense of our own identity—and the social networks we are a part of. We find it interesting to note in this regard that the number one request for help around the world today has to do with relational difficulties—for example, "Can you help me fix my marriage?" or "Can you help me fix my son or daughter?"

So where does this all leave us with the current emphasis on empirically supported treatments (EST) or evidence-based treatments (EBT)? Tremendous pressures are being exerted on all human-service and health-care providers to use only techniques that have been scientifically validated. This is a most difficult challenge in actual practice. A close examination of the vast literature on the topic will suggest that the most effective treatments are often a combination of CBT and psychopharmacology, or a cognitive-behavioral intervention alone, with evidence growing in support of a number of the experiential, psychodynamic or family approaches.

From our perspective it appears that these pressures are often exerted in an effort to control rising costs—and we can appreciate that. But it does concern us that so much of this same emphasis runs the risk of being rather reductionistic—that is, complex problems are biological, or psychological, or sociocultural, or spiritual. Our theological anthropology tells us that whole persons are not just mindless bodies or disembodied minds (see chap. 2). It is also the case that many of these empirically based treatments are tested on relatively "pure" populations that screen out the kinds of complex, messy cases that are actually more the norm in day-to-day practice for mental health practitioners. The research trials are run in university settings that advertise for particular kinds of clients and screen out all those that did not fit tight experimental criteria. In contrast, caring professionals in the community are seeing individuals with multiple diagnoses in complex situations that all too often would never make it into those tightly defined clinical trials. Thus, the EBTs are being validated on patient populations that differ from those individuals seen in practice. On what basis, then, would a practitioner completely restrict her or his practice to these techniques?

Returning back to the pie chart of McMinn and Campbell (2007), a strong argument can be made that we are not looking close enough at the factors that influence outcomes other than "technique." For example, how best do we understand hope and expectancy effects? To what extent does authentic and credible therapist modeling impact this? How do our attempts to make meaning out of suffering help people grow—and potentially heal? How are we to best understand the dance of anger, intimacy and deception that goes on between the provider and recipient of services (McLemore, 2003)? To use an analogy from the computer-driven world, what part of the healing process simply cannot be outsourced? And with reference to the real world in which clients actually work, love and play, how can we increasingly appreciate the contextual and situational realities that are so much of their lives—and so incredibly relevant to making sense of their self-report and our often incomplete observations of them in our offices?

We certainly do not want to minimize the importance of using specific strategies and interventions in our work. But we do want to state that all the work on ESTs or EBTs might be missing some extremely important factors that must be a part of the integrative conversation. We remain convinced of the absolute primacy of relationships in the healing and helping process (Bilezikian, 1997). We believe strongly that we need to have a construct of health, happiness and holiness—and especially a construct of realistic biblical hope. In short, our awareness, comprehension and understanding of the world in which struggling persons actually move could not be more relevant to our attempts to image God's character, his compassion and his concerns (see chap. 12).

The wise and discerning therapist faces a number of challenges in working with hurting persons in the real world. First, the helping process should begin with a comprehensive and thorough assessment of both presenting concerns as well as potential resources to draw upon in the change process. Careful thought should be given to the biopsychosocial formulation (cf. Schwartzberg, 2000) as an appropriate and realistic treatment plan (cf. Jongsma, 2004; Cohen-Posey, 2000; Jongsma & Peterson, 2003; Schultheis, 1998). Consultation with such seminal works as Norcross (2002) or Nathan and Gorman (2002) can yield constructive guidance for how best to proceed. We should keep in view that those interventions should not be utilized without an appreciation for expectancy effects, relational variables and, perhaps most importantly, for specific contextual or situational variables. Surely we should expect nothing less than those of us who aspire to be men and women of depth and substance—and exemplars of compassion, competence and conviction.

Despite the concerns that have been raised by the recent emphasis on outcome-based treatment strategies, a number of themes have emerged that have some fascinating implications for thoughtful and disciplined thinkers (cf. McMinn & Campbell, 2007). We know, for example, that hope and expectancy effects need to be an important part of the conversation—perhaps even as important as the strong emphasis on technique. It is rare, however, to hear serious conversations about these matters in education, training or professional circles. Since hope is such a central part of the Christian gospel (cf. Smedes, 1998), it seems more than appropriate to ask therapists and their clients about what ultimately gives them meaning and purpose in life (cf. Pargament, 1997).

It has also become abundantly clear that potentially *all* dimensions of the relationship between client and therapist are important indicators of successful outcomes (cf. Nathan & Gorman, 2002). How we treat one another—in word and deed—is clearly foundational in all concerted efforts to promote healing and helping. Thoughtful theological anthropology (cf. chap. 2) supports and encourages such a focus. But perhaps the most profound and challenging finding is the growing understanding of the powerful influence of contextual and situational factors that the client deals with on a daily basis in shaping outcomes of the counseling process (cf. chap. 10). It would not be an exaggeration to say that it nearly equals the combined factors of technique, relationships and hope (cf. McMinn & Campbell, 2007). The implications of these findings for training, supervision and professional practice will be explored later in this volume.

How Effective Is Psychotherapy Generally?

On the whole, it continues to be true that scientific studies show that participation in psychotherapy is better than no psychotherapy at all for most individuals with a wide variety of problems, and that the general effect is "significant" (the classic references are Smith, Glass & Miller, 1980; Brown, 1987; these findings are revalidated by Nathan & Gorman, 2002; McMinn & Campbell, 2007). The research to date has failed to show the superiority of one therapeutic approach over another for *all* disorders, even under controlled experimental conditions (Nathan & Gorman, 2002). Therapies within the major traditions have demonstrated a wide range of usefulness in treating a variety of psychopathologies. The few studies on specifically Christian approaches to counseling tend to be poorly designed and executed from a methodological perspective, so optimistic statements about their effectiveness should be taken with a grain of salt. In our judgment, these are largely based on anecdotal observations and therapists' judgments, hardly the criteria demanded in contemporary research. There needs to be a more serious commitment to outcome research on the part of all clinicians. In the interim we must be cautious in our claims about clinical effectiveness and exercise some much-needed humility.

Even though psychotherapy overall has been shown to be effective, we still believe that the Christian clinician needs to answer the question, How do *I* know that what *I* do is effective? To answer this question the clinician needs to know about both the qualitative and quantitative options available for the assessment of the effectiveness of a particular theory or technique. One should view with particular caution the use of self-report by clients or therapists to judge effectiveness, because of the obvious possibilities of distortion and response bias. The human science methodologies mentioned earlier use a variety of self-report and interview strategies to generate broad-range data about human behavior and experience. These methodologies are more rigorous than uncontrolled testimonials or single-case reports and introduce a higher degree of accountability than mere subjective judgment. In conjunction with more traditional measures of evaluation (e.g., clinical observation, objective and projective tests), these strategies can be useful in promoting more of an ongoing assessment of the people-helping process (cf. Nathan & Gorman, 2007).

There are some specific conclusions about the varying effectiveness of certain approaches or strategies with certain populations that have been firmly established in recent decades. For example, a recent meta-analysis claimed to demonstrate the superiority of cognitive-behavioral interventions with most disorders of childhood and adolescence (Christophersen & Mortweet, 2001). At this stage in the research, however, extreme caution must be exercised in drawing too much from such conclusions (i.e., a "one size fits all" mindset). For example, one could argue that the Christophersen and Mortweet study was an analysis of published studies in professional journals and that those journals tend to require experimental rigor that favors behavioral studies because those therapy methods are most easily rendered into acceptable scientific form. Further, one could argue that the clients treated in these experimental studies could not represent the breadth and complexity of the kinds of child and adolescent problems seen in a community counseling clinic since, as we discussed earlier, those clients who do not fit the narrow definitions of the study population are screened out of experimental studies. We do not feel that these considerations should lead one to a crippling skepticism about the use of such research on comparative effectiveness. But we must be careful about impulsively jumping to strong conclusions that are "merited" by the research. Not all of the "heart and soul" of counseling and psychotherapy can be assessed in objective and neutral ways.

Each of the eight chapters on the specific theoretical approaches included recent research updates on that approach's effectiveness. Those presentations do not take us much further in answering the core specificity question—that is, What strategies work best with what populations and problems under what conditions? Briefly put, cognitive-behavioral strategies seem to have made the greatest contribution to our knowledge about outcome-based treatment strategies (cf. Yarhouse, Butman & McRay, 2005). Advances in creative and unique research strategies have helped us to increasingly see the value of certain psychodynamic strategies (cf. chap. 4 in this volume). Humanistic and experiential therapies are clearly moving beyond a strong preference for phenomenologically oriented, single case study approaches. Especially encouraging has been the attempts made by clinicians committed to advancing emotionally focused strategies (EFT) for working with partner conflicts and parent-child conflicts (cf. chaps. 8-9).

What we could not have predicted twenty years ago was the striking increase in the biological understanding of crucial aspects of mental illness (cf. chap. 2 in Yarhouse, Butman & McRay, 2005). Briefly put, biological factors appear to play a significant role not only in problems of anxiety and mood, but in problems of personality and psychosis as well. The cognitive neuroscience revolution has given us a renewed appreciation for the risks of seeing others as a mindless body or a disembodied mind (cf. chap. 2 in this volume). Christian assertions about the fundamental unity of mind and body seem more relevant than ever in our increased understanding and awareness of the etiology and maintenance of mental illness (cf. chap. 2 in Yarhouse, Butman & McRay, 2005).

What this all means is that when seeking the best possible practices in our work with troubled individuals, couples or families, CBT, psychopharmacology (medication) and some form of interpersonal therapy is almost always generically recommended (e.g., Jongsma & Peterson, 2003). Whether or not this constitutes a new form of biological, cognitive or behavioral reductionism remains to be seen. Yarhouse, Butman and McRay (2005) argue that we have increasingly lost touch with some of the rich traditions of historic pastoral care—not the least of which is increasing reliance on high-tech rather than more incarnational and interactional approaches. As McLemore (2003) has warned, few things in life are more toxic than consulting a technician when you are in serious pain. In a day when it seems like well-intentioned efforts for bringing about health care reform have gone awry, a growing number of recipients of services seem to be complaining about what they perceive to be "managed abandonment." Problems in living are exceedingly complex (i.e., everything seems to be a combination of biological, psychosocial, sociocultural and spiritual factors). Obviously, our models of personhood, psychopathology and psychotherapy need to reflect that reality (cf. chap. 2 in Yarhouse, Butman & McRay, 2005).

It is simply unrealistic to expect that most counselors can know so many theories well enough that they can be a cognitive therapist one hour, a behavior therapist the next, an object-relations psychotherapist the third, an experientially oriented gestalt therapist before lunch and so forth. The only practical way this position could be worked out would be for groups of professionals of varying approaches to work together and freely refer clients to each other according to empirically determined effectiveness; this is an attractive ideal. We seriously doubt that would ever happen since the incentives to compete are stronger than the motivations to collaborate in the mental health field.

We are certainly encouraged by the return to basics we have seen in the outcome-based literature in the past two decades. It appears to be moving beyond a "one size fits all" mindset of CBT, medication and interpersonal therapies, where the only real debate appears to be about how best to triage the triad of therapeutic strategies. As McMinn and Campbell (2007) have so clearly noted, a reasoned case can be made for including "head, heart and hands" (i.e., the cognitive, affect and behavioral domains of personality). That makes our understanding of the nature of persons more important than ever. It is not only acceptable to talk about distinctively and decidedly Christian notions of personhood—but vitally essential.

Drawing on what we are learning (relearning) from the community psychology movement, we also need to take seriously what we are learning about coping and resiliency (e.g., Pargament, 1997). Both short-term and long-term, we know social support systems matter deeply, as does an individual's sense of meaning and purpose. These assertions are certainly foundational in both systemic as well as humanistic and existential psychologies.

Further, that same conversation needs to return to such foundational issues as the nature of hope (expectancy effects) and the primacy of authentic and credible relationships in our work (McLemore, 2003). As the psychodynamically-oriented clinicians have claimed for nearly a century, "we are our own best technique" (cf. chap. 4 in this volume). Now that we are well into the twenty-first century, it becomes more important than ever to recognize we are world citizens as well as world Christians. Hence, contextual and situational variables become absolutely essential in making sense of the "calamities of the soul" (cf. chap. 1 in Yarhouse, Butman & McRay, 2005). All these factors are well worth revisiting as we re-vision what it means to promote development, growth and healing.

CONCLUSION

Given the relative merits of eclecticism, common factor approaches or theoretical integrationism, we believe that *theoretical integrationism* is the approach of choice for the Christian counselor. We take this position because we regard the Christian faith to be one that emphasizes coherence and truthfulness of belief. The faith has a core message about human nature, as discussed in chapter two, which can serve as an organizing foundation for our approach to persons in pain. With such a cohesive core, we have a basis from which to critique theories as we have in this book, and from which to build an integrated approach to therapy. We applaud the recent work of Tan (2011) and McMinn and Campbell (2007) in this regard.

We have described the many strengths and weaknesses of the various approaches to psychotherapy, and feel that each model has problems that need to be remedied. Probably the two models that come closest to true comprehensiveness and have the least problems are the newer and broader psychodynamic approaches (chap. 4) and cognitive-behavioral therapy (chap. 6). The approaches to family therapy based on either psychodynamic or cognitive-behavioral models are useful extensions of these approaches, but do not themselves represent a comprehensive approach. It is our judgment that the work being done by faith-based clinicians in community psychology (i.e., prevention) and the family therapies offer some rather intriguing possibilities for how best to extend our understanding of theoretical integrationism.

Even so, as we have shown, the recent psychodynamic and cognitive-behavioral approaches have serious drawbacks from a Christian perspective, and each needs to be fundamentally modified, conceptually and in practice, to be suitable for enthusiastic use by the Christian professional.

At the very least, each needs to seriously confront the greater respect for what is distinctly personal and human as understood in the humanistic-existential perspectives (especially emotionally focused psychotherapies). And each of these models has much to learn from the strengths of the other psychotherapy approaches as well.

As a brief example, we might note that Christian counselors who have clarified their theological foundations could ably use cognitive-behavioral therapy (CBT) as their predominant orienting theoretical approach. Precisely because of their commitment to a Christian understanding of persons, they would recognize many deficits in this working orientation. They would begin with the Christian foundations in resolving these deficits. They may recognize the inattention that cognitive-behavioral therapy manifests to existential issues of meaning to which Christianity speaks, and draw from existential therapy to better understand this dimension of life. From the psychodynamic therapies they could learn much about the likely influence of early relationships on emotional and personality development, and about the deeply conflictual nature of human motivation and its role in the phenomenon of human self-deception. A study of family therapy and community psychology could expand their understanding of the influence of family and social networks, as our faith would indicate the importance of these. Finally, the study of gestalt therapy and the emotionally expressive therapies may yield insights about the emotional dimensions of healthy personality, as this dimension is minimized by cognitive-behavioral therapy.

Following Corey and Corey (2011), Prochaska and Norcross (2010), and Rychlak (1981), we would note some of the following dangers in making integration of counseling theories occur successfully. First, the development of well-articulated, comprehensive Christian models will not be facilitated by the presence of divisiveness, territoriality and claims of exclusive possession of the truth ("My way is Yahweh," as a colleague has said). Humility and a commitment to community interaction and feedback are vital for progress to occur. Second, the effort must be interdisciplinary both in spirit and reality. The exclusion of certain groups from the dialogue will be counterproductive. Third, the effort must emphasize a balanced commitment to conceptual integrity and rigorous research. Finally, and most importantly, those making this effort must seek to be thoroughly biblical and faithful to the historic orthodox Christian faith while being appropriately ecumenical in spirit.

Dimensions of a Comprehensive Christian Counseling Approach

What will a comprehensive approach to Christian counseling embody? Drawing from chapter two and our discussions in each of the chapters, we would suggest the following skeletal and nonexhaustive outline. Although this typology was first introduced in the first edition almost twenty years ago, our students have consistently told us it is a useful "creedal statement" to get them to think in a more disciplined way about how we all need to stretch in order to be more consistent between our truly Christian beliefs and behaviors. A comprehensive theoretical approach to Christian counseling would embody:

- a deep appreciation of the value of being human and of individual human beings

- a vision of our need for a love relationship with our Creator, attainable only through the forgiveness offered through the death of Jesus Christ

- an understanding of the essential place of the work of the Holy Spirit in ultimate healing

- an understanding of our intrinsic purposefulness and need for meaning

- an understanding of our fundamentally relational natures and need for love and acceptance, including the importance of family and community for us all

- a balance of emphasis on thinking, feeling and behaving, as each has a clear and important place in human life

- an appreciation of the power of sin and evil

- an understanding of the influence of the spiritual world on day-to-day human functioning

- a respect for human freedom and agency, yet one that recognizes limitations to human choice as well

- an appreciation of habit, skill and learning

- a balanced attention to within-the-person and external-to-the-person influences on human action

- a vision of life that suggests there can be meaning to suffering and that we are called to pursue something more than our personal gratification

- a respect for individuals that is grounded in God's love for each person, yet without worshiping the individual disconnected from others

- a commitment to holism in understanding the person, but with a sufficiently developed set of specific postulates about molecular processes in personality to guide actual intervention and the change processes

- a respect for our intrinsically moral natures and the value of obedience to appropriate authority, preeminently to God and his Word

- a respect for physical and nonphysical aspects of existence; an appreciation but not a deification of rationality, balanced with an equally appreciative understanding of our "transrational" aesthetic, symbolic and story-telling natures

- a recognition of our need to worship and be committed to the one who transcends all that we can know or imagine

- a love for Christ's body, the church, and a commitment to furthering the church's work in this world

Such a well-articulated, comprehensive and integrated approach to Christian counseling does not exist today. We cannot offer the definitive model. We hope, along with our readers, to be involved in the development of such a model in the years ahead.

FOR FURTHER READING

Christophersen, E., & Mortweet, S. (2001). *Treatments that work with children.* Washington, DC: American Psychological Association.

Garfield, S. (1980). *Psychotherapy: An eclectic approach.* New York, NY: Wiley.

Hubble, D., Duncan, D., & Miller, S. (1999). *The heart and soul of change: What works in therapy.* Washington, DC: American Psychological Association.
    A solid work on core themes that are central to effective psychotherapy.

McMinn, M., & Campbell, C. (2005). *Integrative psychotherapy: Toward a comprehensive Christian approach.* Downers Grove, IL: IVP Academic.
    The best book available on theoretical integrationism from a faith-based perspective.

Nathan, P., & Gorman, J. (Eds.). (2002). *A guide to treatments that work* (2nd ed.).

New York, NY: Oxford University Press.

Respectively, the best presentations on EBT with children and adults.

Norcross, J. (Ed.). (2002). *Psychotherapy relationships that work*. New York, NY: Oxford University Press.

The "foil" for Nathan and Gorman that stresses the primacy of relationships.

Norcross, J., & Beutler, L. (2008). Integrative psychotherapies. In R. Corsini, *Current psychotherapies* (8th ed., pp. 48-151). Belmont, CA: Brooks/Cole.

A helpful introduction to the challenges of responsible eclecticism.

Smith, M., Glass, G., & Miller, T. (1980). *The benefits of psychotherapy*. Baltimore, MD: Johns Hopkins Press.

Strupp, H., & Binder, J. (1984). *Psychotherapy in a new key: A guide to time limited dynamic psychotherapy*. New York, NY: Basic Books.

Three classic responsible eclecticism references that have stood out over time.

Sue, D., & Sue, D. (2008). *Foundations of counseling and psychotherapy: Evidence-based practices for a diverse society*. Hoboken, NJ: Wiley.

A respected work for those who want to face the challenges of living in a complex and pluralistic world.

REFERENCES

American Psychiatric Association (2000). *Diagnostic and statistical manual of mental disorders* (4th ed.). Washington, DC: American Psychiatric Association.

Barlow, D. (2008). *Clinical handbook of psychological disorders* (4th ed.). New York, NY: Guilford Press.

Bender, S., & Messner, E. (2001). *Becoming a therapist*. New York, NY: Guilford Press.

Bilezikian, G. (1993). *Christianity 101*. Grand Rapids, MI: Zondervan.

Bilezikian, G. (1997). *Community 101*. Grand Rapids, MI: Zondervan.

Brown, J. (1987). A review of meta-analyses conducted on psychotherapy outcome research. *Clinical Psychology Review, 7*, 1-23.

Christophersen, E., & Mortweet, S. (2001). *Treatments that work with children*. Washington, DC: American Psychological Association.

Cohen-Posey, K. (2000). *Brief therapy client handouts*. New York, NY: Wiley.

Comer, R. (2007). *Abnormal psychology* (6th ed.). New York, NY: Worth.

Corey, G. (2009). *Theory and practice of counseling and psychotherapy* (8th ed.). Belmont, CA: Thomson/Brooks Cole.

Corey, M. S., & Corey, G. (2011). *Becoming a helper* (6th ed.). Belmont, CA: Brooks/Cole.

Corsini, R. (2008). *Current psychotherapies* (8th ed.). Belmont, CA: Brooks/Cole.

Dueck, A., & Reimer, K. (2009). *A peaceable psychology: Christian therapy in a world of many cultures.* Grand Rapids, MI: Brazos.

First, M., & Tasman, A. (2004). *DSM-IV-TR mental disorders: Diagnosis, etiology and treatment.* New York, NY: Wiley.

Fonagy, P., Target, M., Cottrell, D., Phillips, J., & Kurtz, Z. (2002). *What works for whom: A critical review of treatments for children and adolescents.* New York, NY: Guilford Press.

Frattaroli, E. (2001). *Healing the soul in the age of the brain.* New York, NY: Penguin.

Garber, S. (1996). *The fabric of faithfulness.* Downers Grove, IL: InterVarsity Press.

Gonsiorek, J., Pargament, K., Richards, P., & McMinn, M. (2009). Ethical challenges and opportunities at the edge: Incorporating spirituality and religion into psychotherapy. *Professional Psychology: Research and Practice, 40*(4), 385-395.

Gurman, A., & Messer, S. (Eds.). (2003). *Essential psychotherapies: Theories and practice* (2nd ed.). New York, NY: Guilford Press.

Halgin, R. (1985). Teaching integration of psychotherapy models to beginning therapists. *Psychotherapy, 22,* 555-563.

Hood, R., Hill, P., & Spilka, B. (2009). *The psychology of religion: An empirical approach* (4th ed.). New York, NY: Guilford Press.

Hubble, D., Duncan, D., & Miller, S. (1999). *The heart and soul of change: What works in therapy.* Washington, DC: American Psychological Association.

Jones, S. L., & Butman, R. E. (1991). *Modern psychotherapies.* Downers Grove, IL: InterVarsity Press.

Jongsma, A. (2004). *Adult psychotherapy homework planner.* Hoboken, NJ: Wiley.

Jongsma, A., & Peterson, L. (2003). *The complete adult psychotherapy treatment planner* (3rd ed.). Hoboken, NJ: Wiley.

Kronenberger, W., & Meyer, R. (2001). *The child clinician's handbook* (2nd ed.). Boston, MA: Allyn & Bacon.

McLemore, C. (2003). *Toxic relationships and how to change them.* San Francisco, CA: Wiley.

McMinn, M., & Campbell, C. (2007). *Integrative psychotherapy: Toward a comprehensive Christian approach.* Downers Grove, IL: IVP Academic.

Meier, S. (2008). *Measuring change in counseling and psychotherapy.* New York, NY: Guilford Press.

Meyer, R., & Weaver, C. (2007). *The clinician's handbook* (5th ed.). Long Grove, IL: Waverland Press.

Nathan, P., & Gorman, J. (Eds.). (2002). *A guide to treatments that work* (2nd ed.). New York, NY: Oxford University Press.

Nelson-Jones, R. (1985). Eclecticism, integration and comprehensiveness in counseling theory and practice. *British Journal of Counseling and Guidance, 13*, 129-138.

Norcross, J. (1985). Eclecticism: Definitions, manifestations, and practitioners. *International Journal of Eclectic Psychotherapy, 4*, 19-32.

Norcross, J. (Ed.). (2002). *Psychotherapy relationships that work.* New York, NY: Oxford University Press.

Norcross, J., & Beutler, L. (2008). Integrative psychotherapies. In R. Corsini, *Current psychotherapies* (8th ed., pp. 48-151). Belmont, CA: Brooks/Cole.

Norcross, J., Karpiak, C., & Liser, K. (2005). What's an integrationist? A study of self-identified integrative and (occasionally) eclectic psychologists. *Journal of Clinical Psychology, 61*(12), 1587-1594.

Norcross, J., Karpiak, C., & Santoro, S. (2008). Clinical psychologists across the years: The division of clinical psychology from 1960-2003. *Journal of Clinical Psychology, 61*, 146-1483.

Paloutzian, R., & Parks, C. (Eds.). (2005). *Handbook of the psychology of religion and spirituality.* New York, NY: Guilford Press.

Pargament, K. (1997). *The psychology of religion and coping.* New York, NY: Guilford Press.

Patterson, C. (1985). *The therapeutic relationship: Foundations for an eclectic psychotherapy.* Monterey, CA: Brooks/Cole.

PDM Task Force. (2006). *Psychodynamic diagnostic manual.* Silver Springs, MD: Alliance of Psychoanalytic Organizations.

Plate, T. (2005). *Contemporary clinical psychology* (2nd ed.). Hoboken, NJ: Wiley.

Pliszka, S. (2003). *Neuroscience for the mental health clinician.* New York, NY: Guilford Press.

Post, B., & Wade, N. (2009). Religion and spirituality in psychotherapy: A practice-friendly review of research. *Journal of Clinical Psychology in Session, 65*(2), 131-148.

Prochaska, J., & Norcross, J. (2010). *Systems of psychotherapy: A transtheoretical analysis* (7th ed.). Belmont, CA: Brooks/Cole.

Rychlak, J. (1981). *Introduction to personality and psychotherapy* (2nd ed.). New York, NY: Houghton Mifflin.

Schultheis, G. (1998). *Brief therapy homework planner.* New York, NY: Wiley.

Schwartzberg, S. (2000). *Casebook of psychological disorders: The human face of emotional distress.* Boston, MA: Allyn & Bacon.

Shedler, J. (2010). The efficacy of psychodynamic psychotherapy. *American Psychologist, 65*(2), 98-109.

Smedes, L. (1998). *Standing on the promises*. Grand Rapids, MI: Eerdmans.

Smith, M., Glass, G., & Miller, T. (1980). *The benefits of psychotherapy*. Baltimore, MD: Johns Hopkins University Press.

Sue, D., & Sue, D. (2008). *Foundations of counseling and psychotherapy: Evidence-based practices for a diverse society*. Hoboken, NJ: Wiley.

Swift, J., & Callahan, J. (2010). A comparison of client preferences for intervention empirical support versus common therapy variables. *Journal of Clinical Psychology, 66*(12), 1217-1231.

Tan, S. Y. (2011). *Counseling and psychotherapy: A Christian perspective*. Grand Rapids, MI: Baker Academic.

Van Leeuwen, M. (1987). *Personality theorizing within a Christian world view*. Downers Grove, IL: InterVarsity Press.

Yarhouse, M., Butman, R., & McRay, B. (2005). *Modern psychopathologies: A comprehensive Christian appraisal* (1st ed.). Downers Grove, IL: InterVarsity Press.

12

CHRISTIAN PSYCHOTHERAPY
AND THE PERSON OF
THE CHRISTIAN PSYCHOTHERAPIST

Richard E. Butman and Stanton L. Jones

*I*n the last chapter we elaborated on ways to integrate the key findings of clinicians, researchers and theoreticians into a coherent approach to psychotherapy and counseling. In a sense that chapter culminated our discussion of theories of psychotherapy and counseling by suggesting how we might move toward a Christian theory of counseling. A Christian psychotherapist may use any one of a number of therapy techniques, approaches and strategies when such approaches are suitably criticized and modified to conform with the central tenets of Christian faith. The importance of that deliberate and intentional reflection can hardly be overstated (Gurman & Messer, 2003). Chaotic or pragmatic eclecticism runs the risk of leading to a kind of counseling approach that can be formulaic, naive or highly reductionistic (Frattaroli, 2001).

A counselor is not thoroughly Christian merely by virtue of being anti-Freudian or antibehavioral, but we would also argue that a counselor is not thoroughly Christian merely by virtue of throwing around a few Bible verses. None of the existing counseling theories, religious or nonreligious, adequately plumb the depths of the complexity of human character and of the change process. Likewise, no one approach to studying the "calamities of the soul" seems to grapple adequately with the wide variety of biological, psychosocial and sociocultural variables that can lead to the development of mental illness (cf. Yarhouse, Butman & McRay, 2005). So there are many theoretical options open to counselors who desire to be distinctively Christian in what they do. Christian counselors may operate very differently from each other. This seems to be especially true when we face the challenges of pluralism as global citizens and world Christians (Sue & Sue, 2008).

But we would argue that there will be or should be certain commonalities across all therapists who are attempting to be distinctly Christian in practice. Simply put, there should be a depth of character, an obvious presence of compassion, and certain core convictions that ought to characterize their attempts to speak grace and truth into the lives of hurting persons (cf. McMinn & Campbell, 2007; Sanders, in press) It is these commonalities we wish to develop in this chapter.

The basis for these commonalities is the special claim the gospel has on the counseling process compared to work in other vocations, such as medicine, accounting or construction. We agree with Christian critics of psychology who say that the counseling processes are of such a nature that they must be thoroughly reconceptualized from a biblical foundation to lay claim to the adjective "Christian." Indeed, the biblical mandate to seek and promote shalom ("until justice and mercy embrace") can't somehow be peripheral to the mission and task of the Christian counselor (Dueck & Reimer, 2009).

This assumes that there is something special about the field of psychology specifically, and the mental health professions generally, that demands that we put unusual efforts into making our work an extension of the Christian faith and of God's redemptive activities in the world. We would argue that the theoretical appraisal process, of which this book is an example, is only part of the process of adjusting the nature of the counseling process in a way to allow it to be honoring to God. And we would add that we have a growing conviction that this can't just be done in isolation, but rather must be conducted in the context of the communities in which we worship, fellowship and serve (cf. Bilezikian, 1993, 1997). It is on this process of adjustment that this chapter focuses.

THE COUNSELING VOCATION

Persons who hold to rigid sacred-secular distinctions, and who claim that mature Christians go into the ministry while people of lesser faith go into secular work, are quite wrong. They are also wrong to think that God has different values for different types of work, such that the work of a farmer or engineer is less honoring to God than that of a minister of the gospel. Christ redeems all of life and gives everything honor and goodness and meaning, whether it be plowing a field, counseling a suicidal person or administering the sacraments. All work is to be done under the lordship of Christ, as unto him (Col 3:23), and this lordship commitment means different things in different vocations. We must work creatively and diligently to effectively discharge this lordship responsibility. Put succinctly, this is a vocation where discernment should be taken *very* seriously—both individually and corporately (Sittser, 2004). Not only is this good stewardship of human talent and resources, but it should be a matter of ethical integrity (Sanders, in press).

While almost all careers are good potential options for Christians (though we might rule out prostitute, drug dealer, assassin, etc.), and God honors all righteous vocational commitments, nevertheless the claims of the gospel on different vocations vary in kind and extent. The claims of the gospel over our vocational lives express themselves both in the area of character and concerns (including our ethical standards) and in the area of the structure and content of the work.

We can take farming as one example. Christian farmers are called to be patient, honest, just, compassionate and generous. They are called to farm in accord with kingdom ethics, looking on what they do as an exercise of stewardship over the earth. Thus they might think carefully about the ecological and sustainability implications of their planting, watering, fertilizing and pest control procedures. But with regard to structure and content of the acts of farming itself, the gospel does not have very much to say, except perhaps at the very broadest level of seeing the earth as God's creation and so forth. The faith simply does not dictate the way farmers are to plow a field, fertilize, harvest and so forth. The gospel does not change their understanding of what they work with—corn is still corn and a pig is still a pig. The gospel exerts its claims almost exclusively over their character and concerns, but has less to say of the structure of their work.

At the other extreme we might take the gospel ministry. Here, as with farming, the claims of the gospel over the character of ministers are clear and total, demanding that the minister of the gospel exhibit the same virtues that God desires in Christian farmers. But the gospel also directly dictates much, but not all, of the structure and content of the work of ministers. The gospel dictates the general form of worship, of the sacraments, of pastoral ministry, of doctrine and hence the content of Christian education. The faith prescribes the core of how we understand salvation and sanctification, and how we understand the people that are to be saved and growing. The gospel does not dictate all that ministers can or should do; they can profitably learn from social science studies of church growth or small group dynamics, from recent studies of innovative educational methods or from administrative studies of office management (e.g., Kauffmann, 1999; Paloutzian, 1997). But ministers' work, if it is honoring to God, should clearly bear the mark of God's revelation in his Word in its very structure and content (McMinn & Campbell, 2007).

We would argue that the work of counseling and psychotherapy is much more like that of the ministry than farming. It is a clear example of a group of vocations that are just one step back from the professional ministry in terms of the demand for transformation of our work by the gospel. And we share many of the same risks and responsibilities of those in the professional ministries. Frankly, the recognition of the awesome responsibility should motivate us to excellence in all that we do and say (Sittser, 2004).

The claims of Christian truth should fundamentally transform, at a basic and profound level, the ways we conceptualize and understand our human subject matter, as well as our problems, our goals and the processes of change. That is what the bulk of this book has been about: how Christians can interact thoughtfully with secular psychotherapeutic theory and transform these approaches to conform with Christian revelation (cf. also McMinn & Campbell, 2007; Tan, 2011). We would argue that it does not stop there. It is not just our theories, our understanding of our subject matter, that needs to be transformed, but our very understanding of the contours of the profession as well.

Why is this so? The reason is because of the undeniable relevance of God's revelation for the work of mental health professionals, and because Christian marriage and family therapists, clinical social workers, psychologists, psychiatrists and pastoral counselors are doing part of the work of the church. The mental health field mirrors in some striking ways the redemptive work of the church when it strives to foster the salvation of its members (cf. Bilezikian, 1997).

Salvation is biblically more than a one-shot harvesting of the ephemeral souls of the believers in one instantaneous conversion. Biblically, salvation refers to the healing and restoration of wholeness to the entire lives of believers, though especially in their relationship with God (White, 1984). Mental health workers, then, whose work is so often seen in our society as facilitating growth toward wholeness, are mirroring and partaking in the redemptive or salvific work of the church whether we like to think so or not. As Ray Anderson (1982) says, "The cure of souls . . . is a ministry and service of the Christian community" (p. 202). A huge literature in the psychology of religion has certainly demonstrated the importance of social support in not only effective coping with the demands of everyday living— but in the promotion of physical, emotional and mental well-being (Hood, Hill & Spilka, 2009).

Even though many mental health professionals do not style themselves evangelists or pastors, the truth is that our work often penetrates to the personal core of the life of our clients. In that core, there is often very little distinction between the religious/spiritual component and the personal/ emotional/psychological component. Because our work so closely intersects with kingdom concerns, we must be about the task of structuring our work deliberately and thoroughly in ways that are honoring to the kingdom and are compatible with God's own efforts on behalf of his people (Anderson, 1987). If we don't make this a premier concern, we run the risk of contributing to a system competing with the church of Christ for servicing the welfare of God's people. We ought to supplement or complement the work of the church, not offer an alternative to it (cf. McMinn & Campbell, 2007; Dueck & Reimer, 2009).

When we work to bring healing and wholeness to the hurting, Christ is present in a unique way. He is present in the one seeking help, for he promised that anyone ministering to the suffering was ministering to him (Mt 25:31-46). And he is present in the one ministering and attempting to heal, for he is the source of all growth and healing and comfort (2 Cor 1:3-5). Some have even called psychotherapy an incarnational ministry (Benner, 1983). If in the healing encounter, then, both persons are partaking of the presence of Christ, how can we argue that there is nothing special that distinguishes the therapeutic vocation from many other professions? Indeed, the study of the history of pastoral care has taught how vitally important it can be to "incarnate" these core truths—and "interpersonally mediate" them in word and deed (cf. chap. 1 in Yarhouse, Butman & McRay, 2005).

IMAGING GOD IN THERAPY

In chapter two we discussed the centrality of the concept of the *imago Dei* and its implications for our personality theories. Understanding the nature of the *imago Dei* has been an important concern of theology off and on throughout the last two millennia. Theological anthropology usually looks at the image as our common denominator or denominators, the image as shared necessarily by all persons, asking what it is that we all share that makes us individually and corporately imagers of the Most High. We are all responsible moral agents; we are all rational beings; we are all gender differentiated and thus intrinsically social beings; and so forth. We might call this the descriptive or de facto dimension of the image, because these things and more are true of us all as a matter of our existing as humans because we are made in God's image. We exert no special efforts to manifest this aspect of the image. In fact, no matter how we run from it, we are always imagers of God in these fashions. We *cannot not* image him in these ways.

But there is another side of the imaging reality that is captured in numerous biblical verses: "Be imitators of God, therefore, as dearly loved children" (Eph 5:1); "Put on the new self, which is being renewed in knowledge in the image of its Creator" (Col 3:10). From this perspective we are to be continually striving to actualize the image we have been entrusted with in an ever more conspicuous and pure fashion, to work diligently and deliberately to image our Maker. As Dallas Willard (1990) said in an article titled "Looking Like Jesus": "As disciples (literally students) of Jesus, our goal is to learn to be like him" (p. 29).

The image of God in us, from this perspective, goes quite beyond the more passive common-denominator approach we often take when discussing the image of God. It has suddenly become something we must strive to become or actualize, and we can fall painfully short in the process. The image, rather than being just a passive characteristic, a birthmark as it were, is also a declaration of life purpose, a binding agenda for action and a map for necessary growth, which we as believers are obliged to follow. It is, in fact, the entire goal of the process of our sanctification. This is the *prescriptive* or *normative* dimension of the image-of-God concept.

The very nature of the mental health professions dictates that we must work at this prescriptive aspect of actualizing God's image in building our mental health professional identities in a way that few professions share quite so extensively. When we are reflecting on what we are to become, we must look beyond the de facto image and get a vision for what we are called to be—in our case, how we can actualize the image of God more clearly in our work in the mental health professions. We will explore three aspects of imaging that are relevant to the field of counseling, namely, actualizing the image of God's roles or offices, God's character and God's concerns.

Imaging the Offices of God

By "offices" we refer to the functional roles God assumes in interacting with his people. There are a number of these roles that are relevant to our work in the mental health field. Not all of his offices, however, are ours to assume; some may be impossible for us to assume. God's office as the King and sovereign Lord of the universe is an obvious example of this. Another would be his function as the Redeemer of humanity through sacrificing himself as the Lamb of God. But what are some of the roles he fills that are instructive to us and perhaps in some sense binding on our professional identities?

The first is that of God the Holy Spirit functioning as the Paraclete, the one who draws alongside of us to help, comfort and encourage. In some contexts (1 Jn 2:1), the concept of Paraclete means an "advocate," one who pleads for us before the Father when we sin. In other contexts the concept of Paraclete clearly takes on a more emotionally supportive meaning, as in 2 Corinthians 1 (especially v. 4) where we learn that God comforts us through the Holy Spirit so that we might be able to comfort others around us. In some contexts the Paraclete helps concretely by equipping and providing to enable us to meet the deficiencies in our lives (as when he functions as the teacher who relieves our ignorance).

What rich instruction we can draw for our professional roles from this office that God discharges! Advocacy is a function counselors are called to fill from time to time, when we are dealing with persons who have been robbed of their choices, their hope or their rights. What a loop of beauty and purpose we have in suffering when we know that God entered into our sufferings so that he might perfectly meet our needs, so that we in turn can give comfort to others and in that process be ministering directly to Christ himself! The comforting thus flows in all directions when we image Christ and the Holy Spirit (or are allowed to be his image) by being paracletes ourselves, drawing alongside another with hope and comfort. This function adds new meaning and validity to the concept of the "wounded healer" that we hear so much of today (developed often in the writings of Henri Nouwen; see also Dawn, 2008; Miller & Jackson, 1985; Crabb, 1988). Finally, as providers of that which was lacking, we act as the image of God in comforting by taking part in making up what is lacking in the sufferer.

One aspect of being an advocate may involve prophetic ministry. We are greatly encouraged to see growing numbers of Christian mental health professionals act on this biblical mandate to be both "priest" and "prophet" in this broken and often confusing world in which we live (Dueck & Reimer, 2009). Compassion and justice ministries are flourishing around the world—especially with respect to the "widows and orphans" (Paloutzian & Parks, 2005). We know many individuals (some of whom are former students) who are working in difficult and challenging situations in the global East and South (or domestically) with the "least of these"—that is, persons who are so often invisible, isolated or ghettoized. In our more than three decades of work with aspiring people-helpers, we have never sensed more interest and desire to work with persons who feel so hopeless, helpless and powerless. We firmly believe that they sincerely desire to incarnate this office of paraclete or advocate in word and deed—even if it will cost them dearly (Hybels, 2007).

A second role or office of God that is instructive is his work as the Reconciler. Second Corinthians 5:18-21 instructs us directly that Christ reconciles each believer with God, and that we are in turn to become his agents of reconciliation, "Christ's ambassadors" (v. 20), who take seriously the call to draw others into reconciling relationships with the Father and the Son. The reconciliation called for by the gospel is not merely spiritual (God to person), however; the reconciliation that God works in our hearts is also intended to spill out into our human relationships as well, leading Christians to be bridges of healing between estranged persons wherever possible (Mt 5:24). Clearly, reconciliation between persons is designed to follow the spiritual reconciliation that the gospel brings between God and us.

There are two implications of this work of reconciliation. The first is the eternal value of the personal reconciliations that are so often achieved as a result of psychotherapy (cf. McLemore, 2003). The second is that evangelism will always play some role in counseling, because there should be some dimension of our professional lives that draws people toward reconciliation with God. This does not mean that counseling becomes a scam to lure to us emotionally distraught people who think they are going to be helped when our real motivation is to save their souls. Rather, Christian concern for the whole person will lead to a transparency for and centeredness on Christ that could lead others to a saving knowledge of the gospel. For balanced discussions of the perceived tensions between evangelism and the consulting room, see recent works by Tan (2011) or McMinn and Campbell (2007). Learning to expose our values—without imposing them—requires some essential knowledge about the relationship between persuasion and healing (cf. Kauffmann, 1999).

A third vital office of God is that of Healer, the "Great Physician." When the Lord's virtues are extolled in the Scriptures, his healing grace is often mentioned prominently, as in Psalm 103:2-4:

> Praise the LORD, O my soul,
>   and forget not all his benefits—
> who forgives all your sins
>   and heals all your diseases,
> who redeems your life from the pit
>   and crowns you with love and compassion.

A narrow evangelicalism can focus exclusively on forgiveness of sins and neglect God's healing intent. Healing is an intimate part of God's identity in relating to his people. This implies that he has a heart of compassion for suffering and a passion for wholeness for his afflicted children, which we would do well to cultivate.

The final office of God is that of his being the source of all wisdom; he is in fact the beginning of wisdom (Prov 1:7) and wisdom incarnate (Prov 1:20-33). Derek Tidball (1986) points out that before the coming of Christ, there were three types of "pastors" in ancient Jewish society: priests, prophets and wise men. We had never understood the term *wise men* to refer to an institutionalized role in Old Testament society. It seems to us that there are many parallels between the wise man role in ancient Jewish life and the role mental health professionals serve in contemporary American life. Tidball (1986) writes, "The objective of the wise men was to provide down-to-earth counsel about the ordinary affairs of life. . . . Their approach was to consider, with steady logic, the truth which was hidden within human nature and creation in order to discover the regularities which could form the basis of their lives and counsel" (p. 43). Certainly the provision of such wisdom is a prime duty of the psychotherapist. And it is vital to remember that true wisdom begins with "the fear of the LORD"— and the recognition of our creatureliness (Prov 1:7).

Tidball (1986) suggests that the wise men did not often work according to explicit divine revelation in any direct sense, as they were grappling with practical matters that simply were not a preoccupation of God's revelatory energies. In other words, they dealt with matters for which no simple recourse to "the Bible says" was possible. Nevertheless, they were guided by the notion that "it is only a commitment to [God] which will reveal truth, as there can be no reality except that which he controls" (p. 44). This need to ground wisdom in the word of God is further demonstrated by Jeremiah 8:8-9:

> How can you say, "We are wise,
> 　for we have the law of the LORD,"
> when actually the lying pen of the scribes
> 　has handled it falsely?
> The wise will be put to shame;
> 　they will be dismayed and trapped.
> Since they have rejected the word of the LORD,
> 　what kind of wisdom do they have?

Like the wise men of Israel, contemporary counselors must be cautious in delving into psychotherapeutic theory and practice to remain carefully, deliberately and courageously Christian in our core commitments, lest we merit the same condemnation that Jeremiah pronounced.

We are humbled when we read the recent literature on professionals who commit serious ethical violations and potentially abuse that sacred trust that has been placed in them (cf. Corey, Corey & Callanan, 2011;

Sanders, in press). Briefly stated, such abusers tend to be arrogant, isolated and rather disconnected from either a faith-based community or peer-accountability network. Further, they tend to be poor at self-care or setting appropriate boundaries (Norcross & Guy, 2007). One way to connect the painful reality of moral and ethical failures is to insist that education, training, supervision and service must all be placed under the lordship of Jesus Christ (cf. Bilezikian, 1993). Those who strive to image God simply cannot be "lone rangers" or "rugged individualists." So we need to ask: To whom will I be held accountable? (after Sanders, in press).

Unique spiritual resources are available to the Christian counselor and psychotherapist who is striving to live out the images of God's offices— resources for our ministry of growth and healing, such as prayer, the use of the Scriptures, the sacraments, fellowship and worship (cf. Foster, 1978). These resources must always be used judiciously, in recognition of the complex intricacies and dynamics of the personal and professional relationship of counselor to counselee, the diverse and varied ways that psychodynamics and faith can interact (cf. Fowler, 1984; Parks, 1986), the reality of healthy and unhealthy forms of religious experience, and the different personalities, worldviews, faith and value beliefs of counselor and counselee (Dueck & Reimer, 2009; Sue & Sue, 2008).

As Malony (1982) has warned, religious "God talk" and practice can be used and misused, so a concern for timing, tact and sensitivity must always be present (Clinebell, 1965). Competent and committed clinicians will always attempt to assess accurately and examine the needs and wants of their clients prior to all interventions. Religious interventions that are not part of the societally defined role of the psychotherapist, and for which many therapists have not received formal training, should be cautiously used if at all (cf. Tan, 2011, for helpful discussions of these tensions).

Counselors have a special obligation to intentionally live out the image of the comforting, advocating, healing, reconciling and wise God in their practice. Following and intentionally imaging his work is not an elective process if we claim the name of Christ. By learning all we can from how God himself has exercised these offices, we can be more faithful servants in this field (cf. Anderson, 1990, for helpful discussions of these challenges). This work can be difficult and demanding, so we would be wise to incorporate and internalize what we know about resiliency and effective coping (after Paloutzian & Parks, 2005; Hood, Hill & Spilka, 2009). Briefly stated, those providers of service who have strong social support systems, a clear sense of efficacy, and a sharply focused sense of meaning and purpose in life seem to not merely "survive" but "thrive." To use more explicitly biblical language, they seem better able to stay *faithful* to a "long obedience in the same direction" (Garber, 1996).

Imaging the Character of God

We cannot image God's work without imaging his character, for God's work emanates from his character. Psychotherapy research seems to be converging on the finding that while psychotherapeutic technique per se is not unimportant, it is nevertheless the relationship with the client that carries significant power for at least initial change in the client (cf. Norcross, 2002). Coupled with that therapist's ability to communicate hope in word and deed, as well as with the capacity to fully appreciate the world in which the client moves (contextual or situational factors), the personal qualities of the therapist carry an inordinate potential for positive or negative impact on the client (cf. McMinn & Campbell, 2007).

The list of personal traits we are called to "put on" in Colossians 3:12 is a powerful prescription for a healing influence on the life of another. We are called to "clothe yourselves with compassion, kindness, humility, gentleness and patience. Bear with each other and forgive . . . as the Lord forgave you" (Col 3:12-13). Even Patterson (1985), a leading secular psychotherapist and theoretician, has described the essential character of an optimal therapeutic relationship as that of "love in the highest sense, or agape" (p. 91). More recent works (e.g., Corey & Corey, 2011; Gurman & Messer, 2003) essentially concur that authentic and credible relationships are truly the "heart of the matter."

More than two decades ago, Al Dueck (then of Mennonite Brethren Seminary and now of Fuller Theological Seminary) and Siang Yang Tan of Fuller jointly presented with us a symposium in which we explored ten themes regarding the character of the therapist and his or her practice (Jones, Butman, Dueck & Tan, 1988). We suggested that the Christian counselor is called to virtues that are often in sharp contrast to those that might pay off in the professional world. All these years later, we suspect our convictions are even stronger (cf. Dueck & Reimer, 2009; Tan, 2011; Yarhouse, Butman & McRay, 2005). What has changed, however, is the growing recognition of how economic, political and social forces have strained or even severely tested our then emerging core convictions. We could not have predicted how much subtle and insidious forces of professionalism could have co-opted so many of our colleagues and students (cf. excellent critique in Dueck & Reimer, 2009).

We believe:

We are called to compassion as opposed to elitism. The lordship of Christ always issues forth with compassion for the poor and downtrodden. A counseling practice that is established without a concrete concern for the poor is elitist and less than ideal. Guy (1987) states that the truly outstanding clinician has something in addition to skill and expertise; he or she possesses "a deep sense of caring and compassion that results in a level of empathy and sensitivity that touches others in a very extraordinary way" (p. 294). We must in some way be committed to relieving human misery at a corporate as well as an individual level. If our work never addresses structural or systemic evils—or attempts to be proactive and preventative—it is less than credible.

We are called to servanthood as opposed to superiority. Do we subtly elevate ourselves over our clients, or do we see ourselves when we look deeply into their lives? What is our ground motivation for practice? Christians are called to have servanthood as a ground motive, and this has special implications in therapeutic practice where control and power issues can so easily be intertwined with our practice. We would be wise to look to the history of pastoral care for keen insights as to what this might mean for the context and format of our work (cf. chap. 1 in Yarhouse, Butman & McRay, 2005).

We are called to community as opposed to isolation. We should seek out the give and take of life in unity with other believers. Since counselors are asking their clients to take an honest look at themselves and to make choices concerning how they want to change, it is crucial for counselors to be brutally honest with themselves. Because of the reality of self-deception, this cannot be done in isolation. It becomes difficult to "give yourself away" if you don't know who you are or what you really believe. Counselors must be rigorously committed to their own growth and development in the context of a confessional community if they expect to facilitate that process in others. Isolation also is a major threat to the well-being of psychotherapists

(Guy, 1987), but the radical call of the gospel for the establishment of community stands in opposition to this tendency. We applaud the growing emphasis we see in many churches to reduce the sense of isolation and loneliness so many feel in contemporary society (Bilezikian, 1997). The recent work done on professionals who make serious errors in moral judgment clearly demonstrates that strong accountability networks are morally and ethically imperative (cf. Sanders, in press; Corey & Corey, 2011). There is simply no empirical evidence that credentials ensure that an individual will be competent or above moral reproach.

We are called to accountability as opposed to independence and autonomy. Counselors should not be lone rangers operating by their personal idiosyncratic standards. Guy (1987) mentions independence as a major reason for attraction to the profession, yet we would argue that accountability, first to Christ and then to his church, is a vital dimension of Christian distinctiveness that makes independence as commonly conceived (e.g., "I walk to my own standard") destructive. If we are to speak the truth in love to others, we must find others who are willing to do the same for us. For some psychotherapists, this might involve careful supervision, personal therapy, the utilization of a spiritual mentor or director, or greater accountability to a local church. This need for accountability has been recognized more clearly in the secular discipline with each passing decade (e.g., Norcross & Guy, 2007). In reflecting on this concern of late, we can confidently state that we think it is absolutely essential that a Christian mental health professional commit him- or herself to a lifelong process of continuing education and supervision (cf. suggestions in Sanders, in press). Even those who work overseas or in low-resources settings must seek out creative ways to make those connections occur *even if that cannot be done "live"* (Kauffmann, 1999). The Headington Institute in Pasadena, California, for example, provides consultation, continuing education, supervision and direct services for the relief and development community from a faith-based perspective in some of the most difficult and challenging environments in the world.[1]

We are called to transparency as opposed to impression management. We are called as Christians to be radically transparent to Christ within us in

---

[1]For more on the Headington Institute see www.headington-institute.org.

all aspects of life. The livelihood of counselors, though, often depends on impressing others so they will refer clients to us. This increases the risk that the therapist will engage in impression management (Palmer, 1993).

We are called to love as opposed to Rogerian positive regard. Positive regard supposedly accepts all and is totally indiscriminate. It must overlook evil and sin because it is based in the presumption of the worthiness of the person to be loved. God's love sees the negatives clearly and loves in spite of them. *Agape* love, while indiscriminate, is not relativistic and is wedded to a firm notion of the good for the beloved. Thus, true love can be strict or harsh in its pursuit of the good for the other.

We are called to stewardship as opposed to profit maximization. We should be seriously committed to the real effectiveness of the helping relationship rather than merely judging our success by the size of our referral base and our monthly gross. As was noted earlier, arrogance and pride so often seem to be "triggers" when it comes to lapses in moral judgment and inappropriate behaviors.

We are called to holiness as opposed to anonymity or wholeness. Holiness most basically applies to anything set apart for God's use, and we can be holy in this sense in spite of our own brokenness. A counselor who deserves to be called Christian, or an approach which is distinctively Christian, has to be grounded in a deep understanding of what it means to be intrapersonally or personally integrated. Tan (1987) describes this in terms of the servant's spirituality. As Carter and Narramore (1979) have argued, "Unless we are open to the impact of a relationship with God in our lives and unless we are open to seeing our maladaptive ways of coping, we will find it necessary to shut ourselves off from certain sources of truth and block any real progress in integration. In fact, this is perhaps the biggest single barrier to integration" (p. 117). More recently, both McMinn and Campbell (2007) and Tan (2011) have stressed the development of our character as well as our convictions. The need to be humble, honest and humane has never been more pressing in the work of the Christian mental health professional (McLemore, 2003).

We are called to wisdom as opposed to mere secular brilliance. Wisdom is practical intelligence applied to good and godly ends. The pursuit of wisdom is essential for the Christian therapist. We should be wise in God's eyes, even if that seems old-fashioned, rather than seeking to dazzle with empty brilliance. As Foster (1978, p. 1) has lamented, superficiality is the curse of the modern age; what we need is people of depth. Hurting persons in our world today desperately need to see (and experience) men and women of depth who can truly speak (and model) grace and truth in all their relationships (Garber, 1996).

Finally, *we are called to integrity as opposed to mere ethical compliance.* The fleshly person is merely constrained by ethical codes. The spiritual person should be transformed at a deep level by the Spirit and law of God, and strive for a deep integrity that transcends mere compliance. Rather than ethics being a fence that barely constrains us, we should be exploring new frontiers of integrity and honesty in our practices (cf. Sanders, in press).

Above all else the Christian counselor should be characterized by a *true depth of spirituality*, the foundation for what Farnsworth (1985) has called "wholehearted integration." According to Tan (1987, pp. 36-37), such deep spirituality would have at least the following characteristics: (1) a deep thirst and hunger for God, (2) a love for God based on intimate knowledge of God that leads naturally to worship and obedience, (3) being filled with the Holy Spirit and yielding to God's deepening work of grace in our lives and not to the flesh, (4) acknowledging and using the gifts of the Spirit for God's purposes and glory, and manifesting the fruit of the Spirit, (5) developing biblical thinking and a worldview that is consistent with God's perspective as revealed in the Scriptures, (6) being involved in spiritual warfare, requiring the use of supernatural power and resources available only from God, and (7) being attuned to the "mystical" aspects of our faith that defy easy rational description (see Tan, 2011, for a more recent formulation of these core assertions). These will be the ultimate roots of the good we are able to do, or more accurately that God is able to do through us.

Imaging the Concerns of God

What are God's concerns? What does he care about deeply and passionately? In our contemporary parlance, what are his values? We are told clearly that God loves the world (Jn 3:16), and specifically his bride, the church. The book of Revelation is filled with imagery of the wedding feast of the King and his redeemed bride, and the Song of Songs tells in passionate metaphor of God's pursuit of his beloved. But nowhere is this clearer than in Ephesians 5, where we are instructed about Christ's dying to cleanse his bride to be. A Christian counselor will thus passionately care for both the individual and the church.

At the individual level good counseling or psychotherapy ought to seek to promote a client's spiritual and psychological maturity. We need to be clear about what we are trying to promote as counselors and psychotherapists, which requires us to examine not only the function of symptoms and sickness in a person's life, but the deeper meanings of the counselee's problems in living. As Foster (1978) has noted, the counselor is not unlike a spiritual guide in the process of deepening faith and understanding. Healers can take clients no further than they have been taken themselves (Mangis, 2008). We can only love persons we know, and we can only love another if we have been deeply loved ourselves. Clients can only grow if they have felt heard, understood, appreciated and valued. With the necessary skills, competencies and motivation, the process of growth and development can be facilitated.

Malony (1985) describes an attempt to capture some of the essence of understanding mature spirituality in his "religious status interview." The eight dimensions of his semi-structured interview include (1) awareness of God, (2) acceptance of God's grace and steadfast love, (3) being repentant and responsible, (4) knowing God's leadership and direction, (5) involvement in organized religion, (6) experiencing fellowship, (7) being ethical, and (8) affirming openness in faith. In an excellent volume Malony (1995) also explored the implications of this model for ministerial effectiveness, and the development of a more robust and mature faith commitment. Together with the notions of spiritual wellness postulated by Carter (1985), Clinebell (1965) and White (1985), we have rich resources available to help us understand what constitutes healthy spirituality in the Christian counselor. And the development of such a faith is part of our most profound concerns.

But while God unquestionably loves individuals, there is a special status to the corporate church. It has its own identity that is more than the sum of its individual parts, and God's passion in a special way is for the corporate entity (Bilezikian, 1993). Similarly, Christian mental health professionals must see the welfare of Christ's bride, the church, as a premier concern in their lives. No doubt, we should all see this as an awesome responsibility.

A focused and passionate concern for the welfare of the individuals in our caseloads or churches is not the same thing as concern for the church itself. Earlier we asserted that counselors are inescapably doing the work of the church in being agents of personal healing in the lives of our clients. If we are preoccupied exclusively with the individual impact of our work and not its corporate effect on the church, we may not have the effect of building up the body of Christ that we should have. This is not to argue that individual growth and healing is unimportant—it is in fact vital. But we live in an era when many influences are draining the vitality of the Western church. In the same way that those seeking to minister in the electronic media must grapple with the unintended fallout of utilizing a medium that specializes in unreality, superficial appearances and personal isolation, so also we in the mental health field must realize that not all of the effects of our work necessarily contribute to the benefit of the church. We need to ask hard questions about the corporate effects of our work.

Counseling that deserves to be called Christian will promote the kingdom of God in word and deed. It will stand in marked contrast, at times, to the modernity of Western culture. The church, not the profession, will be its source of accountability, as well as its wellspring for healing and helping. Its practitioners will be disciples, not independent practitioners or technicians, and its driving force will be shaped by the rituals and discernment of the confessional community (cf. Dueck & Reimer, 2009).

CONCLUSION

There are many subtle and not-so-subtle influences that work against the Christian mental health professional effectively actualizing the image of the Father in his or her work. Psychotherapy is a culturally defined activity, and we all work in fashions that we have not adopted deliberately out of a desire to be an effective imager but rather unreflectively by "going with the flow." In the give and take of daily life, mental health professionals face many preoccupying concerns: there is fierce competition for the mental health dollar; interdisciplinary friction is rampant; financial stability for families and businesses (not just ideas) is at risk; and there is probably greater overall stress and insecurity than at any other time in recent history. In this context, counselors often feel already overloaded with the mundane concerns of maintenance and advancement of their practices and professional careers to take on the additional burdens of grappling with imaging God better.

But this is precisely what Christian counselors are called to do at this point in history. The Christian mental health establishment is far from being the effective handmaiden of the church that it ought to be. Pastors, when they are honest, often feel that they are mainly seen as a referral source by the mental health professional, people to be romanced by the psychotherapist to yield the obvious payoff of paying clients. Pastors are happy about the frequent positive outcomes of therapy, but are perhaps more skeptical about psychotherapy than they have been in past years. They are bombarded with "Christian Psychology Is Apostasy" literature on the one hand and "99 Reasons to Refer Your Parishioners to Us" literature on the other. Pastors are more aware than ever that it cannot be taken for granted that psychotherapy is advancing the cause of the church, because there is often too much slippage between therapy goals and the church's needs.

What are we advocating? Obviously, we must start with urging a renewed commitment to serving God and his church, a commitment to imaging the Father through our professional work. If this isn't a foremost commitment, then the rest hardly makes sense.

Second, we advocate the need to think with Christian clarity about the theoretical approaches to understanding and changing people, which provide the background for all counseling practice. It is our prayer that this book represents an advancement of that enterprise.

Further, it is essential to be informed biblically and theologically about God's caring for his people and about the instruction he has given us for the care of souls in the church. Too much of what passes for integration today is anemic theologically or biblically and tends to be little more than a spiritualized rehashing of mainstream mental health thought. The church has a rich corporate history in the field of pastoral care, which we need to know about if we are to be Christian psychotherapists. Psychology was a division of practical theology long before it became a separate field, and the pastoral care tradition has rich resources to digest (cf. Yarhouse, Butman & McRay, 2005).

Pastoral ministers were far from ineffective and uninsightful before the advent of Freud. The mental health professions often unwittingly believe and promulgate the fable that nothing significant occurred in the psychological care of persons before modern times—just look at the coverage in a typical introductory psychology text, where discussion of religion is typically paired with pictures of spinning chairs, straitjackets and inhumane insane asylums (Kirkpatrick and Spilka, 1989). But premodern pastoral care was not ineffective. Thomas Oden (1984), well-known pastoral theologian and former enthusiastic advocate of several psychotherapeutic methods, has for the last three decades devoted his time to the study of the riches of the ancient church, including his first emphasis on the pastoral strategies of the ancients, including the pastoral care techniques of Pope Gregory the Great (from the early so-called Dark Ages) and other historical pastoral care experts. The more we understand the rich history of pastoral care, the greater our appreciation for the richness of the Christian tradition for informing our contemporary practices will be.

Finally, we recommend that Christian counselors be in explicit, ongoing dialogue with responsible members of their own faith community about how best to be distinctively and appropriately Christian in their work. We can be dangerously myopic when we dialogue only with other mental health professionals about these matters, because this lessens the chances that we will be able to see effectively beyond our disciplinary blinders. We know of several Christian psychologists who have formed accountability groups within their local churches. These groups of clergy and laypersons do not oversee or supervise their work at a specific level, but they are accountable to them at the broader level for the Christian distinctiveness and integrity of their functioning as therapists. We are impressed by their courage and openness in committing themselves to a deeper level of accountability than most of us would find comfortable or convenient.

Christian counselors will probably arrive at a diversity of conclusions on how to be accountable for their Christian distinctiveness, but our concern is not so much with the conclusion as the process by which we get there. Have we engaged in an intentional dialogue whereby we put in practice our desire to be responsive to and centered on the will of God and the welfare of the church over and beyond our individual professional welfare? That is the question we must seriously and regularly ask ourselves.

FOR FURTHER READING

Clebsch, W., & Jaekle, C. (1975). *Pastoral care in historical perspective.* New York, NY: Jason Aronson.

Holifield, B. (1983). *A history of pastoral care in America.* Nashville, TN: Abingdon.

Oden, T. (1984). *Care of souls in the classic tradition.* Philadelphia, PA: Fortress.

Tidball, D. (1986). *Skillful shepherds: An introduction to pastoral theology.* Grand Rapids, MI: Zondervan.

Four excellent starting points in broadening one's understanding of the church's historical ministry in the "care of souls." Each has thought-provoking implications for rethinking the psychotherapeutic task.

McMinn, M., & Campbell, C. (2007). *Integrative psychotherapy: Toward a comprehensive Christian approach.* Downers Grove, IL: IVP Academic.

Tan, S. (2011). *Counseling and psychotherapy.* Grand Rapids, MI: Baker.

Two exceptional recent reflections on what it means to be a Christian psychotherapist.

REFERENCES

Anderson, R. (1982). *On being human.* Grand Rapids, MI: Eerdmans.

Anderson, R. (1987). *For those who counsel.* Unpublished manuscript, Fuller Theological Seminary, Pasadena, CA.

Anderson, R. (1990). *For those that counsel.* Grand Rapids, MI: Zondervan.

Benner, D. (1983). The incarnation as a metaphor for psychotherapy. *Journal of Psychology and Theology, 11,* 287-294.

Bilezikian, G. (1993). *Christianity 101.* Grand Rapids, MI: Zondervan.

Bilezikian, G. (1997). *Community 101.* Grand Rapids, MI: Zondervan.

Carter, J. (1985). Healthy personality. In D. Benner (Ed.), *Baker encyclopedia of psychology* (pp. 498-504). Grand Rapids, MI: Baker.

Carter, J., & Narramore, B. (1979). *The integration of psychology and theology.* Grand Rapids, MI: Zondervan.

Clinebell, H. (1965). *The mental health ministry of the local church.* Nashville, TN: Abingdon.

Corey, G., Corey, M., & Callanan, P. (2011). *Issues and ethics in the helping professions* (8th ed.). Belmont, CA: Brooks/Cole.

Corey, M., & Corey, G. (2011). *Becoming a helper* (6th ed.). Belmont, CA: Brooks/Cole.

Crabb, L. (1988). *Inside out.* Colorado Springs, CO: NavPress.

Dawn, M. J. (2008). *Being well when we're ill: Wholeness and hope in spite of infirmity.* Minneapolis, MN: Augsburg.

Dueck, A. (1986, January). *The ethical context of healing.* Paper presented for the Finch Symposium at Fuller Theological Seminary, Pasadena, CA.

Dueck, A., & Reimer, K. (2009). *A peaceable psychology: Christian therapy in a world of many cultures.* Grand Rapids, MI: Brazos.

Farnsworth, K. (1985). *Wholehearted integration.* Grand Rapids, MI: Baker.

Foster, R. (1978). *Celebration of discipline.* San Francisco, CA: Harper & Row.

Fowler, J. (1984). *The stages of faith.* San Francisco, CA: Harper & Row.

Frattaroli, E. (2001). *Healing the brain in the age of the soul.* New York, NY: Penguin.

Garber, S. (1996). *The fabric of faithfulness.* Downers Grove, IL: InterVarsity Press.

Gurman, A., & Messer, S. (Eds.). (2003). *Essential psychotherapies: Theories and practice* (2nd ed.). New York, NY: Guilford.

Guy, J. (1987). *The personal life of the psychotherapist.* New York, NY: Wiley.

Hood, R., Hill, P., & Spilka, B. (2009). *The psychology of religion: An empirical approach.* New York, NY: Guilford.

Hybels, L. (2007). *Nice girls don't change the world.* Grand Rapids, MI: Zondervan.

Jones, S., Butman, R., Dueck, A., & Tan, S. (1988, April). *Psychotherapeutic practice and the lordship of Christ.* Symposium presented at the National Convention of the Christian Association for Psychological Studies, Denver, CO.

Kauffmann, D. (1999). *My faith is ok: Yours is not.* Goshen, IN: Goshen College Press.

Kirkpatrick, L., & Spilka, B. (1989, August). *The treatment of religion in psychology textbooks.* Paper presented at the annual convention of the American Psychological Association, New Orleans, LA.

Malony, H. (1982, August). *God-talk in psychotherapy.* Paper presented at the annual convention of the American Psychological Association, Anaheim, CA.

Malony, H. (1985). Assessing religious maturity. In E. Stern (Ed.), *Psychotherapy and the religiously committed patient* (pp. 25-34). New York, NY: Haworth Press.

Malony, H. (1995). *The psychology of religion for ministry.* Pasadena, CA: Integration Press.

Mangis, M. (2008). *Signature sins.* Downers Grove, IL: InterVarsity Press.

McLemore, C. (2003). *Toxic relationships and how they work.* Hoboken, NJ: Wiley.

McMinn, M., & Campbell, C. (2007). *Integrative psychotherapy: Toward a comprehensive Christian approach.* Downers Grove, IL: IVP Academic.

Miller, W., & Jackson, K. (1985). *Practical psychology for pastors.* Englewood Cliffs, NJ: Prentice-Hall.

Norcross, J. (Ed.). (2002). *Psychotherapy relationships that work*. New York, NY: Oxford University Press.

Norcross, J., & Guy, J. (2007). *Leaving it at the office*. New York, NY: Guilford.

Oden, T. (1984). *Care of souls in the classic tradition*. Philadelphia, PA: Fortress.

Palmer, P. (1993). *To know as we are known*. New York, NY: Harper.

Paloutzian, R. (1997). *Invitation to the psychology of religion*. New York, NY: Guilford.

Paloutzian, R., & Parks, C. (Eds.). (2005). *Handbook of the psychology of religion and spirituality*. New York, NY: Guilford.

Parks, S. (1986). *The critical years*. San Francisco, CA: Harper & Row.

Patterson, C. (1985). *The therapeutic relationship: Foundations for an eclectic psychotherapy*. Monterey, CA: Brooks/Cole.

Sanders, R. (Ed.). (in press). *Christian counseling ethics* (2nd ed.). Downers Grove, IL: InterVarsity Press.

Sittser, G. (2004). *The will of God as a way of life*. Grand Rapids, MI: Eerdmans.

Sue, D., & Sue, D. (2008). *Foundations of counseling and psychotherapy: Evidence-based practice for a diverse society*. Hoboken, NJ: Wiley.

Tan, S. (1987). Intrapersonal integration: The servant's spirituality. *Journal of Psychology and Christianity, 6*, 34-39.

Tan, S. (2011). *Counseling and psychotherapy*. Grand Rapids, MI: Baker.

Tidball, D. (1986). *Skillful shepherds: An introduction to pastoral theology*. Grand Rapids, MI: Zondervan.

White, F. (1985). Religious health and pathology. In D. Benner (Ed.), *Baker encyclopedia of psychology* (pp. 999-1002). Grand Rapids, MI: Baker.

White, R. (1984). Salvation. In W. Elwell (Ed.), *Evangelical dictionary of theology* (pp. 969-971). Grand Rapids, MI: Baker.

Willard, D. (1990, August 20). Looking like Jesus. *Christianity Today*, pp. 29-31.

Yarhouse, M., Butman, R., & McRay, B. (2005). *Modern psychopathologies: A comprehensive Christian appraisal* (1st ed.). Downers Grove, IL: InterVarsity Press.

Author Index

Subject Index